Books by Michael R. Beschloss

KENNEDY AND ROOSEVELT: *The Uneasy Alliance* (1980)
MAYDAY: *Eisenhower, Khrushchev and the U-2 Affair* (1986)
THE CRISIS YEARS: *Kennedy and Khrushchev, 1960–1963* (1991)
AT THE HIGHEST LEVELS: *The Inside Story of the End of the Cold War*
(with Strobe Talbott) (1993)

TAKING CHARGE

The
Johnson White House
Tapes,
1963–1964

EDITED AND WITH COMMENTARY BY

Michael R. Beschloss

SIMON & SCHUSTER

SIMON & SCHUSTER
Rockefeller Center
1230 Avenue of the Americas
New York, NY 10020

Designed by Edith Fowler
Manufactured in the United States of America

10 9 8 7 6 5 4 3 2 1

Library of Congress Cataloging-in-Publication Data is available.
ISBN 0-684-80407-7

For
ALEXANDER MASHAYEKHI BESCHLOSS
AND
CYRUS ANDREW MASHAYEKHI BESCHLOSS

Contents

Prologue

THE FATAL TRIP TO TEXAS

THREE YEARS after John Kennedy was murdered in Dallas, Lyndon Johnson was alarmed by early reports about the soon-to-be-published book *The Death of a President*,[1] by William Manchester. Inspired by Jacqueline Kennedy, who wanted a single authorized history to overshadow other books being written by authors she distrusted,[2] Manchester's book was said to show a Johnson eager to seize power and insensitive to the dead President's family.[3] While privately asking for advice on how to muffle the political damage of Manchester's book, LBJ offered his own memories of November 22, 1963, and its prelude.[4]

In Manchester's narrative, the fatal trip to Texas is foreshadowed when President-elect Kennedy visits the LBJ Ranch eight days after he and Johnson win the 1960 election.[5]

LBJ: I didn't force him to come to Texas. Hell, he wanted to come out there him-*self!* Called up and he came. He didn't bring Miz Kennedy, and he may have told her that he didn't want to come because he brought some other people.[6] [chuckles darkly] But it is a hell of a note.

> Manchester writes that although Kennedy believed that "all killing was senseless," Johnson cajoled him into a deer hunt at dawn, during which Kennedy "looked into the face of the life he was about to take . . . fired and quickly turned back to the car."

[1] Harper & Row, 1967.

[2] Such as Jim Bishop, author of *The Day Lincoln Was Shot* (Harper, 1955).

[3] Some of the early published and hearsay reports on Manchester's book that reached Johnson exaggerated its hostility to him. These included a report by a Johnson aide who had obtained the galleys (Assassination File, Lyndon B. Johnson Library).

[4] Johnson's remarks in this Prologue are heard in taped conversations with Attorney General Nicholas Katzenbach (December 6, 1966, and January 25, 1967), Supreme Court Justice Abe Fortas (December 16, 1966), Press Secretary Bill Moyers (December 26, 1966), and Special Assistant Robert Kintner (December 20, 1966).

[5] William Manchester, *The Death of a President*, pp. 118–19.

[6] Johnson may allude to the presence of at least one unattached woman in the Kennedy traveling party.

LBJ: Forcing that poor man to go hunting? Hell, he not only killed *one* deer. He insisted on killing a *second!* One took two hours and then, by God, he insisted on killing one for Torby O'Donnell and we just worked so hard. It took three hours and I finally gave up. I said, "Mr. President, we just can't do it."[1]

. . . .

Poor little deer—he saw it in his eye and he just could not shoot it? Well, hell, he wasn't within 250 yards from it. . . . He shot it and he jumped up and hoorahed and put it right on the fender of the car so he could kill another one. . . . Most of them have got a rule—they will not let you kill but one. But he was the President[2] . . . and we wanted him to have whatever he wanted. . . . He wasn't competent to be President if he—I think it is the greatest desecration of his memory that an "impotent" Vice President[3] could force this strong man to do a god-damned thing.

>   As Manchester had it, based on his interviews with Jacqueline, Kennedy told his wife the "distressing" story in order to "rid himself of the recollection" and "heal the inner scar." Johnson had the deer's antlers and head mounted. After Kennedy became President, Johnson persistently suggested that JFK display his trophy in the Oval Office. Although "inwardly appalled," according to Manchester, the President, as a "favor" to Johnson, allowed it to be hung in the nearby Fish Room.[4]

LBJ: My calling him up and making him put a deer head in his outer room and he didn't want to? I never called him in my life on it. He had his fish up there that he caught on his honeymoon.[5] He put his deer head up there.

. . . .

[sarcastically:] But even if we had made the *tragic* mistake of forcing this *poor man* to put up a deer head here along with his fish—I do not know who forced him to put up the fish in the Fish Room that he caught on his honeymoon, but *I* damned sure didn't force him to put up anything. It is just a manufactured lie.

>   Manchester wrote that Kennedy came to Texas in November 1963 because Johnson had failed to resolve the "petty dispute," which threatened the 1964 Kennedy-Johnson ticket in Texas, between LBJ's old protégé, Governor John Connally, and their political enemy, the liberal Democratic Senator, Ralph Yarborough.[6]

LBJ: My forcing him to go to Texas! I never *heard* of it. Matter of fact, I tried to *postpone* it. Told him our popularity was too low.

[1] Johnson confuses the names of Kennedy's companions—his old Harvard roommate Torbert Macdonald, a Democratic Congressman from Massachusetts, and his aide Kenneth O'Donnell. It was Macdonald who had trouble with the deer.
[2] Actually President-elect.
[3] Manchester referred to Johnson as "virtually impotent in his own state" by 1963 (p. 3).
[4] The Fish Room was later renamed the Roosevelt Room by President Richard Nixon.
[5] Kennedy had also hung a sailfish he had caught on his 1953 Acapulco honeymoon.
[6] Manchester, *The Death of a President*, p. 3.

. . . .

Kennedy insisted for two years that he come and make five money-raising speeches and he[1] finally told him in my presence, said, "Mr. President, they are going to think that all the Kennedys want out of Texas is money. . . . I would suggest you make one money-raising speech and whatever else you do totally nonpolitical." And he told him that in the spring—April[2]—and he told him that in June, and then, because I would not encourage it, by God, he called him up and would not let me know he was calling him and he came up here and had a secret meeting with him.[3] . . . And he told John the reason he didn't tell me: "The Vice President is not enthusiastic."

. . . .

That's a great myth, that he came here to settle things for *me*. He came down here because he wanted to raise a million dollars and try to improve *him-self.* And he'd been to Massachusetts and done the same thing.[4] I put him off several months and Connally put him off several months. Didn't want him to come. Told him it was a mistake for him to come. And he finally called Connally . . . secretly to the White House, and he didn't tell me a thing about it. And Connally agreed that if he'd wait two or three months, he would help him with a dinner. And he didn't want to. . . . And I . . . had to call my personal friends long distance to get them to put up in order for 'em to even have a respectable crowd.[5]

> At the Rice Hotel in Houston, on Thursday evening, November 21, 1963, Johnson had his final private meeting with Kennedy. In the next room, Jacqueline was rehearsing her Spanish, preparing to speak downstairs to a Hispanic-American group. According to Manchester, the First Lady heard "raised voices" —Kennedy complaining, "expressing himself with exceptional force," about LBJ's treatment of Yarborough in Texas—and that when Johnson departed, the hotel manager thought that he "looked furious."[6]

LBJ: This Manchester stuff about Kennedy and I having an argument—I never had an argument with him in my life.

. . . .

All I can remember was Miz Kennedy was practicing, talking about her Spanish and about . . . whether she would go or not to this Spanish thing. The President . . . told me that he just thought that it was an outrage, that he had heard what Yarborough had done, that he had told him that Yarborough had to ride with us or get out of the party.[7] There was no disagreement of any kind and no violence

---

[1] Connally.

[2] 1963.

[3] The "secret meeting" between President Kennedy and Connally was on October 4, 1963, in the Oval Office.

[4] In October 1963, Kennedy had staged a fund-raising dinner in Boston.

[5] Tickets for the scheduled fund-raising dinner, planned for the evening of November 22, 1963, in Austin, were so slow-selling that LBJ flew to Texas early to ensure that the President would not be embarrassed in Johnson's home state.

[6] William Manchester, *The Death of a President*, p. 82.

[7] Asked to ride in the Johnson motorcade car to demonstrate unity among Texas Democrats, Yarborough had refused.

of any kind. A very friendly thing. And he and I had a drink together, and he sat there with his shirt off and left. We had no debate or no argument or no report and I had not asked to see him anyway. If she heard anybody having a disagreement of any kind, it was the President talking about Yarborough.

> The next day came the assassination. According to Manchester, after Kennedy's death was announced at Parkland Memorial Hospital in Dallas, Johnson's "slumped figure" was seen "sniffing from a vapor inhaler." Manchester wrote that a "dazed, silent" LBJ was "far readier to take orders than issue them." Presented a choice between flying back to Washington on *Air Force One* or the vice presidential backup plane, Johnson chose the President's aircraft and was taken in an unmarked car to the Dallas airport, Love Field.[1]

LBJ: One place they say I slumped, had a vapor inhaler, and would not take any leadership, and the next day I was so arrogant I was bossing everything.

. . . .

What raced through my mind was that if they had shot our President, driving down there, who would they shoot next? And what was going on in Washington? And when would the missiles be coming?[2] I thought it was a conspiracy and I raised that question, and nearly everybody that was with me raised it.

. . . .

And the thought that I should go to a plane that did not have the Bag[3] and did not have the communication—by God, after this terrible thing had happened—is inconceivable to me.

> At 1:33 P.M., heeding a Secret Service agent's shouted order, Johnson ran up the steps to *Air Force One*, where he prepared to take the oath as President.

LBJ: The reason I went to the airport and didn't take it in the hospital was, first, I wanted to be able to talk to the Attorney General[4] and get the oath. And the second thing was McNamara[5] had always told me that . . . if you got a warning [of possible nuclear war] . . . the thing they ought to do is get as high in the air as you can because you was least vulnerable there. Flying, a missile doesn't get you. A plane doesn't get you. You have time to think and you have adequate communications.

> With the shades on the plane yanked shut, Johnson sat in the Presidential bedroom on Jacqueline Kennedy's bed and made telephone calls. One was to the late President's brother, Attorney General Robert Kennedy, at his home in Virginia. Johnson later insisted that RFK advised him to take the oath immediately. According to Manchester, drawing on interviews with Robert, no opinion

[1] William Manchester, *The Death of a President*, pp. 229–32.
[2] Johnson suspected that the assassination might be the forerunner of a surprise, Pearl Harbor–style attack by the Soviet Union against the United States.
[3] The "Black Bag," containing instructions for Presidential use in case of nuclear war, is supposed to accompany the President at all times. Actually, as Johnson knew, the "Bag" could have been carried onto any aircraft.
[4] Robert Kennedy.
[5] Robert McNamara, Secretary of Defense.

was offered by the Attorney General, who would have sentimentally preferred that Johnson wait until he landed in Washington so that John Kennedy could return to the capital one last time as President.[1]

LBJ: I thought the most important thing in the world was to decide who was President of this country at that moment. I was fearful that the Communists were trying to take us over. . . . I think that Bobby agreed that it would be all right to be sworn in. He said he wanted to look into it and he would get back to me, which he did.

. . . .

There's also an implication that Bobby didn't want us to take the oath, when the implication made to me was that he thought it was better to take it there, that he would have somebody call me to give me the oath, and he did.[2]

. . . .

"He sprawled out on the bunk"?[3] I didn't sprawl. I sat and talked on the phone.

> According to Manchester, when Mrs. Kennedy boarded the plane, she found Johnson "reclining" on her bed and "came to a dead stop." LBJ "hastily lumbered past her," followed by his secretary, Marie Fehmer, while "the widow stared after them." Then Johnson returned to offer condolences and "called her 'Honey.' "[4]

LBJ: "He lumbered out of the room as she came in"? Well, now, lumbering—I don't know, I guess that's their way of saying I walked out. But he didn't see me walk out or he doesn't know whether I lumbered or trotted or walked or anything else.

. . . .

You know, if I call some guy's office to get him, I say to his secretary, "Honey, have him call in." I don't think that I said that to anybody. And I don't think that I called Miz Kennedy "honey." I think that's their idea of "you-all" and "comin' " —C-O-M-I-N—and this stuff they write about Texas.

. . . .

I think I would call people "honey" if I felt they *were* "honey." And I might have very well said that to Miz Kennedy, although I never felt that way about her and never believed it. I have held her kind of up on a pedestal and been very reserved with her, as her letters to me will indicate—very proper, very appropriate, very dignified, very reserved.[5]

[1] William Manchester, *The Death of a President*, pp. 238–39, 266–72.
[2] The somebody was Deputy Attorney General Nicholas Katzenbach.
[3] This sentence does not appear in the final version of Manchester's book, only in an early report that made its way to Johnson.
[4] William Manchester, *The Death of a President*, pp. 310, 316. In a 1964 oral history interview for the John F. Kennedy Library, which was sealed for fifteen years, Robert Kennedy said that "the treatment of Jackie" was one matter "which made me bitter—unhappy, at least—with Lyndon Johnson."
[5] Jacqueline Kennedy wrote Johnson by hand in January 1967 that she too had heard that Manchester had disparaged his calling her "honey." By then, the former First Lady was suing Manchester's publisher to remove material from his book that her advisers thought too personal or too anti-Johnson. (The suit was withdrawn later that month.) Mrs. Kennedy told Johnson

On Manchester and his book:

LBJ: I took the position when Manchester was selected that he was a fraud.[1] I refused to see him. I asked my people not to see him. . . . Just as I asked them not to see Teddy White.[2] I think they're agents of the people who want to destroy me. And I hate for them to use my friends to do it. . . . My friends don't know it, and they want to be popular and they just do it. And I don't say it's so much popularity. I don't think my wife wants to be popular. But I think she wants to be—accommodating would be a good word.[3]

. . . .

I am just going to keep my counsel and try to endure it. But it is vicious, mean, dirty, low-down stuff.

. . . .

All of it makes Bobby[4] look like a great hero and makes me look like a son of a bitch.

. . . .

My feeling on the Manchester book is . . . that we[5] are not equipped by experience, by tradition, by personality or financially to cope with this. I just do not believe that we know how to handle public relations and how to handle advertising agencies, how to handle manuscripts, how to handle book writers. . . . So I think they're[6] going to write history as they want it written, as they can buy it written. And I think the best way we can write it is to try to refrain from getting into an argument or a fight or a knockdown, and go on and do our job every day, as best we can.

---

that Manchester's reference to his calling her "honey" was so typical of how the author had twisted everything. Honey was a "loving" word, and she hoped he would call her that again. She added that no matter how his feelings toward her might change, she would always remain fond of Johnson: Once she decided that she cared about someone, nothing could ever make her change (Jacqueline Kennedy to Lyndon Johnson, undated, January 1967, Johnson Library).

[1] Johnson was right to be worried that Manchester was no LBJ fan. But as a World War II hero and the author of seven books before *The Death of a President*, Manchester was not a fraud.

[2] Journalist and author of *The Making of the President: 1960* (Atheneum, 1961) and its successors.

[3] Lady Bird Johnson did agree to be interviewed by Manchester.

[4] Kennedy.

[5] The Johnson circle.

[6] The Kennedys.

Chapter One
NOVEMBER 1963

FRIDAY, NOVEMBER 22, 1963

ROSE FITZGERALD KENNEDY
Mother of John F. Kennedy
3:15 P.M.[1]

      Twenty-eight minutes after *Air Force One* leaves Dallas for Washington, the new President makes his first telephone call after the swearing-in to the mother of his murdered predecessor.[2] Rose Kennedy is summoned to the telephone from a walk outside the Kennedy house at Hyannis Port. The sounds on this tape proclaim emergency—the shrill cries of the telephone operators and steward, the quavering voice of the dead leader's mother, the new President and First Lady shouting through static and over the shriek of jet engines.

VOICE: *AF-1, AF-1*, please stand by. We have Mrs. Rose Kennedy.... I'm going to put Mrs. Rose Kennedy on the line now.

ROSE KENNEDY: Hello? Hello? Hello?

VOICE: Just a moment, Mrs. Kennedy.

VOICE: Roger, one moment now, please.

ROSE KENNEDY: Hello?

VOICE: Stand by *One*, now, please.

VOICE: *AF-1, AF-1, AF-1*, from CROWN,[3] come in.

---

[1] Central Standard Time. All times provided in this volume are local, based on where Johnson was at the time.

[2] Unbeknownst to Johnson, his conversation with President Kennedy's mother and the one that follows were recorded by the Signal Corps, which monitored them from Andrews Air Force Base, outside Washington.

[3] Secret Service code name for the White House.

SGT. JOSEPH AYRES:[1] CROWN, this is *Air Force One*. Do you read us, over?

VOICE: I'm reading you loud and clear. I have Mrs. Kennedy standing by. Are you ready with VOLUNTEER?[2] Go ahead.

AYRES: Yes, we are ready. Can you put her on and I'll turn over to him, over.

VOICE: Roger, roger, she's coming on now.

VOICE: *AF-1* from CROWN. Mrs. Kennedy on. Go ahead, please.

AYRES: Hello, Mrs. Kennedy. Hello, Mrs. Kennedy. We're talking from the airplane. Can you hear us all right, over?

ROSE KENNEDY: Thank you. Hello?

AYRES: Yes, Mrs. Kennedy, I have—uh—Mr. Johnson for you here.[3]

ROSE KENNEDY: Yes, thank you.

LBJ: Mrs. Kennedy?

ROSE KENNEDY: Yes, yes, yes, Mr. President.

LBJ: I wish to God there was something that I could do and I wanted to tell you that we were grieving with you.

ROSE KENNEDY: Yes, well, thank you very much. That's very nice. I know. I know you loved Jack and he loved you.

LADY BIRD JOHNSON: Mrs. Kennedy, we feel lucky—

ROSE KENNEDY: Yes, all right.

LADY BIRD: We're glad that the nation had your son as long as it did—

ROSE KENNEDY: Well, thank you for that, Lady Bird. Thank you very much. Goodbye.

LADY BIRD: —thought and prayers—

ROSE KENNEDY: [weeping] Thank you very much. Goodbye, goodbye, goodbye. [she hangs up]

NELLIE CONNALLY
Wife of Texas Governor John Connally
3:30 P.M.

> NEXT JOHNSON calls the wife of the close friend who had become his congressional secretary in 1939, who was also wounded in Kennedy's limousine.

AYRES: *Air Force One.* VOLUNTEER would like a patch to Governor Connally of Texas—Mrs. Connally. That's the Governor's wife. Go ahead.

VOICE: VOLUNTEER would like a patch with Mrs. Connally, Governor Connally's wife. Is that a roger?

---

[1] Chief Steward on *Air Force One*.
[2] Code name for Lyndon Johnson.
[3] Ayres later recalled that he almost slipped and said "the President," but that, wary of hurting Mrs. Kennedy's feelings with a brutal reminder that her son no longer held that title, he simply said "Mr. Johnson" (William Manchester, *The Death of a President*, p. 371).

AYRES: Is a roger.

VOICE: Roger, roger, stand by *One.*

VOICE: Stand by for the Connally call.

VOICE: Oh, roger, roger, we have Dallas on the line, and we are trying to contact her now. Stand by, please. . . . *Air Force One* from CROWN, the Connally residence in Dallas is on the line, and Mrs. Connally is available to speak with Mr. Johnson if he can get to the phone patch.[1] Go ahead.

AYRES: Roger, he wants specifically to speak with her. Go ahead.

VOICE: Roger, stand by just a moment. *AF-1, AF-1,* from CROWN, would you put VOLUNTEER on, please? Mrs. Connally is on the line, standing by for his call.

LADY BIRD: Nellie? Can you hear me? We are hearing some reassuring news over the TV. We are up in the plane, but the surgeon speaking about John sounded so reassuring. How about it?

NELLIE CONNALLY: The important thing was true. That was the surgeon that had just gotten done operating on him. John is going to be all right, we are almost certain, unless something unforeseen happens— [static]

LADY BIRD: Nellie, I can't hear you too well.

VOICE: Uh, Mrs. Johnson—

LBJ: [shouting into telephone] Nellie, do you hear me?

NELLIE CONNALLY: Yes!

LBJ: I love you, darling, and I know that everything's going to be all right, isn't it?

NELLIE CONNALLY: Yes, it's going to be all right.

LBJ: God bless you, darling.

NELLIE CONNALLY: The same to you.

LBJ: Give him a hug and a kiss for me.

NELLIE CONNALLY: Good luck!

DWIGHT EISENHOWER
Thirty-fourth President of the United States
7:10 P.M.

> AFTER *Air Force One* lands at Andrews Air Force Base, Johnson flies by helicopter to the White House. From his old vice presidential office, Room 274, in the Executive Office Building, west of the White House, he telephones the living former Presidents—Herbert Hoover, Harry Truman, Dwight Eisenhower. As Democratic leader of the Senate throughout the Eisenhower years, Johnson had an amiable relationship with Ike. In 1963, unlike Hoover or Truman, the Supreme Commander of World War II in Europe still had a vast

---

[1] Actually Mrs. Connally was contacted not at the "Connally residence" in Dallas but Parkland Memorial Hospital, to which the wounded Kennedy and Connally had been taken.

national following which Johnson coveted. LBJ knows that Eisenhower, whom Kennedy had resented and generally avoided, will be charmed to know that the new President is so eager for his advice.

LBJ: This has been a shocking day.

EISENHOWER: My heart goes out to you.

LBJ: It has been tragic. I appreciated so much your thoughtful message. . . . It meant a lot to me.[1]

EISENHOWER: Thank you very much. That is the way I felt.

LBJ: I've needed you for a long time, but I need you more than ever now.

EISENHOWER: Anytime you need me, Mr. President, I will be there.

LBJ: I am going to rely on your good, sound judgment and will be calling on you, but I wanted you to know how touched I was by your message. It was typical of you and you know how much I have admired you through the years.

EISENHOWER: The country is far more important than any of us. I am going to be there[2] at eleven o'clock. They have invited ex-Presidents to come right after you and the other officials. . . .

LBJ: Why don't you give me a call right after the service is over?

EISENHOWER: I will. If you would like, I can just step over to see you— wherever the secretaries tell me to go.

LBJ: I wish you would do that.[3]

ARTHUR GOLDBERG
Associate Justice, U.S. Supreme Court
9:00 P.M.

AFTER MEETING with leaders of Congress, Johnson calls Goldberg, formerly JFK's Secretary of Labor, whom LBJ had spotted at Andrews Air Force Base when *Air Force One* landed.

LBJ: I want you to be thinking about what I ought to do to try to bring all these elements together and unite the country to maintain and preserve our system in the world, because if it starts falling to pieces—and some of the extremists are going to be proceeding on the wrong assumption—why, we could deteriorate pretty quick.

GOLDBERG: It won't. I have no doubt about that.

LBJ: . . . Just think, think, think.

GOLDBERG: Anytime, anytime.

---

[1] Eisenhower had sent Johnson a message of support through White House National Security Adviser McGeorge Bundy.
[2] At the White House, to view Kennedy's casket in the East Room.
[3] Eisenhower indeed spent an hour with Johnson the next day at noon, scrawling recommendations on a yellow legal pad.

LBJ: I want to give some thought, by the way, whether we ought to have a Joint Session of Congress after[1] and what would I say to them.

GOLDBERG: I think we ought to.

LBJ: I want you to think about . . . how I ought to do it without—I mean, with dignity and reserve and without being down on my knees, but at the same time letting them know of my respect and confidence. . . . I'm totally inadequate, but I'll do my best. . . . I had a general meeting with the leaders tonight and, needless to say, the Republicans are really more united than the Democrats. Mansfield[2] didn't say a word.

RICHARD MAGUIRE
Treasurer, Democratic National Committee
9:10 P.M.

ONLY HOURS after becoming President, Johnson is already thinking of the 1964 campaign. Although Maguire is scarcely of the stature of a former President, Supreme Court Justice, or the others with whom Johnson has touched base this evening, LBJ makes sure to call Kennedy's chief fund-raiser at the Democratic National Committee, with whom, unlike many other Kennedy aides, he has always had good relations.

LBJ: I know what a great personal tragedy this is to you, but it is to me too. And you have been so wonderful to the President. And I want to rely on you more than he did.

MAGUIRE: Just tell me what you want, sir.

LBJ: I just want to say that I want the same relationship tomorrow as I had yesterday. And I've been on your team[3] ever since I got here. And I just want you to know that you've got to be candid and frank and come in and tell me what we need to do and how we need to do it. I know how saddened you must be tonight, and so am I. We're in the same family, and one thing I know he would want us to do is to carry on—be effective—and that's what we're going to do. And you be giving some thought to what needs to be done, and we'll get together in the next day or two.

[1] Meaning after the Kennedy funeral. As Johnson well recalled, Harry Truman had addressed a Joint Session of Congress after FDR's death.

[2] Mike Mansfield of Montana, Senate Majority Leader, was laconic under any circumstances, but this night he was stilled by the death of Kennedy, of whom he had been very fond back to their days in the Senate.

[3] The Kennedy team.

SATURDAY, NOVEMBER 23, 1963

J. EDGAR HOOVER
Director, Federal Bureau of Investigation
10:01 A.M.

> THE LEGENDARY Director of the FBI, who detested Kennedy, reports to Johnson, his friend of decades and longtime Washington neighbor, on what the FBI knows about the murder. Hoover is eager to impress the new President with the Bureau's efficiency, partly out of concern that Johnson and the public might blame it for lapses that might have made Kennedy's assassination more likely. Forty minutes before this call, Johnson had been briefed by CIA Director John McCone. The CIA had information on foreign connections to the alleged assassin, Lee Harvey Oswald, which suggested to LBJ that Kennedy may have been murdered by an international conspiracy.

HOOVER: I just wanted to let you know of a development which I think is very important in connection with this case—this man in Dallas.[1] We, of course, charged him with the murder of the President. The evidence that they have at the present time is not very, very strong. We have just discovered the place where the gun was purchased and the shipment of the gun from Chicago to Dallas, to a post office box in Dallas, to a man—no, to a woman by the name of "A. Hidell." . . . We had it flown up last night, and our laboratory here is making an examination of it.

LBJ: Yes, I told the Secret Service to see that that got taken care of.

HOOVER: That's right. We have the gun and we have the bullet. There was only one full bullet that was found. That was on the stretcher that the President was on. It apparently had fallen out when they massaged his heart, and we have that one.[2] We have what we call slivers, which are not very valuable in the identification. As soon as we finish the testing of the gun for fingerprints . . . we will then be able to test the one bullet we have with the gun. But the important thing is that this gun was bought in Chicago on a money order. Cost twenty-one dollars, and it seems almost impossible to think that for twenty-one dollars you could kill the President of the United States.

LBJ: Now, who is A. Hidell?

HOOVER: A. Hidell is an alias that this man has used on other occasions, and according to the information we have from the house in which he was living—his mother—he kept a rifle like this wrapped up in a blanket which he kept in the house. On the morning that this incident occurred down there—yesterday—the man who drove him to the building where they work,[3] the building from where the shots came, said that he had a package wrapped up in paper. . . . But the important thing at the time is that the location of the purchase of the gun by

[1] Lee Harvey Oswald.
[2] The official view later had it that the bullet was on Connally's stretcher.
[3] Wesley Frazier drove Oswald to the Texas School Book Depository.

a money order apparently to the Klein Gun Company[1] in Chicago—we were able to establish that last night.

LBJ: Have you established any more about the visit to the Soviet embassy in Mexico in September?[2]

HOOVER: No, that's one angle that's very confusing, for this reason—we have up here the tape and the photograph of the man who was at the Soviet embassy, using Oswald's name. That picture and the tape do not correspond to this man's voice, nor to his appearance. In other words, it appears that there is a second person who was at the Soviet embassy down there.[3] We do have a copy of a letter which was written by Oswald to the Soviet embassy here in Washington, inquiring as well as complaining about the harassment of his wife[4] and the questioning of his wife by the FBI. Now, of course, that letter information—we process all mail that goes to the Soviet embassy.[5] It's a very secret operation.[6] No mail is delivered to the embassy without being examined and opened by us, so that we know what they receive. . . . The case, as it stands now, isn't strong enough to be able to get a conviction. . . . Now if we can identify this man who was at the . . . Soviet embassy in Mexico City. . . . This man Oswald has still denied everything. He doesn't know anything about anything, but the gun thing, of course, is a definite trend.

LBJ: It definitely established that he—the same gun killed the policeman?

HOOVER: That is an entirely different gun. We also have that gun. . . .

LBJ: You think he might have two?

HOOVER: Yes, yes, he had two guns. . . . The one that killed the President was found on the sixth floor in the building from which it had been fired. I think that the bullets were fired from the fifth floor, and the three shells that were found were found on the fifth floor.[7] But he apparently went upstairs to have fired the gun and throw the gun away and then went out. He went down to this theater.[8] There at the theater was where he had the gun battle with the police officer.[9]

LBJ: I wonder if you will get me a little synopsis and let me have what developments come your way during the day and try to get to me before we close up for the day.

[1] Actually Klein's Sporting Goods Company.

[2] A CIA memo written that day reported that Oswald had visited Mexico City in September and talked to a Soviet vice consul whom the CIA knew as a KGB expert in assassination and sabotage. The memo warned that if Oswald had indeed been part of a foreign conspiracy, he might be killed before he could reveal it to U.S. authorities (National Archives).

[3] The tape and photograph came from CIA surveillance. The discrepancy has yet to be fully explained.

[4] After defecting to the Soviet Union, Oswald had married Marina Prusakova in Minsk in 1961. Then he returned to the United States.

[5] In Washington.

[6] Between 1953 and 1973, although the CIA was forbidden by law to engage in domestic operations, mail from the Soviet Union to the United States was covertly opened and photographed by the Agency in concert with the FBI.

[7] Actually the three empty cartridge cases were found on the sixth floor.

[8] The Texas Theater in Dallas, where Oswald was apprehended.

[9] Hoover's early information was wrong. J.D. Tippit was killed on a Dallas street.

EVERETT DIRKSEN
Senate Minority Leader, Republican of Illinois
1:50 P.M.

IN THE 1950s, Johnson and Dirksen had worked together amiably in the Senate—particularly after Dirksen in 1959 became LBJ's counterpart as Minority Leader. Here Johnson moves to recement the old relationship.

LBJ: I'm rather of the opinion that it might be a good thing the day after the funeral—assuming the one in Boston[1] is Tuesday . . . to have a Joint Session and make a brief statement. We've been talking it over. I thought I ought to. And the boys on the staff thought I ought to.[2] And I wanted to get your thoughts on it.

DIRKSEN: I think it would be reassuring to the country.

LBJ: I think every chance you get to say like you did this morning and let them know that you're part of this partnership and your country comes first would be good too.

DIRKSEN: You know I will.

LBJ: The President spent a couple of hours and we reviewed a good many things including staffs and other things.[3] I won't make it definite. I'll have to see when the funeral is. . . . We'll just tentatively shoot at probably Wednesday.

GEORGE SMATHERS
Democratic Senator from Florida
2:10 P.M.

ALONG WITH CIVIL RIGHTS, one of the two chief pieces of unfinished congressional business left by Kennedy is a proposal to stimulate the economy by cutting taxes. Sent to Congress in January 1963, Kennedy's bill intended a major reduction in individual and corporate tax rates, as well as tax reform, chiefly the closing of loopholes. In September, the House passed the bill, with most of the reforms, unsurprisingly, deleted. In October, Senate Finance Chairman Harry Byrd of Virginia opened hearings that were expected to end on November 27.

A strong fiscal conservative who hated the deficit spending that was in vogue in the Kennedy administration, Byrd disliked the bill but was convinced that it would probably pass. Just before Kennedy left for Texas, he told the Secretary of the Treasury, Douglas Dillon, that he would not report the bill unless the budget for the coming year was $100 billion. Kennedy said that if that was necessary, he would comply.[4] Now Johnson asks Smathers, a Senate

---

[1] At this moment, Johnson assumed that a funeral would be held for Kennedy in Boston after official ceremonies in Washington, after which JFK would be buried in his home state.

[2] By citing Kennedy's staff as authority for his suggestion, Johnson shows how seriously he took the need to keep the JFK people friendly.

[3] Here Johnson hastens to mention Eisenhower, knowing that this will score points with Dirksen and remind him of their days of bipartisan cooperation, which Johnson now hopes to duplicate.

[4] See Douglas Dillon and Kermit Gordon oral histories, Johnson Library, and Irving Bernstein, *Guns or Butter* (Oxford, 1996), pp. 28–35.

chum of both Kennedy and himself, a shrewd tactician and member of the Finance Committee, where things stand. In doing so, he discovers that Smathers and Hubert Humphrey of Minnesota, the Senate Majority Whip, are already conspiring to make Humphrey LBJ's running mate in 1964.

LBJ: Tell me, what is the situation on the tax bill? I am going to meet with the Cabinet at two-thirty and I—

SMATHERS: . . . I made a deal, just confidentially . . . that Ribicoff and Long and myself and Fulbright[1] would vote against any motion to take the bill away from the Chairman.[2] . . . He would agree to . . . close the hearings. . . . Now, I asked 'em the other day what Byrd was really trying to accomplish. It's to hold up the tax bill until he could prove that Kennedy was going to have the budget . . . over $100 billion. So he could then argue, you know, that we are financing these tax amendments with debt. So I . . . told him that . . . if we, the President would come out and tell him now in December what he thought his budget was going to be, would Byrd cooperate and help them to get the clearance in the Executive Session over with? . . . He said, "I don't have any problem." . . . Now at the last legislative breakfast—you were not there[3]—I very strongly said that I thought we had enough votes on the floor to pass the tax bill this year. But . . . we were going to have to go around Harry Byrd in the committee. . . . I don't know if you want to do it or not, but the smart thing to do, in light of developments, would be for you to get the appropriation bill through real quick[4] and then just—

LBJ: No, no, I can't do that. That would destroy the party[5] and destroy the election, and destroy everything. We've got to carry on. We can't abandon this fellow's program, because he is a national hero and there are going to be those people want his program passed and we've got to keep this Kennedy aura around us through this election.

SMATHERS: Yeah. Well, in that connection . . . I had a most interesting visit with Hubert last night, after we met with you. He invited me over to his office to have a drink. . . . Hubert and I think that the new President has just got to have a liberal running with him as VP candidate and—I am just speaking for myself—I think, my God, that most of the Southerners would be for Hubert. . . . He was not at all averse to the idea. . . . He jumps for it. . . . I says, "Can you hold Joe and . . . Paul[6] and can you keep them lined up?" And he said, "I'm sure I can. This is going to be the problem. . . . They are going to try to make the new President look immediately like he is an old Texas oilman and . . . he is now the President of everybody."

---

[1] Senators Abraham Ribicoff of Connecticut, Russell Long of Louisiana, and J. William Fulbright of Arkansas, all Democratic members of the Finance Committee.
[2] Byrd.
[3] This refers to John Kennedy's last regular breakfast with congressional leaders at the White House the day before his death. Johnson had already departed for Texas.
[4] By this, Smathers means push Kennedy's tax bill to the side.
[5] Democratic party.
[6] Joseph Clark of Pennsylvania and Paul Douglas of Illinois—two eminent liberal Democratic Senators.

JOHN McCORMACK

Speaker of the House, Democrat of Massachusetts
3:54 P.M.

LBJ: I would guess that Wednesday would be the best day for us.[1] . . . I will know within the next hour what the family thinks. . . . They may have a Mass there.[2] I am not sure. . . . Very frankly, Mr. Speaker . . . I can't sit still. I've got to keep the government going. . . . But I don't want the family to feel that I am having any lack of respect, so I have a very delicate wire to walk there.

McCORMACK: . . . You make your own decisions. It is a delicate field for us all.

McGEORGE BUNDY

Special Assistant to the President for National Security Affairs
5:52 P.M.

KENNEDY'S—and now Johnson's—chief foreign affairs aide advises the new President on meeting key foreign leaders after the funeral.

BUNDY: There will be de Gaulle, Erhard, Douglas-Home.[3] Separate category: Mikoyan.[4] If you were to say that you needed Tuesday morning to restate in brief meetings the basic position of the United States and to pick up threads of your own personal acquaintance of these men . . . I think it may be a worthwhile thing to do. . . . It's going to be awful difficult to pick and choose. . . . To have them come and go and not meet with them would be equally foolish.

LBJ: Why don't you talk to the State Department . . . and tell me what you want me to do?

EDWARD KENNEDY

Democratic Senator from Massachusetts
7:40 P.M.

KENNEDY: Mr. President, I tried last night to get you and you had just gotten home, so I didn't think I would wake you up.

LBJ: Well, you shouldn't be taking your time now. But I did want you to know that you are in my prayers and I am so proud of the fact that I know you and I've been a part of his memory.

KENNEDY: I just want you to know how much I appreciate your thoughts— well, my mother and family.

---

[1] For a Joint Session.
[2] In Boston. In the end, the Kennedys decided that the only funeral should be in Washington.
[3] President Charles de Gaulle of France, Chancellor Ludwig Erhard of West Germany, and Prime Minister Alec Douglas-Home of Great Britain.
[4] Soviet Deputy Prime Minister Anastas Mikoyan.

LBJ: You give her a hug for me and you and Joan[1] keep one for yourself and know that God Almighty in his wisdom works in mysterious ways and we will just bear it together.

SUNDAY, NOVEMBER 24, 1963

JACK BROOKS
Democratic Congressman from Texas
4:53 P.M.

NEAR THE END of a day on which Johnson lays a wreath at John Kennedy's bier in the Capitol Rotunda and also learns that Lee Harvey Oswald has been murdered in Dallas, Johnson unwinds by talking to a close congressional friend from Beaumont, Texas, fourteen years his junior, who two days earlier had stood alongside the Johnsons at Parkland Memorial Hospital and while LBJ took the oath aboard *Air Force One.*

BROOKS: It's not going to be an easy job, but there isn't anybody better prepared to do it than you. I told them on ABC Television yesterday that you're the best prepared Vice President we ever had in the history of the country by training, temperament. . . .

LBJ: Well, good.

BROOKS: We've got to start being—not to be cold-blooded, but I mean to be realistic. We ought to be pointing out that we've got a fine President that can do the job and is because it's good for the . . . continuity of the country.

LBJ: Where are you eating dinner?

BROOKS: Anywhere. Where are you going?

LBJ: I thought maybe I might send a car up there for you when I get ready to leave here. . . . Might drive out to the house[2] and have a drink, a sandwich. Potluck.

BROOKS: All right. What time you think you're going to be?

LBJ: I would guess I'd be through 'tween six and six-thirty. Maybe six. I'll . . . have somebody call you and pick you up and then take you home.

BROOKS: With Charlotte?[3]

LBJ: Oh, yes, sure, sure, sure!

[1] Kennedy's then-wife.
[2] Until Jacqueline Kennedy vacated the White House a fortnight after the assassination, Johnson remained at his large house, The Elms, in the Spring Valley neighborhood of Washington.
[3] Mrs. Brooks.

McGEORGE BUNDY
5:10 P.M.

BUNDY: The reception[1] is tomorrow. It is getting in good shape. Mrs. Kennedy wants to receive the heads of delegations herself very briefly right after the burial and then the State Department would have you, if you would receive more seriously and have a chance to talk to some over there. That would be very agreeable to the family and I think that the doubleheader, in a way, is graceful for both parties and allows you to transact some presidential business. . . .

LBJ: Yeah, that's right.

BUNDY: Now, Tuesday appointments, I think, should not be decided or announced until you and I have had one more talk because there's a good deal of conflict between us and some of the State Department bureaus on it.[2] [chuckles] I'm sure we're right, but I want you to be satisfied.

LBJ: All right.

WHITNEY YOUNG
Executive Director, National Urban League
5:55 P.M.

       IN JUNE 1963, President Kennedy sent a comprehensive civil rights bill to Congress[3] and declared that granting black Americans full citizenship was a "moral issue." LBJ's genuine and emotional passion for civil rights had been considerably submerged while he was a Senator. Texas was scarcely in the forefront of the battle for equal justice. He was known in 1957 for weakening a modest civil rights bill passed by the House, the first in eighty-two years, in order to thwart a Southern-led filibuster.

       Ironically, when Johnson became Vice President and wished to speak out for civil rights, Kennedy was displeased because he wanted LBJ to help hold the South and border states in 1964. For this reason and under JFK's general policy of excluding the old Senate master from his legislative strategies, Kennedy's men wished to keep Johnson at the edges of the fight. Two days before the assassination, the House Judiciary Committee endorsed Kennedy's bill, with minor changes. Now some black leaders who do not know Johnson well worry about his Southern background, his performance in 1957, and the possibility that the old wheeler-dealer might emasculate the bill to get it passed. LBJ is eager to reassure even those leaders he knows, like Whitney Young, of the full depth of his commitment to civil rights.

    [1]A reception at the State Department after the funeral for government leaders who have come to Washington.

    [2]This refers to the Tuesday meetings with de Gaulle, Erhard, Douglas-Home, and Mikoyan.

    [3]The bill had seven major titles: (1) voting rights (completion of the sixth grade would be sufficient proof of literacy and ability to vote); (2) public accommodations (access for all to hotels, places of amusement, stores, restaurants, and other public facilities); (3) school desegregation; (4) a Community Relations Service to help resolve local disputes over discrimination; (5) a four-year extension of the U.S. Commission on Civil Rights; (6) withholding federal funds from discriminatory local and state programs; (7) a Commission on Equal Employment Opportunity.

YOUNG: Negroes . . . have one hundred percent confidence in you.

LBJ: Well, you're mighty—

YOUNG: I've been saying this on television and radio, and I'm quite sincere about it.

LBJ: I know that. You've been wonderful. I want you to come in during the next few days as we get this behind us. . . . Of course, I'm going to urge the Congress to go ahead and act now. But I don't know what we're going to get out of them in the way of tax and civil rights in the next three weeks. . . . But we're just beginning to fight. I want you to give some thought to what our approaches ought to be and who we ought to talk to . . . and let's all try to go in the same direction, kind of like we have with Equal Opportunity[1]. . . . I'm going to call Roy[2] as soon as I hang up talking to you and I don't know who else to call. . . . What about Phil Randolph?[3]

YOUNG: Phil is in Chicago.

LBJ: Would you call him if you were me?

YOUNG: Yeah. I think this is real strategic. . . .

LBJ: . . . Let's try to not move with that ball until we know where we're going and then let's go and go right on through that goal line. . . . Might get run out of bounds a time or two, but they'll keep coming. And kind of like that fellow said, "What's the difference between a Texas Ranger and a Texas Sheriff?" Said, "Well, when you hit a Ranger he just keeps coming." [both laugh] So, that's kind of the fight we want to get in. . . .

YOUNG: I've got some ideas and I'd be happy to sit down and talk with you— the sooner, the better. . . .

LBJ: I've got to get this funeral behind me and I've got all these heads of state coming. . . . I'm going to the Joint Session and I think I ought to just tell them we're carrying on and ask for passage of his civil rights bill and his tax bill. . . . Humphrey told me yesterday that they're all going home Thanksgiving and not gonna come back to taxes until December 10th and said everybody is so worn out, mad, and tired, they're not going to pass anything between now and December 18th, when they quit for Christmas. So I've got to get in behind them pretty quick.

YOUNG: Let me make a quick suggestion. I think you've just got to . . . point out that . . . with the death of President Kennedy . . . that hate anywhere that goes unchecked doesn't stop just for the week. And the killing at Birmingham[4] —the people feel that they can react with violence when they dissent. So this thing is now bigger.

---

[1] As Vice President, Johnson had chaired the President's Committee on Equal Opportunity, which acquainted him with many national black leaders and which, under the civil rights bill, would be replaced by a commission.

[2] Wilkins, executive secretary, National Association for the Advancement of Colored People (NAACP).

[3] A. Philip Randolph, founder of the Brotherhood of Sleeping Car Porters and vice president of the AFL-CIO.

[4] On Sunday morning, September 15, 1963, four black girls were killed when a dozen sticks of dynamite set off an explosion at the Sixteenth Street Baptist Church in Birmingham, Alabama, during a celebration of the integration of the city's public schools that week.

LBJ: [agrees:] I dictated a whole page on hate—hate international—hate domestically—and just say that this hate that produces inequality, this hate that produces poverty, that's why we've got to have a tax bill—the hate that produces injustice—that's why we've got to have a civil rights bill. It's a cancer that just eats out our national existence.

YOUNG: Right, right. That's wonderful.

LBJ: God bless you, and I was thinking of you.

YOUNG: One thing more—and I haven't heard anything about it—we sort of expected an invitation to the funeral. How are they handling that?

LBJ: I have no idea under the sun, but let me inquire on it. I'd sure—I'm taking my family and I'd almost take you as my guest if I can get an extra ticket. Let me see about it. I don't know. Bobby[1] is handling it. But I'll check it.

WHITNEY YOUNG
6:23 P.M.

LBJ: That invitation will come through to you and Roy[2] tonight. . . . We talked to Sargent Shriver[3] and he said that he'd work it right out.

YOUNG: Thanks so much. What time is that?

LBJ: Damned if I know. [aside, to aide:] What time—when will the invitations come through, tonight?

YOUNG: Well, I mean, what time is the service?

LBJ: [back to Young:] Noon. . . . Now, if you don't, you can call Bill Moyer [sic] through the White House switchboard. . . . M-O-Y-E-R [sic]. He's my assistant.[4]

YOUNG: Yes, I know him. Had him speak at our conference last summer.

LBJ: [joking:] No wonder he hasn't been worth a damn to me! He's running around with you all the time. [both laugh]

[1] Robert Kennedy.
[2] Roy Wilkins.
[3] The late President's brother-in-law, Director of the Peace Corps, who is organizing the ceremonies on behalf of the Kennedy family.
[4] Johnson sometimes referred to Moyers, his old Senate aide who had become Shriver's Deputy Director under the Kennedy presidency, as "Moyer."

MONDAY, NOVEMBER 25, 1963

OFFICE CONVERSATION
10:29 A.M.

VOICE: Yes, sir.

LBJ: [angry:] Everybody just keeps coming on. Now I can't work with an office like that 'cause I'll get right talking with J. Edgar Hoover and you and Juanita[1] will start talking and saying hello. If the telephone system can't work, will you just tell 'em I'll have to go home? I've asked you for three days to do it!

VOICE: Yes, sir. . . . Mr. Hoover on 2383.

LBJ: Let me find it—

J. EDGAR HOOVER
10:30 A.M.

PRESIDENT KENNEDY's funeral ceremonies are to begin in an hour. Johnson, in a bad humor, is under pressure to appoint a presidential commission to investigate the Kennedy assassination. He would prefer to leave the investigation to the FBI and state of Texas.[2] Knowing that Hoover will agree, he asks the FBI Director for help.

LBJ: Apparently some lawyer in Justice[3] is lobbying with the *Post*[4] because that's where the suggestion came from for this presidential commission,[5] which we think would be very bad and put it right in the White House. We can't be checking up on every shooting scrape in the country, but they've gone to the *Post* now to get 'em an editorial, and the *Post* is calling up and saying they're going to run an editorial if we don't do things.[6] Now we're going to do two things and I wanted you to know about it. One—we believe that the way to handle this,

---

[1] Juanita Roberts, a Johnson secretary.

[2] Suspecting that Kennedy was killed by a conspiracy, Johnson wished to close off public speculation about Oswald's foreign connections to forestall public outrage that might lead to pressure on him to wage some kind of revenge assault against Cuba or the Soviet Union. On his first night as President, horrified to learn that Dallas prosecutors were threatening to charge Oswald with killing Kennedy to further "a Communist conspiracy," LBJ ordered aides to get the Dallas district attorney in line and to encourage a Texas Court of Inquiry (*Washington Post*, November 14, 1993).

[3] Robert Kennedy's Justice Department, which, as Johnson knows, is Hoover's nemesis.

[4] The *Washington Post*.

[5] To investigate Kennedy's murder.

[6] Indeed the *Post* ran an editorial the next day saying that to investigate the assassination, "no state or local inquiry" would be enough: "The Federal Government must prosecute this inquiry by means that assure the most objective, the most thorough and the most speedy analysis and canvass of every scrap of relevant information. The disclosures and conclusions must be so sweeping and extensive that they leave no room for the imagination of the morbid, the propaganda of the left or right, or the sheer fantasy of the irresponsible."

as we said yesterday—your suggestion—that you put every facility at your command, making a full report to the Attorney General and then they make it available to the country in whatever form may seem desirable. Second—it's a state matter, too, and the state Attorney General[1] is young and able and prudent and very cooperative with you. He's going to run a Court of Inquiry, which is provided for by state law, and he's going to have associated with him the most outstanding jurists in the country. But he's a good conservative fella and we don't start invading local jurisdictions that way and he understands what you're doing and he's for it. . . . Now if you get too many cooks messing with the broth, it'll mess it up. . . . These two are trained organizations and the Attorney General of the state holds Courts of Inquiry every time a law is violated, and the FBI makes these investigations. . . . You ought to tell your press men that that's what's happening and they can expect Waggoner Carr, the Attorney General of Texas, to make an announcement this morning, to have a state inquiry and that you can offer them your full cooperation and vice versa. . . .

HOOVER: We'll both work together on it.

LBJ: And any influence you got with the *Post* . . . point out to them that . . . just picking out a Tom Dewey lawyer from New York[2] and sending him down on new facts—this commission thing—Mr. Herbert Hoover tried that and sometimes a commission that's not trained hurts more than it helps.[3]

HOOVER: It's a regular circus then.

LBJ: That's right.

HOOVER: Because it'll be covered by TV and everything like that.

LBJ: Just like an investigating committee.

HOOVER: Exactly. I don't have much influence with the *Post* because I frankly don't read it. I view it like the *Daily Worker.*[4]

LBJ: [laughs] You told me that once before. I just want your people to know the facts, and your people can say that. And that kind of negates it, you see?

JOSEPH ALSOP
Columnist, Washington Post
10:40 A.M.

> JOHNSON PRODS one of the most powerful columnists of the time to turn *Washington Post* colleagues against the notion of a commission.

ALSOP: You know what I feel about you and you know how I—well, I put it all in the letter.[5] . . .

---

[1] Of Texas.
[2] Thomas Dewey, former New York Governor and twice Republican nominee for President, was Johnson's image of a Wall Street lawyer.
[3] Former President Hoover chaired two presidential commissions for Harry Truman that, contrary to Johnson's memory, were generally accounted a success.
[4] The old American Communist Party gazette.
[5] Alsop wrote Johnson a letter of praise on his succession to the presidency.

LBJ: [reading from notes:] "He has ordered—or will order during the day, probably right after the funeral—a state Court of Inquiry headed by the Attorney General[1]. . . . He will have associated with him one or two of the outstanding civil liberties jurists in the country." Perhaps Jaworski, who represented the Attorney General in the Fifth Circuit Negro case,[2] or the head of the trial lawyers of America or Dean Storey,[3] or—

ALSOP: You mean, somebody from outside Texas?

LBJ: No, they're going to have FBI from outside Texas, but this is under Texas law[4] and they take all the involvements and we don't send in a bunch of carpetbaggers. That's the worst thing we could do right now.

ALSOP: You think so?

LBJ: I *know*. . . . If there's any question about a Texas operation, they've got an FBI that's going to the bottom of it. . . . But paralleling that is a blue-ribbon state Court of Inquiry headed by the brilliant Attorney General[5] and associated with him, somebody like, say, John Garwood, Will Clayton's son-in-law, who was a brilliant Supreme Court Justice, that's retired[6]—somebody like Roberts did at Pearl Harbor.[7] . . . Now, if we have another commission, hell, you're gonna have people running over each other and everybody agrees. Now I know that some of the lawyers—they thought of the blue-ribbon commission first, at Justice, and we just can't have them lobbying against the President, when he makes these decisions. We decided that the best thing to do to counterattack is, number one, to put the FBI in full force, number two, to put the state[8] in full force.

ALSOP: Nobody, nobody, Mr. President, lobbied me. I lay awake all night.

LBJ: No, not you. [irritated:] They lobbied *me* last night! I spent the day on it. I had to leave Mrs. Kennedy's side at the White House and call and ask the Secret Service and FBI to proceed immediately. I spent most of my day on this thing yesterday. [more shrill:] I had the Attorney General from Texas fly in here. . . . And the FBI is of the opinion that the wisest, quickest, ablest, most effective way to go about it is for them to thoroughly study it and bring in a written report to the Attorney General[9] at the earliest possible date, which they've been working

[1] Of Texas.

[2] Leon Jaworski of Houston prosecuted the first major war criminal at Nuremberg in 1946 and resurfaced in 1973 as the second Special Prosecutor to pursue Richard Nixon's Watergate scandal. In 1960, Jaworski defended LBJ's right to run simultaneously for Vice President and Senator from Texas. On behalf of Robert Kennedy's Justice Department, Jaworski had also prosecuted Mississippi Governor Ross Barnett for defying a Fifth Circuit Court order to allow black students to enroll at the University of Mississippi.

[3] M. Robert Storey, former president of the American Bar Association and dean of Southern Methodist Law School in Dallas.

[4] Assassination of a President still fell under state law in 1963. Only two years later did Congress declare presidential assassination, kidnapping, or assault to be federal crimes.

[5] Of Texas.

[6] Will Clayton was a wealthy Texan who served in the Roosevelt and Truman State Departments. His daughter, Ellen Garwood, appeared during the Iran-contra hearings in 1987 as one of those who had raised private funds in league with Colonel Oliver North for the Nicaraguan rebels. Clayton's son-in-law, John Garwood, was a Texas Supreme Court Justice.

[7] U.S. Supreme Court Justice Owen Roberts chaired a commission established by Franklin Roosevelt to investigate the Japanese attack on Pearl Harbor.

[8] Texas.

[9] Robert Kennedy.

on since twelve-thirty yesterday. Number one—and they have information that is available to *no one*, that has not been presented thus far. . . . Number *two*, to parallel that, we're having a blue-ribbon Court of Inquiry . . . in Texas, where this thing occurred.

ALSOP: Mr. President, just let me give you my political judgment on the thing. I think you've done everything that could probably be done—

LBJ: We just don't want to be in a position—I'll make this one more statement and then I'm through—I want to hear you. We don't want to be in the position of saying that we have come into a state, other than the FBI. . . . Some outsiders have told them that their integrity is no good and that we're going to have some carpetbag trials. We can't haul off people from New York and try them in Jackson, Mississippi, and we can't haul off people from Dallas and try them in New York.

ALSOP: I see that, Mr. President, but let me—

LBJ: It is their constitutional right. Go ahead now.

ALSOP: Let me make one suggestion because . . . I think this bridges the gap which I believe and Dean Acheson[1] believes still exists. . . . Friendly[2] is going to come out tomorrow morning with a big thing about a blue-ribbon commission, which he thought of independently. . . . I'm sure you're right except there's one missing piece. I suggest that you announce that as you do not want the Attorney General to have the painful responsibility of reporting on his own brother's assassination, that you have authorized three jurists . . . to review all the evidence by the FBI and produce a report to the nation for the nation. . . . If you'll get out such an announcement this afternoon, you're going to make a marvelous—well, you've already made a marvelous start. You haven't put a damned foot one quarter of an inch wrong, and I've never seen anything like it. . . . I'm sure that if Moyers calls Friendly, you'll have terrific support from the *Washington Post* and from the whole of the rest of the press instantly.

LBJ: I'll ruin both procedures we've got, though. . . . My lawyers, Joe, tell me that . . . the President must not inject himself into local killings.

ALSOP: I agree with that. But in this case it does happen to be the killing of the President. . . .

LBJ: I know that.

ALSOP: Mind you, Mr. President . . . I am talking about a body which will take all the evidence the FBI has amassed. . . . That, I think, you see, that is not an interference in Texas.

LBJ: No, but it's—

ALSOP: Wait a second, now. That is a way to transmit to the public . . . and in a way that will carry absolute conviction what the FBI has turned up.

LBJ: Why can't the FBI transmit it?

ALSOP: Because no one . . . on the left—they won't believe the FBI. And the FBI doesn't write very well.

LBJ: They'd believe Nick Katzenbach?[3]

[1] The Truman Secretary of State had become a Washington lawyer.
[2] Alfred Friendly, managing editor of the *Washington Post*.
[3] Robert Kennedy's Deputy Attorney General.

ALSOP: I just wouldn't put it on Bobby and Nick Katzenbach. . . . I think it's unfair to put it on Bobby. It is his own brother's death.

LBJ: I'm not going to put it on Bobby. [growing more irritated:] We're putting it on the finest jurists in the land. . . . Then we're putting it on the top investigative agency and asking them to write a report.

ALSOP: . . . I'm just suggesting . . . this very small addition to the admirable machinery that you've already set up. . . . And I now see exactly how right you are and how wrong I was about this idea of a blue-ribbon commission.

LBJ: Now, you see, Katzenbach suggested that and that provoked it. The lawyers that counsel me just hit the ceiling. Said, "My God Almighty!" . . .

ALSOP: . . . What I am suggesting is not at all what Katzenbach suggested. . . . I worry about this *Post* editorial. I'd like you to get ahead of them.

LBJ: I worry about the *Post*, period, but— [chuckles]

ALSOP: . . . If you make this decision and have Moyers call Friendly or Kay[1] . . . they'll be flattered. . . . And I *hate* to interfere, sir. I only dare to do so because I care so much about you.

LBJ: I know that, Joe.

ALSOP: . . . What I'm really honestly giving you is public relations advice and not legal advice.

LBJ: Well, I'm not grounded. I don't have the depth in the civil liberties picture that some of the folks that have worked on this with me. I had a lawyer[2] left my house around midnight and spent, I guess, three or four hours going over this thing from A to Z . . . and we thought that this was the best way to handle it.

ALSOP: Mr. President . . . I must not keep you because you'll be late getting into your trousers.

McGEORGE BUNDY
4:00 P.M.

> JUST AFTER KENNEDY'S BURIAL at Arlington National Cemetery, Johnson returns to the White House anxious about what will happen when the national day of mourning is over.

LBJ: The Securities Exchange, commodity markets, and so forth—I'm a little worried about them tomorrow. You know what they did—they dropped—after Eisenhower's heart attack.[3] So that's the main reason we really wanted to speak[4] Tuesday. We hoped that we could hold 'em. But I wonder if you wouldn't mind talking to Dillon and Martin[5] and seeing if they've got any suggestions.

[1] Katharine Graham, Washington Post Company president since her husband's death by his own hand in August 1963.
[2] Johnson's longtime friend and close counselor Abe Fortas.
[3] Eisenhower suffered a massive coronary in September 1955.
[4] To a Joint Session of Congress.
[5] Secretary of the Treasury Douglas Dillon and Federal Reserve Board Chairman William McChesney Martin.

BUNDY: I talked in a general way to Doug yesterday and he was not worried, but let me check again, because that's twenty-four hours old.

LBJ: I think both of them might make some kind of statement about the continuity, stability, or something, and express their confidence—it might help. They ought to be imaginative enough to find something that they think could stabilize it.

BUNDY: Your Latin American idea[1] is regarded a ten-strike and we're going to organize that for tomorrow afternoon. There's some problem of where, but we'll have a recommendation on that for the morning. De Gaulle is the senior of these three men you're seeing this evening.[2] I think you probably ought to see him first. You'd be seeing them all three in order. He's very protocol-aire and the other two don't care. The other two, you see, are not heads of state.

LBJ: All right.

BUNDY: Does that bother you?

LBJ: A little.[3] I thought I'd sandwich him in, but if you think it'd be disagreeable. You see, he urged—what time do we have to see him?

BUNDY: Well, we hope you'll be through with the reception and certain private interviews, and you could see him at seven and then have Pearson and Ikeda[4] right after that. They're both tickled pink.

LBJ: All right, I'll follow your judgment on that.

LAWRENCE O'BRIEN

Special Assistant to the President for Congressional Relations
4:04 P.M.

> JOHNSON MAKES his pitch to Kennedy's congressional liaison, who has returned from the Kennedy burial with a fellow member of JFK's "Irish Mafia," Kenneth O'Donnell, in a deep state of melancholy.

LBJ: Needless to tell you, I'm most anxious for you to continue just like you have been, because I need you a lot more than he did.

O'BRIEN: Mr. President, Ken is here with me. Do you have any immediate problem?

LBJ: No, no, I just wanted you to know how strongly I felt about you and Ken and all the rest of the staff, and I had talked to some of them individually, but I hadn't had a chance to run into you, and I think you know the confidence I have in you and admiration I have for you.

---

[1]Johnson had asked Bundy to arrange a special meeting with a hundred representatives of Latin American nations to reaffirm his commitment to Kennedy's Alliance for Progress, designed to improve relations among the Americas.

[2]At the aforementioned State Department reception.

[3]De Gaulle's relationship with the United States was rocky in 1963, thanks in part to his opposition to British membership in the Common Market and to the American-Soviet-British partial nuclear test ban treaty.

[4]Prime Ministers Lester Pearson of Canada and Hayato Ikeda of Japan.

O'BRIEN: I know that, Mr. President.

LBJ: I don't expect you to love me as much as you did him, but I expect you will after we've been around awhile.

O'BRIEN: Right, Mr. President.

LBJ: . . . I wanted to congratulate you, too, on that Mundt vote up there.[1] I think it would be a terrible thing to Kennedy's memory to have this wheat sale thing repudiated. . . . I did tell Mansfield that I thought it would be . . . a hell of a way to launch a new administration.

O'BRIEN: Right, I agree.

LBJ: And so I want somebody to give it a little attention and let me know tonight or in the morning if there is anything that I need to know about it if it's not well taken care of. . . . And then you let me know any suggestions you have because we're in this thing up to our ears.

MARTIN LUTHER KING, JR.
President, Southern Christian Leadership Conference
9:20 P.M.

LBJ: A good many people told me that they heard about your statement, I guess, on TV, wasn't it?[2]

KING: Yes, that's right.

LBJ: I've been locked up in this office and haven't seen it, but I want to tell you how grateful I am and how worthy I'm going to try to be of all your hopes.

KING: Well, thank you very much. I am so happy to hear that and I knew that you had just that great spirit and you know you have our support and backing. We know what a difficult period this is.

LBJ: It's just an impossible period. We've got a budget coming up that's . . . practically already made and we've got a civil rights bill. . . . We've just got to not let up on any of 'em and keep going. And I guess they'll say that I'm repudiated. But I'm going to ask the Congress Wednesday to just stay there till they pass 'em all. They won't do it, but we'll just keep them there next year until they do and we just won't give up an inch.

KING: Uh-huh. Well, this is mighty fine. . . . I think one of the great tributes that we can pay in memory of President Kennedy is to try to enact some of the great progressive policies that he sought to initiate.

LBJ: I'm going to support 'em all and you can count on that. And I'm going to do my best to get other men to do likewise and I'll have to have you-all's help. I never needed it more'n I do now.

[1] Republican Senator Karl Mundt had sought to block JFK's financing of the sale of surplus wheat to the Soviet bloc through the U.S. Export-Import Bank. At Kennedy's death, the administration lacked the votes to defeat him. By casting the issue as a vote of confidence in the new President, Johnson managed to turn around nine Democrats and one Republican to thwart the Mundt bill by 57 to 35.

[2] Stating confidence in Johnson's leadership.

KING: Well, you know you have it and just feel free to call on us for anything. . . . Regards to the family.

LBJ: Thank you so much, Martin. Call me when you're down here next time and let's get together and any suggestions you've got, bring them in.

THEODORE SORENSEN
Special Counsel to the President
10:10 P.M.

> JOHNSON HAS ASKED Kennedy's chief wordsmith, Theodore Sorensen, to work on his address to the Wednesday Joint Session of Congress. Before starting work, Sorensen wants to know LBJ's opinion of other drafts submitted by Harvard economist John Kenneth Galbraith (previously JFK's Ambassador to India) and others. Sorensen is chagrined to learn that Johnson is already straying from Kennedy's intentions. The new President has decided to cut the budget considerably in order to win conservative support for the tax cut bill and has reversed Kennedy's provisional decision, made at his final congressional leadership breakfast before Dallas, to give civil rights priority over the tax bill.[1] Told how powerfully a tax cut could stimulate the economy just in time for the 1964 presidential election, Johnson did not wish to wait to get it until after what he expected to be a long struggle over civil rights. As with the rest of the Kennedy team, Johnson is working hard to keep Sorensen friendly, fearing that a resignation would bespeak a lack of confidence in the new President.

BILL MOYERS: Ted . . . he'll be with you in just a minute. Trying to get rid of some people. . . .

SORENSEN: How'd your meeting go?

MOYERS: . . . He feels we ought to try a tactical move of talking about a budget of a hundred to a hundred and a half[2] . . . until we get the tax cut. . . . He wants the tax bill and he wants it before January. . . . He thinks if we go into the civil rights bill now, you won't get the tax bill until three or four months from now. And these fellows all tell him the tax bill now will mean an immediate upsurge in the economy, which ought not to be delayed until next April, May, June.[3] . . . So he asked Gordon[4] to go out and restudy $101.5[5]—through the use of gimmicks or through an actual withholding of some plans. . . .

SORENSEN: . . . If it's done by cutting anything out of the budget that's solid muscle, I think that's a mistake.[6] . . . I *know* you can get the tax bill without

---

[1] Byrd had been insisting that the Senate deal with civil rights before the tax cut bill. Treasury strategists presumed that this was to hold the tax bill hostage to rejection of civil rights.

[2] Billion dollars.

[3] At which time it would be too late to be of great help to Democrats in the 1964 election.

[4] Budget Director Kermit Gordon.

[5] Billion dollars.

[6] Sorensen and other Kennedy people, including RFK, suspected that Johnson would be more conservative than Kennedy on domestic policy. LBJ assured Walter Heller, Chairman of the Council of Economic Advisers, that he was "a Roosevelt New Dealer" and that JFK had been "a little too conservative to suit my taste" (Heller memorandum, November 23, 1963, Heller Papers, Kennedy Library).

doing that. . . . There are some gimmicks you can use. There are some ways you can hold things back or conceal them. The budget, after all, is only a schedule of estimate and estimates can vary by a billion dollars one way or the other without much trouble. . . . But I don't want to see some good programs knocked out.

MOYERS: Right. . . . I don't think we ought to say anything specific about the budget in the address—do you—on Wednesday?

SORENSEN: No, no.

MOYERS: Here he comes.

LBJ: [picks up telephone] Yes, Ted.

SORENSEN: Hello, Mr. President.

LBJ: I apologize for being late in calling you, but I had this group—I just got Doug Dillon out of here—that's on the budget. . . . They're not going to give us the tax bill unless we get our budget down to a hundred billion. It's a question of whether you take a billion and a half out of your budget or eleven billion out of taxes. That's the way they put it to us and I guess we'll have to sweat 'em and see what we can do. . . . Byrd's just not going to . . . report any bill unless somebody gives him assurance it's not going over a hundred billion. And he's still going to be against the tax bill. But he'll let the others like Talmadge[1] and Ribicoff and our beloved friend, Mr. Morton,[2] vote to report it if we get him that kind of assurance. . . . They've got a half-billion gimmick so it gets down to 101 pretty quick. . . . They think McNamara can squeeze two or three hundred billion more out of his. So it gets it down to a hundred billion, eight hundred million, they think, without endangering any of the programs that are in there. . . . They think that a hundred-billion budget is going to be awful bad, and I do too. But I don't think a hundred billion with the tax bill is as bad as a hundred and two without one.

SORENSEN: . . . I'm not convinced that *is* the choice.

LBJ: . . . We've been working on it since January.[3] What can we do? . . .

SORENSEN: You have to bear in mind the fact that the fellows who told you that happen to be giving you a fact which justifies the conclusion with which they sympathize. I'd like to check with Larry.[4]

LBJ: I think that's right. . . . How you coming along on the stuff they sent you? Any of it any good?

SORENSEN: One of the reasons I called you earlier was to ask you if you'd had a chance to read it.

LBJ: Yes, I read Galbraith's and I rather liked it. I agree with everything he said. I think maybe that we ought to add two or three little things to it. . . . I think we ought to have a sentence on being frugal and thrifty and at least talk like we're going to watch expenditures[5]. . . . I'd like to have a little more on the "hate"

[1]Democratic Senator Herman Talmadge of Georgia.

[2]Senator Thruston Morton of Kentucky, whose partisan attacks when he was Republican National Chairman have earned him the facetious sobriquet from Johnson "our beloved friend."

[3]Johnson here alludes to Kennedy's ten-month failure to get a tax bill.

[4]O'Brien.

[5]Appealing to the liberal Sorensen, who wants more social spending, Johnson implies that his talk about thrift and frugality is just talk.

stuff.[1] . . . I don't know whether we ought to ask for civil rights and taxes with any given date. I think we just ought to urge the Congress to pass them. I think if we have a given date, we're going to fall on our face. I think they'll say the Kennedy program was defeated and next Johnson is defeated and then, since we've repudiated him, let's don't take it up anymore. Don't you see what I mean?

SORENSEN: Yeah.

LBJ: I want to keep it alive, and Dillon says there's no way in the world they can get a tax bill before January 10th. . . .

SORENSEN: . . . I think before you decide on this budget you should decide on which comes first—taxation or civil rights. . . . You weren't at our last leadership breakfast.[2]

LBJ: That's right.

SORENSEN: And, actually, we tentatively decided then to move civil rights before taxes.

LBJ: Well, Humphrey tells me that it's got to be done. . . . If you do, you won't have a tax bill for four months, my friend.

SORENSEN: . . . I think that it would probably be a good idea to take the whole thing and hear what the reasons are.

LBJ: . . . We'll just have to try to do that maybe Thanksgiving, if you haven't quit me completely by then. This is a mighty hard life. You didn't tell me it was this kind of job when you[3] made me Vice President.

SORENSEN: [chuckles] It *is* a hard life. It is going to get harder. On the other hand, I think you ought to think about going away for Thanksgiving.

LBJ: I'm afraid to. I don't have enough grasp of this, Ted.[4] I just—I haven't read one third of the stuff I need to read and I read until two o'clock in the morning. All these Ambassadors—I bet I saw twenty of them this afternoon. I mean, heads of state—de Gaulle and Pearson and all this crowd. Then they're running fifteen more in on me tomorrow. And then I've got this speech.

SORENSEN: If you go down to your ranch though you'll get a lot more reading done than you ever will here.

LBJ: Yeah, yeah, right, right, right.

SORENSEN: Well, anyway, you liked Galbraith.

LBJ: Yes sir, I did.

SORENSEN: Well, you see, I *didn't* [laughs sardonically], so, uh—

LBJ: [backpedaling fast:] I didn't think it was any ball of *fire*. I thought it was

---

[1] Johnson's desire to inveigh against "hate" in America owes to his earlier conversation, above, with Whitney Young.

[2] Democratic congressional leadership breakfast.

[3] Meaning John Kennedy and his people.

[4] Johnson here tries to score points with Sorensen by feigning a sense of inadequacy as President, implying that he modestly worries that he cannot measure up to Kennedy. He is making such an effort with the man who is now his subordinate because he wants Sorensen to do for his speeches what he did for Kennedy's and because he is so adamant that to preserve public confidence in him, he must keep the Kennedy team intact and satisfied.

something that you could *improve* on.[1] I thought it was a bunch of general statements. But I liked the compassion in it. I don't reject it as a philosophy. No, I read it about three minutes while the economic counselors were coming in here. Then they got me in a debate and I had to quit it. But I think a much better speech could be written. I'm expecting you to write a better one.

SORENSEN: [sensing victory] Ha-ha. All right. I'll give you another one and I'll give you Galbraith at the same time and you can take a look at the two of them.

LBJ: I'll see you in the morning. Thank you, my friend.

TUESDAY, NOVEMBER 26, 1963[2]

HUBERT HUMPHREY
Senate Majority Whip, Democrat of Minnesota
1:11 P.M.

> HUMPHREY'S FLATTERY OF Johnson does not contradict the notion that he is campaigning for Vice President.

LBJ: —thoughts of our country that the Congress is in session at this time that the legislation concern is and that's all up to now.[3]

HUMPHREY: That's marvelous. That's marvelous.

LBJ: ... In light of what you said ... I still think ... that we ought to get that tax bill out of that committee, and we ought to get that civil rights bill passed through the House, and we ought to get started in the Senate, and we ought to just have a minimum of time.

HUMPHREY: I think, Mr. President, when we get a chance to sit with you, so that I can get some directions from you, I'll guarantee you we'll deliver it out there.

LBJ: God bless you.

HUMPHREY: And I think what you've said here is so very—just so appropriate. ... I know that you're going to say something, of course, in the area of foreign policy. You saw my memo about the Alliance?[4] ... Your words on this, Mr. President, mean more than anything. Your connection with ... López

---

[1] Johnson is obviously worried that he has offended Sorensen by praising the other speechwriter.
[2] On this day Johnson moved into the Oval Office.
[3] As with several other conversations in this volume, the tape recording of this exchange begins in mid-sentence.
[4] Kennedy's Alliance for Progress with Latin America.

Mateos of Mexico[1] and all mean just that you will pick up that cudgel for them. It's going to have a tremendous effect.

LBJ: I've got a meeting with them at four o'clock this afternoon, and they'll have a very strong statement that will be publicized all throughout the hemisphere.

HUMPHREY: Last night Walter Reuther[2] and your friend Hubert met with the Scandinavian people,[3] and he gave them all—

LBJ: [cuts him off] By the way, it reminds me. I've got to call the fellow from Denmark. What's—

HUMPHREY: Krag.[4]

LBJ: What's—Krag?

HUMPHREY: Krag.

LBJ: [trying to pronounce the name:] Krag, Krag. I want to see him today or tomorrow.

HUMPHREY: Yes. He's fine. And I want you to know that we met with the Norwegians, the Swedes, the Danes last night and Willy Brandt,[5] and Walter did a marvelous job for you. Really, he was just eloquent in terms of the commitment and reassurance that any of these people might need. You're—we're on the way.

WEDNESDAY, NOVEMBER 27, 1963

NELLIE CONNALLY
1:35 P.M.

> JOHNSON HAS JUST returned from his speech before a Joint Session of Congress[6] to the Oval Office, where he is lunching with Lady Bird and their daughters, Lynda Bird and Luci Baines. Mrs. Johnson dictated into her diary that LBJ's ascension to the Presidency had created something of a "gulf" be-

---

[1] Adolfo López Mateos was President of Mexico.

[2] United Auto Workers president.

[3] Humphrey, whose Minnesota was heavy with Scandinavian-Americans, joined Scandinavian officials who had attended the Kennedy funeral.

[4] Danish Prime Minister Jens Otto Krag.

[5] Mayor of West Berlin.

[6] "All I have I would have given gladly not to be standing here today. The greatest leader of our time has been struck down by the foulest deed of our time. . . . For thirty-two years, Capitol Hill has been my home. . . . In this moment of new resolve, I would say let us continue. . . . No memorial oration or eulogy could more eloquently honor President Kennedy's memory than the earliest possible passage of the civil rights bill for which he fought so long. . . . No act of ours could more fittingly continue the work of President Kennedy than the early passage of the tax bill for which he fought all this long year. . . . I profoundly hope that the tragedy and the torment of these terrible days will bind us together in new fellowship, making us one people in our hour of sorrow. So let us here highly resolve that John Fitzgerald Kennedy did not live—or die—in vain."

tween her and her husband: "If there was anything of a gulf between me and him, there never was anything of a gulf between Lynda Bird and him, so I wanted her to be there." [1] Thus she had called her elder daughter to Washington from the University of Texas, where she had been a student. LBJ calls Mrs. Connally, whose seventeen-year-old son, John III, had attended the Kennedy funeral as his father's representative.

LBJ: Hello, sweetheart! I'm so proud of your boy when he was up here and I'm sitting here in my office with Lady Bird, Luci, and Lynda, and we wanted to find out how our boy was getting along.

NELLIE CONNALLY: Wait a minute. I know this is irreverent to tell the President to hush, but I want to tell *you* I have *never* been prouder of anybody than I was of you a while ago. Can you hear me?

LBJ: I sure can. And I've always been mighty proud of you, darling. I appreciate it. I'd rather hear that from you than nearly anybody.

NELLIE CONNALLY: I was trying to decide whether to try to get in touch with you or not, but Lyndon, you just made me feel so wonderful.

LBJ: Well, you're a wonderful girl. How's my boy?

NELLIE CONNALLY: He's doing real well.

LBJ: Is he in much pain?

NELLIE CONNALLY: Considerable, but not too much. He's doing real good. He's not talking on the phone yet or anything 'cause as soon as he is he'll talk to you.

LBJ: Here's three little chubblies want to say a word to you.

NELLIE CONNALLY: All right. Don't you forget how proud we all were of you today.

LBJ: Give him a hug for me and tell him I'll call you every day or so. I want to keep up with him.

NELLIE CONNALLY: I will. You tend to your big business and we want to help you whenever we can.

LBJ: Sure have been proud of little Johnny. He's a chip off the old block—and the little blonde block too. He had all the grace and charm of Nellie and all the wisdom of John and the poise—he made the nicest statement to Mrs. Kennedy that any seventeen-year-old boy could have.

NELLIE CONNALLY: Oh, that makes me feel wonderful. You were wonderful to tend to him.

LBJ: He didn't need any tending to. He can be on his own, honey. You can turn him out to pasture.

NELLIE CONNALLY: Okay, I'll send him to *you*.

LBJ: Here's Lady Bird.

[1] Private Diary of Lady Bird Johnson, November 24, 1963, Johnson Library. Mrs. Johnson regularly dictated diary entries into what she called "my talking machine." Excerpts were published as *A White House Diary* (Holt, Rinehart and Winston) in 1970. Virtually all of the quotations from the diary in the current book, however, are from passages in it that have heretofore been unpublished.

LADY BIRD: Nellie, I *finally* got to see you on television.

NELLIE CONNALLY: Oh, well, that was a pitiful little appearance, wasn't it?

LADY BIRD: I was so glad I got to see you and you looked beautiful and so feminine and you looked so distraught and full of compassion for everybody that was hurt—well, you couldn't have been better.

NELLIE CONNALLY: I just finished listening to Lyndon and I just couldn't have been prouder of him. I know you are.

LADY BIRD: Yes ma'am. I sure am. And thank you.

NELLIE CONNALLY: Wonderful, wonderful. I know you're having hard times yourself right now.

LUCI JOHNSON: Hi, Aunt Nellie, this is Luci.

NELLIE CONNALLY: Hi, honey, how're you?

LUCI JOHNSON: Oh, I'm doing pretty well. I sure did enjoy getting to see Johnny.

NELLIE CONNALLY: You-all were mighty sweet to Johnny. He'll never, never forget it.

LUCI JOHNSON: He was real good to me. I sort of needed somebody 'cause my sister wasn't up here and he was the best brother anybody could want.

NELLIE CONNALLY: Aren't you dear to say so? You all looked mighty pretty today. I just finished watching you and listening to your daddy and they'd flash over to you pretty girls every now and then.

LUCI JOHNSON: Thank you very much and you take care of my Uncle John —and yourself and your children. And we love you.

NELLIE CONNALLY: Now you-all help your mother and daddy now.

LYNDA BIRD JOHNSON: This is Lynda. I just wanted to tell you that I love you too.

NELLIE CONNALLY: Thank you Lynda, you sweet, sweet thing. We're awful proud of your daddy and your mother and you and Luci.

LBJ: Nellie, did little Johnny get home with a lighter?[1]

NELLIE CONNALLY: Yes, he did.

LBJ: Call me, honey, if there's anything I can do in any way.

ADAM CLAYTON POWELL, JR.
Chairman, House Education and Labor Committee, Democrat of New York
2:22 P.M.

JOHNSON TOUCHES BASE with the flamboyant rapscallion Harlem Congressman, preacher, and civil rights leader. In 1960, Johnson's mentor, House Speaker Sam Rayburn of Texas, had quietly brokered a deal under which Powell

[1] Johnson loved to hand out ballpoint pens, cigarette lighters, and other gimcracks adorned with the seal of his office and/or his signature.

would support LBJ for President in exchange for ensuring that Powell would become Education and Labor Chairman.

LBJ: Did I do all right on civil rights?

POWELL: My friend, I just finished with CBS and it was unequivocally the finest, I said. It was more than I hoped for. And it was the finest that anyone could say. Forthright. You were really wonderful, at your best today. Absolutely superb. I don't know when you get the time to do it though.

LBJ: Well you-all were generous. You had thirty-four applauses in twenty-four minutes.[1]

POWELL: I know you had good ghostwriters but, brother, that was Lyndon Baines Johnson! That wasn't any ghostwriter. That speech was absolutely magnificent. . . . Now I want to get in touch with you about politics. It's not too early.

LBJ: Okay, we will.

POWELL: You know what I'm talking about.[2]

JOSEPH ALSOP
4:01 P.M.

LBJ: I want to tell you how grateful I am for that most beautiful, wonderful article.[3] . . . I'm not as frustrated as that Baptist preacher when he showed up one morning and they gave him a car. . . . He said, "I just want you all to know that I don't appreciate it, but I do deserve it." [laughs] But I *do* appreciate it and I *don't* deserve it!

ALSOP: . . . I sent a wire to Lady Bird. It moved me so, watching her there,[4] thinking about Phil[5] with a couple of my colleagues. Started out, you know, eager [for the speech] to be a failure and remained to applaud a triumphant success and I came back to lunch with Kay.[6] All I can say is we both had a darned good cry.

LBJ: [aside, to Moyers:] Don't let the Governor get away from me there now, Bill![7] [to Alsop:] Well, I had to restrain myself all during the period. . . . Jackie[8] came over and visited me this afternoon, told me about being at your house one

---

[1] After his speeches to Congress, Johnson loved to boast about how many times he had been applauded.
[2] Two months later, Powell sought a meeting with Johnson about the 1964 campaign—"what to do now in order to avoid snags later." One such snag was likely to result from Powell's volatile relationship with the Harlem boss J. Raymond Jones. (See Charles V. Hamilton, *Adam Clayton Powell, Jr.*, Atheneum, 1991, pp. 333–36, 423–25.)
[3] Alsop had written in his *Washington Post* column that Johnson was "an almost pure man of action, in the way that his predecessor never was," was acknowledged by congressional leaders as "the great master of their craft," and had "the qualities that are most wanted in a President."
[4] In the Gallery at the Joint Session during Johnson's speech.
[5] Katharine Graham's late husband, Philip, a Johnson friend and mentor, who had seen LBJ's potential for national leadership.
[6] Graham.
[7] Georgia Governor Carl Sanders was waiting to see him.
[8] Kennedy.

night at dinner and how what you and Phil had said about me and how touched she was, and how she remembered it and what the President had said to her several times about it. We just kind of had a real lovely session for about thirty minutes here. We're going to name Cape Canaveral Cape Kennedy[1] and—

ALSOP: Yes, Kay and I after your speech this morning—she lunched with me —and we both sort of had a ridiculous cry because Phil wasn't there to see how right he'd been.

LBJ: Did you see what she sent me that he had written?

ALSOP: No, I didn't.

LBJ: We'll have to have you and Susan Mary[2] some night.

ALSOP: Your speech was a triumphant success, Lyndon.

LBJ: Was it?

ALSOP: And I have to tell you because I'm going to write it. I've never thought that speaking was your long suit. I've thought that acting was your long suit— action, not oratory. But it was everything that one hoped. . . . And good luck to you and let me come and see you.

LBJ: I sure will, sure will.

THURSDAY, NOVEMBER 28, 1963

JAMES EASTLAND

Chairman, Senate Judiciary Committee, Democrat of Mississippi
3:21 P.M.

NOW JOHNSON is swinging around to the idea of a presidential commission, suggested by Katzenbach and the *Washington Post*, that will hold
closed-door hearings into the Kennedy assassination. He believes that a commission may have the best chance to preempt other investigations that might
get out of control, exciting the public about Oswald's Cuban and Soviet ties.[3]

[1] At Johnson's suggestion, after Mrs. Kennedy asked him to do something to commemorate
JFK's support for the space program.
[2] Mrs. Alsop.
[3] On November 25, Katzenbach had written Moyers, "It is important that all of the facts
surrounding President Kennedy's assassination be made public in a way which will satisfy
people in the United States and abroad that all the facts have been told and that a statement to
this effect be made now. 1. The public must be satisfied that Oswald was the assassin, that he
did not have confederates who are still at large and that the evidence was such he would have
been convicted at trial. 2. Speculation about Oswald's motivation ought to be cut off, and we
should have some basis for rebutting that this was a Communist conspiracy or (as the Iron
Curtain press is saying) a right-wing conspiracy to blame it on the Communists" (Johnson
Library).

He calls Eastland to talk him out of holding separate Senate hearings on the assassination.

LBJ: Jim, on this investigation—this Dallas situation—what does your committee plan to do on it? . . .

EASTLAND: We plan to hold hearings and just make a record of what the proof is. That's all. Show that this man was the assassin. . . . We've had a great number of Senators that have come to us to request it, beginning with Morse.[1] . . . Now if you want it dropped, we'll drop it.

LBJ: I had this feeling—this is very confidential and I haven't proposed it to anybody and I don't know that I would—but we've got a pretty strong states' rights question here and I've had some hesitancy to start having a bunch of Congressional inquiries into violation of a state statute,[2] and it might—

EASTLAND: You see, we've got a bill in to make it a federal—[3]

LBJ: I know it, but you haven't got any law and it might set a precedent that you wouldn't want to have. I talked to some of the fellows about it day before yesterday. Russell[4] was down here for luncheon.

EASTLAND: Now, there's one of them that's urged it.

LBJ: Now my thought would be this, if we could do it—we might get two members from each body. You see, we're going to have three inquiries running as it is.

EASTLAND: Well, I wouldn't want that. That wouldn't do.

LBJ: And if we could have two Congressmen and two Senators and maybe a Justice of the Supreme Court take the FBI report and review it . . . I think it would—this is a very explosive thing and it could be a very dangerous thing for the country. And a little publicity could just fan the flames. What would you think about if we could work it out of getting somebody from the Court and somebody from the House and somebody from the Senate and have a real high-level judicial study of all the facts?

EASTLAND: Well, it would suit me all right. Now you'd have—there's going to be some opposition on the committee. . . .

LBJ: If it is all right with you, I'm not worried about your committee. I know what you can handle.

[1] Wayne Morse, Democrat of Oregon.
[2] Knowing that Eastland is a strong champion of states' rights, especially in blocking federal integration plans, Johnson uses this approach to derail the Senator's intentions on the Kennedy assassination.
[3] Eastland was considering a bill making an assassination attempt on a President or other high administration officials a federal offense.
[4] Senator Richard Russell, Democrat of Georgia.

FRIDAY, NOVEMBER 29, 1963

HALE BOGGS

Assistant House Majority Leader, Democratic Congressman of Louisiana
11:35 A.M.

BOGGS: You were magnificent last night.[1] We sat down—Lindy[2] and I, and a few of our warm friends—and just cried. God, what a job you've done and you were utterly magnificent.

LBJ: You're mighty wonderful. Bird wants Lindy to help her on a good many things. So tell her to be as charitable with my little girl as she can because she's got to be careful who she asks to help.

BOGGS: Don't worry. She's got a flock of letters and things she's working on right now.[3]

EVERETT DIRKSEN

11:40 A.M.

LBJ: I want to talk to you and Charlie[4] in the next day or two about how in the world we're going to get some little action between now and the time we go home. If we don't, why, we're going to get a bad press.

DIRKSEN: Yeah.

LBJ: . . . Now Harry Byrd is very interested in seeing what this budget'll be before he reports this tax bill out. . . . I've already done everything that I humanly can to keep that within bounds. . . . Everett . . . we can pass the tax bill in a week. . . . They've got the MacGregor Burnses and the rest of them writing about the Congress.[5] . . . There is some merit to some of the things they're saying. And my life is the Hill, as I said the other day,[6] but I do think that if we could, we ought to show some evidence of progress. And you be thinking about how you can help us get that tax bill out. . . . Every businessman I've talked to since I've been in here—from the tops on down . . . says every one of them are waiting to see whether they're really going to pass one. . . . That market went up the other day[7] because they thought that we were going to be stable in business,

---

[1] Boggs refers to Johnson's Thanksgiving evening television speech from the Oval Office.
[2] Mrs. Boggs.
[3] Mrs. Boggs was already working at the Johnson house to help Mrs. Johnson with her avalanche of mail.
[4] Congressman Charles Halleck of Indiana, the Republican House Minority Leader.
[5] James MacGregor Burns had decried what he called "the deadlock of democracy" on Capitol Hill in an influential book of the same name (Prentice-Hall, 1963).
[6] At the Joint Session.
[7] When the stock market opened after the Kennedy funeral, it made the greatest advance on record. This was widely ascribed to the smoothness with which Johnson had taken over the reins of government.

because they think we're going to be frugal. But you've got to help me, my friend.

DIRKSEN: I'll be back there Monday and I'll talk to Harry.

LBJ: . . . If Congress is to function at all and can't pass a tax bill between January and January, why, we're in a hell of a shape. . . . They ought to pass it in a week. Then . . . every businessman in this country would have some confidence. And you'd probably pick up a bunch of Senate seats[1] because you're running the Senate like I ran it, you being pretty patriotic. And you cooperate. . . . We've got an obligation to the Congress. And we've just got to show that they can do something because we can't pass civil rights. We know that.[2]

ABE FORTAS
Washington Attorney and Partner, Arnold, Fortas & Porter
1:15 P.M.

JOHNSON'S MEMPHIS-BORN New Deal friend, intimate counselor, and troubleshooter had defended LBJ after the 1948 Democratic primary for Senator from Texas. When Johnson's opponent, Governor Coke Stevenson, charged that Johnson's fabled eighty-seven-vote margin was due to voting irregularities, a federal district court judge kept Johnson's name off the election ballot. Fortas argued his case before Justice Hugo Black, who ordered it restored. Now LBJ has asked Fortas to help persuade Chief Justice Earl Warren to chair his proposed presidential commission on the assassination.

LBJ: Progress on the Court?

FORTAS: Yes, sir, and I've been trying to handle this with the greatest tact, and so the way we worked it out is that Nick[3] and the Solicitor General[4] are going to call on the Chief Justice, see, instead of my doing it.

LBJ: We need it right quick, though, because they're already announcing it[5] in the House and Senate and all over the damned place. Like talking into a big microphone.

FORTAS: I know. . . .

LBJ: All right. How many men on the commission are we going to have?

FORTAS: If you had Dulles[6] and the general,[7] and two from the House, two from the Senate, then the Chief Justice—

[1] Johnson actually believes the exact opposite.
[2] Meaning that LBJ, at the moment, cannot summon the two thirds of the Senate necessary to invoke cloture and abort the inevitable Southern Democratic filibuster. As in the House, Johnson knows that he must recruit Senate Republicans to support cloture in order to get a civil rights bill, and he is already beginning to work on Dirksen, suggesting that despite the Illinois Senator's old reservations about civil rights, the time was now, Dirksen was going to be left behind, and that this was Dirksen's chance to establish a place for himself in the history books.
[3] Katzenbach.
[4] Archibald Cox, later the first Watergate Special Prosecutor.
[5] The prospect of a commission.
[6] Allen Dulles, former Director of Central Intelligence.
[7] Johnson wants a military man on the commission.

LBJ: Who do you think of as the general?

FORTAS: Only one I can think of—and I don't know many of those fellows—is Norstad.[1] . . . So I thought we'd probably have to take Eastland and the ranking minority member of the Judiciary Committee and similarly on the House. . . .

LBJ: Yeah, but Celler![2] God I hate to—Celler and Eastland! I hate to have them. What would you think about John McCloy[3] instead of General Norstad?

FORTAS: I think that'd be great. He's a wonderful man and a very dear friend of mine. I'm devoted to him.

LBJ: Let's think along that line now. Can we do this by executive order?

FORTAS: Yes, sir.

LBJ: Do we infringe upon the Congress in any way in doing it? Reflect on them in any way?

FORTAS: No, sir. I think on the contrary, you know all these editorials are saying this would be a shame to have all these investigations. I think the country will think the Congress had started acting wisely for a change. I think it would be a great thing, Mr. President, for them and for the country.

LBJ: Who would you think about in the Senate? . . . . I'd a whole lot rather have Russell than Eastland.[4]

FORTAS: Oh, I would too. Yes sir, for anything I'd rather have him. . . .

LBJ: I'd like to have Russell and Cooper[5] be my two.

FORTAS: That would be marvelous—simply marvelous. On the House side, we could get Hale Boggs.

LBJ: Well, he's talking all the goddamned time. He's a good fellow, but he's done announced it in the House.[6]

FORTAS: That's what I mean and I thought maybe this would help get it through.

LBJ: What do you have to get through?

FORTAS: I mean just the agreement that they'll do this in lieu of a Senate and House investigation.

LBJ: He's agreed to that.

FORTAS: That's wonderful.

LBJ: And McCormack has agreed to it, I would guess. What's his name—that

---

[1] General Lauris Norstad had been Supreme Commander of NATO from 1956 until January 1963.

[2] Emanuel Celler, Democrat of New York and Chairman, House Judiciary Committee.

[3] Roosevelt's Assistant Secretary of War, Truman's High Commissioner to Germany, and then head of the Chase Manhattan Bank was identified by the New Yorker writer Richard Rovere in a famous 1962 Esquire article as "the Chairman" of the American Establishment.

[4] Johnson is far closer to Russell than Eastland and sees him as a more large-minded, national figure.

[5] Senator John Sherman Cooper, Republican of Kentucky.

[6] At noon that day, Boggs had irked Johnson by telling the House that he could state "on the highest authority" that there would be a "very high-level" nonpartisan inquiry into the assassination to avert any "unseemly scramble for hearings."

fellow McCulloch—he's the ranking Republican.[1] He's pretty good. Or Jerry Ford.[2] I would think Jerry Ford would be good for the Republicans.

FORTAS: . . . How about little old Carl Albert?[3] . . .

LBJ: . . . It might be a slap at Hale if we did that. . . .

FORTAS: Yes sir, I wonder if we aren't stuck with Hale. . . . Now . . . the Chief Justice may not want to do this, but I'll call Nick immediately and see if he's got a report yet. He should have gone over there right away. I really gave him the hotfoot.

LBJ: They've already announced it. You call him back and see what the hell is happening.

FORTAS: Who's announced it?

LBJ: Hale Boggs got down, you see. I had to tell him what we were contemplating, so he got down on the floor of the House. Some jerk got up and said something, so he thought he had to show his knowledge.

FORTAS: Oh, Lord! I thought you meant he'd just announced the House was going to investigate.

LBJ: No, he announced there was going to be a high-level commission.

FORTAS: I see.

LBJ: . . . I guess we have to talk to these fellows before we announce we're going to appoint them, don't we?

FORTAS: Yes sir.

LBJ: All right. God . . . I think we ought to order them to do it and let them bellyache.

J. EDGAR HOOVER
1:40 P.M.

WHILE SOUNDING OUT the FBI Director about names for the Presidential commission, Johnson is sidetracked by fascination with what the FBI is discovering about the murder.

LBJ: Are you familiar with this proposed group that they're trying to put together on this study of your report and other things—two from the House, two from the Senate, somebody from the Court, a couple of outsiders?

HOOVER: No, I haven't heard of that. . . . I think it would be very, very bad to have a rash of investigations on this thing.

LBJ: Well, the only way we can stop them is probably to appoint a high-level one to evaluate your report and put somebody that's pretty good on it that I can

[1] William McCulloch of Ohio, ranking Republican on the House Judiciary Committee.
[2] Republican Congressman from Michigan, later Vice President and President of the United States.
[3] House Majority Leader, Democrat of Oklahoma.

select . . . and tell the House and the Senate not to go ahead . . . because they'll get a lot of television going and I thought it would be bad.

HOOVER: It would be a three-ring circus.

LBJ: What do you think about Allen Dulles?

HOOVER: I think he would be a good man.

LBJ: What do you think about John McCloy?

HOOVER: I'm not as enthusiastic about McCloy. . . . I'm not so certain as to the matter of the publicity that he might seek on it.

LBJ: What about General Norstad?

HOOVER: Good man.

LBJ: . . . I thought maybe I might try to get Boggs and Jerry Ford in the House, maybe try to get Dick Russell and maybe Cooper in the Senate.

HOOVER: Yes, I think so.

LBJ: . . . Me and you are just going to talk like brothers. . . . I thought Russell could kind of look after the general situation, see that the states and their relations—

HOOVER: Russell would be an excellent man.

LBJ: And I thought Cooper might look after the liberal group. . . . He's a pretty judicious fellow but he's a pretty liberal fellow. I wouldn't want Javits[1] or some of those on it.

HOOVER: No, no, no. Javits plays the front page a lot.

LBJ: Cooper is kind of border state. It's not the South and it's not the North.

HOOVER: That's right.

LBJ: Do you know Ford from Michigan?

HOOVER: I know of him, but I don't know him. I saw him on TV the other night for the first time and he handled himself well on that.

LBJ: You know Boggs?

HOOVER: Oh, yes, I know Boggs.

LBJ: He's kind of the author of the resolution. That's why. Now Walter tells me—Walter Jenkins[2]—that you've designated Deke[3] to work with us, like you did on the Hill, and I tell you I sure appreciate that. I didn't ask for it 'cause . . . I know you know how to run your business better than anybody else. . . . We consider him as high-class as you do. And it is a mighty gracious thing to do. And we'll be mighty happy. We salute you for knowing how to pick good men.

HOOVER: That's mighty nice of you, Mr. President, indeed. We hope to have this thing wrapped up today, but could be we probably won't get it before the

---

[1] Republican Senator Jacob Javits of New York.

[2] Walter Jenkins had been Johnson's close aide since 1939.

[3] Cartha "Deke" DeLoach of the FBI, whom Johnson has known and liked since 1958, when, at Hoover's request, DeLoach called on the Senate Majority Leader and asked him for a bill that would award the FBI Director his salary for life. LBJ was happy to accede. (See Cartha DeLoach, *Hoover's FBI*, Regnery, 1995, pp. 371–75.)

first of the week. This angle in Mexico is giving us a great deal of trouble because the story there is of this man Oswald getting $6,500 from the Cuban embassy and then coming back to this country with it. We're not able to prove that fact, but the information was that he was there on the 18th of September in Mexico City and we are able to prove conclusively he was in New Orleans that day. Now then they've changed the dates. The story came in changing the dates to the 28th of September and he was in Mexico City on the 28th. Now the Mexican police have again arrested this woman Durán,[1] who is a member of the Cuban embassy . . . and we're going to confront her with the original informant, who saw the money pass, so he says, and we're also going to put the lie detector test on him. . . .[2]

LBJ: Can you pay any attention to those lie detector tests?

HOOVER: . . . I wouldn't want to be a party to sending a man to the chair on a lie detector. . . . We've found many cases where we've used them—in a bank where there's been embezzlement—and a person will confess before the lie detector test is finished. They're more or less fearful of the fact that the lie detector test will show them guilty psychologically. . . . Of course, it is a misnomer to call it a lie detector because what it really is is the evaluation of the chart that is made by this machine and that evaluation is made by a human being. . . . On the other hand, if this Oswald had lived and had taken the lie detector test and it had shown definitely that he had done these various things together with the evidence that we very definitely have, it would just have added that much more strength to it. There is no question but that he is the man now—with the fingerprints and things we have. This fellow Rubenstein[3] down there—he has offered to take the lie detector test but his lawyer[4] has got to be, of course, consulted first and I doubt whether the lawyer will allow it. He's one of these criminal lawyers from the West Coast and somewhat like an Edward Bennett Williams[5] type—and almost as much of a shyster.

LBJ: [laughs] Have you got any relationship between the two[6] yet?

HOOVER: . . . No, at the present time we have not. There was a story down there—

LBJ: Was he ever in his bar and stuff like that?

HOOVER: There was a story that this fellow had been in this nightclub[7] that is a striptease joint, that he had. But that has not been able to be confirmed. Now

[1] Silvia Durán, a Mexican woman who was secretary to the Cuban consul in Mexico City, Eusebio Azcue.
[2] While in Mexico City in September, Oswald had talked to Silvia Durán about obtaining a Cuban visa. On November 26, John McCone had informed Bundy by memo that a Nicaraguan named Gilberto Alvarado had told the U.S. embassy in Mexico City that he had seen Oswald on September 18 discussing assassinaton and taking money from someone inside the Cuban embassy. McCone warned that this information was "as yet completely unevaluated." (National Archives).
[3] Jack Ruby, née Jacob Rubenstein, who murdered Oswald with a revolver as the accused assassin was being moved from the Dallas jail.
[4] Melvin Belli of San Francisco.
[5] Legendary Washington attorney and one of Hoover's many pet dislikes.
[6] Ruby and Oswald.
[7] Ruby's nightclub was called the Carousel Club.

this fellow Rubenstein is a very shady character, has a bad record—street brawler, fighter, and that sort of thing—and in the place in Dallas, if a fellow came in there and couldn't pay his bill completely, Rubenstein would beat the very devil out of him and throw him out of the place. . . . He didn't drink, didn't smoke, boasted about that. He is what I would put in a category of one of these "egomaniacs." Likes to be in the limelight. He knew all the police in that white-light[1] district . . . and he also let them come in, see the show, get food, liquor, and so forth. That's how, I think, he got into police headquarters. Because they accepted him as kind of a police character, hanging around police headquarters. . . . They never made any moves, as the pictures show, even when they saw him approaching this fellow and got up right to him and pressed his pistol against Oswald's stomach.[2] Neither of the police officers[3] on either side made any move to push him away or grab him. It wasn't until after the gun was fired that they then moved. . . . The Chief of Police[4] admits that he moved him in the morning as a convenience and at the request of motion-picture people, who wanted to have daylight. He should have moved him at night. . . . But so far as tying Rubenstein and Oswald together we haven't as yet done. So there have been a number of stories come in, we've tied Oswald into the Civil Liberties Union in New York, membership into that and, of course, this Cuban Fair Play Committee, which is pro-Castro,[5] and dominated by Communism and financed, to some extent, by the Castro government.

LBJ: How many shots were fired? Three?

HOOVER: Three.

LBJ: Any of them fired at me?[6]

HOOVER: No.

LBJ: All three at the President?

HOOVER: All three at the President and we have them. Two of the shots fired at the President were splintered but they had characteristics on them so that our ballistics expert was able to prove that they were fired by this gun. . . . The President—he was hit by the first and third. The second shot hit the Governor. The third shot is a complete bullet and that rolled out of the President's head. It tore a large part of the President's head off and, in trying to massage his heart at the hospital on the way to the hospital, they apparently loosened that and it fell off onto the stretcher.[7] And we recovered that. . . . And we have the gun here also.

LBJ: Were they aiming at the President?

HOOVER: They were aiming directly at the President. There is no question about that. This telescopic lens, which I've looked through—it brings a person as

[1] Hoover probably means "red-light."
[2] This refers to Ruby's shooting of Oswald on Sunday.
[3] Escorting Oswald.
[4] Jesse Curry, Dallas Chief of Police.
[5] Fidel Castro, the Communist leader of Cuba.
[6] Searching for evidence of conspiracy, Johnson knows that bullets fired at both the President and Vice President might mean a plot to bring down the government.
[7] Hoover's information here conflicts with the later official view that one bullet missed, another pierced Kennedy's throat and struck Connally, and a third fatally struck the President's skull—and that the bullet found was discovered on Connally's stretcher.

close to you as if they were sitting right beside you. And we also have tested the fact that you could fire those three shots . . . within three seconds. There had been some stories going around . . . that there must have been more than one man because no one man could fire those shots in the time that they were fired. . . .

LBJ: How did it happen they hit Connally?

HOOVER: Connally turned to the President when the first shot was fired and I think in that turning, it was where he got hit.

LBJ: If he hadn't turned, he probably wouldn't have got hit?

HOOVER: I think that is very likely.

LBJ: Would the President've got hit with the second one?

HOOVER: No, the President wasn't hit with the second one.

LBJ: I say, if Connally hadn't been in his way?[1]

HOOVER: Oh, yes, yes, the President would no doubt have been hit.

LBJ: He would have been hit three times.

HOOVER: He would have been hit three times from the fifth floor of that building where we found the gun[2] and the wrapping paper in which the gun was wrapped . . . and upon which we found the full fingerprints of this man Oswald. On that floor we found the three empty shells that had been fired and one shell that had not been fired. . . . He then threw the gun aside and came down. At the entrance of the building, he was stopped by a police officer and some manager in the building[3] told the police officer, "Well, he's all right. He works there. You needn't hold him." They let him go. . . . And then he got on a bus. . . . He went out to his home and got ahold of a jacket . . . and he came back downtown . . . and the police officer who was killed[4] stopped him, not knowing who he was and not knowing whether he was *the man,* but just on suspicion. And he fired, of course, and killed the police officer. Then he walked.

LBJ: You can prove that?

HOOVER: Oh, yes, oh, yes, we can prove that. Then he walked about another two blocks and went to the theater[5] and the woman at the theater window selling the tickets,[6] she was so suspicious the way he was acting, she said he was carrying a gun. . . . He went into the theater and she notified the police and the police and our man down there went in there and located this particular man. They had quite a struggle with him. He fought like a regular lion and he had to be subdued, of course, and was then brought out and . . . taken to the police headquarters. . . .

---

[1] Johnson misunderstands. Presuming that Hoover was correct in arguing that the gunman shot from behind and above, Connally, who sat in the jump seat in front of Kennedy, would not have been in the way.

[2] Like the three empty cartridge cases, Oswald's rifle was actually found on the Depository's sixth floor.

[3] Roy Truly.

[4] Tippit.

[5] The Texas Theater in Dallas, where Oswald was apprehended.

[6] Julia Postal.

LBJ: Well your conclusion is: (a) he's the one that did it; (b) the man he was after was the President; (c) he would have hit him three times, except the Governor turned.

HOOVER: I think that is correct.[1]

LBJ: (4) That there is no connection between he and Ruby that you can detect now. And (5) whether he was connected with the Cuban operation with money, you're trying to—

HOOVER: That's what we're trying to nail down now, because he was strongly pro-Castro, he was strongly anti-American, and he had been in correspondence, which we have, with the Soviet embassy here in Washington and with the American Civil Liberties Union and with this Committee for Fair Play to Cuba. . . . None of those letters, however, dealt with any indication of violence or contemplated assassination. They were dealing with the matter of a visa for his wife to go back to Russia. Now there is one angle to this thing that I'm hopeful to get some word on today. This woman, his wife, had been very hostile. She would not cooperate, speaks . . . Russian only. She did say to us yesterday down there that if we could give her assurance that she would be allowed to remain in this country, she might cooperate. I told our agents down there to give her that assurance . . . and I sent a Russian-speaking agent into Dallas last night to interview her. . . . Whether she knows anything or talks anything, I, of course, don't know and won't know till—

LBJ: Where did he work in the building?[2] On this same floor?

HOOVER: He had access on all floors.

LBJ: But where was his office?

HOOVER: He didn't have any particular office. . . . Orders came in for certain books and some books would be on the first floor, second floor, third floor, and so forth. . . . He was just a general packer of the requisitions that came in for school books for the Dallas schools there and therefore he had access . . . to the fifth floor and to the sixth floor. Usually most of the employees were down on a lower floor.

LBJ: Did anybody hear, did anybody see him on the fifth floor or—

HOOVER: Yes, he was seen on the fifth floor by one of the workmen there before the assassination took place. He was seen there so that—

LBJ: Did you get a picture of him shooting?

HOOVER: Oh, no. There was no picture taken of him shooting.

LBJ: Well what was this picture that that fellow sold for $25,000?[3]

HOOVER: That was a picture taken of the parade and showing Mrs. Kennedy climbing out of the back seat. You see, there was no Secret Service man standing on the back of the car. Usually the presidential car in the past has had steps on the back, next to the bumpers, and there's usually been one on either side standing on those steps. . . . Whether the President asked that that not be done,

[1] Since he presumes that the shots came from behind and above the late President, Hoover is still getting it wrong.
[2] The Texas School Book Depository, from which Kennedy was presumed to have been shot.
[3] Johnson may have seen a report that Abraham Zapruder, Dallas garment manufacturer, had sold his home movie of the assassination to Time-Life for $25,000. Orville Nix had sold his film of Mrs. Kennedy climbing onto the car's trunk to UPI for $5,000.

we don't know. And the bubble-top was not up.[1] But the bubble-top wasn't worth a damn anyway because it is made entirely of plastic and, much to my surprise, the Secret Service do not have any armored cars.

LBJ: Do you have a bulletproof car?

HOOVER: Oh, yes I do.

LBJ: You think I ought to have one?

HOOVER: I think you most certainly should have one. . . . I have one here. . . . I use it here for myself and if we have any raids to make or have to surround a place where anybody is hidden in, we use the bulletproof car on that because you can bulletproof the entire car, including the glass, but it means that the top has to remain up. . . . But I do think you ought to have a bulletproof car. . . . I understand that the Secret Service has had two cars with metal plates underneath the car to take care of a hand grenade or bomb that might be thrown out and rolled along the street. Of course, we don't do those things in this country. In Europe, that is the way they assassinate the heads of state. . . . They've been after General de Gaulle, you know, with that sort of thing. But in this country, all of our assassinations have been with guns. . . . I was very much surprised when I learned that this bubble-top thing was *not* bulletproof in any respect and that the plastic —the top to it was down. Of course, the President had insisted upon that so that he could stand up and wave to the crowd. Now it seems to me that the President ought to always be in a bulletproof car. It certainly would prevent anything like this ever happening again. . . . You could have a thousand Secret Service men on guard and still a sniper can snipe you from up in the window if you are exposed, like the President was. . . .

LBJ: You mean, if I ride around my ranch, I ought to be in a bulletproof car?

HOOVER: I would certainly think so, Mr. President. It seems to me that that car down at your ranch there, the little car that we rode around in when I was down there, I think that ought to be bulletproof. I think it ought to be done very quietly. There is a concern, I think, out in Cincinnati, where we have our cars bulletproofed. I think we've got four, one on the West Coast, one in New York, and one here and I think it can be done quietly, without any publicity being given to it or any pictures being taken of it if it's handled properly. But I think you ought to have it at the ranch there. It is perfectly easy for somebody to get onto the ranch.

LBJ: You think those entrances all ought to be guarded though, don't you?

HOOVER: Oh, I think by all means. . . . You've got to really almost be in the capacity of a so-called prisoner because without that security, anything can be done. Now we've gotten a lot of letters and phone calls over the last three or four or five days. We got one about this parade the other day that they were going to try to kill you then and I talked with the Attorney General about it. I was very much opposed to that marching from the White House.[2]

[1] The "bubble-top" was a clear plastic top that could have been attached to Kennedy's open Lincoln Continental. It was usually used to protect the passengers from rain while allowing onlookers a view of the President.
[2] Jacqueline and Robert Kennedy led a march from the White House to St. Matthew's Cathedral, where the funeral service was held. The press was told that by marching, LBJ had overruled the wishes of Secret Service agents by saying, "I'd rather give my life than be afraid to give it" (William Manchester, *The Death of a President*, p. 573).

LBJ: Well, the Secret Service told them not to, but the family felt otherwise.

HOOVER: That's what Bobby told me. . . . I was very much opposed to it because it was even worse than down there in Dallas—you know, walking down the center of the street.

LBJ: Yes, yes, that's right.

HOOVER: And somebody on the sidewalk could dash out. I noticed even on Pennsylvania Avenue—I viewed the procession coming back from the Capitol, and while they had police assigned along the curbstone looking at the crowd, when the parade came along, the police turned around and looked at the parade—

LBJ: [laughs]

HOOVER: —which was the worst thing to do. They also had a line of soldiers, but they were looking at the parade.

LBJ: Well, I'm going to take every precaution I can . . . and I wish you'd put down your thoughts on that a little bit, because you're more than the head of the Federal Bureau. As far as I'm concerned, you're my brother and personal friend. You have been for twenty-five to thirty years. . . . I know you don't want anything happening to your family.

HOOVER: Absolutely *not!*

LBJ: . . . I've got more confidence in your judgment than anybody in town.[1] So you just put down some of the things you think ought to happen and I won't involve you or quote you or get you in jurisdictional disputes or anything, but I'd like to at least advocate them as my opinion.

HOOVER: I'll be very glad to indeed. I certainly appreciate your confidence.

LBJ: Thank you, Edgar. Thank you.

RICHARD RUSSELL
Chairman, Senate Armed Services Committee, Democrat of Georgia
4:05 P.M.

CALLING RUSSELL at his home seat in Winder, Georgia, Johnson tries to persuade him to join the presidential commission on the assassination. As soon as he reached the Senate in 1949, LBJ had maneuvered himself into a place on the powerful Georgian's committee as the only way "to see Russell every day." Johnson had the shy bachelor home for Sunday meals and had his daughters call the old man "Uncle Dick."[2] Now Russell gracefully treats his old pupil with the deference due a President. Knowing how much Russell dislikes the Chief Justice, LBJ does not mention that he has asked Warren to come to the Oval

---

[1] In December 1968, Johnson told President-elect Richard Nixon, "If it hadn't been for Edgar Hoover, I couldn't have carried out my responsibilities as Commander-in-Chief. Period. Dick, you will come to depend on Edgar. He is a pillar of strength in a city of weak men" (Richard Nixon, *RN: The Memoirs of Richard Nixon*, Grosset & Dunlap, 1978, p. 358).

[2] See Doris Kearns, *Lyndon Johnson and the American Dream* (Harper, 1976), pp. 103–07, and Robert Dallek, *Lone Star Rising* (Oxford, 1991), pp. 378–80.

Office twenty-five minutes from now in an effort to overcome Warren's resistance to chairing the commission.

LBJ: I talked to the leadership on trying to have . . . about a seven-man board to evaluate Hoover's report. . . . I think it would be better than . . . having four or five going in the opposite direction.

RUSSELL: I agree with that, but I don't think that Hoover ought to make his report too soon.

LBJ: He's ready with it now and he wants to get it off just as quick as he can.

RUSSELL: Oh-oh.

LBJ: And he'll probably have it out today. At most, on Monday.

RUSSELL: Well, but he ain't going to publish the damned thing, is he?

LBJ: He's going to turn it over to this group and there's some things about it I can't talk about.

RUSSELL: Yeah, I understand that, but I think it be mighty well if that thing was kept quiet another week or ten days. I just do.

LBJ: . . . They're taking this Court of Inquiry in Texas and I think the results of that Court of Inquiry, Hoover's report, and all of them would go to this group. . . . Now here's who I'm going to try to get on it. . . . I don't think I can get any member of the Court. I'm going to try to get Allen Dulles. I'm going to try Senator Russell and Senator Cooper from the Senate—

RUSSELL: Oh no, no, no, get somebody else now.

LBJ: Now wait a minute, now I want to try to get—

RUSSELL: I haven't got time.

LBJ: —Jerry Ford. It is not going to take much time but we've got to get a states' rights man in there[1] and somebody that the country has confidence in. And I'm going to have Boggs in. . . . I think that Ford and Boggs would be pretty good. They're both pretty young men.

RUSSELL: They're both solid citizens.

LBJ: And I think that Cooper as a Republican and you're a good states rights' man. I think we might get John McCloy . . . and maybe somebody from the Court. . . . Who would be the best then if I didn't get the Chief?

RUSSELL: I know you wouldn't want Clark hardly.[2]

LBJ: . . . No, I can't have a Texan.

. . . .

RUSSELL: Really, Mr. President, unless you really think it would be of some benefit, it would really save my life.[3] I declare I don't want to serve.

LBJ: I know you don't want to do anything, but I want you to. And I think that this is important enough and you'll see why. Now, the next thing: I know how you feel about this CIA, but they're worried about having to go into a lot of this

[1] Johnson resorts to the same approach he had used with Eastland.
[2] Supreme Court Justice Tom Clark, an old Texas friend of Johnson's.
[3] Russell suffers from emphysema.

stuff with the Foreign Relations Committee. How much of a problem would it give you to just quietly let Fulbright and Hickenlooper come into your CIA committee?[1]

RUSSELL: As long as it is confined to those two, it wouldn't present any problem at all.

LBJ: That's all we make it now.

RUSSELL: ... Some of those fellows have got no business there ... and we've had a splendid record. ... I've even kept Margaret Chase Smith[2] off that committee, even though I've got a lot of faith in her.

· · · ·

LBJ: I had a nice visit with your Governor[3] and told him—

RUSSELL: Yes, you didn't tell me you'd invited him up here.[4]

LBJ: I didn't invite him up here.

RUSSELL: Well, how did he happen to get ahold of you?

LBJ: ... I told him that you said he was going to have lunch with you and to get ahold of him and tell him I wanted to see him before going back. Hell, I hadn't invited him up here. Never heard of it.

RUSSELL: Oh, I saw where he was in the box there with Lady Bird.[5]

LBJ: Oh well, they—they heard that he was coming, you see, when you told me that afternoon that he was coming and so they wanted some Southerner, some outstanding Southerner[6]—

RUSSELL: ... I just was surprised you didn't say something about it.

LBJ: No, I didn't know at the time I'd seen you that he was invited. See, Bird got up the list for the folks and I guess we got—

RUSSELL: Well, you couldn't have done better. He's an awful nice young fellow.

LBJ: I just told him how much I loved Georgia and he told the press that his grandpappy came from there. [laughs]

RUSSELL: Yes, well, he's a good boy.

LBJ: Well, Georgia is a good state. That's what I like about it.

RUSSELL: Yes, it *is* a good state, Mr. President. See if you can get someone else.[7]

---

[1] J. William Fulbright of Arkansas was the Chairman of the Senate Foreign Relations Committee, Bourke Hickenlooper of Iowa its ranking member. In those days before the House and Senate established permanent committees on intelligence, high CIA officials would periodically consult quietly with Russell and the ranking Republican on his Senate Armed Services Committee.
[2] Republican Senator from Maine.
[3] Carl Sanders. (See Joseph Alsop conversation, November 27, 1963, above.)
[4] Russell is offended that Johnson had not checked with him before inviting the Governor of his state.
[5] At the address to the Joint Session. Russell is trying to catch Johnson in a fib.
[6] Johnson is getting himself in deeper here.
[7] Rather than Russell for the commission.

LBJ: If I can, I will. But I'm not gonna. This country has a lot of confidence in you and if I had it my way, you'd be in my place and I'd trade with you.

RUSSELL: No, no, that would never do.

LBJ: Well, it would too. The country would be in a hell of a lot better shape.

RUSSELL: You're going to run it the next nine years.[1] I'll be dead in another two or three years.

LBJ: You get your rest. I don't want to bother you anymore, but I'm going to have to be calling you every once in a while.

RUSSELL: Well, you know, I'm always available.

. . . .

RUSSELL: Now you're going to let the Attorney General nominate someone, aren't you?

LBJ: No. Uh-uh.

RUSSELL: Well, you going to have Hoover on there?

LBJ: No, it is his report.

RUSSELL: Oh, that's right, that's right. It wouldn't do. . . . Let me see, if I think of a judge in the next thirty or forty minutes. . . .

LBJ: . . . What do you think about a Justice sitting on it? . . . You don't have a President assassinated but every fifty years.

RUSSELL: They put them on the Pearl Harbor inquiry, you know.

LBJ: I know. That's why he's against it now.[2]

RUSSELL: Afraid it[3] might get into the courts?

LBJ: I guess so, I don't know.

RUSSELL: That's probably the theory of it. . . .

LBJ: Give me the arguments why they ought to.

RUSSELL: The only argument about it is that, of course, in a matter of this magnitude . . . the American people would feel reassured to have a member of the highest Court. . . . If you would have some top-flight state Supreme Court Chief Justice—but they're not known all over the country. . . . This thing in television and radio has narrowed the group of celebrities. I don't know. You've got some smart boys there around you who can give you the name of some outstanding Circuit Court judge.

LBJ: Okay. You be thinking.

[1] Under the Twenty-second Amendment, Johnson was indeed eligible to run twice for President and serve nine years.
[2] This refers to Chief Justice Warren's refusal of the Katzenbach-Cox plea to chair the commission.
[3] The prosecution of Ruby and other aspects of the legal process connected with the assassination.

JOHN McCORMACK
4:55 P.M.

WITH AN EMOTIONAL APPEAL, Johnson has just persuaded Chief Justice Warren to chair what will now be called the Warren Commission. Now he asks the Speaker of the House to help clear the way on Capitol Hill.

LBJ: We don't want to be testifying, and some fellow comes up from Dallas and says, "I think Khrushchev planned this whole thing and he got our President assassinated."[1] . . . You can see what that'll lead us to, right quick. . . . You take care of the House of Representatives for me.

McCORMACK: How am I going to take care of them?

LBJ: Just keep them from investigating!

McCORMACK: Oh that. I've been doing it now. Listen, outside, I had Otto Passman in here.[2] . . . I want to call him in and would like for you to say hello to him.

LBJ: Okay, you betcha. I've got a Pakistan Ambassador waiting on me since four forty-five, but put him on.

McCORMACK: [calls to Passman:] Otto! Otto! Hurry up! The President is here! Mr. President, here's Otto. . . .

PASSMAN: Mr. President, how are you? God bless you and remember that I will cooperate in every way that I possibly can. . . .

LBJ: I wish I could trade jobs with you, Otto.

PASSMAN: I know that you do, but remember that my prayers are with you. . . . I'm not going to make it any harder than I have to. I was in here conferring with our great Speaker[3] a little while ago about foreign aid. It is not going to be an easy thing, but if and when—

LBJ: Otto, remember this. Remember this. This is just between you and me. I don't want you to repeat it to anyone, but you've been my friend. The one thing I've found out since I've been down here: in my relations with a hundred and ten other nations, about all I've got is a foreign aid bill to deal with them with and we've got more damned problems than you ever saw. I just finished talking to the Chairman of the Atomic Energy Committee and he said the only one who knew this was Kennedy and you're the only one that knows it now. And when he walked out, I wished I hadn't known it.[4]

[1] Nikita Khrushchev was the leader of the Soviet Union.
[2] Congressman Otto Passman, Democrat of Louisiana, nicknamed "Otto the Terrible," the chief roadblock to the administration's pending foreign aid bill.
[3] Passman clearly cares more about buttering up the Speaker than the new President.
[4] This presumably refers to Johnson's briefing on the effects of a nuclear war with the Soviet Union.

HUBERT HUMPHREY
6:20 P.M.

SENATOR PETER DOMINICK, Republican of Colorado, has speculated that Humphrey might run against Johnson for President in 1964. Johnson reassures himself by talking to Humphrey.

LBJ: Some damned Republican nominated you against me today and I said, "I didn't know we had them at our convention."

HUMPHREY: [laughs nervously]

LBJ: Fellow named Dominick. Do you know Dominick? [sardonically:] Is he a *pal* of yours? I've got to check.

HUMPHREY: Dominick nominated me today?

LBJ: Yes, he nominated you for President.

HUMPHREY: Well, wasn't that nice of him?

LBJ: He said that you were probably going to run, so you'd better answer it and tell them that.

HUMPHREY: By God, Mr. President, I'll tell you I'm not going to give you any worries. I am not a candidate, so you can sleep better tonight.

LBJ: All right, all right. [both laugh]

CHARLES HALLECK
House Minority Leader, Republican of Indiana
6:30 P.M.

GATHERING SUPPORT for the Warren Commission, Johnson locates the House Republican Leader on a Thanksgiving turkey-shooting trip in Indiana.

LBJ: What are you doing?

HALLECK: I'm going to kill one of these turkeys.

LBJ: [laughs] Well, you kill one for me and bring it back now and don't put any arsenic in it!

HALLECK: [laughs] Arsenic? My friend, I'd fix it up so that it would be real good for you.

LBJ: Charlie, I hate to bother you but . . . I've got to appoint a commission and issue an executive order tonight on investigation of the assassination of the President because this thing is getting pretty serious and our folks are worried about it. It's got some foreign complications—CIA and other things—and I'm going to try to get the Chief Justice to go on it.[1] He declined earlier in the day, but I think I'm going to try to get him to head it. . . .

HALLECK: Chief Justice Warren?

---

[1] Johnson conceals the fact that Warren has agreed.

LBJ: Yes.

HALLECK: I think that's a mistake. . . .

LBJ: I'd be glad to hear you, but I want to talk to you about—he thought it was a mistake till I told him everything we knew and we just can't have House and Senate and FBI and other people going around testifying that Khrushchev killed Kennedy or Castro killed him. We've got to have the facts, and you don't have a President assassinated once every fifty years. And this thing is so touchy from an international standpoint that every man we've got over there is concerned about it. . . .

HALLECK: I'll cooperate, my friend. I'll tell you one thing, Lyndon—Mr. President—I think that to call on Supreme Court guys to do jobs is kind of a mistake.

LBJ: It is on all these other things I agree with you on Pearl Harbor and I agree with you on the railroad strike.[1] But this is a question that could involve our losing thirty-nine million people.[2] This is a judicial question.

HALLECK: I, of course, don't want that to happen. Of course, I was a little disappointed in the speech the Chief Justice made.[3] I'll talk to you real plainly. He's jumped at the gun and, of course, I don't know whether the right wing was in this or not. You've been very discreet. You have mentioned the left *and* the right and I am for that.

GERALD FORD
Republican Congressman from Michigan
6:52 P.M.

LBJ: Happy Thanksgiving! Where are you?

FORD: I'm home, sir.

LBJ: You mean Michigan?

FORD: No, no, I'm here in Washington.[4]

LBJ: Thank God there's somebody in town! I was getting ready to tell Mac-Gregor Burns he's right about the Congress—they couldn't function.

[1] "The railroad strike" presumably refers to the presidential commissions appointed by Eisenhower and Kennedy to deal with labor's opposition to changes in outmoded railroad work rules, such as featherbedding. In March 1963, the Supreme Court ruled that railroads had the right to change such rules, and that railroad unions had the right to strike in protest.

[2] Johnson is arguing that if Americans conclude that Khrushchev or Castro was behind Kennedy's murder, they will demand a retalitory nuclear response against the Soviet Union, which could result in the loss of thirty-nine million Americans.

[3] At the Capitol Rotunda ceremonies the previous Sunday, the reformist Chief Justice had declared, "What moved some misguided wretch to do this horrible deed may never be known to us, but we do know that such acts are commonly stimulated by forces of hatred and malevolence, such as today are eating their way into the bloodstream of American life. What a price we pay for such fanaticism!" This was at the time that some American highway billboards said, "IMPEACH EARL WARREN." Conservatives like Halleck not only considered Warren's words a swipe against them but pointed out that the right could scarcely be held responsible for Oswald, an avowed Marxist.

[4] Ford and his family actually lived in the Washington suburb of Alexandria, Virginia.

FORD: I thought your speech was excellent the other day.

LBJ: Thank you, Jerry. Jerry, I've got something I want you to do for me.

FORD: We'll do the best we can, sir.

LBJ: I've got to have a top blue-ribbon presidential commission to investigate this assassination. I'm going to ask the Chief Justice to head it and then I'm going to ask John McCloy and Allen Dulles and I want it nonpartisan. . . . You forget what party you belong to and just serve as an American. . . . I want somebody on Appropriations who knows CIA over in your shop. . . . I'm going to ask Hale Boggs and you to serve from the House. . . .

FORD: You know very well I would be honored to do it and I'll do the very best I can, sir.

LBJ: You do that and keep me up-to-date and I'll be seeing you.

J. WILLIAM FULBRIGHT
Chairman, Senate Foreign Relations Committee, Democrat of Arkansas
7:11 P.M.

JOHNSON AND FULBRIGHT had been sufficiently close in the Senate that LBJ tried to get the newly elected Kennedy in 1960 to appoint the skeptical Arkansan Secretary of State. Here a relationship that in time will grow badly strained over Southeast Asia begins with warmth.

LBJ: I was talking to Dick[1] earlier today and I expressed the hope that he would invite you and Hickenlooper to sit in with him on his CIA committee for these briefings. . . . I think it is very important that you know all they tell them. And then I want to be talking to you from time to time and get your judgments on it.

FULBRIGHT: Sure, sure. Be glad to.

LBJ: All right. You just wait until he invites you because I told him to extend the invitation because it'd be better for him to do it than for me to be saying who served on his committee. . . .

FULBRIGHT: Good, good, good.

LBJ: How's Betty? Is she still living with you?

FULBRIGHT: Fine, and she and I both want to tell you we thought you were absolutely marvelous at the speech the other day really. 'Course I know you've been told it, but it was absolutely first-rate.

LBJ: Is she there?

FULBRIGHT: Yes.

LBJ: Let me talk to her.

FULBRIGHT: Oh, fine, she'd love to. Hold on a second. You really were wonderful, Lyndon. [apologizes for his familiarity:] I may slip now and then. Don't hold it against me.

[1] Russell.

LBJ: That's all right. I make it myself.

FULBRIGHT: Hope you don't mind until I get used to it.

LBJ: You know I'm like that little Jewish boy. He said, "How can I trust Ikey when I don't trust myself?" [both laugh] I can't blame you for something that I do myself. . . .

BETTY FULBRIGHT: Mr. President!

LBJ: Hi, Betty, how are you, honey?

BETTY FULBRIGHT: I just want to tell you you've never been so eloquent or delivered so beautifully in all your life. I was just sending Bird a note about it.

LBJ: Well, you're a mighty sweet girl and I just wanted to tell you how much I loved you and that old Bill Fulbright is a jealous man, but he just got in there first.

BETTY FULBRIGHT: I know he is.

LBJ: And I'll tell you, he's got a lot of men that are pretty envious of him.

BETTY FULBRIGHT: I hope he's just jealous as can be of you and . . . he has reason to be. You were wonderful.

LBJ: Well, I love you and if you run into any pretty things when you're shopping for Christmas, pick them up and send me a bill 'cause I'll have a lot of women I want to send things to. And men too, so I won't ask you to do all that you do for Dick Russell.

BETTY FULBRIGHT: I'm writing Bird. . . . I know she has lots of friends who she knows better . . . but . . . you tell her I would love to do anything I can any time.

LBJ: Thank you and she'll want you and she'll need you and she's so shy that she'll never tell you. But I'll tell you now she does. And she was asking me yesterday about would it be all right for her to ask a couple of friends to do some things that she just couldn't do because she doesn't get but ten thousand letters a week.

RICHARD RUSSELL
8:55 P.M.

> JUST AS HE HAS TOLD FORTAS, the President has simply announced that Russell will be on the Warren Commission. Learning that he has been outfoxed, Russell reacts with astonishment, indignation, then the weary resignation of one who has been dealing with LBJ for years.

LBJ: Dick, I hate to bother you again but I wanted you to know that I made that announcement.

RUSSELL: Announcement of what?

LBJ: Of this special commission.

RUSSELL: Oh, you have already?

LBJ: Yes. May I read it to you? [reads from statement]

RUSSELL: Now, Mr. President, I don't have to tell you of my devotion to you, but I just can't serve on that commission. I'm highly honored you'd think about me in connection with it. But I couldn't serve on it with Chief Justice Warren. I don't like that man. I don't have any confidence in him at all. . . . So you get John Stennis.[1]

LBJ: Dick, it has already been announced. And you can serve with anybody for the good of America. And this is a question that has a good many more ramifications than on the surface. And we've got to take this out of the arena where they're testifying that Khrushchev and Castro did this and did that and kicking us into a war that can kill forty million Americans in an hour. And you would put on your uniform in a minute. Now the reason I've asked Warren is because he is the Chief Justice of this country and we've got to have the highest judicial people we can have. The reason I ask you is because you have that same kind of temperament and you can do anything for your country. And don't go to giving me that kind of stuff about you can't serve with anybody. You can do anything.

RUSSELL: It is not only that. I just don't think the Chief Justice should have served on it.

LBJ: The Chief Justice ought to do anything he can to save America and right now we've got a very touchy thing. And you wait until you look at this evidence. . . . Now I'm not going to lead you wrong and you're not going to be an Old Dog Tray.[2]

RUSSELL: I know that but I have never—

LBJ: You've never turned your country down. This is not me. This is your country. . . . You're my man on that *commission* and you're going to *do* it! And don't tell me what you can do and what you *can't* because I can't *arrest* you and I'm not going to put the *FBI* on you. But you're *goddammed* sure going to *serve* —I'll tell you *that!* And A.W. Moursund is here and he wants to tell you how much all of us love you.[3] Wait a minute.

RUSSELL: Mr. President, you ought to have told me you were going to name me.

LBJ: I *told* you! I told you today I was going to name the Chief Justice when I called you.

RUSSELL: You did not. You talked about getting somebody from the Supreme Court. You didn't tell me you were going to name *him.*

LBJ: I told you! I told you I was going to name Warren. . . .

RUSSELL: Oh no! . . . I said Clark wouldn't do.

LBJ: No, that's right, and I've got to get the highest Justice I can get. He turned Bobby Kennedy down! Bobby and they talked to him and he just said he wouldn't

[1] Democratic Senator from Mississippi.
[2] A reference to Stephen Foster's ballad: "The morn of life is past / And evening comes at last. . . / Old Dog Tray's ever faithful. . . / He's gentle, he is kind; / I'll never, never find / A better friend than Old Dog Tray."
[3] A.W. Moursund is a Hill Country insurance man, ex-judge, and LBJ intimate with whom Johnson played dominoes, hunted, and dealt in cattle, ranching, real estate, and banking. Russell knows Moursund because just as LBJ made his family Russell's family, he had made his friends Russell's friends.

serve under any circumstances.[1] I called him down here and I spent an hour with him and I begged him as much as I'm begging you.[2] I just said, "Now here's the situation I want to tell you."

RUSSELL: You've never begged me. You've always told me.

LBJ: No, I haven't. No I haven't.

RUSSELL: Mr. President, please now—

LBJ: No! It is already done. It has been announced.

RUSSELL: You mean you've given that—

LBJ: Yes sir. I gave the announcement. It is already in the papers and you're on it and you're going to be my man on it and you just forget that. Now wait a minute. A.W. wants to say a word to you and I'll be back.

A.W. MOURSUND: Hello, Senator. We were just sitting here talking and he says, "I've got one man that's smarter than all the rest of them put together."

RUSSELL: You don't have to butter me up.

MOURSUND: I ain't buttering you up, Senator. You know I'm not that kind of a fellow. I just heard that and I wanted you to know it. Hell, he's depending on you. You know that.

RUSSELL: . . . A.W., I don't know when I've been as unhappy about a thing as I am this.

MOURSUND: I know, but you can take 'em. God Almighty, you've taken it for years and the hard ones and the tough ones, and you can take care of it and you can take care of yourself.

RUSSELL: [changes subject:] How are things down in Texas? Kill any deer down there?

MOURSUND: But you come see us. But don't say you can't do anything 'cause you're the best can-do man there is.

RUSSELL: Oh, no, oh, no.

LBJ: Dick? Now we're going into a lot of problems. . . . I saw Wilkins[3] today and had a long talk with him. Now these things are going to be developing[4] and I know you're going to have your reservations and your modesty.

RUSSELL: [disgusted:] Oh—

LBJ: Now, wait a minute! Wait a minute! Now your President's asking you to do these things and there are some things I want you in besides civil rights[5] and, by God, you're going to be in 'em, because I can't run this country by myself.

[1] Johnson's desire to show that he had succeeded where Robert Kennedy had failed has overcome his strict adherence to the truth: it was Katzenbach and Cox who had appealed in vain to Warren.
[2] Actually the President's meeting with Warren lasted twenty-five minutes (President's Daily Diary, Johnson Library).
[3] Roy Wilkins of the NAACP.
[4] The forthcoming battle over passage of the civil rights bill, which will throw Johnson and Russell into grand confrontation.
[5] In other words, despite their differences on civil rights, LBJ intends to consult Russell on presidential business as no other President ever has.

RUSSELL: You know damned well my future is behind me, and that is not entering into it at all.

LBJ: Your future is your country and you're going to do everything you can to serve America.

RUSSELL: I just can't do it. I haven't got the time.

LBJ: All right, we'll just make the time.

RUSSELL: With all my Georgia items in there.

LBJ: Well, we'll just make the time. There's not going to be any time, to begin with. All you're going to do is evaluate the Hoover report he has already made.

RUSSELL: I don't think they'll move that fast on it.[1]

LBJ: Okay, well then, we won't move any faster than you want to move. . . . The Secretary of State came over here this afternoon. He's deeply concerned, Dick, about the idea that they're spreading throughout the Communist world that Khrushchev killed Kennedy. Now he didn't. He didn't have a damned thing to do with it.

RUSSELL: I don't think he did directly. I know Khrushchev didn't because he thought he'd get along better with Kennedy.[2]

LBJ: All right, but we've—

RUSSELL: I wouldn't be surprised if Castro had.

LBJ: All right then, okay. That's what we want to know. And people have got confidence in you and you can be just surprised or not surprised. They want to know what you think. . . .

RUSSELL: You're taking advantage of me. . . .

LBJ: No, no, no. . . . I'm going to take a hell of a lot of advantage of you, my friend, 'cause you made me and I know it and I don't ever forget. And I'll be going to be taking advantage of you a good deal. But you're going to serve your country and do what is right and if you can't do it, you get that damned little Bobby[3] up there and let him twist your tail and put a cocklebur under it. Where is he?

RUSSELL: I don't know. He's in Atlanta tonight.

LBJ: Well, you just tell him to get ready because I'm going to need him and you just tell him that.

RUSSELL: I saw he and Vandiver[4] this afternoon for about thirty minutes. They came by here.

LBJ: Just tell either one of them that I just would like to use them anyplace because I'm a Russell protégé and I don't forget my friends and I want you to stand up and be counted and I don't want to beg you, by God, to serve on these things. . . .

RUSSELL: I know, but this is a sort of rough one.

---

[1] Russell proved to be right.
[2] Russell means better with Kennedy than Johnson.
[3] Russell's nephew Robert Russell.
[4] Former Georgia Governor Ernest Vandiver, husband of Russell's niece.

LBJ: No, it is not rough. What is rough about this? . . . .They had a full-scale investigation going, Dick, with the TV up there. They had the House Un-American Activities Committee in it.

RUSSELL: . . . They shouldn't have done it.

LBJ: Of course, but how do I stop it? How do I stop it, Dick? Now don't tell me that I've worked all day and done wrong.

RUSSELL: I didn't say you'd done wrong. I just said . . . it could have been stopped some other way. . . .

LBJ: What do you think I've done wrong now by appointing you on a commission?

RUSSELL: Well, I just don't like Warren.

LBJ: Of course, you don't like Warren, but you'll like him before it is over with.

RUSSELL: I haven't got any confidence in him.

LBJ: Well, you can *give* him some confidence. Goddamn it! Associate with him now. . . . I'm not afraid to put your intelligence against Warren's. Now by God, I want a *man* on that commission and I've got one!

RUSSELL: I don't know about the intelligence, of course, and I feel like I'm being kidded, but if you think—

LBJ: Well, if you think—now Dick, do you think I'd kid you?

RUSSELL: If it is for the good of the country, you know damned well I'll do it and I'll do it for you, for that matter. . . .

LBJ: Dick, do you remember when you met me at the Carlton Hotel in 1952? When we had breakfast there one morning?[1]

RUSSELL: Yes, I think I do.

LBJ: All right. Do you think I'm kidding you?

RUSSELL: No, I don't think you're kidding me. [laughs] But I think—well, I'm not going to say any more, Mr. President. I'm at your command and I'll do anything you want me to do.

LBJ: You damned sure going to be at my command! You're going to be at my command as long as I'm here.

RUSSELL: I do wish you be a little more deliberate and considerate next time about it but . . . if you've done this, I'm going to . . . go through with it and say I think it is a wonderful idea.

LBJ: . . . I'm going to have you on a good goddamned many things that I have to decide. . . . I've served under you and I don't give a damn if you have to serve with a Republican, if you have to serve with a Communist, if you have to serve with a Negro, or if you have to serve with a thug—or if you have to serve with A.W. Moursund.

[1]This may refer to a secret arrangement Johnson was said to have made with Russell in 1952, when the Georgia Senator made a quixotic campaign for the Democratic presidential nomination: if Russell failed, he would use his influence to get Johnson onto the ticket as Vice President. (See Robert Dallek, *Lone Star Rising*, pp. 417–18, and Ronnie Dugger, *The Politician*, Norton, 1982, pp. 373–75.)

RUSSELL: I can serve with a Communist and I can serve with a Negro. I can serve with a Chinaman.

LBJ: Well, you may have to serve with A.W. Moursund!

RUSSELL: And if I can serve with A.W. Moursund, I would say, "Mr. Chairman, I am pleased to serve with you, Judge Moursund." But—we won't discuss it any further Mr. President. I'll serve.

LBJ: Okay, Dick, and give Bobby my love and tell him he'd better get ready to give up that fruitful law practice he's got.

RUSSELL: He's been appointed to the Georgia Court of Appeals. Now, you see, I got him on there. He's making as much money as I am.

LBJ: What about Vandiver?

RUSSELL: Well, he's running for Governor next time and he'll be elected.[1]

LBJ: Who in the hell is going to help me besides you?

RUSSELL: Those boys will help you if you need them.

LBJ: Well, I need 'em.

RUSSELL: Goddamn it, they're harder for you than I was—remember?

LBJ: No, nobody ever has been more to me than you have, Dick—except my mother.

RUSSELL: [laughs scoffingly]

LBJ: No, no, that's true. I've bothered you more and made you spend more hours with me telling me what's right and wrong than anybody except my mother.

RUSSELL: You've made me do more things I didn't want to do.

LBJ: No, no, I never made you do anything that was wrong. I never—

RUSSELL: I didn't say "wrong." I said more things I didn't want to do. But Bobby[2] and Ernie[3] are two of the most loyal friends you've got on earth.

LBJ: I know that.

RUSSELL: They both called me up and said, "You've just got to do whatever Mr. Johnson says."

LBJ: No . . . I just want to counsel with you and I just want your judgment and your wisdom.

RUSSELL: For whatever it's worth, you've got it.

LBJ: I'm going to have it 'cause I haven't got any daddy and you're going to be it. And don't just forget that.

RUSSELL: Mr. President, you know—I think you know me.

LBJ: I do. I do. I know you're for your country and—period. Now you just get ready to do this and you're my man on there.

RUSSELL: If you hadn't announced it, I would absolutely be—

---

[1] He was not.
[2] Russell.
[3] Vandiver.

LBJ: No you wouldn't. No, you wouldn't.

RUSSELL: Yes, I would. Yes, I would.

LBJ: . . . Warren told me he wouldn't do it under any circumstances. Didn't think a Supreme Court Justice ought to go on. . . . He said a man that criticized this fellow that went on the Nuremberg trial—Jackson.[1] . . . And I said, "Let me read you one report." And I just picked up one report and read it to him, and I said, "Okay, now, forty million Americans involved here."

RUSSELL: I may be wholly wrong. But I think Mr. Warren would serve on anything that would give him any publicity.

LBJ: You want me to tell you the truth? You know what happened? Bobby and them went up to see him today and he turned them down cold and said, "No." Two hours later, I called him and ordered him down here and he didn't want to come. I insisted he come. He came down here and told me no—twice. And I just pulled out what Hoover told me about a little incident in Mexico City[2] and I said, "Now I don't want Mr. Khrushchev to be told tomorrow—and be testifying before a camera that he killed this fellow and that Castro killed him and all I want you to do is look at the facts and bring in any other facts you want in here and determine who killed the President. And I think you put on your uniform in World War I, fat as you are,[3] and would do anything you could to save one American life. And I'm surprised that you, the Chief Justice of the United States, would turn me down." And he started crying[4] and he said, "I won't turn you down. I'll just do whatever you say." But he turned the Attorney General down!

RUSSELL: You ought not to be so persuasive.

LBJ: I think I ought to.

RUSSELL: I think you did wrong in getting Warren, and I know damned well you did wrong in getting me. But we'll both do the best we can.

LBJ: I think that's what you'll do. That's the kind of Americans both of you are. Good night.[5]

---

[1] As a Supreme Court Justice, Robert Jackson served as chief counsel for the prosecution in the international military tribunal that tried leading Nazis at Nuremberg after World War II. Warren was skeptical of Jackson's decision to accept the dual role.

[2] Oswald's visit to the Soviet embassy and the Cuban consulate.

[3] Warren was of robust physique.

[4] So Johnson claims, anyway.

[5] See the Appendix of this book for release of the Warren Commission report.

SATURDAY, NOVEMBER 30, 1963

DONALD COOK[1]
President, American Electric Power Company
1:16 P.M.

> LBJ NOW FOCUSES on the deepening problem of Vietnam. Four weeks earlier, the South Vietnamese President, Ngo Dinh Diem, and his brother and first adviser, Ngo Dinh Nhu, were assassinated in a coup to which John Kennedy had acquiesced. On Sunday, November 24, LBJ met in his vice presidential office with the U.S. Ambassador to Saigon, Henry Cabot Lodge, as well as Secretary of State Dean Rusk, McNamara, Bundy, McCone, and other officials. During the meeting, Johnson said he approached the problem of Vietnam with considerable misgivings. Strong voices in Congress, he said, felt that the United States should get out of Vietnam. He wondered whether they had taken the right course in toppling Diem and complained that America tried too hard to shape other countries in its own image. The main job now, he said, was to help the South Vietnamese resist those using force against them. After the meeting, Johnson insisted that he was not going to be the President who saw Southeast Asia go the way China did.[2]

LBJ: You're already out spending all that money you fat cats make up there? They tell me you were down at Saks Fifth Avenue.

COOK: I had a youngster in town for the Thanksgiving holidays and I had to take him down and keep him from being naked. . . .

LBJ: . . . Well, I've got a sixteen-year-old girl and she's very unhappy about the Secret Service accompanying her on all of her dates. [chuckles]

• • • •

LBJ: I appreciate your memo[3] very much, and thought it was excellent and I just want to philosophize with you a little bit. . . . I don't want to mess up any of your business, but you try to figure out if you can come down Monday afternoon. . . . Maybe you can have dinner with us. . . . There's not anything, except I'm just lonesome for you.

COOK: . . . May I say something? . . . You've been a magnificent President. . . . Everybody else up here I've talked to says the same thing. . . .

LBJ: I want to be . . . and I want you to start looking for some good people for me because that's the great problem. . . . For instance, we got nobody to run the war in Vietnam for us. We need the ablest man that we've got, the toughest

[1] By now a New York utilities executive, Cook had served sporadically as Johnson's counsel —on a House Naval Affairs subcommittee studying World War II production, when the Senate Rules Committee investigated LBJ's disputed 1948 hairbreadth Senate victory over Coke Stevenson, and when Johnson's Preparedness Investigating Subcommittee investigated the conduct of the Korean War.
[2] Memorandum of conversation, November 24, 1963, and Tom Wicker oral history, Johnson Library.
[3] On the tax cut bill.

Chief of Mission you can have. Lodge[1] is just about as much an administrator as he is a utility magnate. He just—

COOK: He never had to do it.

LBJ: He never had to do it and doesn't know one damn thing about it. Just leaks to the press and keeps everybody fighting each other. We need an able, tough guy to go there as Chief of Mission. Now, that's not anything to be desired by anybody. But I don't imagine those eight, ten thousand boys out there[2] desire it either. But we've got to either get in or get out, or get off. And we need a damn tough *cookie* and somebody that can say, "Now, this is it"—and that's got enough judgment to realize he can't make Vietnam into an America *overnight.* 'Cause if they do, the other damn government will fail.[3] There's just some of the illustration. We need the ablest man you can get to operate Latin America. They're just coming in here and bumping them off one at a time. . . . And we've got Alliance for Progress, but it is being run by an alliance of misfits.[4]

JESSE KELLAM
General Manager, Texas Broadcasting Company
2:55 P.M.

>   IN TALKS with his intimate friend and adviser Kellam, whom Johnson has known since they were fellow students at Southwest Texas State Teachers College in the 1920s, as well as Waddy Bullion, A.W. Moursund, Donald Thomas, and other counselors, the President has discussed the problem of his business holdings. Warning that the broadcast holdings presented "potential conflicts of interest," Johnson's friend lawyer-lobbyist Clark Clifford has advised him to consider divesting himself of them. As Clifford later recalled, Johnson replied, "I'm not going to do that. I don't care what anyone says."[5]

---

[1] One reason that Kennedy had appointed Lodge, whom he had defeated for Senator from Massachusetts in 1952 and who then served as Eisenhower's U.N. Ambassador, was to acquire Republican cover for controversial decisions he might have to take—or failure—in Vietnam. Both JFK and LBJ disdained what they saw as Lodge's imperiousness and less than burning intelligence. They remembered how during the hard-fought 1960 campaign, when Lodge had run with Richard Nixon for Vice President, he had insisted on suspending the effort every afternoon for a nap. Johnson also resented Lodge's leading role in encouraging the coup against Diem, whom he had met and admired while touring Southeast Asia in 1961 at Kennedy's behest. (See, for example, Kenneth O'Donnell and David Powers, *"Johnny, We Hardly Knew Ye,"* Little, Brown, 1972, p. 16; Robert Kennedy 1967 oral history, Kennedy Library; and memorandum of Johnson's conversation with Lodge and others on Vietnam, November 24, 1963, Johnson Library.)

[2] Actually there were 15,500 American "advisers" in Vietnam at the end of 1963.

[3] The regime succeeding Diem was led by General Duong Van "Big" Minh. Johnson's complaint about those who wanted Vietnam made "into an America *overnight"* is a tacit criticism of President Kennedy's reform demands on Diem.

[4] Johnson felt that Kennedy had made a mistake in considering social reform so strongly while looking for allies in Latin America.

[5] See Clifford's 1991 memoir, *Counsel to the President* (with Richard Holbrooke, Random House, 1991), pp. 390–91. In her diary, Lady Bird describes a family business meeting on the day before Kennedy's funeral that included Abe and Carol Fortas and Johnson family business advisers Waddy Bullion, Don Thomas, and A.W. Moursund: "Isn't it odd to think that you have to set about planning how you're going to make a living when you've just . . . become President of the United States? But that's the way it was. We obviously had to separate

KELLAM: If there's anything we can do down here to lighten the load, we want to do it.

LBJ: Sure do.

KELLAM: But before we get on anything else . . . I just must tell you that your message to the Joint Session was as good as it could have been—both its content and delivery.

LBJ: Well, thank you.

KELLAM: On your Thanksgiving message, I thought they put a little bit too much oil on your hair because the light is above and it gives a reflection that isn't good, particularly on television. I think with virtually no oil at all on your hair, the effect is good.

LBJ: All right.

KELLAM: Now, your glasses I'm accustomed to and I think it lends a certain— oh, call it dignity. . . . But might I suggest that the best optometrist that you can get examine the possibility of less color in the rims because of the effect of color on the rims of the glasses on television appearances.

LBJ: The ones I've got are just plain flesh color. I've got some black ones but they always look so damn bad, I thought—

KELLAM: I don't know whether or not a rimless glasses would do it or not for television, but you might want to experiment with that.

LBJ: All right.[1]

. . . .

KELLAM: Larry Winship[2] from Boston has been down here the last two or three days. He's doing pretty much an in-depth study.[3] He's been out to A.W.'s[4] house. . . . He's friendly and we've been trying to be as helpful as possible to him.

LBJ: All right.

. . . .

KELLAM: On Scharnhorst,[5] I thought if it was all right, I'd let one or two hunt up there . . . during the balance of the season.

LBJ: All right. I wouldn't have many though 'cause I'm going to want to do some of that myself.

KELLAM: . . . One night—that'll be about all of it.

LBJ: All right.

---

ourselves from KTBC and say goodbye to a 22-year livelihood and love for a thirteen-month hitch [in the White House], for the good and sufficient reason that Lyndon is now in the position of appointing the members of the Federal Communications Commission, who have the power to license and regulate radio and TV stations. . . . The subject was how to put the stock of KTBC in trust—how to simply, quickly and severely cut off our ties with KTBC until such time as Lyndon emerged from a federal office" (November 24, 1963).

[1] Johnson did.
[2] Editor of the *Boston Globe*.
[3] Of Johnson's business holdings.
[4] Moursund.
[5] The 1,800-acre Scharnhorst Ranch, outside Johnson City, which was part of LBJ's barony.

. . . .

LBJ: How's Jake[1] coming?

KELLAM: It's been awfully quiet.

LBJ: You start a campaign today to see that every person, patriotically, in your organization and everyone you know goes and votes absentee right now 'cause we found out last time Bird missed a vote.

. . . .

KELLAM: Now, I am—can I talk pretty freely on this line?

LBJ: Yeah.

KELLAM: I saw Cliff[2] yesterday, and I'm taking care of him with fifteen hundred. Charlie, I've taken care of. Melvin—is that to be taken care of too the same way?

LBJ: I'd just wait and let's see.

KELLAM: All right, and then the balance of 'em—if there were any envelopes that Cliff gave me, I'm just holding 'em.

LBJ: That's right. That's right. I would just turn 'em back to 'em.

KELLAM: Just turn 'em back to the writers?

LBJ: Yeah.

KELLAM: All right, sir. I'll do that. And as I say, I've taken care of Charlie, taken care of Cliff, and I'll just hold up on the Winters. Those are the things that I've been anxious to chat with you on.[3]

. . . .

LBJ: We didn't have you come up here 'cause we thought it would be better for these trustees to operate independently, and they can meet and hire you.[4]

[1] Johnson's friend Democrat J.J. "Jake" Pickle was running in a special runoff election to succeed the newly appointed Federal District Judge Homer Thornberry as Congressman from LBJ's Tenth District in Texas. Supporters of Pickle's opponent, Jim Dobbs, a radio commentator backed by the Dallas radical rightist H.L. Hunt, had erected signs saying "Scratch Lyndon's Boy Jake."

[2] "Cliff" is presumably Clifton Carter, an LBJ political operative who had served on Johnson's vice presidential staff in Washington, then returned to manage Johnson's Austin office and prepare for the Kennedy-Johnson campaign in Texas in the fall of 1963. "Charlie" probably refers to Charles Boatner, a special assistant in Johnson's vice presidential office in Washington, whom LBJ soon moved to the Interior Department to keep an eye on Secretary Stewart Udall, of whom he was suspicious (Boatner oral history, Johnson Library). Melvin Winters was a Hill Country business and political associate of LBJ.

[3] This secretive, cryptic exchange between Johnson and Kellam, who died in 1977, may not be fully illuminated until scholars gain full access to Johnson's private financial records, and perhaps not even then. The context suggests that on LBJ's behalf, Kellam had been supplementing the salaries of Carter, Boatner, and Winters, all now dead. (Walter Jenkins notes in his Johnson Library oral history that "for a long time" Johnson paid Carter "out of his pocket personally.") The envelopes from Carter to which Kellam refers appear to have contained money (from whom, we do not know) that LBJ may have considered proper to accept while Vice President, but not as President. All of this took place under pre-Watergate campaign finance laws, which did little to regulate the raising, reporting, and spending of political money. (See also LBJ conversations with Clifton Carter of June 5 and 23, 1964.)

[4] To create at least the appearance of a blind trust, Johnson will have the trustees hire his business manager, whom he will continue to see throughout his presidency, to manage his holdings.

KELLAM: I'm in agreement a hundred percent with that. . . .

LBJ: All right. How's your business?[1]

KELLAM: It really went to hell, of course, this week. After Friday,[2] we carried no commercials from Friday shortly after noon till sign-off Monday, but we've been working like hell even during that period. . . . Most of these[3] have been pretty understanding. A few of them have said arbitrarily, "Give me credit." But we're going to go forward from there. I've gotten back into this Muzak thing, which is not on an even keel at all, and do something there.[4]

• • • •

LBJ: Jesse, run one of your little telephone Woody polls[5] on Jake and Dobbs. Get about a hundred calls to keep a secretary busy for about a day or so.

KELLAM: All right, sir.

LBJ: Get about four of them per outfit and be sure that about fifteen of them are out of east Austin.

KELLAM: All right, sir. . . . I talked to Morrell yesterday and Morrell says that . . . there was some conversation of some sort about Home Theatres going public and maybe buying Midwest Video.[6] He was talking in circles, as only Morrell can. As soon as Don[7] gets back, I want him to get on that. . . . I sure want to get on that first thing Monday.

LBJ: Bird wants to give up her option. I told her she's crazy.

KELLAM: Can't afford to give up that option. We might sell or transfer. I discussed that with Don and A.W. a little bit, but we don't want to give it up. Sure don't. I wouldn't mind selling it to A.W. and Melvin.[8] . . . But I sure don't want to give it up, sir.

LBJ: Okay.

---

[1] To distance himself from what he referred to as Mrs. Johnson's radio and television stations, Johnson as Congressman, Senator, and Vice President had publicly insisted that he was aloof from the family business. The following exchange, in which Kellam describes the commercial impact of the Kennedy assassination on the Johnson business, suggests curiosity.

[2] Of the Kennedy assassination.

[3] Customers.

[4] The LBJ Company, rechristened the Texas Broadcasting Company after Johnson entered the White House, owned the Muzak piped-in music franchise for Austin. Practicing what he preached, Johnson had installed Muzak speakers to blare music out from the trees at The Elms and at the LBJ Ranch.

[5] Woody is presumably a reference to Warren "Woody" Woodward, who served for many years as a Johnson political aide.

[6] Midwest Video Corporation of Little Rock, Arkansas, had established an Austin cable television firm, the Capital Cable Company. Thanks to the Austin City Council, much under the Johnson influence, the Texas Broadcasting Company held an option to buy 50 percent of Capital (which it later exercised). This was important to the Johnsons because Capital had the capability to compete with their Austin television station, KTBC, which had thenceforth enjoyed a monopoly. KTBC aired programs from all three national networks, omitting some and showing others at inconvenient times. Austin citizens complained that theirs was one of the few metropolitan television markets with only one station. Asked about this phenomenon, so lucrative for the Johnsons, one told a reporter, "I live in Lyndon's town" (*Newsday*, May 29, 1964). George Morrell was vice president of Capital Cable.

[7] Thomas.

[8] Moursund and Winters. In other words, a friendly party.

JOHN McCONE
Director of Central Intelligence
3:14 P.M.

> McCONE HAD BRIEFED LBJ that morning about Gilberto Alvarado, the Nicaraguan in Mexico City who had claimed to see Oswald taking money and speaking of assassination at the Cuban Embassy in September.[1]

McCONE: We got a phone call from Mexico City that this fellow Alvarado that I was telling you about this morning signed a statement that all the statements he'd made in connection with that matter have been false.

LBJ: [chuckles]

McCONE: . . . Apparently there's no substance in it at all. He explained that he had wanted to ingratiate himself to the United States interests in order to gain admission to the United States and to work with the security forces here. So we're sending down a whole series of questions to be sure this isn't misleading, but this is the opinion of our station[2] and, I guess, the FBI. . . . This looks to me like it probably washes that out entirely.

LBJ: Okay, my friend, thank you.

LUCIA JOHNSON ALEXANDER
Sister of Lyndon Johnson
3:16 P.M.

> JOHNSON HAD LAST SEEN his sister when he took her and her engineer husband, Birge, who lived in Fort Worth, to meet President Kennedy in his eighth-floor suite at the Hotel Texas in Fort Worth, two hours before the assassination. Kennedy had said, "We're going to carry two states next year if we don't carry any others—Massachusetts and Texas." These proved to be the last words JFK ever spoke to LBJ.

LBJ: Hi, my darling. . . . This is the first moment I've had to try to get anybody on the phone and I just wanted to tell you I was thinking of you.

ALEXANDER: Well, you *know* we've been thinking of you.

LBJ: I sure do. I wish you were here.

ALEXANDER: I don't know. I think I'd rather be in my place than yours.

LBJ: [laughs] I'd like to trade with you.

ALEXANDER: I went up to Johnson City and looked at the wallpaper.[3]

LBJ: Uh-huh. . . . It's going to cost a million dollars to rebuild that old $5,000 house, isn't it?

---

[1] See LBJ conversation with J. Edgar Hoover, November 29, 1963.
[2] The CIA station in Mexico City.
[3] Johnson's boyhood home was being re-created.

ALEXANDER: It looks that way. . . . I started to call A.W., but I didn't know where to go from here. . . .

LBJ: . . . He's in the office right now. . . . He and Don Thomas came up to work some of our private business things.

. . . .

ALEXANDER: [anxious:] Lyndon, what am I supposed to do when these news-paper people call?

LBJ: Oh, I'd just tell them as little as I could.

ALEXANDER: That's what I do, but if you don't say anything, they print that you didn't say anything. I just don't know what to do. . . . I'm afraid somebody's going to take a pot-shot at *me!*

LBJ: [laughs] I think I'd just tell them you-all have talked it over in the family and . . . you're not going to be conducting interviews because, just very frankly, you don't have the facilities to handle them and the time either, that you have to do your own work and you just hope they'll understand. Sam Houston and Rebekah[1] gave out a good interview, I see.

. . . .

ALEXANDER: I haven't seen it. . . .

LBJ: . . . The *Press* was the mean one, wasn't it?[2]

ALEXANDER: Yes, the *Press* was the mean one. This woman . . . appreciated my position, but . . . they asked where Birge worked, and I figured if I didn't say something, they'd make something out of nothing. . . . She told me she'd call me before she printed anything . . . and when I came back, why, it was all over the front page. . . .

LBJ: Okay, well, I just wanted to tell you I love you.

. . . .

ALEXANDER: Honey, you know how I felt when everything was happening.

LBJ: I guess you're one of the last ones to talk to him.[3]

ALEXANDER: That's right, but it was you I was worried about—and John.[4]

LBJ: God bless you and I'll see you.

[1] Johnson's brother and other sister.
[2] The *Fort Worth Press* ran a front-page article, headlined "Sister Tells of LBJ Devotion to JFK," two days after the assassination. The Alexanders disliked it.
[3] Kennedy.
[4] Connally.

Chapter Two
DECEMBER 1963

SUNDAY, DECEMBER 1, 1963

WALTER LIPPMANN
Columnist, Washington Post
5:46 P.M.

      LBJ PURSUES his courtship of the press with a call to the most influential American journalist of his time. Lippmann is at his home, next to the Washington National Cathedral.

LIPPMANN: Oh, how do you do, Mr. President?

LBJ: I'm doing as good as I could under the circumstances. How are you getting along?

LIPPMANN: ... I'm very satisfied with *you,* but you know it is a tragic business.

LBJ: ... Could I drop by and bum a drink from you?

LIPPMANN: ... Oh, you certainly could. Come right along.

LBJ: ... I'm at the office and I'm going to be here about another ten minutes, and I'll run by on my way to dinner.

MONDAY, DECEMBER 2, 1963

KATHARINE GRAHAM
President, Washington Post Company
11:10 A.M.

MRS. GRAHAM'S HUSBAND, Philip, who took his own life four months before this conversation, had been close to Johnson since the 1950s, when he saw possibilities in the Majority Leader that few outside Texas and the Senate did.[1] Having taken over the company, which owned the *Washington Post* and *Newsweek*, after her husband's death, Mrs. Graham innocently asks the President to speak at a publishers' dinner, not knowing that she would be treated to an LBJ stream of consciousness.

LBJ: Hello, my sweetheart, how are you?

GRAHAM: Well, I'm fine. Are you?

LBJ: You know, the only one thing I dislike about this job is that I'm married and I can't ever get to see you. I just hear that sweet voice and it's always on the telephone and I'd like to break out of here and be like one of these young animals down on my ranch. Jump a fence. [both laugh]

GRAHAM: Now, that's going to set me up for the month, Mr. President!

LBJ: Now that's true. But . . . we've got to get us together some evening and just three or four of us sit around.

GRAHAM: Anytime.

LBJ: I've been here till after oh, ten, eleven every night.

GRAHAM: I'm worried about you.

LBJ: Not at all, not at all.[2]

GRAHAM: Don't you do that too much. I know you have to now, but I hope we stop it soon. Mr. President, I'm calling you really on behalf of the newspaper publishers.[3] . . . Every year, as you probably remember . . . they have a huge dinner . . . at the Waldorf, and they hope very much that this April 23rd, Thursday . . . you might be willing to speak to them. . . .

LBJ: I would. Who else is speaking? I don't want to get in a debate with Goldwater or Nixon[4] or somebody.

---

[1] Mrs. Graham recalled in her memoirs, *Personal History* (Knopf, 1997), that her husband gave LBJ advice on how to improve his national image, "arguing that the Senator needed to counteract the reputation he had as a conservative, sectional and (oil and gas) interest-motivated politician." She was not pleased when, during their 1956 visit to the LBJ Ranch, Johnson, having "put away a good deal of whiskey," complained about the press, saying, "You can buy any one of them with a bottle of whiskey." Mrs. Graham wrote that her husband's exchanges with LBJ "reflect a relationship in which the press is closer to government than journalists ought to be— at least today. However, for those times, for that decade, it was not unusual" (p. 237).

[2] Johnson once again deflects what he thinks are worries about his heart condition.

[3] The American Newspaper Publishers Association.

[4] Senator Barry Goldwater of Arizona and former Vice President Richard Nixon—two prospective Johnson opponents for 1964.

GRAHAM: Oh, of course, they wouldn't have anybody else.

LBJ: . . . My answer would be I wouldn't hesitate the slightest if you had Phil here. If you'd just go up in heaven, get him, bring him back where he could sit and advise with me awhile. But it's so difficult—I just—it was tragic the other night. I had Abe Fortas in my bedroom till two-thirty 'fore I got my message out to the Congress and I was—I could have just blown everything and fallen on my head—and I'm glad Russ Wiggins[1] said he wouldn't change a word. . . . But it was such agony that I haven't recovered from it. I didn't do that when Phil was here. He'd siddown and write in longhand in thirty minutes what we were going to do and after talking it over and fighting about it and arguing, why, we'd get it. I don't find anybody that's that easy with me anymore. I've got all these temperamental people. And he didn't care if you took half his stuff out. He didn't give a damn whether you took any of it. What he'd do—he was just trying to help a human being and a country and not trying to help himself. But they . . . all go and cry and they say, "Well, Abe Fortas put this paragraph in and took my paragraph out."[2] But Adlai did a wonderful job, bless his heart, and I want you to thank him on behalf of your children for being a big man. He came in here when this happened, he brought in a speech of his own that he had personally written, he said, "I am at your service." And a good deal of it was in the message delivered.[3] I don't want that in the paper.[4] But he was a big man and most of the rest of them were, but—

GRAHAM: Mr. President, can I say one thing on behalf of somebody whom I don't think looked very well but I think is a great man? And that is Ted Sorensen.

LBJ: Yes, I think he's just absolutely indispensable.

GRAHAM: He's marvelous and he is very hurt and I encountered him and I know the mood he was in and I don't forgive him for it[5] but I—

LBJ: He did it to me, going up to deliver it. We spent the whole time arguing and I said, "Well, you've got 80 percent of your stuff in there."[6]

GRAHAM: He was just unforgivable, and yet I think that we all have to just imagine how he feels and he's a man who, instead of crying, he did this really naughty trick, but—of being cantankerous and hurt—because he had that peculiar relationship with President Kennedy.

LBJ: Well, the President[7] took out a good deal of his stuff—

GRAHAM: But, Mr. President, I think he's gonna come around and I think that if you just give him a little love and—

[1] J. Russell Wiggins was executive editor of the Washington Post (and, in 1968, Johnson's final Ambassador to the United Nations).
[2] Johnson here is referring to Sorensen's unhappiness that Johnson did not use his draft for the Joint Session address intact.
[3] Along with Galbraith, Fortas, and Humphrey, U.N. Ambassador Adlai Stevenson, the 1952 and 1956 Democratic presidential nominee, was one of those Johnson had solicited for a draft. Almost certainly the President is making a point of praising Stevenson to Mrs. Graham out of knowledge that Mrs. Graham's mother, Agnes Meyer, was one of Stevenson's closest friends and most stalwart supporters.
[4] Johnson does not want the public to think that the controversial Stevenson (or anyone else, for that matter) is writing his speeches.
[5] This refers to Sorensen's complaints about Johnson's failure to use his entire draft.
[6] Some of this argument took place in Johnson's car on the way up to Capitol Hill.
[7] Kennedy.

LBJ: I'm going to, I'm going to.

GRAHAM: I know you did. Incidentally, that little girl of his[1] said to me that "President Johnson has been an angel to Ted." And so, she knows—

LBJ: I've done as much as I can and have any pride and self-respect left. I just—

GRAHAM: No, I know what you did and I think he's going to come back from the weekend and be all right and I just hope he is. I do think he can be just terrible.

LBJ: Kay, here was our feeling. He did the best job, the fastest job that you ever saw, but I had Stevenson and he had some good things that I wanted to say. Abe Fortas had the action in that speech. He just meant civil rights . . . and "the time for action is now." We are not only just going to continue. Now, the speech that came in was a great tribute to a great man but the Congress expected a little sump'n else.[2] They wanted to know how I was going to *stand* on these things, and I had to say so and I had to say "action now" because—I've got to talk to you about it, and no better time than right this minute, although I am thirty minutes behind on my appointments and I've got the Cabinet waiting out here.[3] But I've got to ask you this.

GRAHAM: Mr. President, I—

LBJ: [getting more intense, interrupts:] Howard Smith[4] said to the Speaker of the House that—I quietly and judiciously asked to go talk to him about civil rights—that "you'll have to come back and talk next year, January, and we'll all be late coming back in January." . . . He won't even give 'em a hearing, he won't even call a meetin'. He just said, "I'm out at my farm and I can't have any hearings." . . . We thought *Oswald* ought to have a hearing! We are upset. That's why we've got a commission.[5] . . . So they are going to try to sign a petition that will give 'em a hearing in the House so they can discharge the Rules Committee and bring it out.

GRAHAM: Right.

LBJ: Now every person that doesn't sign that petition has got to be fairly regarded as being anti–civil rights. . . . I don't care if he votes against the bill after he gets a chance to vote on it. . . . But I don't think any American can say that he won't let 'em have a hearing either in the committee or on the floor. That is worse than Hitler did. So we've got to get ready for that and we've got to get ready every day. Front page. In and out. Individuals. Why—are—you—a-gainst —a—hearing? And point 'em out and have their pictures and have editorials and

---

[1] Sorensen was seeing a schoolteacher named Sara Ann Elbery, whom he married in June 1964 and later divorced. He had been divorced from his first wife in July 1963.

[2] Sorensen had wanted Johnson to say, for example, "I who cannot fill his shoes must occupy his desk." (See William Manchester, *The Death of a President*, p. 605.)

[3] Here LBJ flagrantly exaggerates. His Daily Diary shows that his Secretary of Commerce, Luther Hodges, was the only one waiting for him, but it was more flattering to suggest to Mrs. Graham that her call was important enough to keep the entire Cabinet waiting.

[4] Chairman of the House Rules Committee, the eighty-year-old Virginia Bourbon segregationist was blocking a House vote on the civil rights bill by saying that he had "no plans" to schedule floor action before the end of the year. This compelled the administration to request a discharge petition, requiring signatures of more than half the House members to bypass Smith's committee.

[5] The Warren Commission.

have everything else that is in a dignified way for a hearing on the floor.[1] . . .
Once we get that, then these cowards will all vote for the bill. But we've got to
try to appeal to the Southerners—a few of 'em in border states—to sign that
petition. We've only got 150 Democrats. The rest of 'em are Southerners. So
we've got to make every Republican. And we ought to say, "Here is the party of
Lincoln. Here is the image of Lincoln." And whoever it is against a hearing and
against a vote in the House of Representatives is not a man that believes in giving
humanity a fair shake. Vote against it if he wants to. Let him do it. But don't let
him refuse to sign that petition! Now, if we could ever get that signed, that would
practically break their back in the Senate because they could see that here is a
steamroller that can petition it out and they'll put cloture on and the psychology
would be just like Texas[2] won every game this year—that they're a going outfit.

GRAHAM: Right.

LBJ: Otherwise—now they're saying Johnson's a great magic man. Well, I'm
not. But you want to bear in mind that Mr. Kennedy was able and he was
popular and he was rich and he had young giants helping him—and much more
enthusiastic helping him than they are me—and he had the newspapers helping
him and he had everything else. But his tax bill? The last conversation I had with
Phil, he said he had asked the President to make me take charge of the tax bill
and pass it because it would never be passed until I did.[3] Ask Gerry Siegel.[4] That's
the last thing he said in a conversation with me, and he—it's almost unbelievable
how prophetic he was, and I'm sitting here today—and the tax bill—he came
and got me and just was real ugly to me.

GRAHAM: [sympathetically:] I know.

LBJ: And he said *mean* things to me. But he was trying to drive me into action
on the tax bill. But the President's tried for a year and he hasn't been successful
in twelve months. Now I hope in twelve months I *can* be. But he tried since
May[5] on civil rights and he hasn't been successful. So they better not be too
quick to judge it. If this Mickey Mantle that's got a batting average of .500 and
is the star of the Yankees—if *he* couldn't do it, how do you expect some plug-ugly
from Johnson City to come in and do it pretty quick?[6] But we're working on it.
. . . So you can tell your editorial board that this Rules Committee has quietly
said they're not going to do anything. And somebody ought to be asking these
leaders. I can't do it. But you know what I tried to do in appointing your commission the other day—the Kay Graham Commission?[7]

---

[1] Johnson is asking Mrs. Graham to have the *Washington Post* vilify those who are blocking
the civil rights bill in the House.
[2] The University of Texas.
[3] Kennedy was not thrilled with the suggestion. From the start of his administration, remembering LBJ's old dominion over the Senate, he was wary of giving Johnson much influence over
his relations with Capitol Hill.
[4] Gerald Siegel, the *Washington Post* counsel in 1963, had worked for Johnson in the Senate
in the 1950s.
[5] Actually, June.
[6] In his current mood of deference to Kennedy's memory, especially while talking to those he
considers to be JFK friends like Mrs. Graham, Johnson is being exaggeratedly self-deprecating
in a way that he does not actually feel.
[7] Johnson refers to the Warren Commission as the "Kay Graham Commission" here in
homage to the fact that the *Post* had been one of those who had originally suggested a
blue-ribbon panel to investigate Kennedy's murder.

GRAHAM: Yeah?

LBJ: I talked all day long and into the night on that, including talking to you, but they—Justice Warren turned . . . the Justice Department down. Nick Katzenbach and them went to him and he wouldn't do it. I had to come in here, plead with him and finally got him to do it. Everybody else wanted to turn it down. Dick Russell—I had to talk to him four times. But we went through with all that thing. Now, you know where I had to talk to 'em? Russell was in Winder. Dirksen was in Illinois. Humphrey was on the beach. Mansfield was on the beach in Miami in houses that people who've become popular have lent to 'em. Charlie Halleck was out hunting turkey. Now there wasn't a human here. And they're not here *now.* And they are not *working* now. And they are not passing *anything!* And they are not *going* to! [growing shrill:] Now *somebody* has got to—instead of just writing the stories about how the pages live or about Bobby Baker's girl.[1] Whether he had a girl or whether he didn't is not a matter that is going to settle this country. But whether we have justice and equality is pretty *damned* important. So I'd like for them[2] to be asking these fellows, "Where did you spend your Thanksgiving holidays? Tell me about it, was it warm and nice?" And write a little story on it . . . because if you don't, they are going to start quitting here about the 18th of December and they'd come back about the 18th of January and then they'll have hearings in the Rules Committee till about the middle of March and then they'll pass the bill and it will get over and Dick Russell will say, "It's Easter and Lincoln's Birthday." And by the time you get him, he will *screw them to death,* because he's so much smarter than they are.

GRAHAM: Yeah, yeah.

LBJ: He advocates going home at four-thirty and Mansfield's wife says he can't meet after five o'clock. And you can't ever beat this crowd doing that. You can't run your *business* doing that! Now you had better take these broad outlines and give to your broad people[3] and say . . . "I don't care what you cover in the sex route, but let's cover some of these folks' vacations." Not in a mean way, but just point up that . . . these things haven't been done and we've paid 'em to do 'em. And if your reporter didn't show up all this time—and, of course, a part of their job's at home, and in an election year they'll be at home, but they oughtn't to go home until they do something to go home to talk about.[4]

---

[1] Reporting on the growing scandal involving LBJ's old protégé and ex–Secretary of the Senate Majority, Bobby Baker, the *Post* told of the women who were habitués of Baker's Capitol Hill town house.

[2] I.e., the *Washington Post.*

[3] At the *Post.*

[4] Mrs. Graham passed the gist of this talk on to her editors but did not ask them to carry out Johnson's wish, believing that for the *Post* to write about congressional vacations in the manner the new President described would have been "ridiculous." The following evening, the Johnsons had her and the Joseph Alsops for dinner at The Elms, telling them over drinks that that day, "the Kennedy men" had come in, one by one, to give him their resignations (*USA Today,* December 12, 1996, and Katharine Graham, *Personal History,* pp. 354–55).

CARL ALBERT
House Majority Leader and Democratic Congressman from Oklahoma
2:50 P.M.

> ON JOHN KENNEDY'S DESK when he left for Texas was a document appoint-
> ing Frank Coffin, a former Maine Democratic Congressman and mid-level
> foreign aid official, as Ambassador to Panama. It was Coffin's bad luck that JFK
> had not signed the document and sent it on, because Johnson had never forgot-
> ten that in 1961, during a conversation about foreign aid in front of fifty guests
> at a Mayflower Hotel cocktail party, Coffin told him, "You're wrong."[1] Here
> LBJ calls his House Majority Leader to ascertain whether there will be any
> serious cost to killing Coffin's appointment.

LBJ: I want to ask you: How much do we need to do for Frank Coffin? How
much influence has he got?

ALBERT: Well, he's a nice fellow. I don't know whether he has influence. You
know, that's just between you and me.

LBJ: Okay, thank you very much.[2]

THEODORE SORENSEN
3:26 P.M.

> IN THE WAKE of Dallas, the seventy-one-year-old McCormack and eighty-
> six-year-old Carl Hayden of Arizona, Senate President Pro Tempore, are next
> in line for the presidency under the Twenty-second Amendment. Johnson asks
> Sorensen to help him devise procedures of the kind LBJ had once created with
> Kennedy to handle the possibility of presidential disability.

LBJ: I think we ought to do it pretty soon. . . . Everybody is getting worried
and talking about it and Miz Johnson says she's had thirty people say, "I looked up
there and saw those men behind you"[3]—and I've got to come home before seven
o'clock at night. I know these wives will use anything on you, but that's a sample
and you think about what we ought to do and give me a page of what you think.

SORENSEN: The first thing you ought to do is take Mrs. Johnson's advice and
take it goddamned easy because that would be a real disaster—with all due
respect to the Speaker.

J. WILLIAM FULBRIGHT
7:01 P.M.

LBJ: You got anything to talk to me about?

FULBRIGHT: Lots of things. What do you have in mind?

[1] See Rowland Evans and Robert Novak, *Lyndon B. Johnson: The Exercise of Power* (New
American Library, 1966), pp. 354–55.
[2] See also LBJ's conversations with Edmund Muskie (December 11, 1963) and Ralph Dungan
(December 17, 1963) below.
[3] Behind Johnson during his address to the Joint Session were McCormack and Hayden.

LBJ: Just anything you want to talk to me about. I want to talk to you.

FULBRIGHT: I don't want to bother you, but if you've got something—

LBJ: You don't bother me. I always feel a little better after I talk to you. Learn something.[1]

FULBRIGHT: [chuckles] I wish that were so. One thing I want to talk to you about—the easiest thing—is this Cultural Center matter.[2] . . . I hope the time is right.

LBJ: . . . I think we ought to . . . be very careful that we do not let some people think that we're using his[3] name to raid the Treasury. . . . Looks to me, our administration of this Alliance for Progress is in pretty bad shape. . . . I wish you'd think about some real top young fellows that might help us. . . .

FULBRIGHT: . . . They're hard to find. . . . My God, I can't even keep a staff. Somebody always is raiding my staff. . . . They all come in here and pay them more than we can pay them.

LBJ: I might take some of them away from you myself.

· · · ·

LBJ: Is Betty living with you?[4]

FULBRIGHT: Yes, just barely.

LBJ: Give her my love. . . . And I wish you'd tell me what you think we ought to be doing in Cuba.

FULBRIGHT: I don't think you ought to stir that up any. I think this election sounds good—what I heard of it today—in Venezuela.[5] I think the goddamned thing ought to be let alone, as of the moment. I think if you stir it up—

LBJ: They're shipping arms all over the damned hemisphere.[6]

FULBRIGHT: *That* we ought to stop. I thought you meant about going into Cuba.

LBJ: No, I'm not getting into any Bay of Pigs deal![7] No, I'm just asking you what we ought to do to pinch their nuts more than we're doing. Why don't

---

[1] Here Johnson caters to the well-developed self-image of Fulbright, a onetime Rhodes Scholar, as a sage intellectual.

[2] Johnson was proposing a bill to rename the proposed National Cultural Center, to be built on the Potomac River, in Kennedy's memory, and enable the government to match public donations for the center.

[3] Kennedy's.

[4] Johnson had already used this line in an earlier conversation with Fulbright. See November 29, 1963, above.

[5] Despite terrorist threats by pro-Castro forces, 95 percent of Venezuelan voters turned out to elect the anti-Castro Raúl Leoni President.

[6] Two days before Kennedy's death, Richard Helms, Deputy Director of Central Intelligence, had brought him a Cuban rifle found on a Venezuelan *finca*, which showed that Castro had not relaxed his efforts to subvert South America. (See Michael R. Beschloss, *The Crisis Years*, HarperCollins, 1991, pp. 666–67.)

[7] The Bay of Pigs invasion was the failed Kennedy attempt to use anti-Castro Cuban exiles to overthrow the Castro government in April 1961. Pressure on JFK to invade the island with full American force continued even after the Cuban Missile Crisis of 1962. It is particularly on Johnson's mind because he worries that if Americans suspect that Castro was behind Oswald, they will demand another invasion of Cuba in revenge. (See Beschloss, *The Crisis Years*, pp. 682, 692–93.)

you give me a one-page memo on what you'd do, if you were President, about Cuba?

FULBRIGHT: [chuckles] You mean, exclusive of any direct interference?

LBJ: I mean what you'd do, if you were President, about Cuba. Inclusive or exclusive of anything. Just what you'd do. And get your good brain to working. I'd like to look at it and see.

FULBRIGHT: I'd better wait until I get this foreign aid out of my hands.[1]

LBJ: All right, now what about Vietnam?

FULBRIGHT: I just think that is a *hell* of a situation. It involves a lot more talk, but I'll be goddamned if I don't think it's hopeless. . . . I'm not really aware of the new characteristics of it, but I think the whole general situation is against us, as far as a real victory goes. I think that this idea of some kind of a semi-neutralized area in which they'll keep out—by that, I mean the Chinese. . . . But you don't want to send a whole lot more men in there, I don't think. I think we ought to give this new man[2] a chance to see what he can do for a little while. . . . I don't think I would do anything.

LBJ: Why did you send *Lodge* out there, for God's sake?

FULBRIGHT: . . . That was political. . . .

LBJ: I just think he's got things screwed up good. That's what I think.

FULBRIGHT: I think it's a hell of a situation. Some things you can't do anything about unless you want to go all-out and I don't believe you want to go all-out. We had that up about Laos, as you remember.[3]

LBJ: Yep.

FULBRIGHT: Everybody voted against thirty thousand troops.

LBJ: [chuckles] That's right.

FULBRIGHT: I think that *is* right. I'm glad we haven't got thirty thousand troops in Laos, bogged down in a damned war there. It's just not worth it.

· · · ·

LBJ: What would happen if I moved Lodge?

FULBRIGHT: I wouldn't do it right away. I don't know. See, I'm not current on the exact situation. . . . I think he was put there partly to conciliate the opposition.

LBJ: Who does he satisfy?

FULBRIGHT: I assume some elements in the Republican party. I assume that was the reason. I wasn't consulted about that appointment.

---

[1] Fulbright refers to the pending foreign aid bill.
[2] General Minh.
[3] In the fall of 1961, Kennedy forswore a plan to send thirty thousand combat troops to the defense of Laos.

TUESDAY, DECEMBER 3, 1963

DEAN RUSK
Secretary of State
10:02 A.M.

RUSK: Wicked story in the *U.S. News & World Report* this morning that was just absolutely wrong on that reception where you received the foreign dignitaries at the funeral. It takes the line that I was very reluctant about this and that you made me do it, that I hovered all over you all evening so that you wouldn't make any mistakes. . . . We're going to hit that, tear it apart today. . . .

LBJ: They're going to do this with us—with you and McNamara and Bundy and everybody. Honeymoon is over, and we're going to have a lot of it.

CARL ALBERT
3:00 P.M.

> IN THE FALL OF 1963, House Republican Leader Halleck and William McCulloch, ranking Republican on the House Judiciary Committee, had made a deal with John Kennedy: they would press northern Republicans to support the civil rights bill, offsetting the staunch opposition of southern Democrats, as long as their party was granted equal credit and if they were given the right to oppose liberal amendments added to the bill in the Senate. But now both Halleck and McCulloch are thwarting Johnson's wish to use a discharge petition to dislodge the civil rights bill from Smith's Rules Committee. Halleck insists that the Rules Committee must first hold hearings. McCulloch complains that the device undermines the House committee system.

LBJ: I gather you're getting some static and backfire. Tell me about Halleck's conversation last night on adjournment and all that stuff.

ALBERT: He just said that, by God, he was going to raise hell if we didn't adjourn by the 14th . . . and that he was going to fuss about this civil rights bill. . . . The truth of the matter is he's wanting to get a little bit of an anti–civil rights aura around himself because his right-wing group really chewed him when he went down . . . to the White House there and agreed with President Kennedy to get that bill out. . . . Halleck is threatening to do anything he can. . . . He's in bad shape and he's hitting the bottle too much. Too early in the day, you know.

LBJ: Um-hmm. . . . I thought Charlie—that night the leaders met with me,[1] he talked very cooperatively. Was he drinking a little last night?

ALBERT: Yes, drinking too heavy, but he's been smart. Do you know he told us to quit bringing up—that he's getting tired of these things being brought up named after the President.[2] . . .

---

[1] On the night of the Kennedy assassination.
[2] Kennedy.

LBJ: I hear a good deal of that, Carl—a good deal of it.[1]

ALBERT: . . . And he says, "It is time for Lyndon Johnson to move into the White House."

LBJ: [sighs, laughs] That's right.

WEDNESDAY, DECEMBER 4, 1963

LAWRENCE O'BRIEN
6:08 P.M.

LBJ: We've just got to let the party of Lincoln get on that goddamned spot and keep them there and carry it right on through the election. If they ain't for civil rights, let's find out about it right now.

O'BRIEN: McCulloch has made a speech up on the floor there this afternoon saying this[2] is just terrible and violates the concept as he saw it of bipartisanship that he had established and this—

LBJ: Yeah, established, hell! He told Kennedy in my presence that he was for this bill. As soon as Kennedy dies, he runs like a damned—

O'BRIEN: . . . Well, if that's the way they want to play it, I'm sure we're capable of playing it hard.

LBJ: We are. We'll play it for keeps, too. And you just let them know that that's what it is. Let every man stand up and be counted.

O'BRIEN: You can give that to Charlie[3] to start with in the morning.

LBJ: Okay, I'm going to. I saw Dirksen this morning and he's loosened up a good deal.[4]

CLARK CLIFFORD
Washington Attorney and Partner, Clifford & Miller
6:25 P.M.

> JOHNSON HAS KNOWN the Missouri-born Clifford since he was a White House political adviser to Harry Truman in 1946. By 1963 Clifford was the premier Washington amalgam of lawyer, lobbyist, and behind-the-scenes adviser to myriad Democratic politicians, starting with John Kennedy and Lyndon Johnson.[5] Now Clifford has positioned himself as a go-between for LBJ and

---

[1] For example, from Fulbright, in the December 2, 1963, conversation above.
[2] The discharge petition.
[3] Halleck.
[4] On civil rights.
[5] In 1968, Johnson appointed Clifford as his Secretary of Defense.

Robert Kennedy. The chilly relationship between LBJ and the man who unhappily now finds himself Johnson's Attorney General is growing icier by the minute. Staggered by his brother's murder, Robert Kennedy has grown angrier at JFK's successor over one incident after another—the dispute over the Dallas oath taking, the awkwardness with Jacqueline on *Air Force One*, LBJ's insistence on the morning after the assassination that his own people quickly take places outside the Oval Office, Johnson's haste (as RFK saw it) in addressing the Joint Session of Congress.[1] Johnson recalls that in Los Angeles in 1960, Robert Kennedy had tried to reverse Johnson's selection as John Kennedy's running mate. He feels that the late President's brother is trying to undermine him in order to ultimately reclaim the White House and Democratic party for his family—perhaps as early as 1964. Robert is considering whether to abruptly quit Johnson's Cabinet. On Johnson's behalf, Clifford has called on RFK to discuss the political future.

CLIFFORD: Mr. President, I've just finished a two-hour session with Bobby. And first, I want to say, he's going to stay.

LBJ: Yeah?

CLIFFORD: . . . We really had it out, and we covered it all. I think there are some arguments that he found unanswerable and I'm just authorized to say now that he's going to stay.

THURSDAY, DECEMBER 5, 1963

JOHN CONNALLY
Governor of Texas
6:40 P.M.

JUST DISCHARGED from Parkland Memorial Hospital in Dallas, Connally has recovered enough to speak to Johnson by telephone. His right arm, shattered by one of the bullets in Dealey Plaza, is still in a cast.

LBJ: Feel good?

CONNALLY: Feel fine. I'm awfully sore, and my right arm is just going to be a damn pain for, I guess, ninety days, but otherwise all right. . . . I'm just happy to be able to talk to anybody. We came home. We're in Austin.

LBJ: Oh, you are. How's Jake[2] getting along?

CONNALLY: . . . Everybody thinks he's in real good shape. . . .

---

[1] Robert Kennedy oral history, Kennedy Library.
[2] Pickle, who is a fortnight away from his runoff to succeed Thornberry in LBJ's Texas district.

LBJ: I just wanted to tell you I loved you. I didn't have a thing in the world—
was just thinking about you, and I wanted to be damn sure you were doing all
right. And I hadn't called you in two days because they been running me nuts
up here.

CONNALLY: I know they have. Looks like to me like you're doing real well.

LBJ: See what happened to the market today?

CONNALLY: No.

LBJ: All-time high in the history of the republic—eight and a half after I met
with the businessmen yesterday and—

CONNALLY: I was just going to suggest, for God's sake, meet with the businessmen. You been getting a little too much emphasis on meeting with the civil
rights boys every day, and labor and—

LBJ: I had all the Advisory Council . . . for an hour yesterday and took every
question they asked.[1] And then took five of them home to dinner with me. . . . I
had Dirksen yesterday for breakfast.

CONNALLY: I think you're getting off on a whale of a start. . . . Give my
love—

LBJ: Same to Nellie. Watch that Jake thing. Make them vote absentee. Get
those heads of your departments—make Nellie call them up and tell them to go
vote absentee.

CONNALLY: We are.

LBJ: If something happened there, we'd be disgraced. I don't think it could
happen, but, you know, it can.[2]

FRIDAY, DECEMBER 6, 1963

B. EVERETT JORDAN
Chairman, Senate Rules Committee, Democrat of North Carolina
5:34 P.M.

JOHNSON IS DEEPLY WORRIED about the Senate Rules Committee's investigation of the spreading Bobby Baker scandal. Don B. Reynolds, a Maryland
insurance agent for the Manhattan Life Insurance Company, has charged that
when Johnson, at Baker's urging, bought life insurance from his firm after his
1955 heart attack, Walter Jenkins[3] demanded that Reynolds provide LBJ with
kickbacks—a Magnavox hi-fi, which Baker passed on to the Johnsons, and

[1] Johnson had met with members of the Business Council in the Fish Room.
[2] Johnson was being excessively cautious. On December 17, Pickle won with 63 percent of
the vote.
[3] Jenkins was serving as the LBJ Company's corporate treasurer at the same time as he served
as LBJ's administrative assistant while Johnson was Senator.

advertising time on KTBC, the Johnson television station in Austin—although such commercials were scarcely useful to Reynolds's business. To forestall charges that he is trying to twist the Chairman's arm in order to curtail the hearings, Johnson has not spoken to Jordan as President before this conversation. Maintaining this image of aloofness, he turns the telephone over to Jenkins as soon as the talk turns to Baker.

JORDAN: I'm mighty glad to be able to call you Mr. President.

LBJ: You did your part, my friend. You've done everything in the world a human could, and I'll never forget you and that sweet wife of yours, all the times we ever needed you. I'm sitting here with Lady Bird right now, and she sends her love.

JORDAN: Well, bless her soul.

LBJ: She just came down to the office, trying to get me away.

JORDAN: I'll tell you one thing. I'm going to join with her and help get you away from that place. I don't want you to get killed in office, not just by work.

LBJ: I'm not, I'm not, I'm not.

JORDAN: It's two ways to die—work yourself to death and let somebody shoot you.[1] But I don't want anything to happen to you, by all means.

· · · ·

[LBJ turns the call over to Jenkins:]

JENKINS: How you doing, Senator?

JORDAN: Walter, fine. Clark Mollenhoff—[2]

JENKINS: Yeah.

JORDAN: You know him?

JENKINS: Yes, sir.

JORDAN: Was in here yesterday afternoon. And he was prodding and bearing down on Bill[3] and me both about all the stuff he knows. . . . He's been talking to this damned fellow Reynolds, and he said, hell, that that insurance was bought by the LBJ Company, that it was $200,000 of it. . . .

JENKINS: No, but what's wrong with the LBJ Company buying it? . . .

JORDAN: Well, I thought Lyndon did. . . . I didn't know that. . . .

JENKINS: No, I told you, I just—I just put him in touch with the people at the LBJ Company, who bought it.[4]

· · · ·

JORDAN: Now, they keep boring in, and they ain't going to get anything out of Everett, I can tell you that.

---

[1] A not precisely graceful reference to Kennedy's death.
[2] Reporter for the *Des Moines Register,* who has been investigating the Baker affair.
[3] William Whitley, an aide to Jordan.
[4] Mollenhoff had discovered that the premiums had been paid by the LBJ Company in Austin on grounds that Johnson was a major employee. The problem for Johnson was that this fractured his contention that the family business interests were run by Lady Bird, without his involvement, in order to keep him free from conflicts of interest while Senator and Vice President.

· · · ·

JORDAN: I'm trying to keep the Bobby[1] thing from spreading. . . .

JENKINS: I know you are.

JORDAN: Because hell, I don't want to see it spread either. It might spread a place we don't want it to spread. . . . Mighty hard to put a fire out when it gets out of control.[2]

SATURDAY, DECEMBER 7, 1963

RICHARD RUSSELL
12:55 P.M.

> JOHNSON IS MAKING a particular effort now to strengthen his relationship with Russell. He knows that the old segregationist will be a formidable Senate bulwark against his civil rights bill in 1964. LBJ presumes that the friendlier he keeps his old mentor now, the more included Russell feels in presidential business such as foreign affairs, the more success Johnson might have in defanging him on civil rights next year.

LBJ: Dick, how are you feeling today?

RUSSELL: I don't feel very good. How do you feel?

LBJ: I'll be damned. I thought the sun was shining and everything.

RUSSELL: I can't get out in it. . . . You destroyed me, putting me on this commission.[3]

LBJ: I did? Incidentally how many times have you been destroyed in your life altogether?

RUSSELL: This is the first time.

LBJ: You told me at least a hundred times that you were ruined.

RUSSELL: No, this is the first time. I can't understand all you said about Warren, and here you're sitting up there by him.

LBJ: You've said a lot about a lot of folks you're sitting by, you know. Everybody we fought in all these wars[4]—you were in that first one, you know. You got to save the country though now. It's not a question of what you think about somebody.

· · · ·

[1] Baker.

[2] If he was listening in, Johnson could not have been pleased to hear Jordan's final comment.

[3] Russell was finding himself more fatigued by his Warren Commission duties than LBJ had suggested he would be.

[4] Germany, Italy, Japan—now U.S. allies.

RUSSELL: You know, I don't feel too kindly toward most of the foreign aid programs though some of it is completely—

LBJ: You know they've got to have ammunition in Vietnam and Korea, don't you?

RUSSELL: Yes, sir.

LBJ: You know we haven't got it there, and we're short now.

RUSSELL: No, I didn't know that.

LBJ: Well, we are. . . . I know that . . . a good many of you are not sympathetic with the foreign aid program, but we're in Korea and we're in Vietnam and we're in a good many of these places, and it's got down to where it's not too much anyway.

RUSSELL: We should get out, but I don't know any way to get out. I tried my best to keep them from going into Laos and Vietnam, as you—you were there, of course—last meeting we had under Eisenhower before we went in there. Said we'd never get out, be in there fifty years from now.[1]

· · · ·

LBJ: You don't feel like coming down here and going swimming? . . . This is good, warm water.

RUSSELL: I know that but I've got this short-winded business.[2] I can't breathe.

LBJ: Why don't you just come and sit then in the warm weather? Have a little sherry with me and eat lunch and go back. Now I'll have a car pick you up in fifteen minutes and you can go on back after your lunch, and we'll get you a good hamburger. You're going to have to eat something anyway, and I want to talk to you about reducing forces in Korea. You see any reason why you shouldn't do that in about twenty minutes?

RUSSELL: No, sir.

LBJ: All right, the car will be at the side door there, waiting for you.

ROBERT McNAMARA
Secretary of Defense
5:03 P.M.

THE SECRETARY OF DEFENSE has recommended closing a number of military installations as needless extravagances. Johnson is torn between his desire to show himself a thrifty President and his worry about throwing men out of work in key states during an election year. McNamara shows that he is not indifferent to LBJ's political anxieties.

[1] Russell said this at a legislative leaders' meeting with Eisenhower on April 2, 1954, when the President asked for discretionary authority to use U.S. air and sea power against Communist aggression in Southeast Asia. Russell and LBJ balked, arguing that the French must first grant independence to Vietnam and that the allies of the United States must join in the effort (Robert Dallek, *Lone Star Rising*, p. 444).
[2] Emphysema.

LBJ: On the installations, my inclination is to do what's right. I'd hate like hell though to be such a statesman that I didn't get elected, because I wouldn't be able to do what's right then. I wouldn't be here. And I'm worried about the Navy yards in Boston, and Philadelphia, and San Francisco. . . . Looks like to me that they would be the three most controversial ones. . . . I want a memorandum from you, assuring me that every person that's employed will be given another job, and that there's not a one of these installations that's required in the national interest.

McNAMARA: I'll certainly get it. Then I'm free to at least discuss the Navy yards? The two we recommended out were Philadelphia and San Francisco.

LBJ: What about Boston?

McNAMARA: Boston and New York are next on the list. . . . The Navy is wavering a little as to whether they'll . . . support us, and I got so much political heat on even two Navy yards I thought I better save the third and fourth until I can get the Navy behind me.

LBJ: I can go for San Francisco. What I'm really worried about is Philadelphia.

McNAMARA: Oh hell, let's take it off the list. . . . I can wait until November of next year. . . . I know damn well we've got too many yards, and we ought to take out Philadelphia, Boston, and New York. But I'm just not in a position to stand up before Congress and prove that Boston and New York ought to go out now. So we might just as well hold Philadelphia.

LBJ: . . . Tell them individually. Tell Ted Kennedy and Saltonstall,[1] and then we'll wind up by letting them pressure us into holding them at least until the first of the year.

McNAMARA: Take all of them out of the program, in other words.

LBJ: They're all in such sensitive states. California could be hell for me. California, Pennsylvania, and Massachusetts—they all could keep me from getting the nomination.

McNAMARA: Okay. . . . Did you mention anything other than the Navy yards to Russell?

LBJ: I mentioned the whole damned thing, went down every one of them.

McNAMARA: 'What was his reaction?

LBJ: He agrees with you. He doesn't say he agrees with you, but he does. I told him that you weren't messed up in this civil rights thing. . . . You were just doing your job.

[1] Leverett Saltonstall, Republican Senator from Massachusetts.

MONDAY, DECEMBER 9, 1963

DAVID LAWRENCE
Former Governor of Pennsylvania
9:55 A.M.

> LBJ ON THE Philadelphia Navy Yard breaks the news to the Democratic leader in vote-rich Pennsylvania and also makes sure that Lawrence is on the reservation for the presidential politics of 1964.

LBJ: Dave, we've got some problems I want to talk to you about. First, we're going to have to close the Boston, New York, Philadelphia, San Francisco Navy yards. Secretary of Defense says he's studied all of them and he cannot honestly spend one federal dollar on any of them. The stuff is running out of our ears, and he'll give everybody that works at them a job, but we cannot talk about savings and just run Navy yards for the benefit of politicians. . . . Now I talked to John McCormack. He said it'll humiliate him, but he'll have to go along. . . . Talked to the Brooklyn boys. They don't like it, but they don't know what else they can do. . . . I thought I better talk to you. And I'm calling Pat Brown[1] now. I think I ought to touch base before it happens. . . .

LAWRENCE: Yeah, well, we have to go along.

LBJ: That's what I say. Now, I thought, what should I do? Call Bill Green?[2]

LAWRENCE: Yeah, I'd call Bill Green.

LBJ: I heard a little disturbing thing yesterday. . . . Alsop[3] tells one of my men that one of the insiders tells him that Johnson couldn't possibly carry Pennsylvania.

LAWRENCE: They don't know what he's talking about.

LBJ: Yeah, I don't believe Bill Green said that, do you?

LAWRENCE: No.

LBJ: You want to find out if he did? . . . Alsop says— [aside, to aide:] Wait a minute. Shut up! Did Alsop say that Bill Green told him that? [back to Lawrence:] No, a very reliable source—one of the boys from the old days here was telling him there's been a little feeling going on . . . among some of the boys around here,[4] all of whom I want to stay on . . . that Johnson wouldn't run quite as well as maybe Bobby[5] or somebody else. . . . One of the stories yesterday in Evans's column.[6] Did you see it?

LAWRENCE: No I haven't.

LBJ: Well, he is kind of a social lion, and he says that Dick Daley[7] and that Bill

---

[1] Democratic Governor of California.
[2] Democratic Congressman from Philadelphia.
[3] Joseph Alsop.
[4] Kennedy holdovers.
[5] Kennedy.
[6] The *Washington Post* column written by Rowland Evans and Robert Novak.
[7] Mayor and Democratic boss of Chicago.

Green and Governor Lawrence and some of the rest of them are not quite as enthusiastic about Johnson as they might be. . . . Now I think you ought to talk to Dick Daley and talk to three or four of them, and then you ought to tell Mr. Evans and the rest of them that, by God, we're in better shape than we've ever been. . . . The Jews have been for me before they were for anybody else. I'm the leader in the civil rights thing with all the Negroes, and every one of them has said so when they come out of here. Labor unions were throwing their hats through the Cabinet Room the other day when I finished with them. . . . And we've got a better chance in the South than we've ever had before. So . . . we're not going to let a few columnists create an image here.

LAWRENCE: That's right. . . . That goddamned Alsop. . . . He's dishonest. And the other fellow is a snob. [pause, then:] My secretary just passed me a note here. . . . Bill Green is in grave condition, operated on last night. My gosh! He was in New York. We were there for the Pennsylvania Society dinner. I didn't see him, but he left before the dinner started. Said he was sick. That's bad.

LBJ: Where is he?

LAWRENCE: He'll be in Philadelphia, I guess.

LBJ: Do you have any idea, what hospital?

LAWRENCE: No, I'll find out and I'll let you know.

· · · ·

LBJ: Well, I'll get on it. On these other things, I just want to turn this kind of stuff over to you, Dave. Mr. Rayburn is not here, and you're the wisest man I got around me.[1] You just check that and then you call in some of these folks and start leaking to them what *good* shape we're in instead of what *bad* shape we're in.

WEDNESDAY, DECEMBER 11, 1963

EDMUND MUSKIE
Democratic Senator from Maine
10:45 A.M.

> AT FRANK COFFIN'S BEHEST, Muskie implores LBJ to reconsider stripping his fellow Maine Democrat of the appointment to Panama that JFK had promised him. The new President is not buying.

MUSKIE: Since President Kennedy had indicated publicly that he was going to appoint Frank, if Frank were not now appointed, this would have adverse political implications for him and, I think, for me.

[1] Here Johnson displays his gift for overstatement.

LBJ: I've got this problem. . . . We are hoping we're going to get a million-dollar man for a twenty-thousand job in all of these embassies in these touchy, delicate areas. And this is one of the most delicate at the moment.[1] There are a good many things, they said, that might have been worked out with the President.[2] Of course, I don't know anything about them. I know that some of his people and maybe the President had given some thought to Frank down there.[3] . . . I have grave doubts about Frank in Panama. . . . They came up with a suggestion and I said, "Now, I really have no obligation to Frank." I have a good many obligations to other folks because of the thirty years I've spent, as you can understand. It's kind of like you have a different obligation to people in Maine than what I do.[4]

THURSDAY, DECEMBER 12, 1963

OFFICE CONVERSATION
2:37 P.M.

LBJ: [to Jack Valenti[5]:] I want it where I can read it.[6] They've got these big wide paragraphs and I just can't *read* 'em that way unless somebody—can you edit it, Jack? [harried and irritated:] Now will you-all keep people out of my office? I don't want anybody coming in here except my most trusted employees and then only when it's an emergency, when you need to.

LAWRENCE O'BRIEN
4:01 P.M.

JOHNSON'S EFFORT to lobby Congressman Otto Passman for his foreign aid bill has backfired.[7]

LBJ: This damned Passman's vicious. He put out a statement that he'd been summoned to the White House and he'd always go when he was invited, but that he wasn't going to give up any of his convictions, and I was trying to whip him in line and "give him a pep talk."

[1] How delicate Johnson will find out in January 1964, below.
[2] Kennedy.
[3] Here Johnson is deliberately ignoring the fact that Coffin's papers for Panama had already been drawn up and sent to JFK's desk.
[4] Johnson gave Muskie a consolation prize the following month by dropping in at a Washington party being held in his honor, saying that Muskie would make a good Vice President.
[5] A World War II hero, Houston advertising man, and *Houston Post* columnist, married to LBJ's former aide Mary Margaret Wiley, Valenti had joined Johnson from Dallas to become a key member of the Johnson White House staff.
[6] An hour hence, LBJ is to speak in the State Department to participants in the Plans for Progress equal opportunity program.
[7] See Johnson's conversation with Passman above (November 29, 1963).

. . . .

LBJ: Oh, he said, "I'll go to the White House when I'm invited and I'll be polite and I'll listen." Son of a bitch, I wish he had listened. He talked all night. . . .

O'BRIEN: Oh, he is the worst. What is your view, Mr. President, on a Joint Session for the President of Italy?

LBJ: I'd be for it, I'd be for it.

O'BRIEN: Yeah, for reasons I'm sure you and I are thinking of.[1]

LBJ: Yeah.

FRIDAY, DECEMBER 13, 1963

ROBERT McNAMARA
7:15 P.M.

JOHNSON WANTS to replace the four White House military aides with one—JFK's old Army aide, General Chester Clifton. The ostensible reason is frugality, but another motive lurks. On November 22, aboard *Air Force One* before takeoff from Dallas, the dead President's Air Force aide, General Godfrey McHugh, had refused Johnson's commands, saying that he would recognize only one President. Now LBJ uses the streamlining of the White House to disguise his retaliation against McHugh.

LBJ: Let Clifton do the briefing and bring all the material from you to me—I mean all the death letters from the sailors and the Marines and the Army and the Air Force . . . and let him brief me, and I'd get a hell of a good command for Shepard,[2] and I'd ask the other guy[3] to retire or do something else. . . .

McNAMARA: I'll arrange it.

LBJ: And I don't want to make it appear that we're doing this, but I'd do it just quietly and centralize it all with him and tell him that he comes in for five or ten minutes a day if he has to and if he doesn't, he doesn't.

McNAMARA: Sure. I'll take care of it. Be delighted.

[1] Namely, the large Italian-American vote in 1964.
[2] Captain Tazewell Shepard, White House naval aide, who enjoyed some measure of protection as the son-in-law of Senator John Sparkman, Democrat of Alabama.
[3] McHugh.

SATURDAY, DECEMBER 14, 1963

J. WILLIAM FULBRIGHT
12:05 P.M.

IN A GESTURE whose symbolic meaning far outweighs the act itself, Johnson has incurred the wrath of Kennedy men like Arthur Schlesinger, Jr., and Undersecretary of State for Political Affairs Averell Harriman by giving the tough-minded Thomas Mann, Eisenhower's Assistant Secretary of State for Latin America, his old job back, with expanded powers.[1]

LBJ: We've got a little flak from Schlesinger and maybe Averell Harriman on Mann. . . . I don't think he'll spend the money quite as fast as they want him to, and they're calling around town objecting. . . . I don't know what to do about it. . . . I don't know about this jungle. What the hell do you do about an Undersecretary who goes to calling around people to lobby you? . . .

FULBRIGHT: Averell ought to have his ears knocked back. That's none of his business.

LBJ: No, but he wants to be the Latin expert.

FULBRIGHT: Oh, God no! You know Averell's a nice fellow, but he's old and dead.

LBJ: I know it, I know it, I know it.

WALTER JENKINS
Special Assistant to the President[2]
12:25 P.M.

THE SENATE RULES COMMITTEE has asked the White House for consent to examine Bobby Baker's tax returns, which will require Johnson to sign an executive order. The President has asked to see the file personally.

---

[1] Harriman feared that Mann's appointment would "reverse the whole direction of Latin American policy" begun with JFK's Alliance for Progress. Schlesinger, who had been Kennedy's Special Assistant, considered Mann "a colonialist by mentality and a free enterprise zealot." Schlesinger wrote in his diary that the appointment was LBJ's "declaration of independence, even perhaps a declaration of aggression, against the Kennedys" (cited in his *Robert Kennedy and His Times,* Houghton Mifflin, 1978, p. 631). The historian shrewdly wrote to Robert Kennedy, "Johnson has won the first round. He has shown his power to move in a field of special concern to the Kennedys without consulting the Kennedys. This will lead people all over the government to conclude that their future lies with Johnson. . . . We have supposed that Johnson so badly needed the Kennedy people for the election that we would retain a measure of power for eleven months. . . . He has understood that the only sanctions we have are resignation and/or revolt—and that both sanctions are meaningless, and will seem sour grapes, unless they are provoked by a really understandable issue—and this LBJ will do his best to deny us" (December 15, 1963, Robert Kennedy Papers, Kennedy Library).
[2] Jenkins's innocuous title belies the centrality of his role on Johnson's staff.

LBJ: Pierre's[1] in here and he's going to be asking about what we are doing about Bobby Baker's income tax. What happened to it? We can't stand it anymore. Can't you find out about it? Do you have to go direct? If Feldman[2] can't do it, why don't you go direct? Say, "Goddamn it, get it over here!"

JENKINS: All right, sir.

LBJ: I just can't sit this one out. Now I told you that yesterday.

JENKINS: All right, sir.

LBJ: Have you done anything about it since I talked to you?

JENKINS: Yes, sir, I talked to Mike and he said they were going to get it over here as quick as they could get it over here.

LBJ: Well, they don't come from *Berlin*, does it? Doesn't it just come across the street?

JENKINS: Well, I think that's right, but I don't know if they had located it or not. Probably comes from—

LBJ: Well, the answer is we're going to give it to 'em. Period. Isn't that it?

JENKINS: Yes, sir, no question about it.

OFFICE CONVERSATION
12:30 P.M.

> SENATE RULES CHAIRMAN JORDAN has announced that he may ask his committee to investigate the reports that the LBJ Company paid the premiums for insurance on Johnson's life. The President coaches aides on how to deal with the newest problem.

LBJ: There's no violation of law if you go to church, take a piss, or buy insurance. The company *did* buy insurance. It bought it on my life. It made the company the beneficiary. It paid the premiums. They didn't take a tax deduction. [laughs] . . . It's still in effect. And that's four or five hundred thousand dollars. The reason is it made Johnson worth four million dollars. If I dropped dead tomorrow, under Texas law, they'd claim I was entitled to half of it. My heirs would. So it'd be two million. She'd[3] have to pay an estate tax on it. She doesn't have forty dollars in the bank. Where would she get the two million? The estate tax would be four to five hundred thousand on it. . . . Not half of this stock would be as big as Kennedy's. My trust is ten times as tight as his. I said, "I want you to take every trust Kennedy's got and be goddamn sure mine's twice as tight."[4]

---

[1]Presidential Press Secretary Pierre Salinger, inherited from Kennedy.
[2]Deputy Special Counsel Myer "Mike" Feldman, another Kennedy holdover.
[3]Mrs. Johnson.
[4]This statement cannot be taken at face value.

McGEORGE BUNDY
1:25 P.M.

LBJ: Mac, Harriman's called up now and is going to get a memorandum in on his outfit.[1] . . .

BUNDY: Harriman's called up?

LBJ: Yeah, he called up Bill Moyer [sic], and he's getting the memorandum over here. I don't give a damn. . . . If he's got any differences here with the Secretary of State or the Acting Secretary of State,[2] let him express them to them and not be calling around town and talking to other people and drumming up a campaign.

· · · ·

LBJ: I think that you ought to talk to Schlesinger . . . and Harriman too. Tell them . . . you think the proper way to do it's to give it to the Secretary of State and not be talking to other people because I don't want to get my stuff from outside sources.

BUNDY: All right.

LBJ: And number two, I think that you ought to talk to Schlesinger now. Tell him that you understood he's talking to Bill Moyer [sic]. Tell him the Secretary of State recommended this. The Secretary of State's for this. The Secretary of State's not here. How many Secretary of States we got? . . . I don't intend to have but one. . . .

BUNDY: . . . The untidiness here of talking to other people around and within the management is not new, Mr. President. It's only when they talk outside that they've been bounced before. Now, you want me to talk to Averell or not? . . .

LBJ: That's what I'd do, and tell him that if he can confine any objections he's got to his boss, to give them to his boss, it would please me mightily.

BUNDY: Right.

LBJ: I just don't like to get them after Rusk has left town and find out that some underling over there's against what Rusk has done.

TUESDAY, DECEMBER 17, 1963

RALPH DUNGAN
Special Assistant to the President
4:38 P.M.

AT MUSKIE'S INSISTENCE, Dungan, a Kennedy holdover, tries to persuade Johnson to retrieve Frank Coffin's appointment to Panama.

---

[1] Complaining about the Thomas Mann appointment.
[2] George Ball, the Undersecretary of State, was functioning in the absence of Rusk, who was attending a NATO meeting in Paris.

DUNGAN: It would be a great loss of face both to him and to Coffin in Maine if you could not get an ambassadorial appointment. . . .

LBJ: . . . That's a lot of baloney. . . . Everybody imagines that everybody in Maine is watching what Coffin gets. Anybody that's been in this racket for thirty-two years knows that most of them don't know Coffin. I had a poll made about myself after I'd been in Congress twelve years. Fifty percent had never heard of me! . . .

DUNGAN: . . . I did talk to him as you asked—to Frank himself last week. His feeling that he doesn't enjoy your confidence and that he feels completely loyal to you and—

LBJ: He *doesn't* enjoy it. I don't want anything about his loyalty, but he told me that I didn't know what the hell I was talking about. We was at the Mayflower Hotel one night, and I told him we had a fight coming on foreign aid. Can't have much confidence in a fellow that tells me that I don't know what the hell I'm talking about in front of fifty guests.

DUNGAN: I didn't understand that. He doesn't remember that incident, I'm sure.

LBJ: I wouldn't be surprised, because it was a cocktail party, but if I tell you that you don't know what the hell you're talking about, you would remember it, wouldn't you?

OFFICE CONVERSATION
6:04 P.M.

> WITH HIS AIDES AROUND HIM, LBJ leafs through newspaper photographs and accounts on the Bobby Baker affair, including the voluptuous women lodged in his Capitol Hill town house.

LBJ: That's a honey, isn't it?

VOICE: That's a pretty bright photographer who did that.

LBJ: That's a Pulitzer Prize boy. What's that call girl there? Is that a call girl? [laughs] They talk about how expensive that damn thing was, that Bobby Baker opening down there.[1] . . . I didn't go on that bus with that champagne and all that expense. I drove in there and I spent five minutes and went out, just like I'd come to your house if you were having a party and you asked me to it. . . . And I went solely because he was a faithful, diligent, competent employee and I went with my wife and Judge Thornberry[2] and his wife and Walter Jenkins and his wife, didn't I?

---

[1] On July 22, 1962, Baker presided over the lavish opening of his new Carousel Motel in Ocean City, Maryland, attended by many Senators, celebrity guests, and the the Lyndon Johnsons, who drove over in the vice presidential limousine.
[2] Homer Thornberry.

GEORGE BALL
Undersecretary of State
6:05 P.M.

AT NOON, LBJ addressed the United Nations in New York, partly to confront charges that he is inexperienced and uninterested in international affairs. Now he tries to generate some favorable press coverage.

LBJ: Can't you get me some reactions from Stevenson up there at our speech today?[1]

BALL: I'm sure I can.

LBJ: We ought to feed some of that out through your press thing because you've got to get this country-hick, tobacco-chewing Southerner off of you[2] and get in there with you intellectuals, you know.

BALL: Yeah, that was a damn fine speech.

LBJ: Thank you. See if you can't get some folks up there quoting. . . . They put out two stories, you know, about they don't know how Johnson stands. . . . See if they know now.

LADY BIRD JOHNSON
First Lady
7:30 P.M.

MRS. JOHNSON CALLS the President from the Executive Mansion.

LADY BIRD: I'm lonesome over here and I wish you'd come home.

LBJ: Why don't you come and go swimming with us?

LADY BIRD: I just can't go swimming. I don't have enough calories left in me.[3]

LBJ: We'll come on over there then.

LADY BIRD: I hope you come soon.

LBJ: We will.[4]

---

[1] Johnson wants U.N. Ambassador Adlai Stevenson to see reporters and praise his speech.

[2] Meaning off of himself.

[3] Mrs. Johnson is tired after her New York trip and the first grueling weeks in the White House. She dictated into her diary, "A blur of fatigue is rather settling in with me. . . . My intake of life and my reaction to life is slow when my vitality is low, and it's within the last three days it's got to the point when . . . a reaction has set in" (December 19, 1963).

[4] That day Jacqueline Kennedy had quietly returned to the White House to view the Christmas play performed by her daughter Caroline's class, which was still meeting there until the end of the year. As Mrs. Kennedy wrote Johnson, she had planned to call on him but then realized from the newspaper that he was going to New York to address the United Nations. She wrote that she felt "so stupid" to have forgotten and would come to see him after the Christmas holidays, as he had suggested (Jacqueline Kennedy to Lyndon Johnson, December 17, 1963, Johnson Library). As it happened, Mrs. Kennedy could not bear to return and did not come back to the White House until 1971, when President and Mrs. Richard Nixon had her and her children for dinner to view her and JFK's official portraits.

WEDNESDAY, DECEMBER 18, 1963

JOHN CONNALLY
11:45 A.M.

> LBJ CHATS with the Texas Governor, then, when the conversation turns to the turbulent Texas political scene, gets off the line to let Walter Jenkins do the talking.

LBJ: They tell me that you've really got a good health policy, that you just go in and out and must be making a profit on it in these hospitals.[1] . . . I'm standing around here with a bunch of your friends—Pierre Salinger and Jack Valenti and George Reedy[2] and Bill Moyers.

CONNALLY: Tell George, goddamn him, next time he comes to Texas, we're going to put up no welcome signs if he doesn't call me.

LBJ: All right. . . . I'll see you in a few days. Hope you've got somebody to go buy me a good Christmas present because I want a real nice Christmas present from you this year.

CONNALLY: What do you want?

LBJ: I don't know, but something real valuable.

CONNALLY: You want a surprise?

LBJ: I want it in a Paul Douglas Rule[3] though.

CONNALLY: [laughs] Not over twenty-five dollars?

LBJ: [laughs] We won't watch it too close. . . . We're just getting ready to have a little press conference.

CONNALLY: Are you? Well, that's good.

LBJ: I just met with the Secretary of Agriculture and the farmers, trying to get 'em to agree on a farm program. That's not very easy.

CONNALLY: No, I'm sure it isn't.

LBJ: They say that these imports of cattle haven't got a thing to do with it. My brain trust say it's 'cause you fellows overproduced.

CONNALLY: Oh, baloney! Baloney!

· · · ·

[Here Johnson gets off the line and puts Jenkins on:]

CONNALLY: Walter, these stories just keep coming out—a hell of a lot of his[4] friends down here—we recognize that he don't want to have any brawl, but at the same time, we have got the son of a bitch refusing to ride with him in a car twice—two different Texas cities—not a month ago, and we haven't forgotten

---

[1] LBJ refers to Connally's continuing treatment for his gunshot wounds.
[2] LBJ's press secretary while he was Senate Majority Leader and Vice President, now installed on his White House staff.
[3] The Illinois Senator made it a point of accepting no gift worth more than $25.
[4] Senator Ralph Yarborough.

he wouldn't support him for President in 1960 and we ain't gonna love Ralph Yarborough.[1]

JENKINS: Of course, he's not either, and you know that. . . . He hasn't said a word.

CONNALLY: . . . But he invites him over to go swimming with him and then he has to go up to the Lehman funeral and Yarborough, of course, just takes advantage of all that and all it's gonna do is make the Johnson people mad.[2] It ain't gonna make the liberals any happier with Johnson.

JENKINS: Well, I don't know what the papers had printed. He wasn't the first man he asked. He asked practically the whole Senate. There were two planeloads and, I guess, about thirty-five Senators and nearly every liberal Senator was asked. . . . And on the swimming, he just happened to be over here with about six of 'em and he said, "Everybody want to go jump in the pool with me?" And about six or seven others. And it lasted about twenty minutes and it was not planned and it was just by chance. . . .

CONNALLY: . . . But Yarborough puts out these things. It just infuriates everybody that really has been for Johnson and against Yarborough. . . . There ain't no power on earth that's going to keep somebody from running against him.

JENKINS: Ain't nobody going to run against you?

CONNALLY: I don't think so.

JENKINS: I can't imagine that they'd be fool enough.

CONNALLY: And if they do, I don't think they're going to win.

JENKINS: I don't think you'd have to . . . say anything. . . . I don't think you would have anyway. [laughs] But if you had before, you wouldn't now.[3]

CONNALLY: I'm leading a politically charmed life, as of this moment. I don't know how long it'll last.

JENKINS: Well, it's pretty costly.

CONNALLY: Yeah, it sure as hell *is* costly. I don't want to do it again.

EDWIN WEISL, SR.
New York Attorney and Partner, Simpson, Thacher & Bartlett
5:06 P.M.

JOHNSON HAD BEEN INTRODUCED to the Chicago-born Weisl in the 1930s by FDR's aide Harry Hopkins, who told him that Johnson was going places. Weisl served as chief counsel on LBJ's Senate investigation of the defense

[1] Complaining about LBJ's desire to declare a truce with Ralph Yarborough for the 1964 election year, Connally is trying to inflame Jenkins by reminding him of Yarborough's combativeness during JFK's trip to Texas and his refusal to support LBJ for President in 1960.

[2] Yarborough had been one of a group of Senators who went swimming in the White House pool after a meeting. At Johnson's invitation, along with other Senators, he also flew with the President to the New York funeral of former Senator Herbert Lehman. To Connally's ire, Yarborough made certain that both events were heavily publicized in Texas.

[3] Jenkins refers to the fact that Connally's wounding in the Kennedy motorcade has raised him, at least for the moment, to semi-legendary status in Texas, making him virtually unbeatable in 1964.

establishment. Now a Wall Street lawyer and chairman of the executive committee of Paramount Pictures, Weisl, twelve years older than Johnson, is one of the President's closest confidants.

Their subject today is Theodore Sorensen, who has decided to quit the White House staff. Johnson wishes to keep occasionally using Sorensen for speechwriting, which he considers to have been a large part of JFK's magic. Johnson knows that maintaining his ties to Sorensen might also keep the public from viewing Sorensen's resignation as a sign of no confidence in him. Thus, in one of his customary three-carom shots, Johnson has found what he thinks is the perfect solution. Sorensen will become President of the Motion Picture Association of America, Hollywood's embassy in Washington. Since the MPAA's offices are but a few blocks from the White House, it will keep Sorensen nearby to write speeches for Johnson, which LBJ intends to be a condition of Sorensen's gaining the job. With Sorensen sitting at his side in the Oval Office, the President asks Weisl by telephone to use his influence to win the post for Sorensen.

LBJ: I've got some bad news for you and some good news too.

WEISL: What's the bad news?

LBJ: My friend Sorensen's sitting here at my desk, and he's decided he's going to write a book.

WEISL: Yes?

LBJ: And he's the most competent man we've got on the staff, and he's going to write a book about the President.[1] But I don't see how I can get along without him.

WEISL: He mustn't do that.

LBJ: Well, he's got to do it, and he doesn't want too many memories around here. They just live with him every hour, and he's almost as emotional as I am, sentimental as I am. So he wants to go out and go to work for the motion picture producers, and I told him I thought maybe I might get you to help him and he could still work for me, too.

WEISL: I certainly will do that.

LBJ: He's the most competent man we have as a lawyer, as a counselor, as an adviser, he's got all the contacts, and by far the most skillful writer. He did a good part of that speech yesterday.[2] . . . I just think he'd be the best one available, and I believe you could do that job for me if you really tried at it.

WEISL: I will do it. There's nobody like him, you know. . . . What does he want to do for the—

LBJ: He wants to take Eric Johnston's[3] job.

WEISL: Oh. Uh-huh. Has he been approached on it?

LBJ: No, no, uh-uh, doesn't know anything about it. . . . You just go on and get it for him.

WEISL: I'll do my very best.

[1] The book was Sorensen's *Kennedy* (Harper & Row, 1965).
[2] At the United Nations.
[3] The previous president of the MPAA.

LBJ: Okay, pardner, and you call me back, will you?

WEISL: Yes, sir. What's the good news?

LBJ: The good news there is that you're getting him, and the bad news is I'm losing him!

WEISL: Oh. I see. . . .

LBJ: I imagine you'd let him write a speech for me, wouldn't you?

WEISL: And how! You bet.

LBJ: And he could come over here and get a little advice from me once in a while, and maybe I'd get some from him?

WEISL: Wonderful.

LBJ: And I think it'd be good for all of us. . . . [aside, to Sorensen:] He said, "I think I can get it going."

. . . .

LBJ: If I had the money, I'd give this fellow two hundred thousand dollars a year myself. Now, he's not interested in any plug job unless he can be the head of it. There'd be twenty people on him for anything, but I just thought that we had some friends in this outfit, and I didn't think they could find anybody better than one of my best men.

WEISL: You bet. I think it's a favor to the industry, and I'll get right on it. . . .

LBJ: . . . You just tell them that they can draft him if they want to because I'm going to lose him either to this outfit or some other outfit that I control.[1] I'm not going to just turn him out in the pasture.

FRIDAY, DECEMBER 20, 1963

EVERETT DIRKSEN
1:35 P.M.

> THIS EXCHANGE shows how LBJ doles out high-level patronage to powerful political players. First he makes it clear that he is granting the appointment purely on the basis of the friend's recommendation and that if left to his own devices, he would appoint someone else. Then he asks aloud whether the friend wants the person appointed, so that the friend will have to say yes, which makes more explicit the friend's debt to Johnson.[2]

DIRKSEN: Now, on the other thing—Bill What's-his-name, your newly appointed ambassador.

LBJ: Who?

[1] The last six words of this sentence are the germane ones here.
[2] For another example of this, see Johnson's talk with Richard Daley, January 20, 1964, below.

DIRKSEN: Bill what? Oh, what the hell is his name? He's just—he used to be down there in the State Department as a legman for Foster Dulles.

LBJ: Oh— What's this man that used to be a legman for Foster Dulles on the Hill? Bill Somebody—Ambassador—Macomber.[1]

DIRKSEN: Macomber.

LBJ: Do you want him appointed ambassador?

DIRKSEN: Well, he's a damned good guy.

LBJ: I don't care if he's a good guy. There are a million Johnson men that are good guys, but he's a Republican, and if we're going to appoint a Republican ambassador, it'd better be *your* Republican ambassador. I'm not going to be appointing him just out of the skies. Do you want this guy appointed?

DIRKSEN: Yeah.

LBJ: All right, he'll be appointed. Period. But don't you think I'm going to be appointing Republicans around without talking to Republicans. There are all kinds of Republicans.

DIRKSEN: Yes, sir.

LBJ: You're my kind.

DIRKSEN: Yes, sir.

LBJ: Goodbye!

JOHN McCORMACK and CARL ALBERT
6:30 P.M.

> WITH GROWING ANGER and depression, Johnson inveighs against the foreign aid deadlock in the House and what he considers to be his double-crossing by Passman.

McCORMACK: Hell of a situation you're in.

· · · ·

LBJ: Why haven't we Democrats got somebody over there in the House that can do it?[2] Is Passman the only one?... They can't use their head? They just go along with him?...

McCORMACK: I agree with you.... Blast us with it if it comes to you. I'm simply reporting to you what the situation is. I pleaded the three billion one.

LBJ: Much obliged.... I don't want to argue.

McCORMACK: What am I going to tell them?

[1] William Macomber, Assistant Secretary of State for Congressional Relations under Eisenhower's Secretary of State, John Foster Dulles, had briefed Johnson on foreign affairs as Senate Majority Leader in the 1950s.
[2] This is an unsubtle hint that McCormack and Albert are not exercising enough leadership. LBJ felt that both of his House leaders and both of his Senate leaders—Mansfield and Humphrey—were less than fully competent. At some level, this was no doubt because they did not measure up to Johnson's memory of his own mastery over the Senate in the 1950s.

LBJ: Tell them I think we ought to have 3.6. . . . I think they're endangering their country, and I think it's a shame that a caveman like Passman does like he does. . . . That's the way I feel. It's nothing personal to me. I'm just trying to do a job the best I can . . . and we're going to have lots of trouble, and I just don't think we can do it on that. I haven't found a man that thinks we can, and if he wants to demagogue with it . . . he's a bigger power than we are and got more leadership than we have, why, there's not a thing we can do about it.

McCORMACK: They had—apparently they had tentatively agreed on three billion. When they went back this afternoon, that's when the blowup came.

LBJ: I never agreed on anything less than 3.6. That's all I've ever agreed to.

McCORMACK: They won't go that. . . .

LBJ: And I just took his agreement. . . . Mr. Eisenhower told me that he wasn't a dependable man, and Mr. Kennedy told me he wasn't a dependable man. . . . I think that they're seriously endangering the future of their country. And I think it's bitter, unwise, and I don't want to say it's unpatriotic, but it's almost that bad. And I don't think this man knows much about our country, and notwithstanding his great facility with figures, I think he's got a real mental problem. I think that we ought not let our country go that way. I love it too much to see a fellow like that leading it. And I just wish there was some way that we could have enough leadership to—

McCORMACK: Well, I don't want to get caught in any box.

LBJ: We are. We're going to get caught in a bad one. This is bad for our country. You still don't have ammunition in Vietnam right now. You've got McNamara coming in here tomorrow at noon after flying all night.[1] And this country is not in very good shape, and we haven't got anything to brag about. And we oughtn't to just let a mental case take us from 3.9 to 3 billion.

• • • •

LBJ: I think we just got ourselves in a mess talking to this fellow. . . . I think we ought to just go out there and appeal and let them vote it down. . . . I don't want people to think I'm a part of this kind of thing on the country. I just have to speak out. I have to go to them. I have to tell them. I know foreign aid is unpopular. But I didn't want to go to the Pacific in '41 after Pearl Harbor, but I did. And I didn't want to let those Japs shoot at me in a Zero, but I did.[2] And if I can't take a little Passman and let him beat me, that's all right. I'm going to be right, even if I get beat. And I get just as much pension after eleven months as I do after eleven years.

[1] At the request of Johnson, who was worried about the quality of the information he was getting, McNamara had returned from a NATO meeting in Europe by way of Saigon.
[2] For which Johnson received a Silver Star, the Army's third-highest medal, from General Douglas MacArthur. In June 1942, during a fact-finding mission, Congressman Johnson was allowed by MacArthur's headquarters to join a raid against the Japanese. Johnson's bomber, the *Heckling Hare*, lost power and was besieged by eight of the Japanese fighter planes known as the Zero. See Robert A. Caro's account in *Means of Ascent* (Knopf, 1990), pp. 34–53. Robert Dallek wrote in *Lone Star Rising* that LBJ "made more" of his medal "in future political campaigns than the facts warranted, repeatedly exaggerating what had actually happened" (p. 241).

• • • •

LBJ: Just fight him. We've got an expression down in my country that just says, "Fight him till he's shitty as a bear." . . .

ALBERT: I don't think that's the point, though. He's got too many troops with him.

LBJ: All right. Just let him go with them, just divide them up, and we just take our little squad and then—I think that's all we can do. . . . We can never agree to this any more than he can agree to cut a hundred missiles out. I think when we sat there and looked at Mr. Castro with him looking right down our eye, why, we had to look at him, and I think that it's a lot worse than this. . . .

ALBERT: . . . We're dealing with impossible people.

LBJ: Well, then, we've just got to let 180 million people know that we've yielded to Mr. Passman.

ALBERT: We're not yielding. . . . All we've done is twisted arms all day long trying to get more.

LBJ: Well, you can't do any good that way.

ALBERT: We tried and tried and tried to get more and more and more, and I have been up and down. . . . People just say they're out on a limb on this thing. . . . They've promised to cut out the Communist sales and all that sort of thing. . . . You've seen times when you just couldn't get the votes for a certain issue, haven't you? . . .

LBJ: . . . I've said all I know to say, Carl. . . . I don't think we can turn this country over. I'm not letting Khrushchev have it, and I think it's almost as bad to let Passman have it. That's the way I take it, that seriously.

• • • •

LBJ: I'll talk to the Secretary of State about this wheat amendment.[1] . . . Please, let me take the rap. And then they can call me a Communist all over this country —Nixon can—and that will satisfy them.

CARL ALBERT
8:01 P.M.

LBJ: He's a pretty slick operator, this Passman is. . . . I think he's a mental case. I honestly do.

ALBERT: I agree with you a hundred percent, and I think it's time to do something about it.

LBJ: . . . We Democrats are a not very united party, and we haven't got much real reason to want the people to follow us if our people won't follow us. If they won't follow the President and they won't follow the Speaker and they won't follow the Majority Leader, why, they follow Passman—well, by God, they ought to elect *him* President!

---

[1] Republicans were once again pushing a ban on U.S. government financing of commodities sales to the Soviet bloc.

JOHN McCORMACK, CARL ALBERT, ALBERT THOMAS,[1] JACK BROOKS, and MIKE MANSFIELD
10:36 P.M.

> SITTING WITH House and Senate leaders at the end of the long day of failed bargaining, McCormack informs Johnson that Passman has made a tiny gesture —an increase of $200 million, which clears the way for a $3 billion foreign aid bill. The measure will allow Johnson to finance commodities sales to the Soviet bloc, but only if he notifies Congress that it is in the national interest. More dejected, Johnson worries that a 25 percent cut in foreign aid from what Kennedy was given will suggest that Congress has less faith in him than in JFK. Nevertheless, he advises the Speaker to pretend for the benefit of the press that this is a victory.

LBJ: You ought to get the reporters around and tell them you're pleased and happy so they don't think that we suffered a big defeat and that this guy Passman ran the Speaker and the Majority Leader and the President in the cave. That's the kind of impression—

McCORMACK: Well, I don't want to say that—

LBJ: No. . . . I want you to leave the impression, though. . . . See that Carl and Albert and the rest of them that talked to him—Albert Thomas—that they tell everybody that.

·   ·   ·   ·

LBJ: I think this is the best we could do, pardner, and I thank you for all you did.

ALBERT: I wish we'd have done better. . . .

LBJ: . . . They rolled us good. But the time is going to come when we're going to learn how to beat them. . . . I don't know what to do, but I know this—that they make us report, and that makes us advertise it, and that makes the Russians mad every time we do.

ALBERT THOMAS: Mr. President, don't be upset over that language.[2] . . . It says all you got to do is notify them . . .

LBJ: Every time you notify them, though, Albert, they write a story that you're pro-Russian. . . .

THOMAS: Well, Mr. President, you can notify them and put it in the mail. That's notification.

LBJ: . . . And then they say that you're yielding to the Soviet Union, and H.L. Hunt[3] puts out a news release. . . . I don't want to debate it with you, my friend. I love you. But you know goddamn well when I ask them not to make me notify them publicly so it wouldn't be in the papers—you know I know what I'm doing. . . . And we screwed it up. This damn fool Humphrey put that paragraph on.[4] . . .

[1] Democratic Congressman from Houston.
[2] Requiring the President to notify the House and Senate that a commodities sale to the Soviet Union was in the national interest.
[3] The Dallas radical right oil tycoon.
[4] Requiring a presidential report.

THOMAS: ... He told me he's going to do his damnedest to take it out. Have you got the language in front of you?

LBJ: Yes, sir. I got it in front of me. And it oughtn't to be in there. . . . Why should I want to report to everybody that I screwed a girl? You screwed one last night, but you don't want to report it.

THOMAS: I wish I did!

LBJ: You know what I'm talking about. That made it come home to you, didn't it?

THOMAS: It ain't gonna—

LBJ: Well, don't you think I'm a damned idiot now?

THOMAS: Now, now, now, of course not. But I don't think it's going to hamstring you a bit.

LBJ: It doesn't hamstring me. It just publicizes that I'm pro-Russian, right when Nixon is running against me. . . . You just don't ever agree that that's a good clause because you know goddamn well it ain't. Don't try to shit me because I know better.

THOMAS: ... I've worked with it in the—

LBJ: Yeah, you've worked with it, but you've been working with it under Republican Presidents, not under Democrats. When a Democratic President has to report that he makes a determination that it's in his interest to go with Russia, it's not good when you're running for office.[1] Now, you know that, don't you?

THOMAS: Oh, now, I think you're letting your imagination run there.

LBJ: Now, Albert, don't you demagogue in there with the audience!

. . . .

LBJ: I'm really humiliated that I'm President and I've got a friendly Speaker, and I've got a friendly Majority Leader, and I've got a friendly Albert Thomas, I've got a friendly Jack Brooks, and Otto Passman is king. I think that's disgraceful. . . . I want to tell you when I see you the next time, confidentially, what we're looking at in the world. And it's a hell of a lot worse than it was last year. . . . I think it's awful that a goddamn Cajun from the hills of Louisiana has got more power than all of us. . . . If I ever woke up in the cold of the night and a rattlesnake's out there about ready to get him, I ain't gonna pull him off. I'll tell you that. . . . Now you just go and tell all these Texans that want to hit Russia that I want to put those sons of bitches in uniform. Let 'em go fight the Communists for a while. They like to talk a big game, but they don't want to do a damn thing about it.

. . . .

LBJ: [to McCormack:] Hubert's got his damned amendment drafted wrong. You just tell him to quit talking first and thinking afterwards.

. . . .

[1] Johnson shows his sensitivity to the soft-on-Communism charge that Democrats had feared since the days of the anti-Communist demagogue Joseph McCarthy, Republican Senator of Wisconsin from 1947 until his death in 1957.

LBJ: [to Mansfield:] I need to sit down and just talk with you about what's happening in Brazil. I need to tell you what's happening in Vietnam that I don't think you know.... I don't think you know how serious it is.[1] ... I sure wish that you had a day in there to come to Texas.... I'll have a jet pick you up anytime and haul you anyplace. I'm not going to have you riding any other way. I just think that sometime before we get back up here, I ought to have a quiet two or three hours with you to philosophize and see what you think about some of these hot spots, 'cause they're hotter than I think you think they are.[2]

MONDAY, DECEMBER 23, 1963

EDDIE SENZ
New York Hairdresser
11:38 A.M.

JOHN KENNEDY drew sharp distinctions between upstairs and downstairs. Not so LBJ. Family, aides, and secretaries sat side by side at the Johnson dinner table. LBJ extended this solicitude to matters of hair and dress. Here he arranges with a hairdresser to fly from New York to Washington and work on Lady Bird, their daughters, and several of the President's secretaries so that they will be up to LBJ's aesthetic standards over the Christmas holidays.

LBJ: Can I talk to you now without getting it in the paper and getting it advertised?

SENZ: Oh, surely.

LBJ: If not, I want to talk to somebody else, but I hope I can. But I don't want it in any of these columns now, and I don't want it to get out and Mr. Roosevelt said that one of the most valuable men he had in his vicinity destroyed his usefulness because he had to advertise it.

SENZ: Mr. Johnson, I give you my solemn word as a gentleman.

LBJ: All right, now I'm a poor man,[3] and I don't make much money, but I got a wife and a couple of daughters, and four or five people that run around with me, and I like the way you make them look, now how much—

SENZ: I'm most flattered. I promise you, just take my word for it that this is in confidence.

---

[1] As Johnson knew, Mansfield, who had made Asia his specialty, had repeatedly cautioned Kennedy against extended involvement in Vietnam.

[2] Lady Bird dictated into her diary that at about midnight "Lyndon came in and fixed him some oysters and two helpings of dessert—and darn reducing—and we ate it at the kitchen table in the White House." She was worried that he was overstraining himself: "I felt like asking him, 'Who do you think you are? Majority Leader?' " (December 20, 1963).

[3] The Johnson family's net worth at the time was probably in the eight figures.

LBJ: Well, this is your country, and I want to see what you want to do about it. Now how can you come down here and make them look better?

SENZ: When do you want me to come?

LBJ: That depends first on how much it'll cost me.

SENZ: It won't cost you anything to worry about, sir.

LBJ: All right, because I just have to live off a paycheck, and I'm in debt. But I want to see if you can't come. I don't know whether the planes are flying this morning, but if you can't come and stay until five or six o'clock this evening—if you can't do that, I'll have to wait until next year.

SENZ: No. . . . I have a very important appointment, but this I'd be very happy to cancel, and I will come by myself.

LBJ: All right. Now bring whoever you need, and we'll pay their transportation, but we can't pay you much else.

SENZ: [nervous:] Don't you ever worry about that, Mr. Johnson, you know I was telling Miz Carpenter[1] . . . that just things didn't look right to me, and I was a little worried about this. . . . I'm sure that you will at least acknowledge one thing. I have a sense of dignity. I've done nothing heretofore in any way to have violated your confidence in me, and I don't intend to at this particular time, but I called her sincerely, to make this suggestion—an offer.

LBJ: We'll work it out some way, in a proper time, in an appropriate way, in a dignified way where people will know it, but I want you to get down here, and not give her too much of this makeup, but give her enough to do it, and Luci and I got two or three friends, then you'll have to see what we'll have to buy in the way of a dryer or something here, so that when you do come, maybe once every month, why you can do it, and we'll work it out all right.

SENZ: . . . I'm going to try to get a plane out this morning.

LBJ: You just come right on, and call Miz Roberts in my office and tell her what time you'll arrive, and I'll have a White House car meet you. . . . There's a shuttle every hour. They're landing here now, and I think they will be—I had a bunch of friends come in.

SENZ: . . . I'll leave as fast as I can.

LBJ: Okay. Now bring all your stuff with you. And you better bring some packages for them. And I'm going to leave you a hundred-dollar bill, and I'll pay your transportation, but I can't pay you like we normally do.

SENZ: Mr. Johnson, don't even worry about that.

ROSWELL GILPATRIC
Deputy Secretary of Defense
11:45 A.M.

JOHNSON'S FIRING of three White House military assistants has turned out to be messier than he had hoped.

---

[1] Liz Carpenter, Staff Director and Press Secretary to Mrs. Johnson.

LBJ: We've got a big blowup on our aides. They're all hurt because they haven't been notified personally, and they've got Senator Sparkman calling early this morning:[1] "This is an awful Christmas present." . . . I tried to check with McNamara.[2] He told me he had it all worked out and all taken care of, but I guess . . . the poor man just didn't have the time to personally suck up to them. And I think the best thing for you to do is for you to ask each one of the Chiefs of their services to go to them and say that they're already making a study of the number of people in the White House, and there's 1,074. Tell them not to tell the aides that, but I've got an aide named Colonel Jackson[3] and I've got one named General Clifton, and I've got one named Captain Shepard and McHugh and air staff. Now we really think we need one aide instead of four. . . . I just can't talk to 1,074.

GILPATRIC: No.

LBJ: We thought the Secretary had explained that they'd all have good assignments. I particularly asked that we keep the senior man, which is Clifton.

GILPATRIC: Bob did talk to the Service Secretaries, Mr. President. . . . but . . . once the word got down, they began calling up their friends.

LBJ: Well, that doesn't have any weight on me at all—not the slightest effect, except for me to want them to have a poor command instead of a good command. . . . Tell the generals that if they're little men like that, that believe they can pressure their Commander-in-Chief on what his strategy ought to be in war or what his decision ought to be in peace, they don't know the Commander-in-Chief.

GILPATRIC: [laughs] They're gonna learn.

LBJ: . . . The only way I know to avoid four is take the senior one. And I've been around here a lot in three years and I never noticed they paid one damn bit of attention to me before.[4]

GILPATRIC: [chuckles] That's right. Well, Admiral McDonald[5] is coming in here in a few minutes.

LBJ: Well, you tell him that I want him to get that young man to straighten out his backbone right quick and if he's going to lobby about what kind of assignment he's got . . . or if McHugh is . . . see that the Chief of Staff of the Air Force gets ahold of 'em.

GILPATRIC: I will.

LBJ: They're already starting their little tune on the Chief of Staff of the Air Force and I don't want any of that either. . . . And I've been the subject of lobbyists that are professionals, that are paid for that purpose—thirty-two years.

GILPATRIC: You recognize them when you see them.

LBJ: [annoyed] I sure do. Just tell them that we got to watch it now because this man[6] thinks more of the military than any President they've had since Roosevelt.

[1] On behalf of his son-in-law, Captain Shepard.
[2] McNamara has just returned to Washington from his visit to Saigon.
[3] William Jackson was Johnson's vice presidential military aide.
[4] Here another hint that LBJ is using his new station to rectify the slights of his vice presidential years.
[5] D.L. McDonald, Chief of Naval Operations.
[6] Referring to himself.

GILPATRIC: Done more for them over the years.

LBJ: And, I mean, I respect them. I've had the Joint Chiefs of Staff in more than they've been in this year. . . .

GILPATRIC: That's right.

LBJ: Tell them that. But the best way in the world for them to do it is for the Navy to start lobbying for its carrier and the Air Force to start putting out its problem about how many more missiles they need, because when I see that, I know it didn't come from me. I don't want to make my decisions on prejudice, but sometimes a fellow can't make them otherwise, if you just get so damn mad. . . . Tell them I saw two stories this morning—one on the nuclear carrier, and one on the missiles. . . . I don't know whether I'm going to give you fifty more Minutemen or a hundred more, or cut some you got. But I want to let them talk to me man to man, not through Rowland Evans or some of these little pipsqueaks. Now just tell them that. Tell them I called you and I gave you a good going-over. You just make it appear that I just chewed you up.

GILPATRIC: All right.

. . . .

LBJ: You tell them that I was cruel and inhuman with you, that I blamed you for this story on the aircraft carrier, I blamed you for this story on the missiles, and I blamed you for the hellraising about aides, and we had a disagreement and that I told the Secretary of Defense before he went to Vietnam that I do not want to start the New Year with forty military people around me, that they get in my way, they all want to come in, they all want me to sign letters that I can't sign. And I want this Situation Room cleared up. I don't need all those people running around down there.

GILPATRIC: Yeah, I know. Too much.

LBJ: And I'm just not going to do it . . . with communications, Secret Service setup—I cleaned them from the thirty-two to eight in my own outfit, when I was Vice President. Now President, it's a different thing, in light of what happened. But I'm just going to save money here.

WALTER HELLER

Chairman, Council of Economic Advisers
12:00 P.M.

> TRYING TO GET CLOSE to a balanced budget, Johnson is disappointed that estimated tax revenues are not as large as he had wished.

LBJ: I thought you told me we gonna have the damnedest economy we ever had if we had a tax cut.

HELLER: That's right.

LBJ: Well, I just got ninety-two billion in receipts here. I thought there'd be ninety-four or -five. Hell, you had nearly ninety last year.

HELLER: Mr. President, you aren't going to do this overnight.

LBJ: No, I'm going to do it in a whole year, but . . . we've got business confidence. We've got everybody wanting to invest. We're going to have them going into Latin America. They're already lining up. . . . We've got businessmen that— Advisory Council voted the other day, after they . . . met me, they voted 90 to 2 to support us. Only two men that said they wouldn't support the Democratic ticket. That's what Sidney Weinberg[1] said last night and said he'd raise the money for the campaign. So I want you to . . . talk to the Treasury. I'm going to have to get my estimates up here, and I don't want to be too low on my estimates on what we gonna do with these receipts if we get a tax bill. I'd rather be on the high side, like every President has from Hoover. I'd rather say they're going to be ninety-four and have them ninety-three than say they're ninety-two and have them ninety-three.[2]

HELLER: Right. Agreed.

LBJ: You talk to Treasury and see what your estimates look like, and I want this deficit just as low as I can. And my estimate is a news story. And I don't mind being a little optimistic. Hell, I'm an optimist by nature.

HELLER: I hear you.

LBJ: You know, I don't want to be too much of an exaggerator, but I sure want to be optimistic, and I want to assume that things are going well, and I believe . . . business is pretty safe in this country and labor too.

· · · ·

LBJ: You go on and get me a good, solid program that Harry Byrd will look upon with pleasure, and I'll approve it.

HELLER: Boy, you're setting a tough standard.

LBJ: . . . You just get me not over two pages, short sentences, short paragraphs, and let's have something good for this State of the Union. . . . You talk to *Face the Nation*[3] and tell them what a good year we're gonna have.

HELLER: . . . I'm confident, and I think with good reason.

LBJ: And compliment labor a good deal for being decent and appeal to their patriotism for not raising wages, and say that every time you read of a price increase, you don't want to indict the fellow, but you just wonder if he thought about his country before he made it. . . . When their profits jump thirty-seven and a half percent, they ought to let them absorb a little less price increase.

HELLER: Exactly.

· · · ·

LBJ: You just tell them that we're cutting out archaic, out-of-date installations teaching boys to fly. And we don't need them flying. We're going to use missiles. We're not going to make more atomic bombs than we need because that makes

[1] Partner, Goldman, Sachs & Company, New York.
[2] Inviting Heller to exaggerate his estimates on the side of optimism, Johnson here provides a precedent for President Ronald Reagan's "rosy scenarios" in the 1980s.
[3] The CBS Sunday morning interview program.

Russia make more. And besides, we don't want to operate a WPA[1] project for atomic bombs. . . . We're going to have the tightest budget that anybody's had since—to your knowledge. But it's going to be full for human need.

· · · ·

LBJ: You just get ready, and I'll get you on some television. You can just—you brag on the economy, and brag on us, and let's have a good year, and let's have people feeling optimistic. . . . I've got a lot of this old populist doctrine in me.

MIKE MANSFIELD
Senate Majority Leader, Democrat of Montana
1:10 P.M.

WITH THE FOREIGN AID BILL now unexpectedly stalled over the credit restrictions on Soviet bloc trade, Johnson has been advised to defer the matter into the new year. Many members of Congress have already left town for the Christmas holiday. Johnson refuses to delay, believing that if he relents now, he will be powerless in January. He demands a vote this afternoon, infuriating members who have to choose between spoiling their holidays or being criticized for not returning to Washington. To smooth feathers, LBJ decides to invite those Senators and Congressmen in town to a White House reception with crackling Yule logs, to be held after the vote.

LBJ: We would like to invite you and . . . all the Senators to come by and have a cup of coffee. . . . We're going to invite all the House and all the Senate at five o'clock.

MANSFIELD: Now you know where I'm talking from?

LBJ: No, where are you?

MANSFIELD: Florida.

LBJ: Well, I'll be damned! You didn't clear this with me, Mike.[2] . . . You didn't clear leaving with me. I'm going to call your father and tell him you've been a bad boy. . . .

MANSFIELD: Listen, we heard that speech that you gave at the candlelight. . . . That was really a magnificent speech last night.[3]

LBJ: You're mighty nice to say so, but I was the first one that called you a saint. Now Dirksen's saying saying you're a saint. Tell him, by God, he ought to write his own stuff. I'm not his ghostwriter.

---

[1] FDR's Works Progress Administration, which gave government jobs to the unemployed.
[2] Johnson greets the news that Mansfield has decamped early to Florida with humor. But one can imagine how he really feels, as a President who is angry about an absentee Congress and who thinks his Senate Majority Leader is too lackadaisical.
[3] On the evening of December 22, LBJ oversaw a candlelight memorial service for Kennedy at the Lincoln Memorial to mark the end of the month of national mourning.

LAWRENCE O'BRIEN
2:21 P.M.

O'BRIEN INFORMS the President that they have failed to get the two-thirds vote necessary to allow the foreign aid bill to be passed any earlier than seven tomorrow morning.

O'BRIEN: Christ, they've got seventy Republicans absent, and we've got fifty-six Democrats absent.[1]

LBJ: That's right. But let's take the fifty-six, and let's let each one of them know that we really needed them and we love them and we're sorry. Tell them when Grandma died, we saw they couldn't come in and help us, and that these folks that got snowbound this morning remind me of Magnuson.[2] One time Mr. Rayburn asked me to pick a man that he could depend on. . . . And I told him Magnuson—he was young, and he was liberal, and he was courageous, and he had lots of guts. But he got whored up there with a movie star out in Palm Springs, and they had a big vote, and it was a tie vote, and we had to get Magnuson, and they told me to get him. And Maggie[3] told me he was snowbound. And two, three years later, I came up and wanted Maggie to be head of a special committee, and Mr. Rayburn said, "I never put a snowbound man on a committee twice."

O'BRIEN: Damn good.

LBJ: The damn fellow that gets snowbound is just out of luck, and I don't care. It may have been God Almighty's fault that the snow fell. . . . What happened to those fifty-six? They ought to have been here.

O'BRIEN: Yeah. I agree with you.

LBJ: Let's be over there[4] and smile and shake hands and thank everybody, and then just cut their peter off and put it in your pocket when they do us this way.[5]

LADY BIRD JOHNSON
8:35 P.M.

PENNSYLVANIA CONGRESSMAN William Green has died after the illness that LBJ was informed of while talking to David Lawrence.[6]

LBJ: Darling, we need to go by Bill Green's funeral. If we leave here at nine-thirty, ten o'clock we can go by Philadelphia—and we need all the bosses to see us there, and see that he was a good friend of mine—and then go on to Texas. Do you have any objection?

[1] Because of the Christmas holiday and the snow.
[2] Senator Warren Magnuson, Democrat of Washington, previously a Congressman.
[3] "Maggie" was Magnuson's nickname.
[4] At the White House reception for Congress.
[5] The House passed the foreign aid bill without the offending credit restrictions the next morning by 189 to 158.
[6] See conversation of December 9, 1963, above.

LADY BIRD: No, and I can go, dear.

LBJ: Okay. Is he working on your hair?[1]

LADY BIRD: Yes, I was under the dryer just this minute.

LBJ: All right. Will he work on Luci's hair too?

LADY BIRD: On Luci's and on Marie's.

LBJ: Marie over there?

LADY BIRD: Marie is over here.

LBJ: And Yolanda?

LADY BIRD: No, not Yolanda. And he's going to hopefully—well, I don't know what we can do about Juanita.[2]

LBJ: Has she been told? Is she there?

LADY BIRD: She has been told and she says that he combed her hair, and that he liked the way that she was doing it. . . .

LBJ: All right. When he gets through with Marie, tell him I want him to do Yolanda, because she's got to have about a bale cut off if I'm going to look at her through Christmas.

LADY BIRD: Yolanda? Do you want me to get her down here tonight?

LBJ: She's over here now, working like hell with me and Walter and Jack.

LADY BIRD: All right. Then ask her to come over here at her earliest convenience. . . .

LBJ: She ought to come over there once she gets through with you, Luci, and Marie. . . .

LADY BIRD: All right, darling. And I'm eating on a tray. Do you want them to send you some supper on a tray, or what?

LBJ: Yeah, just save me some supper in the kitchen . . .

LADY BIRD: . . . And are you going to bring anybody with you?

LBJ: Jack Valenti is all I know.

LADY BIRD: All right. Probably two people for dinner at a very indefinite hour—

LBJ: Say three people and tell the central service, and they'll set it up.

LADY BIRD: Okay, love. All right, darling.

OFFICE CONVERSATION
Approximately 8:45 P.M.

LBJ: [to Jack Valenti and Walter Jenkins:] You ought to let nothing come to me for an appointment that you haven't checked and you ought to have 'em and you ought to swear 'em in to loyalty and devotion and do or die—every man

---

[1] Eddie Senz is in action.
[2] Johnson secretaries Marie Fehmer, Yolanda Boozer, and Juanita Roberts.

that's appointed. That's your job. Take 'em out and just say, "Do or die, right or wrong."

WALTER REUTHER
President, United Auto Workers Union
9:18 P.M.

LBJ: I've got this civil rights coming up and Dick Russell says he's got seventy votes against cloture. I think he has. So we've got to get going on civil rights.[1] And the first thing we've got to do is get that tax bill out of the way so it won't be defeated. . . . I think I can get it out in two weeks, maybe three weeks, and get it passed maybe in another week or ten days and then, I think, we'll debate civil rights . . . around the clock—if you fellows can put a little steel in Mansfield's spine. . . . That's the only thing that's ever going to beat Dick Russell.

FRANCIS VALEO
Secretary for the Majority, U.S. Senate
9:35 P.M.

LBJ: Frank, I didn't know that you-all had quit. Why in the hell don't you tell me when you're leaving?

VALEO: We haven't quit.

LBJ: Well, I'm keeping everybody in the United States here to pass the foreign aid bill and you-all are scattered out all over the United States. You came to pass it tomorrow. When you gonna pass it?

VALEO: Uh, it looks like Friday or Monday, Mr. President.

LBJ: . . . You mean, I can't have any Christmas while I'm waiting on you-all? . . . I want to see these bills passed. Hell, I'm responsible for this country!

VALEO: You're going to get this bill passed, Mr. President.

LBJ: Not if you-all don't get at it. . . . The whole world is looking at us. Our Ambassadors are warning us that they're wondering whether a strong man or a weak man is leading this country. . . . They're reading all this and everybody's on vacation. We had three goddamn weeks at Thanksgiving. Sixth vacation we had this year. I do want to go home and just lay there, but at the same time, I sure—

VALEO: I think you should go, Mr. President. . . . When I spoke to Senator Mansfield earlier, he said we should be thinking in terms of Friday or Monday.

LBJ: Well, Friday is the day. . . . Help me, because I've got more than I can carry.

VALEO: I'll do everything I can, Mr. President.

LBJ: Now what are we going to do about Vietnam? We're going to look at that war. Do you want that to be another China?

[1]On December 18, Howard Smith had caved in and promised Rules Committee hearings on the civil rights bill, to begin on January 9, 1964.

VALEO: No, I certainly don't.

LBJ: Will you give me a memo on it?[1]

VALEO: [chuckles] Yes, sir, I shall.

LBJ: . . . I don't want these people around the world worrying about us, and they are. . . . They're worried about whether we've got a weak President or a strong President.[2]

VALEO: They oughtn't to worry about that. We can tell them.

PIERRE SALINGER
Press Secretary to the President
9:45 P.M.

THIS CONVERSATION with the portly, cigar-smoking ex-newspaperman from San Francisco who had served as John Kennedy's Press Secretary shows the difficulty of depending on people who have dual loyalties. During the 1960 campaign and the Kennedy presidency, LBJ had given Salinger credit for the adulation of a leader who Johnson considered so short on accomplishment. He wants Salinger to do for him what he thinks Salinger did for Kennedy, but also worries about Salinger's continuing friendship with the Kennedys.

SALINGER: We're taking some of Billy Green's friends,[3] including some people who worked in the White House—Kenny O'Donnell, Ethel Kennedy, and people like that. I just wondered whether we want to put them on our plane.

LBJ: Sure. Love to be on our plane. Any plane I'm on, Kenny O'Donnell, Ethel Kennedy, anybody else that ever even knew the Kennedys can go with me, if you've got room for them.

SALINGER: That's why I was calling Jack[4]—to see who he's got on there already.

LBJ: He's got thirty-two people on it, and we'll just scatter them all.

VOICE: Forty-one.

LBJ: We've got forty-one on one and thirty-two on the other, but we'll just put them on mine. Here's who we've got. On *Air Force One*, the President and Mrs.

[1] Johnson is really asking whether Mansfield would give him a memo. Mansfield did, writing that as LBJ had told Valeo on the telephone, "we do not want another China in Vietnam. . . . Neither do we want another Korea. It would seem that a key (but often overlooked) factor in both situations was a tendency to bite off more than we were prepared in the end to chew. . . . We are close to the point of no return in Vietnam." At LBJ's request, McNamara replied to Mansfield's memo that "the stakes in preserving an anti-Communist South Vietnam are so high that . . . we must go on bending every effort to win. . . . I am confident that the American people are by and large in favor of a policy of firmness and strength in such situations" (Mansfield to Johnson and McNamara to Johnson, January 6 and 7, 1964, Johnson Library).
[2] Here Johnson suggests that he sees Vietnam as a test by leaders around the world of his strength as President.
[3] To Green's funeral in Philadelphia.
[4] Valenti.

Johnson, Luci Johnson, LeRoy Bates.[1] . . . Mr. Salinger and General McHugh.[2] So we put him on the second one, that's one place. Sue Vogelsinger[3]—who is she?

SALINGER: She's not going tomorrow.

LBJ: All right, scratch her off there. That's two places you've got. Dr. Burkley—he can be on the follow-up.[4] . . . Eight Secret Service—I'll take four of them off for these people. Four press men—they've got to go. . . . Now how many you want?

SALINGER: I'm going to find out right now, and I'm going to call back, Mr. President.

LBJ: Whatever you want, you get. But goddamn it, don't let Ken O'Donnell and Ethel Kennedy go without because they're members of the team.

SALINGER: The only thing I was thinking about is it's better that they ride with you than ride on a separate plane.

LBJ: Damn sure *is* better to ride with me than a separate plane!

SALINGER: Mr. President, can I ask you another question?

LBJ: . . . Just let them go with me. Wherever I go, Kenny O'Donnell and Ethel Kennedy go and anybody else named Kennedy—or anybody that's ever *smelled* the Kennedys. This is one team. Period.

SALINGER: Mr. President, when you had the conversation with Mrs. Kennedy, apparently there were some newspaperwomen present?[5]

LBJ: Yes.

SALINGER: Did you know they were going to write stories about it?

LBJ: Yes. Uh, I didn't know they were—I told them they couldn't say anything, except I called her.

SALINGER: Apparently Frances Lewine[6] has filed a very lengthy story about the conversation.

LBJ: Well, she shouldn't have. Not anything wrong with it, though, is it?

SALINGER: I'd better find out. I'll get it read.

LBJ: I told them to write nothing, except I talked to her, because I didn't want a private conversation to be recorded.[7] All I said to her was I just wanted to wish her a Merry Christmas and we were thinking of her and I wanted her to tell Caroline and John hello for me. And I'm sure that she didn't say anything beyond that. If she did, she violated a confidence. But anyway, that was all that was said, anyway.

SALINGER: All right, sir.

---

[1] One of Luci's beaus, later killed in a Navy flight-training accident.
[2] Johnson's Air Force aide, whom he has fired.
[3] Of the White House Press Office.
[4] Presidential physician George Burkley. A month after Dallas, it can only be considered cavalier for a President with a history of serious heart trouble, with two old men next in the line of succession, to banish his doctor to a separate plane.
[5] Sounding almost like a policeman, Salinger refers to a Christmas call from LBJ in the Cabinet Room at 7:18 that evening to Jacqueline Kennedy. Unbeknownst to the former First Lady, Johnson had four female reporters standing over his shoulder.
[6] A UPI reporter.
[7] Johnson says this while recording this conversation without Salinger's knowledge!

LBJ: [growing irritated] And I see nothing wrong with the President calling Mrs. Kennedy and the children and wishing them a Merry Christmas.[1]

SALINGER: There's nothing wrong with it. It was given to me as much more than that.

LBJ: Well, I'll check it and—

SALINGER: No, let me check it for you, Mr. President.

LBJ: If there's anything more than that, why, it's wrong, but anyway I want to be as nice and affectionate and considerate and thoughtful of Miz Kennedy as I can during these days. And I just think that's good politics.

SALINGER: Right, sir. I'll get back to Jack on the number of people on this other plane.

LBJ: All right. Now did you get anything, any stuff, is anything *wrong* with my talking to Miz Kennedy?[2]

SALINGER: Not a thing!

LBJ: All right. Okay.

GERALDINE WHITTINGTON
White House Secretary
9:50 P.M.

> As EVIDENCE of his commitment to civil rights, Johnson has decided to hire a black secretary who has been working in Ralph Dungan's office. When he telephones her late at night, she at first thinks the call is a prank.

LBJ: [annoyed by delay in placing call] How long does it take me to get her? ... Gerri? ... Where are you?

WHITTINGTON: I'm at home. Who's this?

LBJ: This is the President. ... What're you doing?

WHITTINGTON: Oh, I think someone's playing with me.

LBJ: No, no you're not. I want to talk to you about our work, honey. Where are you? At home?

WHITTINGTON: Oh, yes, I am.

LBJ: Are you busy?[3]

WHITTINGTON: No, I'm not.

LBJ: Can you come down here immediately?

WHITTINGTON: Oh, I'd be glad to.

LBJ: Come on down. I've got Jack Valenti here and we want to talk to you about a little reassignment.

---

[1] Part of Johnson's irritation seems to come from his annoyance that in this exchange, Salinger seems to be more loyal to the Kennedys than to him.

[2] Translation: how angry is Mrs. Kennedy about the call having been reported?

[3] At 9:50 at night!

WHITTINGTON: Oh, yes sir.

LBJ: I'm in my office, and you grab a cab and come to the Southwest Gate, and I'll tell them to let you in and if you need a car sent for you, I'll get one, but you can get a cab quicker, can't you?

WHITTINGTON: Well, I can, Mr. President, but inasmuch as the weather is so bad—

LBJ: I'll get one now. Give me your address.

WHITTINGTON: My address is 3807 J Street, Northeast. . . . And the name of the apartment is the Mayfair Apartment. That might help the driver. . . . My telephone number is 399-6293.

LBJ: . . . How far are you away from the White House?

WHITTINGTON: Oh, just about twenty-five minutes.

LBJ: Twenty-five minutes? Hell of a long way! Do you walk to work?

WHITTINGTON: [laughs] No, sir. I don't.

LBJ: All right, okay: 399-6293, Mayfair Apartments, 3807 J Street, Northeast. Okay, get ready now and get your walking clothes on.

FRANCES LEWINE
White House Correspondent, United Press International
9:54 P.M.

> WORRIED THAT Jacqueline Kennedy is angry about the report on their telephone conversation, Johnson calls the reporter who wrote it. Concerned about his own press coverage, he is careful not to alienate Lewine by complaining.

LBJ: You didn't say anything except I talked to her, did you?

LEWINE: That's all.

LBJ: Okay, they said there was a much longer story and a private conversation was revealed and I got some kickback from the family and I don't want to get hurt, honey.

LEWINE: I did not reveal any of the conversation at all. I simply said after the party you placed a call to Mrs. Kennedy.

LBJ: And I just wished her a Merry Christmas.

LEWINE: That's right, and said that you'd been calling her every day or two, when you could.

LBJ: All right. That's sweet of you. Thank you, darling. I appreciate it and I knew it was true, but I got a call from the news office and they were upset.

LEWINE: Aha. Well, I haven't done anything.

LBJ: I know it, but I have and I didn't clear it and I'm not gonna clear things around here. I'm gonna do some things once in a while. So you help protect me.

LEWINE: Well, we certainly appreciate it and I certainly will protect you.

LBJ: . . . I just don't want to be carrying on my private conversations in public and have her think I'm using her or something. All I want to do is just to be as sweet and wish her a Merry Christmas and I hope you didn't say any more than that.

LEWINE: That's all I said, Mr. President.

LBJ: Thank you, Frances.

ROBERT BYRD
Democratic Senator from West Virginia
9:55 P.M.

> FOR A PRIVATE REPORT on the Bobby Baker investigation, Johnson calls a Democrat whose appointment to the Rules Committee he had supported as Vice President.

LBJ: Now, listen, Bob. You think I'm in good shape in your committee, your Rules Committee?

BYRD: Aw, darned if I know. I think so.

LBJ: [irritated:] Well, if you don't know, what the hell you're doing up there on that committee? I put you *on* that so you *would* know!

BYRD: I know. Well, we're doing our best to keep things from getting out of hand. . . . I'm going to do my best. You know.

ANDREW HATCHER
Assistant White House Press Secretary
10:15 P.M.

> JOHNSON COMPLAINS to a Kennedy holdover, the first black man to work in the White House Press Office, about criticism of LBJ in the black press—and asks for a reference on Gerri Whittington.

LBJ: Andy, I read the stuff you sent me on Simeon Booker.[1] . . . It looks like he's awful rough on us. . . . He said that we wouldn't have a picture made with a single one of the Negro leaders, and I thought we had them with every one. . . .

---

[1] Washington bureau chief for the black magazine *Jet*. Booker claimed that Johnson had refused to be photographed with black leaders who called on him and ominously noted the new President's meetings with "Southern guests." Booker wrote that when LBJ was sworn in, "a wave of pessimism and dejection began to build across Negro Americans." Unlike JFK, Johnson lacked a "civil rights image" or a "wide clientele of Negro admirers" and as Vice President had "turned down suggestions for meeting with Negro reporters" on grounds that Kennedy was the administration's spokesman. During the struggle for a civil rights bill, Johnson "didn't get involved." (December 13, 1963).

I called five of them in here and had every one I could think of. . . . I had Bob Weaver[1] go up with me to the United Nations. I had Miz Watson[2] ride in the car with me along with the Mayor, and I had to throw out even his wife to get room. . . . I don't know what more I can do.

. . . .

LBJ: Simeon Booker says that we wouldn't pose with a Negro, and we posed with all of them. Now what do we do about that? Nothing? . . . Is he working for Rockefeller[3] or somebody, you reckon?

HATCHER: No, no, no, sir.

LBJ: . . . Now, what Southern guests are he talking about? When I get Harry Byrd here to talk the tax bill? . . .

HATCHER: . . . He has to write this type of column that's supposed to be a smart-alecky type of Washington column.

LBJ: But he didn't talk about all of them that I've seen. I'm catching more hell for seeing Farmer[4] and . . . all that group than I ever caught from anybody. . . . I don't know what the hell else I could do. I put civil rights first in my State of the Union[5] message. It's my first priority. They tell me they've got enough votes to never allow cloture. . . . They say that they can never get the seventy votes we need, but I'm still fighting. . . . I'm not going to agree to a goddamned amendment. They've got to beg me before I ever let them touch it.[6] I don't think we'll pass a bill without something, and Kennedy didn't either. He said we'd have to give on two things, but I'm not going to give.

HATCHER: . . . Everybody recognizes that this is sort of a controversial type of column that this fellow writes, and everybody that reads it knows how inaccurate he is most of the time. But we're winning on the overall story.

LBJ: I wonder if you couldn't get Martin Luther King and Farmer and Randolph to tell them that everyone had their picture made, and they were published. We sent them copies of them.

HATCHER: All right. I'll take care of that.

LBJ: . . . I guess I'm the first President who just went out of my way to have every one of them come in and have a picture made, have coffee, and sit down and talk to them, and then go to bat for them.

. . . .

LBJ: I think I'll take this girl if I can get her—used to be in Ralph Dungan's office—and just put her in my personal office. . . . I've already got a good Italian —Jack Valenti. . . . I wish you'd point that out to all the minority groups—the

[1] Administrator, U.S. Housing and Home Finance Agency.
[2] D'Jaris Hinton Watson was a member of the President's Committee on Equal Employment Opportunity during LBJ's chairmanship.
[3] Governor Nelson Rockefeller of New York, another possible Johnson foe in 1964, whose relations with the black community are perhaps the best of any prominent Republican's.
[4] James Farmer, national director, Congress of Racial Equality (CORE).
[5] Johnson means his first message to Congress.
[6] Johnson is trying hard to scotch suspicions that in the end he will wheel and deal and produce a watered-down civil rights bill.

first man I hired is Jack Valenti. . . . Anyway, what's this girl—do you know this Wilkinson girl?

HATCHER: Gerri Whittington.

LBJ: Whittington. Is she any good?

HATCHER: She's really good.

LBJ: Well, now, why don't we just put her outside here and be my secretary? . . . She's got good character?

HATCHER: She's good.

LBJ: Good ability?

HATCHER: She's good.

LBJ: Respected by all her employees?

HATCHER: Yes, sir.

LBJ: Okay. I'm just going to offer her a job and put her out here in my office.

OFFICE CONVERSATION
10:50 P.M.

VOICE: That girl is here—Harriet Wilkinson or whatever her name is.

LBJ: I want to talk to her and keep everybody else out of here. Now, listen—

VOICE: It's Gerri Whittington. It says Wilkinson here. Oh, it's Whittington. I'm sorry.

LBJ: Now how in the hell do they expect me to be nice—look at that. These dumbbells! Who in the hell—tell Cliff[1] if he can't get people that spell better than that—and all of them are the same way. . . . They don't know how to spell Gronouski.[2] They'd better find out how to spell it. . . . They obviously don't know how and they can't read. . . . Sign that one out there tonight to Martin Luther King, so be sure and get it. [signing pictures] And get her in here. Here, take these. Tell Cliff he can go on home.

VOICE: Gerri? Here, Mr. President, this is Miss Whittington.

LBJ: Come in, honey. Pull up a chair. . . . [to aide:] Whoever you get down here to spell names again, you get them, they can't spell their own name.

VOICE: Well, I told the boys be sure and check.

LBJ: Well, they didn't check anything. They don't know how to spell.

---

[1] Clifton Carter, soon to be Johnson's man on the Democratic National Committee.
[2] Postmaster General John Gronouski.

WEDNESDAY, DECEMBER 25, 1963

DWIGHT and MAMIE EISENHOWER
1:16 P.M.

HAVING ATTENDED the Green funeral in Philadelphia, the exhausted Johnson has flown to Texas to spend Christmas with his family at the LBJ Ranch.[1] Johnson wishes the Eisenhowers a Merry Christmas at their winter home in Palm Desert, California.

EISENHOWER: Mamie and I are just so old, we've just finished opening our presents, and we're just exhausted.

LBJ: Well, I got one for you, but I haven't sent it. I had to get it leather-bound and put your initials on it, but that "Frugality and Thrift and Economy" speech,[2] I just had it made up to send to you for a Christmas present.

EISENHOWER: Why, thank you very much indeed.

LBJ: I think you're going to enjoy the budget more, though, than you did the speech.

. . . .

LBJ: I tell a story about when America gets in trouble and people close ranks and we lost the President,[3] I said President Eisenhower just came down on his own and even borrowed a plane, wouldn't let me send for him, and got a yellow pencil and a yellow tablet and got in the back room and wrote out some things, and I don't want to give him credit for all the message[4] because he wouldn't want it, but I'll tell you, the good parts of it he helped me on.

EISENHOWER: . . . I'm delighted it started off that way.

LBJ: Well, what are we going to do, Mr. President? We can't get our budget down as much as you'd like, but we're going to—the Kennedy administration has added 133,000 employees in three years. And we're cutting it enough that we're going to have less employees in '65 than we had in '64, although every department has asked for substantial increases.

EISENHOWER: They always do.

LBJ: Particularly the mail people and folks like that. But I got the Post Office Department today to cut out five thousand employees they'd asked for. For the first time in fifteen years, we've got the Pentagon under a million civilian employees, and we're just talking it every day and trying to make each one of them set

[1] Lady Bird wrote in her diary of watching her husband and A.W. Moursund driving away in the Hill Country sunset: "How often I had seen that picture—how much I like it—and what a real release—it's just like getting out of jail finally. I'm sure they had a gun in there—they expected to do a little deer hunting, but more talking" (December 24, 1963).

[2] On Ike's advice, Johnson in his first speech to Congress had said, using Eisenhoverian language, "I pledge that the expenditures of your government will be administered with the utmost thrift and frugality. I will insist that the government get a dollar's value for a dollar spent. The government will set an example of prudence and economy."

[3] Kennedy.

[4] Johnson's first message to Congress.

an example and making them compete with each other. And I don't know whether it'll do any good or not, but that's what you wanted done.

EISENHOWER: Mr. President, don't forget your own baby there. Now, that space can take a little bit of contraction.[1]

LBJ: We moved them down a good deal, and we've still got an item that we're debating about to take up to come down here this week that involves a few hundred million. So I think that you're going to be pleased with it. I honestly do. . . . Here's Lady Bird.

EISENHOWER: Well, how are you, Miz Lady Bird?

LADY BIRD: Mr. President, I just wanted to say two things. One, that one of the nicest times that I myself had when I was living at The Elms was having your sweet wife there for lunch, and her pretty daughter-in-law.

EISENHOWER: . . . She remembers and talked to me about that luncheon the other day.

LADY BIRD: . . . The second thing is that I remember, with a great deal of pleasure, the constructive way that you and Lyndon worked together from different sides of this country when you-all—when you were President and he was running his side of the show. And I sure hope that we can have more of that in time to come. And I appreciate your cooperation and your kindness to him during this last very dreadful month.

EISENHOWER: . . . Any little thing I could do, I'd have cheerfully done. And I think it's going pretty well. Mamie would like to, Miz Johnson, say Merry Christmas to you.

MAMIE EISENHOWER: Well, good morning!

LADY BIRD: Good morning! And I hope you're having just as beautiful and sunny a day. Are you in Pennsylvania?

MAMIE EISENHOWER: No, darling, we're here at Eldorado[2] in Palm Desert. The palm trees are blowing around here, and the sun's shining. Oh, it's gorgeous. We flew out of Pennsylvania two weeks ago.

LADY BIRD: We're here in about 70-degree weather in Texas with about thirty-two kinfolks. . . . Have a happy, happy Christmas.

MAMIE EISENHOWER: Same to you, dear.

JAMES RESTON
Columnist and Washington Bureau Chief, New York Times
8:12 P.M.

ON CHRISTMAS NIGHT, the President describes his day to Reston, his Hill Country accent a bit more pronounced than when he was in Washington.

[1] Eisenhower was a major critic of the Kennedy-Johnson space program, especially the moon landing project. He considered JFK's pledge to land a man on the moon before the decade was out unnecessary and too expensive. (See Stephen E. Ambrose, *Eisenhower: The President,* Simon & Schuster, 1984, pp. 640–41.)
[2] Country Club.

LBJ: We had about 75-degree temperature. Had forty-three of my kinfolks in. We talked about our days as youths. [laughs] And we had a lot of cornbread dressin', and I've had indigestion ever since. [laughs] Had good turkey and went out in the boat this afternoon—a little motorboat—and got a little sunshine on me, and got my two daughters here and my wife. And my good friend Buford Ellington from Tennessee[1] . . . is going hunting with me in the morning. And I just called you to tell you that I was thinking of you and hope you had a Merry Christmas, appreciated your friendship and want your advice and counsel in the days ahead because, God A-mighty, I've got so much to do.[2] I don't know how I'll ever do it. And I've got to have some friends who will speak with candor. The main reason though that I called is that Lady Bird wanted to thank you for your column that appeared today.[3] . . . We get it out here in the morning and wish that you could be down here with us during this good weather.

RESTON: I wanted to come down . . . but I've got to go west, and I just may go through there on my way back.

LBJ: . . . If you do, let me know and you can come out here in the 'copter. Just fifteen minutes from Austin. Come out and have a meal with me.[4]

• • • •

LBJ: My Christmas is very empty since I don't have my Mama. . . . Here's Lady Bird that wants to talk with you before we run up a phone bill. . . .

LADY BIRD: Mr. Reston? What I really don't understand is how you know so much about it, without having lived it? . . . If I wished for two virtues, it would be elasticity and compassion. . . . Sometime I would like to show you, quietly and serenely, if possible, the wonderful country which has made our life, and which

[1] Governor of Tennessee.

[2] These are almost exactly the same as the last words of one of Johnson's heroes, Huey Long, before his death by gunshot in 1935.

[3] Reston had written, "Christmas is no time to tell the truth about the politicians in Washington, so maybe it is the time to tell the truth about their wives. . . . Everybody knows about President Johnson's transition from the Vice Presidency to the Presidency. . . . Mrs. Johnson was there too, always trying to be just a step behind the President, but with that steady sympathetic look. Nevertheless . . . family life in Washington does not stop when official life changes. How . . . for example, do you explain to teenage daughters that Secret Servicemen now have to go along with them on dates? How do you adjust Christmas at the LBJ Ranch to a couple of hundred reporters trying to find out whether you had grits for breakfast, and meanwhile, how do you take care of the Chancellor of West Germany or the Joint Chiefs of Staff who have flown in to discuss the future of the human race?"

[4] Reston and his wife accepted. They and their son Richard stayed overnight at the LBJ Ranch. The Restons flew back to Washington with the Johnsons on *Air Force One* on January 5. The *New York Times* columnist had been in Arizona to interview Barry Goldwater, who had just announced his candidacy for the Republican presidential nomination. Reston recalled in his memoirs, *Deadline* (Times Books, 1991), that Johnson "didn't particularly want to see me, but he wanted to know how the press had reacted to Goldwater's announcement. When we got there, he was worried, not only about Goldwater, but also about all the appointments he would have to make and the first budget he would have to present to the Congress in a few days." When they arrived in Washington, Johnson took the Restons to the White House, saying, "I want to show you something." In the upstairs presidential bedroom suite, LBJ knelt and pointed at an inscription on the fireplace keystone installed by Jacqueline Kennedy saying that she and her husband had lived there, with the dates. Reston wrote, "Johnson nodded to it . . . and raised his eyebrows but didn't say a word. Then he let us go. The stone has since been removed. By whom, nobody seems to know" (pp. 313–14).

has made Lyndon whatever he is because it is the Lord's blessedest pieces of real estate. [laughs]

. . . .

LBJ: Scotty,[1] I want to tell you something real good that's come out of all this to me, and that is the great comfort and strength that I got from Bill Fulbright.[2]

RESTON: He's a wonderful man.

LBJ: I've been in with him a dozen times, and whether it's recognizing the Dominican Republic or Honduras or what it was, or the foreign aid bill, he's just been marvelous, and I don't know how we would have made it without him.

ROBERT McNAMARA
8:27 P.M.

LBJ: Bob, you're one of the nicest things about this Christmas, as far as I'm concerned, and I just wanted to call and tell you and Marg[3] that we were thinking of you, that we hope that you have a wonderful New Year, and you've made our year mighty comforting to know that you're around.

McNAMARA: I can't tell you how grateful I am for your thoughtfulness in calling. . . .

LBJ: We've talked all day and had a delightful day. The weather's 75, and the sun's shining bright, and had all the family around us that meant so much to us, and there's nobody in the government that means more than you, and I just wanted to say that to you. Here's Lady Bird, Bob.

LADY BIRD: Mr. Secretary? . . . Anybody like you who would take time to say a word to me, not to Lyndon—I wouldn't be surprised if you were talking to him, but to me the other day—you don't know how impressed I was.

McNAMARA: You don't know how much we are thinking of you, and how delighted we are that you both are down at the ranch. I hope that he has a very restful day. . . .

LADY BIRD: Serenity is my goal, and contemplation is my greatest desire, and, and next to that, you-all are [laughs] the big staff that we lean on, so we hope that you two get strength and happiness and a good time with all the kinfolks and we will see you in January.

AMON CARTER, JR.
Publisher, Fort Worth Star-Telegram
8:39 P.M.

LBJ: You just tell your crowd over at the *Star-Telegram* that you want to be damn sure that you've got as competent a man . . . as the *New York Times* has got in those press conferences, because you want the President's home state to

[1] Reston's nickname.
[2] Johnson knows, of course, that Reston is a Fulbright admirer.
[3] McNamara's wife, Margaret.

be represented by real intelligence. . . . Just get the best damn fellow for the *Star-Telegram.* Whether you spend a hundred dollars a week more or not, you'll never remember a year from now. . . . If you have to, you can go out . . . and get Sears, Roebuck and them to buy a few more pages of ads. . . .

CARTER: All right sir, I will.

LBJ: 'Cause I'll guarantee you, I'll play ball with him, and I wouldn't be there if it hadn't been for the Carters.[1]

GOULD LINCOLN
Columnist, Washington Star
8:50 P.M.

LINCOLN: I certainly am glad you made those people come back and vote.[2] . . . That's what they need.

LBJ: Well, they *had* to. They had to. You see, Gould . . . the whole Communist world was watching to see any sign of weakness or temporizing or compromising or running on the part of the President. . . . If I'd let it go unchallenged, they'd have said, "Well, he's a weak sister. He hasn't got any steel in his spine, and hell, we don't need to pay any attention to him. He's a pushover." So I just thought I had to go to bat on it, and I hated like the devil to ask people that had run off to come on back, but . . . I just thought you had to stand up and be a man or a mouse.

THURSDAY, DECEMBER 26, 1963

HOUSTON HARTE
Owner, San Angelo Standard Times, *San Angelo, Texas*
9:42 P.M.

HARTE: How did you get along with those *New York Daily News* boys?[3]

LBJ: Got along pretty well. Had a wonderful lunch. They wrote a mean editorial the next day, saying that I was a no-good son of a bitch. I don't understand it. But I got along with them fine and they seemed to be happy. But the next day they wrote an editorial that said that Johnson is selling out the country to Russia. . . . Why don't you call 'em and ask them tomorrow how *they* got along? Tell 'em that I saw all of 'em and I spent two hours with them. I just leaned over and did everything I could.

---

[1] The Carters had been old Johnson political financiers.
[2] For the foreign aid bill.
[3] Johnson had lunched on Saturday, December 21, at the White House with the publisher, managing editor, and Washington bureau chief of the *Daily News.*

TUESDAY, DECEMBER 31, 1963

DEAN RUSK
11:30 A.M.

LBJ: I sure wish you'd find out who's leaking all that stuff out of that Latin American division every day. The *New York Times* is getting these editorials and putting the heat on me. . . . They had all this information before you and Mann[1] got it to me, and I sure don't think that many ought to have that kind of information. . . .

RUSK: That's right. Now, are you thinking of . . . this morning in particular?

LBJ: No. I'm talking about Tad Szulc's story the day before yesterday. . . . There are just so many leaks coming out of there, I don't know how we run a government that way. And I don't know who it is, but there must be some way to see who he's seeing.

RUSK: Let me get onto that.

LBJ: It just almost makes me veto appointments if they say they're already made. I just don't want to confirm that they're that close in my administration, and if they are, why—

RUSK: Something ought to be done about it, right.

LBJ: Sure. Khrushchev may even know more about the government than I do.

[1] Thomas Mann, the State Department's new man for Latin America.

Chapter Three

JANUARY 1964

WEDNESDAY, JANUARY 1, 1964

HELEN GAHAGAN DOUGLAS
Former Democratic Congresswoman from California
Exact Time Unknown

JOHNSON HAD AN INTIMATE relationship with the vivacious, progressive ex-actress when they were both in the House in the 1940s.[1] LBJ never forgave Richard Nixon for his 1950 Senate campaign against Douglas, in which Nixon falsely implied that she was a Communist. Now Johnson invites her to perform a ceremonial chore. He knows that this will score him points with liberal Democrats who remain suspicious of him, but he would also sentimentally like to help relieve whatever cloud lingers over Douglas in the public mind from 1950.

LBJ: Happy New Year, sweetheart!

DOUGLAS: Happy New Year! Oh, Lyndon, you're doing wonderfully.

LBJ: I don't know, I don't know.

DOUGLAS: Yes you are. I sat in absolute admiration and, oh, it's just, you know, everything is just right.

LBJ: I'm cutting down the military bases—some of these archaic, old, out-fashioned things, and Khrushchev's cutting his down too[2] . . . and I'm taking that money and putting it into poverty.[3] Then I'm going to have a budget that's lower than they've ever had it.

[1] Joseph Califano, LBJ's domestic adviser from 1965 to 1969, notes the Douglas relationship in *The Triumph and Tragedy of Lyndon Johnson* (Simon & Schuster, 1991), citing an interview with longtime Johnson aide Horace Busby (p. 337).
[2] On December 13, 1963, Khrushchev had announced plans to cut Soviet military spending and the size of his armed forces.
[3] Johnson was preparing an anti-poverty proposal for his State of the Union.

DOUGLAS: That's wonderful! That's terrific!

LBJ: ... I want you to do something for me. I want you to go as my representative ... to Liberia for their hundredth anniversary of the relations between the United States and Liberia. I'd like to go myself. ... But I can't do it. And it's this Saturday.

DOUGLAS: This *Saturday?*

LBJ: Yeah, it's this Saturday. What you shouting about? That's four days longer than you usually have.

DOUGLAS: Oh, Lyndon.

LBJ: C'mon, chicken. Now don't chicken on me! This'll be good for you. I want you to get back in the public eye a little bit. ... You won't have to be gone for three or four days. You just get your little tennies ready.

DOUGLAS: Wait till I call Mel. [calls to her husband, the actor Melvyn Douglas:] Melvyn! Come here, dear.

LBJ: I thought you ran your own house. Don't tell me that you got to clear things with Sidney.[1]

DOUGLAS: Of course, I have to clear things with Sidney!

· · · ·

DOUGLAS: [consults husband, then:] Lyndon, all right ... and that's Liberia?

LBJ: That's Liberia. ... You just go and see how they're doing, and I'll see you after you get back. We're going to have to run against Nixon.[2] ... I'm just going to have *you* running against him, 'cause he treated you so unfairly.

DOUGLAS: Lyndon, you know I've set that time aside. ... One last thing—don't overdo yourself. ...

LBJ: ... You quit lecturing me, or I'll put you back in the Army![3]

DOUGLAS: [laughs] Wait a minute. ... You know what Mel said to me the other night? ... He suddenly looked at me—you know, he never knew you the way I did.

LBJ: Yeah.

DOUGLAS: He said, "You know, he just might be one of the really great ones."

LBJ: [laughs]

MELVYN DOUGLAS: Hello, sir.[4]

LBJ: Hi, Melvyn. How are you?

MELVYN DOUGLAS: ... I said, "This man might turn out to be one hell of a President."

---

[1] A reference dating back to 1944, when Republicans accused Franklin Roosevelt of requiring that major decisions be "cleared" with the labor leader Sidney Hillman.

[2] LBJ is not really so sure that Nixon will be his opponent but he is trying to motivate Douglas to do his bidding.

[3] In July 1941, five months before Pearl Harbor, Franklin Roosevelt had appointed Douglas to a volunteer committee under the Office of Civilian Defense to help prepare for air raids, sabotage, or other disasters that might come with war.

[4] Melvyn Douglas had once campaigned for Johnson in Texas at Franklin Roosevelt's request.

LBJ: [laughs] Well . . . I hope I'm as hell of a good President as you are in your profession, and we're mighty proud of you, and I just wanted Helen to get back into the limelight a little bit. . . . I wanted to go myself when I was Vice President, but this tragedy happened and I can't go. And I want somebody that's compassionate and understanding to represent the President. . . . Lady Bird wants to say a word to you and to Helen too.

LADY BIRD: Mel-vyn. . . . One of the nicest things that could happen to us in the New Year would be to get to see you and Helen.

MELVYN DOUGLAS: You're so sweet. . . . We both have sat here with our mouths open in admiration of both of you.

LADY BIRD: Don't worry. Hard times will come and you'll have to take it all back but I'll tell you, you never saw a man try harder. . . .

DOUGLAS: Lady Bird!

LADY BIRD: [sweetly:] Ah, Helll-en, so nice to hear you, and honey, let me—

DOUGLAS: You don't know what praises he's getting out here. . . . Those Republican friends of ours said the first Democratic President they're ever going to vote for is Lyndon Johnson. [laughs]

LADY BIRD: . . . I was out in California. . . . I ran into your friends right and left and liked them all so much. . . . [she listens to LBJ aside, then:] Lyndon sent you this sassy message which—I guess I'm used to it 'cause I like for women to like him, and I like him to like them—but anyhow, he said that he and Roz Wyman[1] hit it off very well indeed—partly because of you.[2]

THURSDAY, JANUARY 2, 1964

GEORGE BROWN
Chairman of the Board, Brown & Root, Inc.
11:55 A.M.

BROWN, one of Johnson's earliest financial backers, whose long and many-layered relationship with LBJ was central to the success of both of them,[3] has

[1] Wife of Eugene Wyman, a prominent Los Angeles Democratic fund-raiser.
[2] During her journey to Liberia, Douglas wrote Johnson, "I am on my way! Believe me, it wasn't easy. Getting the proper attire for the occasion was almost as difficult as trying to get to the moon" (January 4, 1964, Johnson Library). At LBJ's request, she told the Liberian President, William Tubman, to rest assured that, although a Southerner, Johnson was concerned about Africa and civil rights. As Douglas later told the story, Tubman wept (Douglas oral history, Johnson Library).
[3] On Johnson and Brown, see particularly the two published volumes of Robert A. Caro's biography *The Years of Lyndon Johnson* (Knopf, 1982 and 1990). Caro writes, "As Brown & Root became, with Johnson's help, an industrial colossus, one of the largest construction companies—and shipbuilding companies and oil-equipment companies—in the world, holder of Johnson-arranged government contracts and receiver of Johnson-arranged government favors

asked him on behalf of another old supporter, Gus Wortham, a Houston insurance tycoon, and John Jones, president of the *Houston Chronicle,* to ask Robert Kennedy's antitrust officials to suspend antitrust restrictions against a merger they are seeking between two Houston banks.[1] As a master horse trader, Johnson was not averse to asking a political price for doing something he may have privately decided to do anyway.[2] In this case, he wants a written promise from Jones that the *Chronicle* will support him as long as he is President. In the conversation below, LBJ insists that John Kennedy had told him on the evening of November 21, 1963, that he was going to exact the same price from Jones.

LBJ: I've got a lot of trouble on my bank down there. And I'm not going to go through with it. . . . If we approve it at all, it'll have to be later[3]. . . . Albert's[4] a little upset. It looks like it'll probably mean that he and Wortham will be upset. But I just can't do it at this moment. . . . I've got problems of my own. And I'm not going to ruin my presidency[5] just on account of something personal. . . . [I want] John Jones to write me a letter telling me that he is our friend, he enjoyed being up here,[6] and that he wanted me to know that he and the *Chronicle* are the strongest supporters of my administration, sincerely, which is a very simple, dignified letter. I never could get him to say that the other day when he was here. I tried to get him to all morning and he finally came around and said, "Whenever you need anything, call on us." There's a hell of a lot of difference, if you follow me. And I know the Joneses, 'cause I dealt with Jesse in the '41 campaign.[7] And Gus was never able to deliver him, and nobody else was. Including Roosevelt. You remember?

BROWN: Yeah.

LBJ: And they say if I approve the merger in Houston . . . it'll be the first action of this administration . . . and it will set off a round of consolidations among the bigger banks in the nation. . . . They'll say in Minneapolis, where they were

---

amounting to billions of dollars, suave George Brown and his fierce brother Herman became the principal financiers of Johnson's rise to national power" (Volume I, *The Path to Power,* p. xvi).

[1] The National Bank of Commerce and the Texas National Bank, the second and fourth largest banks in Houston.

[2] Johnson's attitude toward corporate mergers was generally tolerant. In 1967, while sounding out Ramsey Clark about being Attorney General, he showed his irritation with what he considered to be antitrust zealots in the Justice Department: "You-all try to run the whole government on those antitrust cases. . . . I think you-all have built an empire where you have the veto power over the President . . . and I think it is outrageous" (conversation with Ramsey Clark, January 25, 1967, 8:22 P.M.).

[3] Presumably Johnson means after the 1964 election.

[4] Houston Congressman Albert Thomas was pressuring Johnson on Wortham's behalf to make the ruling.

[5] To turn up the pressure on Jones, Johnson exaggerates the sacrifice he would be making for him.

[6] On Friday morning, December 27, 1963, Jones and Wortham had ridden with Johnson around the LBJ Ranch. In a Johnson Library oral history, Jones recalled that he and Wortham "had gone up to see him about something. I've forgotten what it was."

[7] John Jones's uncle, Jesse, was chairman of FDR's Reconstruction Finance Corporation and, from 1940 to 1945, Secretary of Commerce, as well as owner of the *Chronicle* and Texas radio stations. Despite pressure from President Roosevelt, he had refused to support LBJ in his losing 1941 bid for the Senate. Jones also opposed Johnson's successful Senate campaign in 1948.

turned down, "Well Johnson's got a little different attitude from Bobby Kennedy." And they say that the Texas case is a very bad precedent to start with. I wouldn't mind overriding that if I was overriding it for anything.

BROWN: To be perfectly honest with you, President Kennedy said he was going to approve it.

LBJ: No, he *hadn't* said he was going to approve it. He told me that he was going to get that *Chronicle* right in his hip pocket to support him for the rest of his life or he wasn't going to give them the time of day.

BROWN: He told John while riding out to the airport.[1]

LBJ: No, he didn't. No, he didn't.

BROWN: Well, John quoted him that way.

LBJ: I don't give a damn what he quoted him to. Everybody's quoting Kennedy on everything, George. But I know this 'cause I was in on it . . . very much. I talked to him that night, and I talked to him the next morning and I talked to him a good deal of times about both Fort Worth and Houston. And nobody has committed anybody to anything, and if they were committed, they oughtn't to be committed—unless it's a *mutual* affair.[2] Do you agree?

BROWN: Yeah. As far as you doing it, I mean, if you want to get out of it, why, you say that though Kennedy already has approved it.

LBJ: I can't do that though. He hadn't done that . . . and the Attorney General hadn't done it. . . . And Mr. Kennedy doesn't have to approve it, you see. It's just these underlings.[3] But . . . I have to order them to do it over their objection. And I'm sure it'll be in the columns the next morning. . . . I think the smart thing to do and the wise thing is—if he doesn't feel like he wants to write a little letter like that—just let it go for a few months and let some others be acted on and then take another look at it.[4] . . . I know damn well it'd be lighter on me. And I love Gus . . . but if his feelings are going to get hurt 'cause I don't approve something for him, why, maybe he—

BROWN: Oh, I think that's Albert talking. . . .

LBJ: . . . We wanted a letter and very frankly, what I was going to do was take the letter and send it to an emissary . . . and say, "Now here, goddamn it. You-all've got jobs as well as we have. This fellow here is important to us and we've got to carry this state.[5] And we've just got to do this. Period.". . . Gus [should] just say, "Mr. President . . . I just enjoyed the lunch with you very much and enjoyed the morning visit with you, and good to see you with Mr. Wortham and with Congressman Thomas, and I just want you to know that we're making arrangements for special coverage in Washington for the *Chronicle*"—which they've already done—"and that so far as I'm personally concerned and the paper's concerned, it's going to support your administration as long as you're

[1] Kennedy and Jones, along with their wives, rode together to the Houston airport on Thursday evening, November 21, 1963, before JFK flew on to Fort Worth and Dallas.
[2] Note the last five words of this sentence.
[3] Antitrust officials in the Justice Department.
[4] Here Johnson tacitly suggests that he may be planning to approve the merger anyway.
[5] Texas.

there. Sincerely, your friend, John Jones." And I would have a little lever to hit Bobby[1] and the rest of them, unless they want to defeat me. Now that's what President Kennedy said he was going to make 'em do. And I don't see a damn thing wrong with that. . . . Gus said well, he didn't know . . . whether he'd get this letter. . . . So this morning Albert calls and says that Gus is upset and Gus is worried and Gus is mad, that he thinks that Johnson ought to do this for *him*. Well now, I'll do anything for Gus. . . . I ain't going to get myself in an indefensible position—and I *am* in an indefensible position. And both Justice and Treasury will uncock me right quick, if I do it. So I don't want you to think—it's not because I don't love you and Gus. I just know when you're dealing with the Joneses, you gotta deal with the Joneses. And if he's not that interested in me and not that loyal to me and not even put me in a position where I can tell the people that are fighting him that I'm getting his support, then I've got nothing to fight *with*. And there isn't a goddamn better reason I know of why I should act, do you?

BROWN: . . . Your friends out here want you to.

LBJ: . . . I ain't going to do it, George, unless John Jones is willing to say to me that he's my friend. Don't you think that's a reasonable position?

BROWN: I think it's all right, except that Albert thought it was too much of a cash-and-carry thing. . . . Too much of a trade. . . . It'd hurt you as well as them.

LBJ: . . . Why doesn't he want them committed to me?

BROWN: He . . . says they are committed. He just doesn't think you ought to do it in writing. . . .

LBJ: We may not be there[2] but a little while, but if they don't want to tell me that they're my friends in writing, why, I don't know. . . . I don't want to be pressuring them. I just wanted to tell you, because I'm not going to do it as long as their attitude's that way. . . . I'm afraid that Albert thinks that if they're committed to me . . . they're going to hurt him. Now we've got to quit that damned childish play.

BROWN: I don't think he thinks that.

LBJ: I know I've been trying to have a good dinner[3] in Houston for three goddamned years. And either he's[4] just getting ready to have one or he wants to put it off or something else, constantly. I know that he played around with Yarborough on this whole damned trip.[5] When he was supposed to ride with me, he had Yarborough back there and he was riding with him. I wouldn't have allowed the son of a bitch to ride with me . . . if the positions had been reversed. I know he just whored all over the lot. I know he's jealous and mean and vicious as hell, and you know he is too. And I ain't going to stick my neck to ruin myself *nationally* just to follow his directions. Now we've told Gus what we want. And we want a very simple, easy little letter and we want 'em to live up to it—

[1] Kennedy.
[2] In the White House.
[3] Meaning a fund-raising dinner.
[4] Thomas.
[5] The Kennedy visit to Texas.

namely, that they're my friends and they're going to support me. And they don't have to be mentioning the goddamned bank or anything else. And we want an argument on these four points, written down on legal stationery, by the best lawyer they've got, as to why this won't kick off a series of mergers . . . so I can take that argument and show it to 'em and send a man with both of 'em and say, "Here, gentlemen, here's the way we think you ought to do." Now I think I know more about how to run my business than Albert does.

BROWN: [laughs] I know damn well you do.

LBJ: . . . You don't want to quote me, but you can just say you know me well enough to know, by God, that as long as that letter ain't there, the approval ain't there. . . . I've got no real interest in John Jones. I can get by without the *Chronicle*. . . . Damned well. I would say in the last week that the most hurtful headline nearly every day has been from the *Chronicle*. . . . [I want Albert told] that till we get that letter, we're not going to act. . . . I want to take John's letter, very frankly, to turn over to one of Bobby Kennedy's strongmen and say, "This guy's supporting us and we've got to quit cracking at him. If you're going to stay in this Cabinet, we've got to do it." Now Albert doesn't know the byplay going on within the administration.

BROWN: He thinks you're going to lose Bobby anyway. . . . He's a very confused person.

LBJ: He may be, but that don't make a goddamn if I've got the Controller that goes on and approves it. And if I need the letter to do it, he ought to let me have it. . . .

BROWN: I wouldn't . . . tell Albert anything. Let me talk to Gus.

LBJ: All right.

BROWN: . . . You know, old Albert wants to take credit for this thing. That's what he's playing for.

LBJ: I sure do. . . . [puckishly:] Why don't he let me have a little?

BROWN: That's the way he is. You know it as well as I do. . . .

LBJ: . . . You just go on and get Gus out there and we'll act in accordance with your instructions. But you be damned sure that you and Gus have that *Chronicle*, and you get me that letter and I'll be sure that I send that over . . . and I'll have him meet with this boy at the National Committee[1] that handles the business and I'll have them sit down with the Controller of the Currency and we'll override the whole goddamned outfit. And they'll do it, to hold their own jobs.

IRVING FRANK
Clothier, Sol Frank Uniforms, San Antonio
12:25 P.M.

JOHNSON PLANS to outfit his White House staff, while they are at the ranch, in casual Western ranch suits identical to his.

[1] Democratic National Committee.

LBJ: Mr. Frank, are you the one that sent this suit up here?

FRANK: Yes.

LBJ: I liked it very very much and I just wondered . . . about what do those wholesale out at—that shirt and trousers?

FRANK: I hadn't figured a price on it. How many would you want?

LBJ: I don't know. I just thought I might put a few of the staff around here in 'em—a dozen or so.

FRANK: I'd be glad to figure out a price. Am I speaking to the President?

LBJ: Yes.

FRANK: Mr. Johnson, it's a real honor to talk to you.

LBJ: Thank you. Good to hear you. You do that and if you can—what'd you guess, if you had to—

FRANK: . . . It'd be a real privilege for us to make some of these garments for you and if you thought—

LBJ: We want to pay you something though. You just tell—

FRANK: Oh, twenty, twenty-five dollars.

LBJ: Why don't you send somebody up here that can take some measurements? Are you going to come yourself?

FRANK: I might come myself.

LBJ: What's your given name?

FRANK: Irving, I-R-V-I-N-G.

LBJ: I'll just tell 'em at the gate to let you in. You come up sometime before five o'clock.

FRANK: Today. That's at the LBJ Ranch at Johnson City?

LBJ: Yep. Now when you get to Blanco, you just ask them how to cut through to Stonewall. There's a back way that saves you fifteen miles and it's a paved road. . . . Bring somebody to measure—and stay out of the newspapers.

McGEORGE BUNDY
3:00 P.M.

LBJ: Mac, I want to make a suggestion that doesn't have any originality, but I wonder why you don't get Rusk and the five ablest men in the State Department and go up to Camp David and lock the gate this weekend and try to find some imaginative proposal or some initiative that we can take besides just reacting to actions and just let Khrushchev wire everybody twenty-five pages every two days[1] and us just sit back and dodge. Now you-all are supposed to be a brains group and have a lot of imagination and be soft on Russia.

BUNDY: [laughs]

---

[1] On New Year's Day, Khrushchev had sent a six-thousand-word letter to Johnson and other world leaders renewing the Soviet call for an East-West nonaggression pact.

LBJ: And yet we act like Adenauer[1]—and I don't think we ought to do anything impulsive. I want plenty of deliberation. But I've been in government six weeks and I've just had people tell me what I couldn't do. So you just tell the Secretary that I would like for you-all to take your wives, if you need to. If not, leave 'em at home. But go around and think and be some wise men and see if you can't come up with some proposals besides just having him run me in a corner and me dodge. . . . Does that make sense to you?

BUNDY: Yes, sir, it does. As a matter of fact, I had an hour with Lippmann[2] at lunch today and he had some quite sweeping proposals that he thinks are just right for '64 and I have been brooding over some myself. . . . Do you want something you can say next week or do you want something you can say before the end of January?

LBJ: I want some I can say next week and some I can say before the end of January and some I can say every Saturday night. I am tired, by God, of having him[3] be the man who wants peace and I am the guy who wants war. And I'm just a big, fat slob that they throw a dagger into and I bleed and squirm just like a Mexican bullfighter.

BUNDY: Mr. President, you're in a lot better shape than that, but I do get the thrust of your argument just the same. [laughs] And we'll do it.

LBJ: Now the headlines are all right but we want to get some substance to our proposals. [reads newspaper headlines aloud:] "Johnson Aims at Further Steps Towards Peace." That's the *Baltimore Sun.* "Johnson Writing Khrushchev." *Washington Post.* "Johnson Seeks Peace Offensive." Now let's *get* us an offensive! McNamara—when I told him we wanted economy, he said, "Mr. President, if you want to give substance to your proposals, here are thirty-four bases in thirteen states." I want Mr. Rusk to say to me, "Mr. President, if you want to give substance to your proposals, here are four of them." If they do not have any, go out and get some young Democratic club to give you some.

BUNDY: All right. Old Walter Lippmann has more per square inch than anybody else.

LBJ: Well, let's have some of them. Put one or two on a ticker this afternoon[4] and let me read them. I would like to have something fresh down here that I would at least like to massage my brain with. I read all about this brain trust that I have over there—all these State Department career men and the foreign service and all that kind of stuff and all they've said is, "This is what we *can't* do, Mr. President."

BUNDY: Well, Mr. President, it is in fact harder than McNamara's business, but it is a challenger.

LBJ: Of course, it's harder. Khrushchev has got somebody that's doing it.

BUNDY: Pretty thin pap.

---

[1] The elderly former West German Chancellor, Konrad Adenauer.
[2] The syndicated columnist had floated some foreign policy ideas with his old friend Bundy.
[3] Khrushchev.
[4] Meaning send them from the White House by written communication lines to Johnson in Texas.

LBJ: That's all right.

BUNDY: We can do better than that.

LBJ: That's right. I thought our system's better than his.

FRIDAY, JANUARY 3, 1964

WALTER JENKINS
2:00 P.M.

> DURING FOREIGN TRIPS as Vice President, Johnson loved to shop for bargains while looking for souvenirs and trinkets usable for political gifts back home. Jenkins breaks the news that he must now pay up for a 1963 trip to northern Europe.

JENKINS: We've got to pay a bill to State, quite a big one.

LBJ: For what?

JENKINS: . . . From Luxembourg, liquor, silver, paintings, jewelry.

LBJ: I didn't know how many—I thought that was already taken care of.

JENKINS: $1,700.

LBJ: Hmmm. . . . And I got one of those frames, the silver frames yesterday. . . . Tell them to look all over the country to buy 'em cheaper. I'm not going to pay $75 for one of those silver frames. . . . Go all over the country and see who builds them and if they won't build some for us.

JENKINS: They've got them at Tiffany's, which is probably the high end—

LBJ: Absolutely don't want 'em.

MONDAY, JANUARY 6, 1964

JOHN MACY
Chairman, U.S. Civil Service Commission
3:30 P.M.

LBJ: I want you to get with Walter Jenkins and do one thing for me, if we have to steal the money from the diplomatic fund. I want the five smartest, best-educated, fastest, prettiest secretaries in Washington. And I want to put them right here under my office where I can get them and dictate. I waited an hour and a half this morning and had the goddamn Cabinet sitting around and waiting to try to get the State of the Union out. And people that can't spell their name are operating and I just don't think a President ought to have to do that.

MACY: Absolutely not.

LBJ: Now, you just start looking. . . . I don't want any old, broken-down old maids. I want them from twenty-five to forty. I want them that can work Saturday and Sunday, I want them that can work at night and not be afraid to go home after the Secret Service takes them out of the gate. . . . I had my missiles leaked on me yesterday from Defense, Latin America leaked on State Department, and pay raises today. So I've got to have some people that I can trust.

WHITNEY YOUNG
3:55 P.M.

JOHNSON ASKS the Urban League leader for help in quashing lingering doubts about him among American blacks.

LBJ: You-all can do something about letting 'em know that I'm not a hater and a bigot. You know that, but a lot of 'em don't. They keep saying I have all this trouble in the Negro community and I've never heard a Negro say that.

YOUNG: I haven't either.

LBJ: I've got a new secretary here. Do you know this little Whittington girl?

YOUNG: Yeah, I heard about that.

LBJ: Well, she's in my office and she's my personal secretary, and I took her to church with me yesterday in Stonewall, Texas, and she stayed in my home down there for two weeks and the most competent person in the world.[1] . . . But I keep reading in the columnists. They don't quote you and they don't quote Roy Wilkins and they don't quote Farmer and they don't quote Martin Luther King and they don't quote Phil Randolph 'cause every damned one of them knows that I'm stronger for them than nearly anybody around this place and have been for all these years.

ROY WILKINS
Executive Secretary, National Association for the Advancement of Colored People
5:12 P.M.

JOHNSON HAS SEEN a story come over the UPI ticker saying that today, at the annual meeting of the NAACP, Wilkins has threatened that if House Rules

[1] On New Year's Eve, Johnson had integrated the Forty Acres Club, the faculty club at the University of Texas in Austin, by escorting Whittington to a party there for his old aide Horace Busby. According to Merle Miller's *Lyndon* (Putnam, 1980), she had asked Johnson, "Mr. President, do you know what you're doing?" He replied, "Half of them are going to think you're my wife, and that's just fine with me" (p. 336). Lady Bird wrote in her diary, "There have been a lot of 'firsts' that we have brought into this country!" (January 5, 1964). Johnson

Chairman Howard Smith continues to delay the civil rights bill, blacks might be "forced" to retaliate against the Democrats. Anxious, the President gets on the telephone to Wilkins.

LBJ: When are you going to get down here and start civil rights?

WILKINS: As soon as I get rid of my board of directors and my annual meeting, which is winding up now.

LBJ: Well, you tell them that I think they've got a mighty good head man. I don't know a better one in the United States or a fairer one or abler one.

· · · ·

LBJ: What I want you to do . . . is get on this bill now, because unless you get twenty-five Republicans, you're not going to get to cloture. . . . I talked to Mansfield for an hour and a half this morning. . . . I told him the only way to do it is . . . either go around the clock[1] or get sixty-seven people—and start working on both. I can't be too much of a dictator but I'll help you in any way I can. I stimulated him as much as I could. He went out and told the press . . . he'd have to adjourn for the convention[2] and come back. That's terrible. . . . You're going to have to persuade Dirksen why this is in the interest of the Republican party.[3] . . . And let him know that you're going to go for the presidential candidate that offers you the best hope and the best chance of dignity and decency in this country. And you're going with a senatorial man who does the same thing. And then you're going to have to get busy and do something about it because they say I'm an arm-twister, but I can't make a Southerner change his spots any more than I can make a leopard change them.

WILKINS: That's right.

LBJ: . . . I'm no magician. . . . If we lose this fight, Roy, we're going back ten years.

· · · ·

WILKINS: You would be surprised at the number of people I ran into over the holiday, among my own folks, I mean, who said to me, "Look, don't you think that Lyndon Johnson is going to be moving better than the other man?"[4] . . .

LBJ: I'm going to put $500 million in this budget for poverty and a good deal of it ought to go to your people.[5] . . . Maybe you can get with Whitney Young or some of your other people and give me a little direction. . . . Now . . . I don't want to appoint these folks to judges unless you-all want them appointed.[6] I've got a hundred Johnson men that were for me for Congress, for the Senate, for

---

wished it known that he had hired a black secretary but feared that issuing a press release to that effect might be unsubtle. Instead he had it arranged for Whittington to appear on the television program *What's My Line?*

[1] Let a Southern-led filibuster proceed.

[2] The party conventions in the summer of 1964.

[3] This is Johnson's key mission in passing the civil rights bill.

[4] Meaning President Kennedy.

[5] Eager as ever to kill two birds with the same stone, Johnson wanted to assault poverty but he also wanted to help his political friends. (See also conversation with Richard Daley, January 20, 1964, below.)

[6] Johnson had consulted Wilkins on judicial appointments.

President when I got defeated, for Vice President and everything else. But I want to be fair to your people. . . . I'm just being damned sure that it is who you want. If you don't, I want to appoint somebody else.[1]

WILKINS: You've got my wire don't you?[2]

LBJ: Yes, but your wire . . . just said that you feel that I would want to. Well, I *don't* want to! I don't know them at all. I have never met either one of them.

WILKINS: . . . Robinson is a top-notch man. Top-notch . . .

LBJ: Am I going to get any credit if I name him?

WILKINS: Certainly will. I'll see to that.

LBJ: All right, now what about Higginbotham? . . . You want him appointed?

WILKINS: I would count it a favor.

LBJ: Well, it'll be done, period. And don't be so damned modest.

RUFUS YOUNGBLOOD
Secret Service Agent
8:05 P.M.

> JOHNSON IS FURIOUS about a memo reporting that his Secret Service agents dislike working for him and wish to be transferred. He is especially angry because the memo was written by a Kennedy holdover on his staff. Here he barks at the Georgia-born agent who shielded him with his body in the vice presidential car during the shots in Dallas.

LBJ: [Reads from memo,[3] then:] I just told Rowley[4] to call all of them in and to take any of 'em's resignations that wanted to. And I'd be glad to have his, if he wants to, yours or anybody else's. And if they don't want to handle it, we'll get the FBI to do it. I'm not going to have a car or a man that's got little enough judgment to be up fifty feet of me, because I've had two members of my family that had their necks knocked out of joint because idiots follow them and then when they stop in a hurry, they get their necks knocked out. . . . So you get ahold

[1] Here Johnson begins to go into his routine in granting patronage, as with Dirksen above.

[2] Wilkins had wired Johnson three days earlier that the NAACP "feels certain" that Johnson would wish to make recess appointments of Spottswood Robinson, who had gotten his start as an NAACP lawyer, and A. Leon Higginbotham of the Federal Trade Commission, the first black commissioner of an independent regulatory agency, as judges in the U.S. Circuit Court "since the Senate failed to confirm these nominees at its last session" (January 3, 1964, Johnson Library).

[3] The memo said, "I'm alarmed at the situation that has developed between the President and the Secret Service. Morale in the Secret Service is at an all-time low. A number of the members of the White House detail have been asking for transfers. This is a great body of men. These men feel they are being prevented from doing their job properly. These men do not want favors. They just want to be accepted. We need them badly especially in campaign years. They must feel the President appreciates their efforts. If they do something wrong, they do not want to be reprimanded . . . in public over a radio system which lots of people listen to." (Johnson Library archivists are unable to locate a copy of the memo, suggesting that LBJ may have disposed of it.)

[4] James Rowley, Chief, Secret Service.

of Rowley and you-all call a meeting of your group and . . . if you want to resign, I'll be glad to accept it forthwith. And if the Secret Service wants to go back to counterfeiting,[1] they can go back to counterfeiting, and I'll get FBI to assign me a couple of men. . . . I don't know who it is bellyaching. . . . I'm sorry it didn't come to me. It had to come through some of Kennedy's staffers.

YOUNGBLOOD: If I may ask, sir, who wrote the memorandum?

LBJ: I don't think I ought to do that, but one of Kennedy's top people and somebody has been bellyaching to him. And there's enough truth in it that somebody talked and I can't have disloyalty and I can't talk in front of people and have them repeat it.

YOUNGBLOOD: You're absolutely right. You cannot have disloyalty and I don't want any transfer, reassignment, or any other damned thing, sir.

LBJ: Well, you talk to Rowley about it because I did say that I was going to puncture your tire if you got up that close to me anymore—and I meant it. And I have told them at least one thousand times . . . not to stay close to me when I'm driving fifty miles an hour, stopping on a dime.[2] And they just haven't got sense enough not to do it. . . . So you find out whose morale is low and get rid of the son of a bitch. And if the whole Secret Service is low, I'll tell Dillon[3] the first thing in the morning that we'll just change the damned law in about five minutes and turn it over to the FBI because Hoover thinks that I could be handled a lot better anyway. . . . I think now's a good time, after Dallas, to make the change, if they want to do it. Now I thought I did pretty well after Dallas and I thought I reflected credit on the Secret Service.[4] I did my damnedest to compliment you and everybody else. But if the appreciation I get is going to be articles like this— Kennedy people coming in and telling me that the morale is the lowest in history —I'm not going to be run by them, you know that.

YOUNGBLOOD: Well, I do know it.

TUESDAY, JANUARY 7, 1964

DEAN RUSK
10:15 A.M.

> To MEET the President's growing worry about State Department leaks, Dean Rusk suggests possibly ordering surveillance on the *New York Times* reporter Tad Szulc.

[1] One of the Secret Service's original duties was to track down counterfeiters.
[2] Johnson liked to drive fast in an open Lincoln Continental on his ranch.
[3] Treasury Secretary Douglas Dillon, who oversaw the Secret Service.
[4] On December 4, 1963, in a Rose Garden ceremony attended by Jacqueline Kennedy, Johnson gave Youngblood an Exceptional Service Award, saying, "Without hesitation, he volunteered his life to save mine."

LBJ: There's somebody in that outfit that's leaking.[1] I don't know who it is, but they're leaking awfully bad. We can't run a government unless we can stop it.

RUSK: I talked to Dave Bell[2] about that this morning. This Szulc story this morning sounds like to me like an AID story.

LBJ: State says it's AID. AID swears it's State. I've got a memo from Dave Bell on my desk that he's confident it doesn't come from them at all.

RUSK: Right, well . . . we may have to put a tail on this man. But then if we get caught doing that, it's going to be rough.

LBJ: Yeah, I'd try to stop it some way. I don't know how I'd stop it, but I don't think we can run a government if they're going to talk about our missiles and our atomic bombs—everything that happens before it happens.

HALE BOGGS
12:45 P.M.

THE HOUSE MAJORITY WHIP ceremonially calls the President to open the second session of the 88th Congress.

BOGGS: Mr. President, we're 340 members present, a quorum. We're ready.

LBJ: Wonderful. You get ready to lead that applause. I'll be there in the morning.[3]

WEDNESDAY, JANUARY 8, 1964

JOHN JONES
President, Houston Chronicle
11:04 A.M.

THE *Chronicle* president has sent Johnson the written promise of support that the President has requested. LBJ duly informs Jones that government permission for the Houston bank merger is on its way.[4]

LBJ: John, much obliged for your letter—that thing was signed this morning.

JONES: Thank you very very much, Mr. President.

---

[1] Johnson has just read a front-page *Times* story saying that the U.S. Agency for International Development (AID), "fighting for its life," was planning reforms to meet congressional criticism.
[2] Administrator of the Agency for International Development.
[3] To deliver his first State of the Union.
[4] Five days after this telephone call, Controller of the Currency James Saxon approved the merger.

LBJ: And if I were you, I'd want to call Gus and George,[1] who are awfully interested in it, and then I'll call Albert[2] and you let him tell you. . . .

JONES: Thank you very much, sir.

LBJ: But I appreciated it very much, give my love to your wife, and from here on out, we're partners.

JONES: Thank you. Sure are.

GEORGE BROWN
11:20 A.M.

LBJ: George, we signed that thing this morning and made them[3] reverse themselves and the consolidations.

BROWN: Fine. Nobody else knows about it?

LBJ: No, I just hung up talking to John Jones. Gus is traveling, and I haven't called Albert. . . . I'd just as soon not let them know I ever talked to you and we'll let him make the announcement. But you did it. The letter came in just like it should have and you handled it in your own wise way, as you always do. I don't know how you can walk barbed wire like you do. . . . I'm going to start working on my speech[4] right now.

BROWN: Kind of late, aren't you partner?

LBJ: I've got it written, but I've got to practice it a little. But I just wanted you to know this and I want you to see that we get the proper credit for it.

BROWN: I'll do my best.

LBJ: Now you tell Gus I tried to reach him and couldn't, but not to let anybody know it.

BROWN: All right.

LBJ: Okay. You feeling all right?

BROWN: Yeah, got a bad cold.

LBJ: Everybody asked about you last night.[5] We had a wonderful meeting. Fred[6] said he believed every man in the room was for me.

BROWN: He did say that?

LBJ: Yeah. My budget today is going to be 97.9[7] expenditures.

BROWN: That's wonderful. Nobody ever thought you were going to get there.

LBJ: [laughs] Nobody did, and . . . I think I've knocked them out of the lot, I

[1] Gus Wortham and George Brown.
[2] Thomas.
[3] The Justice Department.
[4] The State of the Union.
[5] Johnson had held a stag dinner for the Business Council.
[6] Kappel, Chairman and CEO of American Telephone and Telegraph Company.
[7] Billion dollars.

don't know.[1] Bob Anderson[2] said that he and Eisenhower and Oveta[3] are going to have to vote for me now.

DREW PEARSON
Syndicated Columnist
3:20 P.M.

AT NOON, Johnson delivered his State of the Union.[4] He calls his sometime friend Pearson, who had contributed a line to the text.

PEARSON: I've been trying to read your speech, but these benighted Republican papers won't carry any of it.

LBJ: Did you hear it?

PEARSON: No, I've been traveling on the plane. I'm out in North Dakota.

LBJ: Well, I'll be damned! A great author like you—and you run off and do that. You disappoint me. . . . [mildly appalled:] You don't even know what's in it, do you?

PEARSON: I heard you got a tremendous amount of applause.

LBJ: I got eighty-one applauses, in 2,900 words. It was a twenty-five-minute speech, and it took forty-one, because of the applauses,[5] and the biggest one after the introduction and the ovation was "We intend to bury no one, and we do not intend to be buried."[6] Did you ever hear anything like that?

PEARSON: I think that's wonderful.

LBJ: Now don't go home and go to bragging to your grandson.

JAMES RESTON
7:10 P.M.

THAT EVENING, exhilarated by the praise that is flowing in for his State of the Union address, Johnson boasts to the *New York Times* columnist that he has so successfully occupied the political center that the Republicans have no issues left for 1964.

[1] Meaning that he has countered the traditional Republican charge against Democrats as big spenders.
[2] Eisenhower's former Treasury Secretary, whom Johnson had been consulting at Ike's emphatic request.
[3] Oveta Culp Hobby, Eisenhower's Secretary of Health, Education and Welfare, and publisher of the *Houston Post*.
[4] Best remembered for this passage: "Unfortunately many Americans live on the outskirts of hope—some because of their poverty, and some because of their color, and all too many because of both. Our task is to help replace despair with opportunity. This administration today, here and now, declares unconditional war on poverty in America."
[5] Once again Johnson loves to cite the number of times he is applauded during a congressional address.
[6] This line was Pearson's contribution, a reference to Nikita Khrushchev's old threat to "bury" the West.

LBJ: You heard what the young Republican said to the old Republican Senator, didn't you?

RESTON: No.

LBJ: Said, "Senator, he didn't leave much for us Republicans, did he?" And the old Senator said, "Oh yes, he did. . . . We can always declare war." [chortles]

JAMES ROWE

Washington Attorney and Partner, Corcoran, Foley, Youngman & Rowe
7:31 P.M.

LBJ AND THE LAWYER from Butte, Montana, had been friends since they were New Dealers in Washington in the 1930s.

LBJ: I thought the finest compliment was from Goldwater. . . . [aside, to aide:] Get me that Goldwater story on the front page of the *Washington Star*. Yes, take this—hand it, boy. [back to Rowe:] He said, "He out-Roosevelted Roosevelt."[1] I thought that was pretty good. . . . Do you want to talk to one of your girlfriends here? Wait a minute. She's putting her glasses on, looking like Miss Minerva[2] here and come over here to lecture me, trying to make me go home.

ROWE: Hello, Lady Bird. I hope you can get him home. . . . To see your President and see that background of McCormack and Hayden[3] makes me wish he'd work four hours a day and no more. Shocking sight, isn't it?

LADY BIRD: I know. That's one of the . . . sights that I kept my eyes on. . . . I know just what you're talking about.

THEODORE SORENSEN

8:00 P.M.

LBJ: These women are after you. I don't know why . . .

SORENSEN: Which woman is it?

LBJ: Here she is.

LADY BIRD: I'm not exactly "after you" but I just wanted to say a very grateful *merci, spasibo,* and a few more things.

[1] Goldwater had gone on to tell an audience in New Hampshire, where he was running in the presidential primary, "I can't think of a single field in which he is not going to move to do things for you that you should be doing for yourselves. I don't think the idealism and initiative and drive of the American people has to be replaced overnight just to perpetuate in power those who want to change our way of life." He denounced the "Fast Deal and the Old Frontier" (*Washington Post*, January 9, 1964).
[2] Johnson refers to the title figure in Frances Boyd Calhoun's novel *Miss Minerva and William Green Hill* (Chicago: Reilly and Britton, 1909), which he no doubt read as a boy. Based in a small Southern town, with egregious portrayals of African-Americans, the novel shows a schoolmarmish spinster trying to keep her rambunctious orphan nephew in line.
[3] During the State of the Union, on television.

SORENSEN: . . . It was certainly helped along a lot by the wonderful hospitality you extended to me and my children.[1]

LADY BIRD: Well, I feel a few years younger and a few pounds lighter right now and I know completely how temporary it is. But there was no bigger hurdle than this one. So thank God, we're over it.[2]

FRIDAY, JANUARY 10, 1964

RICHARD RUSSELL
11:25 A.M.

NOW JOHNSON FACES his first international crisis. The previous day, Panamanian students marched in the United States–controlled Panama Canal Zone to protest hoisting of the American flag by Zonian students over a Zone high school. This defied a January 6 order by the United States, in deference to Panamanian sensitivities, that no U.S. flags should fly over schools. Communist agitators helped to turn the protest march into a riot in which more than twenty Panamanians were killed and more than three hundred wounded under gunfire from Canal Zone police. Worried that Communists might exploit the disturbance to launch a revolution and with his own elections coming in May, the Panamanian President, Roberto Chiari, now seeks to outflank them by demanding renegotiation of the 1903 Panama Canal treaty with the United States.

LBJ: Dick, I want to talk to you off the record a minute, about this Panama situation. . . .

RUSSELL: . . . If I were the President, I'd just tell them . . . this is a most regrettable incident. . . . However the Panama Canal Zone is a property of the United States. The Canal was built with American ingenuity and blood, sweat, and sacrifices . . . and that under no circumstances would you permit the threat of interruption by any subversive group. . . . I'd give a little lick to Castro. I don't know what the State Department has said. I suppose they have suggested you make an apology.

LBJ: No, but . . . it doesn't look good from our standpoint.

RUSSELL: It started with a bunch of schoolboys. . . . They've had a chip on their shoulder for a long time.

---

[1] After Christmas, the Johnsons had had Sorensen and his three sons to the ranch, where he worked on the State of the Union address and dined with the President's family.

[2] Mrs. Johnson dictated into her diary, "It was one of those days that you have the feeling that everything that has gone before—in the last two weeks, at any rate—was leading up to. . . . So had Sir [Edmund] Hillary felt when he at last reached the top of Mount Everest" (January 8, 1964). The next day: "Bone tired. . . . If this day has been a black day, I guess the reason is that it is just a sort of climbing down off the mountain—the release from the tension and getting rid of the State of the Union that has made it so. If it is that way with me, what must it have been like with Lyndon?" (January 9, 1964).

LBJ: Yeah, they have and we've known that.

RUSSELL: . . . The people that we did injury to in connection with the Canal is not the Panamanians. We brought them out of the jungles, where they were hiding, thinking that old Cortes was still trying to get them for slaves. . . .

LBJ: . . . Tom Mann says . . . that our students went out and put up our flag in violation of our understanding. They started to put up their flag and we refused it and we made our people take down our flag and the rioters increased. Communists we know there . . . had a lot of Molotov cocktails and they'd planned this thing apparently, just using the flag as an excuse. They would have kicked it off some other way, some other time, but this was ideal.

                              •   •   •   •

RUSSELL: If there's any one thing that is essential to the economic life as well as the defense of every nation in the hemisphere, it is the Panama Canal. We can't risk having it sabotaged or taken over by any Communist group. There's no question in my mind but that that is Castro's chief aim there. . . .

LBJ: I thought I might do this. . . . I might call their President[1] and say I . . . hope he will do everything possible to quiet the situation and I'll do the same and I'm going to send my trusted representative, Tom Mann . . . and other people in there today. . . .

RUSSELL: . . . I'd certainly take a chunk out of the Communists. You're going to have trouble there all through your entire tenure as President in that area down there. Castro is going to pick up the tempo of his activities down there, in his desperation.

                              •   •   •   •

LBJ: They're going to get the President of Panama. I'll call you back.

RICHARD RUSSELL
1:25 P.M.

LBJ: I talked to the President. . . . I've told him that the Mann mission was taking off within thirty minutes . . . that he must bear in mind that the enemies of both of us were exploiting this thing. And he immediately said that he wanted to revise all of our agreements. . . . I told him that we couldn't get into that because I wanted to get the facts of what happened. . . . I was cold and hard and tough as hell.

RUSSELL: That is exactly right.

LBJ: . . . Then I went back in and told our group here that I thought we had to remember that . . . two or three weeks ago I had to tell them in Bolivia I'd send whatever aid I needed in there to make them release one of our people there[2] . . .

[1] Johnson was later said to have told his aides, "Get me the President of Panama—what's his name, anyway?—I want to talk to him" (quoted in Alfred Steinberg, *Sam Johnson's Boy*, Macmillan, 1968, p. 725).
[2] On December 17, 1963, came the release of four United States Information Agency (USIA) and AID officials who had been seized by local miners in Bolivia enraged by their government's arrest of three of their leaders on criminal charges.

and I was damned tired of their attacking our flag and our embassy and our USIS[1] every time somebody got a little emotional outburst, so they'd better watch it.

RUSSELL: I'm so pleased. Now that's a great President. That's a man that will go down in history.

LBJ: ... The old man finally said that he was glad that he's talking to a man that was taking some action.

RUSSELL: ... If they shoot at them, you can't expect our people to stand there and be killed and not fire back.

LBJ: ... It's hot as a firecracker.[2] ... I think that the position we ought to be in on the Hill is ... for God's sake, if we say anything, say we did right and acted promptly and sent the ablest man we've got down there. Now they tell me that everybody in Latin America is scared of this fellow Mann ... because he's a tough guy. ...

RUSSELL: I hope ... he's much tougher than the ones we've had. ...

LBJ: ... And McNamara doesn't act to me like he goes much with these State Department policies. He's the only one that stayed with me on Indonesia. Now we got it down from $35 million to 15 million ... and they say well I'm going to ... cause us to not have any relations at all. ... I turned it all down though, and concluded that Bobby Kennedy would have to give us a legal opinion on whether this money in the pipeline constitutes a violation of the act of Congress. I don't think it does. ... And I couldn't stop that without going out there and sinking the ships. And now I'm going to send Bobby Kennedy to Indonesia and just put it right in his lap.[3]

RUSSELL: Tell him to be tough too.

LBJ: I think he will.

RUSSELL: Like he was in Los Angeles.[4]

LBJ: Hell, he wasn't so tough last time he saw Sukarno. He took away from the Dutch and gave it to Sukarno, didn't he?[5]

RUSSELL: Yeah, he sure did.

[1] United States Information Service, meaning the external portion of USIA.

[2] That day, a mob assaulted the U.S. embassy in Panama City.

[3] The Indonesian President, Sukarno, furious about the British creation of the Federation of Malaysia, had started guerrilla warfare against the new state. On November 19, 1963, John Kennedy had agreed to resume economic aid and visit Indonesia in 1964 if Sukarno settled the conflict. Taking office, Johnson refused to find that aid to Indonesia was in the American interest but agreed to one more effort to start negotiations between the Malaysians and Sukarno, whom the United States did not wish to drive further into the arms of Beijing. Averell Harriman, Undersecretary of State for Political Affairs, hoping to rouse Robert Kennedy from his depression over his brother's death, recommended that RFK see Sukarno as Johnson's emissary. Johnson reluctantly consented, feeling, as McGeorge Bundy observed, "that he had been sort of maneuvered into approving by staff people who weren't thinking about the Johnson interest" (oral history interview, Kennedy Library).

[4] Russell refers to the fact that at the 1960 Democratic convention, after JFK offered Johnson the vice presidency, RFK went to Johnson's hotel suite to ask him to withdraw.

[5] In 1962, Kennedy had seen Sukarno in Djakarta in an effort to avert an Indonesian war with the Netherlands over West New Guinea, which ultimately went to Indonesia.

LBJ: But I think I'll just put it in his lap. . . . Let him go out there and have whatever row it is with Sukarno. . . . If we're going to have a break, I'll just let him break it.

RUSSELL: That's exactly right. I'm proud of you.

GEORGE SMATHERS
9:01 P.M.

JOHNSON FEELS Smathers out about a tape recording being privately discussed by the Senate Rules Committee. It is said to implicate high U.S. officials in the ring of fast-living women who frequented Bobby Baker's Capitol Hill town house and the Quorum Club, the private suite in the Carroll Arms Hotel across from the Senate office buildings favored by members of Congress and lobbyists.

The particular woman in question is Ellen Rometsch, wife of an airman attached to the West German military mission in Washington, who was under surveillance by the FBI. In the summer of 1963, told of what the Bureau was discovering about her, Robert Kennedy had arranged her immediate expulsion from the country. On October 26, 1963, Clark Mollenhoff reported in the *Des Moines Register* that Rometsch had been "associating with Congressional leaders and some prominent New Frontiersmen." RFK asked J. Edgar Hoover to help persuade Dirksen and Mansfield to scotch a Senate investigation. Balking at first, the FBI Director went to Mansfield's home and persuaded the two Senate leaders to hold the Senate's fire.[1] Nevertheless, in December 1963, Senator Jordan announced that his Rules Committee would look into reports of "party girls" in Bobby Baker's circle.[2] Still, when a committee member asked one witness what he knew about "girls," Jordan ruled him out of order. Spotting a powerful campaign issue that might be used against the Democrats in 1964, Republican Senators Hugh Scott of Pennsylvania and Carl Curtis of Nebraska are challenging Jordan's ruling.

LBJ: Have you heard about this tape recording that's out?

SMATHERS: No.

LBJ: Well, it involves you and John Williams[3] and a number of other people.

SMATHERS: You mean, some woman?

LBJ: Yep.

SMATHERS: Yeah, I've heard about it. And it involves Hugh Scott.

LBJ: But it's a pure made-up deal, isn't it?

SMATHERS: I don't know what it is. I never heard of the woman in my life. . . . But she mentions President Kennedy in there.

LBJ: Oh yeah, and the Attorney General and me and you and everybody. And I never heard of her.

[1] See Taylor Branch, *Parting the Waters* (Simon & Schuster, 1988), pp. 906, 911–14.
[2] Baker insisted in his memoirs, *Wheeling and Dealing* (Norton, 1978), that he "drew the line at furnishing professionals" (p. 47).
[3] Republican Senator from Delaware, who styled himself "the conscience of the Senate," and was the main senatorial goad to investigate Baker.

SMATHERS: Thank God, they've got Hugh Scott in there. He's the guy that was asking for it. But she's also mentioned him, [laughs] which is sort of a lifesaver. So I don't think that'll get too far now. Jordan's orders.

LBJ: Can't you talk to him? Why in the living hell does he let Curtis run him? I thought you were going to talk to Dick Russell and go talk to Curtis and make Dirksen and them behave.

SMATHERS: . . . Jordan has assured me over and over again.

LBJ: Well, he's not strong enough though, unless someone goes and tells him now.

SMATHERS: That's right. Now Dick Russell is the man that ought to do it. And I've asked Dick to do it and Dick has told me that he would. . . .

LBJ: They had this damned fool insurance man[1] in and they had him in a secret session and Bobby gave me a record player and Bobby got the record player from the insurance man. I didn't know a damned thing about it. Never heard of it till this happened. But I paid $88,000 worth of premiums[2] and, by God, they could afford to give me a Cadillac if they'd wanted to and there'd have been not a goddamned thing wrong with it. . . . There's nothing wrong with it. There's not a damned thing wrong. So Walter Jenkins explained it all in his statement.[3] This son of a bitch Curtis comes along and says, well, he wouldn't take any statements not sworn to. They had their counsel come down and Walter Jenkins handled it, told him exactly what was done. . . . A fellow said Manhattan is the only company that would write on a heart attack man. . . . Bobby[4] said, "Hell now, wait, let my man handle it and he'll get a commission off of it." So we said all right. . . . Now he said—Walter—"I'll swear to it." "No, I want a public hearing so I can put it on television."[5] Now that oughtn't to be. Now George, I ought not to have to get into that personally.

SMATHERS: Absolutely not. . . . And Dick Russell has got to exercise his influence. He *must* do this and I think you've got to talk to him about it and just say *you've* got to do it. I'll talk to Jordan. Jordan thinks *I'm* guilty of something. So he thinks I may be covering up trying to protect myself. Hubert[6] has been really good in this and, believe it or not, Joe Clark[7] has finally gotten the picture and *he's* trying to stop it now. But Hugh Scott and Carl Curtis are going wild, and Jordan doesn't have enough experience or enough sense to gavel them down and shut them up. But if Dick will talk to him—*really* talk to him—and say—

LBJ: I think he needs to talk to Curtis too. Why don't you tell Dick to do that?

SMATHERS: I will. I've already talked to him.

LBJ: I hate to call him. . . . Get Dick to go see Curtis in the morning and just say, "Now quit being so goddamn rambunctious about this, Carl."

[1] Don Reynolds.
[2] To Reynolds's company.
[3] Jenkins had given a statement to the committee's staff.
[4] Baker.
[5] Rules Committee Republicans wanted Jenkins to testify under oath on television, which would inflict more damage on Johnson.
[6] Humphrey.
[7] Democratic Senator from Pennsylvania.

SMATHERS: Can I tell Dick this is not right and you know about it? And naturally it makes you apprehensive and you've got all these damn problems and to have this little nitpicking thing. It's just not fair.

LBJ: It's not.

SMATHERS: So I'll do it.

LBJ: Tell him he's the only one can do it. And he *can* do it. And if *he* was involved I'd damned sure walk across the country and do it.

SMATHERS: Exactly. All right, that's a damned good thought and I'll do it. I've already talked to him about it, but I—

LBJ: The FBI has got that record.[1] Now you know I think you ought to leak it. I don't know who you can leak it to. But I've read the goddamn tax report and I've read the FBI report[2] and there ain't a goddamn thing in it that they can even indict him on.[3] The only thing that they can do is that he puffed up the financial statement, which everybody's done. If he pays that off, they couldn't convict him on that. . . .

SMATHERS: They won't print that 'cause I tried to leak that the day before yesterday to . . . two different sources and it hasn't been printed. They just want to print this . . . ugly stuff. . . . That Curtis is mean as a snake. Dirksen sat in the room the night of the day after you became President with me and Humphrey and agreed that this thing ought to stop and that he would get Curtis to stop it. . . . You know, there's some statement about Dirksen and Kuchel[4] with this German girl.[5] So he said, "It is just ridiculous and it ought to stop.". . . . I think we can handle everybody on our side. Howard Cannon[6] is the smartest fellow over there, but he's a little afraid to do anything because he himself figures he was involved out in Las Vegas. So he's a little afraid to be as brave as he ought to be. . . . I'll tell Dick this. I've already told him once, but—

LBJ: Tell him he ought to talk to Dirksen and Curtis both. Please do it, and also Jordan. He's just got his work cut out Monday 'cause they're going to meet Tuesday and they're going to want a public hearing.[7] And then that's a television hearing, and then a television hearing about my buying some insurance. And what in the goddamn hell is wrong with my buying *insurance?* I paid cash for it, wrote them a check for it, made my company the beneficiary, and they didn't deduct it. No tax deduction. We'll do it after we pay our taxes. We pay the premium—only reason being if I died, my wife would have to pay estate tax on me on account of she'd have to sell her stock and they want the company to have some money to buy her stock so she doesn't have to lose control of her company. . . . This son of a bitch Mollenhoff said, "Well he couldn't deduct it for tax purposes unless she was a key employee, so that means Johnson was a key

[1] Of damaging information on Reynolds.
[2] On Baker.
[3] Johnson had called for Bobby Baker's income taxes and FBI files to see how vulnerable Baker might be to criminal action.
[4] Thomas Kuchel of California, the Republican Senate Whip.
[5] Rometsch.
[6] Democrat of Nevada.
[7] With Jenkins as witness.

employee and . . . he oughtn't to have been an employee." . . . The son of a bitch thought I was as crooked as he was. I didn't deduct it 'cause I had a tax opinion showing that I couldn't deduct it because I wasn't a key employee, and I *wasn't* a key employee. So we just paid our taxes and then what money we had left out of our forty-eight percent, we paid the premium.

SMATHERS: Right. I'll get ahold of Dick. I'll just make it a special project and hunt him down tomorrow and just absolutely put him under the gun 'cause he's got to do it, 'cause this is so silly and so stupid that it ought to stop.

SATURDAY, JANUARY 11, 1964

RICHARD RUSSELL
1:05 P.M.

LBJ: [tired, sighs] Oh . . . we're getting ready to send some instructions out to Mann and I'm a little bit dubious. I'm afraid that we're going a little bit further than we ought to go. But it's pretty difficult to say to people that you just won't talk. I mean, it won't be courteous if you won't listen to 'em. . . . Say, what are you going to do tomorrow?

RUSSELL: I hadn't planned anything.

LBJ: I know you're against this, but I thought I might get Lady Bird and Marjorie [sic] McNamara[1] and Bob McNamara and fly up to Camp David this evening and have a quiet dinner in front of the fireplace and a drink or two and philosophize a little bit and then lay around there and sleep in the morning . . . and come on back tomorrow afternoon late. Now why wouldn't you join us?

RUSSELL: For one reason, I've got a date for tonight.

LBJ: This is Saturday night. You have your dates on Friday night.

RUSSELL: I had to call off one I had last night because I thought I was catching a cold. I put it off until tonight and I've already bought two big steaks and got them in the icebox. Of course, I never lose hope. [chuckles] I sometimes don't accomplish a great deal.

LBJ: Well now, how about coming up in the morning and having lunch with us?

RUSSELL: All right.

LBJ: . . . I'll just have a helicopter pick you up in the morning here at the White House pad and you can just fly up there and come back with us tomorrow afternoon for a quiet lunch. Have you ever been up there?

RUSSELL: No, never have.

LBJ: You'd enjoy it. Is there any lady you'd like to bring?

---

[1] Mrs. McNamara's first name was actually Margaret.

RUSSELL: No.

LBJ: Is there any—you got any kinfolks? Anybody around? . . . No companion you'd like to have?

RUSSELL: No, no, no.

LBJ: Damn. You're just going to be a bachelor, aren't you?

RUSSELL: [laughs] Well, I think I'm about past the point of no return on that!

WEDNESDAY, JANUARY 15, 1964

RICHARD RUSSELL
4:30 P.M.

LBJ: [sounding very tired:] De Gaulle's going to recognize Communist China and the question comes whether *I* ought to protest it rather strongly or whether I ought to just let the government protest it. . . . Our disposition is to just let the government protest it. . . . He'll pay no attention. . . .

RUSSELL: . . . I wouldn't go too strong on it, Mr. President. If he ain't going to pay much attention to it, it would look bad when he goes ahead. . . . We've really got no control over their foreign policy.

LBJ: That's right. None whatever.

RUSSELL: . . . We can't talk about it now, but the time's going to come when we're going to have to recognize Red China.

LBJ: . . . I don't think there's any question about that.

RUSSELL: I ain't too sure but what we'd been better off if what we'd recognized her three or four years ago.

LBJ: I think so.[1] . . .

RUSSELL: Politically, right now, it's poison, of course.

LBJ: I didn't want to wake you up last night . . . but we stood pretty well to our original line we had with . . . the President of Panama. . . . They came back immediately and said that we had to . . . have a complete revision of all treaties which affect Panama. . . . I told him ain't nothing we could ever do that justifies violence. . . . He and Secretary Mann ought to get together and let's talk quiet and calm and we'd be glad to listen to them on anything they wanted to discuss.

[1] Had Johnson's private view that the United States should have recognized Communist China in 1960 or 1961 become known to Americans at the time, it would have started a national firestorm among conservatives for whom support of Taiwan was sacrosanct. For example, when Eisenhower met with President-elect Kennedy on the day before JFK's inauguration, he promised to abstain from criticizing Kennedy's foreign policy, with one exception—if Kennedy ever proposed recognizing Communist China, Eisenhower would emerge from retirement to rally public support against him. (See memorandum on the Eisenhower conversation in Kennedy Library, and *Counsel to the President* by Clark Clifford, who was present at the meeting, pp. 344–45.)

... Now when they got down there, they said, "We can't pee a drop until you revise the treaty." So they came back with instructions from me.... "You tell the President we cannot negotiate under the pressure of violence." ... So Mann held to that, and they broke up relations and told him to get the hell on out of there—now.... They came in—this damn Peace Committee[1]—with a statement that we agreed to negotiate the revisions with them ... because of the situation created by the Panama Canal.... I just didn't like the word "negotiate" so I struck "negotiate" wherever it appeared and said we'll be glad to discuss as we're always willing to discuss with anybody—Khrushchev, anybody else—any problem ... and if ... we've done something wrong ... we of course, will be glad to correct it. But ... we're not going to do it by implication, or innuendo, or connotation that this means that ... there's something wrong with the treaties. ... The Peace Commission [sic] considered that until midnight. Then they came back in and agreed to my deletions.

· · · ·

LBJ: I honestly think that being firm with them caused them to cave....

RUSSELL: ... We just had to do it.... They're going to blackmail us and we'll have to give them a little increase once in a while....

LBJ: Why don't we build another canal? We're always going to have this hell.

RUSSELL: I'm in favor of it, but you're talking about a $200 million project....

LBJ: ... Why don't you have a few folks up there call on me to build another one?

RUSSELL: I'll be glad to make a statement on that. We've had surveys made, you know. And it's feasible through both Nicaragua and Colombia....

· · · ·

LBJ: You do a little talking ... now while it's hot. Mr. Nixon's trying to butt into it.[2] I think we cut his water off pretty quick by settling it.

RUSSELL: Maybe so, but it would be ridiculous having him trying to advise anybody.

LBJ: No, but he is.

THURSDAY, JANUARY 16, 1964

RICHARD RUSSELL
4:15 P.M.

BYRD'S FINANCE COMMITTEE is still dragging its feet on Johnson's tax cut bill, despite the fact that LBJ asked his Budget Director, Kermit Gordon, to deliver a freshly minted copy of the new trimmed-down $97.9 billion budget

---

[1] Panama and the United States had asked the OAS (Organization of American States) Inter-American Peace Committee (Argentina, the Dominican Republic, Chile, and Venezuela) to recommend ways to settle the conflict.

[2] In speeches, Nixon was warning Johnson not to retreat on Panama.

personally to Chairman Byrd at his apartment. Here LBJ accuses Russell of conspiring with Byrd to draw out consideration of the tax bill as a means of stalling on civil rights.

LBJ: Looks like to me you're not being very wise in your southern strategy. It's not up to me to tell you how smart you are—for a son to tell the father— but looks like you and Harry Byrd and Albert Gore[1] ought to let that damned tax bill come on out.

RUSSELL: I've been begging them.

LBJ: What you're going to wind up doing—you're going to have all the businessmen giving you hell. . . . You'll have every businessman in the country messing into your civil rights fight.[2] . . .

RUSSELL: I'm not wholly unaware of that. . . .

LBJ: Herman Talmadge and Harry Byrd could get that bill out tomorrow. They've got every damned thing through and we could take it up.

RUSSELL: I wouldn't be surprised if we didn't take it out this week.

LBJ: But they're going to screw you and you're going to be standing there doing the fighting and they're going to be home asleep. Harry Byrd goes home about five-thirty. I've seen these fights. And don't be quarreling with me when it happens. Just say, "Uncle Lyndon told me so."

RUSSELL: He has got more credit and done less in that civil rights fight.

LBJ: [laughs] He's going to come in those white shoes—

RUSSELL: And gives a little twenty-minute speech somewhere along the line and says Thomas Jefferson[3] says this is all bad.

LBJ: You're going to come in and tell me like you used to, "I'm going home for the night. Now I'll see you tomorrow." And then you call a quorum on me about two-thirty. When you do, don't lay it on me. Lay it on to Byrd now 'cause he's the one that's held this damned thing up since September. I got a letter today from Tom Watson of IBM and the head of Merck Company. . . . They're getting their men to want to put . . . $150 million in big investments and . . . they're uncertain . . . and the bill has been in committee since September. . . . You're going to get it up there and we get up civil rights and then they are going to raise unshirted hell.

RUSSELL: I'm well aware of that.

LBJ: So it's not up to me to advise you, the old master. But I would tell Harry Byrd.

RUSSELL: I'm slipping and I'm getting senile but I'm not that bad. I saw that way back yonder last fall and I got after Harry about it.

LBJ: You can't tell me you saw something last fall and nothing has been done about it, 'cause you've got that committee loaded.

[1] Democratic Senator from Tennessee, member of the Finance Committee (and father of the future Vice President), who was telling his poor constituents that the measure was nothing but a "rich man's bill."

[2] In other words, businessmen engaged to oppose Russell to get the tax bill passed might also stay active to oppose him on civil rights.

[3] Byrd's fellow Virginian.

RUSSELL: Well, I was watching civil rights too, you understand.[1]

LBJ: [laughs]

JOHN McCLELLAN

Chairman, Senate Government Operations Committee, Democrat of Arkansas
4:20 P.M.

> JOHNSON IS PLANNING to appoint a black journalist, Carl Rowan, whom
> JFK had appointed Ambassador to Finland, as Director of the U.S. Information
> Agency. To help clear the way, he tries to disarm a key Senate segregationist.

LBJ: John, I've got a little problem. I don't want to embarrass you in any way,
and the best way to avoid it is talk to you about it beforehand so you know what
the problem is. Mr. Ed Murrow[2] is dying with cancer of the lung. . . . I've got a
good solid man that's went around the world with me.[3] . . . He's a good administrator and he'll listen to me. But he's a Negro. His name is Carl Rowan. He's
Ambassador to Finland.

McCLELLAN: I doubt if I'm going against this. You do what you want to.

LBJ: . . . I wouldn't expect you to endorse him or be for him, but . . . I didn't
want to do it without you wondering why in the hell your friend didn't tell you.
I don't want to make any fight on him or anything like that. . . . I know what
your problems are. . . . I don't want you to cut his guts out because he's Negro.
And I've seen you operate with a knife and I have seen a few people get de-nutted.

McCLELLAN: I wouldn't say that.

. . . .

LBJ: I didn't want you to . . . send him home one day without his peter.

McCLELLAN: I'm not going to do that.

LBJ: . . . I've seen you operate, John.

FRIDAY, JANUARY 17, 1964

ROSWELL GILPATRIC
11:12 A.M.

LBJ: Unless somebody is engineering a coup in the government, I just sure
wish you'd get on the phone and tell them to shut up. USIA yesterday said we'd
taken a terrible shellacking on Panama. This morning Saigon says we're taking a

---

[1] Meaning that Russell had also to spend his time and attention opposing Kennedy and
Johnson on civil rights.
[2] JFK had appointed the pioneering CBS broadcaster to head USIA.
[3] Rowan had served as Johnson's press adviser when the Vice President flew to Southeast
Asia in 1961.

terrible shellacking there. We can't stand up anywhere if our own people are going to join the enemy[1] and start putting this stuff out. . . . See that you and State do what you need to do to stop that. And fire whoever did it. Tell me who it was.

GILPATRIC: All right.

ABE FORTAS
7:40 P.M.

JOHNSON CONSULTS Fortas about the Bobby Baker problem. Fortas had been Baker's lawyer until the Kennedy assassination, when Baker gave him up so that he could work for the new President. Today the Senate Rules Committee has voted to release to the public Don Reynolds's secret testimony on his sale of insurance to Johnson and his charge that LBJ required a kickback in return.[2] LBJ is discussing at what moment the transcript might be released in order to do him the least political harm.

LBJ: Walter[3] is in here. . . . He and Pierre Salinger have had a big debate over this release. . . . Al Friendly[4] . . . that little son of a bitch is always causing us trouble. . . . He thinks we ought to go up and try to get the committee to release this thing tomorrow.

FORTAS: . . . The committee has already voted to release it, and the question is at what time. . . .

LBJ: . . . Every paper in America has got twice the circulation on Sunday than it's got any other time.

FORTAS: That's true.

LBJ: Monday, we've got an economic message and Tuesday, we've got the budget and I don't believe it would be in but over one paper. I believe it would be just that son of a bitch Friendly. . . . George[5] said he's had one inquiry.

FORTAS: No, he's got more than that. . . . The Hearst papers have a story and various other papers have the story.

LBJ: No the Hearst papers haven't. They're here now, asking me about it, and I'm showing them the FBI.[6] . . . [to Jenkins:] Go on and ask George to quit lying and tell us how many he's got. He told you one, didn't he? [to Fortas:] Walter just walked into the office and said the only inquiry he had was from Al Friendly.

FORTAS: I got the impression that there were more, Mr. President.

LBJ: . . . I'm sorry George can't handle this. But I guess it's *above* him.

[1] Here, the first appearance on these tapes of a turn of phrase that Johnson's intimate circle will hear many times when U.S. involvement in Vietnam begins in earnest.
[2] Republicans had wanted Reynolds instead to appear at a public hearing.
[3] Jenkins, who is sitting beside Johnson as he speaks on the telephone.
[4] Of the *Washington Post*.
[5] Reedy.
[6] Johnson was leaking damaging FBI information on Reynolds to Hearst's and other reporters.

GEORGE REEDY
Special Assistant to the President, and
WALTER JENKINS
8:00 P.M.

> JOHNSON PURSUES the question of when to have the Reynolds transcript released.

LBJ: I believe that . . . on balance . . . it would be better for the Tuesday morning. . . . We can talk to Salinger in the morning and see what he thinks. . . . Who is leaking this out? Reynolds?

REEDY: Reynolds is leaking part of it, and Senator Scott is leaking another part. Of course, what Scott is leaking is the stuff about D.C. Stadium—McCloskey.[1] I don't think what comes out tonight is going to be too significant.

LBJ: What do you think will come out tonight?

REEDY: . . . That this involved a gift of a stereo set to you, and that there was some hanky-panky about the insurance for the D.C. Stadium. And that there was an abortion ring involved.[2] Wasn't actually a ring, of course, but there's testimony about abortion. And I think it'll be mostly hints. Now what really concerns me is not tonight. It's what comes out tomorrow when they start digging.

MONDAY, JANUARY 20, 1964

RICHARD DALEY
Mayor of Chicago
6:10 P.M.

> JOHNSON ENTICES the nation's most powerful Democratic boss, who helped swing Illinois decisively to the Kennedy-Johnson ticket in 1960, with the prospect that the War on Poverty announced in his State of the Union could mean federal booty for the Mayor to dole out in Chicago.

DALEY: We love everything you're doing. You're doing great. We're very proud of you out here.

[1] Reynolds said that in writing insurance on the performance bond for the builder of the new D.C. Stadium, McCloskey & Company, owned by Matthew McCloskey, a large Philadelphia Democratic donor whom JFK appointed as Ambassador to Ireland, he had been compelled to kick back $35,000 to the 1960 Democratic campaign fund. Reynolds said that Baker had brought him the business.
[2] Baker was rumored also to be running an abortion service. This he denied.

LBJ: Somebody told me I was supposed to come out there and collect some money for you and try to make a speech.[1]

DALEY: If you do, we'll have a reception and you know we put 'em on out here. . . . We'd surely love to see you and Mrs. Johnson out here the 23rd.

LBJ: [laughs] I'm a Dick Daley man. We'll be there.

DALEY: We're Johnson men because, by God, Mr. President. I really mean it. All I hear is everything wonderful about you. You're doing a great job and may the Lord continue to give you health to carry out the responsibilities the way you're doing. . . .

LBJ: . . . I never forget how you treated me in the '60 thing and I always have a warm spot for you.

DALEY: . . . My wife said that never did we meet a finer couple than you and Mrs. Johnson and we've never forgotten it.

LBJ: Are you looking out for things for me in the Middle West?

DALEY: You're looking great . . . and I'm not flattering you because you know I'd say it if we weren't doing so well. I think your conduct of the office, your ability, your courage, your determination, that program—that fight on poverty has got them all swirling around—the opposition. . . . You put it out in concise language so that everybody could understand it. We're picking it up out here tremendously—in every ward organization, every town organization, and this is our program for 1964.

LBJ: We've got to have some real demonstration in Chicago on this anti-poverty program, that we can coordinate.

DALEY: . . . This is all a part of what we're trying to do under your leadership.

LBJ: . . . I wish you'd get your local people together to—local initiative—and let us cooperate and establish the coordinating mechanism of the planning and developing. What you think ought to be done for it there in Chicago. And when we get this money, we can drop a hunk of it in there and do it.

DALEY: That'll be great.

LBJ: But get your planning and development people busy right now to see what you can do for the crummiest place in town—the lowest, the bottom—and see what we can do about it and we'll get our dough and then you'll have your plan ready and we'll move.

DALEY: Wonderful. I appreciate it very much. And I wanted you to know we're very much interested in the appointment of Ed Hanrahan as District Attorney.

LBJ: Is that what you want?

DALEY: He's a great Democrat. He ran for Congress. He was defeated. He's a graduate of Notre Dame, of Harvard. But more than that, Mr. President, let me say with great honor and pride, he's a *precinct captain!*[2]

LBJ: Well, that's wonderful.

DALEY: . . . He's got a family and he's got integrity and decency.

[1] Daley had invited the Johnsons to a fund-raising dinner of Chicago Democrats on April 23.
[2] Here Daley shows his definition of what is really important in politics.

LBJ: Is he your man?

DALEY: Yes, he is.

LBJ: Do you want him?

DALEY: We surely do.

LBJ: You got him, you got him.

. . . .

DALEY: You're doing a great job and don't let them tell you any differently. And the people are with you—the fellow on the bottom rung—and the people that elect Presidents[1] are with you.

LBJ: Will you call me when I need to know otherwise?

DALEY: I surely will. You know that.

LBJ: This will be done today. We'll send it up in the morning, and you just get me good men because I want your kind.

RICHARD RUSSELL
7:20 P.M.

LBJ: Things are going like hell. We're in trouble in Indonesia and we're in trouble in Tanganyika and we're in trouble in Zanzibar[2] and we're in trouble in Panama.

. . . .

RUSSELL: There was an English journalist that . . . had an article that was carried in today's *Washington News.* . . . He said that . . . we had suffered one great defeat in Cuba, and we ought not take another one down there. . . .

LBJ: Well, we're not going to. But I'm going to take a lot of heat, I'll tell you.

. . . .

LBJ: Do you know anything else good for your country?

RUSSELL: No, sir. Wish I did.

LBJ: What have you done for Georgia today?

RUSSELL: Haven't done a damn thing. Not one thing.

LBJ: I'm going to name Carl Rowan, now. I want you to hold your hat.

RUSSELL: If he's a very good man, that's all right.

LBJ: He's the best man that's available anywhere. . . .

RUSSELL: Well, when he just pitches in giving the South hell—dirt eaters, ignoramuses, and all[3]—we're in mighty good shape down there now, but this one thing might tear—

LBJ: He's going to lean over backwards.

[1] Namely himself.

[2] On January 20, the army of Tanganyika overthrew the government in Dar es Salaam. On January 12, the Zanzibar government was overthrown by a group considered to be pro-Communist. Later in 1964, the two nations united to form Tanzania.

[3] Rowan had written some tough articles about the white South.

RUSSELL: I personally don't care, I said.

LBJ: He's going to lean over backwards. The South doesn't listen to USIA.

· · · ·

RUSSELL: . . . You'll never get a kickback on it at all unless he does just go to slaying the South. Then if he does that, it'll upset our applecart down here.

LBJ: Well, he's not going to do that. He's a Tennessee boy . . . and he's got more sense than that. . . . I asked Roy Wilkins about him and he said his articles in the *Saturday Evening Post* indicated he didn't think the Negro was ready for everything, and that's where I might get a kickback—that he's Uncle Tom.

RUSSELL: I don't know about that. . . . He's a pretty able fellow.

LBJ: I know he is. I took him around the world with me for a month. I lived in close quarters with him and he's able, respectful, and a gentleman.

RUSSELL: . . . But if USIA goes to tearing off down there . . . and you know, they did that to start with on the Kennedy assassination. They started giving the South hell, on the first announcement of it—southern racists.

LBJ: Not by USIA.

RUSSELL: Yes, it did. . . . You check it. . . . We got a mighty tranquil situation down there at present, but he's got enough sense not to ruin it, if he hasn't got some great ambition that he's going to take over and be the spokesman for the Negroes by denouncing the South before the world.

· · · ·

LBJ: I looked at this movie last night that they published on the March to Washington.[1] . . . It's not bad, from the South's standpoint. . . . It shows that the Negro has a right to be heard and is heard and has a voice and can petition, and doesn't get shot for doing it. . . . This damn son of a bitch Mollenhoff, who's on the advisory board—Bobby Kennedy put him on there[2]—he ain't worth a damn, and he's called them all over the country trying to . . . get 'em to raise hell. So I just ordered it brought in last night, and I watched it. Lady Bird watched it, and she thought it could have been a better-edited movie. . . . But it was showing that . . . they can come right up here—a hundred thousand of 'em—and march down the street and get in front of . . . Lincoln.

RUSSELL: Damn sight rather they'd show that than show some of these things where they violate the laws by laying down in the road, and all that stuff.

LBJ: It's a whole lot better.

MARY LASKER
Philanthropist
7:50 P.M.

THE JOHNSON TREATMENT is applied to one of LBJ's favorites, a large New York Democratic giver and champion of medical research.

[1]Called *The March*, the film was produced by USIA.
[2]Johnson suggests his suspicion that RFK had been feeding Mollenhoff, his nemesis in the Bobby Baker scandal, with information to damage him.

LBJ: What are you doing running around with these other men?

LASKER: [laughs] Abe Fortas is just leaving the room. We've had a lovely day.

LBJ: I've been watching Abe Fortas most of my life, and . . . I'm very jealous. I'm sitting down here at the desk working like hell and you're up there running around with Abe Fortas.

LASKER: Yes, that's it and we wish you were with us.

LBJ: Listen, I've got something I need for you to do for me. . . . I want to make you Ambassador to Finland.

LASKER: Oh my God! I can't move to Finland!

LBJ: Yes, you can.

LASKER: Oh! [laughs] I can't do that. I wouldn't be good enough. I can't speak.

LBJ: You can take anybody you want . . . with you and you can do a good job. . . . I'm gonna have the FBI check your record and I'm going to tell the President out there that I'm going to send him the most glamorous woman, the ablest person, the most gifted humanitarian and a real patriot. And you can go out there and serve until you get lonesome. . . . I need somebody that's got some brains and some charm and besides, I want a good female. . . . And you can just take off and let Adlai Stevenson run around with that Marianne Means—or whatever her name is—for a while and you come on and run around with me.[1]

LASKER: Listen. [laughs] That would be a long way to go. Lyndon, I wouldn't be good.

LBJ: No, you will. Now don't tell me—

LASKER: I want to get the answer to the different kinds of cancer there are and I've got to ride herd on these boys. . . .

LBJ: Do that after this year. I need you there now, though, because there won't be anybody doing any research if Russia takes over everything. And this is right on the border of Russia, where I need a very able woman, period.

LASKER: You should send—

LBJ: Don't tell me now. I've picked out the woman that I want.

· · · ·

LASKER: [laughs] Oh, Lyndon, let me think until tomorrow.

LBJ: I'm going to let you *think*, but I'm not going to let you say *no*. . . . Mary, four soldiers died last week in Panama trying to save us. I'm not asking you to do anything like that. I'm just asking you to—

LASKER: I know, but . . . I don't know if I have the energy and the knowledge to do it. . . .

[1] Here Johnson is being disingenuous. Means, the White House correspondent for the Hearst papers, was one of his current favorites. On the previous three weekends, she had been a guest at the LBJ Ranch and at Camp David, dining with the President's family, bowling, watching films, and attending church with them. Lady Bird observed jocularly in her diary that Means "is somebody that Lyndon and all men, in fact, have their eye on as considered an extremely attractive woman. So I guess I'll have to look her over harder! At any rate, her articles about Lyndon have all been very favorable and that is at least pleasant" (February 26, 1964). LBJ also refers to Lasker's status as one of the adoring New York women who surrounded Stevenson.

LBJ: . . . I asked Dean Rusk. I said, "What do you think of Mary Lasker for Ambassador to Finland?" And he said, "Perfect."[1]

LASKER: He doesn't know me. You know me better.

LBJ: Well, I said, "More than perfect." . . . Now, Mary, don't make me beg you, honey.

LASKER: It is like being—well, like being exiled.

LBJ: Don't you make me do something now. That is one of the greatest honors ever came to a woman and don't you make me beg you and you get your suitcase fast and . . . you get ready to go to Helsinki.

LASKER: Oh, God![2]

WEDNESDAY, JANUARY 22, 1964

OFFICE CONVERSATION
6:45 P.M.

> As the 6:30 news blares out of Johnson's television set over the tinkling of glasses and cups, LBJ hands Valenti a sheaf of papers.

LBJ: I'm going to give you these back. That one isn't worth a damn, so I made another one. Did you get a transcript of my Plans for Progress speech edited?[3]

VALENTI: I did not write this. It came down—

LBJ: It ain't worth a damn.

VALENTI: It came down from Reedy and Taylor[4]—

LBJ: Tell 'em I said—tell both of 'em I said it wasn't worth *a* shit. They'll understand that. Tell 'em both I said that. . . . I called about the Pennsylvania poll. What does it show Johnson-Scranton?[5]

JENKINS: Just a minute. I have it right here. And it shows he's the weakest one, I believe, in the whole bunch. Let me get it open to that page. No he's not the weakest one, but awful weak.—79.8 to 20.2.

LBJ: All right. What's Goldwater? . . .

JENKINS: . . . Rockefeller, 78.4 to 21.6. Goldwater, 82.1 to 17.9. Nixon, 75.2 to 24.8.

---

[1] Actually Rusk had merely said that Lasker would be "fine" (conversation with Rusk, January 20, 1964, not included in this volume).
[2] Mrs. Lasker managed to wriggle out of the appointment.
[3] Two days hence, Johnson was to speak to participants in the Plans for Progress program, a vestige of his days as Chairman of Kennedy's Equal Employment Opportunity Committee, in which large corporations signed agreements not to discriminate against blacks.
[4] Johnson aide Hobart Taylor, Jr.
[5] The liberal young Republican Governor of Pennsylvania, William Scranton, was a possible 1964 opponent.

LBJ: Now get somebody, whoever our researcher is, get Rowland Evans's column.[1] . . . He was up talking with Scranton the other day, and he said Johnson would have great trouble in Pennsylvania. . . .

VALENTI: Evans is going to put this in his column. He told me about this poll.

JENKINS: This is Joe Napolitan, who is a qualified pollster that's done this in all the states in this part of the country for a good number of years.

LBJ: Well, I want to be damn sure that Rowland Evans eats it 'cause he's been raising hell about it.

VALENTI: He told me he had it, and he said that the significance of this thing is that you beat Scranton in his own home state.

LBJ: That's right, and he's been writing all this stuff and talking about all how weak I was in the Northeast.

JENKINS: And you beat Scranton among the Republicans, Mr. Johnson. Among Republicans, you're 35, he's 28, and Undecided's 36.

LBJ: I beat him among the Republicans?

JENKINS: Yes, sir. Democrats, you've got him 79 to 3.

VALENTI: [laughs]

LBJ: Better go to work on the stereo,[2] hadn't he?

JENKINS: Catholics, 70 to 8. Protestant, 47 to 21. Jewish, 77 to 2.

VALENTI: How about the Catholics?

JENKINS: 70 to 8.

LBJ: What about the Eye-talians?

VALENTI: [laughs]

JENKINS: I'll give you that—69 to 11.

LBJ: I'm doing better with the Catholics than I am with the Eye-talians. Then I need to get an Eye-talian member.[3] I've got a Frenchman.[4] What about the French?

JENKINS: They have German, Irish, Polish, Slavic, Italian, and English.

LBJ: Where did I run the best?

JENKINS: The Slavic, 77 to 7. And the worst—English-Scotch, 48 to 20 and German 50 to 19.

RICHARD RUSSELL

6:55 P.M.

THE POLITICAL SON tries to show his political father how tough he is being on Panama, while also sounding Russell out about possible peace gestures as well as the Bobby Baker scandal.

[1] Evans and Novak had written that day that "Republican pros" were "quietly moving toward" Scranton.
[2] The issue of the gift from Bobby Baker.
[3] This is presumably a joking reference to the fact that Johnson's appointment of the Italian-American Valenti does not seem to be helping him sufficiently with Italian-American voters.
[4] The "Frenchman" is Salinger, whose mother was of French descent.

LBJ: They think they can put that Canal out of commission six months mighty easy and we got to be awfully careful about security, and they're not going to let any mobs come in there, and they're not going to let Castro set up a new government, although every night they think he's going to, and we're trying to get the thing back.

RUSSELL: I wish to hell Castro'd seize it. Then maybe, damn it, those people in the State Department and these weeping sob sisters all over the country would let us go in there and protect our rights.

. . . .

LBJ: That damn propaganda is all against us and it's just everywhere and it just looks—

RUSSELL: I read a piece in the *Manchester Guardian* and one in this London paper. And they both said that we ought to have learned by one mistake in Cuba not to make another now by surrendering here in Panama.

LBJ: Well, we're not surrendering, but I think that there are a good many chicken things that we can do and should do. . . . For instance, we think that we've got a very archaic board—Panama Canal. We think our Governor[1] is no good. He's an old ex-military fellow . . . that's not up to it. . . .

RUSSELL: We've been retiring them off down there for a long time.

LBJ: We know our Ambassador[2] wasn't worth a damn. He was just sold out to the Panamanians a hundred percent. Came back and denounced everybody, and that's why he got fired—because he wanted to run for Governor of West Virginia on the Republican ticket. . . . Now we've got a list of things that—two pages long —that we can do and we ought to do, and that don't sacrifice anything. But there is some merit to their side—not in violence, not in shooting people, but . . . I don't think I can get by with a press conference . . . without this question coming up. I just think it's as sure as the sea. I've got to see the Peace Commission in the morning. . . .

RUSSELL: . . . Withdrawn their aid yet?

LBJ: Yeah, we're not giving them a damn thing, and furthermore, just confidentially, I've moved all of our dependents . . . out to South Carolina.

RUSSELL: If you've done that, you'll hear from Chiari[3] before long and he'll be on his knees. I just wouldn't be too precipitous about it.

LBJ: I'm not. . . .

RUSSELL: . . . You've got all the cards, and this damn yapping over here by this OAS don't amount to a thing. Just because they feel like they've got to stick together. . . . Underneath the bedsheets, they'll say, "I don't blame you a damn bit."

LBJ: Now, Dick, I came back here last night from the Canadian Embassy and

[1] Major General Robert Fleming, Jr., Governor of the Canal Zone. Under a 1912 Act of Congress, the Canal Zone government, under the Secretary of the Army, was charged with "the civil government, including health, sanitation and protection, of the Canal Zone."

[2] Joseph Farland, an Eisenhower-appointed Republican, who had resigned in August 1963 with a blast against AID and Kennedy's Alliance for Progress.

[3] The Panamanian President.

Rusk and the whole outfit met with me[1] and I stayed up until two o'clock . . . and I was the only man in the room that said no. . . .

RUSSELL: But of course, Rusk belongs to the *New York Times, Washington Post.*

LBJ: I said. . . . "As long as I'm President, which is going to be for eleven months, gentlemen, I'm not about to get on my knees and go crawling to him and say, 'I want to apologize to you.' You're shooting my soldiers, by God. I ain't going to do it. And I wasn't raised in that school." And they hushed up and didn't say anything, so we busted up the meeting. . . .

RUSSELL: . . . There's a little flurry here at State—Rusk and that crowd, I imagine Cousin Adlai.[2] . . . But the people of this country are just one million percent back of your position. . . . You just go on and do what is in this country's interest, and tell Rusk and these other fellows to jump in the lake. . . . The American people have been crying for somebody that had some of the elements of Old Hickory Jackson in him. They thought they had him in old Ike, but Ike had to be captive of those people because he didn't know what else to do. You're not in that position. . . . You know this government. You know the world. Ike was limited in his experience and afraid of himself, so he leaned completely on John Foster Dulles.[3]

LBJ: Well, everybody is when you get his job.

RUSSELL: I know, but somebody down there has just got to take the bull by the horns and play the part of old Andrew Jackson, and say, "Gentlemen, this is it."

LBJ: How much does our stereo hurt?

RUSSELL: What stereo?

LBJ: Our record player—Bobby Baker.

RUSSELL: Oh, that ain't going to hurt nothing.

LBJ: Son-of-a-bitching Williams[4] got up today. . . . Because I took a record player from an employee—

RUSSELL: You got to quit letting things like that get under your skin. . . . He's mean as hell.

LBJ: I know, but he didn't say a word about Ike taking that tractor or those bulls or anything like that, and they were from private people.[5]

RUSSELL: Or those oil fellows paying all the expenses of his farm.

LBJ: . . . I took mine from a public employee working for me, and I thought it was all right.

RUSSELL: . . . It ain't going to hurt you. Of course, if a fellow wants to be

---

[1] From 11:05 until midnight.

[2] "Cousin Adlai" Stevenson was, in Russell's mind, the very image of American softness.

[3] Eisenhower's Secretary of State from 1953 until his death in 1959. Later historiography has strongly disagreed with Russell's assessment of Eisenhower and Dulles.

[4] Of the Senate Rules Committee.

[5] Eisenhower had allowed wealthy friends to give him animals, farm equipment, and other goods and services for his Gettysburg, Pennsylvania, farm.

against you, he's going to find some reason for it. . . . My bet will be it'll be
forgotten about before the campaign is over. We'll have other issues that'll be so
big that that fellow Baker will be in the background.

THURSDAY, JANUARY 23, 1964

THEODORE SORENSEN
10:32 A.M.

> JOHNSON IS PLANNING to face the press about Panama in the Fish Room at
> 5:00. Sorensen is worried that the questioning will degenerate into a free-for-all
> on Bobby Baker for which LBJ is insufficiently prepared.[1]

LBJ: This may just be a taste of raw meat and they may want more. . . . Let me
go out and make this statement[2] and then let them ask me any questions they
want to about it. . . . They might ask on our stereo thing because it looks like . . .
the Republicans are all lined up unanimous on it. Though I might say that the
President—although I wasn't President—but I know no reason why he can't buy
insurance. Competitive people agreed that they wanted to sell insurance at a rate,
and that they were advertising with our station and this fellow said that he'd get
us a little more insurance and meet the same conditions. . . . As far as I knew, he
had no connection with the stereo, but we spent $88,000 with his company. . . .
A couple of years later, Bobby Baker sent me a hi-fi record player and we didn't
embarrass him by sending it back. We kept it, and he wasn't a private person
wanting anything. The government wasn't asking anything of me. And we'd
given him gifts. So we accepted it. And those are the facts. You got any improvement on that?

SORENSEN: I think we could discuss that last part a little bit further. But
Mr. President, I'm of the opinion that . . . you're holding a press conference . . .
without enough discussion ahead of time with a lot of us. . . . I think you can go
out there and read your statement before the cameras and—period. Let the
statement speak for itself.

LBJ: Don't you think though that they're going to ask you some of these other
questions pretty soon?

SORENSEN: Yeah, I'm in favor of a press conference pretty soon, but I'd like
to have . . . a little more thoughtful meeting before you have a press conference.

---

[1] Sorensen had sent Johnson a letter of resignation on January 14, to be effective on February 29.
[2] Thanking the Peace Committee and restating the U.S. position on Panama—defending "our
obligation to safeguard the Canal against riots" while being willing, thirty days after diplomatic
relations were restored, to have "a full and frank review and reconsideration of all issues
between our two countries."

ABRAHAM RIBICOFF
Democratic Senator from Connecticut
1:14 P.M.

> DIRKSEN HAS JUST INFURIATED Johnson by pushing through the Senate Finance Committee a surprise amendment to Johnson's tax cut bill, repealing excise taxes on luxuries such as jewelry and furs. This will increase the proposed tax reduction by about $450 million. LBJ worries that Dirksen's gambit will open the way to other excise tax repeals that could destroy the entire bill, just as the committee seems about to pass it. He calls committee members to plead for help.

LBJ: Abe, can't you go with us on this excise thing and let us get a bill? Goddamnit, you need to vote with me once in a while, just one time! . . . We were ready to report this bill, and now we got it just good and screwed up, and the Democrats are going to be a miserable failure in the eyes of the whole country. Now why can't you-all meet at two o'clock and let's leave this excise like we had it before you met this morning?

RIBICOFF: I don't know how you're going to get it. The thing is overwhelming.

LBJ: No, it's not. No it's not! Clint Anderson[1] is going to help us, Hartke will help us, and if you'll help us, we'll have it over and I'll appreciate it and I'll remember it. . . . We've had that damn bill there since September and every day it's costing us $30 million in consumer income. Every single day.

RIBICOFF: One of my problems is one of the amendments in there is for something in my home state that's already been announced.

LBJ: I know it, but every one of them has got it in there, my friend. . . . God Almighty, I think about the problems I've had, and when you wanted to go on that committee, I just stood up and said, by God, it's going to be.[2] Now I just want one vote, and I want to get that bill out of there, and I got to have it, Abe. You've had problems, you've been in the Executive,[3] and you can find a way to help me. They've asked me to call you forty times this year, and I've never done it, but this time, when it means 400 or 500 million dollars[4] . . . don't let . . . Everett Dirksen screw me this way.

RIBICOFF: Mr. President, I wish you had called me. . . . The great tragedy to me . . . and I want to be very frank with you, is that Dillon[5] doesn't know the politics.

LBJ: I think that's right, and he's sick, and I don't know them either, but I want you to know them this afternoon, and go in there. Either don't vote one way or the other, but let them put these damn things back and vote with us. . . .

---

[1] Democratic Senator from New Mexico.

[2] Johnson is implying that he had helped Ribicoff join the coveted Finance Committee in 1963—a highly dubious claim, given the low state of LBJ's power in the Senate and the Kennedy administration by the third year of the Kennedy presidency.

[3] Ribicoff had been Governor of Connecticut and JFK's first Secretary of Health, Education and Welfare.

[4] The Dirksen amendment would increase the tax reduction by $445 million.

[5] Treasury Secretary Douglas Dillon.

RIBICOFF: Let me see how I can save my face. I've got—

LBJ: Don't you worry about saving your face. Your face is in damn good shape and it's going to be better when I get with you. I'll save your face. You save my face this afternoon, and I'll save your face tomorrow.

RIBICOFF: Sometime, I would really like to talk to you.

LBJ: You can do it. Any hour, any hour. I've had fifty-six days in this job, and they've been the most miserable fifty-six I've ever had.[1]

RIBICOFF: You're doing good, sir.

LBJ: And my people are going opposite directions, and that damn Harry Byrd goes one way, and he says, "Cut your damn budget, and I'll help you get your bill out." He called me yesterday, and said, "It'll be reported tomorrow." I thought it was all settled. . . . Will you go in there and help me this afternoon?

RIBICOFF: Let me try. Let me see how I can work it out.

LBJ: You just work it out. Don't say how. I don't give a damn about the details.

HARRY BYRD

Democrat of Virginia, Chairman, Senate Finance Committee
1:17 P.M.

NOW JOHNSON APPEALS to the Finance Chairman's fiscal conservatism.

LBJ: That just throws everything out of caboodle if we lose $450 million on those things. . . . You can't justify your viewpoint, losing $450 million in the Treasury when I'm trying to get this budget down.

BYRD: Yeah, I'll do the best I can.

LBJ: Help me, Harry, help me!

HARRY BYRD

5:40 P.M.

AFTER JOHNSON'S LOBBYING, the Dirksen amendment has been reconsidered and defeated by 9 to 8.

LBJ: Harry, you're a gentleman and a scholar and a producer and I love you.

BYRD: Yeah, we only had one vote. We got by.

LBJ: I know it. That Harry Byrd, though. He can do anything. You've learned how to count since I left up there. . . . God bless you. You're wonderful. Now you make 'em write that report over the weekend, Harry. . . . And I'm going to give 'em hell about economy every day until that last budget dollar is spent, and I'm

[1] One may take this comment with a mineful of salt.

going to prove to you that I can live within my budget if something like haywire don't go wrong.[1]

FRIDAY, JANUARY 24, 1964

PIERRE SALINGER
11:25 A.M.

> As SORENSEN HAD WARNED, Johnson's Fish Room press conference the previous afternoon proved a disaster, inflaming the Bobby Baker affair.[2] Reporters are battering Salinger with follow-up queries.

LBJ: I think there's a good deal of danger in that question on advertising. . . . Why don't you just say that we've said all on this we're going to say?

SALINGER: Right. Then I think I'd go off the record and say nobody suggested that the President—

LBJ: I'd go off the record and say this—and completely off the record: "Now fellows . . . with the problems we got, we're not going to descend to the Republican level of debating a $400 stereo the rest of the year—or $1,100 that was bought in advertising. The witness[3] did not claim that Mr. Johnson did anything improper on insurance or did anything improper on the stereo. He didn't do anything on advertising. . . . Furthermore, we didn't rush out of the room. We stood and talked to them. Tom Wicker had us dashing out, refusing to stop and answer questions and all that kind of crap."[4]

---

[1] That day, the Finance Committee sent the full tax cut bill to the Senate floor by a vote of 12 to 5.

[2] Without waiting to be asked about it, LBJ told about the purchase of insurance from Reynolds by "the company in which Mrs. Johnson and my daughters have a majority interest." He added, "There is a question also which has been raised about a gift of a stereo set that an employee of mine made to me and Mrs. Johnson. That happened . . . five years ago. The Baker family gave us a stereo set. We used it for a period, and we had exchanged gifts before. He was an employee of the public and had no business pending before me . . . and so far as I knew, expected nothing in return any more than I did when I presented him with gifts. . . . That is all I have to say about it and all I know about it." Whereupon Johnson abruptly ended the session. In his memoirs, *Wheeling and Dealing*, Bobby Baker charged that Johnson's statement had been a "lie": "He took the stereo, and he required Don Reynolds to buy that $1,208 worth of advertising on his Austin radio station, as a condition of Reynolds's writing the insurance. It was a kickback pure and simple, though Reynolds himself had originally volunteered to waive his cash commission on the policy and then had reneged. The stereo was supposed to be in compensation for that" (p. 196).

[3] Reynolds.

[4] Wicker's page-one lead story in the *New York Times* that morning said that Johnson "pictured as innocent" his receipt of an "expensive" stereo from Baker: "But he did not comment on charges that have been made in the Baker investigation that the agent who sold the insurance was forced to buy advertising on the Johnson family television station." Wicker noted that Johnson "left the room" before reporters could question him.

SATURDAY, JANUARY 25, 1964

ROBERT McNAMARA
11:50 A.M.

WALTER REUTHER, president of the United Auto Workers union, has proposed to Johnson that the government help create a new American company to produce small cars, competing with Volkswagen, the West German carmaker that has enjoyed phenomenal success in the U.S. market. This would improve the U.S. balance of payments and employ idle American workers. Reuther suggested a joint venture by major U.S. auto manufacturers or a subsidiary of one existing company, with the others pledging not to compete. In either case, the Justice Department would have to suspend antitrust restrictions.

Even if LBJ were not intrigued by the idea, he is eager to keep Reuther as a key ally on civil rights and in the 1964 campaign. He hopes that cooperating with Reuther on his small car idea might also move the labor boss to dampen wage demands that could cause an automobile strike in September 1964, endangering Johnson's election. Johnson has asked John McCloy and McNamara, who was Ford Motor Company president before coming to Kennedy's Pentagon, to explore the possibilities for Reuther's idea.

LBJ: John McCloy called and said he's already talked to the heads of the companies.[1]

McNAMARA: I've already talked to some of them myself. . . . I think some progress is being made.

LBJ: Let's get it made before Reuther goes and knocks 'em in the head. . . . I think Reuther's going to . . . demand the world with a fence around it in wage negotiations. . . . He's going to push 'em to the wall and it's going to be murder on us. I think though that he's vain enough that if we could get some company to . . . put this little car on the market . . . it'd be real novel. . . . And have the Justice Department behave and let it be his idea. . . .

McNAMARA: Mr. President, not until a company decides. Christ, they'd decide *against* it just because it's Reuther's idea.

LBJ: I understand that. But I think if we could . . . get it where we could . . . really compete with Volkswagen, I think that he would be vain enough—I'd say, "Now damn you, we're already doing this to take care of your people. Now please behave on us." . . .

McNAMARA: . . . It's at the point now where Justice could profitably spend a little time thinking about what might be done here to grant some protection possibly to one or two companies, if they were interested.

LBJ: We just have to. . . . I'd like you to talk to Nick and Bobby[2] both, soon as he gets back here. I want to see how much influence you've got with Bobby.[3] I'll

---

[1] Automobile companies.

[2] Katzenbach and Kennedy.

[3] Johnson says this half jokingly, but the joke contains a barbed reference to the fact that, as LBJ knows, McNamara has remained on friendly terms with RFK.

just test that right now 'cause I think it ought to be done. . . . I'd stretch anything that we needed to do. . . . How many cars you buy a year?

McNAMARA: I don't buy any now.

LBJ: Oh the hell you don't. You buy Chevrolets and Fords and—

McNAMARA: Oh you mean in the department. Oh, sure.

LBJ: You're the biggest users. Why don't you give 'em a contract, instead of running around in these damn big old waterboats you gotta haul? Why couldn't you buy a hundred thousand?

McNAMARA: We just couldn't buy this small a car. I really believe it's not right for the military.

LBJ: I see these sergeants come down here every day from Andrews Base—all these White House drivers and everything else and they're all whirling around in Mercurys. I don't know why the hell you've got a sergeant that's delivering a message for the general down to the chamber of commerce, why he's got to have a Mercury or a Chevrolet.

· · · ·

LBJ: [changing the subject to McNamara's congressional relations:] Now you give Russell credit and Vinson[1] credit for every damn thing you can without being soapy or overeffusive. You be sure that you look for things that they suggest that you can go along with 'em on. Because I'm trying to make both of them really go all out[2] and I think Russell has come a long ways in the last sixty days. . . .

McNAMARA: I'll surely do that. I personally put a hospital on his air base, Moody Air Base, that he very much wanted and I found a way to do it.

· · · ·

LBJ: [changes the subject to the Baker scandal:] Did you see Scott's statement on the hi-fi?[3]

McNAMARA: I did.

LBJ: Scott said that we were working for the Republicans. He hated to get messed up in it. He's been the one that's been messing it up and raising all the hell. Goldwater said that he got a miniature television.[4] [bitterly:] But his was miniature and mine was major.

McNAMARA: But even Goldwater said he wouldn't say it was improper.

LBJ: [darkly:] Oh, he's a son of a bitch.

McNAMARA: [laughs]

LBJ: Your woman still living with you?

McNAMARA: Yes.

LBJ: Well, give her my love. . . . You'd better give me your thinking too on what we're going to do with these wage negotiations, how we're ever going to

---

[1] House Armed Services Committee Chairman Carl Vinson, Democrat of Georgia.
[2] On McNamara's defense budget.
[3] Scott had said that the Baker scandal was helping Johnson's opposition so much that he hesitated to interfere.
[4] Goldwater's office staff had given him a $160 miniature television set as a gift.

keep old Reuther before he gets wild 'cause he's talking about taking those moneybags away from them. . . . If Reuther makes his unreasonable demands, they'll shut down, won't they?

McNAMARA: Yes, that's true.

LBJ: And that'll ruin our economy, won't it?

McNAMARA: It won't ruin the economy but it'll ruin the political—it'll ruin September and October.

LBJ: It'll ruin my budget too, won't it?

McNAMARA: Not enough to worry about. I don't think the effect on the economy or the effect on the budget is as important as the effect on the psychology of the country in September and October. It'll just be hell.

LBJ: How are we going to get by that?

McNAMARA: I don't know.

LBJ: Well, that's your problem.

EDWIN WEISL, SR.
12:00 P.M.

LBJ: I've got a hi-fi set on my hands and they're giving me a lot of hell in your *New York Times* and *Washington Post* and *St. Louis Post-Dispatch*. . . . Goldwater says he got a television set, but it was more miniature than mine.

WEISL: Goldwater also got some checks from some gamblers in Las Vegas. He'd better be careful.

LBJ: Uh-huh.

WEISL: Don't let that worry you. Nobody takes that seriously, really. That's the biggest joke of them all.

LBJ: I don't understand though why the *Times* turns on me so. They gave me a mean editorial yesterday morning on retreating on foreign aid, and I asked for $400 million more than we got this year. Every morning, even when I do something good, they've got to find something wrong with it. This morning, they had some little chickenshit editorial. I've forgotten what it is.

WEISL: They call them the "Uptown Daily Worker."

LBJ: I don't understand though.

WEISL: No one understands them.

LBJ: This morning—no, I guess it was the *Post*. It was on Panama. They said if Johnson had been reasonable all the way through, it would have been better. They want to give away the Panama Canal! I don't understand them.

WEISL: [laughs] They don't reflect the views of the people though.

LBJ: They will if they keep publishing that. . . .

WEISL: The *News* had a fairly good editorial. Did you read it? They said that this hi-fi business is a joke. . . .

LBJ: Now how did you and Ted[1] get along?

WEISL: We got along splendidly. Everything is all set.[2]

LBJ: Now you make him understand now, please, to give me first call when I need him for two days on a message to Congress that's real important—that he's just got to do it, even when he's writing that book.

WEISL: That was the understanding we made with him, that you would have first call. Now what he said about the book was this—that he was going to shack up in some little cottage in Cape Cod for a few weeks to write that book. . . . He seems to be a nice man and I think he likes you.

LBJ: He's the most wonderful, capable man you'll ever run into, except he's a vain man and he's got to be told by somebody. . . . "You've got to be available to him when he calls you to be there in thirty minutes." . . . So that he doesn't have any ideas, because he may get this big job and then he just gets as independent as hell.

WEISL: That's the trouble, once you put him in.

· · · ·

LBJ: I had a talk with Buckley,[3] and Buckley said he was a thousand percent for me and he was going to see you. This damn Paul Scott and Bob Allen[4] wrote a column that said that Buckley tried to get a meeting with me up there in New York and I wouldn't see him and I went to a cocktail party given by a woman publisher, which is a lie. I haven't been to any cocktail party in New York at all. . . . You tell him that he can hitch to us just like a Rock of Gibraltar. . . . Buckley and Wagner[5] are at each other's throats, aren't they?

WEISL: . . . If it isn't settled, you'll have some nasty primary fights there in June . . . which could result in a lot of bad feeling and loss of votes. . . .

LBJ: I don't know enough to mess in it. I'll ask Ken O'Donnell to look into it for me.

WEISL: Now how can I impress Ted Sorensen more? I said to him . . . "We want you to know that we want the President served first."

LBJ: Just tell him, "I want it clearly understood, when he wants you, you be available in thirty minutes for three or four days when he needs you."

GEORGE REEDY
2:25 P.M.

JOHNSON HAS JUST HELD another press conference in the Oval Office. Reedy is filling in for Salinger as Acting Press Secretary.

---

[1] Sorensen, who had officially resigned from Johnson's staff. In his formal reply, LBJ had said he would not let Sorensen forget his promise "to be available for future tasks."
[2] For Sorensen to become president of the Motion Picture Association.
[3] Bronx Democratic boss Charles Buckley, a former Congressman who had served with LBJ.
[4] Syndicated columnists.
[5] New York Mayor Robert Wagner.

LBJ: That was all right, wasn't it?

REEDY: Yes, I felt like an acrobat back in the days of vaudeville. It went very easily.

LBJ: What were the leads today?

REEDY: I would say your comments about the Republicans, in which you said you were accustomed to Republican criticism and it didn't particularly bother you.[1] . . .

LBJ: What did you think about the Baker thing?

REEDY: I think you may have recouped on what I believe we lost by the statement Thursday.[2] Because this was offhand. . . . This was just normal.

LBJ: And they can't say that I ran out of the room without answering questions. As a matter of fact, I told any of 'em to ask me any questions they wanted. The next time, we've got to tell somebody to cut it off. It went too long. I was afraid to stop it, on account of the Baker thing.

· · · ·

LBJ: Let's have the best briefings next week we've ever had, so we can get the Johnson team admired and respected. . . . I want you to do better than anybody else does and look nicer and take your shirt and bring it down and change it at lunch so that you've on a clean shirt and a big enough suit for you. . . . Try to leave a good impression on 'em. . . . I want to try to build you up, build you up gradually. . . . You're entitled to prestige. You've worked for it harder than anybody else. . . . But you've got to help yourself. You don't help yourself. You come in those damned old wrinkled suits and you come in with a dirty shirt and you come in with your tie screwed up. I want you to look real nice. Get you a corset, if you have to.[3]

REEDY: Okay, sir.

LBJ: But look like a top-flight businessman. You look like a goddamned reporter and I want you to look better.

GEORGE REEDY
4:40 P.M.

LBJ: [irritated] Trying to locate you ever since our press meeting! Why don't you leave word where you're going to be? I couldn't get you at the Press Office. Couldn't get you at your office. Nobody had ever heard of you. And I need to talk to you once in a while, and you should have a bomb dropped on there. You

---

[1] Asked about "Republican criticism of the stereo set" given him by Baker, Johnson said, "I have learned to expect Republican criticism, and I have endured it for about 32 years. . . . I think it is kind of a hallmark of their party. . . . I am a little amused when you talk about the stereo and the miniature television [received by Barry Goldwater]. I don't know what the difference is, but I guess there is some difference."

[2] Reedy was wrong. Much of the press lambasted Johnson for comparing the stereo from Baker with the miniature television given Goldwater by his staff.

[3] Reedy was stout.

just tell your girl, your secretary, where you are and where you're going to eat or drink or screw or whatever it is you're doing and let me get in touch with you. I don't need to know the number. You just leave word.

WALTER REUTHER
5:39 P.M.

JOHNSON ASKS REUTHER to cool his wage demands before the fall Presidential election and to discuss with Robert Kennedy the antitrust dimension of his idea of starting a small American carmaker.

LBJ: I don't want you raising hell[1] until I get elected. I don't mind how many times you march after November, but don't do it in September.

• • • •

LBJ: McNamara . . . got a spark out of them[2] and they're waiting on Bobby Kennedy.[3] So I told him to go to Katzenbach.[4] And I think you ought to say—I don't mind telling you because you've got to be a good influence in this administration—Bobby and I are going to be pulling together, but he's got some kids over there that have been disillusioned by me because they didn't know me. And I'm willing to be patient with all of them, but I think . . . you ought to tell him that they got to figure out some way that we can keep all of them from going in and messing up the party. . . . You call his office and tell 'em you want to talk to him about it. . . . Your lawyers have been looking at it and you want him, as a can-do man, to find some way it can be done. . . . Just say you've been beating Johnson over the head and what I'm trying to do is not just help solve the balance of payments. It's a damn shame of our boasting that we're the greatest industrial nation in the world and then just let 'em whip the socks off us here and have a bunch of men idle. . . . If we need to amend a law, let's amend one. But if I had an Attorney General that'd interpret one right, I'd interpret it.

REUTHER: I'll go to work on that.

ELMER STAATS
Deputy Director, Bureau of the Budget
5:45 P.M.

AMERICANS WHO IMAGINE LBJ as the incarnation of heedless liberalism will be startled by the following screed.

LBJ: Bob Byrd's just raising hell about us putting in this money . . . in the D.C.[5] budget for all these illegitimate kids. I told you to take that out. . . . They want

[1] Making inordinate wage demands.
[2] Out of the automakers on Reuther's idea.
[3] LBJ is happy to poison Reuther's mind against RFK by suggesting that the Attorney General has not sprung into action behind Reuther's idea.
[4] The Deputy Attorney General.
[5] Washington, D.C., which, before home rule, was administered by Congress.

to just stay up there and breed and won't work and we have to feed them. . . . I told you we don't want to take care of all these illegitimate kids and we want to make 'em get out there and go to work. . . . I don't want to be taking any taxpayers' money and paying it to people just to breed. . . . This is a program of what they call welfare chiselers. Take 'em from the relief rolls. . . . We're financing it and you-all have got me on record for it after I told you not to. . . . I told you to cut the damn thing out.

MONDAY, JANUARY 27, 1964

WALTER JENKINS, BILL MOYERS, ABE FORTAS, JACK VALENTI
8:55 P.M.

> JOHNSON PONDERS whether they should try to stanch the pressure for Jenkins to testify before a televised session of the Senate Rules Committee by having the White House issue a statement in his name.

LBJ: Ted Sorensen said that we're the biggest damned fools he's ever dealt with —first, to make the first statement[1] and then second, to make the next one.[2] But I guess we got to do it. I talked to him a long time about it tonight and he said everybody that is experienced in this thing thinks that we're just . . . blowing it up ourselves. O'Donnell, O'Brien, Sorensen—all of 'em agree that we're building a case against ourselves. . . . He thinks that we just made a terrible mistake coming out the other day.[3] . . . It gave them a chance to say that we ran out on the questioning. He said that's the memory that people have— that the President ran. . . . You got these people in the *Washington Post* and *Newsweek*. And that fellow Friendly[4] over there is really playing this thing for keeps.

VALENTI: Why does Walter have to make a statement, Mr. President?

LBJ: You-all answer that.

FORTAS: I think he ought to make a statement because he's got a great big hole here and it's gonna be very difficult to live with it between now and the election. He's got a story to tell. I think you can fill the hole with that story and then Walter can live with it.

LBJ: Abe, I wish you'd talk to Sorensen about this before we do it. 'Cause just every political adviser we've got that's been winning campaigns is against these

---

[1] The Thursday, January 23, 1964, press conference, in which Johnson had tried to explain the stereo set and then abruptly ended the questioning.
[2] Johnson's comparison on Saturday, January 25, of his stereo from Baker (and Reynolds) with the miniature television Goldwater was given by his employees.
[3] At Johnson's January 23 press conference.
[4] Alfred Friendly of the *Post*.

things. They think that we just came out and reopened it up and built it up and got all the Congressmen and Senators all slushing away, just because we met over there at lunch the other day and decided we had to have a statement.

FORTAS: Well, Humphrey and Mansfield—

LBJ: Humphrey didn't. Humphrey told me the opposite, and Mansfield is not astute anyway. Carl Albert told me not to do it. Everybody whose judgment I really respect. And I knew it. I just knew it was bad. I just *knew* it—*instinctively*. I think it is building up now to where I think we're building it up again and I just don't like to go against your judgment 'cause you've got to defend me. If I don't follow your advice, I'm going to be in a hell of a shape. But if I *do* follow it, I'm going to *jail!* And that's the way I look at it. My instinct tells me that we're just *begging* for trouble. Just out there opening my arms by issuing these damned statements. I thought the one the other day—I just started to turn around when I started to walk out of there and I just couldn't do it because you and Clark Clifford thought it ought to be done. But I just sure think it was a terrible mistake.

. . . .

VALENTI: I'm just going on instinct too and I know nothing about the facts. But here's another front-page story. . . . When they smell blood, they're not going to stop with this statement. Just like the President thought he finished it off the other day. But he hasn't. He just added fuel to the fire. I think every time you issue a statement on it, it just adds to it and the jackals begin to want more blood. . . . Really, the only people exercised about this are the people in Washington.

. . . .

LBJ: I think that anything we say is going to be misinterpreted, misconstrued and the least we say, the better. And I'd just give anything in the world if I could retract my statement the other day. . . . I thought I got by with it fine. I walked in the room and stood there and talked to Helen Thomas[1]—she said, "Are you going out to Liz Carpenter's party?" And I said yes. She said, "Are you going to see Queen Frederika?"[2] And so and so. And we talked about that. Then the sons of bitches had me running out of the room. I was loping. . . . People like that you can't deal with. I've almost got to be as mean with them as Truman was. Tom Wicker of the *New York Times,* who's reputable, honest, presumably a gentleman—yesterday he asked Howard Smith [LBJ does Wicker impersonation:] "Is there a Southerner here on civil rights? Johnson's a Southerner." Well, that son of a bitch is from North Carolina himself. But they're just wicked men and I just think anything you give them is trouble. Now the main thing you got to do is use your power on 'em and hope you get the votes. I wish you and Clark Clifford would spend your time on six Senators,[3] instead of on statements.

[1] UPI White House correspondent.
[2] Of Greece.
[3] Democratic Rules Committee members.

FORTAS: Um-hmm.

LBJ: . . . Tell the Republicans to go straight to hell. And maybe write some statements to answer them on the House floor and Senate floor. But I'd never be answering them out of the White House because, God, that blows it up. . . . I think the most tragic mistake we've made since we've been in the White House was walking out there the other day and making that—we were going to be frank. We were going to be candid. We were going to be open. We answered them all and then what did they do? They said we ran. So we're just children, just getting burnt with this press corps over here.

JENKINS: What would you think . . . having a columnist like Bill White[1] say that, after all, it didn't have anything to do with the government one way or the other, and that it doesn't make a whole lot of difference. . . .

LBJ: I think it would be very good if you get Drew Pearson and Bill White to do it, to just say that the Republicans had canned speeches and "shame on you."

FORTAS: I think I may be able to get Drew to do it.

LBJ: . . . I think if you sit on your ass with a statement—I just tell you the smartest man I've met in the White House is Sorensen. He just told me tonight he just thought I was a big, fat, cigar-puffing, pot-bellied numskull by following the advice to get out here in front of the press. He said, "That's all they want you to do. I told you the other day and I'm going to tell you that again." Now maybe we've got a hole. Maybe we need to fill that hole. But I think we ought to fill it with those six votes up there. . . . But I sure don't think tonight is any night to put it out. I honestly don't.

MOYERS: I would raise a question, Mr. President, about using Bill White for this particular message. . . .

LBJ: Well, who in the hell are you going to use?

MOYERS: Pearson is by far the best choice on this. But White is beginning to be thought of as a private channel.

LBJ: He's always been thought of, and that's all right. . . . He reaches a lot of people and reaches the conservative group you want to reach. Who do you suggest, Bill? Who do you know who would write a column like you want it written, period? Don't be negative. Just be affirmative and knock one off and I'll get you a woman to sleep with yourself. [joking]

MOYERS: . . . You won't believe it, but I think you could get Rowland Evans to do a story like this after what you did to him Saturday night.[2]

LBJ: Oh hell, no!

JENKINS: I'm afraid these people have to have the hooker at the end of it.

LBJ: I think Bill White is respected in the United States. I think he's really about as respected a columnist as you got. I don't think here in Washington, with

---

[1] William S. White of Texas was pro-Johnson to the point of being considered by some as a semi-official spokesman. (At the end of the administration in 1969, Johnson gave him the Presidential Medal of Freedom.)

[2] Johnson had joked about Evans at the annual closed-door dinner of the Alfalfa Club.

your liberals and your radicals and your who-done-its and what-nots. But I think over the country he is.

• • • •

LBJ: Abe, why don't you call three of your best friends ... and ask them whether they think Walter ought to answer this tonight or not.

FORTAS: Well, it's a little difficult, you know, to convey background on this thing.

LBJ: ... Just talk to two or three on what they see and I'd say nothing tonight. ... But I'd write it, and I'd wait until tomorrow, and let's meet on it in the morning. After I get through with Bobby Kennedy. [sardonically:] *That* is going to be a pleasant assignment.[1]

TUESDAY, JANUARY 28, 1964

HUBERT HUMPHREY
6:15 P.M.

LBJ: Hubert, you got a hell of a good interview on this UPI ticker about the civil rights bill and about answering Republican National Chairman Miller.[2] Goddamn, that couldn't be better. That's as fine a statement as I ever saw in that few words.

HUMPHREY: Why, thank you.

LBJ: ... And that tax bill ... you want to bear in mind, my friend, that we get the real impact six months from the time this goes in. That's when it hits us. And this is March—March, April, May, June, July, August. So we'll be needing it about September.

HUMPHREY: ... We're going to find out how many people we've got locked up here without amendment, and if we can rack up forty Democrats or forty-five, well, we're in business.

[1] Johnson was to see Robert Kennedy the following morning to receive a report on his trip to Indonesia. By now, his relations with RFK had deteriorated enough that he is dreading it. When RFK arrived at the White House the next morning, he was astonished to find that he would not see Johnson in private but in a mass meeting with ranking members of the Senate Foreign Relations and Armed Services Committees. Kennedy felt that Johnson had not given a "damn" about his effort. (See Edwin Guthman, *We Band of Brothers,* Harper & Row, 1971, p. 253; Arthur M. Schlesinger, Jr., *Robert Kennedy and His Times,* p. 635; and Kenneth O'Donnell oral history, Johnson Library.)

[2] The Republican National Chairman, William Miller, had denounced the Johnson administration as the "Wheeler Deal" and predicted that Bobby Baker would be "a very big issue." Humphrey had replied, "The issues are pretty well set out already. They include War on Poverty, economic growth, world peace, security, Medicare, human dignity, human rights, education and opportunity for the young, and the issues of the smear and fear are not worthy of this Republic and of these days and the Republicans want to spend a great deal of time on that. So while they're digging there we'll just be building a better America."

. . . .

LBJ: Now this ought to be the party line. . . . The reason the Republicans haven't won any elections except Eisenhower—and Eisenhower didn't mess around with this trash—he was a national hero—but the reason they haven't won one since Hoover is because they spend all their time on Roosevelt's boy Jimmy and on his dog,[1] and . . . Truman and Margaret and the music critics[2] and . . . Kennedy and his relations. . . . And if they don't stand for something—hell, if they just come out here and talk about revival of the corn tassel or . . . Tom Watson[3] watermelons, it would be something, but they're just, by God, against things—against everything and trying to smear and fear.

. . . .

LBJ: Just every day you ought to say the Democratic party is the one party left for America because the other fellows don't stand for anything. Just God pity them for they know not what they do. I just feel sorry for them because—what do they stand for? You can't look at a single one of their candidates. Rocky's for divorce. Goldwater's after him.

HUMPHREY: By the way, I had a talk with Joe[4] and I confided in him vis-à-vis our little paper,[5] and it's very good. We're in fine shape there.

LBJ: All right.

HUMPHREY: The other man[6] I didn't get ahold of today, but there'll be no problem. By the way, I took the liberty—I hope you won't feel badly about it—of sharing that with George.[7]

LBJ: No, that's all right. I think you ought to share it with anybody that you can to let them know that these guys[8] got themselves tied in with a bad egg, and they're relying on him, and they're supporting him . . . and they're out trying to prove now . . . a lot of stuff that if they proved it, there wouldn't be anything wrong with it, but they're tied in with a guy[9] that flunked out, that busted out, that's retired, that's Old Man McCarran, that's anti-Jew.[10] And that's who they've lined up with, and that ought to kill any Republican that lines up with him.

[1] Republicans of FDR's time questioned the business dealings of Roosevelt's eldest son, James, and famously accused him of sending a destroyer to retrieve his dog, Fala, from Alaska.
[2] When the *Washington Post* critic Paul Hume criticized Margaret Truman's singing, Truman replied with a notorious blistering letter.
[3] The nineteenth-century Georgia populist.
[4] Clark of the Rules Committee.
[5] Johnson's private memo on the damaging information in Reynolds's government files.
[6] Claiborne Pell.
[7] Smathers.
[8] Republicans on the Rules Committee.
[9] Don Reynolds.
[10] Johnson's reading of Reynolds's private files led him to believe that Reynolds was a cheerleader for the witch hunts by Joseph McCarthy and Senator Pat McCarran, Democrat of Nevada, in the 1950s, as well as an anti-Semite.

GEORGE BALL
6:30 P.M.

THE PREVIOUS MONTH, Cyprus had erupted into violence over its 1960 constitution, which granted the newly independent island's 18 percent Turkish minority a veto over legislation and empowered both Greece and Turkey to oversee the island. In early January, the Cypriot President, Archbishop Makarios, threatened to cancel the treaties binding Cyprus to Britain, Turkey, and Greece. The British government threatened to withdraw its troops, putting pressure on the United States to replace them. Turkey threatened to intervene on Cyprus. Greece threatened to retaliate.

BALL: Mr. President, we have been working all day on this Cyprus matter. We have a plan which I think is a pretty good one . . . which would involve our putting a small unit in, but in a manner where we would have agreement in advance so we would not get in the middle . . . and then there would be mediation machinery set up.

LBJ: . . . I'd like to move you or Harriman or somebody, Bobby Kennedy or Bob McNamara, somebody—I'd like to move them over there and let them make an all-out diplomatic effort. Maybe put an airplane carrier or two there. . . . And say to those people, "Now we're going to make preparations and we're ready for a quick entry and we're not going to support you Turks if you pull anything like this. . . . We're not going to give you aid and back you up to fight you on the next breath and you just behave yourselves." Tell the Greeks the same thing and let somebody go in there—you or Averell Harriman or some of these other fellows that may be traveling around now—and say to them, "Now we've got to work out an agreement here." . . . And then have a couple of carriers off there, where you could move people in if you needed to, but just not let these damned British run us in there. They're just in a habit of doing this kind of stuff.[1]

WALTER JENKINS
7:30 P.M.

JOHNSON'S EFFORTS to have damaging information found on Don Reynolds that can be leaked to reporters in order to discredit the insurance man have had new results.

JENKINS: I've got considerably more detail on Reynolds's love life . . .

LBJ: Well, get it all typed up for me.

---

[1] Lady Bird wrote in her diary, "Cyprus, unhappily, along with Vietnam and Panama, is my husband's diet these days and that's why I must try to be both strong and understanding" (January 28, 1964).

WEDNESDAY, JANUARY 29, 1964

RICHARD RUSSELL
10:30 A.M.

LBJ: Dick, we're going to have to have a little meeting[1] this afternoon on Panama.... They're insisting that ... we agree to renegotiate and revise the treaties.

RUSSELL: That's so unreasonable.

LBJ: And we're not going to do that. So I thought that if they're going to charge us for breaking it up ... then they may get all their Latin friends with them, you know.

RUSSELL: I'm not too sure about that.

LBJ: ... I wanted to have a meeting of the leaders because I wanted them to know what we're doing, because I think ... the *Washington Post, New York Times,* and Milton Eisenhower[2] and a good group of them would raise hell—that we've been arbitrary and arrogant, and a big tough guy.

RUSSELL: ... You know ... there's such a thing as making an ass out of yourself and after you've agreed to discuss anything and in advance make some agreement to rewrite a treaty in some way....

LBJ: ... I'm going to try to get the leadership in ... just in the hope that I can get them unified so they won't go off in all different directions—the Morses,[3] and the Fulbrights, and the rest of them.

MIKE MANSFIELD
11:11 A.M.

LBJ: Mike ... don't repeat this, but there's no question but what the Republicans in the House group—this fellow Miller[4]—is trying to get our Democrats to involve Walter Jenkins ... and I'm not going to be sending my assistants up to testify before these committees. And they've talked to Joe Clark and Pell, but you ought to talk to 'em again today, and just tell them that there's nothing improper or illegal with my buying insurance or buying advertising.... But don't let those Republicans get them to panic and start trying to summon White House assistants because that's all they want to do. That's the only the issue they got.

MANSFIELD: They want another Sherman Adams.[5]

[1] With the congressional leadership, in the Cabinet Room.
[2] The former President's brother, an outspoken liberal on Latin America.
[3] Referring to Oregon Senator Wayne Morse.
[4] William Miller, the Republican National Chairman.
[5] Eisenhower's chief aide, Sherman Adams, was forced to resign during the 1958 congressional campaign after charges that he had used influence on behalf of Bernard Goldfine, a businessman who had given him money, goods, and favors.

LBJ: And so, you just see that those two boys stand firm with Jordan because Jordan's pretty weak anyway.

MANSFIELD: Yes, sir.

LBJ: . . . They want this committee to start a television show and have a White House assistant on it, and this is not a question of a private company doing something. . . . This is a question of our buying insurance ourselves and there's no reason why we shouldn't, and no reason why we shouldn't sell advertising.

MANSFIELD: Yes, sir.

LBJ: The government is not involved anyway and that resolution oughtn't to be involved. [angry:] And if they *were* involved, I wouldn't let one of my assistants come up and testify. That goes back to George Washington.

MANSFIELD: Yes, sir.

WALTER JENKINS
11:45 A.M.

JOHNSON SUSPECTS THAT Humphrey is trying to escape getting involved in LBJ's defense against the Bobby Baker charges.

LBJ: You never did get Humphrey?

JENKINS: Nope. Called his office back, said they'd tried to reach him downtown, he'd left that place and was on his way back to the office. We just checked again, he's not back yet.

LBJ: Check on the floor, see if he's there, and then when you get him, tell him, goddamn it, let 'em know where we can reach him in an emergency. If we had this country bombed, he'd be in a hell of a shape to be a leader.

WALTER JENKINS
12:25 P.M.

LBJ: You just can't get Hubert on the phone, can you?

JENKINS: Haven't yet, but we're still trying.

LBJ: Think he's dodging you? Sounds like it.

JENKINS: I don't think so. I don't believe he would. I think we just haven't been able to reach him. But I think we will in the next few minutes 'cause his office said he was going to be on the floor right away. They were apparently coming there from somewhere else.

GEORGE BALL
6:12 P.M.

BALL ALERTS JOHNSON that in South Vietnam, a cabal of young military officers led by the 37-year-old General Nguyen Khanh, trained at Fort Leavenworth, Kansas, has just overthrown General Minh and the hapless junta that assumed power in November 1963 after the Diem assassination.

BALL: It looks as though a fellow named General Khanh, who's very close actually to our people and is very anti-neutralist, has gotten the situation in his hands, that he's moved against Generals Don and Kim and Xuan,[1] who have been flirting with the French on the neutralist line . . . and that he is trying, among other things, to get Prime Minister Tho[2] out of the government, and to take a much stronger anti-neutralist line than has been the case out there in the past few weeks. So that if this works and there's a bloodless affair . . . it's probably a good thing. . . .

LBJ: How much of this is in the paper?

BALL: . . . Nothing on the regular ticker, so far, I'm told.

LBJ: Will it be in the morning papers?

BALL: Yeah, I'm sure. It's bound to be.[3]

JACK VALENTI

Special Assistant to the President
6:50 P.M.

VALENTI: Drew Pearson said that in Detroit, Eisenhower said something about that he was unhappy that the President accepted that stereo set, and Eisenhower was asked about his gifts to the farm.[4] He denied receiving the gifts by saying they were all a tissue of lies. . . . Drew Pearson also said that he thinks that we ought to get a reporter to go to Mortimer Caplin.[5] Caplin made a ruling, I think —you may know about it—that three men—W. Alton Jones, W.G. Byars, and George Allen—contributed to the total support of the Eisenhower farm.

LBJ: Let's let that go till tonight. I'm in a CIA meeting here.

[1] Generals Tran Van Don, who had been Defense Minister and Commander-in-Chief of the South Vietnamese Armed Forces, Le Van Kim, Secretary-General of the Military Revolutionary Council, and Mai Huu Xuan.

[2] Nguyen Ngo Tho was Prime Minister and Minister of Economy and Finance.

[3] Although Johnson was later assured that Khanh was more reliably pro-American and competent than the toppled generals, who had been flirting with pro-neutralist forces and direct negotiations with the National Liberation Front, organized by Vietnamese Communists in 1960, he was unhappy about the appearance of disorder in Saigon.

[4] Referring to Johnson's gift from Bobby Baker, Eisenhower had on January 29 told reporters in Detroit, "Someone sends you a set of woods for your golf. Now are you going to send it back and say, 'Well, you so and so.' Are you holier than thou?" (*New York Herald Tribune*, January 30, 1964). The former President was responding to a January 25 Drew Pearson column about the financing of expenses on Eisenhower's Gettysburg farm during his presidency by his wealthy friends. In a later column, Pearson ominously noted that the Senate Rules Committee had the power to investigate the gifts to Eisenhower along with the Bobby Baker scandal.

[5] Chief of the Internal Revenue Service.

THURSDAY, JANUARY 30, 1964

ROBERT ANDERSON

Former Secretary of the Treasury, Eisenhower Administration[1]

4:05 P.M.

ANDERSON: I've seen people that have never voted the Democratic ticket in their life—strong Republicans—and for the first time in their life, they're going to vote for you. Now this is something that's very scarce, even in Eisenhower's time, and he was a national war hero, but you captured the imagination.

LBJ: He made a hell of a good statement yesterday on the stereo set. I just want you to let him know that about two weeks ago, folks came in here and wanted me to authorize or get some information from Internal Revenue on something about maintaining his farm and some kind of an outfit ruling that they'd made over there . . . and said it involved Pete Jones[2] and somebody—Byars or Byler or somebody. And I said, "I don't know anything about it, and I don't want to know anything about it. I served under this man eight years and all the goddamn gold in Fort Knox wouldn't cause him to inch one minute toward me if he didn't think it was right. And so you just as far as I'm concerned, get out of here, and don't ask for anything because I'm not talking to anybody. I just—I don't want to see it, never heard of it, don't want it, wouldn't ask for it under any circumstances."[3] And then a week later, ten days later, by God, they'd ask him out at Detroit and he'd say the same thing. [laughs]

ANDERSON: I talk to him once a week or ever so often and you absolutely won the guy. He'll remain a Republican because—

LBJ: He ought to, because he may be getting them to stand for something positive, so if they win the election we'll have a good administration.

ANDERSON: In any event, he's just as strong as he can be. Nothing disgusts him worse than the stereo set[4] and all these other things.

LBJ: Well, I'll tell you what I did, Bob. This kid, after the '57 fight,[5] we'd been up 37 days and nights and he'd done a good job—and I knew nothing, he had no business dealings till after I left the Senate. But in '57 I took he and his wife and three children and took them to the ranch. Bought them an airplane ticket down there and back and they stayed a week . . . and I've done that with a good many people in my life—invited them to come and see me, made it possible. . . . He felt

---

[1] Anderson was Eisenhower's private first choice for President in 1960. After the Kennedy assassination, Ike had urged LBJ to consult him frequently. Coincidentally, Anderson had been one of the owners of KTBC in Austin when Lady Bird Johnson bought it in 1943.

[2] Oilman W. Alton Jones.

[3] Johnson here is presumably using Anderson to send a message to Eisenhower that since he is working to prevent investigation of the gifts to Eisenhower (potentially more embarrassing than Baker's gift to LBJ, since they were given during Eisenhower's presidency), Ike should use his influence with Republican Senators to thwart the Bobby Baker probe.

[4] Meaning the commotion over the stereo set.

[5] Baker, after the struggle over the 1957 civil rights bill.

a little bit generous about it and this guy[1] owed him some money on insurance he'd never paid him. So he made him get him two sets, and he got one for himself and one for me and sent it over. Never told me he had anything to do with an insurance man, but an insurance man had given it to him. If he'd given it to me, wouldn't been anything wrong with it. We spent $88,000 with him. Why shouldn't he spend $400 with us?

ANDERSON: Not a thing in the world. Look, these are just the kind of things that just gripe the hell out of you.

LBJ: They're trying to make Walter Jenkins a criminal, and he's the best man that ever lived.

ABE FORTAS
5:47 P.M.

STILL SUSPECTING that Humphrey is dodging his pleas to intercede with Rules Committee members on the Bobby Baker problem, Johnson has assigned Fortas to find the Minnesota Senator.

FORTAS: He[2] left on the four-thirty American.[3] I can't understand why they haven't gotten him yet 'cause that plane should have landed. He will be at the Commodore[4] in New York. The guy just ducked out of town.[5]

LBJ: Well, you can't do anything. We're just going to wind up here being unable to do anything. . . . And I just hate to call these people myself but, by God, you-all just don't seem to be able to get anybody on the telephone.

FORTAS: Oh, Senator Humphrey is on the other line. Can I call you right back?

LBJ: [angry] Yes, sir, and ask him what in the goddamned hell he's doing off there in the middle of the week—and why that information he gave us about both of these men is exactly wrong[6] and what they're going to do tomorrow. And, for God's sake, don't let them be voting, be calling people. . . . Number one, we do not want Reynolds called back. Number two, we do not want Jenkins called back. See what the hell he can do about it. If he can't do anything, tell us, so we can get somebody that can!

ABE FORTAS
5:55 P.M.

FORTAS: Hubert said that these two fellows[7] say they strongly believe that Walter ought to testify voluntarily. He said he told them he wasn't going to do

[1] Reynolds.
[2] Humphrey.
[3] American Airlines flight to New York.
[4] Hotel.
[5] Fortas feeds Johnson's suspicions that Humphrey is dodging him.
[6] Humphrey had assured Johnson that Pell and Clark were in line.
[7] Clark and Pell.

it. Then I said, "Well, damn it, that isn't good enough. . . . They've got to stand firm . . . that they're going to close the lid on this thing, that they will not call Reynolds, will not call Jenkins, not call them for any purpose in any way—private, public interviews, hearings or whatnot." And he said . . . he can prevent either of them being called. . . . I said, "Hubert, now can I tell the boss that?" And he said, "Yes, you can tell him that." I said, "Now damn it, that means absolute, positively, and no corners on the thing." And he said, "I want to call you back." That's the damn kind of guy we're dealing with, Mr. President, and he said he'd call me back in just a few minutes. I got him caught out there at the airport. American Airlines guys have got him at La Guardia. I've talked to them about as rough as I've ever talked to anybody in my life.

LBJ: Well—

FORTAS: And he's going to call me back. Now, there he is back again, so I'll talk to him again, and call you back, sir.

OFFICE CONVERSATION
6:00 P.M.

> IN THE OVAL OFFICE, Johnson gripes to Clark Clifford and Walter Jenkins that Humphrey is refusing to help him.

LBJ: He's not going to do anything. You can see. He's full of grits. He's not gonna do anything. He had all this thing worked out here yesterday, and didn't know it. . . . We can't turn these things over to other people. You know them very well.

JENKINS: Yes, sir.

· · · ·

LBJ: [picks up telephone to talk to Reedy:] Have you talked to Hayden's[1] man?

REEDY: Yes sir.

LBJ: What did he say?

REEDY: They will do it.

LBJ: What'll he do?

REEDY: He will pin down the fact that it was not Walter but the station personnel.[2]

LBJ: Did you read him the testimony and make him write it down, where he'll have it?

REEDY: No sir, I didn't go that far.

LBJ: I asked Walter to tell you to do that. George, you do it exactly now, 'cause I can't get through a message to the people and I can't call him myself, so I asked Walter to call him and he designates you to call him and you call him and then you call him and you screw it up. . . . Take that statement of Walter Jenkins out

[1] Carl Hayden, Democratic Senator from Arizona.
[2] Who asked Reynolds for advertising.

of the transcript where he says, "I did not have anything to do with the arrangement." Read that to him. Say, "This is what he says," and take the statement that it presumably conflicts with and point out that Reynolds didn't have a damned thing to do with the advertising himself. So we couldn't have any arrangements with a man that had Young doing it, that Young worked it out with the station. . . . Write out a statement that he[1] can make and if it's not written out and typed out, he won't use it. He's eighty-six years old. And I can't tell you all these things over three times!

REEDY: I'll call him right back, sir.

LBJ: Now who else have you talked to, besides him?

REEDY: I talked to Whitley.[2]

LBJ: All right, now what's he say? You go over the same thing with him?

REEDY: Yes, sir.

LBJ: But didn't read him the testimony?

REEDY: No sir.

LBJ: That's what you've got to do. . . . You've got to get six votes in the morning and I don't believe you boys know how to count six.

ABE FORTAS
6:30 P.M.

LBJ: I don't know where we're going to get our five votes.

FORTAS: Now Humphrey swears to me that he's going to do this job for us.

LBJ: When's he going to do it, and where?

FORTAS: He says he'll be back[3] tomorrow night and, if necessary, will come back earlier. They said they won't be able to meet next week anyway.

LBJ: No, but they'll determine tomorrow who they're going to call and we'll be confronted with a fait accompli. They'll say, "We thought you wanted him[4] called." Like they did yesterday. They're doing this on the basis of our wanting it done.

FORTAS: The hell they are.

LBJ: That's what they said.

FORTAS: That's just a lot of—you know how people are, Mr. President. *Damn* it!

LBJ: Well, I know this—that I talked to Mansfield yesterday and I told Mansfield, goddamn it, I wasn't going to let Walter Jenkins come up there and testify. . . . And "help us." And he said all right he would. And in five minutes, the next

[1] Hayden.
[2] William Whitley, an aide to Senator Jordan.
[3] To Washington.
[4] "We" refers to Clark and Pell. "Him" refers to Jenkins.

thing I heard was Mansfield had talked to 'em and told 'em that we wanted Walter to testify.

FORTAS: I can't control the minds of these damned guys that can't understand the English language. Sherman Adams refused to appear on the Dixon-Yates contract.[1] . . .

LBJ: But all of this happened before I was President. Does that have any weight bearing on it?

FORTAS: . . . We can make a respectable argument that there's an immunity that flows from status. For example, they sure wouldn't compel the President to testify. I don't care on what. The point is that the immunity that applies to the President applies to the President's assistants, just as I've got a lawyer-client privilege, you know, if the client's my secretary. . . . It's not airtight, by any means, but we've got a hell of a good argument for it. . . . The question has never been presented squarely before, but that's what I think the courts would hold. . . . They're not going to subpoena Walter, but the question is whether they'll make it embarrassing. . . .

LBJ: . . . The Attorney General thinks Walter ought to go do it[2] and that whole group thinks that Walter ought to go testify. I know that he oughtn't to do it. And I know that Reynolds oughtn't to do it.

FORTAS: I went back to Hubert. . . . We were talking about Reynolds, and I told him that this guy is a textbook paranoid and he testified very conservatively and convincingly but he's been talking around . . . in a different way, and if they put him back on the stand, the guy's going to blow his top and implicate John Fitzgerald Kennedy and everybody in sight. Hubert said he's been showing around some of the Air Force report.[3] I said, "That ain't nothing. You haven't seen the stuff on this fellow."

LBJ: You'd better see when you can get him back to town and when he can do this.

FRIDAY, JANUARY 31, 1964

WALKER STONE
Editor-in-Chief, Scripps-Howard Newspapers
1:32 P.M.

STUNG BY REPORTS that he is ignoring foreign affairs, Johnson defends himself, off-the-record, to a friendly newspaper man.

---

[1] Citing executive privilege, Eisenhower refused to let Adams, his chief aide, testify during the controversy over the award of a federal contract to build a West Memphis power plant to a utility group headed by Edgar Dixon and Eugene Yates.
[2] Johnson presumes that RFK wants Jenkins to testify because he thinks it will hurt LBJ.
[3] On Reynolds's service in the Air Force.

LBJ: On the Panama thing, I spent three fourths of my time on foreign policy. I added it up this morning. . . . I don't keep statistics, but I had 117 meetings and 188 conversations on the phone on these things. . . . Now we're not throwing our weight around, and we're not whipping anybody. . . . But we're not going to get slugged around any more than we did in Bolivia when they captured our men.[1] We told them we better get 'em back or, by God, we'd come and get 'em.

. . . .

LBJ: We couldn't anticipate the shooting down of the plane.[2] These T-39s are not worth a damn. . . . They got in the wrong territory and they had no business there. . . . You may not be sleeping with my wife, but if I catch you with your britches down and you're coming out of her bedroom, and she's in bed, God, I might do something bad.

. . . .

LBJ: Now let's see . . . Vietnam. . . . This Khanh is the toughest one they got and the ablest one they got.[3] And he said, "Screw this neutrality, we ain't going to do business with the Communists, and get the goddamned hell out of here. I'm pro-American and I'm going to take over." Now it'll take him a little time to get his marbles in a row, just like it's taking me a little time. But it's de Gaulle's loss[4] and the neutralists' loss, not the Americans' loss, and we're going to try to launch some counterattacks ourselves. . . . We're going to touch them up a little bit in the days to come.[5]

JACK BROOKS
6:47 P.M.

BROOKS: Boss . . . you about ready to wrap it up?

LBJ: No, I will be in a few minutes. Would you like to come down and bring that girl of yours and throw her in the swimming pool, or would you like to have a drink, or what would you like to do?

---

[1] See January 10, 1964, LBJ conversation with Richard Russell above.
[2] Soviet MiG fighters had downed an American T-39 jet trainer after it crossed the East German border.
[3] By now Johnson has been fully briefed on the new man in Saigon.
[4] That day the French President had repeated his insistence that North and South Vietnam be unified and neutralized, with all foreign forces withdrawn.
[5] Johnson had approved a covert action plan against North Vietnam called Operations Plan 34-A-64, or Op Plan 34-A. Guerrilla raids against the Ho Chi Minh Trail, used by the Communists to infiltrate South Vietnam, would be expanded. Reconnaissance planes would fly over Laos. There would be commando raids along the North Vietnamese coast and naval shelling of military installations in the Gulf of Tonkin. "Progressively escalating pressure" would be applied to North Vietnam—"punishment" designed to "convince the North Vietnamese leadership, in its own interest, to desist from its aggressive policies." (See Lloyd C. Gardner, *Pay Any Price*, Ivan R. Dee, 1995, pp. 112–13; Stanley Karnow, *Vietnam*, Viking, 1983, p. 364; and Robert S. McNamara, with Brian VanDeMark, *In Retrospect*, Times Books, 1995, pp. 104–05.) Although supervised by the U.S. military, Op Plan 34-A was to be framed as South Vietnamese retaliation for the North's support of the National Liberation Front in the South. General Minh had been unenthusiastic about the program. But when Ambassador Lodge on January 31 briefed the newly installed Khanh about 34-A, the general was delighted.

BROOKS: I might get that girl dressed. I might come down there and we could go swimming. I don't think she will.

LBJ: Well, if she won't go swimming, I won't go either. I ain't going to do anything she won't do. Bring her on down and come down in thirty, thirty-five minutes.

BROOKS: All right. We'll be on down. Bless your heart.

RALPH DUNGAN
7:50 P.M.

LBJ: Now, the story is all over town that you and Schlesinger are disappointed in Mann.[1] . . . They said, well, Dungan thinks he's not liberal enough.

DUNGAN: That's a goddamn lie.

LBJ: So, they're just cutting us up all over town. Did you see the *Herald Tribune* story on the White House?[2]

DUNGAN: I did see that. That's a disgrace.

LBJ: Yeah, who in the White House would do that to us?

DUNGAN: I really can't imagine.

LBJ: They don't know. You see, I counted the meetings. I've had 117 meetings and 188 conversations. . . . But they just don't know it. These people wouldn't be giving it if they knew it. . . . I thought Kennedy's people would be loyal to me if I was loyal to them. I don't understand it.

. . . .

DUNGAN: I'll tell you this. Look, they've given you a honeymoon, and now their knives are out.

---

[1] Thomas Mann.

[2] In the *New York Herald Tribune*, Douglas Kiker had depicted Johnson as disorganized and disengaged in foreign affairs: "In at least one recent instance, word of fresh foreign trouble was somewhat delayed in reaching Mr. Johnson because he was busy discussing old troubles with outsiders and his aides were hesitant to interrupt. . . . Longtime acquaintances of Mr. Johnson point out that he has always run pretty much of a one-man show." Kiker added that McGeorge Bundy found Johnson inaccessible and "difficult to work for" and that he was pondering resignation (January 29, 1964).

Chapter Four

FEBRUARY 1964

SATURDAY, FEBRUARY 1, 1964

SARGENT SHRIVER
Director, Peace Corps
1:02 P.M.

JOHNSON WANTS Sargent Shriver, a roaring success as founder of the Peace Corps, to be head of the new War on Poverty.[1] Only yesterday, on Shriver's return from a world tour, did LBJ ask him to "think about" taking the job. As a further enticement, he has been hinting that he might choose Shriver as his vice presidential running mate. But Shriver knows that the new anti-poverty agency, which has no staff, concrete plan, or even a name, could collapse on his head. And he may be more than slightly troubled about what his brother-in-law Robert Kennedy will say about his joining the enemy.

LBJ: Sarge, I'm gonna announce your appointment at that press conference.

SHRIVER: What press conference?

LBJ: This afternoon.

SHRIVER: God, I think it would be advisable, if you don't mind, if I could have this week and sit down with a couple of people and see what we could get in the

---

[1] In the fall of 1963, concerned that the poor would not benefit directly from his tax cut and by the failure of the new prosperity to elevate their living standard, President Kennedy had asked aides for an anti-poverty program, but was told just before leaving for Texas that his request was falling victim to bureaucratic infighting. Johnson had gained his political start striving to bring the Texas Hill Country into the twentieth century. When he learned of JFK's growing interest in battling poverty, LBJ said it was "my kind" of program: "Give it the highest priority" (Walter Heller memorandum of conversation, November 23, 1963, Heller Papers, Kennedy Library). Five hundred million dollars was inserted into the new budget with little idea of how it would be spent, along with $1 billion for local community action programs. To overcome bureaucratic warfare, Johnson decided to create an independent anti-poverty agency, reporting directly to him.

way of some sort of plan. . . . You announce somebody . . . and they don't know what the hell they are doing. . . . Then you're in a hell of a hole because they are going to call you up and say, "Well now, what are you going to do?" And you don't know what you're talking about.

LBJ: Just don't talk to them. Just go away to Camp David and figure it out. We need something to say to the press. . . . I've got to tell them what I talked about yesterday. And you can just . . . work out your Peace Corps any way you want to. You can be head of the committee and have some acting operator. . . . I'll do anything. But I want to announce this and get it behind me, so I'll quit getting all these other pressures. . . . You've got to do it. You just can't let me down. So the quicker we get this behind us, the better. . . . Don't make me wait till next week, because I want to satisfy this press with something. I told them we were going to have a press meeting.

SHRIVER: Can I make just one point?

LBJ: They're going to have all these damn questions and I don't want to seem indecisive about them.

SHRIVER: . . . Number one: I'm not going to let anybody down, last of all you. You've been terrific to me. Second. . . . I would like to have a chance to prepare the Corps, not only my top people in Washington, which I can do, but I got four or five guys coming back here from abroad right now.

LBJ: But that'll leak out over forty places. . . . Why don't I tell them you are not severing your connection with the Corps . . . and the details of what you'll do there can be worked out later, and you'll announce them? . . .

SHRIVER: . . . Could you deny this, that you have asked me to study how this thing should be carried out? . . . What I will propose, of course, is what you want to have done, but at least, it doesn't look as if I have left the Peace Corps.

LBJ: . . . Let me say that I have asked you to study this, and I'm going to you to direct it. . . .

SHRIVER: Could you just say that you've asked me to study this?

LBJ: Hell, no! They've studied and studied. They want to know who in the hell is going to do this, and it's leaked all over the newspapers for two weeks that you're going to do it, and they'll be shooting me with questions. . . .

SHRIVER: Yes, yes, I'm all set on that. That Shriver is going to be the person that is going to organize this thing, he's going to study it, come in with a report to me on what he wants to do with it, within the two or three weeks. . . .

LBJ: I want to say that you're going to be Special Assistant to the President and executive-in-charge of the poverty program, and how that affects your Peace Corps relationship . . . you'll be glad to go into that at a later date. . . .

SHRIVER: The problem with it is that it'll knock the crap out of the Peace Corps.

LBJ: Not if you tell them you're not severing your identification with the Peace Corps.

SHRIVER: . . . I think it would be better if you would say . . . that I'm going to continue as Director of the Peace Corps.

· · · ·

LBJ: I am going to make it clear that you're Mr. Poverty, at home and abroad, if you want to be. And I don't care who you have running the Peace Corps. You can run it? Wonderful. If you can't, get Oshgosh from Chicago and I'll name him. . . . You can write your ticket on anything you want to do there. I want to get rid of poverty, though. . . . The Sunday papers are going to say that you're Mr. Poverty, unless you've got real compelling reasons, which I haven't heard. . . .

SHRIVER: As I look over the papers, it seems to me this is a thing which really ought to operate out of HEW.[1] . . .

LBJ: . . . You wait till we get by an election before we go to operating out of HEW. We've got to get by this election. . . . I've got an election ahead of me now.[2]

SHRIVER: . . . But of course, there's these Peace Corps people.

LBJ: Well, go talk to them, go talk to them.

SHRIVER: . . . This ought to be a bombshell.

LBJ: No, hell, it'll be a promotion! . . . I don't know why they would object to that. Unless you've got some women that think you won't have enough time to spend with them.

SHRIVER: [laughs]

LBJ: You've got the responsibility, you've got the authority, you've got the power, you've got the money. Now you may not have the glands.

SHRIVER: The *glands?*

LBJ: Yeah.

SHRIVER: [with mild annoyance:] I got plenty of glands.

LBJ: Well, all right. . . . I'd like to have your glands, then. . . . I need Dr. Burkley myself—get some of those goat glands.[3]

· · · ·

SHRIVER: I would have much preferred to have had forty-eight hours.

LBJ: . . . You've known this the whole time. It's been in every paper in the United States.

SHRIVER: . . . I didn't know beans about it, because I've been overseas.

LBJ: Well, you don't need to know much, you just go. . . . You'll have an international Peace Corps—one abroad and one at home.

---

[1] Shriver may be gently suggesting that he should be Secretary of Health, Education and Welfare (later renamed Health and Human Services). A Cabinet position would be far more desirable than to be head of an as-yet nonexistent program that may fail.

[2] Johnson fears that putting the War on Poverty into HEW will look like a subterfuge for expanding HEW, which could be politically damaging in his current mood of "thrift and frugality."

[3] By saying that Shriver might not have the glands, Johnson means that he might not have the energy to run both the Peace Corps and War on Poverty. But the metaphor was not the most diplomatic one LBJ could have used. As Johnson partisan John Connally charged during the 1960 nomination campaign against John Kennedy, JFK had Addison's disease, which meant that his adrenal glands did not function. Shriver's wife, Eunice, had the same malady, which Johnson may have known. (See Clay and Joan Blair, Jr., *The Search for JFK*, Putnam, 1976, p. 579.) Johnson, perceiving Shriver's annoyance, makes it up by joking that he will ask the White House doctor, George Burkley, to inject him with goat-gland serum—the legendary Swiss cure for exhaustion and old age.

SHRIVER: . . . About Bill—Bill can come back if we need him?[1]

LBJ: For just as little as you can spare him. I need him more than anybody in the world right here. And you need him here too. He's good for Shriver here.

SHRIVER: . . . I know he's very valuable to you. But you don't want this whole damn thing to go down. You know, I don't want to give you a whole lot of sap about it.

LBJ: . . . He'll help you and work with you, and he's on your team. He reports to you.

SHRIVER: . . . He couldn't come and take on the acting direction of this thing while I'm on the other thing?

LBJ: Not and run the White House too. . . .

SHRIVER: How about Feldman?[2]

LBJ: No, now don't go to raiding the White House! Go on and get your own damn talent.

SHRIVER: The trouble is, he's got three of my people in the White House now.

LBJ: Well, they're not people that you have to rely on. Peace Corps—hell, you've got a baby-sitter for every ten!

SHRIVER: [laughs]

LBJ: For Christ's sake, if your wife—if the Kennedys had—they wouldn't have this fortune if they had as many baby-sitters as you've got in the Peace Corps. You've got ten thousand people and you've got 1,100 administrators. . . . There's not a Kennedy compound that's got a baby-sitter for ten. And you've got it in the Peace Corps around the world. All right, I'll see you later, and good luck to you. And happy landing!

FRANK ERWIN
Austin Attorney and Democratic Leader
1:25 P.M.

JOHNSON IS NOW FEUDING with John Connally, who is furious about LBJ's truce with Ralph Yarborough, their archenemy until the moment Johnson became President. Connally has been urging conservative Texas Democrats to find an opponent for Yarborough in 1964. LBJ is worried that a party split will endanger his own presidential campaign in Texas. Anguished by Connally's refusal to listen to him, he asks their mutual friend Erwin to intercede.

LBJ: If I ever knew anything in my life I know it that we oughtn't to have a contest[3] this summer. John's not physically able to have one . . . and I can't take one. I can't win forty-nine states[4] if they're fighting at home. . . . Hell, I don't

---

[1] Shriver would like to retrieve Bill Moyers, his Peace Corps Deputy Director until November 22, 1963.
[2] Myer Feldman, Deputy Special Counsel.
[3] Among Democrats for the governorship and U.S. Senate seat from Texas.
[4] Johnson here shows the extent of his ambitions for November 1964.

know why they're so interested in what the votes are up here.[1] If *I* could get along with the Senator from Texas, it looks like *you*-all could. And he's insulted me more than he has anybody else. . . .

ERWIN: Mr. President . . . a lot of people love you and John both . . . but are in the middle, being pulled both ways to where it's a disaster for anybody. . . . If you and John could talk and maybe get all whatever it is that each one of you is upset about out of the way, maybe you could sit down and work something out.

LBJ: I don't have John's confidence. He doesn't call me and ask me any of these things. He goes off with Shivers[2] and plans these things. And Shivers has been an anti-Johnson man that got defeated at my hands. And John doesn't show me respect enough to say, "Now I know you're going to be running for President and I don't want to do anything but help you and I don't want to embarrass you." He goes off to Sid Richardson's island[3] and the paper comes out that he and Shivers and Joe Kilgore have met and plotted.[4] . . . He never has called me and asked me "what should I do" about anything. When he was in private life I called him and asked him what should I do about everything. But he's sensitive about being independent.

· · · ·

LBJ: John has got a good image here with the Negroes and the Mexicans and with being a pretty moderate fellow. And now, by God, he starts meeting with the Citizens Council.[5] . . . I think what we ought to do is make every effort we can . . . that we will not have any opposition for Ralph Yarborough. . . . And I think that's what you ought to ask the Governor to try to do. If the Governor is just hell-bent on having opposition, then we can't help it. . . . But I begged them all to do this . . . and I think everybody is willing to do it, if the Governor is willing to do it for me. If he hates so bitter and he's so vindictive that he's got to have a man up here to pull out this fellow that's voting with me, then I can't help it.

· · · ·

ERWIN: It just made me sick to see here when everything ought to be at the very zenith of everybody's career, to have this kind of problem.

LBJ: It's unthinkable that a boy that would work for me for twenty years[6] would do this without ever talking to me, and run off with Shivers. . . . I just can't understand it.

ERWIN: . . . Well, sir, his answer to that . . . would be that you've turned your back on your friends and gone off with Ralph Yarborough, who's been your lifelong enemy.

---

[1] Many of Connally's friends are demanding a Democratic opponent to Yarborough because of Yarborough's liberal votes in the Senate.
[2] The ultraconservative LBJ foe, former Governor Allan Shivers.
[3] Sid Richardson, who died in 1959, was a Texas oil, gas, ranching, and real estate tycoon for whom Connally had worked in the 1950s. His private island was in the Gulf of Mexico.
[4] Congressman Kilgore was a conservative old LBJ protégé eager to run for Yarborough's seat from the right.
[5] The Dallas Citizens Council included highly conservative members of the city's power elite.
[6] Connally.

LBJ: Ralph Yarborough has voted for me every time my name has been on the ticket. . . . I'm ready to talk to the Governor anytime the Governor feels like talking.

ERWIN: . . . He says. . . . "The President knows my views, and I know the President's views, and there's nothing to talk about."

· · · ·

LBJ: I've worked with John a long, long time . . . and I think I love him more than any other white man. . . . I've heard him pretty adamant on the Negro question.[1] I've heard him pretty adamant on the labor question. . . . He ought to be happy he's Governor. I ought to be happy I'm President. We ought to be able to work together, and meet together, and talk. And I'm anxious to. And all the talking that has been done, I've initiated. . . . I think the record will show, since the assassination, I've called fifteen times to talk to him or his family. . . . I'm willing to talk, walk, scoop—nothing proud about me. . . . I never did understand why he had to do what he did on public accommodations.[2] . . . I didn't think that was a state matter. . . . But he did, and that got some national publicity and . . . cut me a little bit. But I took it like a man, and smiled.

· · · ·

LBJ: Just because we've got a little pique, a Little Boy Blue personality get mad about something—hell, John and Nellie . . . wouldn't ride in the same car with him.[3] So I guess he got mad too. . . . I laughed. I thought it was little boy stuff and both of 'em wound up together riding with each other. . . . We just talked big but when the nut cutting was done, why, we got in the car and bowed nice. I didn't think it hurt me a damned bit to ride with Yarborough.

· · · ·

ERWIN: I'm just very much afraid that the Governor isn't going to run for reelection. I don't think he's bluffing.

LBJ: I think that'd be the best thing that could happen to him and to all of us. . . . If he's sick and doesn't feel like it . . . that would suit me fine. I wouldn't beg him a minute. I think it is a terrible imposition. I wish I didn't have to run for this job. I may *not* run for it. I don't know how to get out of it. . . . If it was as easy for me as it is for him, I wouldn't be running. 'Cause you can imagine how, if I spend this much time on Texas, how I'm handling the world. And I've got right at this moment a press conference at three o'clock. I've got Zanzibar. I've got Cyprus. I've got Panama. I've got a plane shot down in Berlin. . . . And I'm talking to my best friend, begging him please not to get an opponent for a man that's supporting me. That's a hell of a thing to have to do, isn't it?

ERWIN: Yes, sir.

LBJ: I just don't know what's happened to the boy. So maybe it would be better if he didn't run. Encourage him not to. Just let him say that he's not going to run. . . . If he's sick, the last thing I want to do is to kill him.

[1] Connally was no particular friend of civil rights.
[2] Connally had complained about the section of the Johnson civil rights bill that would ban discrimination in public places such as hotels, restaurants, and theaters.
[3] Yarborough, during JFK's Texas tour.

SARGENT SHRIVER
2:25 P.M.

THIRTY-FIVE MINUTES FROM NOW, Johnson's press conference is to start. Shriver tries again to dissuade him from announcing his appointment to the War on Poverty. When Johnson takes the call, he is in the Cabinet Room, preparing for the session with a group of his aides and officials. In front of this audience, Johnson speaks guardedly.

SHRIVER: The more I think about this, the more I really would like to suggest once again that you give me a few more days to get this thing straightened out. . . . If I get in it, I want to do it successfully for you and I just feel that if I get stuck out there today in a position where I am completely exposed—

LBJ: Why don't you let me leave it where we were? Now I'm here with all this staff trying to get ready for the three o'clock meeting, and I haven't had my lunch. . . . I need it for very personal reasons.

SARGENT SHRIVER
Approximately 4:10 P.M.

JOHNSON'S NEWS CONFERENCE is over. Shriver calls the President after hearing his appointment announced on television. Having bagged his quarry, LBJ now tells Shriver how many of his supposed friends (especially RFK allies who might not have wanted Shriver to be a Kennedy family hostage to Johnson) had opposed his selection. One reason Johnson does this is to explain to Shriver why he had been so anxious to announce Shriver's name. But in the classic LBJ manner, there is also a hint of paying Shriver back for playing hard to get. By telling Shriver how hard he has had to fight to ram Shriver's nomination past his enemies, he may hope to make Shriver feel all the more obligated to him.

SHRIVER: [to Bill Moyers, while waiting for LBJ:] What I'd like to do sometime is talk to him and find out where I stand. . . . You know, I have to earn some money and I don't want to go screwing around doing one job after another in Washington. I don't have that need. I'd like to know where I go.[1] . . . It would have been great if I were Secretary of HEW. Or this Vice President thing. I don't know whether I maybe ought to go out to Illinois and run for Governor.[2] . . .

LBJ: Sarge, I couldn't talk to you freely.[3]

SHRIVER: Oh, excuse me.

LBJ: This is Lyndon Johnson.

SHRIVER: Yes, sir.

LBJ: I had the Secretary of State and everybody—fifteen in the room, pep-

---

[1] Shriver presumably means to what future job the anti-poverty position might lead.
[2] In the 1950s, Shriver and his family had lived in Chicago, where he managed the Kennedy family's Merchandise Mart and was president of the Chicago Board of Education.
[3] During their last call, before the press conference.

pering me with questions. Now I don't want to make you feel bad, because you're too successful and I'm too proud of you to ever pour cold water on you. But up to one minute before I appeared, I was meeting violent protest to naming you. Now I couldn't let that grow and continue. I've had other folks recommended and other people pressed. . . . I got another recommendation immediately that it had to go to a fellow in HEW. And it comes from about as powerful people as we have in this government.[1] Now they all think it's terrible to have the Peace Corps and this[2] together. They all think that you're a wonderful man—*but*. . . . One of them said this morning, "He's never had anything to do with anything like this. . . . As a *public relations expert,* he's the best."[3] But I think that as an administrator and as a *candidate*[4] that you have great potentialities. . . . Waiting two hours got me some hell of a pressure that's made people mad and would probably get me some resignations because I just had to ride roughshod over them. But I couldn't tell you that when some of them were sitting there. . . . I was trying to be as gentle as I could with you. . . .

SHRIVER: [sounding downhearted:] Yeah.

LBJ: So now don't go trying to figure out who it is, 'cause it's nothing to worry about. It's done. The decision's made. Water's behind us. Now . . . let's figure out how we're going to get this money through[5] and get you the brains of this government and I'll support you all the way. To the hilt. . . . This is the best thing this administration's done. I've got more comments and more popularity on the poverty thing than anything else. But they'll defeat it and kill it if we let 'em do it. . . . McNamara's got more brains than anybody I'm dealing with, and you picked him, didn't you?[6]

SHRIVER: Yes.

LBJ: I wouldn't want to be President if he weren't here. . . . You could have the damned job—tomorrow. And we got few of them we can rely on that way, Sarge. So you just quit worrying about the little personal items and just take the position that you didn't apply for a goddamned thing. . . . You have courted no favor. Nobody's promoted you with me. . . .

SHRIVER: . . . I didn't want to get into a situation where I don't know what I'm doing and blow it and cause some difficulty for you. . . .

LBJ: . . . We're going to have a lot of hell and a lot of problems, but . . . if it can be done, you'll do it. If it can't, why, we'll find something else for you to do and make a hero out of you for failing. That's the kind of team we play on.

SHRIVER: . . . Who were they proposing?

LBJ: Boisfeuillet Jones[7] was the last one. The Attorney General was the first one. . . . I've got a fellow named Moyers here who handles some of my business

[1] LBJ hints that it was RFK.
[2] The anti-poverty program.
[3] Here Johnson is driving in the needle.
[4] For Vice President. Once again Johnson is playing with Shriver.
[5] Through Congress.
[6] In 1960, Shriver, who was scouting talent for Kennedy's incoming Cabinet, had discovered and interviewed McNamara, a registered Republican, the new president of Ford Motor.
[7] Special Assistant to the Secretary of HEW.

and he has a talking acquaintance with you, so you just tell him you're on your way and he'll work it out for us to meet in a dark alley somewhere.

DEAN RUSK
4:32 P.M.

RUSK CALLS after watching Johnson's press conference.[1]

RUSK: I thought it went well, Mr. President. As a purely technical matter, I think you might want to try varying the pace and the speed at which you answer particular questions just to give it a little more—

LBJ: A little boring to be slow?

RUSK: A little more variety and pace. Now, on the point about de Gaulle,[2] I've dictated to Bill Moyers and Bob Manning,[3] who are over in Pierre Salinger's shop, a suggested clarification because I think we put the emphasis on what de Gaulle's proposals were taken to mean in Southeast Asia and that's the thing that's caused all the anxiety. Because you see, he hasn't made any specific proposals. All he's talked about in very vague terms is neutralization of Southeast Asia, and this is taken to mean, in South Vietnam, some device for neutralizing South Vietnam alone and turning it over to the other side. So I think we shift the burden to the absence of any specific proposals from de Gaulle and to make it quite clear that what you're concerned about is the effect of the talk in South Vietnam.

LBJ: I think that's good. I had the impression from our comments both to the Senators and to the thing here today, your comments, that if they neutralized all of it, that'd be fine, but that . . . I concluded that his proposal was *not* to neutralize all of it.

RUSK: Oh, I see. Now he's talked very vaguely about the neutralization of Southeast Asia. But in probing that point with the Russians, it's been very clear that the Communist side is not about to neutralize North Vietnam. . . .

LBJ: I think what we'll have to say, if we can, is if you neutralize Southeast Asia that's well and good, but it's very obvious that there's no possibility of neutralizing just South Vietnam.

RUSK: Right, and there's no willingness on the other side to neutralize North Vietnam.

---

[1] In an opening statement, after announcing Shriver's appointment, Johnson read aloud from a message to General Khanh in Saigon that "we shall continue to be available to help you carry the war to the enemy, and to increase the confidence of the Vietnamese people in their government."

[2] A reporter had asked whether Johnson ruled out any neutralization of Vietnam, "such as General de Gaulle suggests." Johnson had replied, "If we could have neutralization of both North Vietnam and South Vietnam, I am sure that would be considered sympathetically. But I see no indication of that at the moment." Another reporter asked whether de Gaulle's "proposal for neutralizing Southeast Asia" interfered with American objectives. Johnson replied yes.

[3] State Department spokesman.

SARGENT SHRIVER
6:28 P.M.

PERHAPS FEELING that he had hit Shriver too hard during their last conversation, Johnson now massages his ego by citing enthusiastic news coverage of the appointment.

SHRIVER: What are you doing down there?

LBJ: By God, because there's nobody else working. . . . Somebody's got to tend the store.

SHRIVER: You should be taking a swim now.

LBJ: It looks like you got all the headlines.

SHRIVER: I'm sure of that.

LBJ: That's right. "Popular, personable businessman." [to Valenti:] Get me some of that stuff they've been writing about Shriver over there, Jack, right quick. . . . [back to Shriver, reading from afternoon newspapers:] It says, ". . . The President . . . said Shriver will continue to serve as Director of the Peace Corps." Incidentally Sorensen says that's terrible.[1] "He called Shriver an eminently qualified man for the additional assignment.". . . Didn't say he nearly declined the honor yesterday. . . . "Johnson . . . said the Peace Corps Director . . . had outstanding qualities of leadership." God Almighty! I wish *I* could buy that kind of advertisement! . . .

SHRIVER: Sounds good.

LBJ: I *was* good. Now . . . you've got to . . . see how in the hell you're going to administer this thing. Then, you're going to have to get that bill and that message[2] together. . . . And you got to get on that television and start explaining it. . . . Let's find out any dollar that's appropriated, how we can use it for poverty. And you can have advisory committees in every place, and you can have county commissioners, courts, you can have mayors. Each one of them have to be sponsors. And you'll have more influence in this administration than any man in it. . . . You'll have a billion dollars to pass out. . . . So you just call up the Pope and tell him you might not be on time every morning for church on time, but you're going to be working for the good of humanity.

· · · ·

LBJ: The sky's the limit. You just make this thing work, period. I don't give a damn about the details. . . . And anybody you want us to meet with, we'll do it on our spare time, when we get a night off. Because this is number one on the domestic front. Next to peace in the world, this is the most important. . . . Get all the damn publicity you can, get on all the televisions you can, as soon as you know enough to talk about it. . . . I can't show you much more, with you and Moyers both dragging your feet. I've never had such a hard time. You're a reluctant bride. Moyers has been attacking me around here for weeks, and then I

[1] LBJ is delighted here to pit Shriver against another Kennedy man, Sorensen, by letting him know just who had opposed him.
[2] Johnson would have to propose anti-poverty legislation in a special message to Congress.

got ready to go in and say yes, and then God Almighty, you called him up and he just started having the willies.[1]

SHRIVER: . . . See, the thing we were worried about is this Peace Corps because it's sensitive about—

LBJ: Why in the hell didn't he worry about that two weeks ago? He's been telling me that the only guy in the world that can do poverty is Shriver. And then, by God, I agree on it, and then he wants to unsell me.

. . . .

LBJ: Now, Moyers. I don't know where Moyers is. [joking:] He's probably off with a woman or drunk. [aside, to Valenti:] See if you can find Moyers around here. [back to Shriver:] He went home, Jack Valenti thinks. He was probably wanting to come see God before he went home. But you weren't here, I guess. . . . I was giving him hell about telling me here for two weeks something, and then he got the willies when you called him and barked at him, just once, and he went in the basement.

SHRIVER: You can trick me a lot, but you can't trick me on that because Moyers never goes to the basement.

LBJ: Haven't you seen one of those little feisty dogs, just run and bark like hell like he's going to cut you up and you just turn and stomp your foot once and watch him run? That's the way Moyers does when you talk to him.

SHRIVER: I wish that were true.

LBJ: He stands up and sasses me all day long, until *you* call him, and then in a real low voice—why, I think he thinks there's something to this Kennedy dynasty. . . . It scares the hell out of people.

SHRIVER: The great thing is, though, is that I notice who he's working for.

LBJ: [laughs] Well, I just borrowed him when you were out of town, and he just happened to be there.

. . . .

LBJ: He's been working for you about one hundred percent of the time, I'll tell you that.[2]

SHRIVER: [laughs]

LBJ: He hasn't got any delegates[3] in the field for you. . . . He's got more judgment than that. And he hasn't got your name on any tickets, because he's got more brains than that.[4] But he's in there swinging every hour, I'll tell you that.

SHRIVER: Did you see what I said about the—

LBJ: Yeah, I saw that you eliminated yourself from the race[5] completely. We'll get you back in it, though.

SHRIVER: That's all right.

[1] In counterpoint to his reference to Sorensen, LBJ is glad to let Shriver know that Moyers was his champion.
[2] Meaning that Moyers has been praising Shriver to LBJ.
[3] Democratic convention delegates.
[4] Johnson is mildly lampooning Shriver's interest in the vice presidency.
[5] For the vice presidency. Shriver had told the AP, "I'm not running for anything," adding that RFK would be "terrific."

LBJ: Yeah, that's all right. You just don't go to nominating any candidates. I think that a man runs for Vice President is a very foolish man. Man runs away from it's very wise. I wish I had run further away from it than I did. And I never was a candidate for it, I'll tell you that. And don't you ever be a candidate, and don't let anybody else be a candidate. Tell them anybody ever runs for it never gets it.[1]

SHRIVER: That was a great decision though that day, when you decided to do that.[2]

LBJ: Well, you just come on now. We've decided this, and I'm with you till the end. Death do us part. We're not going to let anybody divide us, so just bear that in mind.[3] And when everybody else has quit you and gone and through with you, I'll still be standing there by your side. So let's get going now.

MONDAY, FEBRUARY 3, 1964

JOHN S. KNIGHT
Chairman of the Board, Miami Herald
5:45 P.M.

LBJ: What do you think we ought to do in Vietnam?

KNIGHT: . . . I never thought we belonged there. . . . That's a real tough one now, and I think President Kennedy thought at one time that we were overcommitted in that area.

LBJ: Well, I opposed it in '54.[4] But we're there now, and there's one of three things you can do. One is run and let the dominoes start falling over.[5] And God Almighty, what they said about us leaving China would just be warming up, compared to what they'd say now.[6] I see Nixon is raising hell about it today. Goldwater too.[7] You can run, or you can fight, as we are doing, or you can sit down and agree to neutralize all of it. But nobody is going to neutralize North

[1] Johnson intends this as a message to Robert Kennedy.
[2] When LBJ accepted JFK's invitation to run for Vice President in Los Angeles.
[3] Another message to Robert Kennedy.
[4] In April 1954. See LBJ conversation with Richard Russell, December 7, 1963, above.
[5] Here LBJ asserts his firm belief in the "domino theory"—that when one Southeast Asian country fell to international Communism, it would help to topple the next. For Johnson, the metaphor may have had special force because one of his chief private pastimes was to play dominoes.
[6] Johnson here shows his great sensitivity to the danger that the appearance of weakness in Southeast Asia will give Republicans a new opening, like those after the fall of China to Mao Zedong's Communists in 1949 and the pursuit of Communists in the Truman administration, to call him and other Democrats soft on Communism.
[7] In North Carolina, Nixon had complained about Johnson's lack of firmness against de Gaulle's neutralization proposal. Goldwater had told a Minneapolis audience that the President was "fiddling with his political promises" and U.S. foreign policy "fumblers" were "napping" while the war in Vietnam "is drifting toward disaster" (UPI, February 3, 1964).

Vietnam, so that's totally impractical. And so it really boils down to one or two decisions—getting out or getting in.[1]

KNIGHT: . . . France wants none of it.

LBJ: None. They just want to create problems, France does.[2]

KNIGHT: . . . I hope we don't get involved in anything full-scale. . . .

LBJ: I sat down with Eisenhower in '54 when we had all the problem. But we can't abandon it to them, as I see it. And we can't get them to agree to neutralize North Vietnam. So I think Old Man de Gaulle is puffing through his hat.

KNIGHT: Long-range over there, the odds are certainly against us.

LBJ: Yes, there is no question about that. Anytime you got that many people against you that far from your home base, it's bad.[3]

EVERETT DIRKSEN
5:57 P.M.

> SUFFERING from a bleeding ulcer, the Senate Minority Leader is confined to Sibley Memorial Hospital in Washington.

LBJ: How are you feeling?

DIRKSEN: I'm doing pretty good. That ulcer hit me last night about midnight.

LBJ: If you quit drinking that damned Sanka and get on a good Scotch whiskey once in a while—

DIRKSEN: I think you got a point there.

LBJ: Remember old Hatton?[4] Used to break his arm and his leg and everything. Remember old Tuck Milligan?[5] Tuck came up to him one day about three or four sheets in the wind. . . . Hatton was down with his crutches and Hatton would always eat spinach and drink Sanka and strain his soup very carefully and never put any ice in his water. . . . And Tuck said, "Hatton, you always got your leg in a cast, your arm in a sling, or you're on crutches. What you need to do is go out and get you about three good half glasses of bourbon whiskey. Then go down to the Occidental and buy a red beefsteak, and then get you a woman." So maybe that's what you need, instead of drinking Sanka.

DIRKSEN: [laughs] You've got an idea!

[1] Did Johnson actually see the choice as starkly as this, so early in his presidency?

[2] Rather than see de Gaulle's proposals as a fig leaf for a possible U.S. backdown in Vietnam, LBJ views them as a disturbing sign to the world of division within SEATO, the Southeast Asia Treaty Organization, of which France and the United States are members, and which has pledged itself to protect Laos, Cambodia, and South Vietnam.

[3] Even at this early moment, Johnson shows no illusion about the odds against victory in Vietnam.

[4] Hatton Sumners, Democratic Congressman from Dallas from 1913 to 1947, who had served with both Johnson and Dirksen in the House of Representatives.

[5] Jacob Milligan, an anti–New Deal Missouri Democratic Congressman who came in third in the 1934 Senate primary that Harry Truman won.

BILL MOYERS
Special Assistant to the President
6:28 P.M.

MOYERS HAS BEEN DEALING with a new complication in the Bobby Baker fracas. Drew Pearson's collaborator Jack Anderson has been asking for permission to quote from the derogatory secret government files he has obtained on Don Reynolds.

LBJ: Oh, this son of a bitch you saw this morning[1] is going to get you in more trouble than four mess of fish. He says that you told him to go get Zuckert[2] to give him permission to quote all these things direct. . . . Now we think that this story ought to be killed any way we can.

MOYERS: I didn't tell him that, Mr. President. He asked me to try to get permission for him, and I said, "That's something I can't do. The White House can't give permission to do that."

LBJ: Well, we're going to get tied in with doing it now and we oughtn't to. . . . Who did you talk to?

MOYERS: To him. He's the only person I talked to.

LBJ: All right. What did you say to him?

MOYERS: . . . I sat down at the breakfast table, and he had a document beside him, and he said, "I want to show you a story that I wrote seven or eight years ago about Don Reynolds." And he read me a paragraph from the story which quoted Reynolds as saying before the Senate Judiciary Committee that the State Department . . . the people handling . . . immigration . . . and visas were infested by Communists, Jews, and sexual deviates. . . . And then he said . . . "Now I've gotten from sources that I want to remain confidential the full Army–Air Force file on it. . . . The problem is that it was given to the Senate and they don't want it, and I think that's the story." I said, "That's very interesting." And he said . . . "If I could have permission to . . . to quote from this . . . it would be much more authentic." And I said, "I certainly can't give you permission. The White House can't give you permission.". . .

LBJ: You better call McNamara and tell him that he asked you to get permission, and you told him you couldn't do it. . . . I talked to him two or three times today, and he just told me that Anderson had been in saying that you told him to tell Zuckert to give you permission to quote it.

JOHN CONNALLY
8:25 P.M.

THE GOVERNOR OF TEXAS feels double-crossed. Through Walter Jenkins, LBJ has pressured Joe Kilgore to keep out of the Senate race against Ralph

[1] Anderson.
[2] Secretary of the Air Force Eugene Zuckert.

Yarborough with the tacit assumption that in exchange, Texas liberals would keep the liberal Democrat Don Yarborough (no relation to Ralph)[1] from challenging Connally. Connally has discovered that, contrary to plan, Don Yarborough has just filed against him for Governor. An irate Connally calls Johnson, who is sitting in the lounge adjoining the Oval Office with his friend Judge Moursund, Valenti, and Salinger. LBJ declines to take the call, letting Valenti try to calm the Governor down.

VALENTI: According to the latest poll I saw, Mr. Yarborough[2] may be clobbered so bad that he'd never be fit for public office again.

CONNALLY: I'm going to do my goddamnedest to clobber him and anybody that's for him, I'll tell you that! And I hope that Mr. Ralph Yarborough will just open his mouth one time 'cause I'd like to run against him at the same time—cut him up a little bit for the next go-around.

JIM WRIGHT
Democratic Congressman from Texas
9:15 P.M.

NOW, WITH ONLY three hours left before the midnight primary filing deadline, Johnson tries to persuade Congressman Wright, of Fort Worth, to run against Ralph Yarborough for the Senate.

LBJ: John . . . was just trembling when he called a while ago. Just trembling. . . . He hates Yarborough.[3] . . .

WRIGHT: Lyndon . . . I just can't believe that Don Yarborough is going to give John any serious trouble at all. . . . Is John anxiously trying to get somebody to run against Ralph now?

LBJ: No, no. He just said, "I want the President to know"—he talked to Jack Valenti—"that all of his labor friends and all of his liberal friends are no good sons of bitches and I want him to know he's been sucked in . . . to give Ralph a free ride, and he's got me opposition."

· · · ·

LBJ: You got an opponent in Fort Worth?

WRIGHT: . . . I've had a fellow there. I don't know how serious he's going to be. . . . First time I've ever had one. . . . I can't believe that it's going to be extremely serious, but anytime you got anybody with his name on that ballot, it's a situation that you don't want to take too much for granted.

LBJ: Why didn't *you* announce for Senate? Couldn't get the money?

WRIGHT: I sure couldn't, Lyndon. . . . And so Saturday I announced for re-

[1] Don Yarborough had come within a percentage point of beating Connally in the 1962 Democratic primary for Governor.
[2] Don Yarborough.
[3] Ralph Yarborough.

election, thinking at the time that Joe[1] was running for the Senate. . . . They tell me now he's not going to run at all.

LBJ: No, he announced today he wouldn't.

WRIGHT: What do you think, Lyndon? . . . Do you think it would be better to have an opponent, or no opponent?

LBJ: . . . I wouldn't be against a Connally-Wright ticket. . . . There're a lot of things I can do for you. I can take care of you here if you lost,[2] and you wouldn't be gambling. . . .

WRIGHT: . . . From a practical standpoint, I made a statement and it was carried out over the state pretty wide giving my reasons for staying and trying to contribute to the harmony of the party, and I would be somewhat out of character to aid and abet Connally. . . . Doggone, though! [laughs] Here we are about, what, four hours before?

LBJ: Less than that. Two or three. . . . Now I may be wrong, but I think that you get on that ticket with John and let him keep his arm in a sling and you keep your tongue in your mouth and I think you could go places. And I always have thought so. I just think you just quit shaking hands, and dodging and darting around every place in the country, and stay on that television every time somebody give you a dollar.

WRIGHT: That's the way it would have to be. Actually, it's such a short campaign. Not but three months . . . before the primary. Just can't get much exposure any other way.

LBJ: How much you willing to gamble? At all? You want to come back to the House or you want to shoot the works, if you can, with John—and if you lose, get something else?

WRIGHT: Lyndon, a week ago—

LBJ: [impatient:] Don't go talking about a week ago. Talk about now! Now come on here. Eliminate all that superfluous stuff. You know I got that knife right in your belly, and I want—

WRIGHT: Yeah, I can feel it. . . .

LBJ: . . . I'm not going to recommend it. I'm just trying to explore it, because I like you.

WRIGHT: Damn, I appreciate that, Lyndon. . . .

LBJ: I think you're the only man in Texas can beat Yarborough . . . and I think you'd vote right if you got elected. . . . And I think the only thing that could keep you from doing it is if John didn't embrace you and put his arm around you and help you get some of this rich, fat-cat money. If he did that and it was a . . . Connally-Wright ticket, I think that things would really go to town. . . . If he'll buy you, take you, I suggest you do it. . . . I'd rather have Connally and Wright than Yarborough and Yarborough.

WRIGHT: I'll buy that.

[1] Kilgore.
[2] Meaning that Johnson, presuming his reelection, could give Wright a federal job.

LBJ: Well, if you buy it, you got a seat in the Senate! What the hell you waiting on?

WRIGHT: [chuckles] Goddamn! . . .

LBJ: . . . Maybe you and Connally are not as good campaigners as I think you are. . . . But . . . I'd damn sight rather have a six-year term in the Senate than where you are. If you lost, I'd take care of you in something else. Whatever you wanted.

WRIGHT: . . . Let me do some checking down home. I want to find out . . . what this guy said who's running against me. I sure don't want to look like I'm running away from that.

LBJ: No, I wouldn't do that. . . . If you run for the Senate, you're shooting the works. You just think about it coolly and don't you tell anybody you talked to me at all. But I'm going to take a swim for about twenty minutes. Then I'm going over to the House. But they'll be deciding in the next hour. . . . John may have Joe Kilgore there wanting to run right this minute, for all I know.[1] . . .

WRIGHT: . . . Lyndon, it's tempting as hell, but I—

LBJ: Of course, it's tempting. I'd do it in two minutes. I wouldn't hesitate one second. . . . You think about it. I'll talk to you in twenty, thirty minutes. Now don't quote me to anybody.[2]

TUESDAY, FEBRUARY 4, 1964

RALPH YARBOROUGH
Democratic Senator from Texas
5:10 P.M.

> SPARED A PRIMARY OPPONENT (despite LBJ's quiet eleventh-hour effort to push Jim Wright into the race), Yarborough thanks his old political foe.

YARBOROUGH: I want to thank you for many kindnesses. I've been told about them by Albert Thomas, Jack Brooks, and others. And I'm so grateful to you.

---

[1] LBJ mentions Kilgore to get Wright's competitive juices flowing.

[2] Lady Bird dictated into her diary, "For the success of the Administration, it would be so much better if there were no fight, no split, no bloody knockdown, drag-out in Texas. . . . Though John's going to win it—I bet *anything*—it's going to be an exertion of strength that he really doesn't have to spare right now. . . . This is not a good night for us, or for him." At 10:30 P.M., LBJ finally called Connally (in an unrecorded conversation). Lady Bird wrote, "I'm glad he did. It must have been a hard call for Lyndon to make. It must have been about like climbing one of the Himalayan peaks without your shoes on" (February 3, 1964). In the end, Congressman Wright refused to run against Ralph Yarborough, leaving the Senator only two token opponents in the Democratic primary.

LBJ: You're gonna come singing near the river and get your prayerbook out when they bury me because I'll need a lot of help. They're awful mad at me down there.[1]

YARBOROUGH: They're doing a lot of cussing of me too, Mr. President.

LBJ: I know I did the right thing. You just keep on representing the people and we'll come out of it some way.

YARBOROUGH: I really appreciate that Mr. President. I really appreciate it.

LBJ: You serve humanity,[2] and I want to help you any way I can.

YARBOROUGH: . . . The *Congressional Quarterly* shows that after I got here, as long as you were Majority Leader, I had the highest percentage of voting with you of any Senator in the Senate. . . .

LBJ: That's wonderful. I'm mighty proud of it. I just told them that . . . if you had a man come up here—I don't care how friendly they are—against the program, didn't believe in the people, why I'd just have two Towers[3] against me and they'd have to do that over my dead body. I was going to support you all the way and I said, "I don't get in primaries, but I'm going to get in this one if a man gets in that won't support me."[4]

YARBOROUGH: I want you to know, Mr. President, anytime I don't vote with you, I'm looking for ways to do so. . . .

LBJ: I know it. . . . The Republicans want to stir up all this trouble. They wanted you to have a knockdown drag-out. And George Bush[5] is around telling everybody all these stories, and they unfortunately—they misled some people, and I'm sorry they misled Don.[6] I didn't want to get him in there and that'll just make it hard. . . .

YARBOROUGH: . . . I did everything I could to keep him out. I had a special reason. His name's Yarborough. [laughs] Some people get us confused.

LBJ: You take care of yourself. . . . We'll get together, and we'll go to the mat with them in November.

YARBOROUGH: You have a tremendous job, Mr. President, with the Communists around the world in Vietnam, Cuba, Panama, and everywhere, and I'd like not to stir up any trouble against you, if I can help it.

LBJ: You're going to help me.

[1] Meaning Connally and his allies.
[2] This is how LBJ spoke to liberals.
[3] John Tower, Republican Senator from Texas since 1961.
[4] Johnson refers to his driving Kilgore out of the race.
[5] The future President was a front-runner to be Yarborough's Republican opponent for the Senate in 1964.
[6] Johnson blames George Bush and other Republicans for nudging Don Yarborough into the race in order to stir up Democratic troubles.

WEDNESDAY, FEBRUARY 5, 1964

WALTER JENKINS
10:25 A.M.

LBJ COMPLAINS of news stories.

LBJ: They're going to do this every day . . . and I don't know what to do about it. The Okamoto thing[1]—everybody is disloyal around here. I just don't trust anybody anymore. Here's Bobby running a man in New Hampshire getting his name up there,[2] and this Okamoto story.

• • • •

JENKINS: What did you think on the Pearson story?[3]

LBJ: I thought that it was just absolutely awful that the *Post* would allow this son of a bitch to take that story and read it and answer it.[4]

JENKINS: I did too. His answer wasn't too good.

LBJ: Not at all, it was very evasive. But I think that when you talk to Gerry,[5] just say we sure hope that you send up Pearson's column in advance so we can answer them in advance.

EDWIN WEISL, SR.
6:24 P.M.

IN NEW YORK, from his suite at the Carlyle Hotel, Johnson calls his close counselor before attending a Joseph P. Kennedy, Jr., Foundation awards dinner.

---

[1] Just as Johnson was trying to establish his reputation for frugality, *Newsweek* reported in late January that he had secured Yoichi Okamoto, a USIA photographer who had traveled with LBJ while Vice President, to join Salinger's staff as a full-time presidential photographer. *Newsweek* reported (January 27, 1964) that since the President's second week in office, Okamoto had photographed virtually all of Johnson's waking moments, yielding eleven thousand stills. Angry at the needling about his vanity and extravagance, Johnson had Salinger announce on February 4 that Okamoto had merely been "on loan" and that his "mission was completed." But after the 1964 election, Okamoto was back at the White House.

[2] Johnson has heard that RFK is running a vice presidential campaign for himself in the New Hampshire primary. (See John Bailey and Richard Maguire conversations, February 11, 1964, below.)

[3] That morning, Drew Pearson and Jack Anderson had published their findings on Don Reynolds in the *Washington Post*. From LBJ's point of view, it fractured Reynolds's reputation. The column noted that Reynolds had flunked out of West Point and lied about it. In October 1952, he had pursued "personal grievances" by charging people who had crossed him with being Communists and sex deviates. The FBI had found in 1953 that Reynolds, as a U.S. consular official and Air Force officer in Berlin, traded visas for sex with German girls and made anti-Semitic remarks.

[4] With his tendency to focus on the half of the glass that is empty, LBJ here harps on the fact that Pearson and Anderson have followed standard journalistic practice by allowing Reynolds to comment on their charges.

[5] Siegel, of the *Washington Post*.

LBJ: Just got in. Taking a shave before I went to this dinner and I wanted to say hello. . . . I've got to be there at six-thirty.

WEISL: Have you got one minute?

LBJ: Yeah.

WEISL: I had a talk with Ted Sorensen twice telling him that we all wanted to be sure that he would be available to you all the time.[1] And he didn't make any reply to that. . . .

LBJ: He didn't give you any reaction?

WEISL: . . . I made it pretty strong.

LBJ: Well, just leave the job and *I'll* take it.

WEISL: [laughs]

LBJ: I'm about ready for it anyway, with their cutting me the way they do. They're all slashing me to pieces down there.

WEISL: I know they do. God, Lyndon, my heart really bleeds for you. I don't know how you can take it.

LBJ: You've got to have trust in people. You can't trust a good many of them. . . . I'm serious. If he doesn't know whether he wants the job or not—if he's not available to us, well, there's no point in our—

WEISL: . . . I didn't want to offend him, but I said, "You know, all of the presidents of the companies[2] expect you to serve the President first." That was the condition that I made, and he didn't respond. . . .

LBJ: Can you get the job for me?

WEISL: I'll say I can!

LBJ: You just hold it open then and I'll take it. We'll just let them have it about July—we'll just let them have it.[3]

WEISL: And you and I'll have a good time.

LBJ: No, no, we'll let Bobby[4] and them take over and let him run against the Republicans and let a Republican beat him.

WEISL: And how they would beat him.

LBJ: But we don't have to have it, and there's no use. It's miserable. You just have no idea how it is 'cause—

WEISL: Oh, I do. I think about it and I just wish there was some way I could help you, Lyndon.

LBJ: You just read the *Herald Tribune* every morning, you'll see how they leak these stories and what they do. . . . Maybe you ought to come down next week and visit a little bit.

WEISL: I'll do anything you want me to do. Anything.

[1] Weisl and Sorensen are still haggling over the Motion Picture Association job.
[2] Motion picture companies that are members of the MPAA.
[3] Courting sympathy for his troubles, LBJ periodically suggests that he might turn down the Democratic nomination that summer.
[4] Kennedy.

LBJ: [back on the Sorensen matter:] I'd just do nothing on this. I'd just hold it until I got a commitment. I'd play this one hard. . . . Just tell him that you may want it for me. If I get defeated or if I don't run, I'd like to do it myself. I'd make a good man for 'em, wouldn't I?

WEISL: I'll say you would. As a matter of fact, I don't think we ought to make a long-term contract with him anyway, do you?

LBJ: No. I sure wouldn't.[1]

THURSDAY, FEBRUARY 6, 1964

FRANK STANTON
President, Columbia Broadcasting System
12:30 P.M.

> STILL IN NEW YORK, LBJ asks his old friend,[2] who is in Washington, for advice on a visit to the *New York Times* editorial board. Stanton is in the White House, where, as a favor to Johnson, he is supervising the remaking of the President's desk to allow for Johnson's height.

LBJ: This morning I'm going to the *New York Times.* What should I tell the *New York Times?* Looks like to me they're pretty anti-Johnson. . . . Do you get that impression?

STANTON: I do. And you saw the editorial this morning.[3]

LBJ: . . . They don't know a damned thing about it.

STANTON: And the one on the consumer thing they had too today.[4]

LBJ: I didn't see the one on the consumer—I didn't read it. Anti-Johnson too?

STANTON: It was sort of saying, you know, this is old stuff and nothing is going to happen and so forth. I was surprised you did this luncheon with them.

LBJ: I shouldn't have. That was a mistake. Somebody else arranged it and I wasn't on top of it. I don't think there was anything to be gained by it. Who runs it?

---

[1] After declining the MPAA job, Sorensen joined a New York law firm.
[2] Not averse to cultivating an influential member of Congress, Stanton, as CBS director of research, had helped to give the Johnson radio station in Austin its crucial CBS affiliation. David Halberstam wrote puckishly in *The Powers That Be* (Knopf, 1979) that "among the documentaries that CBS did not make in the sixties . . . was the study of how Lyndon Johnson . . . became a very rich man." He added that the Johnson-Stanton relationship "made people in the CBS News Division very uneasy when Johnson was President. They knew that Stanton was in touch with Johnson, and they were sure that in his own mind Stanton had his priorities straight, that he was helping a friend who happened to be President, helping CBS in Washington. . . . But they did not like it" (pp. 438–39).
[3] "Fiddling as Panama Burns," which complained that the conflict was "being drawn out too long."
[4] The *Times* said that consumer protection required more than the "lofty sentiments" recently expressed by Johnson.

STANTON: Young Sulzberger.[1]

LBJ: Does he really run it or—

STANTON: Yes, he really does. His father is a very sick man—Arthur Hays,[2] I think, will be there, but don't be surprised if he doesn't remember your name. You know, he's almost senile.

LBJ: What fix would you give? Just general reserve and aloofness?

STANTON: I certainly would. You've got one very strong friend there in a man by the name of Oakes,[3] and he's a gray-haired, curly-haired—

LBJ: I know him. He and his family have been down several times, but, hell, he runs the editorial page—

STANTON: . . . I'm not sure that he runs it to that extent. This is a committee operation over there. How long will you be there today?

LBJ: . . . Be here tonight. Be at the *Times* from one o'clock, I guess, till three o'clock. Then I go to a four o'clock meeting with businessmen. . . . Back tonight.

• • • •

LBJ: What do you think about the Republican candidates?[4] What are they doing? Are they making any headway?

STANTON: I don't think they're making any headway at all.

LBJ: You think we have been hurt any in the last ten days, on account of the stereo set and the television set?[5]

STANTON: Yes, sir.

LBJ: What can we do about it?

STANTON: I'm not sure I've got the advice on what to do, but I think there is some hurt and there is an awful lot of loose talk about Bobby[6] and TFX and so forth.[7]

LBJ: Last I heard, Republicans had a $250,000 fund for investigating buying a lot of land at NASA in Houston.[8] . . . What do you think this does? Create doubt? Or just generally smear you? Or give the Republicans strength? Or what?

STANTON: . . . There's no question in my mind but that this is creating a sort of a question mark. . . . People are beginning to say, "Now, what is there to this?"

• • • •

[1] Arthur Ochs Sulzberger, the *Times* publisher.
[2] Arthur Hays Sulzberger.
[3] John Oakes, editor of the *Times* editorial page and member of the Sulzberger family that owned the *Times*.
[4] For President—Goldwater, Rockefeller, Lodge, Nixon, Scranton.
[5] Meaning revelation of the gift from Baker and Reynolds and Johnson's clumsy attempt to equate it with the miniature television Goldwater received from his staff.
[6] Baker.
[7] In 1961, Johnson had lobbied for the award of a government contract to build the TFX fighter plane to General Dynamics of Fort Worth. It was rumored, without evidence, that LBJ had gotten kickbacks for his efforts.
[8] This rumor had it that just before the government announced that NASA would locate a space flight center in Houston (thanks largely to LBJ), Johnson had bought up nearby land in order to resell at a vast profit.

LBJ: Now, what is the trouble about the TFX? That Bobby Baker is supposed to have had something to do with it? Or I'm supposed to have had something to do with it?

STANTON: Either that he had and that that is going to come out and embarrass you or . . . that you had something to do with it.

LBJ: Well, neither is true.

STANTON: I'm sure of that.

LBJ: But it could be very easily, because it was natural and normal, except that my judgment was that the first thing I ought to do was just say to them,[1] "I won't ever discuss any contract with you." So that's what we said to Webb[2] and that's what we said to McNamara and that's what we've done. Everybody that talks to us about it, we just say, "Talk to your Congressman about it. We can't help you or hurt you on this one." . . .

STANTON: How long is this thing going to drag out?

LBJ: Oh, until the tax bill gets out of the way. The Republicans want to drag it right up until the election and use it. . . . I don't see that it makes any difference whether Reynolds gave me a $500 set or Baker gave me a $500 set. If Reynolds gave it to me, well, we'd spent $90,000 on insurance. So what? If Baker gave it to me, he worked for me, and we'd paid $600 to haul him down to see us.[3] So what? They're talking about something that happened in '57. If that's the strongest thing they've got, I don't believe that appeals to people much. . . . But a good many people wouldn't tell me. That's why I'm just trying to find out. I'm not concerned, because a poll in California, finished January 31st, showed I had more Republican votes than any Republican except Nixon, and damned near as many in the Republican group as he had. And I got 91 percent of the Democrats. Michigan shows the same thing. In Pennsylvania, I got more Republicans than Scranton. Now, of course, you've got these *Literary Digest* polls—you can't believe them.[4] But I think the Republican community got hit awfully hard by the budget,[5] and they don't know what the hell to do, and they've got no positive, affirmative program. They're not *for* something. I'm for a tax bill. They're against it. I'm for a civil rights bill. They're against it. I'm for a medical care bill. They're against it. And all they're for is Bobby Baker and investigation.

STANTON: That's right. . . . They haven't got a strong man in the whole group. . . . What you hear in business circles everyplace is that they've got a new confidence and it just comes out of you. And they are going ahead and doing things that they were just sitting on the edge of their chairs on just three months ago.[6]

[1] Defense Department officials.
[2] James Webb, Administrator of NASA.
[3] At the LBJ Ranch in 1957.
[4] In 1936, the *Literary Digest* notoriously predicted that Alfred Landon would defeat Franklin Roosevelt, who won by a landslide.
[5] Johnson's new $97.9 billion budget.
[6] This was just what Johnson had hoped. (See conversation with Walter Heller above, December 23, 1963.)

1. Vice President Lyndon Johnson, Jacqueline Kennedy, and President John F. Kennedy, Fort Worth, Texas, Friday morning, November 22, 1963.

2. On *Air Force One*, two hours after John Kennedy's murder, the new President, flanked by Lady Bird and Jacqueline Kennedy, at his swearing-in.

3. The new President and First Lady, followed by House Speaker John McCormack, next in line of presidential succession, outside Johnson's vice presidential chambers, Saturday morning, November 23, 1963.

4. Lady Bird and Lyndon Johnson leave the White House East Room after viewing the casket of John Fitzgerald Kennedy, November 23, 1963.

5. Johnson speaks to a Joint Session of Congress, November 27, 1963. Many Americans were frightened at the sight of the two elderly men next in line for the presidency behind LBJ, who had once suffered a massive heart attack—House Speaker John McCormack (left) and Senate President Pro Tempore Carl Hayden.

6. Luci Baines Johnson picks lint from her father's shoulder as they ride up in the President's private elevator to their new White House quarters, just vacated by Jacqueline Kennedy and her children, December 7, 1963.

7. LBJ kisses Lady Bird as they arrive in the White House family quarters. She carries a photograph of Johnson's mentor, former Speaker Sam Rayburn. At left are Johnson aide Bill Moyers and Congressman Albert Thomas.

8. Johnson swims in the White House pool under the Virgin Islands landscape mural donated by Joseph Kennedy.

9. LBJ is about to take a nap in a room off the presidential office.

10. Johnson receives aides and prepares to have his hair cut in the Oval Office. At left is his chief secretary, Juanita Roberts.

11. Johnson holds a news conference in the Oval Office, December 7, 1963. Press Secretary Pierre Salinger is at left.

12. LBJ consults two of his liege men, Jack Valenti (left) and Bill Moyers.

13. Johnson has a private chat with his lawyer and longtime confidant Abe Fortas, who will quietly guide him through controversy.

14. LBJ gives instructions to JFK speechwriter Theodore Sorensen (left) and Senator Hubert Humphrey of Minnesota.

15. During a meeting with a foreign visitor, Johnson shares a joke with his Defense Secretary, Robert McNamara (right), whom he wants to make his Vice President.

16. The Johnson treatment is applied to LBJ's old Senate patron, Richard Russell of Georgia. On the tapes Johnson tells Russell, "I haven't got any daddy and you're going to be it." Both men are about to oppose each other in a titanic struggle over Johnson's civil rights bill.

17. Johnson tries to convince Martin Luther King, Jr., that he is serious about civil rights, while using the FBI to monitor King's movements and intentions.

18. LBJ listens to his Attorney General, Robert Kennedy, with obvious skepticism. Johnson's first nine months in office were overwhelmed by his dread that RFK would seize the Democratic presidential or vice presidential nomination for himself.

19. Johnson shows his chemistry with his FBI Director, J. Edgar Hoover. "You're my brother and personal friend," he tells Hoover on the tapes. "I've got more confidence in your judgment than anybody in town."

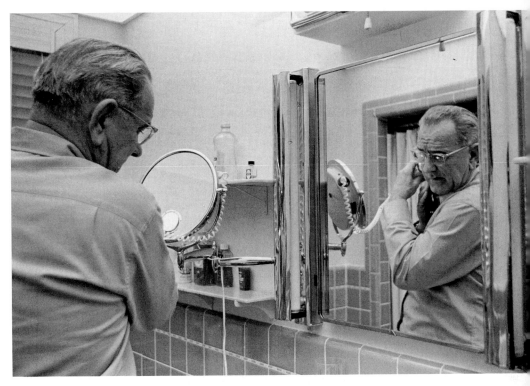

20. Christmas 1963: Johnson shaves in his bathroom at the LBJ Ranch.

21. Lynda Bird Johnson and her father open Christmas presents at the ranch. At right is Gerri Whittington, whom LBJ has just appointed as the first black woman to be a President's secretary.

22. LBJ greets his old Texas comrade Governor John Connally, still recovering from the shooting in Dallas. On the tapes Johnson lambastes Connally's "Little Boy Blue personality" but says, "I think I love him more than any other white man."

23. *Below left:* Bobby Baker, the fun-loving operator who was LBJ's close aide in the Senate. In early 1964, Baker was at the maelstrom of a scandal that Johnson considered to have been invented by Robert Kennedy to destroy his presidency.

24. Campaigning for support among his own people at LBJ's behest, South Vietnamese leader General Nguyen Khanh hands out candy to children, March 1964. U.S. Ambassador Henry Cabot Lodge is at left.

25. LBJ poses with an Appalachian family, April 23, 1964.

26. Johnson lifts his beagle by the ears, April 27, 1964. "When a hound dog barks . . . that's his pleasure," he says on the tapes. "That's not his hurting."

27. With Lynda Bird at his side, LBJ shouts to crowds in Gainesville, Georgia, where he delivers a courageous civil rights speech, May 8, 1964.

28. Secretary of Defense McNamara with the new U.S. Ambassador to Saigon, General Maxwell Taylor. LBJ says on the tapes that he has appointed Taylor "to show that we mean bid-ness" in Vietnam.

29. FBI poster calling for information on the three missing civil rights workers in Mississippi, June 1964. LBJ on the tapes: "I called in Edgar Hoover and told him to fill Mississippi—I can't say this publicly—but load it down with FBI men and put 'em in every place . . . they can as informers."

30. LBJ signs the Civil Rights Act of 1964, a landmark in American history. Despite his exuberant facade, he is deeply worried that African-Americans will riot and that whites will rebel against the new law. "They call me and . . . [say] that the Negroes have taken over the country," he says on the tapes. "They're running the White House. They're running the Democratic party."

31. Republican presidential nominee Barry Goldwater and vice presidential nominee William Miller greet delegates, San Francisco, July 16, 1964. LBJ on the tapes: "I just shudder to think what would happen if Goldwater won it. He's a man that's had two nervous breakdowns. He's not a stable fellow at all."

32. A North Vietnamese torpedo boat in the Gulf of Tonkin of the kind that engaged with the U.S. destroyer *Maddox* on August 2, 1964. LBJ on the tapes: "We're gonna be firm as hell. . . . The people . . . want to be damned sure I don't pull 'em out and run . . . because Goldwater is raising so much hell about how he's gonna blow 'em off the moon."

33. Late at night, Johnson announces that the U.S. has retaliated against North Vietnam, August 4, 1964.

34. At the Democratic convention in Atlantic City, Mississippi Freedom Democratic Party activists sit in seats reserved for the all-white Mississippi delegation in a struggle that makes LBJ privately threaten to withdraw his candidacy for President and retire to Texas. On the tapes he says, "The only thing that can really screw us good is to seat that group of challengers from Mississippi. . . . The Negroes will not listen to me. They're not going to follow a white Southerner."

35. Trying to create suspense about the vice presidency, LBJ flies to the Democratic National Convention at Atlantic City with Senators Thomas Dodd of Connecticut and Hubert Humphrey of Minnesota, August 26, 1964.

36. Robert Kennedy tries to calm a twenty-two-minute ovation by the Democratic convention, August 27, 1964. Johnson had made certain that this scene took place only after he was safely nominated.

37. On his fifty-sixth birthday, LBJ accepts the nomination.

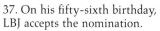

38. The Johnson-Humphrey ticket.

39. Johnson campaigns in Sacramento, California. Exhilarated by his newly won popularity outside the South, Johnson in November 1964 will win 61 percent of the vote, the greatest presidential victory in modern times. But the American position in South Vietnam is collapsing.

LBJ: I had a meeting with a couple of the Cabinet and I said, "Now you keep your foot off of everybody's neck[1] from now . . . till we get elected. . . . I'm tired of people being harassed and getting new bulletins and new questionnaires, just generally irritating 'em." Called in all the regulatory agencies and told them the same thing. I said, "Now . . . let us see if this system will work. Now if . . . they can't provide any jobs and they're just a big bag of wind, we'll come back in here next January after election and we'll give 'em the damndest WPA[2] you ever saw. We'll employ the people of this country. But I'm going to give them a chance to do it first."

. . . .

LBJ: What do you think our answer to the Baker thing is and all the rumors like the NASA land and TFX?

STANTON: . . . I don't have the answer on the tip of my tongue. . . .

LBJ: Looks like the *Tribune* is giving us the works every day. . . . And they don't interview me. . . . I don't know whether Kennedy people are being disloyal and planting it. . . . They wrote a story about when I landed at the airport and asked where Dick Russell was.[3] . . . Pure figment of their imagination, but they'd like to get in the southern Georgia, tobacco-chewing fellow running the foreign policy. The night that I took the oath that I was wondering where Senator Russell was. I wasn't wondering such a thing.

. . . .

LBJ: They are in a contrary mood. Get the President discredited. Looks like it, doesn't it?

STANTON: No, I don't think there is a concerted mood but I think there is . . . somebody doing some talking out of the sides of their mouth down here some-place because these guys are being fed, I think. Did you read Ted Lewis's column this morning?[4]

LBJ: Yeah, and that is pure falsification. I don't have Bobby[5] in all the meetings I have but I have the same identical people. . . . I've had many more of them than Kennedy[6] had for a similar period of time. I believe the State Department shows we've had 188 conversations on it in seventy days. I believe it shows I've met with

---

[1] Meaning ease up on government regulation of business.
[2] Johnson's reference to FDR's Works Progress Administration means a new public works program.
[3] The *New York Herald Tribune* had reported that on November 22, after landing at Andrews, LBJ had looked for his friend Russell.
[4] The columnist Ted Lewis had written in the *New York Daily News* that if the Cyprus crisis had occurred during John Kennedy's time, "he would have a vast store of personal knowledge concerning all aspects of the problem. . . . How much homework on Cyprus—or any other world trouble spot—has President Johnson been doing? . . . JFK was reported to have spent more than 200 hours on the comparatively minor Yemen crisis alone. . . . This is the heart of the sly criticism of Johnson now going on here, particularly as his inherited White House aides move out, one by one. The reports are that they are disillusioned by Johnson's Texas-style operations. The President is said, for example, to be more interested right now in projecting a favorable image before the public than in activities which would improve his knowledge of world problems."
[5] Kennedy.
[6] President Kennedy.

them fifty-one times. [changes subject:] The Cubans have just shut off the water to Guantánamo and says they'll keep it off until we release their fishing boats.[1]

STANTON: Has this been announced yet?

LBJ: No.

STANTON: Boy!

McGEORGE BUNDY
12:52 P.M.

LBJ: I'm meeting with the *New York Times.*

BUNDY: I would hold my fire very carefully, Mr. President. . . . You know as well as I do what kind of a crowd they are.

LBJ: No I don't.

BUNDY: Well, the *Times* editorial page is a soft page, Mr. President. It makes Walter Lippmann look like a warmonger. They're clever, but they don't have a whole lot of judgment. You've got to show them you're a man of peace without letting them call the tune, I think, and you're damned good at that. . . . They've been good to the administration but I think they're going to be watching a little bit. They're not Zionists, but they're influenced by Zionists.[2] They're intelligent men. . . . They're tempted by neutralization in Vietnam, which doesn't make any sense at this stage, any further than you took it last Saturday, which was I think just right on the button.

LBJ: What do we say about neutralization of Vietnam? We have probed and we know that there is no possibility of neutralizing North Vietnam. If they would leave their neighbors alone—

BUNDY: We'd leave everybody alone.

LBJ: Immediately. But they[3] won't do it. And to say that you're going to neutralize South Vietnam and let them take North Vietnam is silly.

BUNDY: That's exactly right, Mr. President. You cannot neutralize the bottom half with the top half waiting to eat it up. . . . And the north half is not about to be neutralized.

LBJ: Well, they say, "What about Laos?"

BUNDY: Laos is different, Mr. President. We had a strength on the scene. There are three different kinds of strength on the scene—ours, the Reds, and the neutrals. . . . What we did was to put a cloak over the division that had existed before and we gained from it.[4] . . . But there's no balance of forces like that in South Vietnam. If the U.S. forces were withdrawn, that thing would collapse like a pack of cards. Maybe when we have a stronger position, maybe when we've

---

[1] Castro had struck back at the United States for seizing seamen aboard four Cuban boats sailing two miles off the Florida Keys by aborting the water supply to the U.S. Navy's base at Guantánamo, Cuba, held under a ninety-nine-year lease.

[2] Bundy did not intend this as a compliment.

[3] The North Vietnamese.

[4] In 1962, Kennedy had acceded to the neutralization of Laos.

pressed through with this and maybe if they can get a government that'll move
. . . there'll come a time when there'll be a balanced force in South Vietnam that
can survive. But anyone who thinks that exists now is crazy and anybody who
says it exists is undermining the essential first effort. And that is the hazard of
what de Gaulle is doing and it's the hazard in what some other people are
suggesting. I wouldn't mention them, but you can look 'em right in the eye.

LBJ: Who is it that you-all . . . and the President[1] formerly consulted on these
things that we're not consulting?

BUNDY: Nobody. I have been up and down this with Kraft[2] and told him it is
sheer nonsense.

LBJ: It's being leaked though. You see Ted Lewis in the *News* today?

BUNDY: No, I didn't see Lewis. I don't even know Lewis and I don't see him,
but it's sheer nonsense, Mr. President. . . . Anyone who's saying it is getting out
of—I know damn well because I've been up and down it . . . not out of my staff,
not out of your immediate staff, and not out of the people who are loyal to you
and I think everybody who's staying on in the White House[3] is loyal to you and
is going to play it that way.

ROBERT McNAMARA
1:01 P.M.

JOHNSON CONSULTS McNamara about Castro's cutoff of the Guantánamo
water supply.

LBJ: What do you think about this Cuba water thing?

McNAMARA: From a military point of view, we're in no trouble. . . . From a
political point of view, I think it's dynamite.[4]

A.W. MOURSUND
Banker, Rancher, Businessman, Johnson City, Texas
7:00 P.M.

LBJ: Khrushchev's threatening us tonight on Cuba[5] and they cut off our water
in Guantánamo. So you've got another crisis on your hands. . . . He said if we
messed with it, he'd let us have it.

[1] Kennedy.
[2] *Washington Post* columnist Joseph Kraft.
[3] I.e., Bundy's fellow Kennedy people.
[4] Interestingly, McNamara had the same immediate reaction when told that Soviet missiles
had been discovered in Cuba in October 1962. (See Michael R. Beschloss, *The Crisis Years,* p.
445, and the tape JFK made of his Cuban Missile Crisis Ex Comm meeting of October 16, 1962,
at 6:30 P.M., Kennedy Library.) McNamara thought that the Guantánamo cutoff was political
"dynamite" because it might ignite the American people to reconsider American military action
against Cuba.
[5] The Soviet leader was supporting Castro's claim that seizure of the Cuban boats was
American "piracy."

MOURSUND: Well, you can just tell him, by God, you're ready.[1]

LBJ: [chuckles sardonically] Wish I was!

FRIDAY, FEBRUARY 7, 1964

RICHARD RUSSELL

11:17 A.M.

> JOHNSON REPORTS on this morning's Guantánamo deliberations. Thomas Mann insisted that Castro's act was a critical Soviet test of the new President. Robert Kennedy demanded that Mann prove it.

LBJ: Dick, these folks . . . haven't got any ideas, or any plans, or any program or anything, except Bobby Kennedy says turn the seamen loose and hold the boats. And they want to put out a little statement that we'd give him twenty-four hours to turn the water on, and if he didn't, we'd supply our own water. I told them, "To hell with that." That was too innocuous. . . . I told McNamara to call you this afternoon before our next meeting, which will be at four-thirty . . . to . . . go over with you the alternatives. . . . He's got a little guts. He's the only one in the meeting that does. He and Tom Mann have a little, but the—

RUSSELL: I ain't as bent on bloodshed and warfare right now down there as some of the people probably are. . . .

LBJ: . . . I suggested . . . that . . . we say . . . we're going to make our base independent of Cuba. . . . So he's got three thousand employees[2] there, and we're going to staff the thing ourselves. We're going to furnish our own water ourselves. . . . We go to searching ships—why, that's an act of war. . . . We're going to cut him off about seven or eight million dollars a year cash that we're financing him. I told them to get ahold of Khrushchev and tell him that this man's[3] playing a mighty dangerous game with his marbles. . . .

RUSSELL: . . . It should be made perfectly clear to him that this man is irrational and that there will be a limit to our patience. . . . Remind him of Hungary[4] a little bit while they're talking to him.

· · · ·

LBJ: The *New York Times* won't want us to take a dime away from them. They think we ought to be feeding Cuba. So will the *Washington Post*.

RUSSELL: I don't think they'll go that far.

---

[1] This was roughly the kind of advice that Johnson's crony Moursund also gave Johnson on Vietnam.

[2] Cubans who worked on the Guantánamo base.

[3] Castro.

[4] The Soviet invasion of Hungary in 1956.

LBJ: Damn near. They'll say you're being punitive, and you're penalizing these poor people.[1]

RICHARD RUSSELL
4:30 P.M.

LBJ: I wanted to talk to you before I went into the meeting.[2] . . . Nobody wants to do much. They think that in the first place these fishermen ought not even have been picked up. . . . We ought to have told them to get on back home and not make a big incident out of it. . . . There's an opposing viewpoint that's pretty well the viewpoint of Rusk and McCone and, I would say, Bobby Kennedy. He wants to turn everybody loose and let them go on home. McNamara feels like the sentiment in this country is such that we've got to do more than that and that . . . we probably ought to do two things—declare the independence of that base . . . saying, "We're going to furnish our own water and we don't want your damn water and to hell with you," and number two, tell the people that are on there that they can pledge allegiance to us and live there—six hundred—and the other 2,500 to go on back and we're going to quit financing. We're going to operate the base independently . . . and it's going to hurt you more by this action than hurts us. . . . He's about the only one that feels that way. That's my feeling. . . .

RUSSELL: That's mine.

. . . .

LBJ: I don't like to see them so split and so divided—State, Defense, and CIA. What do you think the attitude of the country is, the Senate? Are they indignant about cutting this water off? I don't guess many of them feel as strong as Goldwater does. . . .

RUSSELL: . . . They're just tired of Castro urinating on us and getting away with it. They don't like the smell of it any longer. They just want to show that we are taking such steps as are in within our power without involving the shedding of a lot of blood. . . . People don't trust Goldwater's judgment. A lot of them like his independence.

LBJ: You think a lot of people going to think you're hotheaded when you just fire a bunch of innocent Cubans?

RUSSELL: I don't think so. I don't believe that even the *Times* and the *Post* could stir up 5 percent of the people about this.

---

[1] The Cubans who work on the base.
[2] Scheduled for 4:55 P.M.

RUSSELL LONG
Democratic Senator from Louisiana
7:30 P.M.

THE SENATE HAS PASSED Johnson's tax cut bill by a vote of 77 to 21.

LBJ: I wanted to thank you for that wonderful victory on the tax bill. You just really outdid yourself. I saw all your Louisiana folks this morning and I told them you were the greatest man I knew.
LONG: [chuckles] That was awfully kind of you.
LBJ: . . . Just twenty votes against it. Now you go in that conference and get it sacked up. We're losing $80 million a day—that's withholding out of that economy and I want to have a good year, so I can get reelected.

SATURDAY, FEBRUARY 8, 1964

JOHN CONNALLY
9:00 A.M.

THE NIGHT BEFORE, Johnson had abruptly flown to Texas to attend the funeral of Jesse Kellam's wife.

CONNALLY: How are you this morning?
LBJ: Oh-h-h-h, I'm a little bit sad. Just got in late last night.
CONNALLY: . . . I'm sure you are sad. It's a terrible thing. I never saw Jesse so upset. . . . He just doesn't know what to do with himself. . . . I'm sure he's real happy and proud that you-all came down. You were a great help to him. How was your trip?
LBJ: . . . We had this Cuba thing right up until we left and we had a real rough day on it. . . . We told him we didn't need his water and told him to take his men back too. . . . Why don't you and Nellie let me send a plane in and you-all come out[1] and let's ride around?
CONNALLY: [declining the invitation:] I've got a hell of a morning and we're planning on going down to the farm to look at a house this afternoon. . . . We're getting one where we have to do an awful lot of picking out of stuff. Got to pick out marble and brick and tile, fabrics, fixtures, and every other damn thing. . . . They've been building since October. . . .[2]
LBJ: [pretending to ignore the snub by changing the subject:] I bought me a

[1] To the LBJ Ranch.
[2] Here Connally snubs the President of the United States by saying that he cannot come to see him because he must pick out furnishings for a new house.

new little place the other day—the Logan place. . . . But this damned Keller got a thousand[1] adjoining it that I wanted. . . . Kinda squatters' rights.

· · · ·

LBJ: I don't see that they've[2] got anybody that's appealing to people much.[3] Goldwater has gone crazy. He wanted to call in the Marines yesterday.[4] He's just as nutty as a fruitcake. Rockefeller's wife ain't going to let him get off the ground.[5] So I guess that *Time* magazine and the big ones that are really doing this job, I guess they're going to . . . Scranton.[6] I don't believe he's appealing enough or attractive enough. I don't think they can make the image of him enough to get over. All he did was a 5 percent sales tax. . . .

CONNALLY: I don't know how they're going to get off the ground. I think they're going to have to go back to Nixon. Nixon or Scranton. But I don't think either one of them can do any good.

LBJ: Well, I wish you were coming up. If you change your mind, call me. Anytime you want to use this plane, . . . that Lockheed's still over there.[7] You ought to buy it. . . . You're a damn fool if you don't buy it. It's a plane that's worth a minimum of $100,000, without any question. . . . It's got the radio gear that's worth more than it's bringing. . . . By God, we've got plenty of dollars on the inside of it and the only damned thing in the world you have to do is make some of your contributors contribute . . . enough to pay for your gasoline. . . . I'd damned sure do it. Do it in one minute. . . . And the damned committee[8] can sure do it, unless your committee's against you. . . . I'd just say to the committee that in your physical condition, you're not in a position to be traveling unless you have a plane. . . . You can just stretch out. If you feel like working, you've got a damned good office if you're bored, and you can land at 2,500 feet anywhere.

CONNALLY: What are you-all asking for it?

LBJ: I think twenty-nine thousand, thirty thousand. . . . And we've got $65,000 cash that we put in it. Then we put in twenty to thirty on radio equipment and we put twenty to thirty on inside, with all of our furnishings and stuff. . . . We've got four goddamned engines on it, and it just sits down there. . . . You just tell him[9] you want to go to Longview or Floresville. You haven't got a strip down there, have you?

CONNALLY: Building one.

LBJ: I'd damn sure do it. That's the biggest fool thing I ever heard of. You can get a three-thousand-foot strip. . . . Make him take you around somewhere and see if you don't like it.

[1] Acres.
[2] The Republicans.
[3] In the presidential campaign.
[4] To turn on the water to Guantánamo.
[5] Nelson Rockefeller had divorced his first wife to marry a younger woman—heresy for many voters in 1964.
[6] As Johnson knows, the *Time* publisher Henry Luce likes Governor Scranton of Pennsylvania, who happens also to be the brother-in-law of James Linen, president of Time Incorporated.
[7] This refers to the Johnson family's private plane, which he wanted to sell.
[8] Connally's campaign committee.
[9] Johnson's pilot.

CONNALLY: I will.

LBJ: Well, if you change your mind, call me.[1]

CONNALLY: If I can, I will.

BILL MOYERS and WALTER JENKINS
11:25 A.M.

MOYERS: Secretary Rusk called me a few minutes ago . . . and said, "Would you come over right away?" . . . He brought me into his office, closed the door, and said, "Two stories have reached me which I'm not sure are accurate or not but have come to me by means which command my ear. . . . I don't want to be pressed please about how they got to it. But I think that the President should know." . . . Number one, Joe Pulitzer[2] is talking about how, after his meeting over here, he came away shocked that he was read material and others were read material from the confidential files of a government employee.[3] That profoundly disturbed him and shocked him. . . . The second story is that the Hearst people are having great pangs of conscience. . . . Having been offered this material earlier by a White House aide . . . they are discussing if they should not have a story which says that they were offered the material by the White House.[4] . . .

LBJ: I don't believe that's right. I believe that . . . DeLoach at the FBI[5] told 'em. . . .

MOYERS: . . . DeLoach is not a White House aide. . . .

LBJ: . . . I've had that summary . . . which is not a part of the file, just pure notes, which they said they distilled for the Senate committee, although there were facts about this fellow that seriously raised some questions. . . .

MOYERS: Do you think the only course of action would be to have Walter call Dick Berlin,[6] if they really are having pangs of conscience?

LBJ: . . . I'd say as far as we know, we don't have any files and make sure we don't have.

MOYERS: We don't.

LBJ: And all we've had is—we've had interpretations, summaries that this fellow was no good. And that was what I told Pulitzer.

· · · ·

MOYERS: The *Herald Tribune* is one of the papers that asked us—they asked me for this information. I said, "I don't have it, and if I had it, I wouldn't give it to you."

LBJ: I'd remind them of that, Bill.

MOYERS: Yes, sir.

[1] For the third time, LBJ asks him to come to see him.
[2] Joseph Pulitzer, Jr., publisher, *St. Louis Post-Dispatch*.
[3] Don Reynolds.
[4] See Johnson's conversation with Abe Fortas, January 17, 1964, above.
[5] Cartha "Deke" DeLoach, the FBI's liaison to Johnson.
[6] Richard Berlin, chief executive officer of the Hearst Corporation.

. . . .

LBJ: I imagine that I can release anything in any file I want to, can't I?

MOYERS: You can, Mr. President, but releasing a personnel file could have a tremendous effect on the government operations and . . . confidence of the public in the government. . . .

LBJ: I think we take the position we can, we haven't and, matter of fact, we asked that it not be. . . . When we heard that Pearson got it from the Air Force, we expressed the hope to the Air Force that he wouldn't use it.[1] Any of you have any idea where he got it? Did he get it from Zuckert,[2] do you think?

MOYERS: He told me, Mr. President, that he got it from a major. . . . But he said, "I could not have gotten it if it had not been for Zuckert's help." . . . I talked to Zuckert, but I didn't ask point blank 'cause I thought maybe it was better for me not to know.

. . . .

LBJ: I think the position I'd take is . . . we didn't release it, we didn't want it released, and we didn't think it was in our interest to publicize that fellow, to recognize him that much. We don't think so now. We'd have given anything if Pearson hadn't run it. Pearson's libel lawyers called us and we told 'em we hoped he wouldn't run it.

. . . .

LBJ: What I don't understand is why people like the *New York Times* . . . and the *Washington Post* would want to protect a guy like Reynolds. They've been exposing these types of people all through the government always. Now they must have a conspiracy to wreck *us*, or they wouldn't be upset about it. And this must have hurt him and hurt him with the committee. Does Reynolds sound like he's hurt?

MOYERS: Everybody that talks to me thinks that he's hurt. . . . "Glad they exposed this guy." Stuff like that.

LBJ: You'd better have a long talk with DeLoach and see if he's following through on all these leads in the statement. . . . I asked you to do that yesterday, but I'm afraid you didn't get to, did you?

MOYERS: No, sir. I'm not sure that I—

LBJ: Talk to DeLoach and just tell him to be sure that there is an FBI file that Congress will ultimately get. All the material that's in the Air Force file and all the material that's in the State Department file and any leads that they can get from it, they ought to interview him about.

. . . .

LBJ: Now . . . see that you stay close to him,[3] Walter. Every day.

JENKINS: I do. The Director's[4] coming to lunch on Tuesday.

[1] That morning, Drew Pearson reported in the *Washington Post* that State Department and Air Force personnel records showed that the Air Force had tried to expel Don Reynolds in 1953 but was overruled by powerful Senators.
[2] Air Force Secretary Eugene Zuckert.
[3] DeLoach.
[4] Hoover.

LBJ: Tell him about Hearst having pangs of conscience. We haven't talked to him. And remember what he said. We're not going to. But talk to Dick Berlin and Deke DeLoach both about it.

MOYERS: . . . I would hope that, if at all possible, we could avoid saying that this came from the Secretary of State 'cause he doesn't get into things like this and he's doing it, I think, because he really wants to help.

LBJ: Yeah, I think so. . . . I think that it's coming from across the street[1] though. And some of that stuff is being brought to him[2] to try to destroy confidence around and among the Cabinet 'cause otherwise he wouldn't be getting it. What purpose would anybody have in going and telling him? You follow me?

MOYERS: . . . He would not be considered a source of information for the White House on matters like this. So you could make the assumption that therefore the person that told him had in mind to cause him to not believe in the administration, lose confidence in us.

LBJ: . . . I'm much more worried about the reaction that Castro's going to have.

•   •   •   •

MOYERS: Mr. President, I would like to suggest that you really keep pressure on Bundy and Rusk and McCone and others to press forward on what we can do about Cuba—about subversion, espionage, and intelligence. Now there are two reasons for this. One, I think we've got to do it. It's necessary. Cuba has got to be dealt with. But second, the Attorney General did not get any opportunity yesterday either in the session he had last night in the Cabinet Room—or in the Situation Room—where we worked for two hours before coming in there—to say, you know, we're slapping at gnats. The big problems are subversion and the training of guerrillas for Africa.[3] Nobody's giving any thought to that. Nobody seems to be concerned about it. . . . Nobody seems to have come up with a policy. And if we don't keep active on this, sooner or later we're going to start getting some newspaper stories saying that the President's more interested in gnats than he is in the big problems.

LBJ: Well, tell Bundy that. Just tell him to appoint he and Bundy and somebody in the State Department—the three of them—to come up and see what we do about this. I want the Attorney General and Bundy and somebody from the State Department—maybe Averell Harriman, whoever it is that Rusk wants to designate—to get to work and see what we do about this exportation of subversion from Cuba. And also tell Bundy that I really want to press them again, along the lines of that wire, and see what they've got to report on our offensive out there in Vietnam.[4] . . . See what you can get from General Khanh.

[1] LBJ means Kennedy holdovers in the Executive Office Building.
[2] Rusk.
[3] By Castro's Cuba. Not only were subversion and guerrilla training problems in themselves, but Castro's refusal to export revolution was a key condition of the arrangement by which President Kennedy and Nikita Khrushchev had agreed to end the Cuban Missile Crisis. As Johnson and Moyers knew, should it be publicly advertised during the 1964 election year that Castro was flouting this condition (he was also defying the provision demanding on-site inspections of Cuban territory), powerful domestic pressure could be generated on LBJ to turn up the pressure against Cuba, conceivably including invasion. As Johnson says in his December 2, 1963, conversation with J. William Fulbright, above, this he is determined to avoid.
[4] Op Plan 34-A.

PIERRE SALINGER
4:46 P.M.

IN A PAGE-ONE *New York Times* story this morning, Cabell Phillips has reported that Johnson administration officials had tried to use secret government documents to impugn Don Reynolds and his testimony and tried to cover it up with a call to someone at a national newsmagazine.

LBJ: Pierre, anybody in your shop could have talked to any national newsmagazine, like Phillips says about this story?

SALINGER: No, sir.

LBJ: I guess we'll have a White House record of telephone calls. We can find out who called him, can't we?

SALINGER: Yes, sir.

LBJ: . . . Phillips's story says that a White House person—not the President—called a national newsmagazine and attempted to get them not to print the story. Now nobody tried to get them to print anything. . . . Al Friendly[1] is in this thing pretty deep and he's been pretty much misled by Reynolds and it's going to look bad that he's tied up with a McCarthyite and a McCarranite and they're trying to smear the President and Walter Jenkins and everybody else. About what? About a $500 stereo set and $1,200 insurance advertising policy. So he and the *Post* are awfully upset now about somebody leaking something on Reynolds. . . . We've never seen the FBI file. We have seen a narrative based on the file which points up some bad things and shows that he's a no-good character, a page and a half which says he's a no-good son of a bitch. . . . Pearson wanted us to look at the file and try to tell Zuckert to allow him to quote from it. . . . We told him we wouldn't do it. He got mad as hell. We've got a recording of his conversation. He said, "By God, the President won't cooperate. The President's no goddamn good. I'm trying to help the President." . . . The *Times* and the *Post* are upset because of a personnel file, that people have information on it. They're not a goddamn bit upset about *my* personnel.[2]

---

[1] Of the *Washington Post.*

[2] That evening, as Lady Bird dictated into her diary, she and LBJ "had dinner and then the usual walk to Oriole's, which is not participated in by me because instead I had a date with my favorite Saturday night ten o'clock man—Marshal Dillon." Mrs. Johnson was a great fan of *Gunsmoke,* which was carried on the Johnsons' Austin television station. Oriole Bailey was LBJ's cousin.

MONDAY, FEBRUARY 10, 1964

WALTER JENKINS
10:55 P.M.

LBJ: It's about time for you-all to get up and allocate two or three hours for
something that you know I'm very much against. I've been trying to keep these
little tinhorn Ambassadors out of here, ever since I've been in here. . . . You-all
just figure out things for me to do, and that's damned easy to say it, but it's
pretty hard to do. . . . It's awfully easy now this morning to see Justice Goldberg,
but you've got a big bunch of Jews ahead of him that I got to make a speech to,
but I don't feel like making it to them. I've got nothing of interest to them. Ain't
no reason why the President should be seeing them, except we just got lined
into it.

TUESDAY, FEBRUARY 11, 1964

JOHN BAILEY
Chairman, Democratic National Committee
5:20 P.M.

THE PREVIOUS DAY, the House passed the civil rights bill by 290 to 130.
Lady Bird wrote in her diary that that evening "Lyndon came in and although
he had what seemed to me a marvelous victory to rack up . . . he was very
much upset and disturbed—I do not know quite what thing had produced it."
Johnson was furious to learn that Paul Corbin, an eccentric, cynical knock-
about Kennedy operative and assistant to Democratic National Chairman John
Bailey, has been doing independent political chores for Robert Kennedy and
also trying to start a groundswell in New York and New Hampshire for RFK
for Vice President.[1] After a 4:40 P.M. Cabinet Room meeting today, Johnson
asked RFK to withdraw with him into the Oval Office.
Kennedy found it "a bitter, mean conversation . . . the meanest tone that
I've heard."[2] When Johnson asked RFK to get rid of Corbin, RFK refused,

[1] Corbin, of Wisconsin, was such a fanatical Kennedyite that he had converted to Catholicism
in order to make Robert and Ethel Kennedy his godparents. Canadian-born, he had at times
been close to both the Communist Party and Wisconsin Senator Joseph McCarthy. Kenneth
O'Donnell, in a Johnson Library oral history, called Corbin "the Rasputin of our Administration, and what his relationship is with the Kennedys I will never know. . . . He was the fellow
who was telling all the bad stories about Lyndon Johnson as Vice President." Although LBJ
could not believe it, Corbin's efforts for an RFK campaign were essentially his own idea.
[2] He said this in oral history interviews for the John F. Kennedy Library, conducted in March
and April 1964 and sealed for fifteen years.

saying that President Kennedy had "thought he was good." LBJ replied, "President Kennedy isn't President anymore. I am." RFK said, "Don't you ever talk to me like that again." LBJ said he had done RFK a favor by sending him to the Far East. Kennedy replied, "A favor! I don't want you to do any more favors for me. Ever." With that, the Attorney General stalked angrily out of his brother's old office. After the meeting he told an aide, "I'll tell you one thing —this relationship can't last much longer."[1] Worried about the backlash of his confrontation with RFK, Johnson immediately calls John Bailey.

LBJ: John, I want to get you to come on over here tomorrow and bring this fellow Corbin's record with you—everything you have on him and what he does.

BAILEY: All right.

LBJ: He's been up to the New York State Committee[2] and New Hampshire.

BAILEY: He has?

LBJ: Yeah. And I want his travel record, just to see where he's been going, and what he's been doing. What do you know about him?

BAILEY: [laughs] Got an hour?

LBJ: Yeah, but tell me what you know about him in less time.

BAILEY: He came originally from Wisconsin and he got involved in the Wisconsin campaign.[3] . . . During the presidential campaign, he was in upper New York state. And after, he worked with the Attorney General, under his directions. And then when I became Chairman of the party . . . I was given Corbin and told that he was to work here, and shortly thereafter, there were . . . some contentions that at some time or another he had Communist leanings. . . . I have all those records here, if you'd like them.

LBJ: Yeah, I do want them. And if you don't mind, I wish you'd call him in and . . . ask him if he was up in the vice presidential campaign in New York and New Hampshire[4] . . . because we've been getting criticisms that we've had a man from the committee[5] up there running the Attorney General for the Vice President.

RICHARD MAGUIRE
5:27 P.M.

LBJ: Dick, I talked to the Attorney General about Corbin. I told him[6] that . . . we did not want anybody working for the committee to be demonstrating any preference for any vice presidential candidate. . . . I had taken extreme precautions to show my friendship for all of President Kennedy's hierarchy, the top

[1] See Richard N. Goodwin, *Remembering America* (Little, Brown, 1988), pp. 247–48, and Arthur M. Schlesinger, Jr., *Robert Kennedy and His Times*, pp. 651–52.
[2] Democratic Committee.
[3] The 1960 Kennedy campaign in the Wisconsin Democratic primary.
[4] Where there were efforts to encourage voters to write Robert Kennedy's name in for Vice President.
[5] Democratic National Committee.
[6] Kennedy.

men. That when I asked Shriver to take a letter to the Pope[1] and they[2] raised the question, I told them that I had confidence in him and thought that he was an able young fellow. That when the situation arose in Indonesia, I was anxious to demonstrate my confidence in him[3] and I showed it by sending him out there. . . . But I thought that it would be improper for us to raise money from the public and then give it to a fellow that travels around over the country to sponsor individuals. And he[4] said . . . well, he'd[5] had difficulties in his life . . . but that I must understand that he[6] had worked for the President and he worked for him.[7] And I said that "I have no objection to his working for you if you want to take him to Justice and put him on your payroll." . . . He said that he doesn't have a record that he could work at Justice. "But," he said, "the President liked the work he did."

I said, "I know it, Bobby, but *I'm* President and I *don't* like what he's doing, and . . . I don't want him.". . . He said . . . he hasn't been given a fair hearing. . . . I said, "We'll give him a fair hearing . . . but we're not going to have him going around operating independently. . . . Everybody that plays here plays on the team." Tears got in his eyes. And he said he's sorry that I sent him to Indonesia only on account of wanting to show confidence in him. I said, "No, I didn't say that at all. I said . . . I needed someone to go there and I thought you were a competent person to go there and I thought it did demonstrate my confidence." . . .

So he started out of the room and he said, "Then will you talk to Bailey about it? Bailey is the one that is going to have to do it." I said, "Yes, I will instruct Bailey to get rid of him . . . and I hope that we don't have any problems about it." But he went to the door, got about halfway to the door and said, "Well, I don't think that he's had a fair hearing." I said, "I'll authorize Bailey to give him a fair hearing. But if this is true that he's operating independently without anybody's direction . . . I don't think we can tolerate that." . . . So he said, "Very well." So that's it. It's going to be a problem and it's going to be serious.

[1] During his world tour, Shriver had carried a letter from Johnson to Pope Paul VI.
[2] The Vatican.
[3] Robert Kennedy.
[4] Robert Kennedy.
[5] Corbin.
[6] Corbin.
[7] Robert Kennedy.

WEDNESDAY, FEBRUARY 12, 1964

WILLIAM S. WHITE
Syndicated Columnist
9:40 A.M.

WHITE WAS SO CLOSE to LBJ that many in Washington thought of him as a window on the President's thinking.[1] The two Texans had known each other since Johnson came to Washington as a congressional secretary in the early 1930s and grew especially close in the 1950s when White served as Senate correspondent for the *New York Times*.

LBJ: I got a poll from Los Angeles . . . statewide yesterday and it shows that I beat practically all the Republicans in the Republican party and I get 92 and 93 percent of the Democrats. . . . Nixon and Lodge have the best, and they get 20 and 21, something like that. Goldwater gets 17. . . . That's your candidate, as I recall, the man that was going to be nominated. I dare slightly differ with you.[2] . . . The polls look all right, but it looks like they're all hitting at me—Scranton and Romney and Nixon and all the Republican Congressional Committee and the Senatorial Committee. Then it looks like the Bobby Baker editorials and the columnists, the *New York Times* and the *Washington Post*, just making it a personal affair. And this damn Mollenhoff, he's got the *Star* all worked up now and this Reynolds is a no-good character assassin son of a bitch, a McCarthy stooge that pulled this same kind of deal on countless number of people. But if you mention it, why, you're invading his civil liberties. If you question his credibility, they can brand Walter Jenkins as a crook and that's all right. But it looks to me that's bound to hurt in time.

WHITE: . . . I've heard about thirty people mention this Baker affair. . . . Of the thirty I've heard, I've heard about twenty-eight say that "I don't see what the President's got to do with it and why they ask him all these questions." . . . I think your impression of getting a bad press is largely confined to what you're seeing here in Washington and New York. . . . The *Washington Post* and the *New York Times* never do speak for the American press, Mr. President. Almost never.

LBJ: I wonder why they're so much after me? . . .

WHITE: I think it's kind of a glandular reaction to where you're from.

CLIFTON CARTER
Liaison to the President, Democratic National Committee
9:52 A.M.

JOHNSON HAS ASKED his old lieutenant, whom he has just installed on the Democratic Committee, to investigate Corbin.

[1] As Moyers notes in his conversation with Johnson above (January 27, 1964).
[2] At this juncture, Johnson cannot believe that he will be lucky enough to have as extreme an opponent as Goldwater.

LBJ: What did you-all find out about this Corwin?[1]

CARTER: About Corbin?

LBJ: The fellow—you know, that we've been talking about. [annoyed:] Come on!

CARTER: The Chairman[2] is getting together this report to bring over to you right now, pretty quickly.

LBJ: I don't need to see him today. I want him to see Corbin first. . . . We either make him desist or get rid of him.

CARTER: Corbin is not here, sir. He hasn't been in this week and they don't expect him before tomorrow or Friday.

LBJ: Where is he?

CARTER: Nobody knows.

LBJ: They don't know how to reach him?

CARTER: No, sir. . . . The national committeeman from New Hampshire[3]—let me read you my telephone notes just quickly on what he said. [reads aloud:] "There's an organized effort . . . assisted by Paul Corbin for the write-in vote for Bobby Kennedy for Vice President. . . . It could prove quite embarrassing if Bobby could get more votes for Vice President than Johnson gets for President."

. . . .

LBJ: I want Bailey to talk to Corbin. . . . Tell him what they say he's doing there in New Hampshire and tell him that we can't have that. . . . Tell him that we're going to have to give him notice . . . or stop that kind of stuff. . . .

CARTER: He's got this completely un-American activities background. Someone told me that he couldn't work noplace in the government . . . because of his Communist background. Bailey tells me that he's got a file seven inches thick on his un-American activities background.

LBJ: Well, look at that.

KENNETH O'DONNELL

Special Assistant to the President
10:22 A.M.

> IN THE OVAL OFFICE, O'Donnell implores Johnson to keep Corbin on at the National Committee. Since O'Donnell personally detests Corbin, his plea is probably at RFK's behest. O'Donnell's request provokes LBJ's wrath.

LBJ: [with rising anger:] I'm not going to let Corbin. . . . I'll give *up* the damn thing.[4] I'll *quit* it first! I don't want it that much. I just want to do what I know is right and I know this[5] is right. Now you told me that we ought to tell Bailey

---

[1] LBJ, as usual, mispronounces the name of someone at whom he is angry.
[2] Bailey.
[3] William Dunfey, a Kennedy ally.
[4] The presidency.
[5] Removing Corbin.

to stay on.[1] I said, "Okay, we'll tell Bailey to stay on." You said we ought to have the Cabinet stay on. I said, "Okay, we ought to do it." They say Bobby[2] ought to go to Indonesia. I say, "Okay." Now I'm not dragging my feet on anything. I'm playing it just—Pierre Salinger's got more freedom and more knowledge, and you have too, than when Kennedy was *here*. And you've got more power. You want to exercise it. Because I *give* my people power and let 'em use it. . . . I don't know Corbin. All I know is what Dick Maguire says, what Walter Jenkins says, what Cliff Carter says, what you say, and what the New Hampshire man calls down and tells me. I don't give a damn about Corbin. Why do I care about a thousand dollars a month?[3] I'd let him have it. I'm going to raise all I can. But I do think . . . he[4] ought to call Corbin and say, "You oughtn't to do this." . . . Don't let him go around doing what he's doing.[5]

FRIDAY, FEBRUARY 14, 1964

GEORGE BROWN
12:20 P.M.

LBJ: Oh, the papers are being awfully rough on us, and they're being pretty mean. The Republicans have got a smear squad out, investigating and hiring people, and going into all your business, and going into everything you've done for thirty years.[6] Rockefeller's got eight or ten of them and Goldwater's got six or eight of them. . . .

BROWN: . . . I think that the papers have been pretty good to you,[7] and I think that you're really doing all right. . . . You know, six months, eight months ain't very far off.

---

[1] Johnson had asked John Bailey to remain despite the fact that Connally had informed him that Bailey "hates your guts" and that on learning that Kennedy was dead, Bailey had said, "This means that son of a bitch Lyndon Johnson is going to be President" (John Connally, *In History's Shadow,* Hyperion, 1993, p. 194).

[2] Kennedy.

[3] Corbin's salary.

[4] Bailey.

[5] Despite the pleas of Robert Kennedy and O'Donnell, Johnson had Corbin fired that day.

[6] The Republicans were trying to find political vulnerabilities in Johnson's long and mutually rewarding relationship with Brown's company, Brown & Root.

[7] Brown was correct. In general, Johnson was getting an excellent press in the spring of 1964.

SATURDAY, FEBRUARY 15, 1964

MARSHALL McNEIL
Reporter, Scripps-Howard Newspapers[1]
6:30 P.M.

LBJ: The *New York Times* called up down here and said that they wanted us to please come by and meet their editorial board. . . . I spent two and a half hours and we had a wonderful meeting. . . . They even got into the Bobby Baker thing. I gave them an explanation of that and they were happy and pleased with it. Then the next morning, they showed their independence by saying I was a son of a bitch. . . . Now they play it up a good deal that they can't be bought. . . . Now I didn't want to buy them. I didn't want to see them. I just wanted to go on and do my job. But I don't want to be arrogant and unavailable. But when I am available, I don't want to be criticized for being courteous.

McNEIL: You're precisely right. . . .

LBJ: I told Pierre Salinger, "Let's don't ever invite a newspaperman to come in for any reason. Let's just keep them at arm's distance. We don't want to buy them and we don't want them to buy us. Now when they ask to see us, then say to 'em, 'We want you to understand we don't want to promote you and we don't want to lay you. And if you think that by our granting your request to see you that you're going out and tell others to write about how we're courting you, why we don't want to do it.' "

. . . .

McNEIL: You know what they're going to bite on you next? Advertising on this station. . . . Would you give me the story of who has advertising on your station?

LBJ: I imagine that would be the size of an unabridged dictionary. . . . I think that it just blows it up. . . . We have networks that feed us stories. Now when they buy, they don't buy *Gunsmoke*[2] for Austin. They buy it for 180 stations, and . . . we carry it. . . . The only thing we have anything to do with is the local people. . . . Anybody that wants to advertise in the market has to advertise on the station 'cause it's the only one there.[3]

WALTER HELLER
6:50 P.M.

JOHNSON AND HIS AIDES are thrashing out what form the new anti-poverty program should take.

---

[1] McNeil had been a reporter friend of Johnson's for decades, including, in the different journalistic practices of an earlier day, writing at least one speech for him while covering him. (See Robert A. Caro, *Means of Ascent*, p. 276.)

[2] The popular television Western of the time.

[3] Johnson refers to the monopoly that had allowed him to make millions with his Austin television station.

LBJ: You've got this poverty thing heading up and Sorensen just tore Shriver to pieces yesterday. . . . He said it's[1] not going to give a Special Assistant to the President this money in a political year. You're gonna have to handle it through existing agencies. I listened to it for an hour and then I just felt so depressed. . . . I got up and left, but that poverty thing is going to cause us a lot of headaches because we're not going to get it passed if we don't get it in the right channels.

HELLER: . . . Shriver has the idea that if we put these camps under the McNamara umbrella, we'll take a lot of the heat off of you and off of the whole charge that it'll be sort of a slush fund and so forth for the President.[2] . . .

LBJ: . . . We can't start it out with a new political agency, a guy running for Vice President[3] and a President in an election year. Now Walter, I just know that much about politics. . . . If they don't go military, I just don't want a Hitler outfit started over there and McNamara is the smartest guy in the Cabinet. . . . And if he'll buy it—I doubt that he'd buy it—but if Shriver can get him to buy it, he'll go up and swing for it, that is the best chance we've got out of it.

• • • •

HELLER: You didn't get any commitment from Home at all?[4]

LBJ: None whatever. . . . I just told him it was hell. And the trouble, Walter, is everybody just treats us as like we all used to treat our mother. They impose on us. We just know that she's sweet and good and wonderful and she is going to be kind to us and she'll always know that we came out of her womb and we belong to her, and every damned one of them talk to me that way. I don't care who it is. I just talk to 113 nations and they just screw us to death.[5]

[1] Congress.
[2] Shriver was suggesting that planned vocational training camps for poor youths, to be modeled on the FDR-era Civilian Conservation Corps camps, be established under the Defense Department in order to keep the program from seeming as if it was a slush fund from which LBJ could dole out money to political allies in 1964 (which, to some extent, it was, as illustrated by Johnson's talk with Mayor Daley, January 20, 1964, above).
[3] Shriver.
[4] Johnson had wanted a commitment not to trade with Cuba from the visiting British Prime Minister, Alec Douglas-Home, who was eager to sell British buses to the Castro government.
[5] That evening, the Johnsons had the Joseph Alsops, the McGeorge Bundys, and Theodore Sorensen and his date to dinner. Lady Bird dictated into her diary that talking with Alsop, the Washington columnist, was "like thinking I'm reading Madame de Stael's letters or some memoirs of a French count, because he always knows the nice juicy bits about the interior life of the people of this town. . . . Remarkable man, Joe Alsop, so many facets of his character, lover and connoisseur of elegant furniture . . . recorder of the day's events . . . and usually the sort of a feeling that Armageddon is just around the corner. . . . He is one of those people who is the world away from me and Lyndon, and yet I don't find it hard to cross the bridge. . . . As for Ted Sorensen, I see him through a veil, dimly. He's inscrutable. I do not understand him. I think I might even come to like him, although I would always think that he was laughing at me and at Lyndon. His date Sally is a roundfaced, pleasant, sweet-looking schoolteacher (with a Catholic difficulty about getting married . . . to a man who has been divorced). After dinner, we saw *Tom Jones*, which is *hilarious*. . . . Tom Jones jumps merrily from bed to bed with a peculiar and charming innocence, and always headed for the final bed that I—well, that I think is going to be permanent" (February 15, 1964).

WEDNESDAY, FEBRUARY 19, 1964

ORVILLE FREEMAN
Secretary of Agriculture
11:25 A.M.

CONSULTED BY FREEMAN about a high-level vacancy in the Agriculture Department, Johnson restates his interest in appointing women to high office.

LBJ: Why don't you find the greatest farm woman with an international background in this country and give it to a woman, and let these five million more women you got than men think Freeman's a hero? You've got these farm women in every home and let them see that you got one in there. . . . The truth of the business is they've got five million more women voting than men. We've got a Cabinet made up wholly of men. . . . The best thing we've got is sometimes we promote them to . . . a stenographer. And we just can't ever find one that's qualified. Rusk looks to find one for Ambassador, but we just don't ever quite make it. I'll bet you're a can-do man. . . . If I could . . . find some Eleanor Roosevelt with an agricultural background that's good-looking and about forty years old and was outgoing and could talk, I'd damn sure do it. And I'd be the hero. I'll guarantee you, these women will support you. The only press I've got that's worth a damn is these women writers.

ALEX ROSE
Vice Chairman, Liberal Party of New York, and President, United Hatters, Cap and Millinery Workers International Union
1:11 P.M.

JOHNSON IS CONTEMPLATING how he might dramatize the War on Poverty after sending his message on it to Congress in mid-March.

LBJ: I think it'd be a pretty good thing sometime to do like Roosevelt[1] did when he went down into Kentucky into the poor regions. . . . If I could have a tour organized. . . . Just go to the most poverty-stricken places in New York and let the press follow me and let me go there and visit with the people.

ROSE: That would be great!

LBJ: You talk to . . . some of your boys. . . . Get a consensus of opinions and see what they think.

ROSE: You coming down in person, huh?

LBJ: Yeah, maybe I'll go out into Harlem. Maybe I'll go into the East Side.[2]

---

[1] Franklin Roosevelt.
[2] Johnson presumably means the Lower, not the Upper, East Side.

Maybe I'll go somewhere where we have the real slums and the lowest living conditions so we dramatize.[1]

MARIANNE MEANS
White House Correspondent, Hearst Newspapers
6:34 P.M.

IN THE OVAL OFFICE, LBJ chats with one of his new favorites among the press, who has just returned from Texas, where Johnson has arranged interviews with family members.

LBJ: Did you see my sister?[2] Did she give you anything or just clam up?

MEANS: No, she was very good. She kept saying, "Now I'm only doing this because my brother said to." . . .

LBJ: She's very shy and very scared that she'll do something wrong.[3]

MEANS: Yes, she's very conscious of the fact that she doesn't want to be saying anything. But I loved her. I loved all of them.

LBJ: That's wonderful.

MEANS: I really went for Cousin Oriole.[4]

LBJ: We don't know anybody that they'd like more than you.

MEANS: Well, thank you. I certainly enjoyed them. I loved your sister Becky.[5] Gee.

LBJ: Has she moved into her new house?

MEANS: No, she said they still have a couple of weeks to go. . . . But they all sent their love. I assured them I would see you.

LBJ: She have any information to help you? She ought to have a few records.

MEANS: She had some marvelous anecdotes. She said you always liked to play church and you had to be the preacher. [laughs]

LBJ: I don't remember. [laughs]

HUBERT HUMPHREY
6:36 P.M.

THE SENATE MAJORITY WHIP apologizes to LBJ that he must go to California while the Johnson farm bill is pending.

[1] Worried about pushing his anti-poverty bill through white Southern Democrats in Congress, Johnson ultimately opted not to be photographed with the black poor of Harlem but with the white poor of Appalachia.
[2] Lucia Johnson Alexander.
[3] See Johnson's conversation with Mrs. Alexander, November 30, 1963, above.
[4] Oriole Bailey, who lived in a primitive house near LBJ's in Texas and on whom he ritually called when at the ranch.
[5] Rebekah Johnson Bobbitt.

HUMPHREY: I got myself screwed up here. I'm so goddamned—I just may as well be honest with you. I'm really screwed up. I'm supposed to be—

LBJ: [sarcastically:] Got a *bond* drive somewhere?

HUMPHREY: No it's Democratic fund-raising business at Los Angeles. I can cancel the goddamn thing. I'm supposed to be there tomorrow.

LBJ: [exhales] I'd be for you being there 'cause I think that state needs it and I think it's good for you to be out there. But there's not anything happens when you're not. Now George and Mike[1] would stay here and shove' em[2] but—

HUMPHREY: I know that and I'm just sick about it. . . . I've been canceling out everything around here practically, but they've been putting the heat on me. They've got about two thousand people. They're raising a lot of money out there and they figure they need it. . . . I frankly didn't even know I was in it. My damn office runs my life more every day. Christ!

LBJ: [exhales] And this is that liberal group, isn't it?

HUMPHREY: No this is the Democratic State Committee.

LBJ: Damn 'em, they have a fund-raising every month? I was out there a month ago for a fund-raising.

HUMPHREY: I suppose they do. . . . Then I was going to take on that CDC crowd[3] to give them a good President Johnson speech.

LBJ: Well, you know there'll be nothing happening until you get back.

THURSDAY, FEBRUARY 20, 1964

ADLAI STEVENSON
Ambassador to the United Nations
5:00 P.M.

SINCE STEVENSON's national emergence in 1952, Johnson had privately disdained him as an ineffectual, out-of-touch dreamer. He once boasted that at a Democratic dinner, he had bowed to former President Truman so that he could thrust his (large) hindquarters into Stevenson's face. After Kennedy's assassination, LBJ had buttered up the U.N. Ambassador by saying that Adlai should have been President instead of him and that together they would now show those young people how to do things. Never shrewd about people, Stevenson interpreted this to mean that Johnson might appoint him Secretary of State or even Vice President in 1964. With these delusions of grandeur,

[1] Smathers and Mansfield.
[2] On the Johnson farm bill.
[3] The California Democratic Council consisted of liberal Democrats who were skeptical of Johnson.

he now infuriates Johnson by imploring him to renegotiate the Panama Canal treaties.

STEVENSON: I would . . . strongly urge you to get this thing[1] disposed of if you can and not prolong it unduly, because—

LBJ: [conspicuously annoyed:] Governor, I'm not prolonging it at all. They're[2] the ones. We've said to them thirty minutes after it[3] happened that we'd be very glad to discuss anything, anywhere, anytime that affected our relations. Period. But we're not gonna sit down with precommitment on revising or renegotiating a treaty. . . . If I use the word "treaty" or "negotiate" in there I've just got a war and we've got to have—whatever treaty we write, we've got to have it ratified,[4] you know. It's not a single-handed operation.

McGEORGE BUNDY
5:05 P.M.

> JOHNSON WASTES NO TIME in reporting Stevenson's proposal to Bundy, who, as he knows, dislikes Stevenson and who voted against him in 1952 and 1956.

LBJ: Adlai has got a new formula that starts us out where we were on the first day to negotiate a new treaty with the Panamanians.

BUNDY: [disgusted:] Oh, I don't *believe* it!

LBJ: And he doesn't see anything wrong with it! And if he were Secretary of State and President both, he would negotiate. So I thanked him, told him to put it in the mail, send it down and you'd watch for it.

BUNDY: [guffaws] What am *I* supposed to do with it? . . . *Burn* it?

LBJ: Aw-w-w, he was kinda sniffy. He said, "I hope you won't reject it out of hand." . . .

BUNDY: Has he[5] had anything from the Panamanians, or is this just out of his own head?

LBJ: Aw-w, I think he's just getting into a field where he's been down talking to the State Department. . . . Were you in here the other day when we had the Senators here? . . . I wish you'd have been here and heard the hell I caught by just mentioning it.[6]

---

[1] The Panama crisis.
[2] The Panamanians.
[3] The crisis.
[4] By the Senate.
[5] Meaning Stevenson.
[6] A Stevenson-type compromise to end the crisis.

OFFICE CONVERSATION
11:20 A.M.

JOHNSON INVEIGHS some more against newspaper leaks.

LBJ: [to aides:] McCarthy said about the State Department that they have to give these things because of sex or some other reason to these papers.[1] And I'm beginning to believe that. 'Cause whenever they give to the papers—*regularly*—*systematically*—important things before the President even decides them, somebody's got something on 'em. They wouldn't *do* that every day 'cause their name's never mentioned. . . . That happens ev-v-ery day.

ROBERT McNAMARA
11:45 A.M.

DURING A CONVERSATION with his Secretary of Defense, who is to go to Saigon in March, Johnson reveals his current private thinking on Vietnam. He is trying to keep a dangerous and controversial issue on ice.

LBJ: I hate to modify your speech[2] any . . . but I just wonder if we shouldn't tonight still give our relative strengths[3] and still give a very brief summary. . . . Find two minutes in there for Vietnam.

McNAMARA: Yeah, but the problem is what to say about it.

LBJ: All right, I'll tell you what *I* would say about it. I would say that we have a commitment to Vietnamese freedom. Now we could pull out of there. The dominoes would fall, and part of the world would go to the Communists. We could send our Marines in there, and we could get tied down in a Third World War or another Korean action. The other alternative is to advise them and hope that they stand and fight. Now we think that . . . in the period of three years, we can have them trained.[4] And we've removed some there who were guarding the establishments that didn't need to be guarded anymore. . . . We'd put in ten thousand more[5] if they could be useful and if they needed them for training. But

---

[1] Joseph McCarthy claimed that State Department leaks were the partial result of closet homosexuals in the department who were blackmailed to surrender classified information.
[2] Johnson evidently refers to language contributed by McNamara for a speech the President is to deliver in Miami Beach on February 27.
[3] Meaning a comparison of American versus Soviet strength. In the Miami Beach address, Johnson ultimately noted that in the past three years, America had "doubled the number of strategic weapons on alert."
[4] Here Johnson formulates the problem differently from the way he did it in his February 3, 1964, conversation with John Knight, above. With Knight, LBJ said the choice boiled down to getting out of Vietnam or getting in. Now, as he discusses with McNamara what the Defense Secretary should say in public, Johnson suggests a third alternative—advising the Vietnamese and hoping that they would stand and fight. Did LBJ actually consider this a serious option that might work, or was it merely a holding action—rhetoric that would let him get through the campaign year without allowing the hard-liners to charge him with softness on the threat in Southeast Asia or scaring other Americans with the prospect of a vast land war after 1964?
[5] Advisers.

this thousand we didn't need, because they were guarding whatever they were guarding and that's why we pulled them out.[1]

Now we estimate that with the fifteen thousand that we've got left, and all the rest of this year and a large part of next year, that we can just train anybody. . . . And for that reason, we've said that we can reduce that number after they'd trained. Now this nation has made no commitment to go in there to fight as yet. We're in there to train them and advise them, and that's what we're doing. Nobody really understands what it is out there and they don't know, and they're getting to where they're confused. And they're asking questions and saying why don't we do more.

Well, I think . . . you can have more war or you can have more appeasement. But we don't want more of either. And it's their war and it's their men.[2] And we're willing to train them. And we have found that over a period of time that we kept the Communists from spreading. We did it in Greece and Turkey with the Truman Doctrine, by sending them men. We did it in Western Europe by NATO. We've done it there[3] by advice. We haven't done it by going out and dropping bombs and we haven't done it by going out and sending men to fight. And we have no such commitment there. But we do have a commitment to help Vietnamese defend themselves. And we're there for training and that's what we're doing. And they say that the war is not going good. Well, there are days when we win, and there are days when we lose. But our purpose is to train these people and our training is going good, and we're trying to train them.[4]

McNAMARA: All right, sir. I'll get right on it.

LBJ: I don't know if I've said anything there that I shouldn't say.

McNAMARA: No, no.

LBJ: But that's the way you said it to me, and it appealed to me when I say why in the hell—I always thought it was foolish for you to make any statements about withdrawing.[5] I thought it was bad psychologically. But you and the President[6] thought otherwise and I just sat silent. Now you've made them. And I asked for your explanation and you gave a good explanation. Not a damn bit of use to have a thousand people sitting around guarding something that they don't need to guard.

[1] Before the assassination, over LBJ's quiet opposition, JFK had approved McNamara's recommendation to announce withdrawal of a thousand Americans from Vietnam whose mission had become superfluous, to show, as McNamara told Kennedy, "that we *do* have a plan for reducing the exposure of U.S. combat personnel to the guerrilla actions in South Vietnam" and meet "the very strong views of Fulbright and others that we're bogged down in Asia and will be there for decades." (This quote comes from a tape recording of an October 2, 1963, meeting with Kennedy, transcribed by McNamara and cited in his *In Retrospect,* p. 80.) Much later this action was taken by some as proof of Kennedy's intention to withdraw all U.S. troops from Vietnam.
[2] Here Johnson perhaps subconsciously borrows from JFK's comment in an interview with Walter Cronkite of CBS on September 2, 1963: "In the final analysis, it's their war. They are the ones who have to win it or lose it."
[3] In Vietnam.
[4] These talking points for the speech certainly do not reveal the depths of Johnson's doubts about how things were going in Vietnam or his suspicions that the United States might have to commit major forces to the struggle.
[5] Referring to the withdrawal of a thousand troops by JFK.
[6] Kennedy.

McNAMARA: No question about that, Mr. President. The problem is—

LBJ: All right, then the next question comes—how in the hell does McNamara think that when he's losing the war that he can pull men out of it?

McNAMARA: Well, he's—

LBJ: McNamara's not fighting a war. But he's training men to fight a war, and when he gets them through high school, they will have graduated from high school, and will have twelve grades behind them next year, and he hasn't taken on any agreement to keep them for the rest of their life. He's just made a commitment to train them to fight. And if he trains them to fight and they won't fight, he can't do anything about it. Then he's got to choose whether he wants to fight or let them have it.

McNAMARA: That is the problem exactly and what I fear is that we're right at that point. Well, anyhow, I'll get this out to you.

LBJ: We've got to decide who goes with you[1] 'cause they tell me everybody in town is wanting to go, and I wouldn't haul anybody out there, that I just didn't have to have—

McNAMARA: Well, I feel exactly that way.

LBJ: And one man that I want to suggest—I'm sure you can cut him right back right quick and I won't hesitate and if you don't mention him anymore, I'll just know that you haven't used him, but from a psychological standpoint and from a political standpoint, there's one man that I would have with me on that plane,[2] and that's Shoup.[3] I would put a stop to Mansfield's speaking up there[4] every day on it, and Shoup would put a stop to it.[5] I'd have Shoup just go out there,[6] and sit in on these meetings with Taylor,[7] kinda ex officio, and he's out and he hasn't got anything to do, and he's got that medal on his breast, and Mansfield just worships him, and so do the Marines, and the rest of them who are raising hell do the same thing. And I'd use Shoup to go up[8] and tell these boys some things. . . . He's worth a dozen Averell Harrimans to you.[9] And that's my judgment. But I'm not any expert on it. I think that he's quiet enough and humble enough and he's not going to be bossing around and threatening any. He can sit in the back now. You don't have to mess with him, but when he gets back here, you take the McNamara line and sit down with Mansfield and sit down with the rest of them, and say now here's the story and we can get him[10] invited to come to see them.[11]

[1] To Saigon in March.
[2] To South Vietnam.
[3] The iconoclastic David Shoup had just retired as Commandant of the U.S. Marine Corps.
[4] In the Senate.
[5] Mansfield respected Shoup for his intellectual independence.
[6] To Saigon.
[7] General Maxwell Taylor, Chairman, Joint Chiefs of Staff.
[8] To Capitol Hill.
[9] Meaning that the dovish Harriman lacked the prestige lent to Shoup by his military stature.
[10] Shoup.
[11] Members of Congress. In his Miami Beach address, Johnson finally made no more than an oblique reference to Vietnam: "To those who cry havoc and shout for war, we must give them understanding. To those who advocate retreat or appeasement . . . we modestly suggest that . . . on history's face the blotch of Munich is still visible."

WEDNESDAY, FEBRUARY 26, 1964

OFFICE CONVERSATION
Approximately 12 P.M.

IN THE LATE 1930s, Johnson began a dangerous relationship with Alice
Glass, the then-paramour and future wife of one of his most important patrons,
the Austin newspaper publisher Charles Marsh.[1] By now the relationship is
long cooled and the Marshes divorced. Here the President asks an aide to
write a response to a letter from Alice. His nonchalance conceals her onetime
importance in his life.

LBJ: [to aide:] You read this and write her a ni-ice letter. She's an old friend.
She's Charlie Marsh's ex-wife. She's alone—and an alcoholic.

ADLAI STEVENSON
12:31 P.M.

OBLIVIOUS to how much his unwanted butting in on Panama is irking
Johnson, Stevenson suggests language that could be used in a renegotiation of
the Panama Canal treaties.

LBJ: I couldn't get twenty votes[2] for any treaty that substantially rewrote the
present one. . . .
STEVENSON: . . . I think if you were to . . . get this miserable little thing settled on this basis . . . you would not get an unfavorable mention in the *New York
Times.* You'd get resounding applause in an editorial.

LBJ: I think I would—in the *New York Times.* Then I think the *people* would
run me out of the country. . . . What they'll do then is they'll say I'm rewriting
the treaty: "Now, damn it, you're rewriting it!"

STEVENSON: . . . It's awfully important, from your point of view, that you
clear away this little mess because it's affecting the attitude of Latin Americans
way beyond the boundaries of Panama. . . . They feel as though we're stuck on
this dime. . . . If you get it out of the way with language as good as this that's so
far from where we started, you'd be well advised to do it.

LBJ: I could have gotten this language the first morning I talked to him,[3] if I
tell him I'll rewrite that treaty.

STEVENSON: [frustrated, impatient:] But you don't *say* that!

LBJ: That's what he[4] interprets this as saying. . . .

[1] See Robert A. Caro, *The Path to Power,* pp. 479–92, and Robert Dallek, *Lone Star Rising,*
pp. 189–90.
[2] In the Senate.
[3] Panamanian President Roberto Chiari.
[4] Chiari.

STEVENSON: . . . I can't argue with you. I don't think it does. But anyway . . .
we're going to have more goddamn trouble and just get dug in deeper and deeper
on this mess. . . .

LBJ: [disgusted:] It's not our fault, Governor. *They're* the ones that threw out
our Ambassador. . . . *They* didn't come in with a six-shooter and rescue him. *They*
told him to get the hell out.

STEVENSON: [acidly:] Well, I don't know what you want *me* to do.[1]

J. WILLIAM FULBRIGHT
3:06 P.M.

LBJ: Adlai came down and started a heat wave on Panama. He got into negotiations up there without anybody knowing it and he came up with a proposal that
we turned down in the first hour when we talked to the President of Panama. . . .
I had to talk to Adlai an hour and it has got my schedule all kicked up.

ROBERT McNAMARA
3:29 P.M.

> JOHNSON IS SCHEDULED to fly to Florida. The Secret Service has received a
> tip that a suicide pilot or ground-to-air missile launched by pro-Castro Cubans
> in the state might be used to down *Air Force One.* McNamara asks the President
> to accept extraordinary security precautions, including an overhead fighter
> escort. Johnson complains that it will make him look extravagant.

LBJ: I've been trying to defend myself thirty years without too much success.
But if they ask you what they are doing up there and you say, "They're ceremonial," they'll say here is the guy that cuts out lights in the White House and fires
little $1,200 clerks but he's got a big escort. If you say it's to protect his life, they
say, "God almighty, what's happening?" And you notify every other nut in the
country. I think what we ought to do is go to a military airport—and I'm going
to Palm Beach too, to see Mr. Kennedy[2]—and if this fighter escort's up there, it
had better be so damn far that nobody ever sees it.

McNAMARA: Would you be willing to come back in the daytime on Friday?

LBJ: Yeah . . . they'll make me do that.

McNAMARA: Mr. President, I think we can eliminate the honor guard at the
receiving end, which is the visible part of the fighter display. The cap above won't
be detectable. . . . I'll be quite frank with you. If I were you, I wouldn't do a damn
bit of it. . . .

---

[1] What Johnson really wanted from Stevenson was to butt out.
[2] The Johnsons were to call on Joseph and Rose Kennedy in Palm Beach. Lady Bird dictated
into her diary after they did that "though well tanned, well cared for in every medical and
material way," the elder Kennedy was "a terribly sad figure. . . . He does not talk (at least he
did not to us) and I could not help but think . . . that I would hope for Lyndon it would be a
sudden going—although at a very distant time and nicely venerable age" (February 27, 1964).

LBJ: . . . I've got two house detectives up there and they're going to want to play cops and robbers, and boy, they love 'em. I'll tell you. I've got 'em around me here now. . . . You know how many White House police I've got over here? Three hundred! It's unthinkable. You ought to have about three gates, and you ought to have one on each gate and three shifts and you ought to have fifteen. . . . I don't know how many Secret Service, but I know one time they had me about thirty when I was Vice President, till I fired a bunch of 'em. To me, they advertise it, cause more trouble. . . . Do you just say we don't have any honor guard and if your men want to be flying in that area at that time, normal test flights, well that's all right. . . . But I don't want it done on my account.

McNAMARA: . . . I'll be quite frank with you. I don't think that jets and landing are worth a damn in protection against a propeller-driven plane that wants to kamakaze you. . . .

LBJ: Get me out of it some way.[1]

SATURDAY, FEBRUARY 29, 1964

WILLIAM S. WHITE
3:00 P.M.

ALWAYS SEARCHING for techniques with which to improve his performance at press conferences, today LBJ answered questions while sitting behind a low podium. For the first time, Johnson's session was televised.

LBJ: I'm going to have one next week, but I'm going to call them in and give them news when I've got it. I just don't want to say that you got to go at four o'clock, because Kennedy did something in a certain auditorium at a certain place, that you've got to do it the same way, because I thought—I participated in a lot of the Kennedy ones,[2] and I thought that it was . . . vaudeville. . . .

WHITE: Absolutely, it was [laughs] just theater.

LBJ: [laughs] I sat down with them every morning. They'd go over a hundred questions and then plant fifteen of them, and there'd be twenty of them asked and boy, he'd be a great hero.[3]

[1] When Johnson flew into Miami, his plane was shielded from thousands of feet above by fighter interceptors.
[2] Meaning that Johnson would sit with Kennedy and his people the morning before he gave a press conference.
[3] This is said with a trace of resentment and envy. Lady Bird dictated into her diary that "going to the beauty parlor . . . cost me hearing Lyndon's first TV press conference. I did get to listen to the last part of it on the radio and it was strong and good. But I wouldn't say the A-plus performance that he puts in when it's just a face-to-face encounter. . . . TV is still to him a sort of bête noire, and so I feel angry at myself that I didn't somehow work it out to be where I could watch it every moment and give him a critique—honest, if not reassuring" (February 29, 1964).

JACK VALENTI
3:50 P.M.

AT THE PRESS CONFERENCE, a reporter had asked LBJ to clarify a statement he had made in a February 21 speech at the University of California at Los Angeles that those outside South Vietnam who were supplying rebels were playing "a deeply dangerous game."[1]

LBJ: Who was it that asked me that "dangerous game" in Vietnam?

VALENTI: I don't remember, Mr. President. . . . Pierre[2] has it all written down.

LBJ: You know, I wasn't really responsive to this question—"Mr. President, would you further say the situation in the Far East, in line with Mr. Bundy's appointment[3] there and the problems that he may face"—and I just talked about how he was appointed.

VALENTI: That was right, sir. But that was one of the first questions that was given to you, and you hadn't really warmed up.

LBJ: No, no. It was the last question.[4] . . . And he interrupted me. I was still going.

GEORGE SMATHERS
9:00 P.M.

THE *Miami Herald* has broken the story of the Cuban threats against Johnson's life and the measures taken to protect the President in Florida. The *New York Herald Tribune* has fingered Smathers as the *Herald*'s anonymous source. Under pressure from the FBI to track down the origin of the *Herald* story, LBJ angrily interrogates his friend, the Florida Senator.

LBJ: What about this *Miami Herald* that says you told them about the jet?

SMATHERS: The *Herald* didn't say I told them about the jet because I haven't talked with a single soul.

LBJ: That's what it says: "It is known that a principal source to the *Miami Herald* was Florida Senator George Smathers." That's what that son of a bitch told the FBI.

SMATHERS: Well, that's not printed, and you're pulling my leg. [laughs]

LBJ: No, I'm not! I'm reading from Douglas Kiker in the *Herald Tribune*. [reads aloud further from newspaper:] "Behind Johnson's big Miami alert, a tip on a Cuban attack on him in the air. . . . The White House . . . had been told that a Cuban guided missile might be launched toward the President's blue-and-white

---

[1] This line was intended to upbraid not only Ho Chi Minh but also de Gaulle.
[2] Salinger.
[3] William Bundy's appointment as Assistant Secretary of State for the Far East.
[4] Johnson was right.

707. The newspaper story did not say whether the Cuban suicide pilot was an exile or a Castro sympathizer. . . ."

SMATHERS: . . . I have not talked with a single person on the *Miami Herald*. The *Miami Herald* and I are having a feud. . . .

LBJ: He's just laying it onto you.

SMATHERS: . . . I'll give you my word of honor it's a total and complete absolute falsification. . . . I absolutely did not say the first damn thing to anybody about it.

•   •   •   •

LBJ: Well, the FBI wanted to know who I had talked to . . . and they told me to just deny everything and say nothing happened, which I have done up to now. I said, "I'm not going to talk about security." . . . I felt reasonably sure you didn't tell them, but I thought maybe you might have talked to somebody else and they might have told them. You know, someone like Bebe[1] or someone. But it's out and they've got it and they're going to give us hell about it for three or four days, I guess.

SMATHERS: . . . I don't think it hurts you at all. As a matter of fact, I think the net result of it is, when they said that you walked out in the crowds and everything, I think it makes you look good.

•   •   •   •

SMATHERS: Everybody's predicting—every paper in the state—that you're going to carry Florida. . . . How do you feel?

LBJ: Oh, I had my throat sprayed a time or two, and took a long nap yesterday. I was up all the night before and that goddamn fine hotel of yours burned me up. I was so hot that I couldn't sleep.

---

[1]Bebe Rebozo, the Cuban-American Key Biscayne banker who was a chum of JFK's and Smathers's as well as Richard Nixon's closest friend.

Chapter Five

MARCH 1964

MONDAY, MARCH 2, 1964

ROBERT McNAMARA
11:00 A.M.

TWO DAYS after Johnson's press conference, Chalmers Roberts of the *Washington Post* and other reporters are fastening on LBJ's comment in Los Angeles that the North Vietnamese were playing a "deeply dangerous game." They interpret the statement as a threat to invade North Vietnam with force. Irritated that he may have given critics an opening with which to charge that he is secretly plotting a vast land war in Asia, Johnson asks McNamara for specific language for him to use in the future that will suggest to the public that he has made no final decisions on Vietnam.

During this period, Johnson privately shows himself determined, if possible, to defer irrevocable decisions on war in Southeast Asia until the 1964 presidential election is over. Eager to win the presidency in a landslide, he wishes to appear neither soft on Communism nor frighteningly ready to take the nation into a war of unimaginable cost—even if this means leaving Americans confused about his inner inclinations.

Certainly Johnson was reluctant to make crucial decisions amid the heat and pressures of a campaign, if he could help it.[1] But his approach kept Americans from fully knowing whom and what they were voting for in 1964. It also

---

[1] Johnson may have been influenced by memories of how badly critical foreign affairs decisions had been debated in the presidential campaigns of his lifetime. In 1916, during the first presidential race he remembered (see conversation with Isabelle Shelton, March 21, 1964, below), his boyhood hero Woodrow Wilson had campaigned under the misleading slogan "He Kept Us Out of War." In 1940, his adult hero Franklin Roosevelt was not entirely forthright with Americans about his private dealings with Britain and the possibility that he might take Americans into the Second World War. In 1952, Dwight Eisenhower uttered pledges to roll back Communism that he privately did not mean. In 1960, John Kennedy artificially positioned himself as more aggressive than Richard Nixon about saving Cuba from Castro.

tragically foreclosed the possibility of a grand national debate that might have educated both Johnson and the American people as they faced one of the most important presidential decisions of the century—whether the United States should make a monumental commitment to war in Vietnam.

LBJ: I want you to dictate to me a memorandum—a couple of pages . . . so I can read it and study it and commit it to memory . . . on the situation in Vietnam. . . . I'd like for you to say that there are several courses that could be followed. We could send our own divisions . . . and our own Marines in there and they could start attacking the Vietcong. . . . We could come out of there . . . and let 'em neutralize South Vietnam and let the Communists take North Vietnam. And as soon as we get out, they could swallow up South Vietnam. . . . Or we could pull out and say, "To hell with you, we're going to have Fortress America. We're going home." And . . . here's what would happen in Thailand, and here's what would happen in the Philippines and come on back and get us back to Honolulu.

Or we can say this is the Vietnamese's war and they've got two hundred thousand men, they're untrained, and we've got to bring their morale up, and they have nothing really to fight for because of the type of government they've had. We can put in socially conscious people and try to get them to improve their own government . . . and we can train them how to fight. . . . And that, after considering all of these, it seems that the latter offers the best alternative for America to follow. Now if the latter has failed, then, we have to make another decision. But at this point it has not failed. And in the last month, X number of Vietcong were killed, and X number of South Vietnamese.[1] Last year twenty thousand killed to five thousand, while we lost a total of people, in one day in Korea, we lost one thousand, or whatever it is.

· · · ·

LBJ: I would like to have for this period, when everybody is asking me, something in my own words. I can say, why, here are the alternatives and here's our theory, and here's what we're basing it on, how we don't say that we'll win. We don't know. We're doing the best we can. We think we ought to have to train them. Why did you say you'd send a thousand home? And I'd put a sentence saying . . . because they completed their mission. And the illustration is that several hundred were working as military police and they're trained as military police, so we didn't need to keep them there. Why did McNamara say that they were coming back in '65? Because when you say that you're going to give a man a high school education, and he's in the tenth grade, and you've got two years to do it . . . that doesn't mean that everybody comes back, but that means that your training ought to be in pretty good shape by that time. . . . Now this morning— well now, here's a summary. . . . Erwin Canham, editor of the *Christian Science Monitor*, says the President's press conference was placid and calm and noninformative . . . and warned that public opinion is not prepared for a big Vietnam commitment such as the '62 Cuban showdown or Korea. Alexander Kendrick, ABC, says the answer cannot be delayed much longer and he warned that psycho-

[1] The Johnson administration's use of the body count as a measure of progress in Vietnam here begins.

logically, we're approaching the Yalu River again, where Chinese, and possibly Russian intervention must be expected.[1] Now they're all saying that following our speech in Los Angeles where we said that this was a very dangerous business—

McNAMARA: Mr. President, may I interrupt you? Who put the line in? . . .

LBJ: I don't know. . . . "Deeply dangerous game." But I don't see anything wrong with it. . . . I think it *is* deeply dangerous when anybody starts aggression. . . . I blew my top here for a whole damn week. I jumped on you and jumped on Rusk both why you were saying out in Saigon that you were invading North Vietnam—even if you *were* going to invade it.[2] . . . A lot of people in Saigon, they tell me, said that they got it from the State Department here, that Rostow[3] had a propaganda move on to really invade North Vietnam. . . . Now they want to hang it on a little higher person and say that *I* indicated that we're going to invade Vietnam or that we're going to hit the Chinese, or that we're going to bomb Moscow. Now I didn't do any such thing. I said that this is deeply dangerous and it *is* deeply dangerous. It's dangerous for any nation to start aggression and start enveloping neutral, freedom-loving people. And I think it was dangerous to twenty thousand of them that got killed there last year. . . . They're trying to transfer this stuff that's been coming out of Saigon onto this deeply dangerous statement and we're just not doing it. . . . Wasn't this Los Angeles speech cleared with your department?

McNAMARA: No, I didn't see it.

LBJ: Well . . . it should have been.

· · · ·

LBJ: Do you think it's a mistake to explain what I'm saying now about Vietnam, and what we're faced with?

McNAMARA: I do think, Mr. President, it would be wise for you to say as little as possible.[4] The frank answer is we don't know what's going on out there. The signs I see coming through the cables are disturbing signs—poor morale in Vietnamese forces, poor morale in the armed forces, disunity, a tremendous amount of coup planning against Khanh. Not what you'd expect in the situation.

LBJ: Why don't we take some pretty offensive steps pretty quickly then? Why don't we commend Khanh on his operation and try to prop him up? Why don't we raise the salary of the soldiers to improve that morale instead of waiting a long time? Why don't we do some of these things that are inclined to bolster them? I sure as hell don't want to get in the position that Lodge recommended to me. The one thing he recommended was please give us a little more pay for our soldiers, and we turned him down.

---

[1] During the Korean War, Chinese Communist forces had crossed the Yalu River to attack U.N. forces.

[2] This sentence suggests Johnson's preference that even if Rusk and McNamara anticipated large-scale military action against North Vietnam, they should not say so publicly now.

[3] Walt Rostow, Director, State Department Policy Planning Staff.

[4] McNamara here advises that Johnson be cautious in letting the American people know how troubling the situation in Vietnam is.

McNAMARA: Oh no, we've done that.

LBJ: We haven't acted. We said we're going to wait until you go out there.

McNAMARA: He[1] knows that there's money for that. There's no problem on that issue.

LBJ: Why don't we clear it up so we get him answered?[2] . . . I'm not a military strategist, but I think that as long as we've got him there and he makes recommendations, we act on them. Particularly if we act favorably, we're not in too bad a condition politically. But I think when he wires us and says the only damn thing that you can do is give them an increase in pay because morale is terrible, and we say, well wait, then if something happens in between, I think we *are* caught with our britches down. . . .

McNAMARA: That raise has gone through.

LBJ: No, we told him that we'd wait.

McNAMARA: No . . . the Vietnamese people are getting the pay. . . . The only question . . . is whether AID[3] should increase the payment to the South Vietnamese government to offset the increase.

· · · ·

LBJ: Let's make a record on this thing, Bob. I'd like to have a wire out there to him nearly every day or so on something. Either approving what Lodge is recommending, or either trying to boost them up to do a little something extra. Now I've been rather impressed from the news reports of this fellow's[4] social consciousness. He's getting out into the villages and talking to people and offering them something that they claim that the Nhus and Diems[5] never gave them and that this other outfit that took over didn't have time to give them. And I was rather encouraged by Lodge's cable of yesterday, in which he said that he showed more efficiency than either of them.

McNAMARA: That's right.

LBJ: I don't know why his two hundred thousand are not showing some results, and why we keep saying everything is bad, looks blue.

McNAMARA: This is a question, Mr. President. We're not seeing the results yet. Maybe they'll come, but it's a very uncertain period. He is behaving properly. There's no doubt about that.

LBJ: Why don't we send Lodge a wire back and reply to the one he sent yesterday that we heartily agree with him? They ought to clear out an area . . . to please tell Khanh that we think this is absolutely essential to our continued morale here—or our continued support or something.

[1] Lodge.
[2] Johnson is especially worried about keeping Lodge mollified because Republicans are waging a Lodge-for-President write-in campaign in New Hampshire. He does not wish to give his Ambassador in Saigon a pretext for resigning in protest, coming home, and running against him for President, complaining to Americans that LBJ is doing too little to save South Vietnam.
[3] The U.S. Agency for International Development.
[4] Khanh.
[5] Ex-President Ngo Dinh Diem and his brother, Ngo Dinh Nhu, both assassinated in the November 1963 coup.

McNAMARA: Sure will do that.

LBJ: And then you get me this other paper on Vietnam, so that when people ask me questions, I have a smattering of information.[1]

ROBERT WAGNER
Mayor of New York
11:15 A.M.

> JOHNSON CALLS the New York Mayor at his official residence, Gracie Mansion, to ask about Wagner's wife, Susan Edwards Wagner, who is dying there of lung cancer.

LBJ: How's my girl doing?

WAGNER: Not very well, Mr. President. The doctor thinks it's just a matter of a few hours.

LBJ: Give her a big hug for me, and know that we're all thinking of you, and grieving with you. . . . I'd walk up there nekkid if there was something I could do.

WAGNER: Nothing we can do right now. It's in God's hands, but it doesn't look very good. The next few hours.

LBJ: Please give her a hug for me. She is a great lady, and you've made her mighty proud of you.[2]

JAMES ROWLEY
Chief, U.S. Secret Service
11:25 P.M.

> JOHNSON RENEWS his complaints about the Secret Service and his other bodyguards. This time he is worried that the press and Congress will castigate him for extravagance.

LBJ: Jim, I want a report of the number of people assigned to Kennedy the day he died, and the number assigned to me now. And if mine are not less, I want 'em less right quick.

ROWLEY: Yes, sir.

LBJ: And I mean a substantial less because I'm staying right in this house.[3] I won't even go to the bathroom if I have to have more people. And I don't know who has charge of the White House Police.

---

[1] McNamara sent Johnson a two-page memo saying, "Our purpose in South Vietnam is to help the Vietnamese maintain their independence. We are providing the training and the logistic support which they cannot provide themselves. We will continue to provide that support as long as it is required" (McNamara to LBJ, March 2, 1964, Johnson Library).

[2] Mrs. Wagner died eighty minutes after this call.

[3] The White House. Johnson is suggesting that he will not commute to the LBJ Ranch the way JFK did to Hyannis Port and Palm Beach.

ROWLEY: Major Stover.

LBJ: They're about ten to one around here for what we need. So you get with him today, and tell him that these hearings are coming up[1] . . . and if I can't ever go to the bathroom, I won't go. I promise you I won't go anywhere. I'll just stay right behind these black gates. But I don't need eight people following me to church, and one man, Secret Service, driving me and one in the car with me and maybe two or three behind me is all right, but yesterday you had six or seven of them in there. And Walter Trohan has got a column this morning, saying that because I turned out the lights you had to increase your security.[2]

ROWLEY: That isn't so.

LBJ: Of course, it's not so. But I want the figures. These boys that need jobs, put them to counterfeiting or something else. Because if you don't do it, I'll commit suicide.

ROWLEY: . . . As you know, we carried Rufus and Lem Johns from your detail.[3] Otherwise we have the same number of people—the exact number.

LBJ: You just get them down now. . . . We've got daughters and we got wives and we've got other things, but I want less when I go into this campaign than you had before the assassination. . . . If you don't want me to go to church, I'll just go to have a preacher come here. . . . I'll have my own little chapel right here in the White House. . . . Just tell them that that is an order from the President.

DEAN RUSK
11:35 A.M.

JOHNSON ASKS Rusk to pursue the policy for containing Henry Cabot Lodge that he has worked out with McNamara.

LBJ: Lodge is a long ways from here, and he's thinking of New Hampshire and he's thinking of his defeats in the Republican party[4] and he's feeling sorry for himself and he's naturally a martyr.

RUSK: Right.

LBJ: . . . And every time he sends us a cable I'd like to get one right back to him, complimenting him and agreeing with him . . . if it's at all possible. . . . In these cables he says that he's told them to clear out an area and let's have a victory. And I want to tell him right back, "Three cheers! I think your suggestion is a good one." And I think that we got to build that record.[5] He says he wants a

[1] Hearings before the Senate and House Appropriations Committees on the budget for the Executive Office of the President and the Treasury Department, which oversees the Secret Service.
[2] Trohan, a *Chicago Tribune* columnist, referred to LBJ's order to reduce White House lights.
[3] Rufus Youngblood and Lem Johns had served on Johnson's vice presidential detail.
[4] Lodge was turned out of the Senate by John Kennedy in 1952 and, as Nixon's running mate, was defeated for Vice President by Johnson in 1960.
[5] In other words, build a documentary record of endorsing or exceeding Lodge's demands for tougher action against North Vietnam, so that in case he resigns and runs for President, Johnson will have evidence with which to show that he had been just as fierce against Hanoi as Lodge, if not more so.

raise for the army[1] out there. If we can possibly get it, I think we ought to give it to him. They're going to say the morale's no damn good. The soldiers won't fight, and then Lodge is going to come up here before some committee, and say, "I sent Rusk a wire here and told him to please do this, and he said, 'Wait until next month.' In the meantime, the thing caved in." I think we've got to watch what that fellow says. Just be Johnny-on-the-spot and have a runner the moment his cable hits come right to you, and before it goes back you write out a longhand one and check it and let's get right back to him so that he knows he's Mister God, and we're giving him maximum attention.

GEORGE BALL
11:50 A.M.

JOHNSON HAS BEEN TOLD that students are marching past the U.S. embassy in Athens, shouting "Yankee Go Home," hoisting posters lampooning LBJ as a stooge of the Turkish Cypriots and demanding removal of the U.S. Sixth Fleet from waters off Greece.

LBJ: Why are they parading over there with my picture and giving me hell?
BALL: They're just steamed up. But I think just as soon as this thing gets settled . . . it'll die down again.

. . . .

LBJ: I think somebody ought to brief the Foreign Relations Committee pretty quick on the Vietnam situation. I notice about four Senators this morning raising hell about the uncertainty and everything and I think we ought to go over the alternatives with them and try to let them see we're doing the right thing.

McGEORGE BUNDY
12:35 P.M.

JOHNSON SPEAKS with Bundy about his balancing act on Vietnam.

BUNDY: I've got a lunch with Joe Alsop. You got any messages for him?
LBJ: No, except—
BUNDY: I think I'm going to stay away from Vietnam. I think he really wants to have a little old war out there.[2]
LBJ: I'd ask him what his program is. I'd ask him if he wants to send people in there and start another Korea. He didn't say the other day in his column. He just said that it's really going to wreck me. But tell him we'd like to have his recommendation.
BUNDY: What is your own internal thinking on this, Mr. President? That we've just got to stick on this middle course as long as there's any possible hope?

[1] South Vietnamese army.
[2] The hawkish Alsop had been writing some columns implying that LBJ was being too timid about Vietnam.

LBJ: I just can't believe that we can't take fifteen thousand advisers and two hundred thousand people[1] and maintain the status quo for six months.[2] I just believe we can do that if we do it right now. I don't know enough about it to know.

BUNDY: God knows, I don't. The only thing that scares me is that the government[3] would up and quit on us, or that there would be a coup and we get invited out.[4]

LBJ: There may be another coup, but I don't know what we can do if there is. . . . What alternatives do we have then? We're not going to send our *troops* in there, are we?[5]

BUNDY: The one thing that I think you might find, that I think Bob[6] ought at least to look at, is whether a stiffener in the sense of another couple of thousand people would have the psych[7]—it's not because they're needed to win the war but only because they're needed to show that we think this damn thing can be done. I think there is a problem that is essentially a state-of-mind problem. . . . We've got to go over the checklist . . . with McNamara and get your sense of what the costs and values are before he goes,[8] so that he has a complete picture of the possible choices.

LBJ: . . . Why don't you get anybody else that you think that's got any fresh ideas or new ones? I'd ask Joe[9] what he recommends.

BUNDY: I will just say we're at a listening stage . . . because I don't want to give him anything to bite on on that area at the moment. He incidentally is all cheered up because he was very wary of Hilsman and thinks that Bill's going in there is in itself sort of a solution to the problem.[10] It's not. No one man is going to solve a headache like this one.

LBJ: No, but if we can keep him aboard, he ought to be aboard. But his two or three columns haven't helped us any now.

---

[1] American and South Vietnamese, respectively.

[2] Or eight months. Johnson here succinctly captures his aim of moving the next major decision point on Vietnam past the next election.

[3] Of South Vietnam.

[4] Bundy's comment does nothing to underscore the insistence of Mike Mansfield, some of President Kennedy's aides, and others that had JFK lived to win a second term, he would have then withdrawn from Vietnam. Kenneth O'Donnell and David Powers, for example, wrote in their 1972 memoirs that when Kennedy told them that he intended to disengage, they asked how he could do so without damaging American prestige, and the President replied, "Easy. Put a government in there that will ask us to leave" (*"Johnny, We Hardly Knew Ye,"* p. 18).

[5] Johnson presumably means that the United States would not respond to another coup by sending in U.S. troops. This is a serious worry because he is getting reports of coup plots against General Khanh. Should the general be overthrown before the 1964 election and LBJ be compelled to send in troops, he would be forced to make exactly the decision during the heat of the campaign that he would prefer to defer.

[6] McNamara.

[7] Presumably Bundy is about to say "psychological effect."

[8] To Saigon.

[9] Alsop.

[10] LBJ had appointed Bundy's brother William to replace the dovish Roger Hilsman as Assistant Secretary of State for the Far East. Johnson particularly blamed Hilsman for pushing the coup against Diem.

J. WILLIAM FULBRIGHT
8:50 P.M.

LBJ: I think we got a good thing working for us economy-wise. . . . I think we got prosperity, and our market hit over 800, and I'm rather pleased, and the thing I'm worried about now is they tell me that some of our boys are afraid our unemployment is going to get down under 3 percent and we may have inflation. . . . I guess a little inflation is good for you in an election year.

FULBRIGHT: Yeah, I wouldn't worry about that yet. . . .

LBJ: . . . So maybe if we can just get our foreign policy straightened out, now, of course—

FULBRIGHT: Yeah, get that damn Vietnam straightened out. Any hope on that?

LBJ: We've got about four possibilities. [aside, to aide:] Go on and get me that memo on Vietnam that I had on my desk.[1]

FULBRIGHT: That's the most difficult one, I think, at the moment.

LBJ: [back to Fulbright:] The only thing I know to do is do more of the same and do it more efficiently. . . . I want to take one minute here to read you what I think is the best summary of it we have, because I had it this afternoon for some folks I talked to. [reading from statement while interjecting his own comments:] Our purpose in South Vietnam is to help the Vietnamese maintain their independence. . . . Without our support . . . Vietnam will collapse and the ripple effect will be felt throughout Southeast Asia. . . . Number two, we can seek a formula that will neutralize South Vietnam . . . but any such formula will only lead in the end to the same results of withdrawing support. . . . Three, we can send the Marines, à la Goldwater . . . but . . . our men may well be bogged down in a long war against numerically superior North Vietnamese, and Chi Com[2] forces ten thousand miles from home. . . . Four, we continue our present policy of providing training and logistical support for the South Vietnam forces. This policy has not failed. . . . Secretary McNamara's trip to South Vietnam will provide us with an opportunity to again appraise the future prospects of this policy, and the further alternatives that may be available to us.

FULBRIGHT: . . . That's exactly what I'd arrive at under these circumstances, at least for the foreseeable future.

LBJ: All right. Now, when he comes back, though, and we're losing what we're doing, we got to decide whether to send them in or whether to come out and let the dominoes fall.[3] That's where the tough one's going to be. And you do some heavy thinking. As the little Jewish boy said, do some heavy thinking, and let's decide what we do. Okay?

FULBRIGHT: Righto.

[1] "Summary Statement on South Vietnam," Department of Defense, March 2, 1964, Johnson Library.
[2] Chinese Communist.
[3] This suggests that LBJ feels he may have to arrive, at least privately, at a major decision on Vietnam much earlier than the fall of 1964.

LBJ: Give Betty my love.

FULBRIGHT: How's Lady Bird standing up?

LBJ: . . . She and my two daughters are against the White House. They want to go back to Johnson City. Say it's too much strain.

WEDNESDAY, MARCH 4, 1964

OFFICE CONVERSATION
1:48 P.M.

> JOHNSON TRIES to track down a new leak to the press.

LBJ: [to aides:] Who is leaking this poverty stuff that's making such a damned mess? Shriver himself is bound to be doing some of this. . . . You read the *Baltimore Sun* story?[1] . . . Well, it must be the Attorney General, 'cause I saw a lot on what the Justice Department's been doing in these various cities. You notice that?

WALT ROSTOW
Director, State Department Policy Planning Staff
6:05 P.M.

> JOHNSON WANTS to ensure that neither Rostow[2] nor anyone in the administration disrupts his carefully constructed public position on Vietnam.

LBJ: Walt, we've got a little discussion that Mr. Rostow has been speaking for the administration and raising hell about having a little war up in North Vietnam, and some of the reporters are quoting around here that Chalmers Roberts[3] . . . on my California speech, on which you pointed out that this meant was going to trigger an offensive in North Vietnam. . . . Have you had any talks with Chalmers Roberts about North Vietnam?

ROSTOW: . . . There have been a set of fellows coming in, sir, to see me over the last three weeks and I've told them all exactly the same story. One, the position of the administration is that we are going to hold Southeast Asia. Two, that we are now proceeding . . . to make the most of the situation within present terms of reference. Three, in accordance with the President's reference in the

---

[1] In a page-one story in the *Baltimore Sun* that morning, Philip Potter had reported that Sargent Shriver's planners were pushing for a new federal anti-poverty agency which, among other things, would encourage community action programs such as the President's Committee on Juvenile Delinquency, chaired since 1961 by Robert Kennedy. Potter went on to describe programs sponsored by RFK's committee in New York and Charleston, West Virginia.
[2] Whom he will appoint to replace Bundy as National Security Adviser in 1966.
[3] Of the *Washington Post.*

State of the Union message . . . to Hanoi and Havana and other remarks, we're obviously thinking about the problem of the crossing of frontiers.[1] But . . . that will await the return of McNamara. . . .

LBJ: [annoyed:] Number one, I wouldn't talk to 'em about it at all. Number two, the President doesn't know the position of the administration, so *you* can't know it. And number three . . . you call them in and you give them this pitch, then they come to me, and I unload on them to tell them they've got no right to be writing it because I don't have any knowledge of any plans this administration has to do that. . . . Until we do, let's don't make ourselves subject to the charge that we're having . . . spokesmen in the State Department saying one thing, and the President saying the other. Elie[2] the night before last went on television . . . and he says that the administration's very cruel to the poor, unassuming reporters because the administration calls them in and tells them we're going to war in North Vietnam, and then Johnson says, "I didn't say any such thing." Which I haven't said.

ROSTOW: . . . I told no one anything of that kind.

LBJ: Well, you just be careful about talking to 'em, because they're quoting you as advocating Plan Six, or Plan Something Else that I don't know anything about.

McGEORGE BUNDY
7:26 P.M.

JOHNSON EMERGES from a session on Vietnam with the Joint Chiefs of Staff. Two days earlier, the Chiefs had advised in a memo that "preventing the loss of South Vietnam" was of "overriding importance" to the United States. They had insisted that the United States be prepared to destroy North Vietnamese military and industrial targets, mine harbors, and wage a naval blockade, even if these measures caused China to intervene in the conflict and even if nuclear weapons might be required to finish the job.[3]

LBJ: I just spent a lot of time with the Joint Chiefs. The net of it . . . is—they say, get in or get out. And I told them, "Let's try to find an amendment that will —we haven't got any Congress that will go with us, and we haven't got any

[1] Johnson had told Congress, "In 1964, we will be better prepared than ever before to defend the cause of freedom, whether it is threatened by outright aggression or by the infiltration practiced by those in Hanoi and Havana who ship arms and men across international borders to foment insurrection."
[2] NBC television correspondent Elie Abel.
[3] Joint Chiefs of Staff to McNamara, March 2, 1964, in *Foreign Relations of the United States, Volume I, Vietnam 1964* (U.S. Government Printing Office, 1992; hereafter cited as *FRUS*), pp. 112–18. After the meeting General Maxwell Taylor, Chairman of the Joint Chiefs, recorded, "It is quite apparent that he does not want to lose South Vietnam before next November nor does he want to get the country into the war. The President is impressed with the danger of another coup. He feels we must make General Khanh 'our boy' and proclaim that fact to all and sundry. He wants to see Khanh in the newspapers with McNamara and Taylor holding up his arms" (Taylor Memorandum of Conversation, March 4, 1964, in *FRUS*, pp. 129–30).

mothers that will go with us in a war."[1] And nine months I'm just an inherited —I'm a trustee. I've got to win an election. Or Nixon[2] or somebody else has. And then you can make a decision. But in the meantime, let's see if we can't find enough things to do to keep them[3] off base, and to stop these shipments that are coming in from Laos, and take a few selected targets to upset them a little bit,[4] without getting another Korean operation[5] started. Taylor[6] doesn't think that there'll ever be a Korean operation. The Marine man does. The Navy man is between the Marine and Taylor. The Air Force thinks that it will be a Korean-type operation. The Army, well, didn't say much.[7] But Taylor thinks that you've got to pick some specific targets.[8] . . . So I told him to make up a list of everything. . . . He's got his ideas now, and let's see what he does after his trip.[9]

BUNDY: All right.

LBJ: Then I think that he ought to meet with us and McNamara before they go tomorrow.

BUNDY: You've got an NSC meeting, and it's on the subject, Mr. President. . . .

LBJ: I think that we ought to meet with him a minute beforehand.

BUNDY: I'm going to have a draft letter to Lodge for you in the morning, and I think it's also important to have a letter of instruction to McNamara, because one thing they're particularly wary on is that they don't want anybody on this trip coming back with two different plans. . . . You don't want people—John McCone, especially, has a way of saving *his* skin—to be blunt about it.[10]

LBJ: That's right.

JACK VALENTI
8:50 P.M.

Valenti calls Johnson at the White House from the Statler Hilton in Washington, where the President is to present the first Eleanor Roosevelt Memorial Award at 9:20 P.M.

VALENTI: This is a real festive crowd. . . . It's packed. I'm going to suggest you may want to reconsider and make some of those appointments[11] tonight.

[1] Here Johnson shows his worry that neither the American people nor Congress favors large-scale involvement in Vietnam. As a critic of Truman's decision to fight the Korean War without a war declaration by Congress, he is suggesting that before he acts, he will want some kind of congressional amendment or resolution.

[2] At this point, LBJ still thinks that Nixon will probably be his 1964 opponent. He cannot believe that he will be lucky enough to get Goldwater.

[3] The North Vietnamese.

[4] Here Johnson refers to Op Plan 34-A.

[5] Meaning U.S. military action in Vietnam on the scale of Korea, 1950–1953.

[6] General Maxwell Taylor.

[7] Johnson refers to Marine Commandant General Wallace Greene, Chief of Naval Operations Admiral David McDonald, Air Force Chief of Staff General Curtis LeMay, and Army Chief of Staff General Earle Wheeler.

[8] In North Vietnam.

[9] Taylor is accompanying McNamara to South Vietnam.

[10] McCone was to accompany McNamara to Saigon, along with General Taylor, Assistant Secretary of State William Bundy, and David Bell, Director of AID.

[11] Of women to administration positions.

LBJ: . . . Festive. . . . But what about this festive bunch of sons of bitches[1]—three hundred of them tomorrow—that'll say we didn't have any biographies and we didn't have any news leads, and Pierre will say, "I told you not to."

VALENTI: . . . As far as the biographies are concerned, Pierre has them.

LBJ: But he's not available tonight. He's going to another dinner.

VALENTI: Kilduff[2] is handling it here over here, Mr. President. . . . The only one that I wouldn't announce is the Ambassador.[3]

LBJ: . . . That's the only one that's worth a damn. . . . And Liz[4] leaked it, and that made me mad as hell.[5]

FRIDAY, MARCH 6, 1964

HARRY TRUMAN

Thirty-third President of the United States

8:45 P.M.

   JOHNSON WAS SITTING in the lounge adjoining the Oval Office with his reporter friend Marianne Means when Lady Bird dropped in at 8:25 P.M. to ask him to come home.[6] With his wife and Means at his side, LBJ calls Harry

[1] Reporters.

[2] Malcolm Kilduff, Assistant White House Press Secretary.

[3] Katherine White was about to be appointed Ambassador to Denmark. Johnson decided to go ahead and announce that she was to be an Ambassador but not which country, saying that "the country to which she is being appointed is being notified tonight."

[4] Carpenter.

[5] When Johnson went to the Eleanor Roosevelt banquet, he spotted Helen Gahagan Douglas and invited her to spend the night at the White House. Lady Bird later dictated into her diary, "He had supplied her, apparently, with my nightgown and robe and there she was on the third floor. So at breakfast I called her to come down in her robe (my robe) and have breakfast with me in my room while we watched Lyndon depart by helicopter from the South Lawn. . . . She is indeed the same vivid person I knew back in 1949–50, somewhere along there. . . . She's an extraordinarily handsome woman, with an enormous appetite for life, an encyclopedic accumulation of information and a regular machine gun way of imparting it—rat-a-tat-tat. I spent a wonderful hour and a half with her, at the end of which I had gotten in probably two dozen words, was exhausted and had simply *loved* it" (March 5, 1964). Years later, after Douglas publicly criticized LBJ's handling of the Vietnam War, she greeted him in a White House receiving line and received back only a silent glare from Johnson (Helen Gahagan Douglas oral history, Johnson Library).

[6] Lady Bird later dictated into her diary that "rather late in the day, I began to wish I could jar loose Lyndon from his office, so I went there, determined to be very pleasant if I couldn't get him to come home and found him talking to Marianne Means. I had a drink with them, asked her to dinner. We picked up Gerri Whittington [the black woman who was LBJ's new secretary]. We stopped off by the pool. We found suits for both of them. . . . Called up Marianne's date and asked him to join us, which he did presently. . . . Lyndon was astonished that Gerri Whittington couldn't swim and in his very forthright way, he said, "What's the matter, couldn't you go in any public pools?" And she, I must say, with very creditable poise, said, "That is right, so I never learned to swim." . . . Lyndon and I and Gerri and Marianne and her date . . . had dinner and Lyndon rushed off, very much against my wishes, to put in an appearance at the Mexican Inter-Parliamentary dinner. It's simply that I wish he would spare himself

Truman at his home in Independence, Missouri. Reminded that the thirty-third President helped to save Greece and Turkey from Soviet aggression in the late 1940s, he wants Truman to represent him at the funeral of King Paul I of Greece. Truman was in 1964 by no means the great American folk figure he became after death. Shadowed by the Korean War and corruption charges, he had left office deeply unpopular. His relations with President Kennedy, whom he had denounced before the 1960 Democratic convention as a stooge of his father, whom Truman loathed, were little more than correct. But Truman has an old and cordial history with Johnson, dating to their years together in Congress. Johnson knows that having the former President ostentatiously in his corner in 1964 will win him friends among old-line Democrats. He is also eager to show the old man some respect and honor in his own time.

LBJ: I hope that I didn't call you too late. . . .

TRUMAN: Oh, no, it's plenty early out here.

LBJ: How are you getting along?

TRUMAN: Oh, just fine. I hope you are. Well, I *know* you are.

LBJ: I'm just catching hell every day.

TRUMAN: That's a sign that you're doing the right thing. I've been through it. [laughs]

LBJ: I was down here talking to Dick Russell today and he was bragging on you at lunch. He said that you make the best decisions that any President ever made, because you just told them that you didn't give a damn. You was going to do what you wanted to do—what's right.

TRUMAN: [laughs] He's wrong about that.

LBJ: Said you just told them you didn't give a damn what they thought. You was going to do what you thought was right.

TRUMAN: That's all I ever tried to do. I got all the information I could before I made 'em. But they seem to have turned out pretty well. I hope that they did anyway.

LBJ: Sure did. . . . How's Mrs. Truman?

TRUMAN: Oh, she's all right.

LBJ: Why don't you take her and Lady Bird, and let me send the presidential plane out there to pick you up and in the next day or two you fly over to King Paul's funeral?

TRUMAN: Fly over where?

LBJ: King Paul's funeral in Greece.

TRUMAN: . . . I don't have anything to do, and I would like very much to do it, if you want me to.

LBJ: I want you to. They want the best people, the biggest people we can get in this country. They think that the President ought to go. Now I can't go. I can't leave.

---

the unnecessary effort and save that effort for top-notch priority things and for hopefully a longer life with me and Luci and Lynda" (March 6, 1964).

TRUMAN: I know you can't.

LBJ: And I figure the two next biggest ones I can get is you and Lady Bird and Miz Truman.

TRUMAN: Oh, well, that's mighty nice. I don't think that she can go either. She's tied up here.

LBJ: Tell her we'll send a maid with her. We'll send somebody to take care of her. She can sleep all the way over. And that Lady Bird will fix her a good old-fashioned—bourbon and water—whenever she wants it.

TRUMAN: [laughs] Let me consult her about it. . . .

LBJ: You consult her and if she can't go, you've *got* to go. Because I can't go. You told me that you would. These Greek people love you. There're a few crackpots, but they love you. . . . It's very serious. There's four times as many Greeks on Cyprus as there are Turks, and they're both our friends. And the Greeks have been killing the Turks over there. And the Turks wanted to invade them. . . . And we told the Greeks, "You've got to quit killing them."

TRUMAN: All right. That's the way to handle it.

LBJ: And they both kinda got a little bit peeved at us. But we worked it out in the United Nations and know they've got a mediator, and we've got it all settled, and they're going to mediate it.

TRUMAN: You handled it perfectly.

LBJ: I want to show them that we love them, and I wired . . . Queen Frederika.[1] . . . She had pneumonia, and her poor husband got a blood clot and now he winds up dying. And I just got to have the best I've got and the best that I've got is you and Lady Bird. She wants to say hello to you.

TRUMAN: I'll be glad to.

LADY BIRD: Mr. President?

TRUMAN: How are you?

LADY BIRD: I'm fine, and it would be so much more of a *meaningful* trip if *you* go along, because everybody remembers what you did in a time of real stress, when you had to put up or shut up over there.

TRUMAN: You tell the President I'll go if he wants me to.

LADY BIRD: That's wonderful and I would so much enjoy being with you.

TRUMAN: . . . I don't know whether the Madame can go or not, but I'll talk to her. . . . May I call the President tomorrow morning and tell him?

LADY BIRD: Yes sir. Just a second.

LBJ: I'll know probably in the morning when the funeral is and I'll call you back. And I'll have a plane pick you up, and you'll have a military aide to take care of you. And you don't need to worry about a thing. You'll be briefed on everything. And just don't run off. Don't stay over there with my wife! Just bring her back. That's all I ask.

---

[1] Of Greece.

SATURDAY, MARCH 7, 1964

JOHN McCORMACK
12:30 P.M.

LBJ: Yesterday they took a poll in North Dakota. And of the Republicans, Nixon had 58 and I had 30. Of the Democrats I had 95 and Nixon had none. So the Iowa poll shows that I run about 60 percent in Iowa today.

McCORMACK: Overall?

LBJ: Yeah. . . . Now they're going to cut us down. They're trying to slander us. . . . This Baker stuff they're working on all day, and, of course, both of Baker's business ventures[1] were after I left the leadership.[2] He worked for Mansfield, but they want to hook it onto me and I've never had any business ventures with him. But they want to do that and they're raising hell about my television and Mrs. Johnson owning a TV station and they're taking every advertiser—

McCORMACK: They haven't penetrated at all.

LBJ: Yeah, but they're trying and they're going to be mudslinging and sometime or other, some of you ought to just say that the Republican party does not add to its stature with its personal attacks and its mudslinging, and while the President made a hundred speeches defending Eisenhower from personal attacks and supporting him on his foreign relations,[3] they do nothing but attack him . . . and an attacker never gets anywhere. . . .

McCORMACK: I wish many times I wasn't a Speaker. I'd like to be on the floor like I used to.

LBJ: . . . You talk to those newspaper boys when they come around, off the record. . . . Just tell them that here's the contrast. Johnson and Rayburn . . . supported Eisenhower and held his hands up when Knowland would go to the back row and attack him.[4] . . . We said we don't believe you ought to be partisan. . . . Now Johnson gets in and the first thing they attack him on Panama, and he's working that out pretty good. So they attack him on Cuba. He's got that solved pretty well. They attack him on Cyprus, and he's got a United Nations resolution on that. Then they attack him on Zanzibar. And they give every enemy we've got a lot of encouragement that we're divided. We've worked Zanzibar out. Now the only thing we haven't got worked out is Vietnam, and Eisenhower got us into that.[5] And I inherited it. And it had three changes of government before I

---

[1] The ventures being investigated by the Senate.
[2] The majority leadership.
[3] While Johnson was Majority Leader.
[4] The 1950s, when LBJ and Speaker Sam Rayburn often protected President Eisenhower against the likes of his Senate Minority Leader, William Knowland of California, were a high-water mark of bipartisan cooperation between the White House and Congress.
[5] Johnson refers to Eisenhower's role in the 1954 founding of SEATO, binding America (as well as France, Britain, Australia, New Zealand, Thailand, the Philippines, and Pakistan) to defend Laos, Cambodia, and South Vietnam, as well as Eisenhower's written promises to help the Diem government defend itself.

even got in here. And I'm doing the best I can to work that out. And they're trying to destroy the morale by saying there ought to be a neutralization.[1] That Nixon is telling them what to do. And Rockefeller's got a different plan. And Goldwater wants to bomb them.

. . . .

LBJ: Bobby is running for Vice President up in New Hampshire and that is causing a lot of embarrassment. They've got an advertisement agency hired and they're trying to get more votes up there than I get.[2] And I can't do anything. So there won't be anybody writing in my name 'cause they assume I'm going to be President.

LADY BIRD JOHNSON
4:10 P.M.

AFTER WATCHING LBJ's 3:30 P.M. news conference, the First Lady dictated into her diary, "It took place in the East Room, the first time one was ever held there. I watched it from my room. . . . When the questions started, he was much more dramatic, much more interesting-looking and really a very creditable performance. Oh, how rough the questions were and how sorry I felt for him. Vietnam, de Gaulle, Bobby Kennedy. . . . I was reminded once more of a remark that Eisenhower was supposed to have said when he started to make a press conference—'Now I mount my weekly cross.' I guess the only way to know how the other fellow feels is to be in his shoes for awhile and I never have been married to a press man. After it was over, I phoned Lyndon to tell him how good I thought he had been."[3]

LADY BIRD: You want to listen for about one minute to my critique, or would you rather wait until tonight?

LBJ: Yes, ma'am. I'm willing now.

LADY BIRD: I thought you looked strong, firm, and like a reliable guy. Your looks were splendid. The close-ups were much better than the distance ones.

LBJ: You can't get them to do it.[4]

---

[1] This presumably means Charles de Gaulle, Walter Lippmann, and other champions of neutralizing Vietnam.

[2] Here Johnson shows his conviction that RFK is actually behind the New Hampshire vice presidential write-in movement and his assumption that RFK's motive is to get more votes than LBJ, in order to embarrass the President and, presumably, increase Kennedy's leverage at the Democratic convention. In a Johnson Library oral history, Kenneth O'Donnell much later denied that the Kennedys were ever behind LBJ's troubles with Bobby Baker. He recalled JFK in 1963 telling George Smathers, "Do you know how that would read if Bobby Baker was indicted tomorrow morning? . . . *Life* magazine would put twenty-seven pictures of these lovely-looking, buxom lasses running around with no clothes on, twenty-seven pictures of Bobby Baker and hoodlums and vending machines, and then the last picture would be of *me*. And . . . 99 percent of the people would think I was running around with the twenty-nine girls, because they don't read the story."

[3] Diary of Lady Bird Johnson, March 7, 1964, Johnson Library.

[4] Meaning that Johnson's press people cannot force the television networks to emphasize close-ups.

LADY BIRD: . . . During the statement[1] you were a little breathless and there was too much looking down and I think it was a little too fast. Not enough change of pace. Dropping voice at the end of sentence. There was a considerable pickup in drama and interest when the questioning began. Your voice was noticeably better and your facial expressions noticeably better.

. . . .

LADY BIRD: Every now and then, you need a good crisp answer for a change of pace and therefore I was glad when you answered one man, "The answer is *no* to both of your questions."[2] I thought your answer on Lodge was good.[3] I thought your answer on Vietnam was good.[4] I really didn't like the answer on de Gaulle[5] because . . . I believe you actually have said out loud that you don't believe you ought to go out of the country this year.[6] So I don't think you can very well say that you will meet him anytime that is convenient for both people.

LBJ: Well, when it can be arranged. I'm not going out of this country. I didn't say where I'd go. I didn't say I'd go out of the country at all, did I?

LADY BIRD: No, I guess.

LBJ: Press has reaffirmed that I wouldn't go.

LADY BIRD: I see. Uh-huh, well, I just didn't get the meaning of it that everybody else did. . . . When you're going to have a prepared text, you need to have the opportunity to study it a little bit more and to read it with a little more conviction and interest and change of pace.

LBJ: The trouble is they criticize you for taking so much time. They want to use it all for questions. Then their questions don't produce any news. And if you don't give them news, you catch hell. So my problem was trying to get through before ten minutes. And I still ran ten minutes today, and I took a third of it for questions and I could have taken, if I had read it like I wanted to, fifteen minutes. But I didn't know what to cut out. . . .

LADY BIRD: Um-hmm. I believe if I'd had that choice I would have used thirteen minutes or fourteen for the statement. In general, I'd say it was a good B-plus. How do you feel about it?

LBJ: I thought it was much better than last week.

LADY BIRD: I heard last week, see, and didn't see it and didn't hear all of it. At

---

[1] Johnson's opening statement.

[2] In reply to a double question on Soviet trade. In giving this answer, Johnson may have been subliminally thinking of the press conference shortly before Kennedy's assassination when JFK was asked whether, despite the Bobby Baker allegations, he wanted and expected LBJ to be on his 1964 ticket. Johnson was delighted to hear Kennedy say, "Yes to both questions."

[3] Asked about a write-in campaign for Lodge in New Hampshire and whether Lodge might resign, Johnson said, "I have every reason to believe that if he had any plans, he would make them known."

[4] Told of Republican complaints that the Johnson administration was "deliberately hiding the facts" on Vietnam, Johnson said, "I am not aware of anything that we are hiding. I don't want to get into any debates on the basis of partisanship. . . . I expect both Republicans and Democrats to work with this administration in attempting to help us do what is best for our country."

[5] Asked about a meeting with de Gaulle, Johnson said he would be happy to meet "anytime that it can be appropriately arranged."

[6] In Johnson's first address to Congress.

any rate, I felt sort of on safe ground—I mean, like you sort of had gotten over a hump psychologically and in other ways. It will be interesting to hear anybody else's reaction, and the Thornberrys[1] anyhow are awaiting a reasonably early dinner with us . . . and you do anything you want to about getting another couple or two to eat with us. And let me know. And I love you very much.

MONDAY, MARCH 9, 1964

PAUL MILLER
Chairman of the Board, Associated Press
4:02 P.M.

JOHNSON CARPS against press complaints about the way he staged his news conferences.

LBJ: When I sat down, they said I ought to stand up. When I stood up, they said I ought to sit down. When I had it in the State Department,[2] Mary McGrory[3] said the room was too dark. When I had it in the East Room, they said it was too light. And I don't give a damn. Just so it is comfortable for them. Arthur Sylvester,[4] who works at Defense—his boy[5] got up and said, "Why do you have us in this uncomfortable room where we're so crowded?" There were ten seats that weren't occupied. . . . When they tape them and play every bit of it without our correcting a word, they say that's not live. So you've got to give them four hours live. By that time, your news is out of date. . . . I counted up and I've been on television fourteen times in a hundred days. Kennedy had been on six. Eisenhower was on three. And I had about a dozen columns giving me hell for not being on television enough!

EDWIN WEISL, SR.
4:15 P.M.

JOHNSON CONFIDES his anxieties about Robert Kennedy's ambitions.

LBJ: Where are you?

WEISL: I'm in my office.[6]

LBJ: It sounds like you're way down in the walls somewhere.

[1] The Homer Thornberrys.
[2] The State Department Auditorium, where JFK met the press.
[3] Staff writer, *Washington Star.*
[4] Assistant Secretary of Defense for Public Affairs.
[5] Johnson probably refers to a Pentagon correspondent.
[6] In New York City.

WEISL: Can you hear me now?

LBJ: Yeah, we must have four or five lines tapped here.

. . . .

LBJ: Say, I don't want to discuss it with anybody. I'll discuss it with you when you get down here. I wouldn't even tell my daddy. But we have a friend. You know, it's kinda New Hampshire.[1] . . . It's . . . a whole lot worse than you could even believe. And he's having lunch today with the *Wall Street Journal*. They're getting a big article on Miz Johnson's TV. They're calling all afternoon to talk to Mr. Kellam.[2] And I found out that pretty definite that is where the Baker thing started.[3] And the *Journal* has gone back and trying to take all the logs[4] and calling everybody that ever had any business transactions and gone over to Frank Stanton[5] and they told Stanton that they'd been to ABC and NBC and that group at NBC had given them a lot of information and ABC had given them a lot of information. They wanted Stanton to. And Stanton said, "I just never had contact with anybody but Mr. Kellam." And they said, "I don't understand how you could do that from what ABC and NBC says."

WEISL: . . . I'd better call up Leonard and David[6]—don't you think?—to find out.

LBJ: . . . I think that'd probably just stir it up more. . . . The *Wall Street Journal* has just been all over Texas, gone into every business transaction we ever had. And this fellow had a big luncheon with them today. . . . He's doing that on the pretext of doing it for the library.[7] . . .

WEISL: . . . That is one of the vehicles they used in keeping the thing alive, you know. Did Walter[8] show you that letter I got from a county chairman?

LBJ: Nope.

WEISL: . . . He expressed great delight in having that particular fellow[9] out of the National Committee.

LBJ: . . . He went up to New Hampshire . . . to get the other fellow's[10] name written in and then had a fellow hotel owner from Florida call up and raise hell with the Governor and just say he'd be anti-Kennedy if he didn't get to work.[11] So the Governor came out. And I don't know how we ought to treat it. I guess, just ignore it.

[1] Johnson is referring to what he takes to be RFK's vice presidential efforts in New Hampshire.

[2] Johnson's business manager, Jesse Kellam.

[3] Johnson here is claiming that Robert Kennedy was behind the investigation of his ties to Bobby Baker.

[4] Of the Johnson television station.

[5] Of CBS.

[6] Network czars Leonard Goldenson of ABC and David Sarnoff of NBC.

[7] John F. Kennedy Library, to be built in Boston.

[8] Jenkins.

[9] Paul Corbin.

[10] Robert Kennedy's.

[11] On March 5, a Kennedy spokesman replied to reports that New Hampshire Democratic Governor John King was backing an RFK-for-Vice-President write-in campaign by saying that LBJ should choose his own running mate. King then announced his support for a joint Johnson-Kennedy write-in.

WEISL: . . . I don't think it means anything, do you?

LBJ: It will mean a lot in publicity 'cause it has already filled the papers here. The *Star* has got a big editorial today saying that the Kennedy name is "magic" and this means that he'll be swept in. And I talked to a fellow today who said that . . . *Newsweek* has a fellow named Iselin[1] and the *Star* has a woman named Miriam Ottenberg and Tony Lewis of the *Times*[2] and say they just sit inside the office[3] all the time. . . . They're directing it all right from there.

WEISL: Don't let it get your goat 'cause you are so strong and so beloved by the vast majority of the people that this isn't going to work. It is better to have gotten this off this early than later on, because I think it will be resented in many places.

LBJ: I don't understand though why the *Wall Street Journal*—I'm more conservative than any man they've had in twenty years.[4] Why they want to be getting me?

WEISL: . . . I can't understand it. Who owns that thing?

LBJ: I have no idea.

WEISL: I'll find out. You think it is this fellow Novak[5] that writes with Rowland Evans?

LBJ: Yeah.

WEISL: . . . I'll find out what is behind it because . . . their readers[6] are pro-Johnson people.

· · · ·

LBJ: I've got Edgar Hoover over today at lunch. They[7] forged a document saying—sent it out all to Latin America . . . saying that Mann[8] is a reactionary and a Wall Streeter and a rich man and trying to get tough.

WEISL: . . . If he'll be as tough as he ought to be and you back him up, why, you'll go down in history as one of the greatest Presidents.

· · · ·

LBJ: Now on Vietnam, when they[9] come back here they're going to make a choice. They're going to want us to go in or something else[10] and I don't see how we can do anything unless—

WEISL: What in the hell would we do there?

---

[1] John Jay Iselin, a *Newsweek* correspondent in Washington.

[2] *New York Times.*

[3] Robert Kennedy's office.

[4] Here Johnson claims that he is more conservative even than Eisenhower. Johnson is showing his 1964 strategy of trying to hold on to traditional Democratic liberals while subtly suggesting his conservatism to independents and Republicans with his overtures to business and his talk about thrift and frugality.

[5] Robert Novak had been a reporter for the *Journal* until 1963.

[6] *Wall Street Journal* readers.

[7] Latin American Communists.

[8] Thomas Mann of the State Department.

[9] McNamara and Taylor.

[10] Johnson has been much affected by the pressure from the Joint Chiefs for a decision. (See the March 4, 1964, conversation with Bundy above.)

LBJ: Now wait a minute. I think what we're going to have to do is have McNamara and about three or four people[1] sit and listen to them.[2] I don't trust many people and it has got to be kind of a private deal.[3] Till we see where we are, I'm not going to move. I'm not going to get this country in any extended area without some other people looking at it.[4]

WEISL: I did not want to go in there. But now that we're in there, I don't know how to get out.

LBJ: That's what you better be thinking about 'cause you're going to be one of the three or four in the meeting. So you go to sleep thinking about it tonight.

McGEORGE BUNDY
4:27 P.M.

LBJ: Mac, how worried are you about Cyprus?[5] Stevenson is down. He talked to me. He was a little worried about it. He's in Florida.

BUNDY: I think he's going on tickers and not anything more powerful than that, Mr. President. . . .

LBJ: He's going out with Miz Meyer[6] on a cruise for a week or so, so I guess our foreign policy will get in trouble.[7] . . .

BUNDY: [laughs] Okay, we'll batten down the hatches!

• • • •

LBJ: Are you handling things in New Hampshire for us all right?[8]

BUNDY: [laughs] Mr. President, I hope there is no misunderstanding on *that* one.[9] But you know what department that is in. That's not in mine. Now, how about this Arab-Israeli package, Mr. President? What do you want to do about that?[10]

[1] People whose judgment Johnson respects.
[2] McNamara and the others on his trip.
[3] Johnson is worried that any private debate within his administration about large-scale U.S. involvement in Vietnam will become public and frighten the American public in the wild atmosphere of a presidential election year.
[4] Johnson here shows how seriously he takes the possibility of large-scale involvement in Vietnam and his desire to get multiple sources of advice.
[5] The previous week, establishment of a new five-thousand-man Greek Cypriot auxiliary police force had provoked a practice landing of the kind that would precede a Turkish invasion of Cyprus by nine thousand Mainland Turks near Iskenderun. The U.N. Security Council responded by creating an international peacekeeping force and appointment of a mediator for Cyprus. Soon thereafter came more fighting and bomb blasts on the island.
[6] Katharine Graham's mother, Agnes Meyer, who was Stevenson's friend and admirer.
[7] With Bundy, who scorns the U.N. Ambassador even more than he does, LBJ jokes about Stevenson as superfluous.
[8] Johnson here tweaks Bundy about his links to the Kennedys and slyly puts Bundy in a position of having to disown the New Hampshire effort for RFK.
[9] In other words, Johnson should not doubt Bundy's loyalty.
[10] During consideration of aid to Israel and the Arabs, Bundy's aide Robert Komer had warned Johnson by memo about Israel's efforts for nuclear weapons and delivery systems: "Israeli acquisition of a missile capability will be highly expensive and, in our view, wasteful. Why should Israel waste its own money this way, while seeking economic and now military aid from us? . . . Our whole stand against nuclear proliferation will be adversely affected if Israel goes nuclear" (March 6, 1964, Johnson Library).

LBJ: I'm inclined to agree with you.

BUNDY: Do you want to talk with Mike[1] about it and then give him a chance to come back at you?

LBJ: Yes. What I would do is tell Mike that right after I came in,[2] we talked about it. First thing, you came in with suggestions and I talked to McNamara about it. I talked to you about it and my own judgment was we wanted to help them, but we better test things a little bit. We tested this desalinization, and said we'd do it for everybody. Then the Arabs just went wild. Now they're denouncing us. I don't know who it was this morning—was it Syria that hit us? Said that Johnson . . . gave a very inflammatory speech in which he said he was going to help them with desalinization. Of course, he said he would help everybody else, but they didn't read that. . . . Just say in the light of that, I think we better go a little slow. I wouldn't say how long, but just slow and slow and slow.[3]

BUNDY: I won't tell him when.

LBJ: Then we'll get him out there[4] and get him back.

BUNDY: Right.

LBJ: And say I'm afraid they'll . . . say that I'm sending him out there for that purpose and I'd rather wait until that is over with before we take any action, that you know I have in mind doing it.

BUNDY: Okay. But I don't want him to pass that to his friends[5] till he gets back and you'll lose the bargaining power.

LBJ: No, that's right. And tell him we've got a lot we've got to expect of them between now and November anyway and I want to wait till then. If they're so goddamned anxious to get me on the line, *they've* got to get on the line.[6]

BUNDY: [laughs loudly] Right!

J. EDGAR HOOVER
4:31 P.M.

JOHNSON EARLIER asked J. Edgar Hoover to investigate a news leak appearing in the first edition of this afternoon's *Washington Star*, which reported that, according to a "high source," advisers drawing up plans for the War on Poverty had recommended that the draft registration age be lowered. This would allow the Army general classification test to be given sooner so that needy youths could be given special education and job training.

[1]Myer Feldman, who was Jewish and well acquainted with Israeli officialdom and was considered by Kennedy and Bundy to be the house expert on Israeli wishes, although this was not his official duty. Privately Robert Kennedy carped, unfairly, in the spring of 1964 that Feldman's "major interest was Israel rather than the United States" (Robert Kennedy oral history, Kennedy Library).
[2]Into the presidency.
[3]Namely, drag out the issue until after the 1964 election.
[4]Send Feldman to Israel.
[5]In the Israeli government.
[6]Johnson wants the Israelis to pressure American Jews to support his election in 1964.

HOOVER: That matter you talked to me about today—that came from Sargent Shriver to the AP. Now the *Star* has printed a retraction, but that first edition, of course, is the copy you had on your desk when I was there. But they have printed a retraction. But I learned from an absolutely reliable source that it was Sargent Shriver who gave it to the AP.

LBJ: Um-hmm. Thank you a lot.

JACK VALENTI[1] and LADY BIRD JOHNSON[2]
8:30 P.M.

LBJ: Jack, I told you to go on home to your wife.[3] Now don't you be giving me hell around here about your being home at ten o'clock. . . . You're not going to tell her you're with me, are you?

VALENTI: Yes.

LBJ: Tell her I haven't seen you since about seven-thirty, that you've been messing around here. Now you go on home now, 'cause I don't want to catch that hell. Now I'll probably go eat with you tomorrow night when my wife gets out of town.

LADY BIRD: [chuckles] I'll talk to him and tell him some plans I've got for while I'm gone.

LBJ: Talk to who?

LADY BIRD: [chuckles] To your friend Jack.

LBJ: Jack, she wants to talk to you.

. . . .

LADY BIRD: I hope sometime that in a quiet way, just two or three couples of us, we would get the following people over so we get to know 'em better and establish a better team basis[4] or decide that we couldn't do it—that is, the Dungans, the Whites, the Feldmans . . . the O'Donnells[5]—

VALENTI: Mrs. Johnson, I just couldn't agree with you more.

LADY BIRD: And I don't want to do it on the basis of more than six people at once and I don't want to be, say, two or three Johnson couples and just one of them. I want it to be kind of even-steven. And there are some people that I consider neutral. A good bridge is Bill Moyers. And I think everybody must like you real well. I don't want to overpower them with Johnson.

VALENTI: . . . I'm much in favor of that 'cause I think it's needed.

---

[1] In the West Wing, with Johnson.
[2] In the family quarters of the White House.
[3] Mary Margaret, who had once been LBJ's secretary. The Valentis lived in Georgetown.
[4] In other words, a better relationship between the Kennedy people and the Johnson people on the White House staff.
[5] The Ralph Dungans, Lee Whites, Myer Feldmans, and Kenneth O'Donnells, all Kennedy White House staff holdovers and their wives.

BILL MOYERS
9:25 P.M.

JOHNSON IS READING a rough draft of his special presidential message to Congress on the War on Poverty, scheduled for a week hence.

LBJ: I don't know who else you can get that we've got that can really make this rhyme. . . . Jack[1] can, if he works on it. He's got a pretty good rhythm to it.

MOYERS: The only person I know who can—and I'm reluctant to ask him to get involved in this because right now it's in our little circle—is Goodwin.[2]

LBJ: I'd just ask him if he can't put some sex in it. I'd ask him if he couldn't put some rhyme in it and some beautiful Churchillian phrases and take it and turn it out for us tomorrow, if you just want to take off a day. . . . Ask him if he can do it in confidence. Call him tonight and say, "I want to bring it to you. I've got it ready to go, but he wants you to work on it if you can do it without getting into a column."

MOYERS: I'll call him right now.

LBJ: Tell him that I'm pretty impressed with him. . . . But can he put the music to it?

MOYERS: Yes sir, he's got good sentence structure. He'll balance it, weigh it, make it rhyme here and there. . . . Not as good as Sorensen, of course, but pretty good.[3] . . . We've got this fellow in town that I don't really trust now though because he's doing interviewing on Bobby Kennedy for the library—that's John Bartlow Martin.[4] He's an awfully good writer.[5]

LBJ: Bobby was up at the *Wall Street Journal*, putting out that article on us today.[6]

---

[1] Valenti.

[2] Richard Goodwin, who had closely advised JFK during the 1960 campaign and served as a White House adviser and Deputy Assistant Secretary of State on Latin America and a Special Assistant to Sargent Shriver at the Peace Corps. At the moment Kennedy was assassinated he was about to appoint Goodwin his Special Consultant on the Arts. Goodwin was sufficiently a champion of the Alliance for Progress, which Johnson loathed, that in December, when LBJ had appointed Thomas Mann as Assistant Secretary of State for Latin America, Arthur Schlesinger, Jr., had sent Goodwin a copy of the briefing transcript with a note: "R.I.P." (Richard Goodwin, *Remembering America*, p. 245).

[3] In his memoirs, *Remembering America*, Goodwin writes that the Johnson people did not call on him for speechwriting help until about a week after this conversation, when he accompanied Sargent Shriver to a Fish Room meeting on the Peace Corps and LBJ pulled him into the Oval Office to ask him to write him a statement on Panama, a slightly altered version of which Johnson read at his March 21 press conference and sent the same day to the President of the OAS (pp. 250–52). In late March, Goodwin joined the White House staff. (See Johnson conversation with Hugh Sidey, June 11, 1964, below.)

[4] Martin, of Illinois, was a magazine writer who had written speeches for Stevenson's presidential campaigns and whom JFK appointed as Ambassador to the Dominican Republic. Having quit the Johnson administration in February 1964, Martin was now interviewing Robert Kennedy and other alumni of the Kennedy administration for the John F. Kennedy Library's proposed oral history program.

[5] Martin was indeed hired to work under Moyers on Johnson's speeches.

[6] The *Journal* reported that Federal Reserve and Treasury officials felt that LBJ "may never develop" JFK's level of interest in their problems.

MOYERS: You told me about that. Be interesting to see what comes out now. You see the *Newsweek* story?

LBJ: Yeah. What'd it say?

MOYERS: It doesn't help any of us. Just a minute. [reads from story:] "The eldest heir to the political name of Kennedy has reached the decision to go after the vice presidential nomination. . . . At best, the LBJ camp figured the campaign could only exert unwanted pressure on the President to pick Kennedy as a running mate. . . . His court jester, a former Democratic National Committee staffer named Paul Corbin, was reported drumming write-in sentiment with or without Kennedy's blessing. . . . The tensions between Mr. Johnson and the Attorney General feed on old antagonisms."

LBJ: Well, I think that's all right. I think that makes Bobby look bad instead of us.

TUESDAY, MARCH 10, 1964

LADY BIRD JOHNSON
1155 A.M.

THE FIRST LADY is contemplating a Southern tour which will include cities that have benefited from the Kennedy-Johnson space program and which will remind Southerners of her Alabama roots.

LADY BIRD: I talked to Senator Stennis about it and he said, "I must with a heavy heart say that . . . I wouldn't go, if I were you, into my state."[1] I'll give you all the reasons if you want to but I've knocked it out so no need to tick unless you want to hear 'em.

LBJ: Yeah, I'd like to hear one or two.

LADY BIRD: The area at present is not a real NASA installation.[2] It's just a bunch of turned-up dirt and bulldozers. About eight hundred families were moved off and the land condemned and a lot of the landowners are very, very angry. There's a town close by that hoped to get the people who would be coming in, you know, to work for NASA. They made application for sewerage and extra school facilities, all sorts of federal help. And none of the applications have been acted on. And they think, right or wrong, that the reason they're not acted on is because of integration. And he said at present it's not a blessing to the community, it's not popular, they're not glad it's there, it may mean a great shot in the arm to them economically but at present—

LBJ: That's good. That's enough.

[1] Mississippi.
[2] In 1961, NASA had established the beginnings of a testing facility near Bay St. Louis, Mississippi, later named after Stennis.

LADY BIRD: Okay, all right. Now we get to Alabama. I still think that Hunts-ville[1] would be an interesting and good place to go because . . . it seems to be really tying the South to the future. . . . Shall I call John Sparkman,[2] whose hometown it is, and just discuss it with him?

LBJ: Yeah, yeah.

WEDNESDAY, MARCH 11, 1964

CLIFTON CARTER
1:00 P.M.

JOHNSON WANTS CARTER to nudge Senator Claiborne Pell, Democrat of Rhode Island, to help reverse Republican demands to expand the Baker investi-gation.

LBJ: What is the problem with Pell? That's awfully dangerous because you know he's on that Jordan Committee and we've been staying away from him. It's almost *breaking* into jail. Be awfully friendly and nice. Try to stay out of the public lime-light as much as you can, 'cause they'll have you up there fixing that thing that they're going to vote on tomorrow, and you just show up at the goddamndest places at the right time. Did he tell you what he wanted to see you about?

CARTER: No, sir.

LBJ: Maybe you'd better not mention the committee and get away as soon as you can. Do you see what I mean? They're going to have a crucial vote tomorrow on whether they continue the Baker investigation or not, and he's going to be a crucial man. And you're having lunch with him today with all the Senators in front of you. You follow me? It's like you're showing up with Baker almost in front of all of 'em. So get in and get out as quick as you can.[3]

DEAN RUSK
1:05 P.M.

LBJ: Say, what's going on in the world this morning? How are things going in Cyprus today?

RUSK: Cyprus is very touchy and explosive. This is the big one at the moment, but I think we'll be able to get some forces moving fairly soon now that we've been able to put up some money. Now it looks as though the Turks themselves on the island are trying to create a situation where Turkey would have to come in. So both sides are at fault there at the moment. But we're working on it.

[1] Home of the Marshall Space Flight Center.
[2] Democratic Senator from Alabama and 1952 Democratic vice presidential nominee.
[3] As it happened, the committee vote was not taken.

LBJ: . . . Anything at all on Vietnam?

RUSK: No, I've looked at the daily operational reports and things are relatively quiet in the field. The ratio of casualties is very heavily against the other side the last two or three days. But we'll have to wait till Bob[1] gets back[2] on that. Now, are you planning a little quickie press conference tomorrow?

LBJ: Today or tomorrow.

RUSK: I would prefer tomorrow because I think we ought to get a little feeling from Bob as to what's—wait a minute, he's not getting back till Friday morning, is he? Then I better knuckle down as to what can be said about Lodge.[3]

LBJ: You sure got to. . . .

RUSK: Because I think that's a tough one. It's a tough one particularly with Lodge's son being as active as he is in this business.[4] I wish we had something personal in from McNamara on any discussion he had with Lodge on this subject. I'll give it some thought.

LBJ: Why don't you ask somebody to ask McNamara to get you anything you've got on him without making it public, without letting him know it?

LAWRENCE O'BRIEN
2:20 P.M.

> JOHNSON TALKS to O'Brien on the day after receiving 15,217 write-in votes in the New Hampshire primary. Robert Kennedy had received 11,897 write-in votes for Vice President.

LBJ: We just wondered if you mind showing that navel of yours over in the swimming pool.

O'BRIEN: Christ, I'll tell you, I'd love to go over. But it just so happens that I'm going to be swimming around here with a couple of Congressmen in about five minutes. But gee, thanks, for the offer.

LBJ: Tell your wife I want her and two or three couples with you here to come over and have dinner with me in the next few nights, and we'll get a free night when Lady Bird gets back where we can just sit down and tell you how much we love you and also get some ideas on how to get people to love us.[5]

· · · ·

O'BRIEN: You know we have a legislative gathering tonight.[6]

LBJ: Yeah . . . I want you to get an afternoon nap so you can dance with those big fat women over there.

[1] McNamara.
[2] From South Vietnam.
[3] The previous evening, Lodge had won the Republican presidential primary in New Hampshire by a write-in vote.
[4] Lodge's son George had abetted the campaign for his father.
[5] This refers to Lady Bird's effort to harmonize the Johnson staff with the Kennedy holdovers. (See conversation with Jack Valenti and Lady Bird Johnson, March 9, 1964, above.)
[6] An East Room congressional reception.

O'BRIEN: [chuckles] All right.

LBJ: Jack Valenti complains that there're too many of them too tall, so if you could get some short ones, he'd dance with 'em.

O'BRIEN: [laughs] I'll bet you're not too displeased that this is the last one tonight.

LBJ: Not a damn bit. They talk about how I love this dancing. I wish those sumbitches that write it would come take my place. But I will say this—that even old Alger[1] had an article in the *Dallas News* about he was treated courteously and the White House was nice to him, and Miz Johnson talked to him about his children and he talked to me about his children. And I didn't even see him! But I don't think they can be quite as mad at us after this. . . . Now they're talking about administrative assistants that are working on civil rights. . . . If you want to have them in for tea on your own, you can always deliver me. Just ask and I'll show up. . . . You can just say I want you to come to the White House and confidentially I think the President will come by but I want you as my guest— and maybe have their wives. . . . What did you think about New Hampshire? Didn't we come out of that pretty clean?

O'BRIEN: It came out all right. Thank goodness. Goddamn it.

LBJ: Your boy Corbin[2] though is operating out in Wisconsin, they tell me, this morning.

O'BRIEN: I had a suspicion when I read the morning paper.

LBJ: He was out there all last week. I talked to a fella.

O'BRIEN: He's a total shit.

LBJ: And they can't even write him[3] in. . . . It's against the law out there.

O'BRIEN: . . . Those fellows got on the right track, but belatedly up there in New Hampshire. . . . [chuckles] I noticed all those columnists started to get the local touch up there.

LBJ: Now you've got to get me straightened out with Mary.[4] Now she's had three mean columns on me in the last ten days and just tell her that she can be in love with me too, that I love her and I think she's the best writer in town. . . .

O'BRIEN: Mary got sold a pretty bill of goods by Bill Dunfey.[5] . . . I know that territory pretty good. I can just picture that one.

LBJ: I want you to know all the territory of this country good.[6] . . . I notice that the only man the Republicans could elect up there is one who works for the Democrats.[7] [laughs] Just carrying out our instructions! Goodbye.

[1] Bruce Alger, the far-right Republican Congressman from Dallas.
[2] Here Johnson needles O'Brien about having worked with Corbin in 1960.
[3] Robert Kennedy.
[4] McGrory.
[5] William Dunfey, a hotelier and Chairman of the New Hampshire Democratic State Committee, had been coordinator of the Kennedy campaign in New York and New England in 1960.
[6] To be able to help in the fall presidential campaign.
[7] Lodge.

THURSDAY, MARCH 12, 1964

CLIFTON CARTER
1:26 P.M.

LBJ: Some of them tell me that there are some anti-Kennedy stories going around the committee.[1] . . . You don't ever participate in anything that is anti-Kennedy. Any of them . . . that does, fire 'em.

CARTER: Yes sir.

CARTHA DeLOACH
Assistant Director, FBI, and FBI Liaison to the President
2:15 P.M.

CHECKING IN with his man at the FBI, Johnson asks about Paul Corbin and Bobby Baker.

LBJ: Have you done anything for me today?

DeLOACH: I talked to Walter[2] earlier this morning about some stuff that is going on up on the Hill in connection with the Attorney General.

LBJ: What is it?

DeLOACH: Seems that Congressman Johansen[3] is going to make a speech on the floor of the House concerning the Paul Corbin thing this afternoon. . . . It is going to be unfavorable to the Attorney General, of course. He indicated the lack of indicting him for perjury in the House committee considering him earlier,[4] and I think it might react very well insofar as you're concerned.

LBJ: Is that thing going to close up tomorrow?

DeLOACH: The Bobby Baker matter?

LBJ: Yeah.

DeLOACH: Yes, sir.

LBJ: The *Star* has got a hell of a mean editorial today.[5] I thought you had better influence in the *Star* than that.[6]

[1] Democratic National Committee.
[2] Jenkins.
[3] August Johansen, Republican of Michigan.
[4] Corbin, in connection with his earlier flirtation with the Communist Party.
[5] The *Star* editorial complained that despite the "grave questions" raised by Don Reynolds about Jenkins's role as go-between in selling Reynolds advertising on Johnson's station, although a Senate employee, Jenkins had never been called to testify. "Why is the committee so afraid to explore the matter?"
[6] DeLoach had sources on the *Star* who fed him backstage information on the newspaper. (See his *Hoover's FBI*, pp. 98–100.)

DeLOACH: The *Star* is closing up its doors too on that. They've called all their boys and reassigned them to other work.

LBJ: Wish you'd point out to them, when you get a chance, what damned difference does it make whether Baker gave a hi-fi or this fellow gave a hi-fi. There's nothing criminal or nothing venal about it. Nobody has influenced the government or tried to get a contract or tried to influence a government policy. It is a matter between individuals. And it may be bad to accept the hi-fi, but it's not important which one gave it.

DeLOACH: Mr. President, I don't think anybody is paying any attention to that.[1]

FRIDAY, MARCH 13, 1964

ABE FORTAS
10:00 P.M.

LATE AT NIGHT, after Johnson has returned from a visit to Pittsburgh and Cincinnati, his friend and confidential adviser telephones with an invitation.

FORTAS: Mr. President, I'm here on a very serious mission. I'm looking at a beautiful lady in red and we've decided that we want to come and go dancing.

LBJ: [laughs]

FORTAS: I'm going to put her on as just a temporary loan.

LBJ: All right.

FORTAS: You send her right back to me now.

· · · ·

[Fortas puts the woman on the telephone; she asks Johnson to sneak off to join her and Fortas. Johnson politely declines, noting that he has just returned from a trip. She puts Fortas back on the line.]

· · · ·

FORTAS: You know there isn't anything more important than this woman.

LBJ: Yeah, well, hope you-all are doing good.

FORTAS: Well, we're doing good and I'm going to try to do *bad* before the evening's over. Can't you come?

LBJ: No, I can't, Abe. I just got in and I've got a stack of stuff here a mile high.

FORTAS: Oh dear. I'm sorry. Well, we'll miss you.

LBJ: Thank you.

FORTAS: [chuckles] Bye-bye.

[1]On March 23, 1964, by a party-line vote of 6 to 3, the Senate Rules Committee defeated demands for Walter Jenkins to testify before it. Senator Hugh Scott cried "whitewash." Carl Curtis stormed out of the room.

SATURDAY, MARCH 14, 1964

GEORGE REEDY
2:44 P.M.

> HOSPITALIZED FOR POSSIBLE GALLSTONES, Reedy has been kept in the hospital by LBJ, who has arranged to pay out of his own pocket for Reedy to stay there until he loses some of his considerable girth.

LBJ: You were down to 230, I remember, and they told me that you had lost twenty-some-odd pounds.

REEDY: Oh, no. Wish I was down to 230 a long time ago. . . . I've got about fifty pounds to go yet.

LBJ: I'll be darned. Why don't you exercise?

REEDY: I am. . . . I take long walks every day.

LBJ: Good. Are you still in the hospital?

REEDY: Yeah, I'm still here. . . . How did the session go?[1]

LBJ: We haven't started it yet. . . . You got any suggestions?

REEDY: . . . I can't stress too heavily on how important it is to be relaxed in this one. Because this should be a conversation rather than a hard news story. And people are going to be a lot more interested in what you're thinking about rather than just plain hard thoughts.

· · · ·

LBJ: Pierre said he wants to know if *he* can get a hospital room . . . to get in.[2]

REEDY: [laughs] Tell him I'll see if I've got any influence with the head nurse.

---

[1] At 3:00 P.M., Johnson is taping "A Conversation with the President" in the Oval Office with David Brinkley of NBC, Eric Sevareid of CBS, and William Lawrence of ABC. The program is to be aired the next day. Lady Bird's diary shows how much of an ordeal the program was for both Johnsons: "The inquisition lasted a full hour on the air. . . . The lights were as hot as the questions and I felt so sorry for Lyndon. . . . At long last *it* was over. . . . I went up and had a quick dinner with Lyndon and Jesse [Kellam]. I knew Lyndon was worrying about the show" (March 14, 1964). The next day: "We were really in a state of tension and waiting . . . just imagining everything that could be wrong, every answer that would come out in an ugly light. Finally at 6:00, we gathered around the TV set like a group going to an execution. At least that's the way I felt, and I wonder if Lyndon did. . . . I think we all watched it with a rising heart. . . . Lyndon looked so strong and reliable and dependable. He looked very handsome too. And his answers were better than I thought they might be, lying awake, worrying about them the night before. There could have been some more humor, some change of pace, a little more lightheartedness, but I felt better watching it than I had any time anticipating it. Jesse stayed on, had dinner with us and planned to leave early the next morning. It took a good deal of persuading but I think we felt like we wanted our near and dear close to us. It's a lonely thing to be on TV in front of 180 million people" (March 15, 1964).
[2] Salinger was also heavyset.

TUESDAY, MARCH 17, 1964

GEORGE REEDY
12:49 P.M.

> REEDY IS STILL CRASH-DIETING in the hospital.

LBJ: How many pounds you lost now?

REEDY: Twenty-seven.

LBJ: What're you going to make it, fifty-seven or sixty? What is it? What'd the doctor say?

REEDY: That I've got another fifty to go.

LBJ: God Almighty!

REEDY: He thinks though that if I can get down to 240 . . . I'll have the will-power and strength . . . to carry on. . . .

LBJ: Have you looked at this Irish speech?[1]

REEDY: Yeah. I just got it.

LBJ: Is it any good?

REEDY: No. I'm trying to give them a few paragraphs . . . but the difficulty—like that opening line, for instance—"My name is O'Johnson." I certainly wouldn't do that. That's an old, old gag. . . . I'm going to try to get a few paragraphs that'll get a little feel in it that means something to the Irishman today.

LBJ: I didn't think that it was worth a damn.

· · · ·

LBJ: This son of a bitch Stew Alsop has got a mean article—"The Texas Mafia Moves In"[2]—and shows that all the intellectuals are gone, and all of Johnson's guys are in, but the only thing they know is Texas. Carter[3] is the politician of the lot, knows Texas politics. I don't guess O'Brien was an authority on national politics when he came in.

REEDY: Hell, no. I think that that's deliberate.

LBJ: Who do you think keeps doing this? He[4] keeps saying they're[5] all getting out, except a few Texas men. Trying to run them all off.

REEDY: I think that's right, and I think there must be some pretty clever Republicans . . . behind this. . . .

LBJ: I wonder if it's not Bobby.[6]

---

[1] Johnson was to speak that evening to the Friendly Sons of St. Patrick in New York.

[2] Stewart Alsop was Joseph's older brother and former partner. His article, published in the February 15, 1964, issue of the *Saturday Evening Post,* was actually called "Johnson Takes Over: The Untold Story."

[3] Clifton Carter.

[4] Alsop.

[5] The Kennedy men.

[6] Kennedy.

REEDY: I think he'd be too smart for that.

LBJ: Why would he be too smart? That's what he wants to do, is divide us.

REEDY: Yeah, but if he tears up the party, dividing us doesn't do any good. It doesn't do him a damn bit of good. The whole show goes smash. . . . His type of operation would be more to try to get you to buy him.[1] . . . Now I think that we're going to try to create this image of sort of a Texas Mafia, moving in and displacing the Irish Mafia. And of course that's the kind of story people will believe, because people think in those terms. . . . So when they get up and read stuff like this in the papers, they'll probably start looking askance on me[2] and Walter and Valenti. . . . This is pretty high-level cleverness—sort of the tactic that a Nixon would think up.

• • • •

LBJ: I've got to go to this dinner from six-fifty-five to nine-oh-five.[3]

REEDY: Oh, that's going to be rugged.

LBJ: White tie. I don't know who in the hell—

REEDY: Oh, you always have to wear white tie on St. Patrick's Day.

LBJ: Well, give us a speech and give us something with a lead something about foreign affairs—something with seriousness in it. . . . Should we put out a text?

REEDY: It depends on when we get the whole thing put together. . . . I can't do a complete speech in the time allowed. I'm just trying to put some depth in—

LBJ: [irritated:] Why in the hell haven't you been working on it? You knew that I was going to have to do it.

WEDNESDAY, MARCH 18, 1964

EDWIN WEISL, SR.
8:09 A.M.

LBJ: Stew Alsop had a story in yesterday. . . . The poor Kennedy men. . . . The big Texans are riding again, and they're taking over—Bill Moyers and Jack Valenti, these tough Texans, and the poor Kennedy people like O'Donnell and Larry O'Brien and Ralph Dungan and Mike Feldman. They don't have any authority. These Texans are taking all over. I'll bet I've got fewer White House men than any President ever had in the history of the republic. And I just cut two or three . . . and I couldn't keep these two. They quit.[4] But they just give me

[1] Meaning compel Johnson to take him as Vice President.
[2] Despite the fact that Reedy grew up in Chicago.
[3] The Friendly Sons of St. Patrick banquet, at the Waldorf-Astoria in New York.
[4] Sorensen and Schlesinger.

hell about it. . . . Stewart Alsop—he's kind of a supercilious intellectual that thinks he's real smart. Joe's pretty good to me—his brother. . . . But it's working out all right. Did you see the Gallup this morning? Sixty-eight–27 Nixon, 68–27 Lodge, Johnson 68.

WEISL: God, Lyndon—

LBJ: And this time, the Kennedy campaign.[1] There's Kennedy 53, Nixon 47.

WEISL: Lyndon, you have no idea what that broadcast Sunday[2] did. . . . I had at least thirty calls. . . . It was a magnificent display. . . .

LBJ: We just got all kinds of wires. Took in a hundred the first ten minutes, and they were real good wires too. Wasn't a single unfriendly one.

· · · ·

WEISL: I wish there was something I could do to ease your burdens.

LBJ: You just look for some of these good people. The main thing is getting the real smart ones so they say my appointments are not like Truman's, that I've got high-quality people. And I don't want to be owned by Wall Street and I don't want to be owned by the Texas oilmen. . . . And you ought to get close to that *Wall Street Journal,* 'cause they're really—

WEISL: We're working on that. I don't think it's quite as bad as you think.

LBJ: He's demanding this week. He called up yesterday.

WEISL: I know. That's this fellow Kohlmeier, the reporter.[3]

LBJ: Yeah.

WEISL: . . . We can soften it up. I noticed Goldwater started some of it.[4]

LBJ: Yeah, that's where it's coming from.

WEISL: I wouldn't worry about that. Hell, that's nothing. That's nitpicking. . . . They can't find any fault with what you're doing for the country so they're going to talk about you personally. It's a lot of—

LBJ: We'll work it out all right. . . . Tell Dick[5] I sure do appreciate what his people down there are doing. . . . This little Marianne Means[6] is the best reporter he's got for the White House. Almost not enough objective.[7] It's just wonderful. You have no idea. . . . The best publicity we get in America is from Hearst. . . . And it's already dribbled down that Dick's my friend. They know it.

---

[1] Gallup had begun polling on a possible Robert Kennedy presidential candidacy.

[2] The Brinkley-Severeid-Lawrence conversation with the President.

[3] Louis Kohlmeier, of the *Wall Street Journal,* who was researching Johnson's business holdings.

[4] On March 16, Goldwater had gibed at Johnson's contention in the Sunday night broadcast that Bobby Baker had not really been his protégé: "That's ridiculous. . . .Everybody in the Senate knows Bobby Baker was Lyndon Johnson's man." He charged that the Johnson White House had "intervened to stop the investigation of the Baker case."

[5] Richard Berlin of Hearst.

[6] The Hearst White House reporter.

[7] Johnson said this about few journalists.

McGEORGE BUNDY
11:06 A.M.

LBJ: They say you're the only intellectual left in the White House.[1]

BUNDY: Oh, Jesus! [laughs] Stop it! Pull out the needle!

LBJ: . . . Last night I said looks like Valenti's got as much time at Harvard as either of the Bundys. I don't know why they can't classify him as intellectual. . . . They said well that's because of his residence. Valenti got a graduate degree there, didn't he?

BUNDY: I don't have a Harvard degree, except honorary, so he's an honest Harvard man.[2]

PIERRE SALINGER
4:02 P.M.

LBJ: Pierre, I've got a problem here. Did we announce some judges today re-signed?

SALINGER: Yes sir.

LBJ: Why did we announce them? . . . Who in the hell sent that around to you?

SALINGER: I just got it through the normal course of business. . . .

LBJ: I'll have a thousand telephone calls, sweetheart, from my friends tonight, all of them wanting the same judgeship. And I'd like to pick them beforehand. So let's don't announce any resignations unless I know about them.

LADY BIRD JOHNSON
7:35 P.M.

LBJ: Yes, darling.

LADY BIRD: How is my dear?

LBJ: I'm going out to John Bailey's, I'll be gone thirty minutes and I'll come back and eat with you. They're having a little meeting I promised to go to.[3]

LADY BIRD: All right. Hope you're going to get an early night 'cause you sound a little bit hoarse.

---

[1] Johnson is referring to the Stewart Alsop piece on the takeover by the Texans.

[2] Bundy is bending over backward to get along with his new boss. To Bundy, the former Harvard dean and great-nephew of Harvard President A. Lawrence Lowell, the Harvard Business School degree that Valenti possessed hardly made one a Harvard man.

[3] A meeting of Johnson's political advisers at Bailey's Sheraton Park Hotel suite.

SATURDAY, MARCH 21, 1964

DEAN RUSK
12:16 P.M.

> JOHNSON ASKS RUSK about a report by ABC diplomatic correspondent
> John Scali that Rusk intended to resign as Secretary of State in November
> 1964.

LBJ: Where did that story get out?

RUSK: I don't understand. . . . John Scali came to see me, and I did not tell him
that I was resigning in November.[1] I said that I had no plans, that I am the
fifty-fourth Secretary of State, and someday, there'll be a fifty-fifth.

LBJ: I hope not.

RUSK: [laughs] Yeah. You and I talked . . . on November 23rd, and that's the
last exchange we've had.[2] You asked me if I would serve and I said that I would,
and that's the end of it, as far as I'm concerned.

LBJ: Then why would he do that?

RUSK: He says that . . . various people are beginning to maneuver for my successor . . . that I am a man of modest resources and couldn't stay forever. . . .
Maybe I'll be the last one to hear it, but he mentioned that Bill Fulbright and
one or two others—

LBJ: I've heard the speculation, but the speculation has been that there's been a
new relationship and that you're more stronger, and have more responsibility
than ever before. That's the speculation that I've heard and what I've tried to
contribute to.

ROBERT McNAMARA
1:07 P.M.

> BACK IN WASHINGTON from his trip to Saigon, the Defense Secretary has
> told LBJ that conditions in South Vietnam were "unquestionably" worse since
> General Khanh came to power in January. The new government, he said, lacked
> wide political appeal. McNamara reported that a majority of the officials in his
> meetings in Saigon had favored starting air attacks against the North, just as
> the Joint Chiefs had wished, but that he had disagreed. So had Khanh, insisting
> that his base in the South lacked the strength to withstand North Vietnamese

[1] When Kennedy appointed Rusk in 1960, Rusk had told him that "under no circumstances"
could he financially afford to serve as Secretary of State for more than one term (Dean Rusk,
As I Saw It, Norton, 1990, p. 204).
[2] After Kennedy's assassination, Rusk gave the new President his written resignation, which
Johnson refused, saying, "I want you to remain Secretary of State as long as I am President"
(*As I Saw It*, p. 327).

retaliation. LBJ approved McNamara's position but ordered him to begin planning for the possibility of such attacks in the future.[1]

McNAMARA: You may remember Dean Rusk and you and I talked briefly for
the need for a Vietnam speech.[2] . . . I sent a draft over to your office last night to
Mike Forrestal.[3] . . .

LBJ: . . . I'll get it from him and read it over the weekend. . . . I think if you
could that you ought to go up and sit down with Gruening and Morse.[4]

. . . .

McNAMARA: I think I can take a lot of the heat off of you on that Vietnam
issue, Mr. President. There's just a lot of misunderstanding on it in this country,
and that's the real purpose for it.

LBJ: Now what are we going to do? Are we going to do more of the same,
except we're going to firm it up and strengthen it, and what else?

McNAMARA: Well, it's really—

LBJ: What is a one-sentence statement of what our policy is out there?

McNAMARA: Our policy is to help Khanh provide the physical security and
the economic and social progress for his people that he needs in order to gain
their support.

LBJ: All right, but that's what we've been doing.

McNAMARA: We haven't done it very effectively, and neither have they.

LBJ: Why aren't the Russians as interested in this[5] as we are? Why aren't the
French and the English? Why do they want the Commies to take over all of
Southeast Asia?

McNAMARA: I think the French are obviously pursuing their own national
aims and they think that we're going to lose out there anyhow and they might
as well advance their national strength and prestige while we're losing.

LBJ: Looks like to me that the Russians would be more interested in saving
Vietnam than we are.

McNAMARA: You can't be sure what their position is, I think.

LBJ: Doesn't it seem logical to you, if they're in the war with them and got a
civil war going on between eight hundred million Chinese and the Russians, why
do they want to see the Chinese Communists envelop Southeast Asia?

McNAMARA: I think the reason that they can't take a strong position against
the Chinese Communists here is that to do so will lose them the support of
Communist parties elsewhere in the world. . . .

[1] McNamara to Johnson, March 16, 1964, and Record of 524th National Security Council
Meeting, March 17, 1964, Johnson Library.
[2] McNamara was planning to speak to the James Forrestal Memorial Dinner on March 26.
[3] Forrestal, son of the first Defense Secretary, who had killed himself in 1949, was being
honored at the dinner; he was an NSC staff member.
[4] Democrats Ernest Gruening of Alaska and Wayne Morse of Oregon, the two Senators most
skeptical of the U.S. commitment to South Vietnam.
[5] Meaning why are the Soviets not interested in saving Vietnam from the influence of their
Chinese rivals.

LBJ: I thought they just thought we had an umbrella over them, just like de Gaulle does, and thought we'd do it and they didn't need to do it.

McNAMARA: I don't think so. I think they are in a very sensitive position for control of Communist parties worldwide and if they appear to be soft in opposing us in Vietnam, they'll be charged with that and lose control. In any event, I've tried to prepare a strong statement here of what we're doing and why we're doing it and what the prospects are.[1]

ISABELLE SHELTON
Social Reporter, Washington Star
3:45 P.M.

INTERVIEWED BY TELEPHONE, Johnson conveys the importance of women in his life and career.

LBJ: I appointed the first woman judge in the country. That story never has been—

SHELTON: Which one was that?

LBJ: Sarah Hughes at Dallas, Texas, that swore me in.[2]

SHELTON: Oh, that's right.

LBJ: That's a beautiful feature if you'd talk to Liz[3] about it. . . . Say this is no recent thing. We believed in women all along.

. . . .

SHELTON: I was so fascinated by your telling me that your mother had pushed you out, sort of, from the highway job, said, "This is all fine to do, but go get an education." . . .

---

[1] In his speech, McNamara said that the situation in South Vietnam had "unquestionably worsened" and that the road ahead would be "long, difficult and frustrating." He wrote in his 1995 memoir, *In Retrospect,* "All true. But then I reviewed the same alternatives I had presented to the President, and a listener would have concluded I offered no answers to our problems" (p. 116). On the day after McNamara's conversation with Johnson, above, the President and Lady Bird had the McNamaras, the Walter Lippmanns, and the J. William Fulbrights over for dinner. Lady Bird dictated into her diary, "The talk was of Vietnam and it's pretty terrifying to hear McNamara speak of how dedicated the opposition soldiers are over there. They apparently have an intensive training in ideals that is lacking on our side. One little odd manifestation is in a determination . . . for cleanliness that causes them as part of their military training to just be forced to brush their teeth every day, and they wear their toothbrush in their pocket! I suppose it's a sort of status symbol of '*We belong to the up and coming*' " (March 22, 1964).

[2] Hughes, who swore Johnson in on *Air Force One* after the Kennedy assassination, had actually been appointed by JFK, at Johnson's instance. In the spring of 1961, Johnson had championed the liberal Dallas attorney and chairman of the 1960 Kennedy-Johnson campaign in Texas as a U.S. District Judge. Robert Kennedy refused her because she was sixty-four. Asked by the Attorney General why one of his anti-crime bills was stalled in the House, Speaker Sam Rayburn replied, "That bill of yours will pass as soon as Sarah Hughes becomes a federal judge." RFK said he had nothing against Hughes but her age. Rayburn glared: "Sonny, everybody seems old to you." Kennedy and his brother hastened to make an exception for Hughes. The story of Rayburn's success where Johnson had failed quickly spread through Washington and Texas. Johnson complained to the President (Rowland Evans and Robert Novak, *Lyndon B. Johnson,* pp. 314–16).

[3] Carpenter.

LBJ: She pushed me into high school, made me take the college entrance exams when I didn't want to do it and came down and stayed all night with me working on plane geometry, and we didn't close our eyes until I had to go to the eight o'clock class. And I just did make it. I mean, I just made a passing grade. . . .

SHELTON: . . . What was she teaching you then?

LBJ: . . . Maybe reviewing my speech with me and saying, "Please emphasize this word."[1] Or maybe going over a geometry problem, which always gave me trouble. . . . I wish I had her now, so that she could go over the questions before I have a press conference that are likely to be asked because she could always think of every one that the teacher might ask.

SHELTON: Mrs. Johnson told me that your mother always had a lot of books around the house.

LBJ: Just had the bed full of them, and she'd just sit up in bed and read all day and all night. . . . She read out loud to all of us all the time. Largely she was a great Browning woman, a great Tennyson woman, and she liked biographies because all the children liked biographies. And it didn't make a difference whether it was about Jim Hogg[2] or Jim Ferguson[3] or Andrew Jackson or Abraham Lincoln. . . . All of them would gather around and she'd read to all of them the same time.

SHELTON: Can you think of anything that she had you read that particularly influenced you?

LBJ: . . . The first President I really loved was Jackson. I had great respect of Jefferson because he believed in the land. . . . Then I loved Jackson because he was a guy that didn't let 'em tread on him. . . . And Wilson. I devoured him, because everything he wrote or said, I memorized nearly because he was President during the time that I was six to fourteen.

· · · ·

SHELTON: Your mother probably didn't help you with your college subjects then, did she, since she wasn't there?

LBJ: Oh yes, she helped me on everything. I went home every few weeks. She helped me on everything until the day she died. She'd be helping me now if she was here and she'd be telling me what not to say in some of these speeches. And my wife does too, on everything. . . . Bird can still write the best speech of anybody in the family. Her judgment is better on reading something and giving it analysis. She can always tell you what she didn't like about the speech at the Armory the other night.[4] The last third was much better than the first third. You

[1] Just as Lady Bird did in later life. (See March 7, 1964, conversation above.)
[2] Governor of Texas from 1891 to 1895.
[3] Governor of Texas from 1915 until 1917, when he was impeached and removed for financial malfeasance. Despite the scandal, Ferguson ran again for Governor and Senator, then saw his wife, "Ma" Ferguson, serve as Governor from 1925 to 1927 and from 1933 to 1935.
[4] Johnson had spoken at a Democratic congressional dinner two nights earlier at the National Guard Armory. Lady Bird had dictated into her diary, "What a strange dinner it was!" She felt that the St. Patrick's Day theme had made it seem as if the Johnsons had invaded a Kennedy event: "Overall there was the particular pall of 'Are we intruders here?'. . . The Irish decorations, the absence of any member of the Kennedy family—all helped to evoke that mood" (March 19, 1964). Two months later, in the same hall, she missed "that wild adulation" she had seen for John and Jacqueline Kennedy: "But his was a magic quality, a different quality that we do not have. We just have to try to contribute, whatever we do" (May 26, 1964).

go too fast, or you go too slow. She's always got the most discerning observations. She's always raising hell about women, and I don't believe you women pay much attention to her, but she's done more for women. I believe that as a result of her persistence . . . there are over three or four hundred women that make over $10,000 a year that have been advanced some way or another in the last thirty days.

SHELTON: I'll approach it from that angle. . . .

LBJ: See, we just don't just reach out and get a new woman. We take a woman that may work faithfully as a char cleaner or as a typist or a secretary. I'm looking for one now to appoint on the bench.

· · · ·

SHELTON: Your mother actually taught you the alphabet at age two from blocks and taught you to recite nursery rhymes at three, and Tennyson and Lowell, and then had you reading by four, and in kindergarten at five. Is that right?

LBJ: Kindergarten at four. . . . I went and sat in the teacher's lap while she taught all the rest of them. I finished eleven grades, and graduated at fifteen.

MONDAY, MARCH 23, 1964

LADY BIRD JOHNSON
9:15 P.M.

LBJ: Darling, you go on and eat a bite and I'll come home when I can but I'm going to be tied up for a little bit on my speech in the morning.
LADY BIRD: Oh you poor blessed man. I'm so sorry.
LBJ: I'll be there before you go to bed.
LADY BIRD: Good night, darling.

TUESDAY, MARCH 24, 1964

McGEORGE BUNDY
10:16 A.M.

PIERRE SALINGER HAD RESIGNED as White House Press Secretary on March 19 to run for the U.S. Senate from California. He gave only two hours' notice to Johnson, who responded by pulling some bills out of his wallet to make the first contribution to Salinger's campaign. At an informal briefing, LBJ said he was "not disturbed" by Salinger's abrupt departure and denied that this was "another sign that supporters of John Kennedy and Robert Kennedy are anxious to leave your administration." To replace Salinger, Johnson has appointed George Reedy.[1]

BUNDY: I told them[2] to put out this little briefing for George Reedy.

LBJ: That's wonderful. Thank you for thinking of George. He needs your help more than anybody 'cause they're[3] going to be asking for little things, and you get him every little thing that you can.

BUNDY: Yes sir, all right.

LBJ: Now, I sent you a little something down there.[4]

BUNDY: Yeah, Jack[5] has just brought it in.

LBJ: We want a little peace-demagoguery for the mothers, and then we want to call attention to the fact that everything that looks black one morning may not necessarily be black a week later.

BUNDY: Right, let me work on that a little bit.

LBJ: And they're[6] making foreign policy the issue, so let's kind of answer them a little bit.

WEDNESDAY, MARCH 25, 1964

SPESSARD HOLLAND
Democratic Senator from Florida
4:20 P.M.

LBJ: I felt mighty blue over Bill Fulbright's speech today.[7]

HOLLAND: I suppose that was done at your suggestion.

---

[1] Lady Bird dictated into her diary, "The bombshell dropped into our lap late this afternoon. Pierre Salinger walked into Lyndon's office about 3, told him that he was going to resign. . . . Lyndon called George Reedy in the hospital, got him dressed, got him over here as soon as possible. They called a press conference and Salinger told . . . of his resignation, leaving immediately after for California. There's such a vacuum in my own thinking of how to cope with this situation that I can't quite describe it—because of all the people from the Kennedy administration, I had felt that he was one of the most clinical, professional—although very close and attached to the Kennedys, we had established a certain simpatico relationship between [us] that made me feel easy around him at the same time that I trusted his confidence completely" (March 19, 1964).

[2] Members of Bundy's staff.

[3] White House reporters.

[4] A request for some speech language.

[5] Valenti.

[6] The Republicans.

[7] In a well-publicized Senate address called "Old Myths and New Realities," Fulbright warned against intransigence on Panama and dramatic expansion of the Vietnam War. Fulbright said it was time "to start thinking some 'unthinkable thoughts' about the Cold War . . . about the underdeveloped countries, and particularly those in Latin America . . . and about the festering war in Vietnam."

LBJ: Oh, hell! . . . We just have gotten over Mike's[1] speech on neutralizing
Vietnam and pulling out and now Bill gets up and makes a speech and says let's
rewrite a treaty with Panama. And I'm . . . just within an inch of getting an
agreement with them. And every time I do, the *New York Times,* the *Washington
Post,* or some damned fool Senator gets up and knocks it off.

McGEORGE BUNDY
4:35 P.M.

LBJ: What does Rusk think about Fulbright?[2]
BUNDY: I haven't talked to him. . . . Let me find out.
LBJ: . . . Spessard Holland called me and thought it was a trial balloon.
BUNDY: I don't believe it! . . .
LBJ: . . . They all assume that Fulbright speaks for the administration. . . .
BUNDY: I do think it is extraordinary. When he saw you . . . he didn't say to
you any of this was going to happen.
LBJ: Fulbright is that way though. He's a very unpredictable man. . . . As Tru-
man said one time, he's "half bright"!

ABE FORTAS
6:05 P.M.

　　　　　FORTAS IS FIELDING PRESS INQUIRIES growing out of Louis Kohlmeier's
　　just-published findings in the *Wall Street Journal,* "The Johnson Wealth."

FORTAS: I just talked to the Judge.[3] I think that we ought to refer everything
to him and not say anything from the White House. . . . It's just terribly important, in terms of the whole trusteeship concept, for the whole White House
to say that this was entirely in Judge Moursund's hands.
LBJ: That's fine.
FORTAS: . . . It seems to me essential that everybody be buttoned up absolutely.

RENÉ VERDON
White House Chef
7:51 P.M.

LBJ: René, we're going to have six or eight for dinner.
VERDON: Six or eight for dinner?

[1] Mansfield.
[2] Meaning Fulbright's speech.
[3] Moursund.

LBJ: Yeah, and it'll be about thirty minutes.

VERDON: Yes, Mr. President.[1]

LADY BIRD JOHNSON
Exact Time Unknown

JOHNSON REACHES Lady Bird at the White House swimming pool.

LBJ: This rabbi from Houston, Schachtel,[2] and his wife—we're going to invite them to eat with us and Jack and Mary Margaret.[3] Is that all right?

LADY BIRD: . . . I'll be up there in five minutes.

LBJ: No, don't be in such a hurry. . . . We'll take a little time for them to get down here. . . .

LADY BIRD: Just long enough to take off my coat and comb my hair. I'll be upstairs in a minute.

LBJ: We're still here. We're over at the office.

LADY BIRD: You are?

LBJ: Yeah. Who're you swimming with?

LADY BIRD: I'm swimming all by myself and I just finished my eighteenth lap and I'll be upstairs and put on a hostess gown and you-all come on over as soon as you can.

SATURDAY, MARCH 28, 1964

GEORGE REEDY
3:06 A.M.

THE JOHNSONS HAVE GONE to the LBJ Ranch for Easter. There, in the middle of the night, Reedy briefs Johnson on a major earthquake in Alaska.

REEDY: The major thing that . . . might still put this in very bad shape is what happens when that tidal wave hits Hawaii. . . .

LBJ: Or San Francisco. . . . I'd see that they notify Bundy of everything and ask him to check to see if there's any instructions that we should get to anyone that hasn't been alerted—the command in the Pacific or Alaska or any people that

[1] The French chef hired by Jacqueline Kennedy soon quit, unable to cope with Johnson's plain eating habits and his last-minute requests, such as this one.
[2] Hyman Judah Schachtel.
[3] Valenti.

haven't been notified, because . . . we'd want to . . . anticipate anyplace that might hit, like our people in Japan. . . . Anything else? How did the boys get along today in Austin?

REEDY: . . . There was a little flak over that trip to Johnson City.[1] . . . Just that UP had it and nobody else did.

LBJ: Well, you've got 'em spying around everyplace up here.[2] . . .

REEDY: I told them that I think the President has a right to go wherever he wishes. . . .

LBJ: What is it? Somebody doesn't want me to ride into Johnson City?

REEDY: . . . The only thing they get panicky about is the thought you would be moving out there around the country exposed and something might happen and they would be sitting back here and not know about it. . . .

LBJ: If I can't . . . go where I'm working on a house, eleven miles, without somebody having flak, I don't know. . . . They're little chickenshits. I saw where they said I was in the area and that meant I was probably with my big trustee of my fortune.[3] That's the goddamnedest chickenshit thing I ever saw of grown men. . . . They're a pretty bunch of chickenshits. . . . I would like to know that I can leave without drawing a press conference. It's just the same as I do if I go out for dinner in Washington. . . . They've got these little peepholes with these long-range cameras and they're peeking around here. This little UP boy was up here riding up and down in front of the house like a little ass. . . . They're just chickenshits.[4]

RALPH DUNGAN
2:05 P.M.

> JOHNSON CALLS DUNGAN, who has just returned from a Catholic retreat, in Washington in quest of White House news to announce at an impromptu press conference at the ranch.

LBJ: Ralph, you gave a summary the other day of the number of women.[5] . . . If you've got it there now, we can take the total. [to Liz Carpenter:] Liz, get on here a minute and take this.

CARPENTER: . . . How we doing with women? How many you got?[6]

DUNGAN: Well, let's see—goddamn—

---

[1] Johnson had visited his boyhood house in Johnson City without notifying the press.

[2] Johnson presumed that reporters were spying on him in search of evidence that he was consulting Moursund about his business affairs in order to circumvent his blind trust.

[3] Referring to Judge Moursund.

[4] Johnson's annoyance with reporters and photographers was spreading to Lady Bird. She had dictated into her diary the previous Sunday that "the press, our nemesis, had apparently laid in wait at every entrance to see if we were going anywhere to church. . . . I'm just beginning to catch this virus of dislike for photographers. Far too much entrance into my private life" (March 22, 1964).

[5] Female appointments by Johnson.

[6] In January, Johnson had promised to appoint fifty women to top jobs.

LBJ: That's an ugly thing for a Catholic—is that the way the Catholics do when they come in off a retreat? Holler "goddamn"? I'm gonna tell Walter Jenkins[1] on you. . . . You get me all the dope on Katherine May.[2] Is she a Republican or an Independent?

DUNGAN: She's a Republican, Mr. President.

LBJ: All right, we want to be sure of that. And how old is she?

DUNGAN: She's forty-seven, as I recall.

LBJ: That's a little old for me.

DUNGAN: [laughs] She's a spry forty-seven.

LBJ: Is she good-looking?

DUNGAN: Uh, no, she's, uh—

LBJ: Well, I'll—be—damned.

DUNGAN: No, we're striking, we're going about three or four out of five.

LBJ: What about Pat Harris?[3]

DUNGAN: She's *very* attractive.

LBJ: All right now!

MONDAY, MARCH 30, 1964

EDWARD KENNEDY
11:45 A.M.

> JOHNSON CONGRATULATES the Massachusetts Senator on the previous day's appearance on NBC's *Meet the Press*. Amid growing conflicts with his brother Robert, LBJ is taking particular care to keep his other Kennedy fences mended.

LBJ: The President[4] would have been so proud of you, and I just thought you just hit a home run every time they asked you a question. . . .

KENNEDY: That's very, very kind of you. . . .

LBJ: I ran into it by accident . . . just before the first commercial. . . . But I just thought that you handled everything perfectly. . . .

KENNEDY: . . . It's just a matter of survival. . . . You want to come out of the program and not have sort of left yourself wide open. . . . It always seems that they have something in there which completely tries to catch you off balance. . . .

---

[1] A devout Catholic.
[2] A Johnson nomination to the Export-Import Bank.
[3] Patricia Roberts Harris (later Jimmy Carter's Secretary of Housing and Urban Development), whom LBJ was appointing to a commission on Puerto Rico.
[4] Kennedy.

LBJ: You can take my job any time that you're ready. . . . I thought that the way you handled it couldn't be improved on—particularly the President's[1] program. That's the first thing that we're dedicated to, and we're going to do that together. And the second thing—which was very obvious to you and I want it to be to every Kennedy and every person connected with them—is the last thing that he[2] would want us to do is to wind up disagreeing with each other. And we're just not going to do that. Nobody is going to come in between us. And anytime something happens that you or the Attorney General or your mother or your father or your sisters feel ought to go differently, you put on your hat and walk in that office[3] and sit down and say your speech.

KENNEDY: That's very, very kind of you.

LBJ: . . . 'Cause I'm just a trustee that's trying to carry on the best that I can, and I'm aware of my problems and my limitations more than anybody else. And when I see somebody do like you did yesterday, my heart goes out to them and I want you to know it.

KENNEDY: . . . Every word was meant there.[4]

LBJ: We're going to put over his program, and he's going to be proud of it, if we all survive. Then we're going to go on to better things, and you'll always have me in your corner.

ANN GARGAN
Kennedy Cousin, and
JOSEPH KENNEDY
Former Ambassador to Great Britain
11:55 A.M.

JOHNSON CALLS THE COUSIN and full-time companion of the late President's father at the Kennedy winter home in Palm Beach. Before he was paralyzed by a stroke in 1961, Joseph Kennedy had had a hearty relationship with LBJ during his years as Senate Majority Leader.[5]

LBJ: How's my friend?

GARGAN: Oh, he's doing pretty well.

LBJ: Did he see Teddy yesterday?

GARGAN: Oh, yes he did. And he enjoyed it very much, sir.

LBJ: I just thought he hit a home run every time they asked him a question.

GARGAN: We thought that he was pretty good too.

[1] Kennedy's.
[2] President Kennedy.
[3] Oval Office.
[4] Kennedy had expressed support for what Johnson was doing.
[5] Joseph Kennedy's backstage intervention had helped move LBJ to put JFK on the Senate Foreign Relations Committee in 1957 and JFK to offer the vice presidency to Johnson in Los Angeles in 1960.

LBJ: I just thought it was the best I ever saw. . . . And I wish you would tell Mr. Kennedy that we miss him a lot and that we need him, and that we're thinking of him.

GARGAN: Oh, Mr. President, could you just tell him?

LBJ: I sure will.

GARGAN: You know he doesn't feel well, but I'm sure he'd be very happy to—

LBJ: I'd love to. Just whatever is all right with him.

GARGAN: . . . Thank you, sir. Could you just hold on for a minute?

LBJ: Yes, ma'am, I have plenty of time.

GARGAN: . . . Just a minute.

KENNEDY: [faintly:] Hello-o-o.

LBJ: I just wanted to tell you that we miss you a lot, and we need you every day, and I thought Teddy just hit a home run yesterday. . . . I hope you're feeling better and I want to come see you sometime pretty soon. We're going to carry out all the program, try to get it passed. And then maybe I can get down and have a little visit with you. I hope you're doing all right.

KENNEDY: No-o-o-o-o.[1]

GARGAN: Thank you very much, sir.

LBJ: So you take care of him and know that we love him, and tell him how proud I was of Teddy, and tell him there's two things we're going to do. One, we're going to pass the program, and two, we're not going to let them ever divide us.

GEORGE REEDY
8:00 P.M.

LBJ: George, we had a good little ride around this afternoon, and they got some spy around here following us. I don't know who it is. But some little fellow with glasses on, in a car. We didn't get in any trouble. Didn't pay any attention to him. But he snuck around like a sheep-killing dog. . . . I just had that briefing from that general that they forced on us.[2] I didn't want him. I didn't ask for him. He brought some pictures and showed kind of a sales talk for the Air Force—the pictures from the various cities—Anchorage and Kodiak and so forth.

GEORGE REEDY
9:35 P.M.

THE CIA HAS WARNED Johnson that a military coup it is supporting against the government of Brazil is imminent. The President tells Reedy that if the overthrow takes place, he will have to rush back to Washington early.

[1] Since suffering his stroke, the old patriarch often said "No" when he meant yes.
[2] An Air Force general had briefed Johnson on the Alaska earthquake.

LBJ: Of course, if it blows tonight, you'll know it in the morning.

REEDY: That's right. Then we just have to react. . . . But if it doesn't blow tonight . . . then I think we've got to make a normal return.

TUESDAY, MARCH 31, 1964

RODNEY WHITE
Nephew of LBJ
3:10 P.M.

BEFORE LEAVING to return to Washington, Johnson has his fifteen-year-old nephew, the adopted son of his late sister Josefa, called from class at boarding school in San Marcos, Texas, to discuss furnishing his Johnson City family house as a historic site.[1]

WHITE: Uncle Lyndon, I talked to Aunt Lucia the other day and she said that you could use some of the furniture.

LBJ: Yeah, we want to get all of it we can to put it in our house . . . so we can turn it over to the historical society to operate. . . . We'll get a truck to haul it up there, if Lucia will pick out what she wants. We'll get— [telephone line is cut off]

OPERATOR: Operator.

LBJ: [annoyed:] Hello. I was talking to Rodney White.

OPERATOR: I'm sorry. We got disconnected from the call. Just a moment, please.

LBJ: [turns to consult his doctor, George Burkley, about medication for a fever blister on his lip:] . . . That damned thing won't do a bit of good. I've put all that on it for an hour today.

OPERATOR: . . . We were talking with Rodney White. The President is calling. . . . Could you put him on this line, please? . . .

OPERATOR: Just a moment. I'm sorry.

LBJ: Rodney? [annoyed:] Is Rodney White there?

VOICE: No, sir, he's in school at the moment.

OPERATOR: Sir, he was talking to the President and—

LBJ: Makes no difference who he was talking to, Operator! . . . I haven't got much time. . . . When we were in the middle of it, they just cut us right off and I just can't come back from work and play while they cut us on and off. . . . If I can't finish a conversation without being cut off, I don't want to— [leaves, then brought back to telephone:] Yes, Rodney?

[1] White died in 1989 from AIDS.

WHITE: We got disconnected.

LBJ: Yeah, I know it.

WHITE: Aunt Lucia said that you couldn't use any of the chandeliers.

LBJ: ... Just leave it up to her, and let her pick out whatever she needs that can be used there. . . . Did she say what she could use?

WHITE: She said that we could use one of the sofas.

LBJ: All right, anything else?

WHITE: And then I told her about the dining room set and the buffet. And she said that it wasn't walnut, so it wouldn't be very good. It's mahogany.

LBJ: ... All right. Now why don't you get to studying down there?

WHITE: Yes sir, I'm doing a lot better this semester.

LBJ: All right. It's costing a lot of money to keep you down there, and you either ought to get out there or go to work for this CCC[1] camp or something because you oughtn't be spending that much money and not making As.

---

[1] Civilian Convervation Corps.

Chapter Six

APRIL 1964

FRIDAY, APRIL 3, 1964

THOMAS MANN
Assistant Secretary of State for Inter-American Affairs
12:06 P.M.

THE CIA-BACKED military coup in Brazil has toppled the leftist President, João Goulart.[1]

MANN: I hope you're as happy about Brazil as I am.

LBJ: I am.

MANN: I think that's the most important thing that's happened in the hemisphere in three years.

LBJ: I hope they give us *some* credit, instead of hell.

MONDAY, APRIL 6, 1964

LAWRENCE O'BRIEN
7:35 P.M.

THE PREVIOUS afternoon, as Lady Bird dictated into her diary, "Something happened that I have been wanting to happen for about nine years or more.

[1] The U.S. plan was code-named OPERATION BROTHER SAM. As the U.S. Ambassador to Brazil, Lincoln Gordon, observed, the Americans had been worried that Goulart's leftist authoritarianism might provoke "a more radical and very likely Communist-led coup against Goulart" (Warren Cohen and Nancy Bernkopf Tucker, *Lyndon Johnson Confronts the World: American Foreign Policy, 1963–1968*, Cambridge, 1994, p. 233).

Lyndon played golf! . . . *Maybe* he'll do it once a week and it would make a lot of difference for him . . . in health, in joy, in life."[1] Johnson's partner at Burning Tree Club was O'Brien's son, Larry Jr., who defeated the President.

LBJ: I've got a bunch of thugs in here waiting on you—O'Donnell and Company. They want to know why you produce boys that go out and embarrass the President. You're supposed to be the politician in the crowd and the first thing you ought to learn—Homer Thornberry played dominoes with me and let me beat him every game. He wound up in clover.

O'BRIEN: I gave all kinds of signals.

LBJ: You bring your boy out, and he beats the hell out of me the first day.

O'BRIEN: No, no, I looked over that card, and I think it was a tie.

LBJ: No, it wasn't. Come on down.

TUESDAY, APRIL 7, 1964

GEORGE REEDY
11:50 A.M.

> *TIME* HAS A STORY this week called "Mr. President, You're Fun," which reports Johnson's beer drinking while speeding in his cream-colored Lincoln Continental across the LBJ Ranch.[2]

LBJ: All of our people talk too much. . . . Just whap-whap-whap-whap-whap—big hydrophobia[3] of the mouth. We've just got to stop opening our mouths. We had four bad columns this morning. . . . On that other thing,[4] I'd just say the President and Miz Johnson were hosts . . . in their home to newspapers, on their land, and so far as you know, neither a *Time* or a *Newsweek* person was in either car with either one of them. . . .

REEDY: Now, got one or two other little problems. . . . You go to Washington

[1] Diary of Lady Bird Johnson, April 5, 1964, Johnson Library.

[2] "Groaned a passenger in the President's car when the ride was over: 'That's the closest John McCormack has come to the White House yet.' . . . At one point, Johnson pulled up near a small gathering of cattle, pushed a button under the dashboard—and a cow horn bawled from underneath the gleaming hood. . . . Johnson talked about his cattle, once plunged into what one startled newswoman called a 'very graphic description of the sex life of a bull.' . . . During the tour, Reporter [Marianne] Means, her baby-blue eyes fastened on Johnson, cooed: 'Mr. President, you're fun.' Through all the fun, the President sipped beer from his paper cup. Eventually he ran dry, refilled once from Marianne's supply, emptied his cup again and took off at speeds up to 90 m.p.h. to get more. . . . Someone gasped at how fast Johnson was driving. Quickly Lyndon took one hand from the wheel, removed his five-gallon hat and flopped it on the dashboard to cover the speedometer" (*Time*, April 13, 1964).

[3] "Hydrophobia" means fear of water. Johnson probably means "diarrhea."

[4] The *Time* story.

National Airport to pay your respects to Mrs. MacArthur.[1] . . . The question I'll get immediately, of course, is will you go to the funeral.

LBJ: . . . I'd just tell them,[2] "Now goddamn you. . . . Don't try to get rough with me. All I can tell you is here's what he's going to do Wednesday. He's going to give up two hours of his day meeting this casket and watching this horse and following it around town. Beyond that, I don't know what he's going to do."

. . . .

REEDY: I wanted to check this resignation of Doherty[3] with you. . . . The only thing on the record is he's leaving for personal reasons. . . . Ken O'Donnell suggests that if they ask me what are these personal reasons, that I go on deep background . . . just say he's a longtime friend of yours.

LBJ: I wouldn't do that at all, because he's not. . . . You don't have to say how long I've known him . . . and how many bastard children he's got. This crowd here[4]—you got to understand that they're not the masters of the White House. They're just the servants and we give them what we want to give them.[5]

GILLIS LONG
Democratic Congressman from Louisiana
7:05 P.M.

JOHNSON CALLS FOR HELP on his cotton-wheat subsidy bill.

LBJ: I've got the ox in the ditch.

LONG: [laughs] Lord, Mr. President. . . . I've got a real problem. . . . I'm going to end up with a substantial opponent if I vote for this bill and if I don't, I'm going to very probably end up with no opponent. It doesn't mean my not getting elected, but—

LBJ: Of course not. Well, what the hell. . . . why do you have to vote? Now you've missed a vote a time or two in your life. . . . Don't join up with Charlie Halleck against Lyndon Johnson, 'cause by God, I'm your friend.

LONG: Oh, I know that, Mr. President.

LBJ: And I'll be joining up with you when you need me, so just don't go vote, or give me a pair.[6] . . . Either of those two. Don't vote or give me a live vote. . . . If you vote to kill this bill tomorrow, if you vote with Charlie Halleck, you're going to add $125 million to the taxpayers of this country. Now you didn't know that, did you?

[1] General Douglas MacArthur had died two days earlier.
[2] The White House press.
[3] William Doherty, former chief of the National Association of Letter Carriers, whom President Kennedy had named as the first U.S. Ambassador to newly independent Jamaica in 1962.
[4] White House correspondents.
[5] Here a succinct version of Johnson's private view of the press, which would get him into trouble.
[6] An absent member of Congress can arrange for his or her vote to be "paired" with that of another absent member casting an opposite vote.

LONG: I've been pretty well through the bill, sir.

LBJ: Hell, I've got a poll coming out tomorrow where I jumped from 73 to 77 percent. [to aide:] Hand me that Gallup Poll. [back to Long:] Here's the heading —77 percent of public approve Johnson handling job. High popularity rating accorded LBJ in all regions of the country. . . . Today it's 77 approve, 9 disapprove. East—81 to 6. Midwest—77 to 9. South—75 to 13.

LONG: Whoo-*hoo!*

LBJ: West—76 to 8. . . . At exactly this same point in the election of '56, Eisenhower's popularity was 60 to 76, although he went on to win 58 percent of the popular vote for the greatest landslide victory in November. . . .

LONG: By your poll, Mr. President, I wouldn't be worried at all. [laughs]

LBJ: Listen now, I want you to vote for me, but if you can't vote for me, I wouldn't ask you to cause yourself to have trouble. But I know damn well that you can say . . . I was paired against it because I've been gone sometimes and I helped him out when he was campaigning in Texas.

WEDNESDAY, APRIL 8, 1964

GEORGE REEDY
11:45 A.M.

REEDY WANTS GUIDANCE on the previous day's Wisconsin presidential primary. The segregationist George Wallace, Governor of Alabama, won 25 percent of the vote for President against Wisconsin Governor John Reynolds, a Johnson-pledged favorite son.[1] Reedy also asks about a *New York Herald Tribune* story by Douglas Kiker about Johnson's irritation at *Time's* story about his speeding and beer drinking.

LBJ: I'd tell 'em, off the record, that I have tried not to show any activity in any of these primaries. Would have been mighty easy for me to let my name go on the ticket and roll up a heavy vote. But I want to try to be President of all of the people and we've got a lot of controversial things coming up where we want to try to appeal to both parties. So I want to be . . . as absolutely nonpolitical as I can. . . . I'd say that we've been in political life in Austin for thirty years. And our vote has usually been, for every office we've ever run for, not over 70 and

[1] RFK had urged Wisconsin voters to support Reynolds to strengthen "the good fight for human dignity" embodied in the civil rights bill. Although maintaining his refusal to campaign in the primaries, Johnson wired a testimonial dinner for the Wisconsin Governor the weekend before the vote that Reynolds was a "patriot." After the ballots were counted, Reynolds said that all Wallace had demonstrated was that "we have a lot of people who are prejudiced." This blunt remark helped defeat Reynolds for reelection that fall. As consolation prize, Johnson gave him a circuit judgeship. (See Dan T. Carter, *The Politics of Rage*, Simon & Schuster, 1995, pp. 203–09, and Stephan Lesher, *George Wallace*, Addison-Wesley, 1994, pp. 270–85.)

not under 60. And we find that a two-thirds vote is a pretty good vote. . . . If we could get two out of three votes in Wisconsin or two out of three in the Senate, we'd be happy. Or two out of three in the nation. . . . The fact that we get more votes than Wallace is pretty satisfactory to us.

· · · ·

LBJ: I'd say[1] . . . "If he has any irritation about it, I haven't observed it. I think that he has been here long enough to understand that *Time* writes about his gold cuff links—as if they expected him to have bronze ones—and about a gold wristwatch.[2] . . . He doesn't consider it anything but pretty political when they talk about his sipping a cup of beer." . . . I don't believe Kiker. I think he's just a little, dirty son of a bitch, don't you?

REEDY: I don't think he's a very good friend of ours.

· · · ·

LBJ: I'd say that you think there's something in the column of Reston's.[3] . . . The point is not the driving that we're talking about, or not the Baker[4] thing, or not the gold cuff links—not any of these things that are a pièce de résistance for Republican campaigns. . . . We've never mentioned a man's name or his family or anything else in any campaign we've ever run. We discuss the issues. But you do think that there is a question whether or not there's bigotry in the North against a Southerner on questions that involve his ability to handle foreign relations, that we think it's a little odd that they would make a big play of that, that we think that our relations are doing pretty well. Mr. Kohler[5] says compared to the problems that Khrushchev has, why, we ought to be joyful. He has 'em in every country, with every Communist Party, and eight hundred million Chinese Communists. We have a little one with Panama and maybe with Cuba that gets worked out pretty easily. But the attitude of the *Post* and the *Times* and *Newsweek* . . . not just the Baker thing or the gold cuff links . . . but on things such as Panama. Whenever we work it out satisfactory, their editorials are still critical— that while it was done the right way . . . the fellow that did it is still a son of a bitch. . . .

We think it shows some of the same attitude toward a Southerner that Mississippi shows toward Harlem, that there is a question as to whether you[6] can bring 'em together like Eisenhower had to. . . . Whether I can bring 'em together on these important issues of the day, whether it's poverty or whatnot. I don't know whether I can lead the world and people like the Prime Minister of Canada, like the Prime Minister of Great Britain and the Chancellor of Germany and Mr. Khrushchev if my own people feel this way about me. . . . It may be that

---

[1] About the *Herald Tribune* story.

[2] Johnson presumed that *Time*'s references to his gold cuff links and other expensive accessories were intended to portray him as a rich Texas operator.

[3] James Reston wrote in the *New York Times* that day that while LBJ was said to be "angry and hurt" over reports of his speeding in Texas, he should remember that he had had "a remarkably good press ever since he came to the White House," and that "the White House press corps has always been concerned about the safety of the President," especially since the Kennedy assassination.

[4] Bobby Baker.

[5] Foy Kohler, U.S. Ambassador to the Soviet Union.

[6] Meaning Johnson himself.

they've got somebody else that can do it better. I know that *Time's* got Scranton. And I don't know who *Newsweek* and the *Washington Post* have got, but I know it ain't us. . . . I'd say we're worried, from a patriotic standpoint, about the future of the country and the world. We've tried to effect the transition and bring labor in and bring business in with a minimum of deep divisions and hate. . . . and we tried to get rid of McCarthy[1] because we thought he promoted that. But we believe that the Eastern press has a feeling. It's kinda like Berryman's cartoons.[2] They always put a string bow tie on me because of where I was born. I never wore one in my life.

OFFICE CONVERSATION
12:13 P.M.

LBJ: [to aides in office:] I have to go to more things I don't want to go to. Have to go to some wedding and the cherry blossoms.

LAWRENCE O'BRIEN
12:14 P.M.

JOHNSON COMPLAINS that Congressman John Brademas, Democrat of Indiana, is refusing to support his cotton-wheat subsidy bill.

LBJ: You haven't got Brademas yet, have you? I was going to South Bend[3] to put my arm around him, say he's my boy and I love him . . . give him plenty of money and do anything. I thought he was a Rhodes Scholar and all this Phi Beta Kappa stuff.[4]

O'BRIEN: Here's a guy that could vote with us and not be hurt a bit.

LBJ: . . . I sent him to Greece.[5] . . . We had him down with the Queen of Greece. We've done every damn thing for that boy you can and he's gonna go off with about twenty or thirty wild men with Halleck. And by God, I'm gonna let Halleck be his leader from now on. I'm gonna be like Truman was one time when Tom Connally[6] came down here and wanted his campaign manager appointed judge. . . . And he said, "Is Lyndon Johnson for it?" He said, "Yes." Said, "Is Tom Clark, the Attorney General, for it?" Said, "Yes." . . . Well, he said, "Of course, I'll appoint him. Just consider it done." So he just took the commission and signed it. They put it on his desk . . . and Connally thanked him profusely . . . and went to the door and said, "By the way, Mr. President. I think I ought to tell you. . . . This fellow, while he did manage my campaign and always has been a lifelong Democrat, I think that he might have voted for Dewey." . . . And Truman just

---

[1] Joseph McCarthy.
[2] Paul Berryman was the *Washington Star's* editorial cartoonist.
[3] Brademas's home town in Indiana.
[4] Brademas was a member of Phi Beta Kappa at Harvard before becoming a Rhodes Scholar.
[5] Brademas's father was a Greek immigrant.
[6] Democratic Senator from Texas (no relation to John).

reached over and took this commission and tore it up right in front of him and said, "Tell him, by God, to get Dewey to appoint him!"[1]

THURSDAY, APRIL 9, 1964

McGEORGE BUNDY
11:30 A.M.

> BUNDY IS TRYING to act as a peacemaker between RFK and LBJ. At the moment, Johnson is not enormously interested.

BUNDY: Mr. President, I saw the Attorney General last night and talked at some length with him. He's in much the best state of mind that he's been in at any time since November, and I think in the next week or two when you find a moment—

LBJ: [perfunctorily:] Anytime he wants to come in, he can come in.

BUNDY: I think it would be very desirable for you and him to talk about civil rights.[2] He is one of the few people who's as wise about this Wallace thing[3] and, of course, as farsighted about it as you are. I think there's some advantage in—

LBJ: Anytime he wants to, I'm ready.

RICHARD RUSSELL
5:01 P.M.

LBJ: We just whipped the living hell out of your friend Charlie Halleck[4] and we had to do it with Yankees.

RUSSELL: You did a great job. . . .

LBJ: I stayed on the phone till midnight, night before last, and I changed people like Edna Kelly and Hugh Carey[5] and your friend Adam Clayton Powell. I just made it a Democratic issue.

• • • •

LBJ: Now the Governor of Mississippi[6] wants to come up here and see me and I think that'll just cause a lot of talk about my trading out, selling out, and

---

[1] Brademas voted against Johnson's cotton-wheat bill, which passed the House that day by 211 to 203.

[2] Bundy knows that on civil rights Johnson and RFK have more current common ground than on any other issue.

[3] The threat from the Alabama Governor.

[4] On the cotton-wheat bill.

[5] Kelly and Carey were both Democratic Members of Congress from New York.

[6] Paul Johnson.

everything else.[1] But they tell me that every family down there is buying a gun and every Nigra family's got a gun and that there's gonna be the damnedest shootings you ever saw on registration[2] and they're sending them in by buses in the hundreds from all over the country to help 'em register and they're gonna try to get 'em all registered in Mississippi and there're gonna be a bunch of killings.[3] Now what do you think about my having the Governor in here? Jim Eastland and John Stennis[4] both say they think I ought to see him.

RUSSELL: I think you have to see any Governor of any state of the union that asks to see you. . . .

LBJ: . . . I told 'em that I didn't think it was wise. It would just put me under attack that I'm conniving with the Governor of Mississippi and gonna try to trade out and there'll be some more compromise talk. . . .

RUSSELL: I think I'd defer it until after this fight's over, if I could.[5]

LBJ: How long's it going to be?

RUSSELL: We ought to get out about the middle of June.

LBJ: Oh, Dick, now you're not gonna keep 'em there till *June!*

RUSSELL: Why not?

. . . .

LBJ: Did you see Walter Lippmann last night?[6] I thought he was wonderful.

RUSSELL: I just wondered what it cost you. [both laugh] God, I know Old A.W. Moursund is signing up the deed to that damned television station. It's a Lippmann station now![7]

LBJ: Now, I want to ask you about that. They're demanding we sell it.[8]

RUSSELL: Oh, I wouldn't do it.

LBJ: I've got it in trust and they can't pay us any dividends. Can't pay us anything. And I don't own a share of it anyway. But now they're demanding my little minor children have to sell it because I'm President.

RUSSELL: Who's demanding? Ain't anybody that's for Johnson demanding it.

LBJ: No, Republicans.

RUSSELL: I wouldn't pay any attention to it a-tall.

LBJ: *U.S. News & World Report* are demanding that I give 'em a financial

---

[1] Despite Johnson's insistence that he would not compromise, his critics had been charging that he would make deals that would water down the civil rights bill to get it passed.

[2] When blacks register to vote.

[3] As part of what they were calling "Freedom Summer," large numbers of Northerners were planning to go to Mississippi in June to register black voters. About the outcome Johnson is chillingly prescient. (See June 23, 1964, conversations and those that follow below.)

[4] Senators from Mississippi.

[5] Meaning the fight over the civil rights bill.

[6] The previous evening, in the upstairs Oval Room, along with the Valentis and his secretary Vicky McCammon, Johnson had watched the columnist interviewed on CBS. Lippmann had called LBJ "a healing man," a "genius" in finding national consensus, adding that "the country is far more united and at peace with itself, except over the issue of Negro rights, than it has been for a long time."

[7] Russell is joking that LBJ has given Lippmann his television station as a bribe for his praise.

[8] The television station.

statement. I don't mind it. All I've got is some ranchland—six or seven thousand acres that may be worth ten to fifty dollars an acre and that television station and some municipal bonds.

RUSSELL: . . . I don't see where any elected officer's got to make any statement about his business interests. That's a matter between him and the electorate.[1] As far as him having to give out a statement every month or two, it's just foolishness.

LBJ: I thought that I'd tell 'em if they'd get one from Rockefeller and one from Scranton and one from Bobby Kennedy[2] and all them, I wouldn't hesitate.

RUSSELL: No, I'd just sit tight. . . . I wouldn't vote for Senators doing it, though I could stand it better than anybody in the Senate.

LBJ: Yeah, I remember. You sold out your stuff before I became President. You got out of the market when Eisenhower came.

RUSSELL: I'd be an object of pity. I didn't have but $19,000 worth, but I did sell that. . . . I just resent the implication that everybody that's in elected office is a damned scoundrel.

· · · ·

LBJ: What do you think about McNamara?

RUSSELL: I'm for McNamara.

LBJ: Think you could nominate a Republican Vice President?

RUSSELL: I think it'd help. Hell, he never has been enough for any party to hurt.

LBJ: He's got a lot of checks that he gave the Republicans, trying to satisfy Henry Ford.[3] He plays on the team.

RUSSELL: I wouldn't be the least bit bothered about that. Hell, Eisenhower—what was he?

OFFICE CONVERSATION
5:20 P.M.

> JOHNSON TELLS AIDES what they should say to reporters about Lady Bird's private finances.

LBJ: [to aides:] She[4] owns 50 percent of the station. It's worth two million, odd thousand, and owes about eight hundred. She owns half. So she'd be worth a million there and owe four hundred, so she'd be worth six, seven hundred thousand. So she's a millionaire and I'm worth about a little under two hundred thousand.[5]

---

[1] Russell here states the general view about financial disclosure among members of Congress before the post-Watergate laws of the 1970s.

[2] All three rich men.

[3] While McNamara was a Ford Motor executive.

[4] Lady Bird.

[5] This valuation was absurd because it was based on the purchase price of Johnson's properties, not the much higher figure for which he could have sold them in 1964. LBJ was always insistent on minimizing public statements of his net worth in order to avoid questions about how his

ROBERT McNAMARA and McGEORGE BUNDY
7:25 P.M.

JOHNSON WANTS PENTAGON OFFICIALS to brief the Secretary of State on Vietnam during a visit to Manila and Saigon.

LBJ: Rusk is leaving in the morning to go to Manila. . . . Maybe they could go ahead of him or maybe they could join him when he gets there[1] on the 17th.

McNAMARA: Why, surely. I think it'd be wise for Bus Wheeler[2] to do it.

LBJ: . . . They can meet him in Manila and go on out with him to Saigon.

McNAMARA: It would probably be wiser for them to meet him in Saigon.

LBJ: . . . I want him to spend a little time with Lodge too. . . . I don't want this to be solely "McNamara's War."[3]

McNAMARA: [laughs] I'm happy to have a partner!

LBJ: I agree with that, Bob. If you're going up in the polls now, I don't want you to be a warmonger. I want to have a peacemaker.[4]

BUNDY: [chuckles] We're going to have the Secretary make a few speeches out there to the crowd.

McNAMARA: [giggles] Don't pull my leg, Mr. President!

MIKE MANSFIELD
7:46 P.M.

IN RETALIATION for new rules reducing outmoded employees, railroad unions are threatening a nationwide shutdown at midnight. Confident of his bargaining powers, eager to succeed where previous Presidents had failed, Johnson has called negotiators for both sides to the White House. He has just emerged from a first meeting.

LBJ: They've determined to have a strike.

MANSFIELD: That fellow Luna[5] is an SOB.

LBJ: Yes, he is. And they couldn't locate him. Didn't get him here until two o'clock this afternoon. Had to send a plane after him. . . . Council of Economic Advisers says the great immediate excitement's gonna be in commuter service in

---

family had made so much money during his years in public service, to avoid the stigma of being a rich Texan remote from understanding people's needs, and also to avoid criticism for refusing to donate his $100,000 salary to charity, as Kennedy had. He certainly did not want it publicly known that although Kennedy had the reputation of being a rich man, LBJ was actually wealthier than his predecessor. *Life* estimated Johnson's net worth in August 1964 as approximately $14 million. The *Wall Street Journal* reported that same month that "some intimates back home in Austin" calculated it as "in the neighborhood of $20 million."
   [1] Saigon.
   [2] General Earle Wheeler, Army Chief of Staff.
   [3] Democratic Senator Wayne Morse of Oregon had publicly branded the American role in the Vietnam conflict, which he opposed, "McNamara's War."
   [4] Johnson here drops hints that he might choose McNamara for Vice President.
   [5] Charles Luna, a Texan who was president of the Brotherhood of Railroad Trainmen.

New York, Chicago, Philadelphia. Food shortages will occur almost immediately in New York. Heavy industry, ship, rail, coal mining will close down almost at once. . . . There'll be speculative price increases. The rails carry 44 percent of the total goods. . . . After the first week, our best guess is where total output, Gross National Product will be down 13 percent. That'll be four times the largest decline in any postwar recession. Six million or more workers, in addition to the seven hundred thousand in railroads, will lose their jobs, raising the unemployment rate to 15 percent or more. . . . You're the first one I've called. I thought I'd call Dirksen and the Speaker and just tell them what happened. . . . We're gonna have to be not impetuous, but I gave 'em until eight o'clock and I think they'll both turn it down.

FRIDAY, APRIL 10, 1964

MARSHALL McNEIL
6:40 P.M.

> JOHNSON'S OLD REPORTER FRIEND McNeil congratulates him. Late the previous evening, LBJ managed to persuade railroad bargainers to postpone a strike for fifteen days in order to allow negotiations at the White House. Then he took the Illinois Central president and the head of the Brotherhood of Locomotive Engineers into the Fish Room, where he announced his achievement on national television.

McNEIL: I thought this railroad thing was about as fine an operation as I nearly ever saw.

LBJ: . . . You haven't been into trouble until you get in between them.

McNEIL: No, sir, but I thought you were just cuter than a pig on that television last night.

LBJ: You know what they did? I told them to come back at eight o'clock. So they came back with a written statement. Wirtz[1] called up and said that they can't get anywhere and I said, "Bring 'em over." . . . I told them that this country couldn't stand this. . . . It meant that everything we've done all year since I came in November would fall back. And that I wanted them to give me twenty days to see what I could do about it and for them to go off till eight o'clock and come back and tell me. They came back. And the carriers said, "We accept your proposal." The labor people said, "We do not accept your proposal. . . . We've been at this four years and Presidents have asked us to postpone time and time again . . . and we just lost our ass every time.". . .

I said . . . "I'm not going to take that kind of no. I'm supposed to be a great healer and a great pleader. You go in that President's private office by yourselves.

---

[1] Secretary of Labor Willard Wirtz.

Talk it over and see if you want to tell the people of this country that you said no to their President when he hasn't had a chance. Now, Kennedy's had chances[1] but I haven't had any. And I want to see if we can't bring this thing about. I've had a lot of tough ones in the Senate and I think maybe we can bring some new faces and I can get some new negotiators, get some new ideas." They said no use in doing that. I said, "Go on in. I want you to see my office anyway." They went in[2] and sat down in the rocking chair and . . . got coffee. . . . Finally I went in there. I said . . . "There's a poll over on my desk—Gallup. Says 77 percent approve Johnson for President. . . . Now look at that, fellows. You wouldn't want me to say to the people of this country that you-all wouldn't give me two weeks to try to do my duty." . . . So . . . they came back and the old boy said . . . "We're going to go with you." They just blew up the whole damned works. Television didn't have their cameras and they didn't know what to do. . . . We just got 'em all excited. . . .

McNEIL: Well, you were cuter than a pig on that television. . . . I get prouder of you—damn your ornery hide, Mr. President—day by day.

LBJ: We got Panama behind us now[3] and if we can get this one pulled out some way—I don't know how. But I got Dean Rusk going to Vietnam.

McNEIL: . . . I hope he keeps that Lodge out of this race, by God.

LBJ: No, let him run from out there. . . .

McNEIL: . . . And you'll kick his ass off. . . . Did I tell you that Dobie[4] is not coming to Gridiron?[5]

LBJ: . . . I don't think *I'm* going. . . . I haven't recovered from that White House Photographers[6] the other night. They told me I could come and stay fifteen minutes and my back is still hurting.

McNEIL: No, Mr. President, by God, you're wrong, you've *got* to come.

LBJ: . . . I can't listen to these damn fellows try to make fun all evening.

McNEIL: They're not going to make fun all evening, but you'll like 90 percent of this show and you'll appreciate it.

LBJ: I don't like shows.

McNEIL: . . . There ain't nobody in Gridiron wrote about you driving a car fast.

[1] As President, JFK had delayed a railroad strike.

[2] To the Oval Office.

[3] Panama and the United States had agreed on an accord signed on April 3, reestablishing diplomatic relations and naming special ambassadors to "seek the prompt elimination of the cause of the conflict." The language pointedly omitted mention of the Panama Canal. Still, meeting with reporters on April 3, Johnson did not exclude revising the 1903 treaty that allowed the United States to control the Canal Zone into perpetuity. In 1977, amid deep political rancor in America, President Jimmy Carter and the Panamanian chief of government, General Omar Torrijos, signed two treaties ceding the Panama Canal to Panama on the last day of 1999.

[4] J. Frank Dobie of the University of Texas was a historian of early Texas and an old Johnson friend.

[5] McNeil was a former president of the Gridiron Club, an organization of Washington journalists who hold a celebrated annual private dinner at which the President of the United States usually gives an amusing speech.

[6] Dinner on the evening of April 2.

LBJ: . . . I don't even like Bob Hope. I went out to hear him the other night. I wanted to go to bed. . . . Don't want to come. I don't like to see those big old long-legged naked boys get up and make fun and trying to be actors. . . . I might for fifteen minutes.

. . . .

McNEIL: I think there's a woman here you gotta say hello to.

LBJ: All right. Let me talk to her.

McNEIL: Here she is. [stutters:] And, and q-quit, *quit* trying to make my *wife!* [1]

JENNIE McNEIL: Hello!

LBJ: How are you, Miz McNeil? [2]

JENNIE McNEIL: I'm just fine, thank you.

LBJ: I enjoyed being in your home the other evening.

JENNIE McNEIL: I am glad you did because we thoroughly enjoyed having you.

LBJ: It was mighty nice and I hope you can come down to see us pretty soon.

TUESDAY, APRIL 14, 1964

McGEORGE BUNDY
12:50 P.M.

THE BRAZILIAN COUP has culminated in the installation of General Humberto Castelo Branco as President.

BUNDY: We've got a message that we want to send out to Castelo Branco on the occasion of his inauguration. They reckon there's a difference between Gordon,[3] who wants to be very warm, and our view in the White House, which is that you ought to be a little careful while this fellow's locking people up. . . .

LBJ: I'd be a little warm.

BUNDY: You would? It'll be published.

LBJ: I know it. But I don't give a damn. I think that there's some people that need to be locked up here and there too. I haven't got any crusade on 'em but I wish they'd locked up some before they took Cuba.[4]

---

[1] Was McNeil joking, or stuttering out of embarrassment in reprimanding the President? Not unknown for his demonstrativeness with women he liked, Johnson had dined on March 24 at the McNeil home with McNeil and his new wife of six months, who worked at the Small Business Administration.
[2] Perhaps as a result of her husband's beseeching, Johnson is extremely formal and polite with Mrs. McNeil.
[3] Ambassador to Brazil Lincoln Gordon.
[4] This statement encapsulates the difference between the Johnson-Mann approach to Latin America and that of LBJ's predecessor.

. . . .

BUNDY: Wasn't Reston helpful on Sunday?[1] It's a new picture. Well, I do get a B-plus on that one.

LBJ: . . . I think you're getting these boys loosened up a little bit and helping George some and helping Bill.[2] . . . They need some leadership in this deal, just like you did your faculty.[3] I'd take 'em and I'd try to have coffee with 'em once every two or three days and say, "Now here's the kind of an image we ought to mold." . . . I think that Moyers has got the capacity and Jack Valenti can learn anything, if you'd just direct him. You just take them like they're teachers of freshman government and you're the dean of faculty and you tell 'em what you think they ought to do. . . . Because they're socially attractive. Everybody wants them out every night.[4]

McGEORGE BUNDY
1:00 P.M.

LBJ: UPI number 19. I'm sure you read it, but I think you ought to watch this with Lippmann. [referring to wire copy:] "Nixon told a joint luncheon meeting he had refused to discuss politics all through the area."[5] That's all he's done. . . . "The United States should take a tougher line toward Communism in Asia and should unleash South Vietnamese troops to extend that country's civil war to 'the sources of the trouble, whether in North Vietnam or Laos.' " Now, I guess he's unleashing 'em like Eisenhower unleashed Chiang Kai-shek.[6]

BUNDY: Just about.

LBJ: But they're done unleashed. What we're trying to do is get 'em to protect themselves. They haven't got much capacity to advance.

BUNDY: Our basic posture now is that General Khanh has told us that he wants to secure his base before he tries any fancy stuff. And we're standing on that position.

LBJ: But that's what he's gonna do. And General Khanh is not popular. You ought to tell Lippmann to knock the tail off of him[7] because he's trying to start

---

[1] Reston had written, "One of the vital natural resources of this country these days is the tireless negotiating skill of President Lyndon Johnson. Without it, the House of Representatives would certainly not have passed the Farm Bill or the Food Stamp Bill this week, and without it, every railroad train in this country would be at a standstill. . . . The emotional content of the Johnson appeal, the total absence of ideology, the passionate insistence on the general welfare, the willingness to talk endlessly through the night if necessary, the vivid earthy American language and optimistic faith that problems can be solved—all this is highly effective under Johnson" (*New York Times,* April 12, 1964).

[2] Reedy and Moyers.

[3] Bundy was dean of Harvard College before joining the Kennedy administration in 1961.

[4] Johnson says this almost as if boasting that Kennedy staff members are not the only ones who are popular at Washington social functions.

[5] Vietnam.

[6] Here Johnson refers to hollow Republican promises in the 1950s to "unleash" Chiang Kai-shek and his Nationalist Chinese on Taiwan to attack and retake the mainland.

[7] Nixon.

another war with China.[1] And he doesn't know what he's doing. And Lodge is not recommending that. Let's be awful damn careful that Bill Bundy and them see if Nixon's speaking for Lodge.

. . . .

LBJ: I sure think we got to tie that up. My judgment, Mac, is that Lodge is coming back. He'll probably be back in June. He's gonna find some trouble. He's gonna fall out with us about something.[2]

BUNDY: He's going to have differences with us and it's gonna be on this area, I'm sure. There're no others.

LBJ: And I'm not gonna let him have any differences. . . . You just better talk to Bill[3] out there in Manila and tell him that Johnson is not going to have any difference with Lodge. He's gonna have to run and catch me before he does. I'm gonna agree with every damn thing he does. That's my strategy.

BUNDY: [guffaws]

FRIDAY, APRIL 17, 1964

HARRY TRUMAN
3:52 P.M.

THE THIRTY-THIRD PRESIDENT will soon be visiting Washington.

LBJ: I called you to tell you that I hoped that you would use the Blair House[4] so you could have all your friends in, and be comfortable and do whatever you wanted to.

TRUMAN: You're just as nice as you could be. I can't tell you how much I appreciate it.

LBJ: . . . I'll have a car meet you and stay with you as long as you want him. . . . You just put your hat on, and come on in whenever you want to. . . . You'll sit at the head of the table at my place as long as I'm here.

. . . .

LBJ: You use the Blair House and have anybody over there you want to, and burn it down if you want to. . . .

[1] Here the wily Johnson wants Bundy to provoke the dovish Lippmann to attack Nixon for excessive hawkishness.
[2] Johnson presumed that Lodge would resign in protest over some aspect of Vietnam policy and return to the United States to run actively for President. Polls showed that of all the major potential Republican nominees, Lodge would give Johnson the closest race.
[3] Bundy.
[4] The official presidential guest house, across Pennsylvania Avenue from the White House, where the Trumans had lived from 1949 to 1952, when the mansion was being renovated.

TRUMAN: [laughs] I'll be careful not to do that.

LBJ: And if they raise too much hell, you let me know and I'll come join you.

MONDAY, APRIL 20, 1964

JACK BROOKS
6:45 P.M.

> BROOKS HAS JUST BEEN in Texas.

LBJ: How's old brother Connally?

BROOKS: . . . That hand business.[1] He's still got a problem with it. . . . He was just like being naked. Nobody was looking after him, so I had to stay right with him and . . . manage him.

LBJ: How's that good-looking girl of yours?

BROOKS: She's fine. . . .

LBJ: Why don't you let me get through with my business here, if I can, and let me call you back and come eat dinner with us?

BROOKS: We'd love to.

LBJ: Lady Bird's out of town. She got in an airplane. . . . Lightning hit it today a couple of times.[2] . . . She's driving back. She got hell scared out of her.

TUESDAY, APRIL 21, 1964

CYRUS VANCE
Deputy Secretary of Defense
8:00 P.M.

> THE CHAIRMAN of the Howard Foundry Company of Chicago has testified in court that a Bobby Baker business partner, Fred Black, took $150,000 to intervene with the Air Force in a $2.7 million claim against his firm.

---

[1] Connally's hand remained disabled from the shooting in Dallas.

[2] On a United Airlines flight to Cleveland. She dictated into her diary, "About an hour out of Washington, something happened—it's the most frightening thing I have ever known in an airplane. Suddenly there was a loud explosion. . . . My mind went back immediately to November 22nd. I thought. 'This is it.' I wondered whether we would go down fast or whether we would have a chance to glide down" (April 20, 1964).

LBJ: There's some testimony in the Black trial today. Are you familiar with it?

VANCE: No, sir, I haven't seen it yet.

LBJ: . . . It says that some company paid . . . Fred Black . . . some money to bribe officers out at Wright Field. . . . You call Sheldon Cohen. . . . He's the General Counsel of Internal Revenue and he's our man.[1] . . . I just want to be sure if there's any bribery going on, we know about it. We got to watch that. We want to double all the efforts we've been making up till now. . . . Notice the Harris Poll? . . . Half of them think that I can't keep corruption out of the government. So I don't want one case of corruption. Don't want anything close to it. That means my mother and my brother and my dead daddy, everybody else. Just say no to them when they come in. . . . It's only on the merits. If it just looks suspicious, kick it out and tell everybody in that department to do the same thing.

WEDNESDAY, APRIL 22, 1964

ROBERT KENNEDY
Attorney General
4:29 P.M.

FOR ALMOST TWO WEEKS, the two sides in the railroad bargaining have been closeted in the Old Executive Office Building. Johnson has frequently popped in to spur them on. After a long deadlock, the railroad presidents are now suggesting that they might be willing to settle the dispute in exchange for certain concessions from the U.S. government. Twenty minutes from now, Johnson will have them to the Yellow Oval Room in the family quarters of the White House, for coffee and a final session of persuasion. To increase the atmosphere of bonhomie, he has invited Lynda and Lady Bird to join them.

LBJ: The railroad owners . . . have raised a question. If they settle this strike— they got some mergers pending at the Department of Justice—they want to know if there's any chance that they'll get sympathetic consideration there. . . . My normal reply would be that the appropriate agency will give everybody . . . a fair shake. . . . But I thought before I did that, I'm going to try to hit them pretty hard and pretty tough. Almost as bad as we were with steel,[2] because I just don't think we can take this now. I just think it's the worst thing that could happen to us. . . . I thought I better talk to you. . . . What are the merger things? How serious are they? . . . Are they in the public interest? . . .

KENNEDY: . . . We've had a number of railroad mergers that we've permitted. . . . We have had a rather—quote—liberal—unquote—point of view. . . .

[1] Johnson had appointed Cohen soon after becoming President.
[2] A reference to the Kennedy administration's brutal confrontation with steelmakers over price rises in 1962.

LBJ: . . . Tell me what you think I ought to say.

KENNEDY: . . . Just say that everybody would make a major effort to try to do what was in the interest.

LBJ: . . . I don't want to give them any false encouragement. At the same time I want to try to settle it.

LADY BIRD JOHNSON
7:47 P.M.

JOHNSON'S MANSION COFFEE with the railroad presidents has succeeded. For LBJ, averting a railroad strike is a particular triumph because he has been much criticized for putting the prestige of the presidency on the line. The previous day Lady Bird dictated into her diary, "Every night Lyndon and I talk about what's happening to the railroad negotiators . . . and I know how much is hanging in the balance for him."[1] He could not give the good news to the nation immediately because in the spring of 1964, technology still did not allow a President to make an instant live broadcast from the White House. Instead Johnson swept four of the railroad bargainers into his limousine and sped to the local CBS affiliate, WTOP, where his friend CBS president Frank Stanton arranged for a three-network broadcast. Now, with Johnson back in the Oval Office, his wife showers him with acclaim.

LADY BIRD: *Pra-a-aise* the Lord! I thought it was *well* delivered and a *great* victory.

LBJ: Thank you, darling. Thank you. I've got to go on movies and some more TVs[2] and sign the mail and I'll be over in a little bit.

LADY BIRD: All right, dear. . . . I'll keep the TV on. I may have a massage and I'll see you whenever you get here.

THURSDAY, APRIL 23, 1964

BILL MOYERS
6:03 P.M.

THE JOHNSONS are in a penthouse of the Conrad Hilton Hotel in Chicago. As Lady Bird later recorded in her diary, they were about to attend "a fund-raising dinner at which Lyndon had blithely promised my presence to Mayor Daley, one of his favorite people. . . . He's a very arch type of political boss,

[1] Diary of Lady Bird Johnson, April 21, 1964 (Johnson Library).
[2] With cameras now ready in the Fish Room, Johnson was about to tape additional statements on the settlement.

ruddy-faced, emanating efficiency and friendliness."[1] LBJ speaks to his Special Assistant in Washington.

LBJ: The Attorney General's calling me out here. Do you know what that's about?

MOYERS: I suspect it's this, Mr. President. Bundy came by to see me a while ago and said, "I'd like to speak to you alone for a little bit."[2] So we closeted ourselves. And he said, "I just had a very frustrating session with the Attorney General and he was very angry when it was all over because he wanted to go to Berlin[3] and feel that he was going on behalf of his dead brother, and that if we want to stop him, then we just are not being faithful to the memory of his brother." And Mac said . . . "I'm a little disappointed in the Attorney General's reaction. . . . It was a very unsatisfactory session and a very unhappy one for both of us." And he was very upset about it. And he said, "I think, Bobby, this is something you ought to talk with the President about directly. If you really want to go because it's a tribute to John Kennedy, then you're the one who ought to tell that to the President." So that may be why he's calling.

LBJ: Well, what do you think I ought to say to him?

MOYERS: I think you ought to say to him that . . . when the assassination happened, everyone was out of the country[4] . . . and while the civil rights is going on, you don't want that to be upset. Just take Shriver, for example. He's in Germany and poverty[5] is up in the air. And you really don't believe he ought to go. . . . You can easily point out that the reason it all came up is that today this poverty situation blew up in our face and Shriver was out of the country.

WALTER JENKINS
6:24 P.M.

JENKINS: A.W.[6] called me. He and Waddy[7] have a wire, quite long, from the *Wall Street Journal.* . . . It's pretty pointed. A lot of questions. You interested in hearing any of them?

LBJ: Yeah, but I'm due to leave right this second.[8] I haven't shaved or put on my tux yet. What's the net of it?

JENKINS: The net of it is that you said that you didn't have anything to secrete and that the trustees were the proper people to get the information from, so

[1] Diary of Lady Bird Johnson, April 23, 1964 (Johnson Library).
[2] Bundy is still trying to act as a go-between for Johnson and RFK.
[3] West Berlin Mayor Willy Brandt had invited RFK to attend a ceremony rededicating the square in which JFK had declared *"Ich bin ein Berliner"* in 1963 as John F. Kennedy Platz. Worried about giving the late President's brother too much exposure, LBJ preferred that Kennedy stay home.
[4] This refers to the fact that Pierre Salinger, Dean Rusk, and five other members of Kennedy's Cabinet were on a plane flying to Tokyo at the moment of his assassination.
[5] The Johnson anti-poverty bill, sent to Congress in a special message of March 16, 1964, asking for $962.5 million, was being navigated through often-rocky hearings before the House Subcommittee on the War on Poverty Program, chaired by Adam Clayton Powell.
[6] Moursund.
[7] Bullion.
[8] For Mayor Daley's fund-raising dinner.

here's the questions they have. . . . Have they considered disposing of the properties since you said they[1] had the authority to? . . . They want the revenues, the
net income for the last three years. . . . What dividends have been paid since the
stock went into trusteeship both to Miz Johnson and the daughters? . . . What
matters were discussed during a conference between Johnson and trustee Moursund?[2] . . . What discussions has Johnson had with Kellam[3] in his repeated sessions with the Johnsons in the White House and in Texas? . . . Pages and pages
in a wire.

LBJ: [quieter:] I'd show it to Abe.[4] . . . Probably just say that here's a copy of
the trust agreement, that they've had no conversations with Johnson mentioning
the business at all. . . .

JENKINS: It's a nasty wire. It says that failure to answer these questions would
also be newsworthy too. I mean, kind of bribery.

LBJ: A little blackmail.

· · · ·

LBJ: Who signed the wire?

JENKINS: It's signed by Henry Gemmill, Washington Bureau Chief. . . .

LBJ: I think that we can give 'em the public records and say that we'd be glad
to consider any offer. We've had none. The dividends have been fifteen thousand.
Been a total of so much invested, and all of it's been reinvested and they've only
had the three years of dividends. . . . It's a matter of the Johnson children, and I
wouldn't like to see 'em driven out of business. We don't know what they've
done that caused this madness to descend. . . . The *Wall Street Journal*'s had a
pretty long article on it and a good more, it looks like, than they've had on the
holdings of other Presidents. And this is not personal holdings. It's a question of
the family, and I don't know what they've done that would cause this attack to
be made. . . . We've had no conversations with Kellam and them. . . . They've
been running it direct.

BILL MOYERS
6:36 P.M.

READING OVER HIS SPEECH TEXT, Johnson notes a passage in which he is to
say how much his plan to provide medical care for the aging will cost an
American worker.

MOYERS: You should say an average of about a dollar a month.

LBJ: That's too much. . . . On the average worker's earnings, it's about a dollar
a month. Something like that. [irritated:[5]] Why the hell don't you get ahold of

[1] Johnson's trustees.
[2] During Johnson's Texas trip at the end of March.
[3] LBJ's business manager.
[4] Fortas.
[5] Johnson's irritation probably stems from Jenkins's call about the *Wall Street Journal* problem.

that damned Jack Valenti? I've asked him and I told you to do it the other day, Bill. I called this to your specific attention.

MOYERS: All right. Then I thought I had it right, but I didn't.

LBJ: You haven't got anything. You've just got a dollar a month, period. Just what I said. [loudly:] Which we know is wrong. The AMA's[1] done attacked it. I'm ready to leave right this second to go to the platform and it's a hell of a shape to get me in. Where's Jack? Has he just gone off socializing again?

MOYERS: I don't know where he is. I've got the White House looking for him.

· · · ·

LBJ: The *Wall Street Journal* sent a long wire to the trustees that was very upsetting. . . . I've got really not anything to hide, but they're going into every grocery store[2] and asking why they're advertising with us. . . . It's something that I've renounced any interest in. . . . Can't get it legally. . . . And all of hers is in trust. They've got to imply the government would be doing something to benefit 'em.[3] And they're not. They're making less than they were before.

ROBERT KENNEDY
10:50 P.M.

>DURING HIS SPEECH before Mayor Daley and six thousand cheering Demo-crats, Johnson named his administration, declaring that Americans had been called upon to build "a Great Society of the highest order."[4] Lady Bird observed in her diary, "The air was full of the sort of euphoria of success—the end of the railroad strike. If you could make a graph of this administration, perhaps this would be sort of a peak."[5] On the way back to the hotel, Johnson was feted in Grant Park with fireworks in the shape of his profile, a Stetson hat, and an American flag.[6] After returning to the Conrad Hilton penthouse for a rubdown, Johnson calls Robert Kennedy at home.

LBJ: Bobby, I'm sorry to be so late calling you. I hope we didn't wake you up.

KENNEDY: No, that was fine.

LBJ: We had six thousand out here tonight and I just got through shaking hands with some of them.

KENNEDY: Oh, I saw it on television. It sounded very good. . . . Said it was the biggest one they had. That was terrific.

LBJ: Thank you.

KENNEDY: I talked to Bill Moyers and gave him a message. . . . It was just on

---

[1] American Medical Association.

[2] In Austin.

[3] Members of the Johnson family.

[4] Many of the Cook County Democrats, unaware or indifferent to the fact that they were hearing history being made, talked through much of Johnson's speech.

[5] Diary of Lady Bird Johnson, April 23, 1964 (Johnson Library).

[6] One must remark on the irony that the Great Society, at least in name, was born in Chicago, next to Grant Park and the Conrad Hilton, and that it died in the same spot, during the anti-LBJ, anti–Vietnam War riots surrounding the 1968 Democratic convention.

the jury trial amendment and we reached a compromise which I thought would be acceptable to you. We're doing thirty days. Senator Dirksen wanted ten. . . . So we reached a compromise of thirty.[1]

LBJ: You think that's all right?

KENNEDY: Yes.

LBJ: All right. . . . If it's okay by you, it's fine by me.

KENNEDY: . . . He was optimistic about getting a bill within the next six weeks —Senator Dirksen. . . . The impression he gave was that he really wants to work it out and wants to get the thing behind everybody.

LBJ: I just think if we don't pass it, I'm getting awfully frightened that if we don't pass it in the next thirty, forty days, I'm afraid these people are going to hurt it pretty bad. Aren't you?

KENNEDY: Yes, I am. On the other hand, the pressure gets greater on Dirksen not to hold out. . . .

LBJ: I tried to put a little of it on tonight, to everybody I talked to out here. I think they can feel some of it maybe in a few days how important it is to go ahead.

TUESDAY, APRIL 28, 1964

JOHN McCORMACK
12:25 P.M.

> LBJ COMPLAINS about delays in passing his government pay raise bill.

LBJ: Magnuson's[2] telling everybody—the damn fool—that he's ready and he wants to meet and he wants to shove it down. 'Course they all run when it's something involving me. If it involved them, they wouldn't do it. But they don't care. . . . It doesn't do anything but help the Republicans. And I guess I expect too much of them sometimes. I ought to just go on and just take it in my own hide.

. . . .

LBJ: We ought to hire some people . . . that can get a count. Goddamn it, I've been trying to get this count now for three or four weeks on three or four bills and we don't know any more every Tuesday than we did the Tuesday before. . . . I used to check these votes. I had a hundred Senators and they're more independent than the House members. And I knew before the McCarthy vote[3] every

---

[1] Kennedy is boasting about his negotiating skills with Dirksen. Senator Herman Talmadge had proposed a jury trial amendment as a new tactic with which to weaken and stall the civil rights bill. (See Johnson's conversation with Mike Mansfield, April 29, 1964, below.)

[2] Senator Warren Magnuson, Democrat of Washington.

[3] The Senate vote to censure Joseph McCarthy in December 1954.

vote in that body was going to be in his chair without a quorum call against McCarthy. Every Democrat. . . . Somebody up there. Goddamn it, if we have to get Bobby Baker back![1]

. . . .

LBJ: They're asking me to try to run a government without a damn thing to keep 'em.[2] I just can't have them come in here charitable. I can get a bunch of rich men who'll come down here and do it and look after their own nests. But Kennedy really put together a hell of a good crowd. And I've just got dozens of 'em, just like sheep. Charlie Murphy over at Agriculture says he's not gonna stay and Wilbur Cohen, top man over at Health-Education.[3] That damn thing would fold up if that man walks out of it. . . . It might be that you and Carl[4] ought to sit down with Charlie Halleck. . . . I'd just say, "Charlie, if you don't make it a political issue and you let ten or twelve of your boys walk off and let us pass it, goddamn it, we'll get you the money." Now he's in trouble out in Indiana.[5] . . . They wanted me to take a little crack at him. . . . I said, "We've got some rules in this thing, and we don't fight each other personally. . . . And Charlie Halleck is a pretty responsible leader and he worked with me. . . . I have to have him." Anyway, you can tell him that, off the record. Just tell him that we don't want him to make a party issue out of poverty—poor people and a pay bill. . . . We'll give him some consideration on some things that he needs.

LAWRENCE O'BRIEN
5:50 P.M.

JOHNSON'S TRANSPORTATION BILL has suffered a reverse.

LBJ: I see where the "Johnson bill" took a big whipping today. They name it "Johnson" when they lose, I guess.

O'BRIEN: Yeah, I suppose.

LBJ: What happened?

O'BRIEN: . . . We made contact with Tip O'Neill[6] yesterday and he said . . . he didn't like the bill. . . . He said, "It looks to me that by the time I get through explaining to people that as far as I know, the Boston Navy Yard will not close down at least for a while, and as long as McNamara is screwing everybody, that keeps me pretty busy in my office answering mail." I said, "Now that . . . is a pretty archaic administration." He said, "Don't give me that shit, Larry. . . . You fellows create 2,200 destitute families." . . .

LBJ: . . . Maybe we ought to close the damn Navy yard if that's the way he wants to play it. [chuckles darkly]

[1] Baker was noted for his vote-counting abilities.
[2] Johnson is complaining about his predicament in the absence of his pay bill.
[3] Murphy was Undersecretary of Agriculture, Cohen an Assistant Secretary of HEW.
[4] Albert.
[5] Halleck had nearly been defeated for reelection to the House in 1962.
[6] Democratic Congressman from Massachusetts and future House Speaker Thomas P. O'Neill, who was a pivotal member of the House Rules Committee.

O'BRIEN: Well, Tip—you know him well. He plays tough. He was the first Democratic Speaker of the House in the history of Massachusetts and boy, he didn't get that way without being a pretty tough boy.

WILLIAM BUNDY

Assistant Secretary of State for Far Eastern Affairs

6:50 P.M.

LBJ: Bill, I got a letter from the wife of the [former] Vietnamese Ambassador, the one that is . . . Madame Nhu's[1] mother.[2] . . . After I came back,[3] all the Ambassadors wanted to give me a dinner to report on my trip and they agreed that the senior one would do it and he happened to be the one. We felt very friendly toward him, and I thought that it was pretty hard for a father to have to be against his daughter at that time. And being a father, I was pretty upset about it. I got a letter from her tonight. . . . "I come to beg you to rescue . . . my only son Tran Van Khiem. . . . I know your kindness. When you invited the camel driver from Pakistan to come here, you gave him great happiness.[4] If you see a bird or a dog, you save him and rescue him. Now my son is in danger, and he . . . did not commit any crime whatever. . . . The present government is going to bring him before a revolutionary court. . . . Please save my son. . . . If you do, I will be grateful to you for all my life." I want him saved. Now what can we do about it? . . .

BUNDY: . . . I'll get cracking on it right away. . . . Do you want to send a personal message?

LBJ: No, I just want you to cable out there and see if they can't prevail on him and let him come and live with his mother in Chevy Chase and tell her that a very high official wants it done. . . . I just want to save the boy, because I love the mother and I don't think he's done anything.

GEORGE REEDY

7:07 P.M.

THE DAY BEFORE this conversation, Johnson created an image for which he is remembered to this day. While greeting a group of bankers and other businesspeople in the Rose Garden, he pulled his beagles upright by the ears, saying, "If you ever follow dogs, you like to hear them yelp. . . . It does them good to let them bark." Johnson was immediately denounced by dog lovers across America.

[1] Madame Nhu was the notorious sister-in-law of the slain South Vietnamese President, Ngo Dinh Diem. In the fall of 1963, she had gone on a U.S. lecture tour, denouncing American liberals as worse than Communists, and Vietnamese Buddhist monks, who had opposed the Diem regime, as "hooligans in robes." Her father, Tran Van Chuong, appointing himself a "one-man truth squad," followed her around the country to rebut her charges and warn that the Diem government had become "unwittingly the greatest asset to the Communists."
[2] Chang Van Sung.
[3] From a trip to South and Southeast Asia as President Kennedy's emissary in 1961.
[4] During Johnson's 1961 trip, he invited a Pakistani camel driver to visit him in the United States, which the man did in a wave of publicity.

The head of the Chicago Humane Society declared, "How painful it is to any living creature to be picked up by the ears." Now LBJ complains to Reedy.

LBJ: Hell, the pictures . . . show that the dog is standing on his hind heels and there's not anything that hurts him doing that. He barks all the time. He's been here barking a dozen times today. Who was it? Doug Cornell?[1]

REEDY: Yes sir.

LBJ: Well, I want to know what that son of a bitch looks like, and I want to give him the silent treatment for a while. Did he carry on interviews with everybody over the nation too? Did he carry on interviews with all the pet experts?

REEDY: No sir. That came in from their bureaus.

LBJ: So he's got a great feeling for hurting a dog, huh?

JOHN McCORMACK
7:18 P.M.

DURING A CONVERSATION about Congressman Tip O'Neill's objection to potential closure of the Boston Navy Yard, the Speaker of the House complains to Johnson about McNamara.

LBJ: Somebody said that O'Neill was awfully upset because . . . McNamara closed something up in Boston. I asked 'em if it was in his district and they said no, somebody else's.

McCORMACK: Yeah, but most of the people who work there live in his district.

LBJ: Well, he can't give all of them a job.

McCORMACK: . . . Mr. President, you know from your own experience they can't do that. They promise it, but they can't do it. There's about 2,400 up there.

· · · ·

LBJ: He tells me though that both of those places in Boston really ought to have been closed. Two in Massachusetts—Watertown[2] and I've forgotten the other one.

McCORMACK: Springfield?

LBJ: Yeah.

McCORMACK: Well, I'll not burden you with headaches. But I had one experience with Bob McNamara and I don't want another one with him. I'll just tell you I had the most uncomfortable experience with him that I ever had in my life. All the thirty-six years that I've been in Congress, I never underwent an experience like what I had with him. I'm not complaining.

LBJ: What was wrong with it? What was it about?

[1] Of the Associated Press, who had written a wire service story on Johnson's infraction.
[2] LBJ means Charlestown, where the Boston Navy Yard was.

McCORMACK: Leverett Saltonstall and Ted Kennedy[1] were interested in some company in Worcester and they asked me to go along. And I went along. And McNamara was so *drastic*. Now he could have said no . . . the right way. But he was so drastic. . . . I finally spoke up and said, "Mr. Secretary, I have a feeling you're putting us in the position of being defendants." If I was alone, I'd have gotten up and walked out. It's awful. I just don't have to take those things. . . . I don't want to have any more conferences with the man. Not that I don't respect his ability. . . . I gave him great organizational powers in the McCormack Amendment[2] and I'm glad that I did. It's a valuable thing.

LBJ: I'm surprised that he treats you that way 'cause I consider him about the best man that I've got.

McCORMACK: . . . I respect him very much for his ability. But I don't want to have any more conferences with the man. I just had one experience.

LBJ: Do you think that entered into this thing with O'Neill, or is it just the port?

McCORMACK: No, I don't think so. O'Neill would be against it anyway. Tom's all right. He's a good fellow. He might bark, but his bark is worse than his bite. . . . Tom's like a big Saint Bernard dog. A very fine fellow. He'll bark, but he's just as loyal as they make 'em.

WEDNESDAY, APRIL 29, 1964

MIKE MANSFIELD
11:32 A.M.

ON MARCH 9, Johnson's civil rights bill arrived on the Senate floor.[3] Senator Richard Russell immediately began his filibuster, insisting that the South was determined to fight "to the last ditch." Determined not to look as if he was being steamrollered by Johnson, Dirksen on April 7 offered forty crippling amendments to the bill's Title Seven, which banned discrimination in employment. But during a meeting with reporters, affecting a droll look, he added, "My position is negotiable."

On April 21, the Senate Republican leader quietly told Humphrey that Johnson's civil rights bill would and should pass the Senate and it was his duty to help. But he wished to avoid a cloture vote. He told Humphrey that the Southerners were wearing out anyway and that it would be difficult for him to summon enough Republicans to stop the filibuster. Humphrey stood firm, unwilling to let Russell and his comrades off the hook. Dirksen relented.

When the news reached Russell, the Georgian privately said, "The jig is

[1] The two Massachusetts Senators. Saltonstall was a Republican.
[2] This presumably refers to the McCormack-Curtis Amendment to the 1958 Defense Reorganization Act, which broadened the authority of the Secretary of Defense.
[3] The House had passed it with modest changes 290 to 130.

up." He lamented his inability to persuade Lyndon Johnson to compromise. Changing tactics, his Georgia colleague, Herman Talmadge, proposed an amendment to Title Six offering a jury trial to anyone charged with willfully defying a court order against an act of discrimination. Talmadge did not need to mention that few Southern all-white juries would vote to convict in such a case. Talmadge's gambit put pro–civil rights Senators in the awkward position of having to seem to oppose trial by jury.

On April 24, Dirksen and Mansfield proposed a victorious bipartisan substitute amendment.[1] Over luncheon with Republican leaders on April 28, Dirksen said he would give the Southerners one week's notice. If they did not stop their filibuster within a week, he would file for cloture. But, unwilling to appear as if he had become LBJ's puppet, he complained to reporters about Johnson's abuse of his beagles and the President's refusal to compromise on the House civil rights bill. He announced that he was about to tell his old friend at the White House, "In my humble opinion, you are not going to get it. Now it's your play. What do you have to say?" Dirksen said that if the President was ready to compromise, Republicans would deliver between twenty-two and twenty-five votes to stop the filibuster.[2]

In the conversation below, LBJ shows his irritation with Dirksen's public posturing, which could force the President to back down on his promise not to wheel and deal on civil rights.

LBJ: Mike, what should I tell Dirksen when he starts trying to put me on the spot down here on this civil rights thing today? Just work it out with the leaders?

MANSFIELD: That's right. Tell him that . . . it would be your suggestion that he and I just keep working together and it is our responsibility now.

LBJ: I'm going to tell him that I support a strong civil rights bill. He gave out a long interview of what he's going to tell me today before he comes, which is not like him. I don't know what is happening to him here lately. He's acting like a shit-ass.

MANSFIELD: Yeah.

LBJ: First thing—he said he wouldn't treat his dog like I treated mine. . . . It's none of his damned business how I treat my dog. And I'm a hell of a lot better to dogs—*and humans too*—than he is.

MANSFIELD: [laughs]

LBJ: I stand my damned dogs up and hold them by the ears so an AP photographer can get a picture and another little guy that didn't know what he was doing,[3] he writes a story that it is cruel to the dogs. Hell, I know more about hounds than he ever heard of! But they've got every dog lover in the country raising hell, thinking I'm burning them at the stake. All just a big play about nothing, 'cause that's all they can get. Dirksen is . . . trying to stir it up. And it is too little a thing for a big man like Dirksen, *but* I gathered from Larry O'Brien that

---

[1] The Mansfield-Dirksen substitute let the judge decide whether a person accused of criminal contempt should be tried by jury or not. If a jury trial was vetoed, punishment could not exceed a $300 fine or thirty-day imprisonment.

[2] For congressional action on the civil rights bill in March and April 1964, see, for example, Robert Mann, *The Walls of Jericho* (Harcourt, 1996), pp. 389–417.

[3] Douglas Cornell.

Humphrey wanted us to tell him that we want to get cloture on the whole bill. But I gather from the paper that you are going with cloture on the jury trial.[1]

MANSFIELD: I raised the question with him after this meeting yesterday and he wouldn't go along with it on the bill. And I would rather go on the bill. But we've got to get those twenty-three to twenty-five votes there and if we can't get cloture on this, at least we'll break the ice. . . .

LBJ: . . . Then . . . I'm going to say to him . . . now these details can't be decided down here in the White House, legislative-wise. I have the Attorney General and he's in constant contact with Senator Mansfield and Senator Humphrey and whatever you-all work out, I'm sure, will be agreeable.

MANSFIELD: Yes sir. Put it back on us and stroke his back.

LBJ: That's good.[2]

J. WILLIAM FULBRIGHT
11:55 A.M.

JOHNSON WANTS the Senate Foreign Relations Chairman to extend a brief planned ceremonial trip to The Hague and Copenhagen in order to perform some additional diplomatic errands with the French, British, and Greeks. Fulbright is worried that Senator Russell will think that LBJ has fiendishly sent him out of the country in order to deprive Southern segregationist forces of a vote on amendments to the civil rights bill.[3] Fulbright suggests that privately he would prefer to vote for the bill, if it were not for his certainty that this would kill him politically in Arkansas.

LBJ: Bill, I've got this thing worked out now. . . . I hit Butler[4] pretty hard on it this morning. . . . I said, "We just, by God, don't want to be open to this charge that our friends are selling anything to Cuba. And Nixon is running around all over the country raising hell and you just find some way to avoid it." So he heard it loud and clear and he's taking it back to Home.[5] . . . If they had to say they had to continue to sell, why, then it would look like we had a failure of a mission whereas if you went in privately . . . you could get them to reduce it and it would be a success. Go to Paris. Go to London. . . . You probably ought to go to Greece and talk to their Prime Minister . . . about Cyprus and tell him not to overplay his hand there now. . . .

FULBRIGHT: You know, one thing bothers me—our mutual friend, Dick Russell. . . . I think you know what he's going to say—that I'm being taken away because of a pending cloture vote.

[1] Only the jury trial amendment instead of the entire bill.
[2] Assured by Mansfield and Humphrey that he could get a civil rights bill now without bargaining with Dirksen, Johnson outfoxed the Illinoisan by refusing to deal when Dirksen arrived at the White House. After Dirksen departed, LBJ told reporters that they had barely even discussed civil rights.
[3] This may have been one of Johnson's motives.
[4] The British Foreign Secretary, R. A. "Rab" Butler, who was visiting the White House.
[5] The British Prime Minister, Alec Douglas-Home.

LBJ: I wouldn't do that. You were going to be away anyway.

FULBRIGHT: I was only going to be a couple of days.

LBJ: You won't have to be but a couple more . . .

FULBRIGHT: . . . It's just about my relations with him. You know what I mean.

LBJ: I don't want to cause that. I'd rather lose the government than to have you and Dick falling out. . . . I don't want him saying that I'm trying to plot though to beat him this way. . . . Just tell him that . . . you've got to make a couple of extra stops and . . . for him to figure out what day he needs you.

FULBRIGHT: The paper says they're about to have a cloture vote. I can't just go off and leave him.

LBJ: That's right. . . . I'd resign before I'd hurt his feelings.

FULBRIGHT: If that cloture vote comes while I'm away, you know it might make quite a difference, the way I understand this thing. Now, personally, if I've got a good excuse, I'm not going to cry about that.

LBJ: I'd tell him . . . not to have his cloture vote the day you're gone. . . . I wouldn't tell him that Johnson has called me because he'll think it is a trick.

· · · ·

FULBRIGHT: These silly statements of Novak's and others, who said I was going to trade my vote on cloture.[1] Goddamned press will find out I'm gone . . . and I want to minimize that. You know damned well I don't want to be Secretary of State. . . .

LBJ: I'd be awful careful. I don't think I'd tell him that I was going to do this administration stuff 'cause he'll think it is a slick trick of Johnson's.

FULBRIGHT: That's just what I'm afraid of. . . . Hell, they've got the whole thing set up.[2] My God, that Ambassador in The Hague. The Queen[3] and all that crap . . . and you know these people abroad take these things very seriously.

· · · ·

FULBRIGHT: . . . I'm going to have to tell him[4] this. . . . It is a kind of embarrassing thing for me. As you know, goddamn it, I'm not very enthusiastic about these fights.[5]

LBJ: I know it, I know it, I know it.

FULBRIGHT: Jesus Christ, I'm really over a barrel on this thing. I wish to hell I could vote with you. You know that.

LBJ: I know that, I know it.

FULBRIGHT: I hope to hell I can get this thing out of the way, but I feel like a traitor, you know. Down in Arkansas, I had all these damned people from the chamber of commerce last night. . . . John McClellan[6] gave them a rousing speech against the civil rights bill. . . . It puts me in a hell of a spot.

[1] This refers to the Evans and Novak column surmising that Fulbright might vote for cloture in order to become Johnson's Secretary of State.
[2] Fulbright's scheduled ceremonial duties in Europe.
[3] Queen Juliana of the Netherlands and Queen Ingrid of Denmark.
[4] Russell.
[5] Against civil rights.
[6] Fulbright's fellow Senator from Arkansas.

LBJ: Sure does. I know it does.

FULBRIGHT: The only thing that really concerns me is my relations with Dick. I don't want him to think I'm welching. That's what really concerns me. The fact is that if I'm out of the country and if they had a vote, as far as my constituency, I'd say, hell, I was on government business. But with Dick, it's a little different from my constituency. [chuckles] I'm awfully afraid of what his reaction is going to be.

LBJ: ... I'm like Sam Goldwyn[1] with you and Dick. I love him so much, and you too. Include me out.[2] [laughs]

FULBRIGHT: Goddamn it. That ain't easy with him.

LBJ: I know it, but I've got to do it, and don't you let me ask you to do anything that would interfere with him. But if you go anyway, I sure want to make you a little more comfortable.

ABE FORTAS
6:26 P.M.

> FORTAS HAS MET with the *Wall Street Journal* reporters who wanted further information on Johnson's business holdings.

LBJ: What was your general reaction with the *Wall Street Journal?*

FORTAS: ... The fellow who is the head of the office seemed to be very friendly. ... The fellow who wrote the articles just sat there and glowered. But I thought it worked out very well. But you know you can never tell, these damned things. The net of it was that everything I was telling them was from a conversation with Moursund and Bullion. I explained to them that these were Texans and that they didn't feel that when they were running a business that they ought to be subjected to any kind of badgering that other people running a business were immune from, and that their position was that this was all politics and from the Republican National Committee. ... When I said that they thought this was political, he said, "Oh, no, no, it's not political at all." And I said, "Of course it's political."

. . . .

LBJ: I see today in the *U.S. News & World Report* that we make $500,000 after taxes.[3]

FORTAS: That was in that original *Wall Street Journal* article.[4] ...

LBJ: [laughs] Exclude the capital gain on sale of the capital assets—162[5] for last year. And if you include that, it's two hundred.

FORTAS: ... I didn't tell 'em about that capital gains though because that just will lead to more questions. ... The next question is what were the assets that

[1] The studio chief who was fabled for his malapropisms.
[2] A command popularly attributed to Goldwyn.
[3] *U.S. News* had reported that this was Johnson's annual income.
[4] In March 1964, by Louis Kohlmeier.
[5] Thousand.

were sold, and then you've got to get into all the rest of the property that Texas Broadcasting Company[1] owns, and I think would be a mistake.

LBJ: No, it wouldn't. . . . I'd just say we sold a television station and a bunch of cattle. That's all. That's very simple. That's not what the outfit earns, though. It earns $165,000 a year, after taxes. And they say it earns $500,000 a year. . . . They ought to quit lying that way.

.   .   .   .

LBJ: They exaggerate all this stuff and it makes it like hell. If we had an estate tax tomorrow, that goddamned examiner would come in. First thing he'd have is a copy of the *Wall Street Journal*. . . . and he'd try to prove that they were low at seven million and the property's worth ten. . . . That's a very great disservice to us.

THURSDAY, APRIL 30, 1964

HUBERT HUMPHREY
12:11 P.M.

> AFTER STANDING UP to Dirksen on civil rights the day before, Johnson is angry to read a UPI story quoting Humphrey as saying that the President might be willing to compromise on amendments to the bill.

LBJ: Hubert, I don't believe you ought to be quoting me on what I'm ready to do on these amendments. Just go on and tell what you-all are doing.

HUMPHREY: [prickly:] Mr. President, that was not my quote and I'm very sorry.

LBJ: It's on all the tickers though and they're raising hell about it. . . . Don't quote me unless . . . you know I want to say it, because . . . I've been saying it at every press conference since I came in here and they would like very very much to say I weakened the bill. And I'm not going to. That's not my position. I'm against any amendment. I'm going to be against them right up until I sign them.[2] . . .

HUMPHREY: That's what I said here this morning. I said the President of the United States wants the House bill and . . . our job in the Senate is to legislate. The President of the United States is not going to tell us what to do and that he's a reasonable man, and we will do what we are required to do here, and then the President will decide what he wants to do.

LBJ: That's good. That's the thing to do. That's the way to handle it.

[1] Johnson's company.
[2] Johnson here privately shows Humphrey that he will accept amendments in the end.

HUMPHREY: One of these reporters last night came out after Dirksen had talked and said to me, "Will the President accept—"

LBJ: They're trying to jockey us into that position, and we just must not be caught in it now.

HUMPHREY: I won't say a word.

LBJ: I'm against any bill except the House bill, and the only bill that I'll sign is one that you and the Attorney General both recommend in writing I sign.[1] And let's don't get divided on it, because Russell says this morning that he thought there was some significance in Johnson's willingness to accept amendments. When the debate started eight weeks ago, he said everyone was saying we had to take the House bill without change. Nobody has ever said that anybody has to take anything. We just said we're going to pass a bill and we favor the House bill.

HUMPHREY: I'll send over exactly what I said.

LBJ: Well, you just tell that damn UPI to correct that impression they put—

HUMPHREY: I gave it to Bill Theis[2] just a few minutes ago and gave him the devil.

LBJ: I just don't want the farmers and the rest of them coming in and saying I've changed my position. Because I haven't. And you tell them. And you know they can do that mighty quick.

HUMPHREY: I know.

LBJ: Okay, pardner.

ROBERT McNAMARA
7:50 P.M.

> McNAMARA HAD WARNED Johnson's National Security Council on April 22 that they were "right on the margin in Vietnam" and that he could not guarantee that the United States would still be there in six or twelve months. During Rusk's mid-April trip to Saigon, General Khanh had insisted that the South Vietnamese situation was deteriorating so fast that the United States should not wait for him to secure his own base before launching major attacks on the North. The Secretary of State had replied that such an action might risk a nuclear war with Communist China. Unfazed, Khanh said that as long as Communist China remained, the United States would never have security.[3]

LBJ: Bob, I hate to bother you but tell me—I saw a little glimmer of hope on Vietnam in some paper today where we'd routed some and killed a few and run 'em out or something. Are you getting good cables on them at all?

[1] Johnson suggests that he will defend himself from public charges of having compromised on the House civil rights bill by waving a written demand from RFK and Humphrey that he sign a compromise bill.
[2] Chief of the UPI Senate staff.
[3] Record of 578th NSC meeting, April 22, 1964, Johnson Library, and Memorandum of Conversation between Rusk and Khanh, April 18, 1964, and Rusk to State Department, April 19, 1964, in FRUS, pp. 244–48.

McNAMARA: I read that article, Mr. President. The official battle report wasn't as good as the newspaper report, for once. . . .

LBJ: Is Carl Rowan getting any of his propaganda people[1] out there now?

McNAMARA: Yes, I think so and I'm going to check again before I go at the end of the week.

. . . .

LBJ: Have we got anybody that's got a military mind that can give us some military plans for winning that war?

McNAMARA: Bus Wheeler[2] is going out with me.

LBJ: I know, but he went out last time and he just came back with planes. That's all he had in mind, wasn't it?

McNAMARA: . . . Whether we should have more planes or not is another question, but it is not going to make any difference in the short run.

LBJ: Let's get some more of something, my friend, because I'm going to have a heart attack if you don't get me something. I just sit here every day. And this war . . . I'm not doing much about fighting it. I'm not doing much about winning it. I just read about it. Let's get somebody that wants to do something besides drop a bomb, that can go in and go after these damn fellows[3] and run them back where they belong. . . . We need somebody over there that can get us some better plans than we've got, because what we've got is what we've had since '54.[4] We're not getting it done. We're losing. So we need something new. If you pitch this old southpaw every day and you wind up as the Washington Senators and you lose, we'd better go and get us a new pitcher.

McNAMARA: I know it.

LBJ: . . . Tell those damn generals over there to find one for you or you're going to go out there yourself.

McNAMARA: That's one reason why I want to go back. A kick in the tail a little bit will help.

. . . .

LBJ: What I want is somebody that can lay up some plans to trap those guys and whup hell out of them, and kill some of them. That's what I want to do. If this Army Chief of Staff[5] is not going to, let's get somebody else that'll do it.

[1] From USIA.
[2] Army Chief of Staff.
[3] The North Vietnamese.
[4] When Eisenhower began aiding the South Vietnamese.
[5] Wheeler.

Chapter Seven
MAY 1964

FRIDAY, MAY 1, 1964

GEORGE REEDY
11:50 A.M.

THE *Baltimore Sun* has reported that the previous day LBJ gave Hubert Humphrey "unshirted hell" for suggesting publicly that Johnson might compromise on the civil rights bill.

LBJ: I'd call Hubert and ask him what to say about that. Tell him that we never said anything to anybody. I didn't dress him down. I just told him that I wouldn't be making any statements about the White House position. I'd just take one position. I didn't dress him down at all.

REEDY: . . . Should I just say you believe it's a good bill? . . .

LBJ: I'd say that I have made my recommendations, and that obviously from time to time, proposals come up that would be considered. . . . That's a matter for the Senate. I'm not going to comment on legislation at this stage, other than to say that I thought the House bill should be passed. I recommended the House bill. I still do.

SATURDAY, MAY 2, 1964

GEORGE REEDY
1:55 P.M.

LBJ: We got a bad one from Roscoe Drummond[1] because you were sleeping on it. . . . We just got to see these columnists. . . . He takes a Republican handout or

---

[1] A syndicated columnist.

a George Reedy handout. And if you don't give him a handout, he's going to take theirs.[1]

HUBERT HUMPHREY
2:14 P.M.

LBJ: [irritated] I got your note here. Nobody was in the room when I talked to you. I read that story and I thought it was just my friend[2] talking too much up there. I thought that was your way of expressing it because I didn't feel like I was giving you "unshirted hell." I was just trying to clear it out.

HUMPHREY: I didn't either. I didn't either.

LBJ: And you just talked when you ought to have been listening.[3] That's the problem that all of us got with dogs and everything else.

HUMPHREY: Well, yes. [laughs]

LBJ: I read the story and it looked like it came right from you and you just said, "Oh, God Almighty, I just caught hell." . . . I've got a diary. It shows that Senator Kennedy[4] came in three minutes after I talked to you but he wasn't in the room and no one else was in the room with me. And I wasn't giving any unshirted hell anyway. I was just clarifying that I want to be awful careful. . . . I think you can get by with repealing the goddamn bill, but I think that if I changed one comma. . . . I want to be awfully careful. And that's all I was saying.

HUMPHREY: I understand that. Listen, I'm not being critical of you.

LBJ: I know it. But I don't want to hurt you. I want to be helpful to you. I'm trying to build you up.[5] I'm trying to make you the greatest man in the world, and I would be the last man in the world to say that I ever corrected you about anything. I might say you corrected *me*. But nobody in this office did it. . . . You better just check and see who was in your own office or if you told somebody that you just caught the devil or you were sweating because Johnson kept you late. I saw a story. One of them said that you held up your ears like a beagle . . . and said they had a debate in the press corps whether you were cupping your ears, trying to hear him, or holding them up like a beagle dog. Of course, they got it wrong on the beagle dog. All I was doing was holding the beagle up so they could get the front of his picture instead of his ass. They got his ass for ten days here and I wanted to show them a good well-formed head. And besides, when a hound dog barks—I don't want to get in the paper on this, but that's his pleasure. That's not his hurting. [laughs]

· · · ·

---

[1] Here Johnson again privately shows his low opinion of journalistic practice and motive.
[2] Meaning Humphrey.
[3] This is one of Johnson's most consistent private criticisms of Humphrey.
[4] Edward Kennedy.
[5] Johnson here drops a hint that he is seriously considering Humphrey for Vice President, just as he has to Shriver, McNamara, and others.

LBJ: [changes subject to civil rights:] Are you making any progress?

HUMPHREY: We are going to start meeting on Tuesday with Mr. Dirksen and see what he has in mind.[1] . . . I've tried to make it crystal clear . . . what your position is. . . . We will just go ahead and do the best we can.

LBJ: God bless you, my friend.

McGEORGE BUNDY
4:30 P.M.

LBJ: You want to go play golf with me? Why don't you come walk around?

BUNDY: I have played tennis, Mr. President.

LBJ: Oh, well, you are such a sissy. What do you want to run out here and play a girl's game for?[2]

BUNDY: [guffaws]

LBJ: I was going to call Rusk. Come on, I've got nobody but Walter Jenkins and Jack Valenti and you walk around and we got some irons for you.

BUNDY: Mr. President, I really think I'd better not. Thank you ever so much. Not today. [laughs] I did enjoy myself fabulously last week. I've cheated the doctors by playing three sets of tennis today and I don't think I'd better.

LBJ: Okay, you better not.

FRIDAY, MAY 8, 1964

LAWRENCE O'BRIEN
6:11 P.M.

EARLIER IN THE DAY, LBJ had closed a tour of Appalachia with two courageous, bravura civil rights speeches in Georgia[3] and won the most enthusiastic welcome thus far of his presidency. Vast throngs lined the streets of Atlanta,

[1] Frustrated by Johnson's refusal to compromise on civil rights, Dirksen has agreed to start full-fledged negotiations with Mansfield and Humphrey.
[2] Here Johnson betrays his inner views about the unmasculinity of the Northeastern well-bred.
[3] At an Atlanta breakfast of Georgia legislators: "Heed not those who would come waving the tattered and discredited banners of the past, who seek to stir old hostilities and kindle old hatreds. . . . I will never feel that I have done justice to my high office until every section of this country is linked, in single purpose and joined devotion, to bring an end to injustice, to bring an end to poverty, and to bring an end to the threat of conflict among nations." At Franklin D. Roosevelt Square in Gainesville: "Full participation in our society can no longer be denied to men because of their race or their religion or the region in which they live."

moving Johnson to depart his limousine a dozen times and shout through a bullhorn.

O'BRIEN: Welcome home! My God Almighty, that must have been fantastic.

· · · ·

LBJ: I've got two hands. I need two hands. My right one is chewed up and fingernails have poisoned it, and I've got it where I can't shake hands.

O'BRIEN: I'll tell you, reading it and watching the wires—my God!

LBJ: I made sixteen speeches and we had a million people, and that's a minimum. I think it's two million, but the goddamn mean Republicans gave us a million. Today we looked up there and just as far as you could see—the Cotton Bowl didn't have anything like they had today, and most of them said sixty-five thousand. Some said one hundred thousand. Old Herman Talmadge[1] got up there after I made two civil rights speeches that he was present at, and said, "I just want to say this, that I have never seen as many people anywhere." If you don't think they're for what you're doing, you ought to get out there and see them.

· · · ·

O'BRIEN: Now Carey is into this religious thing. . . .[2]

LBJ: Oh, the hell with him.

O'BRIEN: . . . Christ, I said to Shriver, "What the hell is the matter? You have some nice Jewish boy from HEW[3] that's been talking to Carey, and Carey has told us to keep him the hell away from him." And Shriver said, "Goddamn it, they sent a fellow up there that doesn't believe in any private schools. He thinks they all ought to be closed." And I said, "That's a great guy to put in with Carey."

· · · ·

LBJ: Now Drew Pearson says[4] I'm mad at O'Donnell for paying attention to politics. I've never seen Drew Pearson. I've never talked to him. I haven't said it to a human. I'm not mad at him. I want him to spend more time on politics. . . . Tell him it's a lying son of a bitch and somebody's trying to make Ken O'Donnell get mad or me get mad at him. . . . He's just a troublemaker. . . .

O'BRIEN: Listen, I wouldn't be a bit surprised to pick up the column any morning and find that President Johnson is very disappointed in Larry O'Brien's activities. Why, hell, those things are going to happen. . . .

LBJ: Tell him there ain't a word of truth in it. I'll take a polygram[5] on it that I don't. I never had that feeling. I never said it in my life. . . . If he's not doing it, we're in a hell of a shape, because I'm not doing a bit of it. All I'm doing is making some speeches.

O'BRIEN: I'm not accusing you of doing any politicking over the last thirty-six hours. [laughs]

· · · ·

[1] Democratic Senator from Georgia.
[2] Congressman Hugh Carey of New York and other Catholic Congressmen were concerned that Johnson's poverty bill would discriminate against parochial schools.
[3] Wilbur Cohen.
[4] In his syndicated column.
[5] Meaning polygraph.

LBJ: Dirksen told me they were going to pass the bill and it was going to be a good bill—on civil rights. Can't you-all get him to agree to come on and go to cloture with you or is he just going to try to keep from passing anything?

O'BRIEN: . . . Somebody's going to have to use the whip.

· · · ·

O'BRIEN: . . . Hubert was shaking his head the other night.[1] That shook hell out of them, you know. I says, "God, look at those votes today and look at your . . . one-vote margin. . . . All the intellectuals that you're talking to all day long, and changing commas and language. . . . For God's sakes, you've got the title of Whip and you just better get a whip out." . . . I think you're absolutely right, Mr. President, that Dirksen will say okay just before the Republican convention— "Boys, let's have a bill." And then he'll sneak out of town. . . .

LBJ: I'm going to call them back too, if they do.

O'BRIEN: I don't blame you. . . . They know you mean business.

MONDAY, MAY 11, 1964

STEPHEN SMITH
President, John F. Kennedy Library Corporation
12:27 P.M.

> SMITH, husband of John Kennedy's youngest sister, Jean, is the Kennedy family business manager and chief fund-raiser for the John F. Kennedy Library, planned for Boston, across the Charles River from Harvard College.[2] Briefly a JFK State Department official, Smith and his wife accompanied Johnson on his Asia tour in 1961. Now Smith wants LBJ to solicit the millions of U.S. federal employees to give money to the Kennedy Library.

SMITH: Is this the President?

LBJ: [laughs] This is what's left of him. . . . I thought you had quit me. . . . You just come in here and pay one little pop call and then you play tennis the rest of your life. . . . Just come to see me the next time you are in town.

SMITH: All right, I'd love to. I just tell you, they are all up here[3] either signing up as Democrats or making drunks out of themselves. You've got to leave those Republicans 2 or 3 percent.

LBJ: Now, don't you worry about that. They'll have 50 percent.

SMITH: I saw Jock Whitney[4] the other night and he was drunk and saying that you Democrats ought to be concerned about the two-party system. . . . He's so

[1] After the four votes on the jury trial amendment.
[2] After protests by local citizens worried about congestion, the Kennedy Library was relocated to Columbia Point, Boston, and opened in 1979.
[3] In New York City.
[4] John Hay Whitney, Republican publisher of the *New York Herald Tribune*.

upset they can't do anything about Brother Goldwater that he wants the Democrats to do something about it now.

LBJ: [laughs] Henry Luce[1] asked me yesterday what I would do for the Republican party, what I'd recommend. I said, "Stand for something. Only thing you-all talking about is beagles and speedometers."

SMITH: I must say it's going awfully well. . . .

LBJ: Well, it will be dark days. We have them back and forth.

· · · ·

SMITH: The federal employee request or solicitation has apparently a tremendous possibility. . . . It would make a major difference, of course.

LBJ: I want to do anything I can by example. I don't want to do anything by compulsion. . . . The Republicans are just laying for it. . . . They would like nothing better than to say that I was trying to shake them down. . . . Terry Sanford[2] suggested that Jackie might . . . decide to go on Sunday.[3] We could fly her down there. Lady Bird and I could make a five-minute real hard pitch with the Billy Graham thing when he speaks to forty thousand. That would be electrifying and there would be enough notoriety connected with it because of Graham's presence and her presence that we could take that and circularize the hell out of it.[4] . . .

SMITH: [disappointed:] Um-hmm. Fine.

LBJ: [persists:] Now the North Carolina thing. . . . If we just flew down there quietly and I made a three-minute speech that could be broadcast and reprinted, that could be put up in every department.[5] . . . I told Mac Bundy to work it out. He just spends 90 percent of his time on the library anyway.[6] . . . I'm not a hesitant guy. I will do more than you want me to do. I just want to do it the right way and we got a few new people in here and I don't want to bungle it. . . . If Jackie will go to North Carolina . . . I'll get a Jetstar and it will take us a hour to get there. . . . Being President, I imagine they would call on me for two minutes. . . . I would say what you could print all over the country. . . . We would get somebody to put in the *Record* and they could frank the damn thing up.[7]

SMITH: All right. Then let me find out about that and get back to Mac.

LBJ: How's my girl?[8]

---

[1] The *Time-Life* publisher.

[2] Democratic Governor of North Carolina.

[3] With Billy Graham as main speaker, a rally is planned for Kenan Stadium at the University of North Carolina for Sunday, May 18, culminating the state's drive to raise $230,000 of the $10 million required to build the Kennedy Library. Johnson understands that if Jacqueline Kennedy decides to join him and pose for photographs with him—at a time when he is anxious about support from the Kennedys and their national following—the Kennedy Library will not be the only beneficiary.

[4] It is hard to imagine that Johnson really thought that Jacqueline Kennedy would actually break her private mourning to appear in a North Carolina stadium before forty thousand people in the company of LBJ and Billy Graham. He probably calculated that though she was unlikely to accept, it was worth a try and besides, it would help to get Smith off his back.

[5] Of the government.

[6] Meaning that Bundy is still loyal to the Kennedys.

[7] Meaning put it in the *Congressional Record* and send out the statement at government expense.

[8] Jean Smith.

SMITH: She couldn't be better.

LBJ: Give her my love and tell her that she's not paying much attention to me. I think these titles scare her. Just tell her if she wants me to be a lone wolf, I would resign my job rather than give her up. How's Mr. Kennedy?[1]

SMITH: . . . He's up at the Cape.[2] . . . Basically about the same. It was a little encouraging there for a while[3] and then he tired. . . .

LBJ: I'll call him. I don't want to bother him and I don't want to be a bore.

SMITH: No . . . I must say it's a great boost for him. . . .

LBJ: Teddy is burning up the league down here. He's the guy that's the hero of the Senate. . . .

SMITH: Yes, he's working hard.

LBJ: Now, you come to see me, Steve. I'm not going to let you off the hook. You just think you can retire? You are crazy as hell.

ANN GARGAN and JOSEPH KENNEDY
12:45 P.M.

> As he had promised Stephen Smith, Johnson calls Joseph Kennedy at Hyannis Port.

LBJ: How's my friend?

GARGAN: He's doing pretty well, sir.

· · · ·

KENNEDY: [faintly:] Hello-o-o!

LBJ: I'm so glad to hear you and I'm so glad you're back home.[4] And I just wanted to tell you that Teddy and Bobby are doing a wonderful job, and we're so proud of them, and I hope you are feeling better.

KENNEDY: Hm-m-m-m.

LBJ: You got so much to be proud of because Teddy is just burning up the Senate. He's the best thing they've got up there. Bobby is doing a wonderful job with the civil rights bill and I know you must be awfully proud of the training you gave those boys.

KENNEDY: I-know-I-know-I-know.[5]

LBJ: . . . And I hope you enjoy Hyannis Port, and maybe I'll get to come to see you before too long, and if there's anything I can do, you please have Ann call me.

· · · ·

---

[1] Joseph Kennedy.
[2] Cape Cod.
[3] Ambassador Kennedy had been undergoing rehabilitation.
[4] From Palm Beach.
[5] This is an approximation of Kennedy's faint words.

LBJ: Ann, I told him, if he didn't understand it, that . . . Teddy is just the most popular thing in America. . . . He's more popular than Jack or Lyndon or anybody ever was in the Senate.

GARGAN: Oh, that's great. . . . Uncle Joe has been very good, but he was a little bit stunned by your call.

JOHN McCORMACK
2:00 P.M.

McCORMACK: Boy, that speech of yours![1] . . . That's just a revelation, what you did down there. Just amazing.

LBJ: You're mighty nice. I wish Old Carl Vinson[2] would put them in the *Record*. If he don't, you put 'em in.

McCORMACK: Phil Landrum put the speech in himself.[3]

LBJ: That's in Gainesville. I had one in Atlanta though, when I talked to the legislature and told them about Georgia's motto being wisdom and justice and moderation and we had to be wise enough to act and we had to be just enough to give everybody a little justice, and we had to be moderate. I got by with it pretty good and six hundred thousand came out and applauded me. . . . That Atlanta speech—I think you will remember it a few years from now.

McCORMACK: . . . It's a historic speech anywhere, but particularly where you made it right down there, and it took guts.

LBJ: [chuckles] It sure did.

McCORMACK: It took guts, with a capital "G."

LBJ: [laughs] You know, they gave me a couple of tigers beforehand, baby tigers.[4] Said that I had beagle dogs . . . and they wanted to give me a couple of tigers. They wanted to name one of them "Lyndon" and one "Lady Bird." I said I'm not unaccustomed to tigers. . . . I was Senate Leader for eight years. And I am going to rename them "Dick" and "Herman."[5] [laughs] That's what got me off so I could say what I said on civil rights.

CARL ALBERT
2:20 P.M.

LBJ: I see where O'Neill[6] threatened us on the Boston shipyard. . . . He's threatening the wrong man when he goes threatening me.

---

[1] In Georgia.
[2] Democrat of Georgia and Chairman, House Armed Services Committee.
[3] This was large of Georgia Democratic Congressman Landrum, for he opposed Johnson's civil rights bill.
[4] Johnson later gave the gift of tiger cubs to the Atlanta Zoo.
[5] Referring to Georgia Senators Russell and Talmadge.
[6] Congressman Tip O'Neill.

LAWRENCE O'BRIEN
2:52 P.M.

LBJ: Larry, Charlie Halleck's going to try to keep us from peeing a drop from now until the session is over. . . . Now he wants to bring the Church into this poverty fight. . . . I've got a Catholic in charge of it. I can't put the Pope in charge of it. I've got the nearest thing to the Pope I can get.[1]

WEDNESDAY, MAY 13, 1964

SARGENT SHRIVER
2:45 P.M.

JOHNSON HAS JUST RETURNED from a private luncheon in the Capitol with the Texas delegation to Congress—Protestants who have filled his ears with complaints about special Catholic influence on the poverty bill.

LBJ: We had a bill for all the country . . . but Spellman[2] rewrote it. He sent down word from the Pope and that's it. I've just been to the Hill and just had lunch with twenty-three of them and they just tore right in. . . . I told them . . . "There's nothing for you-all to get all hot and bothered about now because Moyers[3] is in on this program and he's not going to turn it over to the Pope." . . . Halleck has got it going. He's outsmarted you. . . . He tried the Negro thing and that didn't get off the ground and now he's got the religious thing. . . . And you got no more chance to hold that Bible Belt by changing a comma . . . than you have of just flying to the moon.

· · · ·

LBJ: I know that this feeling is deep. . . . You'd almost have a fistfight if you put Bob Poage and Wright Patman in the room with Jim Delaney and Tip O'Neill.[4]

· · · ·

LBJ: I think what you'd better try to work out . . . is to say please, please give me the discretion. . . . If you can't . . . trust me and Johnson, you can't trust anybody. . . .

SHRIVER: . . . Carey put it to me. . . . "They're closing up my Navy yard, and now they're closing up my schools. What the hell have I got to run with? And I've got a Republican against me."

[1] Meaning the devout Shriver.
[2] Francis Cardinal Spellman of New York, who supported Nixon for President in 1960.
[3] An ordained Baptist minister, Moyers obtained a Bachelor of Divinity degree from the Southwestern Theological Seminary in Fort Worth and held three rural pastorates before joining Johnson's Senate staff. LBJ uses Moyers to reassure the Baptists, Shriver to reassure the Catholics—and perhaps Wilbur Cohen to reassure the Jews.
[4] Two Protestant Congressmen, Democrats from Texas, and two Catholic Congressmen.

LBJ: . . . I've *saved* his Navy yards. . . . He doesn't have to get a religious argument started to do that. . . . I'm the one that kept the Navy yards from closing. No one else but Little Lyndon! They ought to be closed. . . . They're operated for the basis of giving jobs to the people. . . . It's just a poverty program. But I've kept them open in Boston and Brooklyn and Philadelphia. And I did it because Ken O'Donnell came in and said that we can't afford to close 'em. But I'm not closing Carey's Navy yard. And if that's what he's doing on that, why we *can* close it. . . . I don't *have* to have a poverty program. If they want to kill it, they can kill it.

McGEORGE BUNDY
3:35 P.M.

> ON THE SENATE FLOOR, Ernest Gruening, Democrat of Alaska, has demanded that Johnson offer a mutual defense pact to Israel, guaranteed by the U.S. Sixth Fleet, and convene a joint meeting of Israeli and Arab leaders at which the Arabs would renounce their pledge to destroy the Jewish state.

BUNDY: I'm just talking right now to Abe Ribicoff.[1] We would like your authority to say to Abe I've given . . . a pretty clear picture of the story to Abe Feinberg[2] . . . and have them tell the . . . Israeli Ambassador and any Jewish leader that they think necessary that this is no time to rock the boat, because Gruening is out in the *Times* this morning, and Javits[3] has letters making trouble that are circulating on the Hill. And as you know, the one thing that is going to make life tough for our British friends is to have it look as though we were passing the buck to them. Abe said that he understands this proposition . . . and he will try and keep things buttoned up, if that's what you want.

LBJ: Yeah. But I'm afraid that if you tell one of them, it'll be in the paper.

BUNDY: [aside:] He says that if you tell anybody it'll get in the paper. [back to LBJ:] Well, the whole object is to keep it out of the papers, and we won't give the details of the deal.

LBJ: I wouldn't. That's what I would do then. . . .

BUNDY: You've got to make two phone calls—one to Harman[4] and to Feinberg, telling everybody to keep quiet for a week.

LBJ: That's right, and please tell him to tell Javits. . . . I want him to stop everybody that's talking about it.

[1] The Democratic Senator from Connecticut, a Jew, was also a strong supporter of Israel.
[2] Businessman and fund-raiser for Jewish and Israeli causes, as well as the Democratic party.
[3] New York Republican Senator Jacob Javits.
[4] Israeli Ambassador Avraham Harman.

ROBERT KENNEDY
4:05 P.M.

THE ATTORNEY GENERAL has just emerged from a pivotal bargaining session with Dirksen in the Senate Republican leader's office. The Democrats have agreed to changes in the House bill, primarily face-saving, that will allow Dirksen, with his rhetorical gifts, to claim that he has wangled important concessions and allow him to become one of the fathers of the civil rights bill when it passes.

KENNEDY: Mr. President, we had a meeting all day today with Senator Dirksen on the civil rights bill—

LBJ: Good.

KENNEDY: And feel that we have an agreement with him and with Senator Aiken and Senator Russell.

LBJ: *Congratulations!* Congratulations! Congratulations! Now what does he think? Does he think he can get the votes for cloture?

KENNEDY: He's hopeful . . . They're going to have a meeting of the Republicans on Tuesday morning.

LBJ: Are you in pretty good shape with the folks that are interested in the bill?[1]

KENNEDY: We're supposed to meet with them at four-thirty. . . . You know, they're not going to be happy, but nothing makes them happy and so we just have to accept that.

LBJ: I don't know. You did a good job making everybody happy on the House side.

KENNEDY: Well, you remember, in October, they weren't happy when they did it.[2]

LBJ: Yeah, I know it, but they saw the wisdom of it after you did it.

KENNEDY: After it was over. But Senator Humphrey did a fine job. Senator Dirksen was terrific. You might just—

LBJ: Should I call them?

KENNEDY: Yeah. I think it would be nice and should I give you the names? Senator Saltonstall and Senator Aiken and Phil Hart[3] was damned helpful and Senator Magnuson was very helpful.

LBJ: All right. All right.

KENNEDY: And, of course, you've got Dirksen and Senator Humphrey.

LBJ: . . . All right. Thank you, Bobby.

KENNEDY: Righto, sir.

[1] The most zealous pro–civil rights forces.
[2] In October 1963, when John and Robert Kennedy made their deal with Halleck and McCulloch to get a House civil rights bill, some civil rights groups had decried the Kennedy "sellout."
[3] Democrat of Michigan.

EVERETT DIRKSEN
4:30 P.M.

LBJ: Everett, the Attorney General said that you were very helpful and did an excellent job and that I ought to tell you that I admire you. I told him that I had done that for some time.

DIRKSEN: That's very kind.

LBJ: But I'd repeat it, and hope that you go on and let us get the folks get together and do the job.

DIRKSEN: Yeah, well, we set the conference[1] for next Tuesday morning.

LBJ: All right.

DIRKSEN: And so soon as those are out of the way, we will then see what we do about procedure, to get the thing on the road, and buttoned up. I talked to Dick[2] this morning. He gave me no comfort. . . . He said, "You're not going to vote this week, because we're going to keep the show[3] going." I said, "What about next week?" "I can give you no commitment, because we'll have a caucus of our members Monday morning." I said, "Dick, we're either going to have to fish or cut bait, because I think we've now gone far enough and I think that we've been fair." . . .

LBJ: . . . You've got to take care of your own people, and you're doing that. . . . We don't want this to be a Democratic bill. We want it to be an American bill. . . . These schools are . . . coming out the end of this month and if . . . we haven't got a bill, we're in a hell of a shape. We're in trouble anyway.[4]

DIRKSEN: Well, we're going to try.

LBJ: I saw your exhibit[5] at the World's Fair,[6] and it said "the Land of Lincoln." So you're worthy of the Land of Lincoln. And the Man from Illinois is going to pass the bill, and I'll see that you get proper attention and credit.[7]

RICHARD RUSSELL and B. EVERETT JORDAN
5:17 P.M.

> JUST AS JOHNSON is on the verge of his civil rights triumph, the Bobby Baker scandal reemerges, throwing LBJ into the uncomfortable position of asking Russell, his antagonist on civil rights, for help.

[1] A bipartisan Senate meeting to discuss the revised bill.
[2] Russell.
[3] The filibuster.
[4] Johnson is already worried about violence and disobedience across the country in response to passage of the civil rights bill.
[5] The Illinois exhibit.
[6] The 1964–1965 New York World's Fair, where Johnson four days earlier had addressed 1,500 members of the Amalgamated Clothing and Textile Workers Union and held a news conference at the United States Pavilion.
[7] Johnson elsewhere said that to ensure Dirksen's cooperation on the bill, he would erect a pedestal that the Illinoisan could step on top of.

RUSSELL: I'm mighty sorry I couldn't go to Georgia with you but you had a fine reception down there.

LBJ: Aw, couldn't have been better. I missed you. That was the only thing wrong with the trip.

RUSSELL: . . . I had to talk to the junior chamber of commerce. . . . I'm all right with the old ones. I'll never get back in with the young women, but I'm trying to get back in with the young men.

. . . .

RUSSELL: Now listen, I'm down here with Everett Jordan and he's sweating blood about this danged Bobby Baker thing. They had a hell of a big revival of it up here today. . . . It looks to me like they're just trying to keep the damned thing open. . . . Everett is greatly bothered about it. . . . He asked me to come down here, said he had to have some help. I don't know how to help him.

. . . .

JORDAN: I'm worried. They made a hell of a fight on this thing on the floor today. . . . They've already said they're going to drag Walter Jenkins down here. Of course, I know they can't, but you'd have to stop it. That'd be embarrassing. . . . They want to get into campaign expenses, Baker putting out money to Senators, controlling who was going on committees. . . . It's the damnedest mess you ever saw. The press just eats it up. . . . I need some help and I need it bad. . . . If you'd call Mike—

LBJ: I'm not the one to call Mike. . . . If I had any influence with Mike, he never would have fired Bobby.[1]

JORDAN: What about Hubert?

LBJ: . . . I'm afraid to say I'll talk to anybody 'cause they'll say the White House is calling. . . . But I'll do what I can.

. . . .

RUSSELL: Dirksen—of course, if it looks like there's going to be an investigation, he's going to run like hell 'cause he's one of the last fellows up here that wants an investigation.

LBJ: You ought to tell Dirksen that too, Dick. . . .

RUSSELL: . . . I'm doing the best I can, Mr. President, but God knows, I've got a hell of a lot to do. I sat up last night till eleven-thirty reading the FBI reports on some son of a bitch—this fellow Rankin on the Warren Commission.[2] Everybody's raising hell about him being a Communist and all, a left-winger.[3] The FBI was investigating. Eight thousand pages of raw material. There ain't but twenty-four hours a day. [chuckles] 'Course, I know I'm talking to a man that's got a hell of a lot more to do than I have. You's the only man in Washington that does.

[1] Baker.
[2] J. Lee Rankin, the commission's General Counsel.
[3] After serving as Eisenhower's Solicitor General, Rankin had been active as a New York lawyer in civil liberties cases, which may have opened him up to unfounded accusations. Rankin's reputation was otherwise so impeccable that when he moved to New York in 1961, the regular bar examination was waived.

McGEORGE BUNDY
5:35 P.M.

LBJ: I haven't been able to go to the toilet today.[1] Just the moment I start to the toilet, the buzzer rings. I guess I've talked two hundred times.

BUNDY: I can hang up, Mr. President.

. . . .

BUNDY: I don't know whether Juanita[2] had a chance to give you a draft letter to Jackie Kennedy about the library. . . .

LBJ: I've looked at it, and I think it's all right.[3] And I'm trying to decide now whether I'm going down to North Carolina[4] on Sunday. . . .

BUNDY: She, I think, doesn't want to go. . . .

LBJ: That's right.

. . . .

LBJ: I also think I want to make a recording[5] for the library. I just don't know who or when, but I'll decide that.

BUNDY: . . . I think you really ought to make it for yourself, and then decide what parts of it you are willing to have in somebody's else's library, if I were you. . . .

LBJ: I don't give a damn about mine. . . .

BUNDY: Sooner or later you will, Mr. President.[6]

MIKE MANSFIELD
6:28 P.M.

NOW THE REPUBLICANS are trying to enmesh Lady Bird in a mini-scandal. As she has dictated in her diary, "It appears that two Republican Congressmen have made a trip to Alabama . . . to interview some of my tenants, concealed tape recorders in their briefcases, have taken pictures of the houses—and quite miserable indeed they are—and are all prepared to try to prevent Lyndon's

[1] Johnson liked to try to shock Bundy out of his proper Bostonian reticence. The story is often told of his talking to Bundy while sitting in the bathroom with the door opened and, when Bundy tried to keep his distance and his back turned, wondering how Bundy ever got so far in life. (See Richard Goodwin, *Remembering America*, pp. 257–59.)

[2] Roberts, one of Johnson's secretaries.

[3] Bundy had drafted a letter from Johnson to Mrs. Kennedy, which was sent on May 14, enclosing a contribution from LBJ and Lady Bird for the Kennedy Library as "an enduring testament to all that President Kennedy stood for—gallantry and learning, grace and force, excellence and humanity." Jacqueline replied on May 16 that it was "so important" to "build the finest memorial" so that "no one will ever forget him," and that she would always remember that the Johnsons had helped "the cause closest to my heart."

[4] For the Billy Graham fund-raising event for the library. (See May 11, 1964, conversation with Stephen Smith above.)

[5] An oral history recording.

[6] Truer words never spoken.

poverty bill . . . with the flashy, gossipy, ugly information that Mrs. Johnson has tenants who live in squalor."[1]

LBJ: I got a call this afternoon that distressed me a lot. Dick Russell . . . said that . . . Everett Jordan . . . was crying because . . . the leadership had run out on him. . . . They've been down inspecting Miz Johnson's property in Texas, and they've harassed and harangued her every day since we've been here. She's about to have a nervous breakdown. They've gone to her farms and taken pictures of all the Negro shacks on it in poverty. They've harassed Walter Jenkins's life out, and it's just pure cheap politics and are using the Senate as a forum. I said, "Well, you get up and make a speech to that effect." And he said he would. He thought that they ought to take it up and then somebody make a motion to table it and call the roll, and let the Cases and Scotts that are demagogues—let them know where the Senate stood. . . . He said Dirksen would be the first one to run because he didn't want it investigated. If he wanted to go into money, the Republicans have raised more money than anybody else. The FBI can look into their contributions and it won't look very good.[2] . . . Don't let them make a political issue out of it. . . . Jordan's not the man to handle it. . . . It's above him. You'll have to get yourself and . . . Hubert Humphrey and . . . say now this is low-down, dirty, cheap politics.

HUBERT HUMPHREY
7:25 P.M.

HUMPHREY REPORTS that Senators Dirksen, Jordan, Russell, and Mansfield have agreed to quash the attempt to reopen the Rules Committee hearings on Bobby Baker. Then he offers Johnson more good news on the civil rights bill.

HUMPHREY: We don't intend to let anything happen on this thing tomorrow. . . . We'll have a nine-thirty meeting over here and come out with some sort of . . . solution. . . .

LBJ: . . . That committee ought to . . . say that each Senator that has any income from any business that has anything to do with the government or any law practice could file his income with it. . . . I'd make a substantive recommendation. Any of this other stuff, I'd just say that's pure, cheap politics and table the hell out of it.

· · · ·

LBJ: This Williams[3] is mean and he wants to make speeches. And somebody is just going to have to be there and take his britches off. . . . I never handled any money. Nobody brought me any money and I didn't distribute any money. And I told Bobby Baker that he was a damned idiot to ever be close to it. . . . But everybody else was saluting him and he was operating mighty big and he

---

[1] Diary of Lady Bird Johnson, May 13, 1964, Johnson Library. She later added that, "like Lyndon's joke about a jackass in a hailstorm," she would simply have to "hunker up and take it" (May 18, 1964).

[2] Here LBJ is putting his own words into Russell's mouth.

[3] Republican Senator John Williams of Delaware.

was too big for his britches, but he wasn't very big for his britches when I was there. . . . I'd make Russell make a speech. Then you make a good one, and that puts the two of you together. Now you think you've got this civil rights in decent shape?

HUMPHREY: Yes, sir. . . . I had a little trouble. . . . The Leadership Conference[1] people are just up in arms, as they generally are. I must confess that old Joe,[2] God dang it—I thought we had Joe all wired. . . . I stepped out of the room here when I answered the phone for your call . . . and while I was away five minutes, why, Joe gave 'em a lecture about that we'd sold out. . . . Joe . . . said, "Look, I'm not going to cause you any trouble, but I don't want to be here 'cause I'm not sure I want to agree yet, see." But before the rest of us[3] went out . . . I said . . . "If we're going to be for . . . what we've done, we're going to be for it. We're going to resist everything else. . . . And we're going to sell it."

LBJ: That's right. Now can Dirksen get the votes for cloture?

HUMPHREY: Yes, sir. He can get twenty-five votes. I had dinner with him last night. And Mr. President, we've got a much better bill than anybody even dreamed possible. We haven't weakened this bill *one damned bit.* In fact, in some places we've improved it. And that's no lie! We really have.

LBJ: . . . Tell these Leadership people . . . the thing we are more afraid of than anything else is that we'll have real revolution in this country when this bill goes into effect, that I've got to go on television in a fireside chat and say to them, "Now it took us ten years to put the Supreme Court decision into effect on education, but we have got to appeal to all of you to come and put this law into effect." And unless we have the Republicans joining us and helping us put down this mutiny, we'll have mutiny in this goddamn country. So we've got to make this an American bill and not just a Democratic bill. And they've got to be glad that the Republicans have participated, like McCulloch[4] and like Dirksen, because it doesn't do any good to have a law like the Volstead Act[5] if you can't enforce it.

· · · ·

LBJ: Now Dirksen think he can get the Hickenloopers and folks like that?

HUMPHREY: Yes, sir. . . .

LBJ: And how many you got?

HUMPHREY: We've got forty-two or forty-three. We've got forty-one for sure, Mr. President, and that means we've got cloture and we can put this bill out. . . . We're not going to rush anybody here now. But the truth is that Dirksen said today he contemplated about the first week of June.

LBJ: You know, they think they're gonna win with Wallace in Maryland.[6]

---

[1] The Leadership Conference on Civil Rights.

[2] The Washington lawyer and civil libertarian Joseph Rauh was one of the most militant national champions of a strong civil rights bill. At Los Angeles in 1960, Rauh had opposed Johnson's nomination as Vice President.

[3] Humphrey was meeting with Senators Dirksen, Magnuson, Hart, Aiken, and Saltonstall.

[4] House Judiciary Committee member William McCulloch, Republican of Ohio, had been key to the October 1963 compromise House bill.

[5] The Volstead Act of 1919 was the vain attempt to enforce the ban on use of alcohol in America.

[6] Governor Wallace was campaigning for Maryland's May 19 primary.

HUMPHREY: . . . I called the National Committee[1] today. They haven't given any money for the goddamned campaign. I told John Bailey, "What in hell is up? You people have got the fight of your life over here." First of all, our candidate's not a good candidate.[2] Let's face it. Brewster—God Almighty!

LBJ: I was amazed. I didn't know that boy was as dumb as he is.

HUMPHREY: I just figured that it wasn't maybe smart for a fellow like me to get involved in it. I'd have loved to, but it's all a matter of judgment whether carpetbaggers and this sort of thing are helpful.

LBJ: I think you ought to get some reporter though to write . . . that all these years the Southerners have resented people coming into their states and they talk about the do-gooders in the North, and yet now it's the South that's going in, that's stirring up this trouble and these tear gases. Alabama's[3] coming into Maryland. Alabama's going into Indiana. . . . They're fine ones to be talking. They've been raising hell about it all these years. . . .

HUMPHREY: Yes, sir.

LBJ: He's just divide and conquer. That's what he is.

HUMPHREY: And he's clever.

LBJ: Yes, he is.

HUMPHREY: I've watched him on the television. Even his commercials are no damned good.

LBJ: Yeah, at six-thirty tonight he had a lot of stuff on Huntley-Brinkley, nationwide. All the crowds applauding him and the kids applauding him.

HUMPHREY: It just makes me sick.

LBJ: You're doing a wonderful job though. Stay on this one though in the morning . . . Let's kill this off 'cause we can make this a party thing and hold together on it.

GEORGE REEDY
7:35 P.M.

JOHNSON IS PREPARING a defense against Republican attacks against Lady Bird's treatment of tenant farmers on her family land.

LBJ: The total income down there from rent was $1,150 and $400 and some odd of it were taxes on 3,900 acres. That's that "valuable" $150 land that they said they owned—about 10 cents an acre. [chuckles] Didn't even bring $100 a month.

REEDY: [chuckles] It's only valuable when your name's on it—indirectly.

[1] Democratic National Committee.
[2] Democratic Senator Daniel Brewster of Maryland was running as the Johnson stand-in candidate, calling Wallace "a professional liar, a bigot, and an aspiring dictator, and a certain enemy of the Constitution of the United States."
[3] Meaning Wallace.

LBJ: I don't know how far they're gonna get with all this harassing and investigation, but I think that Liz[1] ought to make a martyr out of her if she can. . . .

REEDY: If I were a Republican, I'd rather attack Joan of Arc than Mrs. Johnson.

· · · ·

LBJ: Talk to Phil Potter[2] and see if he can't get that *Baltimore Sun* to . . . expose Wallace. I think they ought to point out that Wallace is now under investigation for frauds, highway contracts in Alabama that are paying his expenses. . . . The FBI is now investigating it.[3]

REEDY: I'll have a long talk with him. I'll look into that.

LBJ: Talk to Walter and see if you can tell him that. I don't want to get another Don Reynolds thing, but see if you can tell him he's under investigation.[4]

THURSDAY, MAY 14, 1964

MIKE MANSFIELD
8:38 P.M.

> THE SENATE MAJORITY LEADER has succeeded in thwarting the reopening of the Bobby Baker investigation.[5]

LBJ: Mike, I just got off the plane and looking at this ticker.[6] Sorry you had all that difficulty today, but I'm awfully grateful to you and I think you're a great man.

MANSFIELD: Thanks, Mr. President, but it had to be done. . . .

LBJ: It sure was and they're going to make all the political capital they can out of it. And we'll just have to go after Mr. Williams[7] . . . He's a mean vicious man . . . I saw him on television. He's emotionally unbalanced and he's so goddamned

---

[1] Carpenter.

[2] *Baltimore Sun* reporter.

[3] Johnson has asked for the FBI's confidential files on Wallace and shows here that he is already eager to leak information from them. In 1970, under President Richard Nixon, who wished to eliminate Wallace as a threat to his reelection, the Internal Revenue Service investigated kickbacks from Alabama state contractors to Wallace cronies, illegal campaign financing by Wallace and possible bribes given to Wallace's brother Gerald. At the urging of Nixon's chief of staff, H. R. Haldeman, this material was leaked to Jack Anderson, who by then had taken over Drew Pearson's syndicated column. (See Dan T. Carter, *The Politics of Rage*, pp. 386–93.)

[4] LBJ regrets the clumsiness of the way his White House leaked damaging confidential information on Reynolds but suggests here that if it can be done more gracefully against Wallace, he would not object.

[5] See Johnson's May 13, 1964, conversation with Hubert Humphrey, above. Although the Baker scandal subsided as an acute political issue, Baker himself was convicted of tax evasion and fraud in 1967, serving seventeen months in prison.

[6] Wire service ticker.

[7] Senator John Williams of Delaware.

interested—he's a member of a big law firm up in New York which one of my friends is in for years. And I don't know why he's so worked up about people's income. But sometimes the holier-than-thou ones are the ones. . . .

MANSFIELD: That's right.

LBJ: God bless you. I wanted to thank you.

FRIDAY, MAY 15, 1964

McGEORGE BUNDY
6:06 P.M.

BUNDY: Joe Alsop is back[1] breathing absolute fire and sulfur about the need for war in South Vietnam. I'm going to see him this afternoon and find out just how alarmed he is. . . . I'll check back with you in the morning for you to see him pretty soon.

LBJ: Be better if you'd get McNamara to see him tomorrow, and then maybe I can see him over the weekend. I've got so many to see that I don't believe I can survive it.

BUNDY: I don't want to add a soul to your calendar from that point of view. Lippmann is back, and I don't yet know his views. . . . They'll be opposite on this issue, of course. Now, I know you've got more than enough people trying to see you.

LBJ: Jack's[2] just got me a great big list. . . . He says that next week is just murder. We got George Meany's German labor leaders and we got two or three Africans in. I like Joe, and I like—

BUNDY: I have a feeling that the best way to keep him on the reservation is for you to have a few words, and I think we may learn something from him, too. . . .

LBJ: . . . Maybe if I don't have anything to do tomorrow night, maybe I can go out to his house. . . . If you and Mary—maybe we could have you all over to our house.

GEORGE REEDY
7:00 P.M.

REEDY: I was called by Tom Collins of *Newsday* today. He called me from Long Island, said that they have a four-part serial ready to go on the operations

[1] From a trip to South Vietnam.
[2] Valenti.

of the ranch . . . past connections you've had with the company . . . the trade-out policy of the station, and the Midwest Video option deal.[1] Now he said that he had a very brief conference with Waddy Bullion. Wasn't able to get any satisfaction. . . . Said he called Walter and Walter referred him to Abe Fortas and Abe didn't know enough about it,[2] and that therefore he's asking whether he and an editor of *Newsday* can see you Monday, so in fairness they can check points in the article.

LBJ: No. . . . Tell them Mr. Fortas will be glad to see them Monday and to answer any question they got.[3]

WEDNESDAY, MAY 20, 1964

WALTER JENKINS
11:40 A.M.

THE PREVIOUS DAY George Wallace won 43 percent of the vote in the Maryland presidential primary against the Johnson stand-in, Senator Daniel Brewster.[4] The President wants to make doubly sure that his ducks will be in a row for the Democratic convention in August. He is worried that while canvassing political leaders across the nation, his strategist Clifton Carter might be giving away information that could be dangerously fed back to Robert Kennedy.

LBJ: Tell Cliff now not to talk to but one man in each one of these places. . . . And he'd better bear in mind that he's always talking to a spy, 'cause you can see there's a spy.[5] And I just shiver at who you talk to and who Cliff talks to and who the rest of us talk to. But I just think they're[6] taking a photostat of everything we say. [exhales] And that's all we can. . . . Just tell him we want to know if we have some spies in our own house. We need to know about it.

---

[1] See Johnson's conversation with Jesse Kellam, November 30, 1963, above.
[2] Fortas had asked Collins "why in the hell" the press would not leave the Johnsons alone: the President was "trying to do his public job" (Walter Jenkins to Johnson, May 11, 1964, Johnson Library, and Bruce Allen Murphy, *Fortas,* Morrow, 1988, pp. 139–40).
[3] Fortas was not very effective in blunting Collins's spear. On May 28, 1964, *Newsday* began publishing a series called "LBJ, KTBC—and the FCC." Collins wrote that despite Johnson's public declarations of "total divorcement" from the Austin radio and television stations, they were actually about as linked "as the corner grocer and his grocery store." Collins asked "how a man whose wife and daughters own a television station can be considered unconnected with a government-regulated industry."
[4] Senator Abraham Ribicoff told reporters that Wallace's "big victory" had proved "that there are many Americans in the North as well as the South who do not believe in civil rights" (quoted in Stephan Lesher, *George Wallace,* p. 305).
[5] Meaning someone who will report back to RFK.
[6] Robert Kennedy's allies in the White House, of which LBJ suspects there is an increasing number.

McGEORGE BUNDY
6:56 P.M.

VIETNAM IS NOW BEING pushed to the forefront of Johnson's anxieties. The Communists are waging an offensive in Laos. On May 15, the CIA warned the President that if the "tide of deterioration" in South Vietnam should not be arrested by the end of 1964, "the anti-Communist position in South Vietnam is likely to become untenable." That same week in Saigon, frustrated by the failure of covert operations, General Khanh told McNamara that since his base was weak, perhaps they should strike the North immediately. Khanh then began to backpedal, but Lodge insisted that the North be struck soon. He told McNamara that another coup might topple Khanh, in which "the U.S. should be prepared to run the country, possibly from Cam Ranh Bay."[1] McNamara told Khanh that there could be no large offensive until he had stabilized his regime.

Frustrated with the Khanh government's disorganization and lack of popular support and pressured by Lodge, LBJ is toying with something akin to a U.S. military government in South Vietnam. Lodge was cabling Washington that week that the United States might have to "move into a position of actual control" in South Vietnam, through "a High Commissioner" or "a man who really gives the orders under the title of Ambassador."[2]

LBJ: What military government setup can we put in charge and how do we get Lodge to do it? ... If we can ... get enough of them there where one good American can run a hamlet ... I think that'll improve that situation a good deal. And I don't know how we're gonna get them to organize their special guerrillas.

BUNDY: I'm not quite at the root of what Bob's[3] hesitation is there.

LBJ: He says that Khanh told him in March that he'd organize guerrilla units and bring some people in ... but he just never has done it. ... We just can't have pure Americans going in and doing all the fighting.

BUNDY: You can't.

LBJ: Gotta have some Vietnamese to go with 'em. But I kinda had the impression that we hadn't been as active in the guerrilla warfare on the ground as we were in the air.

BUNDY: I think this is right, Mr. President. I don't think we do have enough people with a guerrilla and counterguerrilla mentality in that process. And that means Special Forces.[4] That means really saying to Westmoreland[5] very loud and very clear that's the kind of war it is—not napalm from the air, but being in

---

[1] Situated on one of the world's greatest natural harbors, Cam Ranh, once used by the French, Russian, and Japanese navies, was being transformed into a major American base.

[2] Directorate of Intelligence, CIA, Memorandum, May 15, 1964; McNamara to Johnson, May 14, 1964, Johnson Library; and Lodge to State Department, March 22, 1964, in FRUS, pp. 346–48.

[3] McNamara.

[4] Responding to the guerrilla and counterinsurgency methods used by such revolutionaries as Mao Zedong and Che Guevara, President Kennedy lavished attention on the U.S. Army Special Forces, known as the "Green Berets."

[5] General William Westmoreland was about to go to South Vietnam as commander in charge of U.S. military assistance.

there stiffening the troops. Five to a battalion is less than one to a hundred. That's not a hell of a stiffening.

. . . .

LBJ: And I would seriously think about bringing Lodge and them back to Hono-lulah.[1]

BUNDY: . . . Let's make goddamn sure we've got something before we do that.

LBJ: . . . But we got to do something pretty quick now. He's got in his proposals and he's gonna be saying they're not acted on, you know.

BUNDY: I know it. We're only holding the fort on that, at the moment. Just saying we're thinking hard, and that's not good enough.

LBJ: No, it's not. Not when your men are being killed and they won't act here and there's paper shuffling and bureaucrats can't make up their mind and they're procrastinating. . . . I've heard it for thirty years.

TUESDAY, MAY 26, 1964

CARL ALBERT
12:06 P.M.

> JOHNSON'S ANTI-POVERTY BILL was passed earlier this day by the House Education and Labor Committee. The next hurdle is the House Rules Committee. LBJ complains that Chairman Howard Smith is being obstructionist.

LBJ: This is one bill we're gonna *pass*.

ALBERT: This is the most important bill we've got.

LBJ: That's right. . . . Smith has got to understand that I want these people taken off relief and trained to do something. . . . And they'll be tax-*payers* in two years, instead of tax-*eaters*. But if he just lets the thing go on, we're spending $8 billion on relief now and I'm not spending a total of one in my whole poverty program. But I'm gonna cut down that $8 billion, if he'll let me, and put 'em to work.

---

[1] For a strategy meeting with high U.S. officials.

WEDNESDAY, MAY 27, 1964

GEORGE REEDY
10:40 A.M.

LBJ: Dirksen did us awfully dirty. He came down here last Friday . . . and he suggested that we ought to get the three men from each one of these committees[1] and talk to them.[2] So we invite them and after we got them invited . . . he denounced our policy and left the impression . . . that he was so important I called him up.

. . . .

LBJ: You better check with the TelePrompTers. They went wild on us last night.[3] . . . What was wrong with it?

REEDY: It was a short circuit.

LBJ: Now, how many short circuits am I going to have? I saved myself last night but that sure could ruin me.

REEDY: You don't get them often, but they do hit.

LBJ: What caused it?

REEDY: A short circuit, sir, is when a wire gets overloaded because of an overcharge of electricity and the wire snaps. . . . They're hard as hell to locate. . . .

LBJ: Did they find it, and ever get it fixed?

REEDY: Yes, it's fixed.

LBJ: . . . I thought that it was almost sabotage, George.[4]

REEDY: No, that happens, sir. . . .

LBJ: Now, if that happened to me before the convention[5] or something, I'd really be destroyed, wouldn't I?

REEDY: That's why you've always got to have the cards in front of you as an alternative, sir.

LBJ: Yeah, but I can't turn them every time. . . . I'd have to go look for it to see where I was.

REEDY: . . . I don't think that there's any ultimate defense against that because it's one of those odd accidents. Maybe once in a million times. . . .

LBJ: . . . I'm not sure that it was that way. Because it went fast and then it stopped and I was about to catch up with it. Then it run off from me again.

---

[1] Appropriations, Armed Services, and Foreign Relations.
[2] About Vietnam.
[3] Johnson had addressed nine thousand guests at a "Salute to President Johnson" at the D.C. Armory.
[4] Johnson presumably suspects that the RFK forces may have deliberately caused the short circuit to embarrass him or create worries that LBJ is not in full possession of his faculties.
[5] Democratic convention.

ADLAI STEVENSON
10:50 A.M.

AT A MAY 24 National Security Council meeting, Rusk had described the problems of sealing the Cambodian border and preserving the government of Laos. McNamara said that if he were President, he would wish to ask his advisers, "Do I want to use military force in Southeast Asia within the next two or three months?" He added that "where our proposals are being carried out now, the situation is still going to hell. We are continuing to lose. Nothing we are now doing will win. . . . The question is whether we should hit North Vietnam now or whether we can wait. South Vietnam is weaker now than it was in January, but we can ride through for a few additional weeks. . . . We do not have to act now, but we may have to use military force later." Rusk warned that "we must counter reports that the President is not acting because of the upcoming elections."

Rusk, McNamara, and Bundy recommended that Johnson "make a presidential decision that the U.S. will use selected and carefully graduated military force against North Vietnam . . . after appropriate diplomatic and political warning and preparation and . . . unless such warning and preparation—in combination with other efforts—should produce a sufficient improvement of non-Communist prospects in South Vietnam and in Laos to make military action against North Vietnam unnecessary."[1] Pressed to make such a momentous choice, Johnson has demurred in order to consult other advisers, including his U.N. Ambassador, knowing that Stevenson is likely to give him the arguments against this kind of militance.

LBJ: Adlai . . . my wife tells me that you're a mighty high stepper.[2]

STEVENSON: [chuckles] She did a great job up here for us, I'll tell you—really. She's masterful at this business. She not only made a good speech, but she made everybody happy and comfortable and relaxed. . . . In addition to that, I think she kind of liked it.

LBJ: She surely enjoyed it, and she was very complimentary of you. . . . I just wanted to . . . just exchange thoughts with you about this South Vietnam thing and Laos and what you think we ought to do out there.

· · · ·

LBJ: I was just sitting here at the desk thinking about the alternatives[3] and how horrible they are. . . . I expect that we better just talk over the phone. . . . I'm going to be in New York tomorrow evening,[4] but it's going to be one of those madhouses like yesterday.

STEVENSON: . . . Do you suppose that there would be any chance of seeing you afterward?

[1] Record of NSC Executive Committee Meeting, May 24, 1964, in Johnson Library.

[2] On Monday night, after a dinner at which Mrs. Johnson spoke at the opening of the new wing of the Museum of Modern Art in New York, Stevenson had her to a party at his official apartment in the Waldorf Towers.

[3] In Vietnam.

[4] For a Democratic fund-raising dinner and another "Salute to President Johnson" at Madison Square Garden, featuring Bill Cosby, Woody Allen, Joan Baez, Johnny Carson, Mahalia Jackson, and the New Christy Minstrels.

LBJ: I'm going to be flying to Texas with all these reporters at midnight, but probably you could ride with me. Maybe we could get together after the show and go to the Krims'[1] house and you could ride with Lady Bird and me over there.... And you be thinking about it.... I shudder at getting too deeply involved there, and everybody thinks that's the only alternative.

STEVENSON: I've been shuddering on this thing for three years and I'm afraid that we're in a position now where you *don't* have any alternatives. And it's a *hell* of an alternative. And it really gives me the shakes.

RICHARD RUSSELL
10:55 A.M.

WITH HIS OLD COMRADE from Georgia, Johnson comes as close as he does with anyone to exposing his inner ambivalences about Vietnam.

LBJ: Got lots of troubles.

RUSSELL: Well, we all have those.

LBJ: ... What do you think of this Vietnam thing? I'd like to hear you talk a little bit.

RUSSELL: Frankly, Mr. President, if you were to tell me that I was authorized to settle it as I saw fit, I would respectfully decline and not take it.

LBJ: [chuckles]

RUSSELL: It's the damn worst mess I ever saw, and I don't like to brag. I never have been right many times in my life. But I knew that we were going to get into this sort of mess when we went in there. And I don't see how we're ever going to get out of it without fighting a major war with the Chinese and all of them down there in those rice paddies and jungles.... I just don't know what to do.

LBJ: That's the way that I've been feeling for six months.

RUSSELL: It appears that our position is deteriorating. And it looks like the more that we try to do for them, the less that they're willing to do for themselves. It's just a sad situation. There's no sense of responsibility there on the part of any of their leaders that are bearing it. It's all just through the generations, or even centuries, they've just thought about the individual and glorifying the individual and that the only utilization of power is to glorify the individual and not to save the state, or help other people. And they just can't shed themselves of that complex. It's a hell of a situation. It's a mess. And it's going to get worse. And I don't know what to do. I don't think that the American people are quite ready to send our troops in there to do the fighting. If it came down to an option for us of just sending the Americans in there to do the fighting, which will, of course, eventually lead into a ground war and a conventional war with China, we'd do them a favor every time we killed a coolie, whereas when one of our

---

[1] Mathilde and Arthur Krim, President of United Artists and a major Democratic fund-raiser as chairman of the President's Club, whose members gave the party $1,000 or more.

people got killed, it would be a loss to us. If it got down to . . . just pulling out, I'd get out. But then I don't know. There's undoubtedly some middle ground somewhere. If I was going to get out, I'd get the same crowd that got rid of old Diem to get rid of these people and get some fellow in there that said he wished to hell we *would* get out.[1] That would give us a good excuse for getting out. . . .

LBJ: How important is it to us?

RUSSELL: It isn't important a damn bit, with all these new missile systems.[2]

LBJ: Well, I guess it's important to us—

RUSSELL: From a psychological standpoint.

LBJ: I mean, yes, and from the standpoint that we are party to a treaty.[3] And if we don't pay any attention to this treaty, why, I don't guess they think we pay attention to any of them.

RUSSELL: Yeah, but we're the only ones paying any attention to it!

LBJ: Yeah, I think that's right.

RUSSELL: You see, the other people are just as bound to that treaty as we are. I think there're some twelve or fourteen other countries.

LBJ: That's right, but just because somebody else—

RUSSELL: I don't know much about the foreign policy, but it seems to me there were several of them in there that were parties to it, and other than a question of our word and saving face, that's the reason I said that I don't think that anybody would expect us to stay in there. Some old freebooter down in there—I've forgotten his name. . . . He's sort of a hellraiser. . . . I think that if he were to take over, he'd ask us to get out. Of course, if he did, under our theory of standing by the self-determination of people, I don't see how we can say we're not going to go. . . . The thing is going to be a headache to anybody that tries to fool with it. Now you got all the brains in the country, Mr. President. You better get ahold of them. I don't know what to do about this. . . . We're there. You've got over there McNamara. He was up here testifying yesterday before the committee.[4] . . . He's been kicked around on it, so where I'm not sure he's as objective as he ought to be in surveying the conditions out there. He feels like it's sort of up to him personally to see that the thing goes through. And he's a can-do fellow. But I'm not too sure he understands the history and background of those people out there as fully as he should. But even from his picture, the damn thing ain't getting any better and it's getting worse. And we're putting more and more in there. And they're taking more and more away from the people we're trying to help, that we give them. . . .

LBJ: I spend all my days with Rusk and McNamara and Bundy and Harriman and Vance and all those folks that are dealing with it and I would say that it pretty well adds up to them now that we've got to show some power and some force, that they do not believe—they're kinda like MacArthur in Korea—they

[1] Here Russell echoes what President Kennedy was said to have said.
[2] Russell means that with America's newly established arsenal of nuclear-tipped intercontinental ballistic missiles, holding an area like South Vietnam lacked its old importance.
[3] The SEATO treaty that de Gaulle was so happy to interpret in his own fashion.
[4] Senate Armed Services.

don't believe that the Chinese Communists will come into this thing. But they don't know and nobody can really be sure. But their feeling is that they won't. And in any event, that we haven't got much choice, that we are treaty-bound, that we are there, that this will be a domino that will kick off a whole list of others, that we've just got to prepare for the worst. Now I have avoided that for a few days. I don't think the American people are for it. I don't agree with Morse[1] and all he says, but—

RUSSELL: No, neither do I, but he's voicing the sentiment of a hell of a lot of people.

LBJ: I'm afraid that's right. I don't think the people of the country know much about Vietnam and I think they care a hell of a lot less.

RUSSELL: Yeah, I know, but you go to send a whole lot of our boys out there—

LBJ: Yeah, that's right. That's exactly right. That's what I'm talking about. You get a few. We had thirty-five killed—and we got enough hell over thirty-five—this year.[2]

RUSSELL: More than that . . . in Atlanta, Georgia, have been killed this year in automobile accidents.

LBJ: That's right, and eighty-three went down in one crash on a 707[3] in one day, but that doesn't make any difference. . . . The Republicans are going to make a political issue out of it, every one of them, even Dirksen.

RUSSELL: It's the only issue they got.

LBJ: . . . Hickenlooper said[4] that we just had to stand and show our force and put our men in there and let come what may come. And nobody disagreed with him. Now Mansfield, he just wants to pull up and get out. And Morse wants to get out, and Gruening[5] wants to get out. And that's about where it stops. I don't know.

RUSSELL: . . . Frank Church[6] has told me two or three times that he didn't want to make a speech on it. He just wished to God we could get out of there. I don't know whether he's told you that or not.

LBJ: No, I haven't talked to him. . . . Who are the best people we have that you know of to talk to about this thing? I don't want to do anything on the basis of just the information I've got now. . . . I've talked to Eisenhower a little bit.

RUSSELL: I think that the people that you have named have all formed a hard opinion on it.

LBJ: No, Rusk has tried to pull back. . . . But he's about to come to the conclusion now that Laos is crumbling and Vietnam is wobbly—

[1] Democratic Senator Wayne Morse of Oregon, the steadfast foe of U.S. intervention in Vietnam.
[2] According to the Pentagon, from January 1, 1961, through May 16, 1964, a total of 229 Americans had been killed in South Vietnam, 131 of these in combat against the Vietcong.
[3] Boeing 707.
[4] At the above-mentioned meeting with Dirksen and members of three Senate committees.
[5] Senator Ernest Gruening, Democrat of Alaska.
[6] Democratic Senator from Idaho.

RUSSELL: Laos, Laos. Hell, it ain't worth a damn. . . . It's a whole lot worse than Vietnam. There are some of these Vietnamese, after they beat 'em over the head, that'll go in there and fight. But Laos is an impossible situation. That's just a rathole there. I don't know. Before I took any drastic action, I think I'd get somebody like old Omar Bradley[1] and one or two perhaps senior people that have had government experience—not necessarily military . . . Let them go out there and fool around for a few days and smell the air and get the atmosphere and come back and tell you what they think. . . .

LBJ: Now one of our big problems, Dick, the biggest, between us—and I don't want this repeated to anybody—is Lodge. He ain't worth a damn. He can't work with any-bodd-y. . . . We get the best USIA man to put on all the radios and try to get 'em to be loyal to the government and to be fighting and quit deserting and he calls in the USIA and says, "I handle the newspapers and magazines and radio myself, so the hell with you!" So that knocks that guy out. Then we send out the best CIA man we got and he said, "I handle the intelligence. To hell with you!" Then he wants a new Deputy Chief of Mission. We get him to give us some names and we pick one of those, the best we got,[2] send him out to run the damn war and he gets where he won't speak to the Deputy Chief of Mission! Then we get General Harkins[3] out there and we thought he was a pretty good man and he gets where he can't work with him. So we send Westmoreland out. And it's just a hell of a mess. You can't do anything with Lodge and that's where McNamara's so frustrated. He goes out and they get agreements and he issues orders and he sends his stuff in there and Lodge just takes charge of it himself and he's not a take-charge man and it just gets stacked up there.

RUSSELL: He never has followed anything through to a conclusion since I've known him and I've known him for twenty-odd years.[4] . . . He's a bright fellow, intelligent fellow, but . . . he thinks he's dealing with barbarian tribes out there, that he's an emperor and he's gonna tell 'em what to do. There ain't any doubt in my mind that he had old Diem killed out there himself[5] so he could—

LBJ: That was a *tragic* mistake. It was awful and we've lost everything.

RUSSELL: Why don't you get somebody who's more pliant than Lodge, who'd do exactly what you said, right quick? He's living up on cloud nine. . . . Probably the best thing you could do would be to ask Lodge if he don't think it's about time he be coming home.

LBJ: He'd be back home campaigning against us on this issue, every day.

RUSSELL: God Almighty, he's gonna come back anyway when the time comes. I'd give him a reason for doing it. He's going to come back. If you bring him back now, everybody'll say he's mad 'cause Johnson removed him out there. MacAr-

[1]Bradley, a General of the Army, had commanded the U.S. ground contingent during the Normandy campaign that ended World War II in Europe, and from 1948 to 1953 was the first Chairman of the Joint Chiefs of Staff.
[2]David G. Nes.
[3]The eternally optimistic General Paul Harkins had been commander of U.S. military assistance in South Vietnam since 1962.
[4]Lodge had long served with Russell in the Senate.
[5]While Lodge was accessory to the Kennedy administration's championship of a coup against the South Vietnamese President, he certainly cannot be accused of wishing Diem dead.

thur with all his power couldn't hurt Truman,[1] because everybody said hell, he's just mad 'cause he got removed, although a million sympathized with him in it. You needn't worry. Lodge'll be in here. In my judgment, he'll be on that ticket in some way. I don't think they'll nominate him for President, but they may put him on there for Vice President. Whether they do or don't, he'll be back here campaigning before the campaign's over. . . . I better take that back. This thing is so hopeless for the Republicans. . . . He certainly has got enough political sense to know not to get his head chopped off. It would be perfectly foolish.

. . . .

RUSSELL: It's a tragic situation. It's just one of those places where you can't win. Anything that you do is wrong. . . . I have thought about it. I have worried about it. I have prayed about it.

LBJ: I don't believe we can do anything—

RUSSELL: It frightens me 'cause it's my country involved over there and if we get into there on any considerable scale, there's no doubt in my mind but that the Chinese will be in there and we'd be fighting a danged conventional war against our secondary potential threat and it'd be a Korea on a much bigger scale and a worse scale. . . . If you go from Laos and Cambodia and Vietnam and bring North Vietnam into it too, it's the damndest mess on earth. The French report that they lost 250,000 men and spent a couple billion of their money and two billion of ours down there and just got the hell whipped out of them.[2] . . .

LBJ: You don't have any doubt but what if we go in there and get 'em up against the wall, the Chinese Communists are gonna come in?

RUSSELL: No sir, no doubt about it.

LBJ: That's my judgment, and our people don't think so. . . . Now Mike[3] writes me a memo . . . and all he says is that we continue to support the Vietnamese . . . and end . . . "the reflex of pique and face-saving at every essay of de Gaulle's." Well, we're not piqued. We just asked de Gaulle to give us a blueprint and he don't have it. He just says neutralization, but there ain't nobody wants to agree to neutralization. . . . He just says we have to continue to maintain our strength and get into position. . . . "We are in this situation without reliable military allies." Well, hell, I know that. . . . "An exploration of the possibility of the United Nations or some other arrangement." . . . They won't do a damn thing, even on the Cambodia border. We can't get a majority vote in the Security Council. "A willingness to entertain any reasonable proposals for international conferences." Well, we are ready to confer with anybody, anytime. But conferences ain't gonna do a damn bit of good. They ain't gonna take back and give us territory and behave. We tell 'em every week, we tell Khrushchev, we send China and Hanoi and all of 'em word that we'll get out of there and stay out of there if they'll just quit raiding their neighbors. And they just say, "Screw you."

RUSSELL: That's right.

[1] After Truman fired MacArthur as commander of U.S. forces in Korea, the General of the Army returned to America to denounce the Truman Asia policy.
[2] The French vainly fought for most of the decade after World War II to hold their imperial position in Vietnam.
[3] Mansfield.

LBJ: . . . The whole question, as I see it, is, is it more dangerous for us to let things go as they're going now, deteriorating every day—

RUSSELL: I don't think we can let it go, Mr. President, indefinitely.

LBJ: Than it would be for us to move in.

RUSSELL: We either got to move in or move out.

LBJ: That's about what it is.

RUSSELL: You can make a tremendous case for moving out, not as good a one for moving in, but—

LBJ: Well, you now take Nixon, Rockefeller—

RUSSELL: It would be more consistent with the attitude of the American people and their general reactions to go in, because they could understand that better. But getting out, even after we go in and get bogged down in there in a war with China, it's going to be a hell of a mess. It would be worse than where we are now, to some extent, and that's what makes it so difficult. . . . I don't know how much Russia—they want to cause us all the trouble they can—is there any truth in their theory that they are really at odds with China?[1]

LBJ: They are, but they'd go with them as soon as the fight started. They wouldn't forsake that Communist philosophy.

RUSSELL: . . . We might get them to take an active part in getting the thing straightened out.

LBJ: We're doing all we can on that, but she doesn't show any signs of contributing anything.

RUSSELL: They'd be foolish to . . . because we are just continuing to pour money in there and . . . we don't even get goodwill back out of that. . . . McNamara is the smartest fellow that any of us know, but he's got so damn— He is opinionated as hell, and he's made up his mind on this.

LBJ: . . . I think he's a pretty flexible fellow. He's gone out there. He got Khanh to agree that we cannot launch a counteroffensive or hit the North until he gets more stabilized and better set in the South and he thought he was buying us time and we could get by till November. But these politicians got to raising hell. . . . All the Senators, Nixon and Rockefeller and Goldwater all saying let's move, let's go into the North.[2] . . . They can always get an isolated example of the bad things that McNamara says. But that's not generally true.[3] They've helped too many damned people being killed every day.[4] And they're flying the sorties and they're getting some results and they're killing thousands of their people. But we're losing more. I mean, we're losing ground. And he was hoping that we could avoid moving into the North and thereby provoking the Chinese for a few months.

---

[1] Russell still doubts the genuineness of the five-year-old divorce between China and the Soviet Union.

[2] Johnson here demonstrates his worry about the militance of Republican opponents on Vietnam during the presidential campaign.

[3] LBJ is saying it is not generally true that McNamara is opinionated.

[4] Meaning, it seems, that Republican pressures for war are causing too many people to be killed.

RUSSELL: Hell, there ain't any way you can move into the North. You know as well as I do that we've tried that from the infiltration, guerrilla war standpoint, with disastrous results.

LBJ: Lodge, Nixon, Rockefeller, Goldwater all say move. Eisenhower—

RUSSELL: Bomb the North and kill old men, women, and children?

LBJ: No, they say pick out an oil plant or pick out a refinery or something like that. Take selected targets. Watch this trail they're coming down.[1] Try to bomb them out of them, when they're coming in.

RUSSELL: Oh, hell! That ain't worth a hoot. That's just impossible.

LBJ: McNamara said yesterday that in Korea that LeMay and all of 'em were going to stop all those tanks. There's ninety came through. They turned all the Air Force loose on them. They got one. Eighty-nine come on through.

RUSSELL: We tried it in Korea. We even got a lot of old B-29s to increase the bomb load and sent 'em over there and just dropped millions and millions of bombs, day and night, and in the morning, they would knock the road at night and in the morning, the damn people would be back traveling over it. . . . We never could actually interdict all their lines of communication although we had absolute control of the seas and the air, and we never did stop them. And you ain't gonna stop these people either.

LBJ: Well, they'd impeach a President though that would run out, wouldn't they?[2] I just don't believe that—outside of Morse, everybody I talk to says you got to go in, including Hickenlooper, including all the Republicans. . . . And I don't know how in the hell you're gonna get out unless they[3] tell you to get out.

RUSSELL: If we had a man running the government over there that told us to get out, we could sure get out.

LBJ: That's right, but you can't do that. . . . Wouldn't that pretty well fix us in the eyes of the world though and make it look mighty bad?[4]

RUSSELL: I don't know. [chuckles] We don't look too good right now. You'd look pretty good, I guess, going in there with all the troops and sending them all in there, but I tell you it'll be the most expensive venture this country ever went into.

LBJ: I've got a little old sergeant that works for me over at the house[5] and he's got six children and I just put him up as the United States Army, Air Force, and Navy every time I think about making this decision and think about sending that father of those six kids in there. And what the hell are we going to get out of his doing it? And it just makes the chills run up my back.

RUSSELL: It does me. I just can't see it.

---

[1] The Ho Chi Minh Trail, a major supply route.
[2] Knowing that he was taping this conversation, did LBJ ask this in order to put Russell on the (hidden) record as pressing him to defend South Vietnam? (See Editor's Note.)
[3] Those Senators.
[4] Johnson's point is that the American hand could not be concealed and that an American pullout would damage the U.S. world image.
[5] Sergeant Kenneth Gaddis, one of Johnson's valets.

LBJ: I just haven't got the nerve to do it, and I don't see any other way out of it.

RUSSELL: It's one of these things where "heads I win, tails you lose."

LBJ: Well, think about it and I'll talk to you again. I hate to bother you, but I just—

RUSSELL: I wish I could help you. God knows I do 'cause it's a terrific quandary that we're in over there. We're just in the quicksands up to our very necks. And I just don't know what the hell is the best way to do about it.

LBJ: I love you and I'll be calling you.

McGEORGE BUNDY
11:24 A.M.

> WITH BUNDY, LBJ confides his inner anxieties on Southeast Asia. He may be using Bundy as a bellwether of the Kennedy alumni to see how strongly he feels about a major effort in Vietnam. At this moment when he is testing domestic and congressional opinion, Johnson is worried about political damage from not only hawkish Republicans but also, potentially, Kennedy men like Rusk, McNamara, and Bundy—and Robert Kennedy, who, he fears, might conceivably denounce him for softness and betraying Kennedy's commitment to South Vietnam.[1]

LBJ: I'll tell you the more that I stayed awake last night thinking of this thing, the more I think of it, I don't know what in the hell—it looks to me like we're getting into another Korea. It just worries the hell out of me. I don't see what we can ever hope to get out of there with, once we're committed. I believe that the Chinese Communists are coming into it. I don't think that we can fight them ten thousand miles away from home. . . . I don't think it's worth fighting for and I don't think that we can get out. It's just the biggest damned mess that I ever saw.

BUNDY: It is. It's an awful mess.

LBJ: And we just got to think about—I was looking at this sergeant of mine this morning. Got six little old kids over there and he's getting out my things and bringing me in my night reading . . . and I just thought about ordering his kids in there and what in the hell am I ordering him out there for? What the hell is Vietnam worth to me? What is Laos worth to me? What is it worth to this country? No, we've got a treaty but, hell, everybody else's got a treaty out there and they're not doing anything about it. Of course if you start running from the Communists, they may just chase you right into your own kitchen.

BUNDY: Yeah, that's the trouble. And that is what the rest of that half of the world is going to think if this thing comes apart on us. That's the dilemma.

LBJ: But everybody I talk to that's got any sense in there says, "Oh, my God,

---

[1] He may also be trying to get a key Kennedy man on the secretly taped record insisting that LBJ be firm in Vietnam. In his Texas retirement, Johnson told Doris Kearns that if Vietnam had fallen, Robert Kennedy would be "out in front leading the fight against me, telling everyone that I had betrayed John Kennedy's commitment to Vietnam" (Doris Kearns, *Lyndon Johnson and the American Dream*, p. 253).

ple-e-e-ease give this thought." Of course, I was reading Mansfield's stuff this morning and it's just milquetoast as it can be. He got no spine at all. But this is a terrible thing we're getting ready to do.

BUNDY: Mr. President, I just think this is the only big decision in one sense . . . that we either reach up and get it or we let it go by.[1] And I'm not telling you today what I'd do in your position. I just think the most we have to do is to pray with it for another while.

LBJ: Anybody else that we got that we can advise with, that might have any judgment on this question, that might be fresh, might have some new approach? Would Bradley be any good? Would Clay[2] be any good?

BUNDY: No, Bradley would be no good. I do not think Clay would add. I think you're constantly searching, if I understand you correctly, for some means of stiffening this thing that does not have this escalating aspect to it.[3] And I've been up and down this with Bob McNamara and I've been up and down it again with Mike Forrestal. I think there are some marginal things that we can do. . . . Also, Mr. President, you can do what I think Kennedy did at least once,[4] which is to make the threat without having made your own internal decision that you would actually carry it through. I think the risk in that is that we have at least seemed to do it once or twice before. And there's another dilemma in here, which is the difficulty your own people have in—I'm not talking about Dean Rusk or Bob McNamara or me—but people who are at second remove,[5] who just find it very hard to be firm if they're not absolutely clear what your decision is. And yet you *must* safeguard that decision.

LBJ: What does Bill[6] think we ought to do?

BUNDY: He's in favor of touching things up, but you ought to talk to him about it.[7] I've got an extremely good memorandum from Forrestal. . . . He thinks we ought to be ready to move a little bit, mainly the Vietnamese. On the other hand, readiness to do more. He believes really that that's the best way of galvanizing the South, that if they feel that we are prepared to take a little action against the center of this infection, that that's the best way.

LBJ: What action do we take though?

BUNDY: . . . We really need to do you some target folder work, Mr. President, that shows precisely what we do and don't mean here.[8] The main object is to kill as few people as possible while creating an environment in which the incentive to react is as low as possible. But I can't say to you this is a small matter. There's one other thing that . . . I've just thought about overnight. It's on this same

[1] Bundy uses the metaphor of the baseball outfielder.
[2] After World War II, General Lucius Clay was Military Governor of the U.S. Zone in conquered Germany and commander-in-chief of U.S. forces in Europe.
[3] This is a perfect summary of what Johnson is groping for at this moment.
[4] Bundy presumably refers not only to Southeast Asia, but to Kennedy's veiled threat to bomb and invade Cuba during the Cuban Missile Crisis—and perhaps to JFK's avowed intention to use nuclear weapons to retaliate against any Soviet move to take West Berlin.
[5] Bundy perhaps refers to people like Harriman and Ball.
[6] Bundy.
[7] Bundy does not want Johnson to think of him as his brother's spokesman at court.
[8] In other words, the exact nature of a bombing campaign against the North.

matter of saying to a guy, "You go to Korea" or "You go to Vietnam and you fight in the rice paddies." I would love to know what would happen if we were to say in this same speech, "And from now on, nobody goes to this task who doesn't volunteer." I think we might turn around the atmosphere of our own people out there if it were a volunteers' enterprise. I suspect the Joint Chiefs won't agree to that. But I'd like to know what would happen if we really dramatized this as "Americans Against Terror" and "Americans Keeping Their Commitment" and "Americans Who Have Only Peace as Their Object" and "Only Americans Who Want to Go Have to Go." You might change the temper of it some.

LBJ: You wouldn't have a corporals' guard, would you?[1]

BUNDY: I just don't know. If that's true, then I'm not sure we're the country to do this job.

LBJ: [exhales] I don't think it's just Morse and Russell and Gruening.

BUNDY: I know it isn't, Mr. President. It's 90 percent of the people who don't want any part of this.

LBJ: Did you see the poll this morning? Sixty-five percent of 'em don't know anything about it[2] and of those that do, the majority think we're mishandling it. But they don't know what to do. That's Gallup. It's damned easy to get in a war but it's gonna be awfully hard to ever extricate yourself if you get in.

BUNDY: It's very easy. I'm very sensitive to the fact that people who are having trouble with an intransigent problem find it very easy to come and say to the President of the United States go and be tough.

LBJ: What does Lippmann think you ought to do?

BUNDY: . . . What he really thinks is that you should provide a diplomatic structure within which the thing can go under the control of Hanoi and walk away from it. . . .

LBJ: You mean he thinks that Hanoi ought to take South Vietnam?

BUNDY: Yes, sir—diplomatically.

LBJ: Um-hmm.

BUNDY: Maybe by calling it a neutralization and removing American force and letting it slip away the way Laos did— [corrects himself:] would, if we didn't do anything, and will, if we don't do anything. And we would guarantee the neutrality in some sort of a treaty. . . . I'm sorry. I'm not sure I'm the best person to describe Lippmann's views because I don't agree with them.

LBJ: Who has he been talking to, besides you? Has he talked to Rusk any on this? Has he talked to McNamara?

BUNDY: He's talked to George Ball.[3] . . .

LBJ: Wouldn't it be good for he and McNamara to sit down?

BUNDY: I think it'd be very good. . . . I had planned to have lunch with Walter on Monday . . . but I can do it sooner, if you'd like me to.

[1] Meaning that virtually no one would volunteer.
[2] Vietnam.
[3] Along with Stevenson, who was Ball's longtime friend, Ball was the most dovish of the Johnson foreign policy circle.

LBJ: I wish you would. I'd try to get his ideas a little more concrete . . . and I'd like to have him talk to McNamara. I might just have the three of you in this afternoon sometime. . . . I'd like to hear Walter and McNamara debate this thing.[1]

ADLAI STEVENSON
3:45 P.M.

THE U.N. AMBASSADOR offers the advice on Vietnam that Johnson solicited earlier in the day.

STEVENSON: I think many members[2] will view strikes against North Vietnam as aggression. Nevertheless I think there would be a widespread tendency to oppose carrying the war to North Vietnam, largely because of fear of a major conflict with China. But if we don't take the problem to the U.N., somebody else is sure to do so. Therefore I think we should preempt the situation by going to the Security Council first . . . before taking any action. You may remember that that was what I was insisting upon in the days before Cuba.[3]

LBJ: Yeah.[4]

STEVENSON: And that was what Kennedy finally agreed to do. Now in Vietnam, I think some thought should be given to reconvening the Geneva group of 1954.[5] Let the United States come in there and file a complaint against Hanoi for violation of the agreement. If there is no satisfaction . . . we could serve notice that we are going to defend its[6] independence and begin to step up the military activity. For the future in South Vietnam, I think there are an awful lot of refugees who are now in Paris, now in Phnom Penh, now in Bangkok. . . . Sometime these people have to be brought together with the leaders of the government in Saigon to see if they can't form a more broadly based government with broader popular appeal.

. . . .

STEVENSON: Now, if I can add a further postscript, Mr. President. This is politics, which you know more about than I'll ever know. I have some idea of the pressures that you're under or going to get under with that damned Goldwater and so on. However I'm confident that this is the time for restraint. This is a peace-and-war issue. The man who is the peacemonger and not the warmonger will be in the strongest political position. . . . I'd rather see us muddle through with an inconclusive conference. We'll be better off than with a war—especially a war ten thousand miles away in a part of the world that's almost meaningless to the Ameri-

[1] Bundy brought in Lippmann that afternoon at 4:30 for a conversation on Vietnam with Johnson, McNamara, and George Ball in the small lounge adjoining the Oval Office.
[2] Of the United Nations.
[3] Stevenson means during the Cuban Missile Crisis, before President Kennedy imposed a quarantine against Cuba.
[4] Johnson is not exhilarated by the notion of having U.S. action against North Vietnam debated in the U.N. Security Council, especially during an election year.
[5] The 1954 Geneva Conference on Indochina imposed a cease-fire on the French struggle with the Vietnamese, partitioned the country, banned the movement of foreign military equipment into Vietnam, and called for nationwide elections within two years.
[6] South Vietnam's.

can people and which is a quagmire. . . . I told Kennedy that I prayed he would move with the greatest hesitation to undertake this task in Southeast Asia. . . .

LBJ: . . . Can you write all this out for me and have it ready for me when I come up there?

STEVENSON: I'd be delighted to.

THURSDAY, MAY 28, 1964

ROBERT KENNEDY
11:45 A.M.

JOHNSON THANKS his Attorney General for a note on civil rights strategy[1] and consults him on racial disturbances in Cambridge, Maryland, where National Guardsmen had fired tear gas grenades at civil rights demonstrators three days earlier. Then, drawing on a private talk with McNamara, Kennedy gently critiques Johnson's policy-making process on Vietnam.

LBJ: Bobby, I got your note the other day and thought that it was very good— on this civil rights thing. . . .

KENNEDY: Oh, yeah.

LBJ: . . . I want to do anything and everything that is suggested in it. . . . Dirksen told me that he thought that he would have the bill passed by the 15th.[2]

KENNEDY: Yes, that would be wonderful.

LBJ: I doubt that, but that's what he indicated . . . Now I talked to them yesterday about this situation in Maryland. I gather that they got by last night, but they may have trouble tonight. Are you up-to-date on that?

RFK: Yes. . . . In the first place, the Negroes don't know what they want. If we can find out from them exactly what they're interested in—and Dick Gregory's[3] been some help on that. The second thing is that primarily, in my judgment, it must be jobs, because the reason that you've had so much dissension over there is that 33 or 35 percent unemployment. . . . If we could say that . . . there would be some emergency action that could be taken . . . I think that it would calm that situation.

· · · ·

KENNEDY: I have not been involved intimately on Southeast Asia or Vietnam. Just . . . two National Security Council meetings. Bob McNamara about five or six days ago had a talk with me and asked me to come over and I went through it. I think that there's a lot of—and I had the same feeling with President

[1] RFK wrote him "to bring you up to date on problems which may occur over the summer" on civil rights (Kennedy to Johnson, May 21, 1964, Johnson Library).
[2] Of June.
[3] Gregory was a comedian and civil rights activist.

Kennedy—I think there's a lot of people around, such as Douglas Dillon . . . who . . . frequently, based on experience and some judgment, have some good ideas on some of these matters. I think that was the advantage of dealing with the— you know, the problem of the Missile Crisis, and also some of the difficulties over the period of the last three years. And I think, to make the suggestion, to utilize some of those brains and talent to the maximum is helpful. . . . I think that to have those people involved and make sure that there is a full discussion about some of these things, I—again being quite frank about it—based on my two meetings of the National Security Council, I thought that there was—which I have said to Bob McNamara—there was too much emphasis really on the military aspects of it.

I would think that the war would never be won militarily. Where it's going to be won really is the political war. And the best talent, of course, is over at the Pentagon because you have Bob McNamara. But that kind of talent really has to be applied to doing what needs to be done politically in that country. And whether it's setting up an organization for each one of those countries, politically, and what steps have to be taken, maybe dropping a bomb someplace or sending more planes there or someplace, the people themselves aren't interested, as you point out frequently. I'm not sure that they concentrate sufficiently. . . . The military action obviously will have to be taken. Unless the political action is taken concurrently, in my judgment, I just don't think that can be successful.

LBJ: I think that that's good thinking and that's not any different from the way I have felt about it. We spent the whole afternoon yesterday with Lippmann.[1] I assume you saw his column this morning.[2]

KENNEDY: Yes, I did.

LBJ: Bob McNamara and George Ball and Bundy and different ones. I agree with you on Dillon and the council[3] too. The problem that we've had there is very much what you referred to on one of the first days I was in here—that you don't get too much when the President is present in the way of frankness and

---

[1] Johnson had himself sat in for only a half hour with Lippmann, the others longer. George Ball afterward told Rusk that LBJ was "quite clearly impressed by Lippmann's contention that the United States was presenting itself in a bad light to the world by refusing to negotiate and entertaining the possibility of enlarged military action. After Walter's departure, the President returned to the question that has been preoccupying him. (He said that he had not slept more than a few hours the night before.) How could he maintain his posture as a man of peace in the face of the Southeast Asian crisis? How could he carry a united country with him if we were to embark on a course of action that might escalate under conditions where the rest of the world would regard us as wrong-headed?" (Ball to Rusk, May 31, 1964, in *FRUS*, pp. 400–404).

[2] Lippmann wrote that under Eisenhower, Kennedy, and Johnson, there had been no solution available to the Vietnam problem "which any of the three Presidents felt he could be decisive about. . . . In spite of the endless official assurances of how the struggle was being won, there has never been a time when a military victory, or anything like a military victory, has been possible. Even if one of the Presidents had been willing to intervene with an American army on the scale of Korea, even if he had unleashed the Air Force, no acceptable or tolerable outcome was visible. For once the American troops were engaged, there would be no way of withdrawing. The territory they had occupied would be reoccupied by the Asian multitude who would be more fiercely determined than ever to do away with the presence of the Western white man. . . . The original mistake in Southeast Asia has to be repaired. The way to do this is to go to a conference. . . . Even if the prospects of a conference are not brilliant, the military outlook in South Vietnam is dismal beyond words."

[3] National Security Council.

real adventure and imagination.[1] And people are somewhat hesitant, as you said, to give their *i*-deas. So I have been trying to stimulate . . . some diplomatic adventure and some political programs. I've even gone so far as to say . . . take the whole Mayors Conference[2] and put 'em out there in these provinces and give 'em . . . civilian leadership. . . . Now one of our basic problems there is the Ambassador.[3] . . . Almost you have to every three or four weeks get either Rusk or McNamara or somebody to go out and get agreement on four or five specific things, then go back and check a month later to see if he's doing 'em. Now we're gonna have another meeting with him.

We have resolved none of these things. . . . We're not ready to have a declaration of war[4]—or war by executive order.[5] We're trying everywhere we can to soup up what we've got and stabilize it and to find some way to call upon people to help us preserve the peace and have some diplomatic programs and political programs, instead of just sending out twenty extra planes. . . . Rusk is going by there from the funeral[6] with that definitely in mind. He's gonna try to get him to agree that we go into all these provinces, all these hamlets with civilian leadership, that we go . . . with very beefed-up radio programs to the people themselves, that we try to give them some hope, that we launch some offensive in the way of conferences ourselves.[7]

KENNEDY: Well, that's fine.

LBJ: That we get the Canadians to go in and tell Hanoi that our objectives are very limited. That we don't want to take 'em over and we don't want to be the power in that part of the world, that all we want to do is get 'em to leave these other folks alone and then they'll do better by then. And we're going to talk to Pearson today in New York about getting the Canadians to go into Hanoi on that front.[8] We're going to Khrushchev with suggestions as to what we think they

---

[1] RFK had reminded Johnson that President Kennedy had deliberately stayed away from meetings of his rump council "Ex Comm" during the Cuban Missile Crisis, so that people would not feel inhibited in suggesting iconoclastic approaches.

[2] U.S. Conference of Mayors.

[3] Lodge.

[4] Meaning a congressional resolution.

[5] As Truman waged in Korea.

[6] Of Indian Prime Minister Jawaharlal Nehru.

[7] Johnson is trying to rebut Kennedy's criticism that he is neglecting political means of solving the Vietnam problem.

[8] At 6:15 that evening, in New York for a Democratic fund-raising dinner, LBJ quietly met with Canadian Prime Minister Lester Pearson at the New York Hilton. J. Blair Seaborn, the new Canadian member of the International Control Commission for Vietnam, was to visit Hanoi in mid-June. At Johnson's request, Bundy had asked Pearson to let Seaborn privately assure the North Vietnamese that the United States had no intention of trying to overthrow Ho Chi Minh's regime, nor to retain a military position in the South, and wished only that Hanoi abide by the Geneva agreements of 1954 on Vietnam and those of 1962 on Laos—keeping North Vietnamese forces in their own territory and halting dispatch of military supplies to the South. He was also to say that if the North accepted Johnson's peace feeler, the U.S. would be in a position to assist North Vietnamese economic development. Pearson had consented. Johnson now told Pearson that he was "not going to be pushed out" of Vietnam but would "follow a policy of peace" (William Sullivan to Rusk, May 23, 1964, Memorandum of Conversation, Johnson and Pearson, May 28, 1964, in *FRUS*, pp. 351–55, 394–96). When Seaborn made his pitch in Hanoi, he was simply informed that the U.S. should totally withdraw from the South to allow establishment of a "neutral" regime—which would, in fact, be dominated by Hanoi (Lyndon Baines Johnson, *The Vantage Point*, Holt, Rinehart and Winston, 1971, pp. 67, 579).

ought to do and can do. We're going to London with our trying to open some new diplomatic routes . . . which we haven't advertised. . . . Now, just to be perfectly frank with you . . . *you* could be working. I asked the other day if you were. They said no. I said, "You use your judgment but I think that you ought to get him back for this small group that's trying to originate and conceive of some of these approaches." They haven't got 'em yet. That's the trouble. . . . I have suggested practically all the things that are being considered.

KENNEDY: That's a big advance, even on the last five days.

LBJ: If you're gonna be here, I wish you'd get in with Bundy. . . . Now I have talked to the Congress and I'm telling you, it's gonna be very difficult to wage much more effort out there than we are with any of their approval.

KENNEDY: Yes, I can see that.

LBJ: Mansfield is just—you know, he's for pulling out. Humphrey said, "Well, we're not doing any good." The Frank Churches said we don't want any part of it. The Dick Russells and the twenty-odd in that group say we ought not to have ever been in there.[1] The French found that out, and we didn't go along with the '54 accords. And what the hell are we doing in there anyway? And Dulles and Eisenhower got us in there[2] and we oughtn't have stayed. Yet when you go to reason with 'em and say, "How in the world you gonna get out?" they say, "God, if some government would ask to get out, it'd be wonderful."[3] But it's saddening to talk to 'em about it. So summarizing what I think we do, our thinking is very much the same. I always feel comforted by Dillon's approach[4] and . . . I didn't know whether you had been working on 'em or not. I asked Mac Bundy and told him two or three days ago to tell you that we'd like to have you.

KENNEDY: I'd be glad to.

LBJ: I think it's the hottest thing we got on our hands and the most potentially dangerous.

KENNEDY: I just didn't want to, you know, put myself in there.

LBJ: You put yourself into everything that you've ever been doing. Forget that stuff. Now I've told you that about three times. You're wanted and needed and we care and we must have all the capacity we have and all the experience. And you just go and do it like you did it last August.[5] . . . Wear the same hats. And you're even needed more than you were. . . . I wouldn't say that if I didn't mean that. . . . I'd just say, "Much obliged and thank you," if I didn't want it, sincerely want it and genuinely want it. They're never going to separate us, as far as I'm concerned.

KENNEDY: Thank you.

---

[1] Just as in his days as Majority Leader, Johnson has assessed the voting blocs in the Senate for and against war in Vietnam.

[2] After the 1954 Geneva agreement, Eisenhower and his Secretary of State created SEATO, which committed the alliance's members to Saigon's defense.

[3] See LBJ's conversation with Richard Russell, May 27, 1964, above.

[4] Johnson is trying to be polite about Kennedy's suggestion.

[5] President Kennedy had abruptly brought his brother deeply into Vietnam policy-making in August 1963, when factions at the top of his own government were battling over whether or not to undertake a coup against Diem. Johnson had been present at some of the meetings.

LBJ: And if any of my people ever contribute to it, why, I'll get rid of any of them that we can put the finger on.

KENNEDY: That's fine.

LBJ: So I would get into that.

KENNEDY: But I think that—again, I don't know what—speaking frankly about it—when I talked to Bob McNamara, he didn't feel at that time that there really had been any coordination.[1] He's getting his job done, as he always does, but as far as getting the political program and what needed to be done, it wasn't being done at that time. The way you discussed it here, obviously a lot has been accomplished. I think that that group that met on Cuba and some of these other people in government, as you know, are smart people. And if they could perhaps be brought together and just go through some of these matters to see if somebody has an original idea, which would then be presented to you. That could be helpful in stimulating some of this thought.

LBJ: They are going to meet with Lodge the early part of the week. Rusk and the task force and Westmoreland, who's taking Harkins's place . . . they think it'll be a little better relationship with Lodge than it has been and they think that Westmoreland is—they're pretty high on him. Everybody. They ought to have something the middle of the week for people to start chewing on.

---

[1]One might imagine how inwardly angry LBJ might be to hear that McNamara is over having a private meeting with RFK criticizing the way Johnson runs things.

Chapter Eight
JUNE 1964

TUESDAY, JUNE 2, 1964

McGEORGE BUNDY
3:56 P.M.

ON THE HOUSE FLOOR, Melvin Laird, a Wisconsin Republican on the
Armed Services Committee, has threatened to disrupt Johnson's careful public
balance on Vietnam.

LBJ: Laird is saying that McNamara has given them[1] a plan for invasion of the
North. . . . I approved no plan to invade anything.
BUNDY: . . . I'd just leave it alone. I wouldn't get into an argument with Laird.
He's too small.

ROBERT ANDERSON
3:59 P.M.

AT A NEWS CONFERENCE this morning held at his Oval Office desk, Johnson
insisted that his Vietnam policy directly followed that of Eisenhower and Kennedy. He read aloud an October 1954 letter from Eisenhower to President Diem
offering to help the Saigon government build "a strong, viable state, capable of
resisting attempted subversion or aggression through military means." Possibly
at Eisenhower's insistence, Ike's former Treasury Secretary here suggests that
Johnson consult the former President on Vietnam. Although LBJ likes and
admires Eisenhower and wishes to preserve their good relationship, he puts
Anderson off. He may worry that Eisenhower might convey what Johnson tells
him about Vietnam to other Republicans, who could use the information

---

[1] Lodge and the others with whom McNamara is meeting in Honolulu.

against LBJ on this, the most potentially explosive political issue of 1964. Johnson might also worry that Eisenhower will pull the rug out from under him by complaining to him that a letter he wrote ten years earlier offering to help a now-deposed South Vietnamese leader should not be cited now as authorization for massive war in Vietnam.[1]

ANDERSON: I had lunch today with President Eisenhower. From the opposition, you do not have a greater admirer. . . . Why don't you ask him to come down and talk to you about this thing in Southeast Asia?

LBJ: . . . I know we ought to before we make any definite hard plans to do more than we are doing. The situation has not materially changed in the last ninety days under Khanh's operation. It's changed at home because they're writing articles about it . . . kind of promoting a panic. On the other hand, we're not getting anywhere with what we're doing. And I'm restless with that. And I don't want to get tied down in an Asiatic war.

ANDERSON: . . . He's going back to Gettysburg today. This just might be the solution to it, and then you've got both sides because after all, when you get over in a place like that, politics ends.

LBJ: It sure ought to.

ANDERSON: . . . I think he'd be very responsive. . . .

LBJ: Okay, Bob. That's good.[2]

DEAN RUSK[3] and McGEORGE BUNDY[4]
4:55 P.M.

RUSK AND McNAMARA are in Honolulu for a hastily called meeting with Lodge, Taylor, and the new commander in South Vietnam, General William Westmoreland. Some reporters and columnists have predicted that a dramatic decision will emerge from this conference. Wayne Morse has charged on the Senate floor that McNamara and his colleagues are in Honolulu to plan "an American war in Asia."[5] Actually they are discussing possible next steps in Vietnam—a congressional resolution for expanded action, quiet communication with Hanoi, then graduated military pressures culminating in limited air attacks against the North. But they have reached no consensus.[6]

---

[1] Eisenhower was indeed angry about LBJ's use of his letter to Diem and he may have said so to Anderson at their luncheon, which took place just after LBJ's press conference. At a Republican meeting in Philadelphia that Eisenhower attended on June 15, Clare Boothe Luce complained that by using the letter, Johnson was making it appear that American involvement in Vietnam was under Eisenhower's "remote control today." Eisenhower replied, "I agree. It's nonsense." Ike said he did not believe America should "quit" in Vietnam, but that until South Vietnamese morale was much improved, "there is little hope for what we're doing now" (Washington Post, June 16, 1964).
[2] In other words, thank you but no thank you.
[3] In Honolulu.
[4] At the White House, with Johnson.
[5] Congressional Record, June 1, 1964.
[6] Record of Meetings in Honolulu, June 2, 1964, in FRUS, pp. 428–33.

RUSK: Mr. President, Bob McNamara and I feel that we should have a brief backgrounder out here to try to cut down, if we can, some of the excitement about this meeting. . . . One of the questions we need to check with you on is this matter of your press conference statement and the way Laird tried to pick that up. Now this is a phony issue he's raised, because the Departments of State and Defense have a responsibility of always looking at all the contingencies that might develop in any situation. But the truth is that we have not laid before you any such plan as he was referring to for your consideration and approval. . . .

LBJ: . . . I'd say Laird is talking about contingencies and possibilities, potentialities, and Johnson is talking about a program and a decision. And there's a good deal of difference between the two. We have plans for every contingency, but that does not mean that that is an administration plan to go into North Vietnam.

RUSK: That's right. Those contingencies are not policy.

LBJ: That's right. Now McNamara's statement, which I have, in an executive session,[1] he just says we've got a program for going into North Vietnam and we're all ready. And Laird takes that as an administration program. And I imagine that General Taylor has got a plan for Cuba.[2] And maybe he's got one for Hono-lulah and Pearl Harbor, but that doesn't mean that that's this administration. Now . . . Mr. Laird over the weekend . . . declared that the administration is preparing to move the Vietnam War into the North. I don't know whether we're preparing to do that or not.

RUSK: That's right.

LBJ: I've got no preparations to do it on my desk. Now, you might recommend something like that down the road, but not here. That's my feeling. [quotes and paraphrases from transcript of his morning news conference:] So I would say, Mr. Laird is not as yet speaking for the administration. He might next year sometime.[3] . . . Regardless of whether Mr. Laird is spokesman or not, is there any substance to what he said? The President: I know of no plans that have been made to that effect—that is, to move the Vietnam War into the North. [puts down transcript] Now, I think that's a truthful statement. I *haven't* got any plans to move it in there. I don't know what you-all going to do. . . . Now here's what McNamara said. [Johnson reads aloud from McNamara's statement to the executive session of the House Armed Services Committee:] ". . . To the President on March 16 . . . we recommended that preparations be undertaken immediately to be in a position . . . to carry out . . . United States military action against North Vietnam. The action General Khanh was referring to was action by South Vietnamese forces. . . . We are taking many actions to assist him. . . . He believes that he'll be prepared for effective air strikes by the end of the year." Now McNamara is talking about planning on contingency. And a decision being made, I'm talking about. I have no such plans to do that. I might have them this afternoon. I might

[1] Of the House Armed Services Committee.
[2] Meaning an invasion of Cuba.
[3] In other words, a Republican President might make Laird Secretary of Defense. Johnson is prescient, for that is exactly what President Nixon did in 1969.

have them tomorrow. But I don't have them before me. I haven't made them now. He[1] has no right to say that we're going into North Vietnam.

RUSK: Right, right.

LBJ: Now I don't know who's right. It looks like he has a good basis for what he's saying, I think.

BUNDY: I think it's the difference, Dean, isn't it, between—we have a book full of contingency plans, but we have no current plan for action.

RUSK: We've been saying to these congressional committees that we've been looking at . . . these four main alternatives all along. . . . The one we haven't been taking up for any serious study is the alternative of pulling out of Southeast Asia. But the other alternatives we've been looking at. And that we're on the track of supporting the Vietnamese and giving them a chance to win that war. The other alternative of enlarging the war is a very serious one. We don't rule that out. But that is a very serious matter and the President will be in touch with congressional leaders if we have to move that way. Now that's what I've been saying in executive sessions.

LBJ: Now, my statement.[2] It was a little awkward—"I know of no plans that have been made to that effect"—that is, to carry the war into Vietnam. Now, I don't mean that we haven't considered the alternative of going in there. We haven't considered South Vietnamese planes going in there and taking bombs and whatnot. But I have approved no plans to carry and have made no plans at this stage to carry the war into North Vietnam. That's what I was trying to say.

RUSK: Right. Well, I think that gives us the difference. That's the same difference as McNamara and I see out here. And we'll try to give that a little more perspective in a little backgrounder.

· · · ·

RUSK: Now this is one thing you should have in mind back there in terms of this meeting. This is at least the fourteenth meeting that has been held in Honolulu plus . . . Bob McNamara on five occasions, when he's gone to Vietnam.

LBJ: Yeah.

RUSK: So this is not a massive orgasm[3] or something that is wholly new and different.

LBJ: Yeah. We're not playing it any heavier than we can help back here.

RUSK: I think we ought to play down any sort of notion of cataclysmic character of this meeting.

BUNDY: Couldn't agree more.

LBJ: Are you all about through?

RUSK: Yes sir, we'll be leaving here about six this afternoon.[4] Be there the first thing in the morning.

---

[1] Laird.

[2] At the morning news conference.

[3] Rusk's language was far more pungent in private than public. It was only in private during the Missile Crisis, for instance, that he said that the Americans were eyeball-to-eyeball and the other fellow had just blinked.

[4] Honolulu time.

LBJ: Are you reasonably well together?

RUSK: I think I could answer a little better in the afternoon. We want a private talk with Cabot Lodge this afternoon, and we'll try to pull things together with him.[1] But in general, I think that we're at the moment seeing it pretty much the same way. There may be one or two . . . points we've got to straighten out with him and see what he really thinks about it.

LBJ: You try to stay there until you wrap that thing up and you-all have one mind.

THURSDAY, JUNE 4, 1964

HOUSTON HARTE
11:25 A.M.

> LBJ TALKS POLITICS with his Texas newspaper publisher friend. On Tuesday night, Goldwater had defeated Rockefeller in California, bringing him within striking distance of the Republican presidential nomination.

HARTE: What do you think of the California situation?

LBJ: I think that it's a pretty intense, fanatical group and they poured lots of money in and there's a bunch of screwballs in California, kinda like the Dr. Townsend group.[2] They're the Birch Societies. They've got eleven people nominated for Congress on the Birch ticket.[3] I don't know what it'll mean over the country. I think it'd probably mean the death of the Republican party. It'll kill out a bunch of Congressmen and Senators and Governors and things like that if they keep going. He[4] wants to drop atomic bombs on everybody. I don't believe the people will stand for that. They may do it.

HARTE: I think it's a fine thing for us. I think he's the man to beat.

LBJ: I agree.

HARTE: There may be somebody that's easier to beat but I know he's very easy to beat.

LBJ: I think so.

---

[1] Try to ensure a united front with Lodge.
[2] In 1933, Dr. Francis Townsend of Long Beach, California, proposed a $200-a-month pension to any retired American over sixty. Up to thirty million Americans became Townsendites before the movement lost steam after passage of the Social Security Act in 1935.
[3] In 1958, a Massachusetts businessman, Robert Welch, formed the radical right-wing John Birch Society, named for a Baptist missionary killed by Chinese Communists soon after VJ-Day, dedicated to exposing the "Communist conspiracy" controlling the U.S. government. Three Birchers won Republican nominations for Congress in the June 2 California primary.
[4] Goldwater.

FRIDAY, JUNE 5, 1964

RICHARD GOODWIN
White House Speechwriter[1]
12:58 P.M.

JOHNSON IS TO SPEAK the next day to the International Ladies Garment Workers Union in New York. At Johnson's side will be the leaders of the New York Liberal Party, David Dubinsky, President of the Ladies Garment Workers, and Alex Rose, President of the Hatters, Cap and Millinery Workers.

LBJ: Get all this anti-Goldwater stuff out of there. I don't want to bring him[2] up and start arguing with him with all this bluster and bravado. . . . It'll just build him up . . . and that's childish, so tear all that Goldwater stuff out like you never heard of Goldwater. . . . We're not worried about him. We've got a positive, affirmative program. . . .

GOODWIN: All right, fine, we'll do that.

LBJ: You do it. Get a little "fanatic" stuff in there.[3] A little rhythm for me. . . . It's a pretty good speech. Just jazz it up a little bit.

CARL ALBERT
1:00 P.M.

JOHNSON REPORTS a conversation that Sargent Shriver has had with House Rules Committee Chairman Howard Smith on the poverty bill, which was reported out by the House Education and Labor Committee on June 3.

LBJ: Did you hear what Smith told Shriver? . . . Said the leadership[4] wasn't in a hurry to get it out. They had more than they could take care of and he couldn't do anything about it.

ALBERT: That isn't true.

LBJ: That's just a part of his strategy, Carl. They're just screwing us to death every week.

· · · ·

LBJ: [angry:] I don't care whether he votes for it or not. But that's my number one bill. I'd rather have it than all the other bills put together.[5]

---

[1] Goodwin would not be formally announced as a member of the White House staff until December 1964, when Johnson made him a Special Assistant.
[2] Goldwater.
[3] Johnson later thought better of this suggestion. The final speech contained no reference to fanaticism.
[4] Meaning the House Democratic leadership.
[5] Johnson here suggests even greater concern about poverty than civil rights. Certainly this would have flowed out of his early upbringing. As Robert A. Caro wrote in *The Path to Power,*

ALBERT: . . . We're going to get that bill.

LBJ: . . . I've just been suffering here for three damn months while they just screw us to death and I can't ever get it up. And I know when I'm being screwed. . . . Halleck and Smith and them just put us off week after week after week.

. . . .

LBJ: They're delaying it. . . . They say it's a political thing. . . . Hell, 16 percent of our unemployment's among young people! And we're trying to move that 16 percent down and make tax-*payers* out of them instead of tax-*eaters*. But I've been on this thing now for six long months, trying to get this bill up where they can vote on it.

. . . .

LBJ: I just think you and John[1] ought to tell 'em that we just need that . . . to be taken up next week, without fail, if we don't do anything else. If they don't, *damn* it if I'm not just gonna turn this job over to somebody else. Poverty—I just fought my heart out for it and each week Halleck gives me another week's postponement. . . . He's fighting it with all that he's worth and he's out making these political speeches about it. And I just think that we got to take 'em on and say, by God, they stand for poverty and they stand against progress and they stand against helping the people. . . . If I need to, I'll call every Democrat down here and meet in the East Room with them and say, now, goddamn it, let's pass our program or let's quit.

WALTER REUTHER
7:52 P.M.

THE AUTO UNION LEADER has offered to help repair the split in Texas Democratic politics.

LBJ: Now the problem we've got is getting Yarborough[2] to beat this attractive young boy Bush.[3] And he ought to quit fighting with Connally and every Democrat. . . . The only ones he ought to cuss is Republicans. . . . I don't know if I can keep 'em from biting at each other's throats 'cause they're like two big pussycats. . . . I've got to have Connally to carry the state myself. . . . They'll wind up having Tower[4] in the Senate and having Bush in the Senate. That's the way they're

---

"The children of Johnson City were not only poor, they *felt* poor. . . . The Depression came early to farmers, and nowhere did it come earlier than in the Hill Country" (p. 115).

[1] McCormack.

[2] Ralph Yarborough.

[3] The forty-year-old Houston oilman and Republican county chairman George Bush, son of LBJ's old Senate colleague Prescott Bush of Connecticut, won the Republican nomination to oppose Yarborough. The future forty-first President opposed the civil rights bill, saying that he would "hate to see" the Constitution "trampled on in the process of trying to solve civil rights problems." Bush said that the vote for George Wallace in the Democratic primaries "indicates to me that there must be a general concern from many responsible people over the civil rights bill from many responsible people all over the nation" (quoted in Stephan Lesher, *George Wallace*, pp. 311–12).

[4] John Tower, elected in 1961 to Johnson's old Senate seat as the first statewide Republican officeholder in Texas since Reconstruction.

going. Of course, Yarborough is a very weak candidate. Civil rights and union labor and the Negro thing is not the way to get elected in a state that elects Connally by 72 percent. . . . He's handicapped in that state. Now he wouldn't be handicapped in Michigan or New York, but he's handicapped in Texas.

CLIFTON CARTER
8:26 P.M.

JOHNSON COMPLAINS to his campaign strategist about wasting resources in so Republican a state as Ohio.

LBJ: I don't know why you're trying to raise money in Ohio. You can't even elect a constable out there. You oughtn't to use the President on that kinda stuff. That's awful bad judgment. I've been to Ohio and campaigned over it for years and never have made any progress and I'm ready to wipe 'em out as far as I'm concerned. Just tell whoever's telling you on Ohio that Ohio is off the list until they come in with their guarantee[1] and bring it in and show us what they got. So don't get us scheduled any more for Columbus. . . . I don't think you-all know what you're doing when you schedule these things and you just let some damned nincompoop put you in. We're doing too many of them. . . . Don't make any more engagements or consider Ohio until I clear it.

MONDAY, JUNE 8, 1964

RICHARD RUSSELL
4:35 P.M.

AT 4:30 A.M. on June 6, Bundy awoke Johnson with the news that a U.S. reconnaissance plane had been downed over Laos.[2] On June 7, Laotian Communists downed a U.S. armed fighter jet. Now the President talks to Russell from the Cabinet Room, where he is consulting McNamara, General Wheeler, and other advisers on what to do next.

LBJ: You've seen what's happened to these planes the last two days? Our people are pretty unanimous that they ought to go in there and notify Hanoi by taking out this anti-aircraft battery.
RUSSELL: Do they know where it is?
LBJ: Yep.

---

[1] Of campaign money.
[2] With the consent of Prince Souvanna Phouma, the Laotian Prime Minister, such flights had begun in May.

RUSSELL: I thought they already would have taken it out then.

LBJ: They had to get that boy last night and they were shooting the hell out of us all around it and they had to pick him up because he was on that fighter escort armed and we didn't want him prisoner.[1]

RUSSELL: Did they get both the boys?

LBJ: No, they got the one that was armed in the fighter escort, but they haven't gotten the other one yet.

. . . .

LBJ: The Ambassador[2] is very much against it. He says it'll escalate it, that it'll likely cause us to lose the government,[3] but all the Joint Chiefs and McNamara—

RUSSELL: I thought this was in Laos.

LBJ: It is, but they think Souvanna Phouma will be very much against going in with armed planes and starting to shooting. . . . They'd asked us to do reconnaissance but they hadn't asked us to start destroying any batteries. . . . Now the orders have been given and they're about ready to go. . . . The Ambassador feels that you are violating the Geneva Accords[4] and you are now getting yourself in the same position that the other side's in. . . . On the other hand, all of our military people and most of our political people feel definitely and my own instinct is to hit back when I'm hit.

TUESDAY, JUNE 9, 1964

GEORGE REEDY
10:16 A.M.

LBJ: [to aide who walks into the Oval Office without invitation:] Wait a minute. Wait a minute, here! [angry:] Just *call* me now when you want to talk to me. I'm busy. . . . Don't think of what I'm trying to stop with the Kennedy people— butting in here.[5] Haven't I *told* you-all that?

. . . .

LBJ: [shrill:] Don't ever issue anything over two hours in advance anymore. You've accommodated all these folks[6] and ruined me. . . . None of 'em thank you. None of 'em appreciate it. . . . I read every story this morning and in practically

[1] The pilot was rescued after parachuting from his plane over the Plain of Jars.
[2] Lodge.
[3] The Khanh government.
[4] Of 1962, providing for a neutral Laos.
[5] Note how, even at this late date, Johnson differentiates between the "Kennedy" people and the "Johnson" people.
[6] The White House press corps.

every one, the whole story was written on the changes we made in a speech that
I had not approved.[1] . . . You have no right to issue anything that I don't approve
of. . . . Tell these reporters that they damn sure didn't play fair with you, that
you gave it to them Saturday and they wrote the whole story on change and
next time you don't have to give it to 'em at all! All you do is serve their
convenience. [angry] I don't give a *piss* whether I get it in the afternoon paper or
not. I couldn't care less. And anyway, if you can't give it to 'em at 8:00 and get it
in the afternoon paper, I don't know what the hell they're doing. Why do they
go up there? They could, every one of them, file their story. And all you had to
do was hand it to 'em when you got on the plane Monday morning. . . . Every
one of 'em . . . wrote their stories, but wrote the story about—the dumbbell print
reporters—about we're after Barry Goldwater. And also read the speeches very
carefully and if there's anything that can be interpreted as hitting at Goldwater,
call it to my attention.

ROBERT KENNEDY
12:25 P.M.

JOHNSON HAD TOLD Kenneth O'Donnell the previous December that if he
needed Robert Kennedy as Vice President to win the 1964 election, he would
take him: "If I don't need him, I'm not going to take him. I don't want to go
down in history as the guy to have the dog wagged by the tail and have the
Vice President elect me. . . . Bobby and I don't get along, and that's neither one
of our faults, but there's no sense in that."[2]

By now, with the strongly conservative Barry Goldwater as the likely
Republican nominee, it seems that Johnson will not need RFK. Nevertheless
Kennedy is keeping his hat at least nominally in the vice presidential ring,
perhaps imagining that lightning could strike or that he might pressure Johnson to choose a running mate like Hubert Humphrey who would be amenable
to the Kennedy wing of the Democratic party.[3] The conversation below shows
Kennedy tacitly suggesting that he is capable of deference to LBJ and that the
foreign and domestic experience he has gained from three years at his brother's
side could be of use to Johnson.

---

[1] Johnson had given a commencement speech the previous day at Swarthmore College.
[2] O'Donnell oral history, Johnson Library.
[3] RFK had heard that Johnson had said that whomever he selected for number two, "I want
his pecker to be in my pocket." In a mid-May 1964 oral history interview for the Kennedy
Library, he told John Bartlow Martin, "I think he's hysterical about how he's going to try to
avoid having me. . . . That's what he spends most of his time on, from what I understand—
figuring out how he's going to avoid me." He said that if he were forced on LBJ, "it would be
an unpleasant relationship. I would lose all ability to ever take any independent position. . . .
Johnson's explained quite clearly that it's not the Democratic party anymore, it's the all-
American party, and the businessmen like it. All the people who were opposed to the President
[Kennedy] like it. I don't like it very much." He added that Johnson was "able to eat people up,
and even people who are considered rather strong figures—I mean Mac Bundy or Bob McNamara. There's nothing left of them. . . . Our President [Kennedy] was a gentleman and a human
being. . . . This man is not. . . . He's mean, bitter, vicious—an animal in many ways. . . . I think
his reaction on a lot of things is correct. But I think he's got this other side of him and his
relationship with human beings, which makes it difficult, unless you want to kiss his behind
all the time. That's what Bob McNamara suggested to me a couple of weeks ago if I wanted to
get along. . . . I can't do that."

KENNEDY: I was just talking, Mr. President, to Mac Bundy on the phone when I heard of this incident of last night[1] and I asked him if the congressional people had been informed about it, and he didn't think that they probably had. And you know, it's going to come out from the Chinese and it's going to come out in other ways. I thought that it was a matter that would be well if it was handled—

LBJ: Yeah, I think so. Some of them have been. But it hasn't been done as a group and I don't know whether if the Republicans would bring it out and leak it or not and that's a great question.

KENNEDY: But of course, the Chinese will talk about it and the Russians will talk about it. . . . I would think that you can expect that it's going to be within twenty-four hours because it'll be worldwide and if we had done it without telling anybody in the United States, they're all going to wonder, you know. I would think that that's gonna be a problem. The second thing is it seems to me that somebody should be working on how it will be handled with the public because the Chinese obviously will say something about it—what are we going to say and whether we'd repeat it.

LBJ: I raised that question with them and I've got another meeting at one o'clock[2] where I'll raise it again. The boy in the State Department and McNamara have had that question put to them by me. What's the man over there that runs their publicity? . . . State.

KENNEDY: Manning?[3]

LBJ: Manning, yeah. . . . His feeling was that we shouldn't do anything about it. My feeling was that we ought to go ahead and say something. McNamara agreed with him.

KENNEDY: I vote with you.

LBJ: . . . We took the ball the other day and said that we had taken this action and announced it ourselves and I thought got by pretty well with the other two flights. It doesn't look like they got much results last night on what they did. Have you analyzed it?

KENNEDY: I haven't. Just heard about it on the telephone.

LBJ: Are you going to meet with them anytime today or tomorrow? . . . I told Mac Bundy to get you, because we've got to see where we go from here. They have no real plans. McNamara and Rusk were both rather insistent on going through with this one, although the Ambassador[4] raised some grave questions which concern me— (A) The reaction in the world. (B) Souvanna's reaction. But they felt that unless we showed some strength and made some kind of reply that it would be very bad for us and we went ahead. But they were confident they could knock this battery out. They didn't. And think it shows us that we can't rely too much on airpower on some of these things.

KENNEDY: I think that's a real lesson. . . . About four or five days ago, we went though the plan for Vietnam and I had some serious questions about it. . . .

---

[1] The United States had retaliated for the airplane downings in Laos by trying, with partial success, to take out the offending anti-aircraft batteries.

[2] LBJ's "Tuesday luncheon" with Bundy, Rusk, McNamara, and other foreign policy officials.

[3] Robert Manning.

[4] Lodge.

Perhaps they are going to have some other discussions with you. But I mean, for instance, the congressional part of it and getting a congressional resolution.[1] I think this poses all kinds of problems.

LBJ: It will. You can't do anything about that until you get rid of this problem we've got up there now. And the question of whether you ought to try is a difficult one and I don't know how you can conduct much offensive without some authority.[2] We had the United Nations behind us but we had a very divided country and a lot of hell, and we finally really lost—the Democrats did—on the Korea thing.

KENNEDY: Yeah, that's right.

LBJ: I'm fearful that if we move without any authority of the Congress that the resentment would be pretty widespread and it would involve a lot of people who normally would be with us. If we asked for the authority, on the other hand, I would shudder to think that if they debated it for a long period of time, and they're likely to do that. So I don't think the choice is very good.

KENNEDY: Yeah. . . . It seems likely that they'll start asking somebody to spell out what exactly is going to happen and if we drop bombs there, then they retaliate and we eventually bomb Hanoi. . . . And what the answer is . . . to those questions are *so* difficult to give, particularly if you're giving it to a lot of people that are antagonistic.

LBJ: . . . That's all true and you can't go into the details of your plans. But if you take the other route, then they ask you by what authority, what executive order, do you declare war?

KENNEDY: Yeah, well, I guess . . . it's not necessary constitutionally, but the alternative to that—especially if that's going to be very harmful—the alternative, of course, is for you and Secretary McNamara and Secretary Rusk, at the appropriate time, to start bringing in the labor leaders and the business leaders and the congressional leaders and talk with them, sort as if it were a National

---

[1] In recent weeks, while the Departments of State and Defense worked on a plan for gradually escalating political and military action against North Vietnam, a group led by George Ball had drafted a resolution to be submitted to Congress that would endorse "all measures, including the commitment of force" to defend the South Vietnamese or Laotian governments, upon their request. Johnson told his men that Truman had made a mistake in waging the Korean War without congressional approval: only if Congress were in on the "takeoff" would it accept responsibility for a "crash landing." A May 24 National Security Council meeting debated the draft. McNamara insisted that it be withheld from Congress for now, unless Johnson decided to use U.S. combat (not training) forces in Southeast Asia within the next two or three months. Bundy wrote on June 10, "The immediate watershed decision is whether or not the Administration should seek a Congressional resolution giving general authority for action which the President may judge necessary to defend the peace and security of the area. . . . The best available time for such a move is immediately after the civil rights bill clears the Senate floor. . . . On balance, it appears that we need a Congressional resolution if and only if we decide that a substantial increase of national attention and international tension is a necessary part of the defense of Southeast Asia in the coming summer" (Draft Congressional Resolution, May 24, 1964; Record of NSC Executive Committee Meeting, May 24, 1964; and Bundy to Johnson, June 10, 1964, Johnson Library).
[2] From Congress. LBJ told Valenti that when he was Senate Majority Leader, if some President had tried to move in Southeast Asia without getting the Congress aboard, Johnson would have "torn his balls off" (Ted Gittinger, ed., *The Johnson Years: A Vietnam Roundtable*, Johnson Library, 1993, p. 19).

Security Council meeting and that you were briefing them. And this is what we have to do at this time and if you have to take any further steps, that you will inform them and that you'll keep them advised and bring in some of the newspapers and bring in some of the television people.

LBJ: And I think probably talk to the country about why we are there.[1]

KENNEDY: Yeah.

LBJ: And how we're there and what we confronted there and what we may do before you submit a resolution. Because . . . I have doubts about what would happen to it right now.

KENNEDY: That's what I think.

LBJ: I think they'd just talk and develop a big divide here at home.

KENNEDY: That's what I think. And then some people will say we're not doing enough. And the others will say too much. You know all you need is fifteen of them up there that are doing that and I think it's just—unless the ground is laid.

LBJ: Did this jury amendment[2] bother you any this morning?

KENNEDY: No. I think it makes it much more difficult, but hell, we can live with it.

LBJ: Um-hmm. Does it help you any on cloture?

KENNEDY: Yes.

LBJ: You think cloture is decided now, don't you?

KENNEDY: . . . It certainly appears that way. It'd be just a miracle getting this bill. Who could have thought a year ago that we could get this bill?

LBJ: It'll be a wonderful thing. Now are you making your plans on who we ought to call in to follow through on it?[3]

KENNEDY: Yes, we are.

LBJ: Now should we do that between the time that it goes from the Senate to the House and by the time we sign it, or should we wait until after we sign it?

KENNEDY: I think probably at least the feeling has been to wait until after we sign it.

LBJ: All right. Now, you give thought to that, because we could move when the Senate messages it over to the House, because it's a pretty foregone conclusion then.

KENNEDY: That's right.

[1] Here the first appearance of the Johnson administration refrain of the middle and late 1960s, "Why We Are in Vietnam."

[2] To the civil rights bill. Backed by Senator Hickenlooper, who was complaining about Dirksen's acquiescence to Johnson, Republican Senator Thruston Morton of Kentucky wanted to ensure the right to a jury trial for all criminal contempt defendants, except in voting rights cases. Humphrey agreed to the amendment, on condition that three doubtful Republicans—Karl Mundt of South Dakota, Norris Cotton of New Hampshire, and Roman Hruska of Nebraska—promise to vote for cloture.

[3] Johnson, worried about national opposition to enforcement of the bill, was considering calling in the Governors of all states that had not had a public accommodations law.

. . . .

LBJ: [back to Vietnam:] Okay, I sure want you to get with these fellows.[1] . . .
Mac Bundy told me this morning that they were going to have executive meet-
ings until Thursday and come in with some recommendations on Thursday and
I'll get back in touch with you.

. . . .

KENNEDY: The other person, Mr. President, who has got some sense on these
matters is—you know, again, none of us are always right, but who has got some
sense and has had a good deal of experience is Douglas Dillon.
LBJ: Yeah, I told them. I tell them every day.[2]

GEORGE REEDY
12:31 P.M.

> TODAY'S *Washington Star* is running a two-page "special report" by John
> Barron, "The Johnson Money," starting at the top of page one, which estimates
> LBJ's net worth at $9 million, "amassed almost entirely while Mr. Johnson was
> in public office." Barron charges that, despite LBJ's insistence that the family
> fortune was owed to Lady Bird's business acumen, he actually "often was
> personally involved in gaining interests in radio and television stations" and
> was continuing to do private business as President despite his claimed blind
> trust. Lady Bird dictated into her diary that the *Star* exposé "irritates Lyndon
> more than it does me," but she wondered why the *Star* was "more intent" on
> discovering the sources of their family wealth "than any other paper in the
> United States." She scoffed at the $9 million estimate, adding that "unfortu-
> nately there were no offers included" in the *Star*'s story.[3]

LBJ: I think you ought to go away in your bathroom or someplace. Take the
Star and read this Barron story because it's a very vicious, a very mean one
and it's planted and I rather think that we'll have to say that it's untrue, but I
think if we go into getting into it, then we bring it right in here and start debating it.
REEDY: Right.
LBJ: And I don't know how to avoid that. But we have not met with them at
any time. That's a pure planted lie. They claim we met with Morrell and Moses.[4]
Both of them denied it in a telegram . . . Now they've got a presidential aide
telephoning 'em. We didn't do that. That's all untrue.

. . . .

[1] On Vietnam.
[2] Once again Kennedy is pushing Dillon and once again Johnson is not buying. If LBJ had
really told his people to include Dillon, they would have complied.
[3] Diary of Lady Bird Johnson, June 9, 1964, Johnson Library.
[4] The *Star* article reported that according to some sources, LBJ talked business during his
December 1963 vacation at the ranch with C. Hamilton Moses and George Morrell of Midwest
Video. (See Johnson's November 30, 1963, conversation with Jesse Kellam above.)

LBJ: Now we've got to think about the strategy and Abe's[1] in New York. He ought to read the story and then you ought to try to talk to Abe and see what you think ought to be done. What is your reaction to what ought to be done?

REEDY: First of all, the most damaging thing in it is that nine-million figure because that's the sort of thing that's gonna get picked up. The rest of it, I think, is too complicated for anybody to read or understand. But that nine million is going to make a big splash. Second, my immediate impulse is that we've gotta ride it out. . . . There's an awful lot of stuff that I could pick to pieces, even with my limited knowledge. But before I give you a judgment, I really want to sit down and do some thinking because I think this can be serious. But the thing that everybody is going to leak to them immediately is that thing about nine million. 'Cause that sounds like a helluva lot of money to John Doe on the street.

LBJ: And I think the bad part is—I think this is unquestionably these opponents of ours for the nomination.[2]

REEDY: No doubt.

LBJ: I think that there's no question but what Bobby[3] and his group have got the *Star*. They're using it and the play they give it—it's most unusual for the *Star* to do anything like that at all.

JOHN McCORMACK
12:50 P.M.

JOHNSON TELLS the House Speaker how he has retaliated against the plane downings in Laos.

LBJ: We went in there last night to take out this battery that had shot down these two planes and we destroyed some buildings and . . . had a partial success, taking out one of the guns. The Secretary of State and the Secretary of Defense and the Joint Chiefs all felt like that after they'd shot down two planes that we had to make some response. If we didn't, why, we'd just destroy ourselves. So we did that and our planes came back uninjured and are all back at their base. Now we can't say anything about it. . . . I don't know who we ought to discuss this with, if anyone. I imagine the Chinese, who are speaking for them,[4] will issue a press release sometime or other. But we do not plan any further expeditions. We'll make a survey about once a week . . . so we can't get caught off guard. But we have . . . shown that we mean business. I stayed awake most of the night, hoping that these planes would come back.[5] And one-thirty they went off and three o'clock they got back. But there are ten of 'em and they're all back safe. They partially destroyed the battery that was giving us this trouble. . . . That's

[1] Fortas.
[2] Meaning Robert Kennedy.
[3] Kennedy. It is a measure of Johnson's complexity that he could shift immediately from a congenial, cooperative talk with RFK to this kind of discussion.
[4] The Laotians.
[5] Here is the first appearance of a frequent scene as U.S. involvement grows in Vietnam—of Johnson waiting sleepless through the night for word on bombing raids he has ordered.

where we stand now. Would it be your thought we ought to talk to Halleck and any of the Republicans about it?

McCORMACK: It's bound to come out. I would think so.

LBJ: I had the feeling I ought to send McNamara to see the armed services people and I ought to send Rusk to see the foreign affairs people. . . . But we've got to keep it to a very limited group. If we don't, it would greatly injure our interests by their talking about it.

McCORMACK: Yeah, the worst of that is when you get a group like that, you know what democracies are. . . .

LBJ: . . . They ought to be sworn to secrecy. . . . Don't discuss it with anyone. I'm gonna discuss it with you and Carl, Mansfield and Humphrey, and we'll try to keep it to that.

MIKE MANSFIELD
12:56 P.M.

AFTER INFORMING Mansfield of the air strike on Laos, he solicits the dovish Senate Majority Leader's general advice on Southeast Asia.

LBJ: I've submitted all the things that you've suggested to me and I've got Stevenson down here.[1] . . . They don't have very much of a plan.[2] We can't go in there[3] with ground troops. The air forces don't get the job done and can't get it done. We are trying every way we know how to appeal to Hanoi and to Peiping. We have told de Gaulle that we are very anxious to follow any conference route that we can, that we're very anxious to follow any plan of neutralization that we can. . . . But we've got to keep our strength there and show that we will react in order to have them where they'll talk to us at all. Otherwise they'll just think they don't need to. We have—very confidentially—talked to the Canadians . . . and asked them to go to Hanoi and say to Hanoi that we're willing to pull out of there . . . and stay out of there if they'll just quit overrunning South Vietnam, and that we may actually be able to work with them and help them better *their* lot. But we don't want anything over there. . . . We don't want to dominate anybody. If they'll just quit advancing, why, then we can get out. . . . We talked to Hickenlooper and all the Republicans. . . . This is a week or so ago. I told you about it at the time. . . . He thought that we had to go in and show some strength. If we didn't, they'd run us out and that would be a catastrophe. Now I haven't agreed to that yet because I can't see any very firm plans and I don't want to get

---

[1] LBJ mentions Stevenson to show Mansfield that he is receptive to dovish advice.

[2] After the Honolulu meeting, the Joint Chiefs, with the exception of Taylor, had complained to McNamara in a memo that a "militarily valid objective for Southeast Asia" had not been established, nor a "military course of action" to achieve it. They proposed two alternatives— break North Vietnam's will and capability or simply stop the North's support of the southern insurgency. Taylor said that the memo was not "an accurate or complete expression of our choices" and complained that the first option, which the Chiefs preferred, raised "considerably the risks of escalation" (Joint Chiefs to McNamara, June 2, 1964, and Taylor to McNamara, June 5, 1964, in *FRUS*, pp. 437–40, 457–58).

[3] Vietnam.

in a land war in Asia. So I have held it back for three or four weeks. Now I don't know who I ought to discuss what we're doing with up there . . . Do you have any suggestions on who we ought to talk to? . . .

MANSFIELD: I think the best thing to do would be if you would talk to them all together.

LBJ: It always gets out . . . and we don't want to blow it up. 'Cause we sure don't want to give any indications[1] that we're getting involved in a war. I've been playing it down, if you'll notice. . . . After the Honolulu meeting, I tried to draw away from this thing that we're invading the North.

MANSFIELD: And you did it very successfully. But I think, Mr. President, that even if there is a leak, it would be better if you'd do it, rather than the others . . . because it'll get out anyway and it's a matter of ego as far as some of these people are concerned. . . . So far as I'm concerned, I think you've done everything right.

LBJ: You-all are voting[2] this afternoon, aren't you? And if you come down, that'll sure get in the papers and that'll be notifying 'em what we're doing.

HUBERT HUMPHREY
1:06 P.M.

LBJ: We lost these two planes in Laos, and our folks went in there about 3:00 this morning. . . . We had a partial success, and our planes returned safely. . . . We don't want to tell them what we're doing. We felt like we had to respond. The Secretary of State, the Secretary of Defense, and the Joint Chiefs thought that this was the minimum. . . . Thought we ought to do more. . . . I couldn't talk to you publicly with all those people here this morning.[3] I don't want for us to be responsible for escalating this thing and announcing these things and appear that we're on a bombing rampage. Because we're not. We just had to answer their knocking down two planes with some kind of response.

HUMPHREY: Yes, sir.

LBJ: And we did, and we got back, and while we didn't get everything we went after, we didn't lose anything, and we did make the response. Now, the question comes is—what is the wise thing? McNamara is going to talk to Russell and Saltonstall. I've talked to you and Mansfield. Mansfield thinks we ought to call these people to the White House. I think that that escalates it and makes it too important and it announces to the enemy what we're doing. And we're just doing that too much these days.

HUMPHREY: I agree with that.

LBJ: So I rather think that probably I ought to call Dirksen on the phone and Hickenlooper or maybe send Rusk to see Dirksen and Hickenlooper, let McNamara see the two armed services. . . . The leadership of the House has been talked

[1] During the presidential campaign.
[2] On civil rights.
[3] Humphrey had come to the White House for the weekly Democratic leaders' breakfast.

to. But it's kind of like making an atomic bomb. You go around telling everybody and you lose the war.

HUMPHREY: I would suggest that you would send both Rusk and McNamara to those persons together. It just seems to me the two of them coming together is more impressive and has a tendency to kind of give everybody equal treatment. Plus the fact McNamara is a little firmer and Rusk can give a little touch to it.

LBJ: Uh-huh, okay.

HUMPHREY: . . . With Dirksen and Hick. Dirksen is not on the Foreign Relations[1] but he's key.

LBJ: Do you think that they ought to be doing it together? They getting along that well these days?

HUMPHREY: No, I would send them to talk to them separately. . . . I don't think that you could do anything less than you've done right now.

LBJ: Yeah, okay.

CARL ALBERT
4:44 P.M.

ALBERT: The Speaker has talked to Tip O'Neill and Tip's going to leave next Tuesday night if they don't finish that bill[2] on Tuesday.

LBJ: [chuckles darkly] Well, I'll just let 'em nominate somebody else.[3] I ain't gonna kiss any more Congressmen's ass. I decided this morning I don't even think we ought to be meeting at breakfast.[4] We don't do a thing. . . . .Everybody comes in and finds a thing that's wrong. . . . I don't believe we get anywhere. I'm just tired.

ALBERT: I just don't understand. He said he's taking his wife and going to Europe. . . . How are we going to pass a bill out if we don't have our votes?

LBJ: . . . I don't care, Carl. I'm in a humor today to tell 'em I won't have the nomination. I'm just not. My staff's embarrassed to come to those breakfasts. Some of them told me this morning, said they don't think we ought to have 'em anymore. The Speaker starts talking about all the things that are wrong with the pay bill. Then somebody else talks about what's wrong. . . . I have to manage to get the budget. I have to manage to submit 'em to the Congress. Then, by God, I have to go to calling all these Congressmen individually. Now that's the Leader's job and you-all's and I can't do it.

ALBERT: . . . I bet I talk to a hundred Congressmen a day.

LBJ: . . . I'd just go tell the Speaker about it and tell him if he wants the poverty bill to fail because Tip O'Neill is gone, that's all right. . . .

ALBERT: . . . If the Speaker can't do anything with it, what can I do?

LBJ: . . . I'd just let him go and let the whole damn thing go.

[1] Committee.
[2] Anti-poverty bill.
[3] For President.
[4] The weekly Tuesday Democratic legislative leaders' breakfast.

ROBERT McNAMARA
6:20 P.M.

> McNamara has quietly reported to senior Senators and Congressmen on the air strike.

LBJ: How did you get along with the Congress today?

McNAMARA: . . . Saltonstall is concerned as to where we're going. He doesn't think the American people know why we're in Vietnam. He wasn't particularly concerned about the reconnaissance flights. . . .

LBJ: . . . Why don't you tell him Dulles got us in there?[1]

McNAMARA: . . . What he's saying is we ought to tell the American people why we're there and explain to them why Southeast Asia is important to us and many of his constituents think it is not. I think he's right, in a sense. We're going to have to do more work on making clear to the American people why this is important to us.

LBJ: I do too.

McNAMARA: . . . George Mahon[2] is a little timid. . . . He's just worried about the situation in Southeast Asia and the criticism that he thinks is going to be directed at the government because of it. I think in that respect he reflects a substantial body of public opinion. He's a rather timid person anyhow and he's simply reflecting the fears of many of his own constituents.

                               · · · ·

LBJ: We haven't taken any real serious losses and we can't put our finger on anything that really justifies this acceleration and escalation of public sentiment that it's going to hell in a hack since you were out there in March. Is that a buildup of our critics largely? Have we fed that? Where does it come from that we're losing? . . .

McNAMARA: . . . If you went to . . . the estimators in CIA and said how's the situation today in South Vietnam versus three months ago or four months ago, I think they'd say it's worse.

LBJ: That's not what Lodge and Khanh think, is it? They think it's a little better, don't they?

McNAMARA: I don't think they really believe that, Mr. President. No, sir. I think that they both would indicate it's a very weak situation. I think they think . . . it's better to have Khanh there than it was . . . to have that committee running it.[3] But I think Lodge is personally very much concerned about it. The very fact that he's constantly pushing for . . . military pressure on the North. . . . That letter that he sent in today that we read at lunch.[4] . . . What he was saying is

---

[1] Deflecting Republican criticism, LBJ is making ample use of what Eisenhower's Secretary of State did in 1954 to involve the United States in SEATO and the continuing defense of South Vietnam.

[2] Texas Democrat, Chairman of the House Appropriations Committee.

[3] The South Vietnamese junta that had ruled from November 1963 through January 1964.

[4] Lodge had written to Johnson in a letter dated June 5, "Clearly a very strong, if not impregnable, argument can be made for the proposition that Southeast Asia is of vital concern to the United States. . . . I do worry about committing seven divisions of the U.S. Army to the

don't be scared away from my plan to apply military pressure on the North by the thought of putting in seven divisions. . . . It isn't necessary. . . . This is Lodge's way of saying that things are in pretty bad shape. . . . The CIA estimators, Lodge, many of the rest of us in private would say that things are not good. They've gotten worse. You see it in the desertion rate.[1] You see it in the morale. You see it in the difficulty to recruit people. . . . While we say this in private and not in public, there are facts available in the public domain over there that find their way in the press. . . . The Pathet Lao[2] have just advanced on the ground within the last three weeks and have kept their gains. I think it's these two events that lead the people to feel a sense of pessimism about Southeast Asia.

LBJ: While I was talking to you, I have a note from Mansfield, which is interesting. [reads from four-page Mansfield memorandum:] "I do not conclude that our national interests are served by deep military involvement in Southeast Asia. . . . If the decision must be for continuance on the course which is leading to deeper involvement, however, I would most respectfully suggest that the basis for these decisions must be made much clearer and more persuasive to the people of this nation than has heretofore been the case." So what he comes out and says is he thinks we ought to get out of there. Which we can't and are not going to. And if we don't, then we've got to educate the people as to why we're in there.

McNAMARA: I think he's absolutely right. If we're going to stay in there, if we're going to go strictly up the escalating chain, we're going to have to educate the people, Mr. President. We haven't done so yet. I'm not sure now is exactly the right time.

LBJ: Now, and I think if you start doing it, they're going to be hollering, "You're a warmonger."[3]

McNAMARA: That's right. I completely agree with you.

LBJ: I think that's the horn that the Republicans would like to get us on. Now if we could do something in the way of social work, in the way of hospitals, in the way of our province program and the way of our fertilizer and the way of remaking that area out there[4] and giving them some hope and something to fight for and put some of our own people into their units and do a little better job of fighting without material escalation for the next few months, that is what we ought to do.[5]

---

mainland of Southeast Asia, as is contemplated. This goes against the belief that has been held by many Americans, including myself, for a long time. The climate and other conditions in this area are of incomparable difficulty for Americans. . . . This . . . would be neither an encapsulated action . . . with a good possibility of clearly limited results and a quick departure, nor is it a large campaign in which the U.S. provides a small proportion of troops in order to get the command. On the contrary, it is largely a U.S. venture of unlimited possibilities which could put us onto a slope along which we slide into a bottomless pit. I still have faith that naval and air power, with clearly limited and very specific actions on the ground, can give us what we need" (Johnson Library).

[1] Of South Vietnamese soldiers.

[2] Laotian Communist forces.

[3] LBJ need not add that this would be particularly true in the middle of a presidential campaign.

[4] South Vietnam.

[5] Johnson shows how eager he is to hold the line until after the November elections and until Khanh's durability was proven.

McNAMARA: Mr. President, this is what I call my Eight Critical Provinces Program and that is what we'd laid out. We finally sent it out to Lodge by cable three nights ago. . . . Step H and I on there . . . involves the use of 580 additional U.S. personnel in these critical provinces. . . . He said he wanted to make it perfectly clear that he hadn't agreed to it. . . . So we have just got to push like hell on this.

LBJ: I wonder why we don't come right back to a cable to him. Why don't you draft one . . . from State to him or from me to him, saying that we have felt since '61 that one of the great problems there was giving those people something to fight for. And we recommended that to Diem in '61, when I was out there[1] and got his agreement that he would do more of it and he didn't do enough of it soon enough. That's one of the big problems we have. We deeply believe in it and feel that it has got to be done and urge him to carry out what we want done.

McNAMARA: He said in his cable he would respond more fully when he had gone over the detailed plan. I think it might be wise, in view of our relations with him, to give him a day or so to do that.

LBJ: That may be. . . . Just say I personally recommended this in '61 and I want to reiterate what I would like to see done and I hope I can have your cooperation in doing it.

McNAMARA: It gets you on the line though of putting more Americans in Vietnam. And this is one of the issues he could charge against you or the administration—we have got too many Americans there trying to run the country, to take over and causing resentment among the Vietnamese. He has already had a kickback from Khanh and Deputy Prime Minister Hoan[2] on the four men he put in the government and I am sure this is in his mind here on this five hundred.[3] I think it would be better if you kept out of it and let us handle it with him and I will make a note on my pad two days from now if we don't get a favorable reply to go back to him on this.

LBJ: Okay.

HUBERT HUMPHREY
7:03 P.M.

JOHNSON'S SENATE WHIP informs him that after eighty-three days, the longest debate in Senate history, Senators are ready to shut off the Southern-led filibuster against civil rights. The way is now cleared for the Senate to pass one of the most important laws in American history.

LBJ: Hubert, tell me, do you have a reliable count on your cloture?

HUMPHREY: Yeah, I think that my reliable count shows a minimum of sixty-eight votes. And I'm just going to go over it here again with one of the staff fellows, because we're going to be in session practically all night. I guess we got some boys who are going to hold us in session. We had a little parliamentary

[1] As Vice President.
[2] Nguyen Ton Hoan, South Vietnamese Vice Premier for Civil Pacification Affairs.
[3] Actually the 580 additional Americans mentioned by McNamara above.

snafu here, but we got it all cleared up. So I think we're all right. I'm going to be here for some time. Can I call back one of your men and let you know?

LBJ: Yeah. . . . Call Lee White.[1] I'm going to have to be at a dinner at seven-forty to meet the Prime Minister.[2] . . . How are you counting Hayden?[3] Against us, aren't you?

HUMPHREY: Yes sir . . . I'm counting we got some Republicans that come in that sound pretty good—Mundt. . . . I haven't got any commitment out of Edmondson[4] yet, but the boys tell me that it looks good. I've asked some of the people to contact his brother. I've been after Edmondson two or three times and since that jury trial amendment got in, I thought that might pull him through and I think it does, because he was so anxious about it.

LBJ: But you think we're safe?

HUMPHREY: Yes sir. . . . I'm just pawing around here for some papers but as I see it now, we have sixty-eight votes.

LBJ: How many of those are Democrats?

HUMPHREY: Forty-two.

LBJ: The Republicans are doing a little better than we are, aren't they?

HUMPHREY: Yes sir. Dirksen tells me he's got twenty-eight votes, but I don't think he has. I think he's got twenty-six.

LBJ: And how many they have? Thirty-six?

HUMPHREY: They got thirty-three members of the Senate. . . . Losing seven.

LBJ: I know three of them is Mechem[5] and Tower and Goldwater.[6]

THURSDAY, JUNE 11, 1964

RICHARD RUSSELL
12:26 P.M.

JOHNSON HAS BEEN INFORMED that Lodge is about to resign as Ambassador in Saigon. He will come back to America and campaign for "moderation"

[1] Johnson's Associate Counsel.
[2] Krag of Denmark, at a White House state dinner.
[3] Senate President Pro Tempore Carl Hayden of Arizona. Hayden was willing to support cloture only if Johnson needed the vote to prevail.
[4] Democratic Senator J. Howard Edmondson of Oklahoma.
[5] Republican Senator Edwin Mechem of New Mexico.
[6] Several minutes after the Johnson-Humphrey call, Senator Robert Byrd of West Virginia began the final speech of the civil rights debate, insisting for fourteen hours that the bill "cannot be justified on any basis—legal, economic, moral, or religious." After Byrd sat down, at 10:00 A.M. the next morning, Senators began final remarks on the vote for cloture. One hour later, the roll call began. By 71 to 29, Senators shut off debate. An angry Richard Russell complained that Senators had been "confronted with the spirit" of a "lynch mob." Exuberant over the victory, Johnson saw Robert Kennedy at the White House and called out, "Hello, hero!" (President's Daily Diary, June 10, 1964, Johnson Library).

in Republican politics (meaning Scranton). While asking the Armed Services Committee Chairman to suggest a successor, LBJ reveals his abiding inner conflicts about Southeast Asia.[1]

LBJ: I don't want anybody to know this but the two of us. I think Lodge is—he hasn't been willing to do anything out there—I think he's coming out within the next few days or weeks. I need to pick the best man in America to succeed him. I don't know who that is. . . . Rusk is willing to do it. I don't think he's the man. I don't think I can afford to let him go. McNamara is anxious to do it. The same thing. Bundy the same thing. I can't let any of them go here because I got too many damn serious problems. I need a Lucius Clay twenty-five years ago. . . . I can't take anybody from the Cabinet. I've looked over every single Ambassador we've got. . . . The man we need is a man that's a pretty good diplomat and a hell of a good administrator that can help this government make some decisions for 'em and lead 'em . . . and at the same time work with our military. We think we've got the best man we can get in Westmoreland. . . . The best we've got in the government is George Ball,[2] who's probably first, and Averell Harriman. And we just can't send Walter Jenkins, so we've got to send somebody.

•   •   •   •

LBJ: You think it would be very bad for McNamara, don't you? . . . He's the most valuable man I got in the Cabinet on everything.

RUSSELL: . . . All this business about "McNamara's War" would be accentuated. . . . I don't think you can spare him.

•   •   •   •

LBJ: I'm confronted. I don't believe the American people ever want me to run.[3] If I lose it, I think that they'll say I've lost. I've pulled in. At the same time, I don't want to commit us to a war. And I'm in a hell of a shape.

RUSSELL: We're just like the damn cow over a fence out there in Vietnam.

LBJ: . . . I've got a study being made now by the experts[4] . . . whether Malaysia will necessarily go and India'll go[5] and how much it'll hurt our prestige if we just got out and let some conference fail or something. . . . A fellow like A.W.

---

[1] Johnson is also happy to have a reason to ask Russell's counsel, in the hope that it will help smooth over the frictions generated between them by LBJ's victory on civil rights. During the battle, Russell had told Moyers, "Now you tell Lyndon that I've been expecting the rod for a long time, and I'm sorry that it's from his hand the rod must be wielded, but I'd rather it be his hand than anybody else's I know. Tell him to cry a little when he uses it" (Robert Mann, *The Walls of Jericho*, p. 393).

[2] How might history have been changed had LBJ chosen Ball, who soon proved to be the chief dove and skeptic about Vietnam among the highest ranks of the Johnson administration?

[3] Meaning abandon Vietnam.

[4] On June 9, the CIA had responded to Johnson's request for an estimate of what would happen in East Asia were the dominoes of Laos and South Vietnam to fall. The Agency's Board of National Estimates replied that this would be "profoundly damaging" to U.S. prestige "and would seriously debase the credibility of U.S. will and capability to contain the spread of Communism elsewhere in the area. Our enemies would be encouraged and there would be an increased tendency among other states to move toward a greater degree of accommodation with the Communists" (Johnson Library).

[5] In other words, the domino theory.

Moursund said to me last night, "Goddamn, there's not anything that'll destroy you as quick as pulling out, pulling up stakes and running. America wants, by God, prestige and power." . . . I said, "Yeah, but I don't want to kill these folks." He said, "I don't give a damn. I didn't want to kill 'em in Korea, but if you don't stand up for America, there's nothing that a fellow in Johnson City"—or Georgia or any other place—"they'll forgive you for anything except being weak." Goldwater and all of 'em are raising hell about . . . hot pursuit and let's go in and bomb 'em. . . . You can't clean it up. That's the hell of it.

RUSSELL: . . . It'd take a half million men. They'd be bogged down in there for ten years.[1] . . .

LBJ: We never did clear Korea up yet.[2]

RUSSELL: . . . We're right where we started, except for seventy thousand of 'em buried over there.[3]

LBJ: Now Dick, you think, every time you can get your mind off of other things, think about some man.[4] . . . My great weakness in this job is I just don't know these other people. The Kennedys—they know every damn fellow in the country or have got somebody that knows 'em. They're out at these universities and everyplace in the country—New York and Chicago.

· · · ·

LBJ: We're just doing fine, except for this damned Vietnam thing. We're just doing wonderful. Every index.[5] The businessmen are going wonderful. They're up 12, 14 percent investment over last year. The tax bill has just worked out wonderfully. There're only 2.6 percent of the married people unemployed. . . . And 16 percent of these youngsters, and I'll have all them employed. . . . It's kids that are dropping out of school and then they go on a roll. But I'll take care of that with my poverty,[6] just by organizing it all. We've got the money in these various departments—Labor and HEW and Justice. . . . I'm gonna put all of them in one and put one top administrator[7] and really get some results. Go in and clear up these damn rolls. And I'll do it with only $300 million more than was in the budget anyway last year. . . . I was down in Kentucky the other day. We've got fifty kids there teaching beauty culture—how to fix Lynda's hair. And they're all going out and get jobs $50, $60 a week in another three months. . . . That's what we ought to do instead of paying out four billion a year on relief, for nothing, where you don't have to work. To hell with this unemployment compensation. It's relief. But I've got to find a man for Vietnam.

· · · ·

LBJ: I see where you and John Stennis got your pictures all over the paper. You ought to open your eyes, though. God damn 'em. Make 'em quit taking—you took a picture like Lyndon Johnson. I have my eyes shut.

[1] Russell was hauntingly right.
[2] The Korean War had been halted in 1953 only by a truce that required a large, continuing American military commitment to South Korea.
[3] The Korean War saw 33,629 Americans and about 47,000 South Koreans killed.
[4] For the embassy in Saigon.
[5] Of American economic performance.
[6] Program.
[7] Meaning Shriver.

. . . .

LBJ: How did the Congress react to our going in and doing this bombing?[1]

RUSSELL: They[2] don't know about it. . . . I think all of 'em would approve of it if they did.

LBJ: Now we're going to continue these reconnaissance flights as needed, as we must have 'em, and we're going to send in armed people. And if they shoot at us, we're going to shoot back.

RUSSELL: That's just like A.W. told you. That's the American inclination. . . .

LBJ: Now Mansfield's got a four-page memo saying that I'm getting ourselves involved and I'm gonna get in another war if I do it anymore.

RUSSELL: . . . I in a way share some of his fears.

LBJ: I do too, but the fear the other way is more.

RUSSELL: I don't know what the hell to do. I didn't ever want to get messed up down there. I do not agree with those brain trusters who say that this thing has got tremendous strategic and economic value and that we'll lose everything in Southeast Asia if we lose Vietnam. . . . But as a practical matter, we're in there and I don't know how the hell you can tell the American people you're coming out. . . . They'll think that you've just been whipped, you've been ruined, you're scared. It'd be disastrous.

LBJ: I think that I've got to say that I didn't get you in here, but we're in here by treaty and our national honor's at stake. And if this treaty's[3] no good, none of 'em are any good. Therefore we're there. And being there, we've got to conduct ourselves like men. That's number one. Number two, in our own revolution, we wanted freedom and we naturally look with sympathy with other people who want freedom and if you'll leave 'em alone and give 'em freedom, we'll get out tomorrow. . . . Third thing, we've got to try to find some proposal some way, like Eisenhower worked out in Korea.

RUSSELL: . . . I think the people, if you get some sort of agreement all the way around, would understand it. And I don't think that they're so damned opposed to the United Nations getting in there. And I don't think they'd be opposed to coming out. I don't think the American people want to stay in there. They've got enough sense to realize that it's just a matter of face, that we can't just walk off and leave those people down there.

LBJ: But U Thant[4] says he won't have anything to do with that part of the world. . . . Think about my man[5] and I'll talk to you in a day or two.

[1] Of the ground battery that downed the two U.S. planes.
[2] Meaning all but the leaders that McNamara briefed.
[3] SEATO.
[4] Of Burma, the U.N. Secretary-General.
[5] For Saigon.

HUGH SIDEY
Washington Correspondent, Time *Magazine*
3:17 P.M.

AFTER USING THE PHRASE "Great Society" at the April Democratic dinner in Chicago and in other venues, LBJ had given the signature speech of his administration on May 22 at the University of Michigan at Ann Arbor.[1] The address was written mainly by Richard Goodwin, as Goodwin later recalled, in consultation with the President, Moyers, and other advisers. After the speech brought hosannas from Henry Luce, Walter Lippmann, James Reston, and others, Sidey felt he should write about Goodwin's new role as a Johnson adviser and speechwriter. When Sidey called on Reedy, he was immediately whisked into the Oval Office for the monologue below. Sidey began by politely noting that a President's speeches were a product of his own thought and effort, but was there not always a writer who helped put things together and polished the lines? Unwilling to concede his reliance on Goodwin or any speechwriter, Johnson insisted that Goodwin was merely providing the White House with "special research."

LBJ: I can tell you, the Ann Arbor speech came as the result of a book I read by Barbara Ward,[2] if that satisfies you. Dick Goodwin, as far as I know, never saw it. It doesn't make any difference, but I just want to show you that somebody is trying to appear important to you, and I resent that to hell. People on the outside, on the edge, they want to appear that they know something that they don't know. . . . They oughtn't to, because they ought to be working. That's not their job to spend their time telling *Time* about who does what. *I'll* tell 'em, if they want to know.[3]

---

[1] "We have the opportunity to move not only toward the rich society and the powerful society, but upward to the Great Society. The Great Society rests on abundance and liberty for all. It . . . is a place where every child can find knowledge to enrich his mind and enlarge his talents. . . . where leisure is a welcome chance to build and reflect, not a feared cause of boredom and restlessness. . . . where the city of man serves not only the needs of the body and the demands of commerce but the desire for beauty and the hunger for community. . . . where men are more concerned with the quality of their goals than the quantity of their goods. But most of all, the Great Society is not a safe harbor. . . . It is a challenge constantly renewed, beckoning us toward a destiny where the meaning of our lives matches the marvelous products of our labor. . . . Will you join in the battle to build the Great Society, to prove that our material progress is only the foundation on which we will build a richer life of mind and spirit?"

[2] *The Rich Nations and the Poor Nations* (Norton, 1962), which Johnson kept at his bedside.

[3] Sidey later recalled, "As Johnson continued to talk about his staff, I had the notion that he was playing a game. He certainly knew that I was aware that Goodwin wrote his speeches and, indeed, had become his chief writer. . . . Johnson wound up the interview by pulling a felt-tipped pen from his shirt pocket and sketching the table of organization of his men. Down at the bottom under a 'Miscellaneous' category was a man named 'Goodman.' This was the ultimate put-down—misspelling Goodwin's name, as if he were a stranger in the White House" (*A Very Personal Presidency,* Atheneum, 1968, pp. 156–58).

LAWRENCE O'BRIEN
3:55 P.M.

O'BRIEN: The pay bill has passed, 243 to 157.[1]

LBJ: Congratulations! Congratulations! That's wonderful. . . . That gives you your tax bill, your civil rights bill, your farm bill, your pay bill. Now you get me a rule on poverty next week and we're really moving.

STEPHEN SMITH
4:28 P.M.

SMITH HAS INVITED the Johnsons to a Kennedy Library fund-raising dinner, to be held on the roof of the Hotel St. Regis in New York the following week. Honoring Jacqueline Kennedy, it will be the first appearance at a public social occasion by the slain President's widow since Dallas. Lady Bird has told LBJ that he will have to choose between the dinner and a previously scheduled business evening with members of Congress on Capitol Hill. The President floridly assures Smith that nevertheless he and Mrs. Johnson will come to New York.

LBJ: I said,[2] "I believe that President Kennedy is watching everything I do, from heaven. And I think that God Almighty has a way of directing these things. He took him ahead of us so that he could get things lined up for some of the rest of us that haven't got much chance.[3] And they're having this meeting to carry on what he was trying to do and they're calling the roll and they get to Johnson and they say, 'Absent.' And I don't want to ever have that done. So you just call 'em and tell 'em we'll be there." . . . So that's the story and that's the way I feel about it and I'm coming just because I want to. . . . If it was a Johnson dinner in honor of my wife and I had been called ahead, he'd be there and you would too.

ROBERT KENNEDY
6:11 P.M.

RFK HAS SENT LBJ a handwritten letter offering to replace Lodge as Ambassador to South Vietnam.[4] Johnson does not want to accept. Among other

---

[1] With this action, the House had cleared the way for a $535 million annual pay raise for federal employees and members of Congress.

[2] To Lady Bird.

[3] To go to heaven. LBJ is really pouring it on.

[4] "I just wanted to make sure you understood that if you wished me to go to Viet Nam in any capacity I would be glad to go. It is obviously the most important problem facing the United States and if you felt I could help I am at your service. I have talked to both Bob and Mac about this and I believe they know my feelings. I realize some of the other complications but I am sure that if you reached the conclusion that this was the right thing to do then between us both or us all we could work it out satisfactorily" (June 11, 1964, Johnson Library).

reasons,[1] he feels that Kennedy's life might be in danger in Saigon.[2] And if he is tired of dealing with Lodge, with his independent constituency and willingness to stand up to the President, he would scarcely wish to replace Lodge with RFK. Johnson knows that, much more than with Lodge, he would have to worry hourly that Kennedy might resign the job in protest over his Vietnam policies. Still, knowing that RFK's offer, if accepted, would almost certainly remove him as a political threat in 1964, he genuinely appreciates the gesture.[3]

LBJ: I'm with some folks.[4] I just wanted you to know that the nicest thing that happened to me since I've been here is your note, and I appreciate it *so ver-r-r-y much*. Can't think of letting you do that, but you've gotta help me with who we do get and we've gotta get him pretty soon. We'll talk about it in the next few hours, but I think we're in better shape than we've ever been when that letter come in and I wanted you to know it. I'll sleep better tonight.

KENNEDY: Thank you very much, Mr. President.

LBJ: I appreciate it more than you'll ever know.

KENNEDY: That's very nice.

LBJ: You're a great guy or you wouldn't write that kind of letter.

FRIDAY, JUNE 12, 1964

JOHN CONNALLY
4:15 P.M.

>   JOHNSON TALKS to the Texas Governor from his bedroom, where he has just risen from a nap.

CONNALLY: The Belden Poll[5] came out today. . . . Shows you at an all-time high of 84 percent.

LBJ: That's 74 in the nation, Sunday. Gallup's coming out Sunday, 74.

CONNALLY: And shows me at 82, highest of any Governor since they started keeping it in 1940. . . .

---

[1] See Johnson conversation with Bundy, June 17, 1964, below.
[2] Johnson told Valenti, "I would be accusing myself for the rest of my life if something happened to him out there" (Jack Valenti, *A Very Human President*, Norton, 1975, p. 141). LBJ may have thought that some South Vietnamese backer of the Diem regime might try to murder RFK in revenge for the assassination of Diem.
[3] RFK may have been certain that Johnson would reject the offer and may have hoped that it would improve LBJ's view of him as he began to think seriously about the vice presidency.
[4] John Stennis and several Johnson aides.
[5] A major Texas survey.

LBJ: I don't believe we're that good, do you?

CONNALLY: No!

[Both laugh]

MONDAY, JUNE 15, 1964

McGEORGE BUNDY
7:56 P.M.

AT THE FOLLOWING DAY's Tuesday luncheon of his foreign policy advisers, Johnson will discuss candidates for the Embassy in Saigon with Bundy, Rusk, and McNamara. Bundy tries to put in the fix for his own candidate.

BUNDY: Dean and Bob and I all think that your best bet is, in fact, Gilpatric.[1]

LBJ: He's out. I couldn't name him at all. I can't name Gilpatric.[2]

BUNDY: You sure of that, Mr. President?

LBJ: Um-hmm. Yeah, yeah, yeah. I can't name him.

BUNDY: Then we have to go back to the boards.[3] We have assumed that whatever might have been his political troubles before, any man leaving a very fat and fancy practice for the most dangerous job in the government would get more cheers than groans.[4]

LBJ: No. . . . I'm just pretty confident it ought to be Taylor.[5]

BUNDY: [peremptorily:] . . . Rusk and McNamara both think that would be a mistake.

LBJ: I want to hear 'em out on it, but that's who I'd be for. I wouldn't name Gilpatric. I like him and I'm for him, but I wouldn't send him to that job. I think it'd just be harry-karry.[6] Just be political suicide.

BUNDY: [bitingly:] Well, I'm *astonished* at your judgment.[7] We must argue it out again tomorrow.

[1] Roswell Gilpatric, who had resigned as Deputy Secretary of Defense in January to return to his New York law practice at Cravath, Swaine & Moore.
[2] The reason for this is that in 1963, the Kennedy administration suffered a burst of criticism over award of the lucrative contract for the TFX fighter-bomber to General Dynamics, for which Gilpatric had argued and for which he had done legal work. A Senate subcommittee and the Justice Department had cleared him of conflict-of-interest charges, but Johnson does not wish to give the Republicans any more openings to "holler corruption" during the campaign year.
[3] Drawing boards.
[4] Bundy here shows his ignorance of partisan politics.
[5] The Chairman of the Joint Chiefs.
[6] Hara-kiri.
[7] Bundy says this in a tone almost of reprimand.

LBJ: What are their objections to Taylor?

BUNDY: One, that he is physically weary.

LBJ: He'll be less weary there than he is here, running every goddamn day to every conference they got in the world.

BUNDY: He's got—I don't know whether it's a bum ticker,[1] but he's had a warning. Rusk feels that . . . a military man in the one and two spots is a bad signal, both internationally and in some ways locally.

LBJ: That's a military job though.

BUNDY: Bob would agree with you on that. Rusk would not and I would not. . . . I think . . . you'd lose ground and it would be said that you lost it because of a militaristic process and a failure to understand the politics of it. The thing that worries me most though is simply that this is a man of ebbing energy. . . . The fact is you need a hell of a commander on that spot. I would rather put Westmoreland in charge of everything than send Max out. . . . McNamara . . . feels as I do that Ros is first-rate and that there is not a political vulnerability, but we defer obviously to your judgment on that.

LBJ: I've made up my mind on Ros. I don't need anything on him. . . . I think that . . . would make a real partisan war out of it, and I don't want that to happen. And I think we've got to have somebody that's got great stature to avoid it. . . . I just have the feeling that the people of this country have more confidence in Taylor out there than any man that's going to be available to us that I've heard of. . . . The people of the world—I don't think they're gonna think that Max Taylor is a LeMay.[2] . . . They're gonna look at him as a reasonable, fair, good man and has the respect of everybody. And I think it's going to show that we mean bid-ness without having to bluff and bluster a lot. I think it means we got our best man we put out there. . . . I'm gonna have dinner with Fulbright tonight. I'm gonna ask him what he thinks.

BUNDY: [testily:] Well, then it's going to leak.[3] But never mind. If you decide it within twenty-four hours—

LBJ: You think so?

BUNDY: Well, no. I think he can keep his peace for a day or two. That's about all. . . . No, I don't quite think that, Mr. President. Unless he gets asked by some newspaperman he fully trusts. . . . It's happened so many times in the last three or four years.

LBJ: I won't discuss with him then.

BUNDY: [backpedaling:] I think he needs to be in the act. No, I think he'd keep his mouth shut for you—for the length of time you need. . . . You've gotta decide this right away anyhow.

LBJ: If I had to decide tonight . . . I've decided totally on Taylor.

BUNDY: I couldn't pass judgment on the politics of it, but it does surprise me that you're so negative on Ros on that.

---

[1] Meaning coronary problems. One wonders whether Bundy remembered that he was talking to a man who had suffered a major heart attack in 1955.

[2] In other words, a warmonger.

[3] Bundy thinks of Fulbright as indiscreet.

LBJ: ... He's just left and he's going up there and now he's coming back—I think I'd rather have *Ball* than Ros. And they tell *me* that *Ros* is no administrator. ... McNamara told me. ...

BUNDY: ... I think his use of staff I would have thought very well of.

. . . .

LBJ: The way I feel about Taylor is this. I believe, from what I've seen in the seven months I've been in here, that the most challenging and most dangerous military problem we have is out there. He's our top military man. He's respected in the world and here at home. I'm not sure that the administration has as much respect on Vietnam as Taylor would have on Vietnam. I believe anything in his name, signed to, would carry some weight with nearly anyone. ... Maybe Westmoreland can help him if he's got any problem with his age. ...

BUNDY: ... The immediate prestige and safety impact[1] of this is better than any other single appointment you can make. On the real merits, I would say this is a tired man with an uncertain health problem and I myself do not believe that in fact he's ever understood that war. I think this is just the painful truth.

LBJ: It's a good place for him to get to understand it then.

BUNDY: Mr. President, men at sixty-two and a half who are tired are not an easy bet for that. I think what you're getting is great protection and no harm. ... All the people who have watched him operate have been worried about how quickly he tires.

LBJ: I think one of the reasons is that they run him. ... When I go to this damned Los Angeles thing,[2] I'll be constipated, I'll skip three hours, I'll get up at 7:00 in the morning—

BUNDY: We haven't thought of sending *you*, Mr. President, but that's a perfect solution! [chuckles]

LBJ: No, but I'm just telling you that one of the problems of his is just traveling all the time. ...

BUNDY: I'll grant you that.

LBJ: He's touring, and that'll kill anybody—a man that just travels all the time. I believe he'll be easier there than he will fighting with LeMay here. ... We'll talk about it tomorrow.

. . . .

LBJ: I looked at two or three items in *Newsweek*[3] and we narrowed 'em down to only three people knowing 'em around here. They're about as limited as they could be and they know 'em. I'm getting very suspicious. Hell of it is, Mac, that two or three of these are just things that my people knew. Bill Moyers knew 'em and Jack Valenti knew 'em. And the three of us are about the only ones that know 'em and they've got 'em in there.

BUNDY: I bet you a cookie more than those three, Mr. President. It's just not possible, from what I know of your people. ... Sump'n else. Sump'n funny.

[1] Meaning Taylor's ability to provide Johnson with political cover.
[2] Next week, Johnson is to speak in Los Angeles.
[3] *Newsweek*'s "Periscope" section revealed that Assistant Secretary of State Fred Dutton had been "tapped" for LBJ's campaign staff and that Johnson would not name a new IRS chief until after the November election (June 22, 1964).

TUESDAY, JUNE 16, 1964

ROBERT McNAMARA
9:55 A.M.

> TWO DAYS EARLIER, Lodge had formally cabled Johnson that he wished to resign. Now LBJ is earnestly considering a replacement.

LBJ: Taylor . . . can give us the best protection[1] with all the forces that want to make that a political war.[2]

McNAMARA: He's better in that respect than Ros. . . .

LBJ: Oh, they'd just start making speeches on Ros. The lead on the story . . . would be "Former Undersecretary of Defense, who was involved in the TFX contract,[3] was named by Johnson today to succeed Lodge." And then every damn speaker would be up there raising hell. . . . They can't say much about Taylor. . . .

McNAMARA: . . . I think what they'd say is you're putting it in the hands of a military man.

LBJ: Morse[4] and them would say that, but nearly everybody thinks that's what it is.[5]

McNAMARA: I was just going to say I don't think that's bad. . . .

LBJ: I was just staying awake at night thinking about it.

McNAMARA: . . . He[6] told me yesterday . . . that he wanted to be considered for the job. . . .

LBJ: A cable with his name signed to it would have a hell of a lot more weight in a lot of circles than any other name I know of.

McNAMARA: I agree with you.

LBJ: . . . I was with some folks last night,[7] and they think we're about to lose the greatest race that the United States has ever lost, and it'd be the first time that we've ever turned a tail and then shoved out of a place and come home and said we'd given up the Pacific. Now I don't think it's that bad, but a lot of people do, and I think we're gonna have to make a decision pretty promptly and we're

---

[1] Domestic political protection.
[2] In other words, the American leaders who want to have a domestic political struggle over involvement in Vietnam.
[3] Scandal.
[4] The Oregon Senator.
[5] In other words, that Vietnam is a military problem.
[6] Taylor.
[7] The previous evening, the Johnsons had dined with the Joseph Alsops and the Clark Cliffords, after which LBJ, Clifford, and Alsop withdrew. Alsop told the President that if he did not commit combat troops to Vietnam, he was going to preside over the first real defeat of the United States in history. Lady Bird wrote in her diary, "I can't say the evening did anything to solve Lyndon's dilemma—or to smooth his path for the days ahead" (June 15, 1964, Johnson Library).

gonna have to send him out there and then kinda support what he thinks we ought to do.

McNAMARA: I just don't believe we *can* be pushed out of there, Mr. President. We just can't *allow* it to be done. You wouldn't want to go down in history as having—[1]

LBJ: Not at all. But how're we gonna avoid it though? Suppose your government[2] collapsed today and another one came in and said get the hell out. What do we do? See my point?

McNAMARA: Oh, I agree it's a ticklish situation. You know how I felt about it. But I don't think we're quite at that point. I don't believe the government *is* gonna collapse today and I think if we continue to show some signs of firmness in Laos and in that area, it won't collapse. And I think putting Max out there, as a matter of fact, is a sign of firmness. Khanh will appreciate it. The people, I think, in Vietnam will interpret it—

LBJ: I think everybody in the world will look at it . . . and say these folks mean bid-ness.

· · · ·

LBJ: It has a way of getting into columns that I confer with my old congressional buddies, but I know Russell and Vinson[3] can have a lot to do with helping us and I just like to have their feeling. And they all just say right off the bat that they don't go very strong for Ball. They like Gilpatric . . . but they think that that man doesn't have the stature in the United States that that man ought to have following Lodge. They all think *you'd* be the best man, but it would be harry-karry to send you out there—from my standpoint.

McNAMARA: I want you to know, Mr. President, I'm prepared to go. I've talked to Marg[4] about it and Marg is prepared to go.

LBJ: Well, you're not going. . . . You talk to him[5] again today. . . . You ought to tell him that he can write a blank check on us here and just let's get him the best people we can and let's start assembling them.

WEDNESDAY, JUNE 17, 1964

GEORGE REEDY
6:36 P.M.

THE PREVIOUS EVENING, in New York, Robert Kennedy had ridden with the Johnsons and Chief Justice Earl Warren from the Kennedy Library dinner at

---

[1] McNamara is pressing Johnson very hard.
[2] Meaning the Khanh government.
[3] Chairmen of the Senate and House Armed Services Committees.
[4] Mrs. McNamara.
[5] Taylor.

the St. Regis Hotel to what was now known as John F. Kennedy International Airport. Lady Bird later dictated into her diary that "Bobby was easy, relaxed, but he's an enigma to me. . . . I respect Bobby. In many ways, I admire him. But I feel a peculiar unease around him which I did not feel around his brother. . . . He never once used the word 'Jack' or 'President Kennedy.' He always said 'my brother.' I haven't the vaguest idea what is going on in his mind."[1]

REEDY: Tom Wicker[2] came in to see me. He said that the New York papers today carried stories saying that Bobby Kennedy rode back with you last night from the hotel to the airport and had a long conversation. And the New York papers are speculating on politics and that sort of thing.

LBJ: Tell him that wasn't mentioned. I've never discussed politics with him since I've been President.[3]

REEDY: Right. Tom said that both the Attorney General and Ed Guthman[4] told them there was no discussion of politics. What you did discuss was civil rights. But the Attorney General was reluctant to let them even do it for background.

LBJ: No, just tell them . . . that I must be able to ride to the airport without getting in any controversy and there was absolutely nothing said that is of any consequence or of any public interest, and in no way touched on politics of any kind. Never have. He hasn't raised it with me and I've never raised it with him.

REEDY: Right. You don't need to tell 'em.

LBJ: [angry] Hell, no! I don't *want* to tell 'em. I didn't *discuss* civil rights.[5]

McGEORGE BUNDY
6:38 P.M.

> JAMES RESTON HAS BROKEN the news in the *New York Times* that Robert Kennedy volunteered to be Johnson's Ambassador in Saigon. Lodge has still yet to publicly announce his resignation. Bundy reads aloud from a statement he is drafting with Kennedy's staff saying that RFK will not take the job.

BUNDY: "It is known that the Attorney General offered to go. The President is known to have expressed his view that in terms of qualifications, the Attorney General is about the best man for the job—"

LBJ: No, no! I don't want him to say that at all. I haven't said anything like that. I told the Attorney General to please call Scotty Reston and tell him he wrote me and told me if there was a resignation that he was available to go, that he would volunteer to go, that I immediately called him and told him under no circumstances would I consider him for the task, period. That I would need him

[1] Diary of Lady Bird Johnson, June 16, 1964, Johnson Library.
[2] The *New York Times* columnist.
[3] Actually, according to Lady Bird's diary, the conversation was about what LBJ should do after the civil rights bill was passed—perhaps call a meeting of Governors from states that had no public accommodations law.
[4] Aide to RFK.
[5] Here LBJ is not being straight with his press secretary.

here and didn't want him to think of going. That's all I want them to say. I don't want to say that I consider him the best qualified man for it 'cause I frankly don't.

BUNDY: Oh, I thought you'd said that to me one time. . . .

LBJ: No, no.

BUNDY: The other thing he's hanging it on is your unwillingness to put a man whose family have been in such danger in danger himself.

LBJ: Not at all. I don't want to say that at all. That hasn't got anything to do with it. I just told him when I got his letter that it was a fine thing, that I appreciated it very much, but I couldn't under any circumstances consider it.

· · · ·

LBJ: I don't want Bobby or anybody else to get a lot of feeling in the country that I'm trying to send him, banish him to the isle. . . . I want him to stay right where he is. I think he'd just be controversial as hell on the Hill.[1] That's another good reason. But I don't want to say that. I don't want to cut the guy. . . . Same problem as we have on the vice presidency.[2] Bobby is a very, very controversial character in the country. And I don't want this to be a Democratic campaign manager's—a brother's thing.[3] . . . I want this man to be above political matters of any kind and not to have been in any wars with Democrats or Republicans.

JAMES RESTON
6:58 P.M.

> JOHNSON CALLS the *New York Times* columnist personally to correct the part of Reston's story about his refusal to appoint RFK to Saigon.

RESTON: I hadn't thought of the family angle. . . .

LBJ: Without the family—if he was single, I wouldn't send him. And if his name was Brown, I wouldn't. We've got all these problems here with civil rights. . . . There's talk of his running for office, for other things.[4] There's a good deal of speculation about our relationship. They're not gonna ever catch me banishing somebody to the isle. [chuckles]

RESTON: It would be said that you're sending him to Siberia to get rid of him.

LBJ: I didn't let 'em say it a second. When I read your column this morning, I just wished, *God*, I wished Scotty'd called me. . . .

RESTON: I got the impression however that lately you have been talking to him more.

---

[1] Capitol Hill.
[2] Anyone who heard Johnson say this (in private) would know that he had already mentally ruled Robert Kennedy out for Vice President.
[3] Here Johnson reveals what a limited view he actually has of RFK's role in American politics —as a mere partisan campaign manager (as RFK was for JFK in 1960) and "brother." Had RFK heard this, he would have been furious.
[4] Johnson here is happy to keep RFK-for-Vice-President speculation alive.

LBJ: I've been talking to him ever since I came here.[1] All the time. There's never been a month since I've been in Washington I haven't seen more of him than I have of almost any Cabinet officer—and since I've been President, with the exception of Rusk and McNamara. . . . There's never been anything to the thing that we didn't see each other.

. . . .

LBJ: Tell me, what's *your* feeling about Vietnam?

RESTON: Oh, I'd just depress you. . . . I've always thought, you know, that it's always unwise to assume that . . . other great nations would stand for things we wouldn't stand for ourselves. . . . If there was a hostile power in Mexico, a Communist government . . . you wouldn't be able to keep the drunks from flying out of Dallas and Houston and Chicago every Saturday night until we got those bastards the hell out of there. I think the Lord will strike me dead for saying anything in favor of Mr. de Gaulle, but I've always believed that in the long run . . . France's experience is right—that nothing big can be done there over a long period of time without the acquiescence of China. . . . We can't do anything about it except go on doing what we're doing now. . . . We can't get out and we can't go smashing into China, à la Mr. Goldwater.

LBJ: All right, now that's exactly the way I look at it. I never discussed it with you. But President Eisenhower said, here I've got this problem on my hand. Whether good or bad, or whether he was wise or unwise, after he did he wrote Diem a letter[2] and says I want you to help yourself any way you can and I'll help you economically and militarily and spiritually. . . . But you'll have to help yourself. We'll do our best to save your freedom basically because our national honor is at stake. We've got a treaty and, second, we like to see people free. We love freedom ourselves and we've helped other people keep theirs. And third, it's very important to the world. So he writes him then and says our policy will be to do this. Now not to go in with our own . . . ground troops, or with our own air. Not to drop atomic bombs and burn the trees. And not to involve China. But we'll help you. . . . The only thing you've got left is try to make this thing more efficient and more effective and hold as strong as you can and keep this government as stable as you can and try to improve it as you can, and that we're doing, day and night.

LADY BIRD JOHNSON
8:58 P.M.

LBJ: How're you feeling?

LADY BIRD: I'm feeling fine. I'm sitting in here talking on my talking machine[3] and had a wonderful talk with Luci Baines and Lynda Bird and got cut off

[1] Johnson does not want Reston to have the idea that there has been coolness between him and RFK.
[2] In October 1954. See Johnson's conversation with Robert Anderson, June 2, 1964, above.
[3] Mrs. Johnson was dictating her daily diary.

in the middle of a talk with her only to find out that the one she really wanted to talk with was you. . . . So don't be surprised if you hear from her. . . .

LBJ: Did she have any news?

LADY BIRD: No, we'd just been talking a few minutes.

THURSDAY, JUNE 18, 1964

ROBERT McNAMARA
11:11 A.M.

> JOHNSON AND MCNAMARA discuss who should go to Saigon as Ambassador.

LBJ: What we've got to bear in mind as the number one objective is holding there and not seeing South Vietnam and Thailand and Cambodia and all of 'em go under. Now in order to do that, we've got to get the man that will most unite this country. . . . You're still gonna catch hell from the right-wingers. He's not going to alleviate any of that and in addition to that, you're gonna grab the left-wingers here. That troubles me. But I don't see anybody that will make it less and I think he'd[1] be more competent. . . . I believe Khanh's gonna be pretty upset when this man goes out and he gets a second-rater he never heard of. . . . Taylor can give us the cover that we need with the country and with the Republicans and with the Congress. We need somebody to give us cover with the opinion-molders.[2] I don't know how to do that. That worries me. You see Bobby's[3] instinctive reaction—political job, not a military job. . . . There's been a little feeling like that in the State Department. They've got the biggest bunch of leaks in the country. You know damn well they'll start giving backgrounders immediately about the military has won, the Army's taking over. It's all going to be a military operation. . . . That's the type of stuff that the *New Republic* and the *Nation* and the *Reporter,* the *New York Times,* the *Washington Post, Louisville Courier, St. Louis Post-Dispatch*[4]—that's what they're going to say.

McNAMARA: . . . It may be a price we have to pay to get the right man out there, particularly a man that will buck up Khanh and give the country a feeling of strength in our response. . . .

LBJ: The greatest danger we face there now is losing Khanh and being asked to get out.[5]

McNAMARA: That's right.

---

[1] Taylor.
[2] Columnists and other leaders of American domestic opinion.
[3] Kennedy.
[4] This is a roster of what Johnson considers to be the liberal media.
[5] Once again, the hoary specter.

LBJ: The man that can give him the most confidence and the most strength would be Taylor, I believe. I don't believe George Ball, Gilpatric, or Mac Bundy and any of those fellows are going to give him any strength 'cause we're gonna start catching hell the minute we announce him. The only man I really know that's not regarded as a warmonger, that's got a bunch of stars and got standing is Taylor.

McGEORGE BUNDY
5:22 P.M.

> STILL UNDECIDED about Saigon, Johnson[1] has had Bundy sound out the New York banker-lawyer John McCloy, who had served with Bundy's father in FDR's War Department and as High Commissioner to Germany under Truman, about serving as Ambassador.[2]

BUNDY: I saw him. Negative.

LBJ: Yeah, that's what I thought.

BUNDY: . . . I said, "Is this the sort of thing that you think someone in the Cabinet ought to do?" He said no, he really didn't think so. I said I thought it was the most challenging job the government had. . . . I said, "Of course Bobby —we had to tie him down to keep him from going." "Well," he said, "Bobby has never liked that Justice job and he wants to be Secretary of State—and how's he going to get there?" So my guess is that if you said that if he did it for six months and you would promise to make him Secretary of State, he'd probably say yes, but not otherwise.

LBJ: Hm-m-m. Well, I wouldn't do that, so that's that.[3]

ROBERT KENNEDY
8:58 P.M.

> RFK IS ABOUT TO FLY to West Berlin to dedicate John F. Kennedy Platz. This is the trip he had mentioned to Bundy in April,[4] complaining that Johnson

[1] Johnson was by now feeling harassed. Buzzed for Bundy's call, he told his secretary Vicky McCammon, "I can't take any more calls. . . . They're driving me crazy!" (Daily Diary, June 15, 1964).
[2] McCloy later gave vainglorious interviews, insisting that in the early summer LBJ called him to the little room off the Oval Office and implored him, as the "finest proconsul ever" (in Germany, after World War II), to become Ambassador to Saigon, saying, "We're organizing for victory over there, McCloy, and I want you," adding that the job would be "almost as powerful as the presidency" and that McCloy's refusing his patriotic duty might mean "you're just yellow" (McCloy oral history, Johnson Library). But Johnson's daily diary shows that LBJ actually had not seen McCloy in person since April.
[3] After his conversation with Bundy, Johnson asked Rusk to approach McCloy once more. Rusk reported to LBJ two days later that McCloy had told him he was "without independent income" (meaning without family money) and did not feel he could contribute enough in Saigon to justify "making such a drastic personal sacrifice" (Rusk to Johnson, June 20, 1964, Johnson Library).
[4] See Johnson's conversation with Bill Moyers above, April 23, 1964.

was trying to keep him from going. He contemplates stopping in Poland but has been told that Johnson's people are cool to the idea. LBJ speaks with him by telephone from the little room off the Oval Office where he is having drinks with Bundy, Valenti, and Lady Bird.

KENNEDY: I, you know, was going to Berlin and there was some discussion about going to either Kraków or Warsaw for a day and speaking to the university there.[1] But from what I understand, it hadn't been brought up with you. So I didn't want to go or even contemplate going unless you thought it was advisable or helpful.

LBJ: I don't know anything about it. If you think you ought to, go ahead.[2] . . . I wouldn't want to say not to do something, but I don't know anything about the wisdom of it. This is the first I heard of it. But I'd be guided by your judgment.

KENNEDY: I don't know whether it's helpful or not, Mr. President. I've had some conversations with people at the State Department. They thought that it might be. But I don't know that it would be.

LBJ: You just use your own judgment and I'll ride with it.

KENNEDY: All right. Okay.

LBJ: Madame Nhu wants to come in and do a little campaigning between now and November.[3]

KENNEDY: For Barry Goldwater?

LBJ: Yeah, I guess so. She just wants to raise hell with us. That's what she wants to do. Would you let her in? Rusk thinks you ought to and some of the others think you shouldn't. If you get her in, I don't know how we get her out. Lodge says don't let her in. Said it'll hurt you in Vietnam. It'll hurt our war effort out there.

KENNEDY: Where is she now? In Paris?

LBJ: Yes. And Fred Dutton's[4] told the Constitutional Party,[5] or whatever it is that's having her—she's speaking up in Long Island or something—that they're going to approve the visa. But it hasn't been approved. Schwartz[6] is willing to turn it down.

KENNEDY: What is the reason for turning it down?

LBJ: [reading from memo:] "A person about whom there is reason to believe seeks to enter the United States solely, principally, or incidentally to engage in activities which would be prejudicial to the public interest or endanger the wel-

---

[1] The Polish Communist government has refused to invite RFK but has agreed to tolerate a "nonofficial" visit.

[2] This is not exactly the most enthusiastic response Johnson might have offered.

[3] Irate over the fatal November coup against her husband and brother-in-law, Nhu wishes to reinject herself into American politics.

[4] Assistant Secretary of State for Congressional Relations and an RFK friend.

[5] Of Flushing, New York, which had invited Madame Nhu to speak at a "truth rally" on July 7.

[6] Abba Schwartz, another old Kennedy hand, was Administrator of the State Department's Bureau of Security and Consular Affairs.

fare, safety, or security of the United States. . . . The memory is particularly vivid of her deplorable letter to Mrs. Kennedy after the President's assassination."[1]

· · · ·

KENNEDY: I don't think I'd probably let her in.

LBJ: That's my instinct. . . .

KENNEDY: It's not a question of we're concerned about it. We let her in before[2] and she toured the United States, but I'd do it on the basis that we've recognized . . . another government there . . . and they figure it would be harmful to the effort.[3] You know, I'd put it off on something else. . . . She can come in some other time, but she's had her full opportunity here. We've shown quite clearly that we allow freedom of speech.

OFFICE CONVERSATION
9:05 P.M.

AFTER HANGING UP with Kennedy, Johnson makes it clear to Bundy, Lady Bird, and Valenti that he would prefer RFK to stay out of Poland.

LBJ: I don't want to be saying that the President is sending him to Warsaw or directing him to go or approving his going. I think that's a matter for him to determine. I don't want to say . . . "I'm not going to let you go."

BUNDY: No, you can't.[4]

FRIDAY, JUNE 19, 1964

HUBERT HUMPHREY
4:00 P.M.

AT THE WHITE HOUSE this morning, Johnson woke up at 5:30 A.M. for his California tour. Lady Bird dictated into her diary, "The papers don't even come until 6:30, so he did a little more reading on the never-quite-finished big envelope marked 'Night Reading.' Had his exercises. He's been awfully good

---

[1] Madame Nhu had written Mrs. Kennedy from Rome that President Kennedy's death must be particularly unbearable "because of your habitually well-sheltered life": it showed that "extreme graciousness with Communism still does not protect from its traitorous blows"(*New York Times*, November 25, 1963).

[2] In 1963.

[3] In South Vietnam.

[4] Lady Bird dictated into her diary that in the presidential bedroom that night, "when Lyndon's massage was over, I went in and crawled in bed beside him because my conscience was hurting because I was not going to California" for a grueling two-day campaign trip (June 18, 1964).

about them now. And then about ten minutes of seven, left for the helicopter to go to California, but as he got to the door, turned and came back, leaned over real close to me and whispered, 'Get me out of this, won't you?' "[1]

Now Johnson is lying in bed in pajamas in the Presidential Suite of the Fairmont Hotel in San Francisco. He is about to dress and go downstairs to greet a ballroomful of Democratic fund-raisers. He calls Humphrey, whose twenty-year-old son, Robert, has been diagnosed with a malignant growth on his neck, requiring immediate surgery. Because the civil rights bill and his role in it are so vital, Humphrey is staying in Washington to shepherd the measure through final Senate passage, now expected within the hour.

LBJ: Hubert, I heard about your distress . . . and I just wanted to tell you that I was grieving with you.[2]

HUMPHREY: Bless your heart. . . . I think it's going to come along. We're a little worried, I must confess, but it's one of those things. I just don't know. We were so surprised. He's an awfully healthy young fellow. But they discovered a little malignancy there on one of those lymph nodes. . . .

LBJ: Count me in if there's anything in the world we can do.

HUMPHREY: I know that. Lady Bird called. She was so sweet.

LBJ: I asked her to call this morning. I just got in the hotel here in San Francisco. Had a mob out here of 400,000.[3]

HUMPHREY: I'll bet they did. I'm glad you're out there. That's good. They need you out there.

LBJ: Will you know a little more in a few days?

HUMPHREY: Yes, we will. I'm going out home[4] tonight and I'll be back Monday and I'll surely let you know then. . . . So far it's localized, and that's a very heartening sign.[5]

LBJ: When're you going to pass your civil rights?

HUMPHREY: In about thirty minutes, and it's going to go through with about seventy-five votes or more.[6]

LBJ: What's your interpretation of the significance of Goldwater's vote?[7]

HUMPHREY: I think that he really didn't have anything else to do. It would have looked almost completely phony had he done anything else. . . .

LBJ: Will it cost him the nomination?

HUMPHREY: I think it may, if he hasn't got it locked up and I doubt that he's

[1] Diary of Lady Bird Johnson, June 19, 1964, Johnson Library.

[2] Johnson used the same language with Rose Kennedy in their conversation on November 22, 1963, above.

[3] In an open car, Johnson had traveled through cheering throngs in the city at noontime on his way to dedicate a new federal building.

[4] To Minneapolis.

[5] Robert Humphrey's cancer operation was successful.

[6] Exactly a year after President Kennedy had sent a civil rights bill to Congress, the Senate passed the amended version 73 to 27.

[7] The previous day, Goldwater had announced that he would be one of twenty-seven Senators to oppose the civil rights bill, claiming that "the problems of discrimination cannot be cured by laws alone."

got it really locked up. The big money in the East,[1] you know, Mr. President, could move in as they've done before.

LBJ: I've seen 'em do it, like that '52, when Taft had Pennsylvania and Fine arrived strong for Taft and the next morning, when steel got through with him, he turned and flipped.[2]

HUMPHREY: That's right. I think some of that can happen again.

ROY WILKINS
5:20 P.M.

> JOHNSON HAS JUST BEEN TOLD that the Senate has passed his civil rights bill.[3] He calls the head of the NAACP.[4]

LBJ: Feel pretty good?

WILKINS: I do feel pretty good. I haven't the official news yet. I've been at a—

LBJ: Seventy-three to 27.

WILKINS: Seventy-three–27! Mr. President, that's very good news.

LBJ: You're a mighty good man. You deserve all the credit. I sure do salute you. And I'm mighty proud of you. Our troubles are just beginning. I guess you know that.[5]

. . . .

LBJ: We had a half a million on the streets. They said the biggest that anybody ever had in the history of San Francisco.

WILKINS: You deserve twice that many.

LBJ: Just took us two or three hours to get to the hotel and I just came back and put in a call for you.

. . . .

LBJ: I want to take some leadership. I'm just afraid of what's gonna happen this summer, like I saw yesterday at St. Augustine.[6] . . . I thought maybe I ought to call each one of the individual governors. Then I decided it would be too many. There's nineteen states that don't have an accommodation law. So I'm gonna write 'em all a letter. I'm a little afraid to call 'em to Washington 'cause I'm afraid the local demagogues will say that they're selling out to Hubert Humphrey

[1] Meaning Eastern Wall Street Republican interests.

[2] At the 1952 Republican convention in Chicago, Pennsylvania steel interests helped push Governor John Fine from backing Robert Taft to Eisenhower.

[3] In Washington, Lady Bird dictated into her diary. " 'June Teenth'—June 19th—and this is the day that the civil rights bill passed in the Senate! I wonder if anybody but me will remember that June Teenth was always celebrated by all the Negroes in Texas. Nobody's maid worked on June Teenth because it was the day that the Emancipation Proclamation went into effect in Texas a hundred or so years ago" (June 19, 1964).

[4] From San Francisco, Johnson issued a formal statement calling on people "of goodwill and compassion" to join the struggle for "a vision of justice without violence in the streets."

[5] LBJ is bracing for an anti–civil rights backlash across the nation.

[6] White citizens had kicked and beaten civil rights demonstrators after a desegregation march in the northern Florida city, touching off a fortnight of disturbances. Martin Luther King, Jr., was jailed after trying to eat in a white St. Augustine motel restaurant.

and Bobby Kennedy and Lyndon Johnson. And if we get 'em up there, Wallace and Johnson would probably take the lead and start ranting and the other fellows be afraid not to outdo 'em. . . . Maybe I ought to get one or two men representing me that kinda had their viewpoint that would carry my message and go around and see these governors and just tell 'em you've got to call meetings now of all your people and we've got to have observance instead of enforcement. If they'll observe the law, then we won't have to take pistols and enforce it.

WILKINS: That's right. I'll think about that and I'll do whatever I can to help. But nobody can think of as many ideas as Lyndon Johnson. . . .

LBJ: [chuckles] We've come a long ways in six months.

WILKINS: You must have seen that cartoon of the big Texas boot and the little fellow looking up there, the Republican saying, "I know they grow 'em big in Texas, but this is ridiculous!"

LBJ: [laughs]

WILKINS: . . . That speech of yours in Ann Arbor[1]—I mean, I'm supposed to be interested in civil rights and I am. . . . But I'm interested in my country too. And I think that speech in Ann Arbor was simply magnificent. . . .

LBJ: . . . We got some of the nicest compliments on it, but you remember when we were talking when we had to get that petition signed to try and get it[2] out of the Rules Committee? . . . Now we've gone the hard way. Every bit. Cloture and everything else. But we've done it.

WILKINS: It was absolutely magnificent and of course Russell put his finger on two things. First he said it was Lyndon Johnson. And second, he said it was the clergy. He hasn't been wrong—much.

LBJ: I just hope that we can get through the summer.[3]

SATURDAY, JUNE 20, 1964

WALTER JENKINS
9:15 A.M.

THE PREVIOUS EVENING, while speaking to a ballroom of California Democrats, Johnson was told that an airplane carrying Senator Edward Kennedy had crashed in western Massachusetts.

JENKINS:[4]   I talked . . . in the middle of the night to the doctor. He's very serious, but he's holding his own.

---

[1] At the University of Michigan commencement, on the Great Society. See Johnson's conversation with Hugh Sidey, June 11, 1964, above.
[2] The civil rights bill.
[3] Without rioting or other turmoil.
[4] Speaking from the White House.

LBJ:　There's not any question about him dying, is there?

JENKINS:　Doctor said he didn't think so . . . although his pulse was not strong and he was in and out of shock, and that he had a broken back.[1] . . .

LBJ:　What does that mean? Do you recover from that?

JENKINS:　Yes, sir. Perhaps not completely.

LBJ:　What caused it, do you know?

JENKINS:　Fog. They were coming in for a landing at this little airport up there near to where they were having this convention.[2]

ROBERT KENNEDY
6:45 P.M.

> FROM HIS SUITE in the Beverly Hilton in Los Angeles, Johnson calls the brother of the injured Senator at Hyannis Port.

LBJ:　How's Teddy, Bob?

KENNEDY:　He's got a lot of broken bones and his back is in bad shape, but he's not paralyzed. It's going to take anywhere from six months to a year, but he's going to be fine.

LBJ:　Oh, well, thank God he's safe. Looks like you just have more than you can bear, but you're a mighty brave fellow and you have my sympathy and all your family and any way in the world I can help, I'm just as close as the phone. . . . It's so distressing, and I know you're carrying a heavy load and I wished I could do something to help you. Give your mother my love.

KENNEDY:　Jackie just wants to say hello to you too.

JACQUELINE BOUVIER KENNEDY
Widow of John F. Kennedy
6:46 P.M.

JACQUELINE KENNEDY:　Hello, Mr. President.[3]

LBJ:　My dear, it looks like you have more than we can bear, don't you?

JACQUELINE KENNEDY:　Yeah, oh, boy! For a day! But you were so nice to call.

---

[1] Kennedy suffered three fractured vertebrae, two broken ribs, a bruised kidney, and multiple cuts.

[2] An hour after voting for the civil rights bill, Kennedy, an aide, Edward Moss, and Indiana Senator Birch Bayh and his wife, Marvella, had boarded a twin-engine Aero Commander at National Airport, Washington, to fly up to the Massachusetts State Democratic Convention in Springfield. The plane crashed in an apple orchard, killing Moss and the pilot. Johnson ordered four Walter Reed Army Hospital specialists flown to the Cooley Dickinson Hospital in Northampton, Massachusetts, to assist in Kennedy's treatment.

[3] On *Air Force One* before leaving Dallas, Jacqueline had called him "Lyndon," caught herself, then pledged never to call him that again. Johnson said he hoped she would call him that for the rest of her life (William Manchester, *The Death of a President*, p. 317).

LBJ: Well, I'm thinking of you and I wished I could do something.

JACQUELINE KENNEDY: . . . Thank you so much.

LBJ: I talked to Mr. Corriden[1] last night about three or four o'clock. And he thought that it was going to take time, but everything's all right. Is that it?

JACQUELINE KENNEDY: Yes, that's it. . . . At least, you know, everything'll be all right.

LBJ: Give Joan[2] a hug for me.

JACQUELINE KENNEDY: [sweetly:] I will.

LBJ: Thank you, Jackie.

JACQUELINE KENNEDY: Thank you, Mr. President.[3]

MONDAY, JUNE 22, 1964

EVERETT DIRKSEN
6:05 P.M.

HAVING HELPED to push the civil rights bill through the Senate, the Senate Republican leader calls LBJ to begin collecting on a few IOUs.

DIRKSEN:[4]   Hey, I got one or two matters I ought to talk to you about.

LBJ: Walter[5] talked to me about a parole thing this morning.[6] Yeah, you want to come down? . . . I'll call you someday as soon as I get these Turks out of town.[7] You in a hurry?

DIRKSEN: No hurry.

LBJ: . . . Your friend out in Southeast Asia[8] may be coming home.

DIRKSEN: [startled:] Oh-h! [chuckles] Wh-y-y?[9]

[1] Dr. Thomas Corriden was consulting surgeon at the Cooley Dickinson Hospital.

[2] Edward Kennedy's then-wife was at his side.

[3] That evening, Johnson dined in the Embassy Room of the Ambassador Hotel in Los Angeles, the same room near which RFK would be assassinated four years later to the month.

[4] Dirksen's basso profundo voice sounds extraordinarily relaxed, perhaps the result of the Scotch whiskey to which Johnson referred in their February 3, 1964, conversation above.

[5] Jenkins.

[6] As other Senators did, Dirksen used his influence to get the President to arrange paroles for prisoners he wished to help.

[7] The President and Prime Minister of Turkey were in Washington on a state visit.

[8] Lodge.

[9] Dirksen dislikes Lodge for what he considers to be his laziness, lack of intelligence, and supercilious patrician manner. To the Illinoisan, Lodge is the embodiment of the Eastern Wall Street Republicans whom he had denounced at the 1952 Republican convention for twice dragging their party to defeat with Thomas Dewey. He refers to Lodge as one would refer to a silly child.

LBJ: [chuckles] You can imagine.[1]

DIRKSEN: You know, you gave me your word he wasn't gonna come home, and I said to you, well, who *gave* a damn?[2]

LBJ: [laughs]

DIRKSEN: [acidly:] Maybe it's too *hot* out there.[3]

LBJ: [laughs] No, no. I would imagine it has to do with this other thing.

DIRKSEN: [contemptuously:] Send him word. Say it's hot here too.[4]

LBJ: [laughs] Don't say a word about it till I know for sure.

CHARLES HALLECK
6:24 P.M.

LBJ: Charlie, don't you think I ought to try to get my program passed? . . . You oughtn't to hold up my poverty bill.

· · · ·

HALLECK: Goddamn it, did I help you on civil rights?

LBJ: Yeah, you sure did. You helped Kennedy and you agreed with him.

HALLECK: . . . Now wait just a minute, my friend.

LBJ: And you helped yourself. 'Course you-all want civil rights as much as we do. I believe it's a nonpartisan bill. I don't think it's a Johnson bill.

HALLECK: No, no, no, you're gonna get all the political advantage. We aren't gonna get a goddamn thing.

LBJ: No, no. No-no!

HALLECK: Wait just a minute. Now we got a lot of things in that bill. But I don't know what in the hell the Senate put in there. Maybe we ought to kind of take a little look at 'em.

LBJ: Maybe you ought to. I'm not saying you oughtn't to.

HALLECK: . . . I'm just looking at it hard-boiled, and once in a while I can get hard-boiled.

LBJ: You wouldn't want to go to your convention without a civil rights bill, would you?

HALLECK: You know, as a matter of fact, if you scratch me very deep, Mr. President—

LBJ: I wouldn't scratch you at all 'cause I want to pat you! [cackles]

---

[1] Meaning, to thrust himself into the presidential or vice presidential campaign.

[2] Meaning that Lodge is a figure of such little consequence, why worry.

[3] In Saigon. Dirksen thinks of Lodge as someone excessively concerned for his own physical comfort.

[4] In other words, stay out of Washington—and the presidential campaign.

TUESDAY, JUNE 23, 1964

LEE WHITE
Associate Counsel to the President
12:35 P.M.

THREE YOUNG CIVIL RIGHTS WORKERS—Michael Schwerner and Andrew Goodman, of New York, and James Chaney, a young local black man who had been helping them—have been missing, along with their car, since Sunday night in Neshoba County, Mississippi, where white segregationists were seething over the certain final passage of LBJ's civil rights bill. Schwerner and Goodman had come to the state under the aegis of the Council of Federated Organizations (COFO), a civil rights coalition aiming to register four hundred thousand black voters in "Freedom Summer" 1964.

With the civil rights bill almost ready for his signature, Johnson is deeply worried that the South and other parts of the country will explode in anger. Now his immediate priority is no longer getting votes for the civil rights bill but keeping segregationists and civil rights forces across the nation calm. He knows that the Schwerner-Goodman-Chaney incident could touch off a wave of national violence. Told that James Farmer of the Congress of Racial Equality has called to complain that he has not done enough to rescue them, LBJ conveys his anger to White.

LBJ: You ought to quit dealing in these murder cases. Because you make me call him[1] back. I asked Hoover two weeks ago, after talking to the Attorney General, to fill up Mississippi with FBI men and infiltrate everything[2] he could, that they haul 'em in by the dozens. . . . I've asked him to put more men after these three kids. . . . I've asked him for another report today. . . . I'm shoving in as much as I know how. . . . I didn't ask 'em[3] to go and I can't control the actions of Mississippi people. The only weapon I have for locating 'em is the FBI. I haven't got any state police, any constables. And FBI is better than marshals and I've got all of 'em I've got looking after 'em. I can't find 'em myself.

· · · ·

LBJ: Tell him we are doing everything we know how to do with the FBI. . . . If he needs me to talk to him after you've talked to him, you'll get me to call him. . . . I want to be awfully careful what I say to this fellow.

WHITE: He seems fairly responsible, but it's murder dealing with these people on the telephone. But I've got the message and I'll call him right away.

LBJ: Here's what he said to Juanita[4]—"I want to express personally to the President my concern about the disappearance of three people in Mississippi familiar with the case. . . . I'd hoped to be able to chat with the President about

[1] Farmer.
[2] Meaning the Ku Klux Klan and other violent segregationist organizations.
[3] The civil rights workers.
[4] Roberts, LBJ's secretary.

it." Juanita—"Yes . . . how long would you be available?" See, she's trying to promote a meeting with us 'cause she's dumb.

· · · ·

LBJ: What do they think happened? Think they got killed?

WHITE: This morning they had absolutely no trace. There's no sign of the automobile. They have found nobody who's seen the car or the three people. So as far as they're concerned, they just disappeared from the face of the earth. This means murder, as they see it.

GEORGE REEDY
12:40 P.M.

> At 11 A.M., Johnson held an unannounced press conference at his desk in the Oval Office. He announced that Lodge would leave Saigon, to be replaced by General Taylor.[1]

LBJ: [angry:] They always refer to our press conferences as "quickies" but when we have an announcement, we *make* it. We consider that a *compliment*. They ought to quit acting like they're children. I don't know why we ought to give them a day notice to think up a question. They're supposed to be intelligent. If they expect me to answer it on the spur of the moment, they ought to be able to ask it. Besides they can accum-a-late their questions and put 'em in their ass pocket and write on 'em if they want to . . . so when I do call one, they're prepared. There's no reason why I ought to give 'em a day's notice 'cause I don't know a day ahead of time.

JOHN McCORMACK
12:45 P.M.

> JOHNSON EXPLAINS why he has appointed General Taylor, then describes the Mississippi situation.

LBJ: I want the military to work with Khanh 'cause they've[2] got a military President—and try to get his cooperation. If he[3] falls over, as he may any day, and we have another coup, we're through in Asia. And I'm trying to get a man can lead him and give him advice.

· · · ·

LBJ: About three weeks ago, I called in Edgar Hoover and told him to fill Mississippi—I can't say this publicly—but load it down with FBI men and put 'em in every place they anticipate they can as informers and put 'em in the Klan

---

[1] Goldwater responded to the news by saying that Lodge's resignation was "undoubtedly motivated" by the "Johnson-McNamara program of indecision and vacillation" in Southeast Asia (*Washington Post*, June 25, 1964).

[2] The South Vietnamese.

[3] Khanh.

and infiltrate it and get 'em to join up—we can't advertise this. But get all the informers they need so we know what's going on and that we can protect these kids as best we can. We don't recommend it, don't advise it, but they're going to do it anyway. So we're gonna give 'em as much protection as we can. So he's shipped the FBI in there and he's got them joining up on everything and they're trying to get in the position where they can be helpful. When these kids didn't show, night before last, yesterday morning we sent a new bunch of FBI in to supplement 'em. . . . The FBI's got two big groups that've gone in at my request, although I don't want to be appearing to be directing this thing and appear that I'm invading the state and taking the rights of the Governor or Mayor.[1] Nevertheless I've quietly shown plenty of firmness and put plenty of power. That's the only power I have. The marshals couldn't do much about it. The FBI's the best people. Marshals are not investigative in nature and can't locate anybody. We've asked 'em for a report as quickly as they can get it.

. . . .

LBJ: What do you think I ought to do?[2]

McCORMACK: I wouldn't see them. Just diplomatically you haven't got time. . . . In a day or two they'll catch those three. They can't disappear forever, can they?

LBJ: No, unless they've killed them.

. . . .

McCORMACK: The press told me that Lodge resigned.[3] . . .

LBJ: He's coming back to try to rescue the party from Goldwater.

JOHN McCORMACK
1:20 P.M.

LBJ: We're not going to do anything on conventions[4] until after the Republicans meet to see what the story is. . . . We have nobody picked out for anything and I'd like you to be thinking about who you think would be good, and I'm going to talk to some of the boys in the Senate, but I'm not going to until after we see whether it's Goldwater or who it is because we've got plenty of time. We don't have to move until six weeks after they do. We've got the end of August. We really won't do any campaigning till after Labor Day. Kennedy[5] set it back to August and I think he did it very wisely. So we'll let them show all their hole cards and then we'll come in and trump 'em.

[1] As the civil rights bill becomes law, LBJ is very careful to do nothing that will appear as if the President and federal government are usurping states' rights.
[2] LBJ refers to the request that he see the parents of the missing men.
[3] McCormack apparently had not realized that Lodge had publicly announced his resignation that morning.
[4] Arrangements for the Democratic convention in Atlantic City.
[5] President Kennedy.

CLIFTON CARTER
1:36 P.M.

LBJ: I don't think that there's anything to this, but they tell me yesterday a newspaperman who is very reliable says that our friend Bobby[1] met with Pierre Salinger[2] and a whole group two weeks ago, and they decided that they could get about 40 percent of themselves for the top job.[3] . . . They talked to Daley and to the various leaders—California, Illinois, Pennsylvania and Massachusetts and New York—and they could count about 40 percent. . . . They met two weeks ago at Hyannis Port. I would think that it is about the vice presidency . . . I don't know what our contact is with Daley, but we ought to have a friendly one and talk about general things—what we can do to help Chicago . . . and then we ought to see . . . if we can see if he is going to go with us. If he's not, maybe we ought to let them pick their whole outfit.[4]

CARTER: Yes, sir.

· · · ·

LBJ: Now, I think it's bad for you to be in on any money-raising things. You try to stay as far away from it as you can. Let Dick handle that.[5]

CARTER: All right, sir.

LBJ: Just tell him you just don't know, you've never had any experience with it, you don't have anything to do with it.[6] And that he's the best one, and you do other things. Because you got a big write-up in the *Star* here today—about you and Maguire are meeting with a bunch of people from Cleveland, Ohio.[7] Now who let that out?

CARTER: I don't know.

LBJ: Tell them over at the National Committee to quit claiming that they're picking up all this money that they're not picking up. They claimed they picked up a million dollars out yonder. They don't do it. They didn't pick up $500,000 net. And I would put the net figure. Because if we pick up that, people are not going to want to give money. Do you follow me?

[1] Kennedy.

[2] Who has won the Democratic primary for Senator from California.

[3] In other words, 40 percent of the delegates to the August Democratic convention in Atlantic City might support RFK for President.

[4] Meaning that LBJ should drop out of the race.

[5] LBJ is telling Carter to let Maguire, the Democratic treasurer and Kennedy man, raise campaign funds. If Carter had accepted envelopes with political money for Johnson as Vice President and earlier (see conversation with Jesse Kellam, November 30, 1963), LBJ may have been worried that allowing him to be prominent in 1964 fund-raising might draw attention to his earlier role.

[6] This comment underscores the notion that LBJ is worried that people might delve into Carter's fund-raising history.

[7] In the *Washington Star*, Walter Pincus wrote that the Democratic National Committee coffers had "almost doubled in the last few months," thanks largely to "the President's Club, composed of contributors of $1000 or more." Pincus reported that Carter and Maguire had met with sixty Cleveland business leaders in search of members, who "enjoy a 'special relationship' with the President. . . . When federal positions are up for consideration, recommendations of President's Club members are sought. At the Atlantic City convention, members will receive special seats . . . and be invited to a private supper to be given by President Johnson after his speech accepting the nomination for President."

CARTER: Yes sir.

LBJ: And I'd just quit telling them all this stuff that we do tell them. Somebody over at that committee talks too much to these reporters—that fellow Pincus from the *Star*. You look into it when you get back. . . . Have you got any idea how many votes we got, up to now? How many in the convention? Total?

CARTER: Two thousand five hundred eighty.

LBJ: All right, so that means that we got to have roughly 1,300.

CARTER: Yes sir, 1,250.

LBJ: How many do we have?

CARTER: I think over a thousand. Actually you got more than that. But over a thousand, definitely.

LBJ: Let's be positive now we wrap up the number that we need right away.

CLARK CLIFFORD
1:52 P.M.

> JOHNSON TELLS CLIFFORD, his chief intermediary with RFK, about his conversation with the Attorney General about his European trip.[1]

LBJ: Called me up and asked me if I wanted him to go to Poland. He thought I knew about it and I said, "No, I haven't heard about it. Don't know anything about it. Don't know what the merits are. I'd be guided by your judgment. If you think you ought to go, I'll go with you. If you don't think you ought to go, I'd stay." So I just chucked it back to him. I'd called two or three times to ask about his brother, and very friendly. Bill Benton[2] came in just now and said he's been talking to Harriman . . . and that he urged me to send Bobby to Moscow as Ambassador . . . because Khrushchev wanted to get along. And he hoped I'd send Sargent Shriver to Paris. I didn't comment either way. I didn't know whether it was a plant. . . . Harriman and Bobby are pretty close. He may be wanting that kind of world experience. . . . Anyway, that's your department and I just thought you ought to have all this background in case you got called or talked to. I assume he'll tell me about it this afternoon.[3] If he does, I'll just say, "Fine, whatever you want to do. In regard to New York,[4] that's your business. And if you decide you want to do it, I'm prepared to go with you.". . .

A newspaperman came in yesterday and said they had a meeting . . . up at Hyannis Port . . . and they said that they had Massachusetts and New York and Illinois and Ohio and California . . . and they'd meet again about the time of the Republican convention. I don't believe anything like that happened. They *might* have talked about the *vice* presidency. . . . Larry O'Brien told me he[5] *definitely*

---

[1] See June 18, 1964, above.
[2] Former Democratic Senator from Connecticut.
[3] LBJ was to talk to RFK later that day.
[4] RFK was pondering whether he should run for Senator from New York against the Republican incumbent, Kenneth Keating.
[5] Robert Kennedy.

wanted the second place. He has been to California on TV, and meeting with a group out there. And has been in New York a good deal, as you know, and I think has had some contacts in Pennsylvania and Illinois. I think it's something that we ought to look into.

. . . .

LBJ: You might wish him[1] goodbye at least before they leave.[2] They're leaving tonight or in the morning. And you might just say, "I see where you're leaving. Just wanting to pay my respects."

CLIFFORD: And see what I pick up.

LBJ: "What have you decided in New York?" Be good. Call me when you hear anything.

ROBERT KENNEDY
3:13 P.M.

RFK HAS TELEPHONED for Johnson, who is in the Cabinet Room, rereading some of his press conference statements on Lodge and Taylor for newsreel cameras. Valenti takes the call.

KENNEDY: I've just seen these parents, you know, of these kids that have been picked up, lost down in Mississippi. And I think that two things—number one, I think he should probably make a statement about that. Now I've heard he said something at the press conference this morning.

VALENTI: Right.

KENNEDY: But I think that it should really be more formalized, although I haven't seen the statement and perhaps it is satisfactory. Second, I think that he should consider seeing them—the parents. And third, I think that he should consider making a call to Governor Johnson[3] and expressing concern, so it would be said that he had made that call.[4] . . . Now you see yesterday, I told him to use the helicopters, and they've got the FBI as if it's a kidnapping. So we're doing all that we can. But I think that people—well, there's going to be more of this and people are going to wonder.

VALENTI: Let me read you his answer. [reads from Johnson statement:] "Mr. President, do you have any information about those three kids that disappeared in Mississippi?" "The FBI has a substantial number of men who are closely studying and investigating the entire situation. . . . I have had no reports since breakfast, but at that time I understood that they had increased their forces in that area."

KENNEDY: You see, I think that to express sort of concern, you know, personal concern for them and their families. Now, I don't know whether—I've seen their

[1] RFK.
[2] Before Robert Kennedy and his wife, Ethel, leave for Europe.
[3] Paul Johnson, of Mississippi.
[4] RFK not only wishes LBJ to be seen as compassionate but he also remembers that a call by his brother John to Martin Luther King's wife when King was jailed was a decisive moment in the 1960 campaign.

families. And it might not be necessary. But we're going to have more of this. It's a hell of a problem.

. . . .

KENNEDY: I'd like him to say something . . . you know, even if just a paragraph, so that it'll get on television, about his concern about this thing. I think it'll make them feel—that is not as important as that he's on top of all these things. I think it's the human equation that's damn important. For everything.

NICHOLAS KATZENBACH
Deputy Attorney General
3:35 P.M.

WHEN LBJ CALLS Robert Kennedy back, the Attorney General is out, so Johnson speaks to Kennedy's trusted deputy.

LBJ: He[1] thought I probably should make a statement on these three boys that are missing down in Mississippi and I ought to consider seeing their parents. . . . I'm afraid that if I start housemothering each kid that's gone down there and that doesn't show up, that we'll have this White House full of people every day asking for sympathy and Congressmen too 'cause they want to come over and have their picture made and get on TV.[2] . . . There's not anything new I can tell 'em except let this be a forum. . . . I thought Lee[3] ought to come over there and then they don't have this as a bunch of television cameras. . . . I told him to get his tail over there and he messed around here and didn't do it.

. . . .

LBJ: What do you think happened to 'em?
KATZENBACH: I think they got picked up by some of these Klan people, would be my guess.
LBJ: And murdered?
KATZENBACH: Yeah, probably, or else they're just being hidden on one of those barns or something . . . and having the hell scared out of them. But I would not be surprised if they'd been murdered, Mr. President. Pretty rough characters.
LBJ: How old are these kids?
KATZENBACH: Twenty and twenty-four and twenty-two.[4]

. . . .

LBJ: Now if you think . . . they're[5] raising hell, tell 'em to come down and see Lee right now and just let me know. . . . And I may just walk into his office and say a word to them. Would you advise that or not advise?

---

[1] RFK.
[2] With his eagerness to preserve national quiet and his anxieties about the 1964 election, Johnson also wishes to keep some public distance between himself and the civil rights forces.
[3] White.
[4] Goodman, Schwerner, and Chaney, respectively.
[5] The parents of the missing civil rights workers.

KATZENBACH: . . . I think you have a problem of every future one.[1] I think you've got an awful good reason today to be tied up. . . . This is not going to be the only time this sort of thing will occur, I'm afraid.

JAMES EASTLAND
3:59 P.M.

> JOHNSON CONTACTS the Senate Judiciary Committee Chairman at his home in Ruleville, Mississippi, for advice from the segregationist side.

LBJ: You got a lot of sunshine down there?

EASTLAND: We need rain might bad.

LBJ: We're so dry in my country that we're gonna have to sell off all of our cattle if we don't get a rain.

EASTLAND: I'm in the same shape. Got a cotton crop that's burning up.

· · · ·

LBJ: Jim, we got three kids missing down there. What can I do about it?

EASTLAND: I don't know. I don't believe there's three missing. I believe it's a publicity stunt.[2]

· · · ·

EASTLAND: I'll tell you why I don't think there's a damned thing to it. They were put in jail in Philadelphia in east Mississippi, right next to John Stennis's home county, and they were going to Meridian.[3] There's not a Ku Klux Klan in that area. There's not a Citizens Council in that area. There's no organized white men in that area.[4] . . . I happen to know that some of these bombings where nobody gets hurt are publicity stunts. This Negro woman in Ruleville that's been to Washington and testified that she was shot at nineteen times is lying. Of course, anybody that gets shot at nineteen times is going to get hit. . . .[5]

LBJ: . . . They suggested I see these parents. I told 'em I thought that would be a bad precedent. I'm gonna try to get 'em to see an assistant of mine and get by with that, if I can, so that I don't add to the fuel.

· · · ·

[1] Every future such incident.

[2] Cynical about the civil rights workers, Eastland was happy to believe rumors that they had been spotted laughing in a Chicago bar or that they had boarded a plane to Los Angeles.

[3] On Sunday night, Chaney was arrested for speeding and fined $20. All three men were questioned, then released at about 10:30 P.M.

[4] Eastland was correct in that Neshoba County was not considered to be one of the most violent counties in the state.

[5] Cotton sharecropper and granddaughter of a slave, Fannie Lou Hamer, of Ruleville, Eastland's hometown, was a field worker for the Student Nonviolent Coordinating Committee (SNCC) who helped black Mississippians to register to vote and helped to start a political network that became the anti-establishment Mississippi Freedom Democratic Party. In June 1963, after entering a "whites only" dining room in Columbus, Mississippi, she was beaten and jailed. On other occasions, gunshots were fired into her home.

EASTLAND: Let me ask you this question about these three that are missing. Who is it that would harm 'em? There's no white organizations in that area of Mississippi. Who could possibly harm 'em?

LBJ: You might have some crank or some nut. They locked a man up in Minneapolis today for saying he's going to kill me Friday when I go out there.

EASTLAND: It'll take a crowd to make three men disappear.

LBJ: That depends on the kind of men, Jim. . . . It might take a big crowd to take three like you! I imagine it wouldn't take many to capture me.

EASTLAND: [laughs] Well, I'd run.

LBJ: All right, you get that rain for both of us and send it on east when you get through using it. . . . Now we got to appoint a conciliator under this law, Jim.[1] I've got to have some Southerner that knows something about the South and that the Negroes will have confidence in and won't say that I've fixed 'em. If you've got any ideas, anybody that's worth a damn, I wish you'd let me know. . . . One of 'em suggested that I get LeRoy Collins.[2] . . .

EASTLAND: He's a damned cheap double-crosser and a liar and he's strictly dishonest. Now he agreed at the convention to recognize us[3] to vote for you and he went back on his word. I called him a goddamned, lying son of a bitch out there.

LBJ: Well, we don't want him then, do we?

EASTLAND: Hell, no![4]

J. EDGAR HOOVER
4:05 P.M.

> THE FBI DIRECTOR calls Johnson to report that the Schwerner-Chaney-Goodman car, a 1963 Ford station wagon, has been found.

HOOVER: Mr. President, I wanted to let you know we've found the car. Now this is not known. Nobody knows this at all. But the car was burned and we do not know yet whether any bodies are inside of the car because of the intense heat that still is in the area of the car. . . . This is off to the side of the road.[5] . . . Now whether there are any bodies in the car, we won't know until we can get into the car ourselves. . . . But I did want you to know. Apparently what's happened— these men have been killed. . . .

LBJ: Now what would make you think they've been killed?

HOOVER: Because . . . it is the same car that they were in in Philadelphia, Mississippi. . . . This is merely an assumption that probably they were burned in the car. On the other hand, they may have been taken out and killed on the outside.

LBJ: Or maybe kidnapped and locked up.

[1] The civil rights bill provided for appointment of a federal mediator.
[2] Former Governor of Florida.
[3] The Mississippi delegation, which was pledged to Johnson for President in 1960.
[4] In the end, Collins got the appointment.
[5] Highway 21, near a swamp.

HOOVER: I would doubt whether those people down there would give them even that much of a break.

. . . .

LBJ: How long had the car been burning, do you reckon? Six or eight hours?
HOOVER: . . . Maybe five or six hours.

. . . .

LBJ: Looks like those fellows jumped out of the car and burned it.
HOOVER: You'd think they would unless they'd been bound and were locked in that car and then the car set afire.
LBJ: Why wouldn't an agent be able to look at a car and see if there's any bones in it?
HOOVER: . . . The car is so burned and charred with heat that you can't get close to it.

. . . .

LBJ: Now this group's[1] coming down here to see Lee White, my assistant. You think in the light of this that . . . I ought to step in and just tell 'em I've talked to you and you're doing everything you can?
HOOVER: . . . I don't like you having to see these people because we're going to have more cases like this down South and every time it occurs they're going to have these families come on into Washington and, of course, the Congressmen, being politically minded, they'll want you to see them.[2]

LEE WHITE
4:15 P.M.

> IN THE OVAL OFFICE, Johnson advises White on how to handle the relatives of Schwerner and Goodman.

LBJ: Tell 'em to just come down to your office and come in that side door near the EOB.[3] . . . Tell 'em what-all we've done and let me come over and say a word. And I just ought to tell 'em we've found the car. . . . I'd have to tell 'em.
WHITE: That's gonna be rough.

J. EDGAR HOOVER
4:21 P.M.

HOOVER: Agents are endeavoring now to get inside the car. . . . The inside of the car from the intense heat has melted and burned everything into ashes. Now we've got to therefore pry the doors open, which we're doing, and getting into the inside to examine, to see whether there's any human bones inside the car. . . .

[1] Goodman's parents and Schwerner's mother.
[2] Hoover was as cynical about civil rights workers as he was about members of Congress.
[3] Executive Office Building, across the street from the White House West Wing.

Everything has been consumed inside the car, even to the metal inside the car being melted.

LBJ: Much obliged. You have to keep me informed.

JAMES EASTLAND
4:25 P.M.

> EASTLAND REPORTS that he has talked to the Governor of Mississippi, Paul Johnson.

EASTLAND: He says he expects them[1] to turn up with bruises and claiming that somebody's whipped 'em. He doesn't believe a word of it. . . .

LBJ: Now here's the problem, Jim. Hoover just called me . . . five minutes ago and told me that they had found the car. . . . The car is still burning and it's so hot they can't get inside of it and they don't know whether the people are inside of it or not. . . .

EASTLAND: Well, I know nothing about that.

LEE WHITE
4:49 P.M.

> JOHNSON IS IRRITATED to learn that his friend Roy Wilkins's NAACP is about to crank up public pressure on the President for doing too little about the thousands of civil rights workers who have gone to Mississippi.

LBJ: NAACP has just voted to picket the White House tomorrow because they want protection for their people in Mississippi.

WHITE: No kidding! [sarcastic:] That's really great, isn't it? . . .

LBJ: I think you ought to try to get ahold of Roy Wilkins and ask him what in the hell we've done. I've been on the phone all day long. . . . Ask him what else he wants us to do. . . . I don't see what good they think they can do by picketing the White House.

EVERETT DIRKSEN
6:00 P.M.

> DIRKSEN WANTS LBJ's help in getting planning money for the Kaskaskia River Navigation Project in Illinois.

DIRKSEN: The total cost of the project is some $30 million. Now it's in that area of Illinois that's distressed. . . . It's going to be the making of the southern thirty counties of the state.

[1] Schwerner, Goodman, and Chaney.

LBJ: Let me get on it and I'll call you back. Now you're not going to beat me on excise taxes[1] and ruin my budget this year. . . . Don't beat me on that now. You can do it if you want to and you can ruin my budget, but you're hollering economy and trying to balance it and I cut the deficit 50 percent under what Kennedy had it. Now if you screw me up on excise taxes and get that thing going, I'll have hell. Now let my Ways and Means Committee—

DIRKSEN: Now look at the pressure I'm under.

LBJ: Hell, you're not under any—

DIRKSEN: Goddamn trade associations.

LBJ: I know it, but you're also for good fiscal prudence and you know that the way to do this is through the House committee and you know if you put it in, they're not going to let you-all write a bill over in the Senate on taxes.

DIRKSEN: I don't suppose they are.

LBJ: Now please don't press me on that.

DIRKSEN: Well, I've got to press it.

LBJ: Who are you going to take. You going to take all your Republicans? Give me one or two of them and let 'em be prudent. . . .

DIRKSEN: You've got enough votes.

LBJ: No, I haven't. You can beat me and you oughtn't to do it. You see how you're going to let me win by one vote in there and I'll call you back in a little bit on this.

DIRKSEN: You never talked that way when you were sitting in that front seat.

LBJ: I did if my country's involved. I voted for Ike one time when Knowland[2] voted against him. I cast the vote on his foreign aid and brought it out of committee.

DIRKSEN: You're a ha-a-a-ard bargainer.

LBJ: No, I'm not. But you just take care of it and I'll look at this and see what I can do and call you right back.

EVERETT DIRKSEN
6:22 P.M.

JOHNSON INFORMS Dirksen that he has told the Army Corps of Engineers to do whatever is possible for Dirksen's pet project.

LBJ: So don't you tell anybody now that you've got a back door to the White House but you go up there and don't you kill my goddamn tax bill tomorrow. Quit messing around in my smokehouse!

[1] Republican Senators still wished to repeal excise taxes on luxury items.
[2] Senator William Knowland of California, the Senate Republican leader for much of the 1950s.

DIRKSEN: You forget that I bought a tea at Peoples Drug Store that's got a label on it "Packed at the White House."[1]

· · · ·

LBJ: I'm going to lose a bunch of people on my side so I've got to get two or three of your men.

DIRKSEN: You're a hard bargainer.

LBJ: You get 'em for me.

· · · ·

LBJ: Hell, I just got you straightened out $30 million worth.

DIRKSEN: You left me upset for a hundred days on that damned civil rights bill.

LBJ: . . . You're the hero of the hour now.[2] Hell, they've forgotten that anybody else was around. Every time I pick up the papers—Dirksen! Magazines! NAACP is flying Dirksen banners and picketing the White House tomorrow.

DIRKSEN: I couldn't even get you to change your tune about that damn House bill.

LBJ: The hell you couldn't. . . . I said whatever Dirksen and the Attorney General agree on, I'm for. . . . You never got a call from me during the whole outfit, and you know it. But don't mess up that tax bill tomorrow, Everett. Please don't.[3]

CLARK CLIFFORD
6:34 P.M.

> CLIFFORD CALLS TO REPORT on a talk with RFK. Coincidentally, at the very moment of his call, Kennedy is sitting in the Oval Office, talking to Johnson about the lost civil rights workers in Mississippi. Kennedy has issued a statement that he will not run for Senator from New York.

CLIFFORD: I had a brief conversation with the man.[4] He was in a great hurry getting ready to fly to New York to get a plane to Europe. He said the event that had decided him[5] was the accident to his brother Teddy. He says that he wants to spend time with him. He's going to have a very serious morale factor. He's always been so active and he's got to lie there on that fracture bed for maybe six months. And also he expects to devote a very substantial amount of time to campaigning in Massachusetts in Teddy's behalf because Teddy can't do a thing. . . . So he said, "I'm off in a hurry and I just wanted to tell you I thought it all over with great care and I was really continuing to be undecided until this terrible thing happened to Teddy and that decided me. I think I've got to stick closer to him and help him

---

[1] Perhaps Dirksen is suggesting that, as in the Boston Tea Party against the British, he is protesting unfair taxation imposed by the White House.

[2] Thanks to Dirksen's leadership on civil rights.

[3] The Republican excise tax repeal was passed over Johnson's opposition, but, with Dirksen's cooperation, a congressional conference overturned it on June 29.

[4] Kennedy.

[5] Not to declare for the Senate from New York.

and get him through and I'll look after myself later on." . . . That may be part of it. The other part is that sneaking notion that he might be there when the lightning struck for number two,[1] which, of course, was his choice when he came here last week. I thought maybe he'd gotten out of it by the time he left.

LBJ: [unwilling to speak with RFK in the room] Much obliged.

ANNE SCHWERNER
Mother of Michael Schwerner
8:35 P.M.

WITH RFK AT HIS SIDE, Johnson informs Schwerner's mother in Pelham, New York, that the FBI has found no trace of the three men's bodies in the Ford station wagon.

LBJ: We have received word from Mr. Hoover that the investigation in the car indicates that there were no people in the car. And it's very likely that none of them were burned. . . . They've seen some tracks leaving the car. . . . We're flying people in from the FBI tonight. And I just wanted you to know that and that was a little hope that we didn't have earlier and I thought that we would enjoy it as long as we could.[2]

ANNE SCHWERNER: [weeping, glad even for a scintilla of optimism] Thank you so much, President Johnson. I appreciate this. Thank you very much.

WEDNESDAY, JUNE 24, 1964

J. EDGAR HOOVER
5:30 P.M.

LBJ: Edgar, any other news on Mississippi?

HOOVER: No, there's no additional news on that. . . .

LBJ: That sheriff[3] is a pretty bad fellow down there, isn't he?

HOOVER: Yes he is, and we have been going over him pretty thoroughly. There are several theories that have been advanced and, of course, we're running all leads on the cranks. All of them. One is that this may have been done by these fellows in order to create an incident that would inflame the situation. The

---

[1] Meaning in case lightning should strike and LBJ choose RFK for Vice President.
[2] Johnson phrases this very carefully in order not to arouse false expectations that the men were likely to be found.
[3] Neshoba County Sheriff Lawrence Rainey, whose deputy, Cecil Price, had arrested Chaney on Sunday night.

basis for that is that setting this car afire within sight of a highway. It was only a few feet off the highway and burning it, leaving the license tags on the car, was not a thing that a person who had probably committed a murder and killed the three—but that the three fellows may have done it themselves. There are reports which we are running out down there that two white men resembling those two fellows . . . were seen at an airport trying to board a plane going west to Los Angeles. That, of course, is one of these cases where people phone in and imagine they've seen something. But we've got to run all that out anyway. On the other hand, the thing that we lean strongly to here, is that these three may have gotten rather fresh.[1]

LBJ: [interrupts to take call from John Stennis]

JOHN STENNIS
Democratic Senator from Mississippi
5:32 P.M.

JOHNSON TOUCHES BASE with the other Mississippi Senator.

LBJ: I've got Edgar Hoover on the other line. He tells me they've looked in the car very carefully and there's no indication that the bodies were in the car at all.

STENNIS: Yeah, I'm awfully, awfully worried about it, Lyndon, you know. Local colored man[2] has been making himself obnoxious—smart-aleck troublemaker—and I'm afraid somebody is after him and just got the others along with him. Out in those rural areas, you know.

LBJ: Yeah, I sure do. Well, I just wanted you to know, my friend, and I sure love you and I know that your heart is bleeding[3] and mine is too and maybe somehow we'll work out of it.

J. EDGAR HOOVER
5:40 P.M.

LBJ: Edgar, I'm sorry that got interrupted.

HOOVER: That's all right.

LBJ: Walter[4] told me that Deke[5] was upset some because somebody indicated that Dulles was supposed to go down there and be an investigator.[6] I told him that's the furthest thing from my mind. What happened was after we talked

[1] Meaning that they might have said something that struck the locals as insolent.
[2] Referring to Chaney.
[3] For Mississippi.
[4] Jenkins.
[5] DeLoach.
[6] LBJ has agreed to send former Director of Central Intelligence Allen Dulles to Mississippi as his representative to meet with Governor Johnson and provide an independent assessment of law enforcement in the state. He is worried that this will infuriate Hoover, for whom Dulles was a bureaucratic rival while at the CIA.

yesterday and you got the Governor to have that press conference.[1] . . . Gave out a wonderful statement. Then he called Jim Eastland, who is my friend and your friend, and told Eastland that he would like for me to see some of the problems that they were confronted with down there with all these damn fellows parading over everyplace.

HOOVER: That's right.

LBJ: And that he would like for me to send an impartial observer to come and talk to him. And he would like to send him to talk to some of the businessmen to see if we could avoid some of this. Now I felt like if the Governor asked me to send an impartial observer and I didn't send it, I'd be in a little bad shape later on if I had to do something. If I'd have thought for one moment that it was something that would affect you in any way, I would have picked up the phone and called you because I haven't got a better friend in this government than you and I always will have. So I told 'em to plant a question at my press conference today. . . . There ain't nobody here who's gonna take over anything from you as long as I'm living. . . . Nobody's ever going to take anything between us and you just be sure of that. And if I do, I may make a mistake of the head sometimes—I make a lot of them over here every day—but if it is, you just tell Deke what the score is and we'll get it straightened out so damn quick it'll make your head swim. Ain't nobody gonna take our thirty-year friendship and mess it up one bit.

HOOVER: Don't you have any concern about that.

LBJ: [laughs] I won't. God bless you.

THURSDAY, JUNE 25, 1964

OFFICE CONVERSATION
4:52 P.M.

LBJ: [to Jack Valenti:] I imagine they're in that lake.[2] It's my guess. Three days now.

CHESTER CLIFTON
Military Aide to the President
7:45 P.M.

INDULGING HIS IRRITATIONS with the Secret Service, Johnson complains about having to take a large group of agents on his usual Boeing 707 for a

[1] Governor Johnson had announced the day before that Mississippi law enforcement facilities would be mobilized "to prevent acts of violence or public disorder."

[2] Johnson refers to the Bogue Chitto Swamp, near the highway where the charred car was found. The search was expanded to the Pearl River and nearby lakes.

political trip to Detroit and Minneapolis, for which the Democratic National Committee will have to pay. LBJ would prefer to fly in a less expensive Jetstar.

LBJ: They[1] never do anything but endanger you. They notify everybody in town what time you're coming, how you're coming, where you're coming, and how to kill you, if you want to. They do everything except kill you. And if they'll just let us go and get in the car and keep their damn mouth shut, we'll go down a back road and nobody ever knows we're there. But they get the si-renes going, forty cops leading you, and all that kind of stuff. So I don't care about haulin' any more of them than necessary because the most that I've ever been in danger is with a bunch of Secret Service men. They don't know how to operate their guns. Hell, I had ten of 'em out there one day trying to kill a snake and they couldn't kill it. They just emptied the gun. At my ranch. So that argument don't appeal to me—that I need more than three in a Jetstar.

FRIDAY, JUNE 26, 1964

J. EDGAR HOOVER
1:17 P.M.

THE FBI DIRECTOR reports on Mississippi.

HOOVER: I've got about 110 additional men in there now. . . .
LBJ: How're you expanding your search? . . . Away from the lake?
HOOVER: Oh, yes, away from the lake and we've dragged the river. . . . We are gradually going farther and farther away from the place where the burned car was located. I've also issued today a circular with the photographs of the three men that we're looking for. . . . They'll be placed in post offices and local police departments.

WALTER JENKINS
5:30 P.M.

FROM THE SHERATON-CADILLAC HOTEL in Detroit, LBJ checks in with Jenkins at the White House.

JENKINS: I have a memo from Bundy . . . asking to use Camp David on the weekend of the 4th. We're just declining.

[1] The Secret Service.

LBJ: No, go on and let him use it. We can't stop them because we just don't know how to do it, Walter. I give up on our staff. We got the worst staff in the United States.

. . . .

LBJ: What are you going to do about Camp David?

JENKINS: I've told the General[1] to notify everybody that it be not used for staff anymore.

LBJ: And what did he do, say he hadn't notified Bundy?

JENKINS: . . . I'm sure that's right. And I've told all of our people myself.

LBJ: We ought to after the Bundy thing just arrange to close it up and send the people on back somewhere and just maintain it. . . . Clean that whole outfit out. Just have a maintenance man go and take care of it. Tell 'em I want the whole thing cut out and never used unless I personally say so, and I don't plan to use it and don't want anybody else to use it.[2] I think it's a waste and there's no reason we ought to have a luxury hotel for a few special people. . . . Just say we have agreed to close it down. Don't say why. Don't say the President or anything else. Just say it's closed for repairs, not going to be available this summer. I'm not going to have it as a campaign issue.

. . . .

JENKINS: General Phinney[3] came by and said that his man in Dallas is close to the Republican campaign committee and told him that there were three items they were putting out on a quiet basis. One, that George Parr had had a transaction with you that involved $32,000.[4] Didn't know what for. Second, that they've made a deal with Coke Stevenson to make a nationwide campaign—ship him around the country explaining how he lost the election with Box Thirteen.[5] And third, that some people closely related to us had purchased large tracts of real estate near the space center in Houston before the location was announced and then sold it at a huge profit.

LBJ: Well, none of it's true. Coke might do it, but the others—

JENKINS: I doubt he's well enough. . . .

LBJ: Where's he say he gets that?

JENKINS: I asked him. He said it was from a man whose name we wouldn't know and he promised not to use, but he's a high-up fellow in Republican circles in Dallas.

[1] Clifton.
[2] Johnson soon changed his mind.
[3] Carl Phinney, Commanding General of the Texas National Guard from 1925 to 1961, was a lawyer friend of Johnson's.
[4] George Parr was the "Duke of Duval County," Texas, fabled for tipping the 1948 Senate election, won by eighty-seven votes, to Johnson. (See Robert A. Caro, *Means of Ascent*, pp. 268–402, and Robert Dallek, *Lone Star Rising*, pp. 327–48.)
[5] Stevenson, former Texas Governor, was the loser in 1948, thanks, it was said, to the intervention of Parr's crony Luis Salas, the election judge for Box Thirteen in Alice, Texas.

MONDAY, JUNE 29, 1964

HUBERT HUMPHREY
2:35 P.M.

OVER THE WEEKEND, the Johnsons were lauded by large crowds in St. Paul and Minneapolis, where LBJ spoke at a Democratic fund-raising dinner. Lady Bird dictated into her diary, "Dear Hubert is as adaptable as a chameleon. . . . Where is life, there is Hubert, which somehow adds an extra twist of ugly poignancy to his son Bob's desperate illness. . . . All day long there had been crowds lining every street, friendly, cheering crowds. I wonder how much of it is the general air of euphoria in the country or respect for the office of the Presidency or how much of it is an understanding and liking of Lyndon himself. At any rate we have progressed beyond Texas."[1]

LBJ: We had a wonderful day and I just wanted to thank you for it.

HUMPHREY: Ohhh, listen, they just l-l-l-loved it. You ought to see the follow-up stories in the morning press out there.

LBJ: I hope they didn't play that "war" like this paper here did.[2]

HUMPHREY: No, they did.

LBJ: It was a peace speech and I said sometimes we had to risk war to get peace but long as I'm in office, my job's going to be a quest for peace. And damned if they didn't take the sentence right out of the paragraph.

HUMPHREY: . . . The St. Paul paper had you speaking to 150,000. The Minneapolis, just 100,000.

LBJ: Somebody here cut it down to fifty.

HUMPHREY: Oh, that damn outfit here. They don't know anything about it.

LBJ: *Chicago Tribune,* cutting it to fifty. [laughs and snorts]

HUMPHREY: You can expect that. But everybody was—it was such good *feeling.* You know, everybody.

LBJ: They were happy. Better shape than I ever saw'm. I never saw a crowd as good.

HUMPHREY: Well, they loved you.

[1] Diary of Lady Bird Johnson, June 28, 1964, Johnson Library.
[2] The lead story in the June 29 *Washington Post* reported that at the fund-raising dinner, LBJ had said that a nation must be prepared to risk war to keep its freedom and that "in Vietnam, we are engaged in a brutal and bitter struggle for the freedom of a friend. There too we will use the force necessary to help them maintain their own freedom."

RICHARD DALEY
3:00 P.M.

LBJ: This Mississippi thing is awful mean. I'm gonna have to walk a tightwire there.[1] I don't know what in the world is going to happen. . . . I don't have any authority to do anything but send FBI and I've got over a hundred in there now. . . . All these folks going in and no telling what's going to blow up. It really worries me. The war thing—South Vietnam. We think we've got a couple of good men in charge out there and it's really good that Lodge came back. Lodge is going to get in this Scranton thing and I don't mind. I don't believe they can *stop* Goldwater. What do you think?

DALEY: I think you're right. . . . I think he's done his groundwork too well. While all these fellows were sitting on the sidelines, waiting for the moment to be called . . . he was out . . . making his contacts and getting the people that mean something. . . .

LBJ: Will Dirksen wind up going for him?

DALEY: I think he will. Sure. I think that's definite.

· · · ·

LBJ: What are they saying about our Vice President? What are we going to do about that?

DALEY: Everyone is waiting for you. . . .

LBJ: I want you to think about it a little bit and you keep it that way and then I want to talk to you before or after this Republican convention. You tell the missus that we want to pay her back for being so nice and you see if you can't get away one night and come down and visit with me.

J. EDGAR HOOVER
6:47 P.M.

> AN HOUR EARLIER, Johnson had met in the Green Room of the White House with Schwerner's wife, Rita.

LBJ: I saw this Miz Schwertner [sic] this evening—the wife of the missing boy. . . . She came in this afternoon and saw Lee White and he brought her down to see me. She wants thousands of extra people put down there[2] and said I'm the only one that has the authority to do it. I told her I put all that we could efficiently handle. . . . Now I talked to McNamara this afternoon. He said he got plenty of airmen and plenty of Army people in Mississippi without moving 'em in and plenty of Navy people. So if you don't mind, you figure out what we can do 'cause if we don't, they're gonna want us to go in with big troops and stuff like that. And I'd utilize as many as I could and add a few each day until we give up hope. . . . So we show the country that we are really working at it and being

---

[1] Between the civil rights groups and segregationist Mississippians.
[2] In Mississippi.

very diligent and we stay just ahead of the hounds because if we don't, this crowd's gonna demand everything in the world.

HOOVER: . . . We can call on the Governor down there to put in the National Guard. . . .

LBJ: I don't see any harm in it. They might say that it wasn't worth a damn.

TUESDAY, JUNE 30, 1964

EDWARD KENNEDY
5:35 P.M.

JOHNSON REACHES the Massachusetts Senator, recovering from his air crash injuries in Cooley Dickinson Hospital in Northampton, Massachusetts.

LBJ: My friend, I'm sure glad to hear your voice.

KENNEDY: . . . I wanted to call and tell you how much we appreciate it—Joan[1] appreciates everything you've done.

LBJ: I haven't done anything but I'm sure ready and willing.

KENNEDY: You sent all those wonderful people up from the Army—Secretary Vance[2] did, and they made a great deal of difference and everyone's been so kind down there and they've taken great care of me. Really coming along now. Making some progress.

LBJ: You got a bad break, but my mother used to tell me that things like that develop character and it'll make you stronger when you get older. [chuckles]

KENNEDY: I don't know about that. You're ready to trade a little of that. . . . That's what I keep reading in all that mail. They say you get down on that back a little while and think and do a little suffering, you'll be a better man. So I guess I'll take my chances about it.

LBJ: Well, you're a great guy and you got lots of guts and stay in there and pitch and anything we can do, we're ready. . . . And we'll elect you by a bigger vote than you got before.[3]

KENNEDY: I know. Now you're really gonna have to pull me through up there.

LBJ: Just tell 'em that I'll fill your speaking engagements. . . . Give Joan a hug for me.

[1] Mrs. Kennedy.
[2] Deputy Secretary of Defense Cyrus Vance.
[3] For Senator from Massachusetts.

Chapter Nine

JULY 1964

THURSDAY, JULY 2, 1964

CLARE BOOTHE LUCE
Former Republican Congresswoman from Connecticut
10:25 A.M.

       PLAYWRIGHT AND WIFE of the *Time-Life* founder, Mrs. Luce, who served in the House in the 1940s, had once had an intimate friendship with Johnson.[1] Now an intense supporter of Barry Goldwater and foe of the civil rights bill, she has seen news reports that LBJ is planning to pay the measure special homage by signing it on Independence Day.

LUCE: I heard . . . that you were going to sign the civil rights bill on the Fourth of July and it seemed to be such an *appalling* idea. . . .

LBJ: No, I never had any thought of doing that.

LUCE: It was in all the papers.

LBJ: I know it, honey, but— [chuckles] —I don't want to be critical of the press. . . . No human being has ever discussed it with me and I've never given any indication that I would do anything except to sign it the first moment it was available, which would be Thursday.[2]

            . . . .

LBJ: You take my word, there's not one person out of 190 million that ever mentioned the Fourth of July to me and I've not mentioned it to one.

---

[1] LBJ once told Henry Luce that his wife was "the sweetest little woman I ever served with in Congress" (W.A. Swanberg, *Luce and His Empire,* Scribners, 1972, p. 441).
[2] In other words, that same day.

ROBERT KENNEDY
11:19 A.M.

THE ATTORNEY GENERAL has just returned from his trip to West Berlin and Warsaw.[1] With Kennedy campaigning for Johnson to make him Vice President and Johnson worried that he will become an open enemy when he discovers that he will not get the job, both men are striving to be amiable.

LBJ: You're a world traveler. You worn out?

KENNEDY: No, not too bad. . . .

LBJ: Must have been exciting.

KENNEDY: It just makes you feel so good . . . when we talk about all our problems here . . . and . . . then you go to a country like Poland . . . and have the people as enthusiastic about our country as they are. How would we feel if Communists came over—Khrushchev's brother or some high official—and visited the Communist party headquarters and had thousands . . . turning out and cheering for him? . . . It's just a damned inspiring thing . . . I hope that after January that you're able to go to Eastern Europe and perhaps the Soviet Union. I just think it'd make a hell of a difference.

LBJ: I'm sure glad you're back. Anybody that needs a little invigoration ought to leave Washington, oughtn't they?

KENNEDY: Oh boy, what a difference! . . . Also yesterday, Mr. President, I for the first time read that article in *Newsweek*.[2] . . . I just spoke about all of these matters quite frankly and openly, as I always have. . . . I said I thought it was Lyndon Johnson's administration after January and that he would like to have it on his own, so I wouldn't think that he'd like to have a Kennedy directly associated with it. If I were he, I'd feel that way. . . .

LBJ: I thought it was quite unfortunate. . . . Every one of 'em's playing it. I see this morning you've got ABC Radio—"some of the extremists backing Kennedy are challenging Johnson."

KENNEDY: Of course, nobody's doing that.

LBJ: . . . They're going to try to get us fighting. I hope we don't have to.

KENNEDY: You know I'm not. Hell, I haven't done it. You know, I've talked to people for seven months and nobody's ever written anything like that. . . . Because . . . I haven't done it. . . .

LBJ: Well, unfortunate. And let's forget it. There're too few left in the family and let's hold together as much as we can. We got so much more to be thankful for than we ought to be worried about stuff like this. . . . You just tell these people that come to you that that's a matter that we'll all work out.

[1] See LBJ conversation with Kennedy of June 18, 1964.
[2] The *Newsweek* Washington bureau chief Benjamin Bradlee, a close JFK friend, had traveled with RFK to Kansas City in June and written that while the Attorney General was eager to be Vice President, RFK thought that he was "the last man in the world" Johnson would want—"because my name is Kennedy, because he wants a Johnson Administration with no Kennedys in it . . . because I suppose some businessmen would object, and because I'd cost them a few votes in the South" (July 6, 1964).

KENNEDY: I always do.

LBJ: And we'll sit around a table and—

KENNEDY: I don't want to get into a discussion about it now, but I just wanted to explain about that.

· · · ·

KENNEDY: I don't know whether this has gone too far, about the signing of the bill.[1] If it's signed today, we're going to have a rather difficult weekend—a holiday weekend. . . . That Friday and Saturday, with the Fourth of July and firecrackers going off . . . with Negroes running all over the South figuring that they get the day off, that they're going to go into every hotel and motel and every restaurant. . . . If it's possible . . . to postpone it till Monday and sign it. . . . I don't know whether it's gone so far that you feel it's necessary to sign it today.

LBJ: No, I don't think so. Here were the considerations that entered into it. They all announced—and we've gotta stop that. [growing irritated:] You tell your publicity man over there don't say a damned word about what I'm gonna do.[2] . . . The House did the same thing on me. Some of their people up there planned on what the President's gonna do. So they all got it pretty well scattered over the country that he was going to wait till July the Fourth to sign it, so that he'd tie it in with the Declaration of Independence. That was pretty well accepted and generated all over the country before we could stop it. We never mentioned it, never opened our mouth.[3]

· · · ·

LBJ: There's no point of waiting till it's the Fourth of July. I thought that would just irritate a lot of people unnecessarily. . . . So that's kind of how we got off the hook on the Fourth of July—by signing it when it gets to us. Now when it gets to us I don't know, but I think it'll be late today.

ROY WILKINS
12:05 P.M.

> JOHNSON CONSULTS the NAACP leader on whether to sign the civil rights bill that day.

LBJ: The question has been raised now that if we sign it that quick, that Saturday throughout the South is a big day when everybody's in town, shooting firecrackers. It's the Fourth of July and celebratin' and the fellas get a few drinks of beer. We could kick off a wave of trouble that will wind up with a lot of people getting hurt. Maybe we ought to wait until after the weekend. . . . We've already

---

[1] Civil rights bill.

[2] Johnson blamed Kennedy's spokesmen, in part, for telling the press that he might sign the bill on Independence Day.

[3] Johnson is especially eager to scotch the rumor because it has already generated Republican speculation that LBJ wishes to delay signing the bill until Republicans will have left town for Independence Day and their San Francisco convention, to open July 13, so that he can then claim full credit for the Democrats.

tentatively announced that we're gonna do it tonight, if the bill's available. . . . I thought before I did it that maybe I'd better check with one or two of my friends. . . .

WILKINS: . . . I think you have the right hunch here. I think a delay would simply mean that you felt that you ought to delay signing it. . . .

LBJ: . . . The Republicans are leaving for their convention and they're getting out tonight. . . . I don't know whether they'd come or not, but it was bipartisan and I think that we ought to have Republican legislators . . . just like we have Humphrey.

WILKINS: . . . The Republicans do deserve a chance at this.

LBJ: . . . They'd charge me with trying to be cute if we put off signing . . . until after they left town.

• • • •

WILKINS: I thank you for what you did on this bill.

LBJ: . . . We've got a long, hard fight ahead, but if we work together, we'll find the answers. 'Cause we're right. We're right.

GEORGE REEDY
1:44 P.M.

> FINAL PASSAGE of the civil rights bill is expected within the hour. Johnson has opted to sign it that evening.

LBJ: I've got to announce to the Cabinet what time we have the ceremony and where. It's in the East Room, isn't it?

REEDY: The East Room. The networks say six forty-five is the absolute best time, sir. . . . Both NBC and CBS will carry live. . . .

LBJ: I thought seven was what we asked them to do.[1]

REEDY: It was and they'll do it, but we'll get better play at six forty-five, they say.

LBJ: I don't believe that. That's cheaper time. Six forty-five is four forty-five in a good part of our country, George. . . . It seems like it'd be better, to me, in Texas, to have something at five o'clock, when people are getting off.

• • • •

LBJ: I don't want to do this in a hurry and I don't know enough about it and I don't think anybody in our outfit knows enough about the radio-television. And I believe they're[2] selfish bastards. They're like Jesse Kellam.[3] He wants anything carried in the afternoon he can 'cause he don't want to give up that night primary time.

---

[1] Johnson wants to sign it with maximum television coverage across the nation.
[2] Television network executives.
[3] Manager of the Johnson television station.

CARL ALBERT
2:29 P.M.

> JOHNSON IS in the Oval Office, where Robert Kennedy has joined him after a Cabinet meeting. Told that the House has just passed the final version of the civil rights bill, LBJ calls the House Majority Leader.

LBJ: Sitting here with the Attorney General. Looks like congratulation's in order. Want to salute you. I guess you know that probably you'll get more congratulations up here than you'll get at home.[1] Have you finished the bill?

ALBERT: Yes, sir! The Speaker's signed it. It's on its way to be messaging into the Senate right now.

J. EDGAR HOOVER
5:02 P.M.

> NERVOUS THAT the Ku Klux Klan and other whites in Mississippi will rise up in arms against the civil rights bill's enactment, LBJ asks for help from the FBI Director.

LBJ: How many people can you bring in there? . . . I think you ought to put fifty, a hundred people after this Klan. . . . Their very presence may save us a division of soldiers. . . . You ought to have the best intelligence system—better than you've got on the Communists. I read a dozen of your reports here last night, here till one o'clock, on Communists, and they can't open their mouth without your knowing what they're saying.

HOOVER: Very true.

LBJ: Now I don't want these Klansmen to open their mouth without your knowing what they're saying. . . . We ought to have intelligence on that state[2] because that's gonna be the most dangerous thing we have this year. If I have to send in troops, or somebody gets rash and we have to go like what we did in Little Rock,[3] it'd be awfully dangerous. . . . I'm having these demands for five thousand soldiers. And all these groups are meeting all over the United States and sending wires. Farmer's[4] got a group out in Kansas City today. . . . Martin Luther King's getting ready.[5]

---

[1] The civil rights bill was unpopular in Albert's Oklahoma.

[2] Mississippi.

[3] Eisenhower's dispatch of federal troops to Little Rock in 1957 to support the integration of the Little Rock high school.

[4] James Farmer, national director of the Congress of Racial Equality (CORE).

[5] At 6:45 P.M., Johnson signed the Civil Rights Act of 1964 in the presence of Robert Kennedy, Everett Dirksen, Martin Luther King, Hubert Humphrey, and over a hundred others who had had a stake in its passage. He reminded the nation that "an overwhelming majority" of Republicans and Democrats had voted for it and that "its purpose is not to divide, but to end divisions. . . . My fellow citizens, we have come now to a time of testing. We must not fail."

FRIDAY, JULY 3, 1964

JOHN CONNALLY
11:38 A.M.

STAYING at the LBJ Ranch for the weekend, Johnson calls the Texas Governor. Now that the Civil Rights Act is law, LBJ turns his attention to his 1964 running mate.

LBJ: I think we gotta give a little thought to our Vice President. You know who's campaigning for it,[1] and that's gonna be a knock-down drag-out probably. With Miz Kennedy[2] nominating him and all the emotions . . . you can't tell what'll come there. . . . I don't know what the Republicans are going to do, but they'll probably name a Catholic as Vice President. We'll have that problem.

. . . .

LBJ: I believe it'll be somebody like Goldwater and Scranton or Goldwater and Miller,[3] maybe.

CONNALLY: I think it'll be Miller. . . . He a Catholic?

LBJ: Yeah, he's a Catholic. Who would you rather the Republicans nominate— Goldwater or Scranton?

CONNALLY: I'd rather they nominate Scranton.

LBJ: . . . I think from the Southern standpoint, it'd be better.[4] But God, if they nominate Scranton . . . all those newspapers and all that money.[5]

CONNALLY: . . . The only thing that Scranton won't do is he won't make a vicious fight out of it.

LBJ: They say he's the worst in the world. They say he's a real character assassin, but he does it in a Brooks Brothers style.

. . . .

LBJ: [back on Goldwater:] Texas is pretty belligerent, but I don't believe they want a fellow with an A-bomb that's ready to turn it loose like he is.

. . . .

LBJ: I talked to the Attorney General this morning, and we've had these spies in different states watching for trouble[6] and it's very quiet over the country. The response, the wires, are just amazingly good—particularly from the South—on the speech last night. I didn't cuddle up to 'em but I wasn't the least bit critical

[1] Namely Robert Kennedy.
[2] Jacqueline Kennedy.
[3] Congressman William Miller of New York, Republican National Chairman.
[4] Because as a moderate Republican, Scranton lacks Goldwater's conservative appeal in the South.
[5] LBJ refers to the Pennsylvania Governor's popularity among newspaper and magazine publishers and with Wall Street.
[6] Over the Civil Rights Act.

or vicious or demanding. I just appealed for us reasoning together. . . . I had all the Republicans and all the Democrats, had Halleck and Dirksen, and had all the liberals—Javits[1] and Humphrey and all that group. But it was a pretty united group that was there.

JESSE KELLAM
12:43 P.M.

LBJ INVITES his old schoolmate and business manager to join the Johnson family and friends for a boat ride on Lake Wirtz.

LBJ: If you know any other interesting men with good-looking wives that keep their mouths shut and would like to just really drive around and flirt with us a little bit, pick 'em out.

SATURDAY, JULY 4, 1964

JACQUELINE BOUVIER KENNEDY
7:22 P.M.

ON INDEPENDENCE DAY MORNING, LBJ lunched with John Connally, Connally's brother, and their wives, as well as Johnson's Texas friends, the Homer Thornberrys and the Frank Ikards. Then, as Lady Bird dictated into her diary, "The real important session of the day. . . . We discussed the vice presidency. Two of us there were for McCarthy[2]—the Thornberrys. Six were for McNamara—John and Nellie, Merrill and Mary Connally, and the two Ikards. They pretty much all agreed that Humphrey would be their third choice, although they've not forgotten the South's antipathy for him.[3] . . . No voice was raised for Shriver."[4] That evening, in a call to Hyannis Port, after talking with Robert Kennedy about civil rights, Johnson speaks to the former First Lady.

JACQUELINE KENNEDY: Mr. President?

LBJ: Hi, Jackie, how are you?

JACQUELINE KENNEDY: Happy Fourth of July!

[1] Senator Jacob Javits, Republican of New York.
[2] Eugene McCarthy, the junior Democratic Senator from Minnesota, whose name was being suggested by Johnson advisers who felt he must choose a Catholic.
[3] Over civil rights.
[4] Diary of Lady Bird Johnson, July 4, 1964, Johnson Library. On the possibility of Robert Kennedy, Mrs. Johnson later dictated, "It is true that we need more young people . . . with a 'charge hell with a bucket of water' spirit that used to be a trademark of Lyndon. . . . He needs many of the things that Bobby Kennedy has and represents and is able to attract. But as he . . . said . . . 'It would take an agonizing wrench of the spirit . . . [for] either one of us to try honestly to feel close to the other' " (July 12, 1964).

LBJ: Thank you, my dear. Did you have a good day?

JACQUELINE KENNEDY: Oh, yes. Are you in Texas?

LBJ: What did you do? Go out on the boat?

JACQUELINE KENNEDY: Well, no. It's so rainy, nobody could. But General Taylor came up, and then we saw him off.[1]

LBJ: Uh-huh.

JACQUELINE KENNEDY: Are you at your ranch now?

LBJ: Yes, I just came off the lake. I've been out in a boat all afternoon.

JACQUELINE KENNEDY: Oh, I'm so glad. So you'll get some rest?

LBJ: I got a sunburn, and I'll probably be blistered now.

JACQUELINE KENNEDY: Oh, no, no. You'll look marvelous with a sunburn.

LBJ: Well, I hope so. I hope you're doing all right.

JACQUELINE KENNEDY: Yes, I'm fine, Mr. President.

LBJ: How are the children?

JACQUELINE KENNEDY: Oh, fine, thank you, and yours?

LBJ: Good. Lynda's with us. Luci's in Washington having dates.

JACQUELINE KENNEDY: I know. I noticed she didn't come. I thought it was something sinister like that.

LBJ: You know, she came in and said that she wanted a very special birthday present on July the 2nd, and we asked her what it was, and she said she just wanted to go one whole day without an agent.[2]

JACQUELINE KENNEDY: [laughs]

LBJ: What do you reckon happened?

JACQUELINE KENNEDY: Well, did you arrange it?

LBJ: Oh, yeah, I arranged it. What do you reckon happened?

JACQUELINE KENNEDY: [laughs] I'd hate to think!

LBJ: [laughs]

JACQUELINE KENNEDY: [laughs] And don't you!

LBJ: It's sure good to hear your voice, and I hope that you're feeling all right.

JACQUELINE KENNEDY: Oh, yes. It was nice to talk to you. Give my love to Lady Bird.

LBJ: All right. I long to see you.

JACQUELINE KENNEDY: Okay, we'll see you soon.

LBJ: Thank you, dear.

---

[1] Maxwell Taylor, who had been close to John Kennedy as White House military adviser and Chairman of the Joint Chiefs, had called on Mrs. Kennedy at Hyannis Port before his departure for Saigon.

[2] Secret Service agent.

FRIDAY, JULY 10, 1964

ROBERT KENNEDY
10:35 A.M.

KENNEDY: Mr. Hoover is going down to Jackson, Mississippi, and I understand that they have a press conference scheduled there. . . . If he's asked some of the questions about this Communist . . . connection with the civil rights movement and answered . . . in the way that some of the memos have indicated,[1] he might . . . cause a good number of difficulties around the country.

LBJ: . . . Do you want me to talk to him?

KENNEDY: As I've said before, it's quite difficult for me.[2] . . .

LBJ: . . . I'll do it right now.[3]

MONDAY, JULY 13, 1964

ROBERT KENNEDY
3:22 P.M.

LBJ: If you know how to get any votes on poverty,[4] get to work on that. Damn . . . they're going to try to beat us. . . . Halleck[5] and all of them are hitting at us with it.

KENNEDY: Isn't it gonna go through all right?

LBJ: I'm afraid not. . . . We have only two weeks. . . . You have to pass the Senate to put the pressure on the House. . . . You've got to take the Rules Committee away from the Judge.[6] That's never been done on anything but civil rights. . . . Then . . . the House, and the Republicans think they have enough Democrats to go with them to beat it. . . . Then you've got to go get an appropriation. I don't see how you can do all that without bringing 'em back here.[7] I'd be very interested

---

[1] Hoover believed that the civil rights movement was heavily influenced by Communists.

[2] Furious at RFK for his three years of efforts to strengthen oversight over the FBI, Hoover had virtually ceased relations with RFK after his brother's death robbed him of his status as the second most powerful man in the government.

[3] Johnson did not fulfill his promise.

[4] Johnson's poverty bill.

[5] The House Republican Leader.

[6] Dislodge the bill from the dominion of the House Rules Chairman, Judge Howard Smith of Virginia.

[7] Meaning that Congress be brought back into session after the Democratic and Republican conventions, as it was in 1960, to finish dealing with LBJ's program.

in your reaction as campaign manager for 1960—and perhaps '64[1]—whether you think I ought to ask this Congress to come back. I'm kind of scared to.

KENNEDY: God, I don't think so.

LBJ: [laughs] Have you had enough of it?[2]

KENNEDY: Hell, yeah.

LBJ: Are you still bleeding from '60?[3]

KENNEDY: Yeah, I think that was awful.

LBJ: The President[4] . . . said, "Oh, just anything, Lyndon, to get out of here. . . . I'm gonna lose the election if you don't let me get out of here."[5]

KENNEDY: Exactly. God, and I think the record's[6] pretty good.

LBJ: They're gonna say that we got thirty-two bills and fifteen of them we haven't acted on but . . . everything that Kennedy thought was urgent we will have passed.

KENNEDY: I think the impression is that you've done a hell of a lot to Congress. . . . I'd just say we took a lot of positive steps and we can do more in '65.

LBJ: And then get out of it?

KENNEDY: Yeah, I sure would.

TUESDAY, JULY 14, 1964

JOHN McCORMACK
9:50 A.M.

LBJ: I've talked to these leaders, these bosses—Wagner and Daley[7] and the rest of them. They all are for me and every delegation except Alabama[8] has either passed resolutions or endorsed me. And the leaders say they're for me for whatever platform we want and whoever I want as Vice President. I keep hearing rumblings that there's gonna be a big demonstration[9] and that they're gonna try to force me to do this and do that. . . . I don't want the presidency if they do because I don't want to have to sleep with a woman that I don't trust. But I'm

[1] Johnson sneaks in a suggestion that RFK might be the presidential campaign manager in 1964, as he was in 1960, to see if RFK bites.
[2] Congress.
[3] The post-convention congressional session.
[4] Kennedy.
[5] Republicans were using the special session to embarrass Kennedy and Johnson.
[6] Johnson's legislative record.
[7] The Mayors of New York and Chicago.
[8] Home of George Wallace, Johnson's springtime challenger, who was threatening to keep running for President, on a third-party ticket.
[9] For Robert Kennedy.

just trying to be quiet and say nothing about it—just kind of do like you do sometimes—endure things that are kind of problems. . . . Daley had lunch with me this week and Wagner and Dave Lawrence.[1] . . . They rather resent the fact that I'm kind of being pressured. Do you get any sense of that at all?

McCORMACK: Yes. . . . All I just simply said is that the President has to pick his running mate.

LBJ: Yeah, that's right. . . . I've got to talk to you about when I do it and . . . how I do it. . . . We've got to have a loyal team.

McGEORGE BUNDY
5:36 P.M.

LBJ: I wish these high-level spokesmen . . . out in the Vietnam theater would quit giving out interviews as long as a whore's dream about how much trouble we're in and about how all the North Vietnamese are moving in.

· · · ·

LBJ: [reads from a dispatch,[2] then:] He ought to keep his mouth shut. We've got a convention and an election going on, and it's not up to the military to go to talking. Just tell him to submit his reports to the Secretary of Defense and we'll issue them here. Unless it's Taylor[3] himself.

THURSDAY, JULY 16, 1964

GEORGE REEDY
11:04 A.M.

THE PREVIOUS EVENING, Johnson had watched on television as the Republicans nominated Barry Goldwater in San Francisco.

LBJ: Buz[4] says we sure ought to have some kind of comment. I don't agree. . . .
REEDY: I don't either. . . .
LBJ: Somebody got ahold of him.[5] He said I was terrible yesterday morning.

[1] Former Governor of Pennsylvania, who would be head of his state's delegation to the Democratic convention.
[2] Perhaps in the *New York Times*. That morning, in a report of a Vietcong ambush near Saigon the previous day, a South Vietnamese military spokesman was quoted as saying that guerrillas had captured enough weapons during the past week "to arm a battalion."
[3] Ambassador Maxwell Taylor, just arrived in Saigon.
[4] Johnson's old aide Horace Busby, now a Special Assistant to the President.
[5] Goldwater.

Last night he said I'm fine and he's not going to get personal at all in his victory statement.[1] You see that?

REEDY: ... I think he realized he made a boo-boo.

LBJ: ... You ought to say all day long we're not gonna get personal and he's probably tired and angry and got a lot of problems out there when he talks about "fakers and phonies." We spent a hundred years building the presidency up and I'm not gonna try to tear it down. Galbraith said this morning[2] that they spent a hundred years building the institution of the presidency up and here's a wild madman—mad dog that's gonna tear it down in fifteen minutes and then wanting to succeed to the job. ... I'd put that out.

FRIDAY, JULY 17, 1964

A.W. MOURSUND
1:57 P.M.

ABOUT TO FLY to the LBJ Ranch for the weekend, Johnson calls his Hill Country friend and business partner.

LBJ: Oh, I've got more problems than a farmer's got oats. ... I thought we might go over and get on the boat and knock around a little and maybe eat dinner somewhere tonight. I'd like to eat ... some fish dinner if we could. Reckon you can get old Melvin to cook us some, or you reckon Mariallen knows how?[3] ... I've been on a diet so damn long, I'd like to get off of it.

BILL MOYERS
6:20 P.M.

LBJ: It may be that we ought to talk about these pistol-packing, shotgun night riders that shoot people driving up and down the highway.[4] ... It's got to be

[1] That morning's New York Times reported that the previous day, before his nomination, Goldwater had been asked whether Republican refusal to champion civil rights might not help the Democrats. Goldwater replied, "After Lyndon Johnson—the biggest faker in the United States? He opposed civil rights until this year. ... He's the phoniest individual who ever came around." After the balloting that evening, Goldwater told the press that he would not wage a campaign of personal attack.
[2] Johnson had breakfasted with liberal Harvard economist and JFK Ambassador to India John Kenneth Galbraith.
[3] Melvin is Johnson's local friend Melvin Winters. Mariallen is Mrs. Moursund. That night, LBJ did indeed dine on fried catfish.
[4] On July 11, Lieutenant Colonel Lemuel Penn, an African American in the Army Reserve, was shot to death by Ku Klux Klansmen while driving near Athens, Georgia, on his way home from Fort Benning.

stopped and the government is going to see that it is.... We might ought to make a little appeal to the Negroes and say we hope people would be restrained. We've got a law now. Let us try it and let us have it work. Just as the night riders oughtn't to be taking things in their hands, I hope that the people who feel that they've been aggrieved through the years could kinda also be restrained.

.   .   .   .

LBJ: Now you've got to get ... a little God in there ... but you ought to have Hoover[1] prepare you the basic statement.... We really ought to be on record as denouncing both of them,[2] but doing the Klan in a pretty tough way—and all extremists. What'd he say yesterday about extremists?

MOYERS: He said, "Extremism in the defense of liberty is not a vice."[3]

LBJ: Well, I'd just say extremism to destroy liberty *is*.

MONDAY, JULY 20, 1964

RUSSELL LONG
5:32 P.M.

BACK AT THE WHITE HOUSE, in a talk with the segregationist Senator from Louisiana, Johnson privately defends himself against the charge of excessive ardor for civil rights.

LBJ: This civil rights thing—I came in.[4] The bill was up there. I couldn't say, "Tear it down, I'm against it." I haven't called a human being.[5] I haven't done anything that's vicious that I know of. When things get so bad that I can't do anything else, why, I sent in the FBI and they just investigated.[6] I haven't ordered in any paratroopers or any divisions.... I let some Navy boys in little white jackets search around with the FBI and local officers. And I'm getting along reasonably well with ... the Governor of Mississippi,[7] and he and I talk back and forth two or three times a week. I try to cooperate. I had Hoover down there.... I'm doing what I can to carry out my oath of office and at the same time not be ugly and vicious and mean—and be as considerate of my fellow man as I can and still try to lead the nation. I can understand how this thing is in Mississippi and

[1] J. Edgar Hoover.
[2] Black radicals and white supremacists.
[3] In his acceptance speech the previous evening at San Francisco, Barry Goldwater had declared, "Extremism in the defense of liberty is no vice."
[4] Trying hard not to seem radical on civil rights, Johnson makes it sound almost as if the only reason he supported the bill was because it happened to be lying there when he became President and pledged himself to support Kennedy's program.
[5] To lobby for the bill.
[6] The still-unsolved Schwerner-Chaney-Goodman case, in Mississippi.
[7] Paul Johnson.

Alabama and Louisiana and East Texas, Georgia. . . . I've spent fifty-six years in it and living in it and I'm trying my damnedest to walk the tightrope that I got to walk. . . .

LONG: I think if you can just play it low-key from here on until November, it's going to get better for you. This thing[1] had to pass sooner or later. . . . Momentarily it creates a big storm. . . . But it can't go anywhere but up.

GEORGE REEDY
7:40 P.M.

ON SATURDAY EVENING, July 18, a protest march against a Harlem police station erupted into two nights of rioting.

LBJ: It's my considered judgment . . . that we wouldn't carry a state in the South if the vote were tomorrow. . . . These Negro demonstrators at San Francisco[2] got everybody mad. . . . Everybody thinks . . . if we denounce the killings in Mississippi and . . . the shooting in Georgia, we ought to denounce it in Harlem too. And we haven't done a damn thing about it. . . .

REEDY: . . . Goldwater is going to want to keep this stuff—all this rioting and the civil rights—he's gonna wash his hands of it and say that "he's responsible."[3] . . . If we aren't careful, we're just gonna be presiding over a country that's so badly split up that they'll vote for anybody that isn't us.

• • • •

LBJ: What we really want to do with Goldwater is . . . say that . . . we're not gonna do anything to incite or inflame anybody. . . . And let's leave the impression he *is*, without saying so.

TUESDAY, JULY 21, 1964

ROBERT KENNEDY
12:35 P.M.

KENNEDY: Mr. President, Martin Luther King is going down to Greenwood, Mississippi, tonight, and he is going to conduct a mass rally there.[4] . . . The officials down there representing the Governor . . . say that they will not escort him, but they'll have a state patrol there. . . . We asked them about escorting him

[1] The Civil Rights Act.
[2] At the Republican convention.
[3] Meaning that Johnson is responsible.
[4] In support of the Mississippi Freedom Democratic Party, which was challenging the all-white Mississippi delegation, chosen under the state's restrictive procedures.

out of Greenwood and back to Jackson and they said they wouldn't do that, but that they would patrol the highway. . . . So we passed that on to Martin Luther King. . . . It's a ticklish problem because if he gets killed, it creates all kinds of problems. Not just being dead, but also a lot of other kind of problems.

LBJ: Can we have FBI people there . . . keeping their eyes and ears open and preceding him and following him?

KENNEDY: It's difficult. . . . I have no dealings with the FBI anymore but I think maybe if you ask them, perhaps.

LBJ: Didn't he get you that report the other day?[1]

KENNEDY: Yes. I understand that he sends all kinds of reports over to you about me—and about the Department of Justice.[2]

LBJ: Not any that *I* have seen. What are you talking about?

KENNEDY: Well, well, I just understand that—about me planning and plotting things.

LBJ: No, no, he hasn't sent me a report that I remember. . . . He hasn't sent me any report on you or on the department at any time.[3] I get, I guess, a letter every three or four days that summarizes a good deal of stuff. And Walter Jenkins gets eight or ten of them a day on Yugoslavia and various routine things.[4] . . . But, so far as I know, they haven't involved you.

KENNEDY: I had understood that he had sent reports over about me plotting the overthrow of the government by force and violence. Leading a coup. [chuckles]

LBJ: No, no, that's an error. He never has said that.

J. EDGAR HOOVER
12:40 P.M.

> JOHNSON READS Hoover a statement on the New York City riots and other recent violence, to be issued that day, saying, "In the preservation of law and order there can be no compromise—just as there can be no compromise in securing equal and exact justice for all Americans." The statement added that Johnson was asking Hoover to contact New York city and state officials.

HOOVER: Do you want me to go up there personally?

LBJ: I think it'd be a good thing.

HOOVER: I'll do that.

---

[1] Johnson presumably refers to a Hoover report on a civil rights matter.

[2] McNamara and others had told Kennedy that Hoover was currying favor with LBJ and indulging his feud with RFK by sending Johnson damaging FBI material on the Attorney General. In an oral history taken later in 1964, RFK said that Hoover had sent Johnson a report on an alleged meeting "in which we were discussing the overthrow of Lyndon Johnson, to take the nomination away from him" (Kennedy Library). Cartha DeLoach of the FBI confirmed in his memoirs that LBJ "enlisted me in his war to keep Bobby Kennedy from spoiling his reelection campaign" (*Hoover's FBI*, p. 381). (See LBJ conversation with DeLoach, August 15, 1964, below.)

[3] Johnson is making a dubious claim.

[4] Jenkins was the White House contact for the FBI.

LBJ: ... Just tell them that I have directed you to investigate the possibility of law violations and to get me a full report, just as you have in Mississippi and ... Georgia. ... Now we've got another problem. ... Martin Luther King is going to speak tonight down in Greenville, Mississippi.[1]

HOOVER: ... There are threats that they're going to kill him.

LBJ: Yeah. ... I would think it would be a good idea for you to talk to your man in Jackson[2] and tell him that we think that it would be the better part of wisdom, in the national interest, that they work out some arrangement where somebody's in front of him and behind him when he goes over there. ... So that we won't find another burning car.[3] It's a hell of a lot easier to watch a situation like that before it happens than it is to call out the Navy after it happens.

HOOVER: Don't you think I ought to also advise the Governor[4] what we plan to do on that?

LBJ: Yeah, I'd tell him that you want to invite his people to join you, but if they don't ... that you don't want to be looking for bodies after the fact.

ROBERT KENNEDY
1:00 P.M.

KENNEDY: Mr. Hoover just called me and said that you were sending him up there to New York. ... I'd like to just raise a question about it. I think it's a different situation than Mississippi. ... There's no sort of public question about the fact that the Governor ... of New York, the Mayor of ... New York and the police are going to try to do their job. Secondly ... we might have problems in ... some other part of the country, and whether someone then says, "You sent him to Mississippi and ... New York. Does that mean you think this is less serious?" ...

LBJ: What I told him was I wanted him to study it, and he said, "You think it's all right for me to go up there?" And I said, "Yes, if you conduct yourself just like you did other places." ... I see your point of not having him go everywhere, but if he's working with them ... it might put some of these Communist organizations on notice that we are not going to let this stuff go unattended.[5] ... I didn't initiate the suggestion to go, but when he mentioned it, I didn't veto it. ...

KENNEDY: Let me just tell you, between ourselves—he said to me, "I think it's a bad idea, but I'll do it." So he's giving me a little different story.

LBJ: He's the one that initiated it. ... Well, you want the FBI involved, don't you? Isn't that what you asked?

KENNEDY: I want them involved, but—

LBJ: But you don't want *him* involved.

[1] Johnson means Greenwood.
[2] Jackson, Mississippi.
[3] A reference to Goodman, Schwerner, and Chaney.
[4] Of Mississippi, Paul Johnson.
[5] Bolstered by Hoover's memos, Johnson thought that Communists were among those behind the riots.

J. EDGAR HOOVER
1:06 P.M.

LBJ: Edgar, the Attorney General says that he's talked to you and that you think—and he doubts the wisdom of your personally going in there because we'll have requests from . . . every other place where we have a problem. I don't feel strong about it one way or the other. . . . Maybe since I'm putting out this statement, in the light of you-all's feeling, that we just withhold your going up there until we see the reaction to the statement and . . . play it by ear. . . .

HOOVER: I think that statement of the Attorney General is a little bit exaggerated. . . . He said he thought it would be very unwise for me to go. I said, "Of course, I'm merely complying with the orders of the President." . . . Now . . . if you think it's desirable, I may not go, but I can get in touch with Mayor Wagner by telephone.

LBJ: I would, and I'd call Murphy[1] first.

HOOVER: I'll call Murphy.

LBJ: And then tell the Governor[2] the same thing. . . . This is a very unusual situation. We're getting floods of wires and telegrams. . . . Here's one. [reads aloud:] "I'm a working girl. . . . I'm afraid to leave my house. . . . I feel the Negro revolution will reach Queens. . . . Please send troops immediately to Harlem." . . . Just say to them that . . . we got to investigate the possible federal violations and get some people in there that they'll know are FBI. And maybe you can put a quietus on that Muslim X[3] and all that stuff. I think the Communists are in charge of it.

RICHARD DALEY
3:29 P.M.

LBJ: I've got another column this morning—the *New York News.*[4] . . . It says . . . that the Northern people want a certain individual[5]—the bosses—and it's going to be trouble at the convention. . . . I've about concluded that the wise thing for me to do would be to call this fellow over and say, "Now I've looked at Goldwater and I've seen what's happened in Wallace[6] and I see our problem in the South and the Midwest. I just don't believe that . . . I'm going to be able to recommend you." . . .

---

[1] The New York City Police Commissioner, Michael Murphy.

[2] New York Governor Nelson Rockefeller.

[3] LBJ means Malcolm X. As usual, he twists the name of someone he does not like. While visiting Egypt, the black nationalist leader had charged that the "outright scare tactics" of the New York police had caused the Harlem riots.

[4] *New York Daily News.*

[5] Meaning Robert Kennedy for Vice President.

[6] Johnson means that with Goldwater nominated over Scranton, there is no need for LBJ to worry about the Northeast, where RFK might have helped. He also refers to Governor Wallace's withdrawal two days earlier as a presidential candidate, meaning that now the Southern vote will not be divided between Goldwater and Wallace, which would have helped Johnson across the South.

DALEY: . . . I think I'd think a little about that. . . . Assume that he would resign. Then you'd have the thing right out in the open.[1]

LBJ: [forlorn:] Yeah.

DALEY: . . . It's different if you're an old-timer in the ranks, like yourself and myself. But realizing he's not, then you never know what's going to be the consequence of that.[2] . . .

LBJ: My folks . . . think that this campaign[3] is kinda going on, and that if we don't nip it that they're going to say that "you were silent and . . . allowed it to go on."

DALEY: . . . It's a natural thing if a fellow wants to campaign. . . . But I wouldn't be paying any attention to these columnists because they just are trying to foment . . . trouble in Atlantic City. . . . See, the worst city in the United States for rumor and gossip is Washington.[4]

LBJ: Yeah.

DALEY: You know that. You were there thirty-two years. And frankly . . . we out in the prairies . . . don't pay much attention to columnists, the newspapers, or anything else. . . . Now unless someone is misinforming me tremendously, I don't see this thing developing. . . . I don't see any mass campaigning. . . .

LBJ: I think—my people think they're[5] relying primarily on emotionalism. They think that most of these delegates that go there[6] will be delegates that were there in '60 and will be people that like the name and were friendly, and that they'll have a demonstration and they'll say, "Now this man[7] didn't get to finish his job, and he's got a lot of friends, and we need this name, and we just ought to go ahead and give him a vote."

DALEY: But . . . I'm thinking of what happens after the convention.[8] . . . I hope we can work it in such a way that you're not the one to give this information.[9] . . .

LBJ: Don't you think though that . . . I'm going to have to say that I want somebody else?

DALEY: . . . Oh, you will. At the proper time. But I don't think *this* is the time. . . . As long as you keep talking to the heads of the delegations. . . .

LBJ: I haven't talked to anybody but you and Lawrence.[10]

DALEY: . . . I've been talking to them. They don't see it, and Dave doesn't see

---

[1] Daley means that Kennedy might resign from the Cabinet and wage an open fight with Johnson.

[2] Meaning that as a young maverick, RFK does not abide by the political etiquette of the Johnson-Daley generation.

[3] For RFK for Vice President.

[4] Daley's relationship with Johnson at this moment is extraordinarily paternal.

[5] Robert Kennedy and his allies.

[6] To Atlantic City.

[7] President Kennedy.

[8] Daley does not want the convention to erupt in a Johnson-Kennedy split that will harm the party and his own local ticket in the fall.

[9] To Kennedy.

[10] David Lawrence of Pennsylvania.

it. . . . It would be better, in my opinion . . . to do it the day before the nomination or . . . the night of the nomination. . . . I know a lot of people are pushing you to act . . . but . . . I think that you have control of the entire situation at all times.

LBJ: You don't think that anybody of consequence is likely to go away from us by waiting?

DALEY: No. . . . We don't see that. . . . I don't know if you have.

LBJ: No. I hear of it, but not of anything with a fellow like you or Lawrence or somebody that's a powerhouse. . . .

DALEY: He's coming out tomorrow, you know. . . . Out in Chicago.[1]

LBJ: No, what is that?

DALEY: You know, the library exhibit. . . .

LBJ: . . . I want you to handle it for me. You watch it.

DALEY: Maybe I'll do some talking tomorrow night.[2]

LBJ: Do that, and feel around. I think you ought to point out if you get a chance that the problem is the Midwest.[3] . . . And we'll kind of get it away from Boston. . . .

DALEY: I think you're right.

LBJ: You do that and give me a ring.

DALEY: . . . I'll talk to you Thursday or Friday.

ROBERT KENNEDY
8:00 P.M.

> DURING A CONVERSATION on Johnson's statement on the New York riots, LBJ mentions that Goldwater has sent him a message, asking for an unpublicized meeting to discuss how to avoid exacerbating national divisions over civil rights.

KENNEDY: You're not going to be able to have an unpublicized meeting.

LBJ: Of course not. That is silly. But . . . we can't refuse to see him. Now what do you think we ought to do?

KENNEDY: . . . I think maybe the ground rules should be laid quite clearly in advance. . . . Just send somebody down to talk to him to say. . . . "What are you going to discuss and what is going to come out of it?" And it would be damaging perhaps to the country to have the two of you disagree as to what might be done. . . . I don't have great confidence in him.

---

[1] Kennedy was coming to Chicago to open a traveling Kennedy Library exhibit and meet with Daley.

[2] With Kennedy on this subject.

[3] Johnson does not want RFK to be able to say that LBJ and the South had vetoed his nomination. Thus he wants Daley to make the argument that the chief battleground with Goldwater in the fall will be Daley's Midwest, where Kennedy has no particular strength. Under such reasoning, the logical Vice Presidential nominee would be Hubert Humphrey, to whom Johnson is privately beginning to gravitate.

LBJ: I don't have any. No, he was talking about "faker and phony" a week ago and now he's calling up wanting to come down.

. . . .

LBJ: Carl Sanders[1] talked to us yesterday. Says that Georgia is in one hell of shape. . . . That Goldwater had made great progress in Georgia. I think that they had a cut-and-dried deal with this fellow Grenier of Alabama and then they agreed that he would take over his campaign and that Wallace would get out and Wallace could keep his dough. He'd gotten a good deal of money in it.[2]

KENNEDY: I think . . . it's a major mistake to let him[3] choose this battleground now and have the struggle and this election over the question of civil rights. Because if it comes down to the question of civil rights, the Democrats are going to have a very tough time. . . .

LBJ: Yes, of course. . . . What we need to get in on is his impetuousness and his impulsiveness and his wanting to turn the Bomb over to somebody else.[4]

KENNEDY: . . . I think that will scare people and I think that is helpful. But it is difficult sometimes for people to understand . . . turning the Bomb over to the NATO commander. They don't know whether it is already in the hands of the NATO commander. But I think to get into . . . what this is going to mean as far as your lunch pail is concerned . . . when you get sick, what it is going to mean economically. When the country is at peace, as it is now, they're not concerned about Russians as much. . . . There's not a crisis like the Berlin Wall or Cuba.

LBJ: I don't know. A mother is pretty worried if she thinks her child is drinking contaminated milk or that maybe she's going to have a baby with two heads. . . . He's pretty vulnerable. . . . But I certainly agree with you that civil rights is something around our neck.

WEDNESDAY, JULY 22, 1964

ROBERT WAGNER
8:39 A.M.

DRAWING ON Hoover's confidential FBI reports, Johnson speculates to the New York Mayor that behind his city's riots are fanatics of both left and right.

[1] Democratic Governor of Georgia.
[2] John Grenier was a Birmingham lawyer and Goldwater organizer in the South whom Goldwater had just installed as executive director of the Republican National Committee. LBJ refers to a rumor that Grenier had helped to negotiate Wallace's withdrawal from the presidential race by promising that Wallace could pocket the campaign money he had collected.
[3] Goldwater.
[4] Goldwater had said in April 1964 that the NATO supreme commander "should have direct command over a NATO nuclear force" and use it to "meet local invasions on the spot with tactical nuclear weapons."

If true, this will fit neatly with the campaign Johnson is planning against Goldwater's "extremism."

LBJ: It's my own belief that some of these right-wingers—whether they're unmasked or not—are ... financing a little of this and trying to start it. And I anticipate that Harlem is the first place and California will be the next place and Philadelphia will be the next place to prove what he said in his acceptance speech that the cities of this country are going to be in a hell of a shape.[1] ... I notice some of them say, "Oh well, it's the Communists taking over." I have no doubt but that there're some people with those tendencies mixed up in these things, and I have no doubt that there're some extremists of all kinds. I think it's a good thing to raise the question whether some of this stuff is being fomented and contributed from outside. Make ... people stop and think ... particularly Negroes, before they become the tools of some of these right-wing cranks. If the Negroes ... and ... the country and ... the press realize that ... there're some right-wingers plotting and giving a little encouragement to this too, it will not be as dangerous to us as it would be otherwise. ... I'm asking Hoover to particularly watch that.

. . . .

LBJ: The good people of this country don't want this unrest fomented. I think it's already got some of these people upset that they would say extremism is a virtue because that's almost like advocating rioting.

WAGNER: ... Up in Harlem last night[2]—I couldn't believe it until I saw it—they had some of these youngsters with these helmets ... on motorcycles and the two-way walkie-talkies. ... Somebody must be giving them that equipment. I mean, they're not buying that stuff themselves.

THURSDAY, JULY 23, 1964

JOHN CONNALLY
5:31 P.M.

JOHNSON HAD SCARCELY slept the previous night. Already anguished over the Robert Kennedy problem, he is now dejected that the Mississippi Freedom Democratic Party (MFDP) is demanding that at Atlantic City the Democratic convention expel the all-white Mississippi regulars and seat its delegation of sixty-four blacks and four whites. Johnson envisions a convention floor fight that will divide the party and damage his election chances.

[1] Goldwater had said, "The growing menace in our country tonight, to personal safety, to life, to limb and property ... particularly in our cities, is the mounting concern—or should be—of every thoughtful citizen in the United States."
[2] The Mayor had been touring Harlem with his police chief.

LBJ: I don't know how anybody can stop what they're doing on the Freedom Party. I think it's very bad and I wish that I could stop it. I tried, but I haven't been able to. . . . It may very well be that Bobby has started it.[1] Last night I couldn't sleep. About two-thirty I waked up. And I tried to figure what I would do if I were a candidate for Vice President[2] . . . and the bossman would say that "I can't take you on account of the South." I think the first thing I'd do is try to make the South of no value either to him or to me. . . . I believe that's what is happening. . . . Joe Rauh[3] and Martin Luther King and folks that normally run with that crowd are leading 'em. Humphrey is trying his best to put an end to it, but he hasn't had much luck with 'em. . . . It's going to be pretty difficult for a fellow like Donald Russell[4] . . . and you or anybody else from that part of the country with a substantial Negro population . . . to sit by and let their sister states be thrown out when they were duly elected. . . .

On the other hand, I don't see how a fellow like Dick Hughes and Governor Lawrence and Dick Daley[5] . . . can possibly go back to their states and say that they were for seating the Alabama group and the Mississippi group when they won't say they'll support their nominees.[6] . . . So it looks like you just pretty well split the party. . . . Worse than Goldwater and Rockefeller even.[7] And it looks like there are forces that would like to do that. I have no doubt. They claim that they got a Texas oil millionaire messing around up in Harlem. I don't know who it is, unless Old Man Hunt[8] got some money. But Hoover is after it now, and they've got all the Communists in. . . . Both sides are in on these riots. . . . Hell, these folks have got walkie-talkies. . . . Somebody's financing them big. . . . It's Brooklyn one night and it's Harlem the next night and it'll be another section of New York tonight.[9]

· · · ·

LBJ: He went out to Illinois last night.[10] . . . [reading from memo:] "An extremely reliable and perceptive observer reports 'the consensus among the Cook County organization is that Daley favors the Attorney General for Vice President but might not press the matter openly against the President's wishes.' "[11] . . . I have about come to the conclusion that it is just as positive as we're sitting here that he is going to force a roll call on his name for this place or the other place.[12]

---

[1] With no evidence, Johnson wonders whether Robert Kennedy is secretly encouraging the MFDP in order to damage Johnson's election chances.

[2] In other words, as if he were RFK campaigning for the vice presidency.

[3] The Washington labor lawyer and counsel to the Freedom Party.

[4] Democratic Governor of South Carolina.

[5] Governor Richard Hughes, Lawrence, and Daley would be heads of the New Jersey, Pennsylvania, and Illinois delegations at Atlantic City.

[6] The regular delegations from Mississippi and Alabama were balking at signing a required pledge to support the convention's nominees that fall.

[7] Goldwater's nomination was spurring many Republicans from the Rockefeller wing of their party to bolt the nominee.

[8] The Dallas radical right oil tycoon H.L. Hunt.

[9] The Bedford-Stuyvesant black ghetto in Brooklyn had also exploded in rioting.

[10] Robert Kennedy had been in Chicago to open the Kennedy Library exhibit and see Mayor Daley.

[11] This report probably made Johnson suspicious that Daley was some kind of Kennedy double agent.

[12] Meaning the presidency or vice presidency.

... They're going to have an emotional thing with this film and Miz Kennedy.[1]
... Then he's gonna really make a pitch. Now most of my advisers here think I
ought to call him in now, a month ahead of time, so I can get word to all the
leaders[2] and tell 'em how I feel. And if they don't want me, why, it's all right.
They can just take *him*. Because he will have the nomination, if I don't have it.
And so I have about concluded that I would give Daley until tomorrow.[3] He told
me he'd call me Thursday or Friday. ... If I didn't hear from him, then I'd ask
this fellow to come in.[4] ... He'll want to argue about it. ... They say he's very
much against Humphrey.[5] He told Clark Clifford that he would consider that a
great insult to his brother's memory—Humphrey ran against him.[6] ... Most
of them think that he has determined that he wants *this* job[7] and he'll do anything in the world he can to get it. And if by causing a fight, he thinks that
he can probably make me throw the election, he would even like to see me a
defeated man.

· · · ·

LBJ: When this fellow looks at me, he looks at me like he's going to look a hole
through me like I'm a spy or something—Bobby. ... I think if we just go down
and start fighting, maybe the prestige of the office[8] will carry us through. But I
think it'll be like Daley said. Daley says, "Please don't do it—wait until you get
up there."[9] ... Clark Clifford and others say here that if I do that, it'll be too late,
that they'll be in charge up there. ... That I've got to tell him and if I can't stop
him ... he'd probably resign[10] and then we'll just have to see which one can win.
I have the office, but I don't have much to fight with. ... I didn't sleep two hours
last night.

· · · ·

LBJ: It might be this is an easy way maybe to get out[11]—save your face by just
getting beat.

CONNALLY: Aw, you ain't gonna do that.

LBJ: ... Goldwater's coming in tomorrow.[12] ... Nothing good can come out of
that. He wants to use this[13] as a forum. He wants to encourage a backlash.[14]
That's where his future is. It's not in peace and harmony.

[1] A memorial film for President Kennedy was to be shown at the Atlantic City convention.
Johnson was also hearing rumors that Jacqueline Kennedy would attend to rally support for
her brother-in-law.
[2] Democratic party leaders.
[3] Johnson is waiting to hear Daley's report on his conversation with RFK in Chicago on
Wednesday night.
[4] Meaning that Johnson will ask RFK to come in to be told that he will not be Vice President.
[5] For Vice President. Actually, although Johnson did not know it, Kennedy preferred that if
he was not to be the running mate, Humphrey should be.
[6] Humphrey ran against John Kennedy in the early primaries of 1960. RFK may have said
this in an effort to persuade Clifford that he should himself be the choice.
[7] The presidency.
[8] The presidency.
[9] At the convention in Atlantic City.
[10] From Johnson's Cabinet.
[11] Of the presidency.
[12] For the meeting he had sought with Johnson at the White House.
[13] The White House.
[14] "White backlash" was a term much in vogue in the summer of 1964, referring to the
electoral retribution of whites angry at Johnson about the Civil Rights Act.

. . . .

CONNALLY: I think your great appeal and your great strength in this country now is that you're doing what you think is right. . . . If you have to take Bobby on in a goddamn fight, let's take him on. . . . I think you can whup him in a standstill. . . . I don't think he'll make the fight. And I damn sure agree that you ought not give him running room between now and August. . . . I'd get it over with. . . . I'd rather fight with him between now and August than I would the next four years. And I don't think there's any question but that he would be delighted to see you defeated. . . . He's an arrogant, egotistical, selfish person that feels like he's almost anointed. He's so power-mad that it's unbelievable. That's the very reason you can't take him on this ticket.

. . . .

LBJ: I don't see the answer to this damn convention thing on seating.[1]

CONNALLY: . . . That's going to be a tough problem. . . . If they have a hundred thousand Negroes up there—or ten thousand—and they picket this thing because Alabama and Mississippi are being seated and then the convention kicks them out, the impression around the country is going to be that they just got kicked out because the niggers wanted them kicked out.

. . . .

LBJ: Now there are only really three people that have any strength, John, that we can talk about to get nominated.[2] If I . . . could just push a button, I'd put McNamara. Because he just is by far the most help to me of any-bod-y. But that's out. There's not a one that's got a delegation—whether it's Lawrence, whether it's Wagner, whether it's Daley. . . . They say that if we haven't got a Democrat in our own party, we can't do it.[3] So that's that. . . . When you go on the Catholic thing,[4] you don't get anybody really very strong on McCarthy.[5] Clark Clifford thinks we may have to come to him because he just thinks that they[6] will say that they were discriminated against and their man[7] got cuddown . . . and the Protestants took over, and the men that tried to defeat Kennedy in his lifetime have defeated him in his death—Johnson and Humphrey. . . . The labor people . . . and the Negro people and the folks that do the work and got the votes and put up the money . . . they would generally stay with you for Humphrey. . . .

You really need somebody that's a good debater and a good TV performer and can take 'em on because you're tied down so damned hard in this job. I don't want to say so, but I wish I knew some nice, decent way just to let them fight it out and let anybody that wants it have it. Because . . . you got problems with Khrushchev and Castro. Say they're gonna shoot down your planes the minute the election's over. . . . You've just got more damned problems than I can handle.

[1] The Mississippi Freedom Democratic Party challenge.
[2] For Vice President.
[3] When LBJ had floated McNamara's name with the bosses, they had bridled at the notion that Democrats should choose someone with no roots in the party, who was so recently a Republican.
[4] The argument that, especially with RFK out of the running, LBJ should choose a Catholic.
[5] Eugene McCarthy.
[6] The Catholics.
[7] President Kennedy.

I've got old enough and flabby enough that I can't surmount all the obstacles. And I don't have the help and the advice and the counselors and the loved ones around you to do it. Every man in my Cabinet's a Kennedy man. . . . I haven't been able to change 'em and I don't have the personnel if I *could* change 'em. They didn't go to San Marcos Teachers College.[1] . . . It's just agony.

. . . .

LBJ: I just shudder to think what would happen if Goldwater won it. He's a man that's had two nervous breakdowns.[2] He's not a stable fellow at all. . . .

CONNALLY: [laughs]

LBJ: I don't really know how to handle it all. That's the honest truth.

CONNALLY: Oh yes, you do.

LBJ: No, I don't. . . . If I win, I lose. Because I want the South for me. . . . And if I can't offer the ticket the South, I haven't got really anything to offer them.[3] I don't have any standing in Chicago . . . Iowa, Los Angeles, New York City. . . . Now my judgment is we're gonna lose every Southern state, including Kentucky and Oklahoma and Missouri. . . . I just don't think they can take this nigra stuff. . . . And they're[4] gonna pour it in.

CONNALLY: Yeah, I think they will.

LBJ: I think I'll have that conversation.[5] . . . I'll call you afterwards and we probably will have to make a deep pitch to governors . . . and . . . leaders . . . and see if they'll stay with the President. Then I just think I have to say that if they don't, I'm not going to let them put somebody in bed with me that'll murder me.[6] Then I just can't be President. Then that's exactly what he[7] wants. Because then with his having enough support to be Vice President and I got out, he'd have it more than anybody else has.[8] . . . But I don't think my self-respect could suffer a defeat at the convention[9] and then take the presidency. Do you?

CONNALLY: No.

LBJ: So no use in being a crybaby. I just have to say that.

CONNALLY: It's not that bad.

LBJ: I don't know. . . . If this . . . fight against the South gets up, I'm gonna wind up without anything but the South. And the South ain't gonna be for me. But *they're*[10] not gonna be for me on grounds that I'm a Southerner. Because I

[1] Southwest Texas State Teachers College at San Marcos was Johnson's alma mater.
[2] This information appeared in a May 1964 *Good Housekeeping* interview with Goldwater's wife, Peggy, but Johnson may have also received it from more covert sources.
[3] Johnson shows that his mind-set of 1960 has remained intact. In 1960, the Kennedy people had used him in an effort to try to hold the Democratic South, despite a convention platform that was progressive and pro–civil rights. That year he was scarcely permitted to campaign in the North, which made him feel insecure about his Northern appeal. (See Kenneth O'Donnell oral history, Johnson Library.)
[4] The Goldwater people.
[5] With Robert Kennedy.
[6] Meaning force Robert Kennedy on him for Vice President.
[7] Robert Kennedy.
[8] In other words, if LBJ, angry at having RFK pressed on him as Vice President, pulled out, Robert Kennedy would have the strength to win the presidential nomination.
[9] Over the vice presidency.
[10] The Northerners.

have no real rapport or anything in common with those folks. The only thing is I got possession of the office at the moment.

. . . .

LBJ: Who would you pick as Vice President right now?

CONNALLY: . . . What about Abe Ribicoff?[1]

LBJ: Nope. Tom Dodd[2] would like to have it, but you couldn't do it with him. You're gonna have to take either Humphrey or McCarthy or Bobby. And I wouldn't take Bobby. I'd take Humphrey. And I think Humphrey would cause you trouble in the South. I don't think it'd be much better than Bobby. . . .

CONNALLY: Of course, I would take. . . . I really shouldn't say—I don't know McCarthy that well.

LBJ: He'll get a lot of smear. He votes the oil and gas companies. . . . He'll catch you unshirted hell from the Drew Pearsons.[3] . . . They've already told me. . . . He's kind of regarded as a liberal renegade.

CONNALLY: . . . I'd take him simply on the premise that nobody knows him and he's damn little harm, damn little good. . . .

LBJ: . . . You'd really prefer McCarthy to Humphrey?

CONNALLY: Sure.

LBJ: We're not going to carry any Southern states, John, and Humphrey has a lot more appeal in the other states. In the Midwest, he has a lot more appeal than McCarthy.

HUBERT HUMPHREY
6:17 P.M.

> HUMPHREY SHOWS Johnson how he is trying to forestall a convention showdown over the Mississippi Freedom Democratic Party, which he also hopes will improve his chances with LBJ for Vice President.

HUMPHREY: I've asked Walter[4] to contact the key leaders of the civil rights groups. Quietly, unobtrusively, I'm going to meet with them. . . . We'll have Luther King and all of them in. . . .

LBJ: Sure ought to do that, Hubert.

. . . .

LBJ: I think that I will probably, in the next two or three days . . . call him[5] in and tell him how I feel. And that may break it open right there. Then everybody's going to have to be prepared to move heaven and earth.

. . . .

---

[1] A novel suggestion for Connally to make. Ribicoff was a liberal Jewish Senator from Connecticut.
[2] Ribicoff's senior colleague from Connecticut, a Catholic.
[3] Meaning muckraking columnists.
[4] Humphrey's ally, United Auto Workers president Walter Reuther.
[5] Robert Kennedy.

LBJ: You'd be surprised at this—you've got some opposition in the South. A good deal. They want somebody they've never heard of.[1] . . . They just take the position that anything hurts you. I'm afraid we're not gonna carry any of those states anyway. I'm just really worried about it.

FRIDAY, JULY 24, 1964

ROBERT McNAMARA
5:56 P.M.

> JOHNSON CALLS his Defense Secretary from the Oval Office, where he has just had a fifteen-minute meeting with Barry Goldwater.

LBJ: I just finished seeing your friend[2] and it was the damnedest experience I ever had in my life.

· · · ·

LBJ: He said, "You're looking fine." I said, "I never felt better. . . . They won't let you drink. You got a policeman at each gate, so you can't go out with any pretty girls. You can't gamble or play poker. You just have to spend all night reading your intelligence reports and FBI reports.[3] So there's no reason why you shouldn't look good." He said, "I just wanted to come in and tell you that I'm not going to get personal in this campaign. . . . And there are a lot of conservatives in this country—and I can't control 'em—but I want to do the best I can to keep down any riot. It just would hurt me terribly if somebody got killed because of something I said." . . . I thought the more I talked, probably the greater danger I was taking, so . . . I said, "Here's what I'm going to say when you leave, if it's all right." I had a one-sentence statement.[4] . . . He said, "That's fine by me. . . . I'm going out the back way." . . . So I walked out the door with him. He said, "What's the name of this plane that you announced today? . . . I've been trying to get a ride in it."[5] . . . I said, "I didn't think you were very wise flying your own plane around San Francisco."[6] He said, "Oh no, I'm not ever going to quit flying."

---

[1] LBJ is referring to his talk, above, with Connally and Connally's preference for McCarthy.

[2] Goldwater was an outspoken critic of McNamara.

[3] Did Johnson refer to FBI reports in an effort to warn Goldwater that if Goldwater waged a personal campaign against LBJ, Johnson would have plenty of material on Goldwater with which to retaliate?

[4] Actually the White House issued three sentences, saying merely that Johnson had showed Goldwater the steps he had taken "to avoid the incitement of racial tensions" and that Goldwater had agreed that such tensions should be avoided.

[5] At his afternoon press conference, Johnson had revealed the existence of the new swift, high-flying SR-71 reconnaissance plane.

[6] A World War II veteran and major-general in the Air Force Reserve, Goldwater liked to fly his own plane.

SATURDAY, JULY 25, 1964

RICHARD DALEY
10:01 A.M.

ALREADY NERVOUS that Daley might be quietly supporting Robert Kennedy for Vice President, Johnson has grown anxious about why, after meeting with RFK in Chicago the previous Wednesday, the Chicago Mayor has not fulfilled his promise to call Johnson on Thursday or Friday.

LBJ: I thought I was going to hear from you.

DALEY: I was going to call you yesterday, and then I thought I'd call you Monday.

LBJ: Good.

DALEY: I think that maybe your idea that you had last week[1] was a good one.

LBJ: Yeah?

DALEY: . . . I had a chance to talk a little bit[2] . . . Wednesday night. . . . I kept saying . . . that after all, this is a selection that's made by the President. . . . Then I . . . suggested some conversation with you. . . . The only thing is . . . the timing. . . . That's what I was trying to do some thinking about over the weekend.

• • • •

DALEY: We have to have unity in order to win. . . . When would you do it? Next week?

LBJ: I thought so. . . . I was just kind of waiting until I heard you-all's conversation, because I felt he'd[3] raise the question with you.

• • • •

LBJ: Does he feel that he's entitled to it?[4] Does he feel he wants to fight for it, or what?

DALEY: Not the latter.

• • • •

LBJ: Did he give you an indication that he knew of the trend of my thinking?

DALEY: He didn't say that. He kept saying . . . how everyone was depending on some of the fellows to speak out, including myself.[5]

[1] To give RFK the bad news now, rather than wait for the convention.
[2] With Robert Kennedy.
[3] Robert Kennedy.
[4] The vice presidency.
[5] Daley means that RFK expects him and other leaders to openly demand that LBJ name him Vice President.

NICHOLAS KATZENBACH
10:15 A.M.

> JOHNSON TELLS more about his meeting with Goldwater in a talk with Robert Kennedy's deputy.

LBJ: He said that . . . he was a half Jew and that he didn't want to do anything that would contribute to any riots or disorders or bring about any violence. Because of his ancestry, he was aware of the problems that existed in that field. . . . I told him . . . that when I had come into this office, this bill was pending[1] and I thought it was better to handle it in the courts than in the streets. I thought we'd waited for a hundred years to make good on the Emancipation Proclamation. It was a proclamation but it wasn't a fact, and we ought to have this machinery,[2] so I had asked the Congress for it. Eighty percent of the Republicans had given it to me in the Senate—a much bigger percentage than even the Democrats. And I had called all the members of both parties down and made a television broadcast, signed the bill, and appealed to all of them to observe the law. And I didn't want another Volstead Act or Eighteenth Amendment.[3]

EVERETT DIRKSEN
4:45 P.M.

LBJ: I don't expect you to nominate me[4] but I expect you to help me get elected on the basis of having a good record.[5]
DIRKSEN: Yeah, damn you! You didn't even listen to my nominating speech.
LBJ: Oh yes, I did. Yes, I did. I think you do everything well.

• • • •

DIRKSEN: I'm out here in a farm, just puzzling about some speeches that I'm going to be making.
LBJ: [joking:] Don't make any speeches. You've already done enough damage to me. Now just lay off. . . . Go out and plant some roses.
DIRKSEN: Don't you want *any* speeches?
LBJ: . . . I wouldn't mind your going down and making a speech at your daughter's home when you're visiting the family, but I don't want you to take any hard schedule because I want to save you to get my program through. [both laugh] Come see me.
DIRKSEN: If you let me, I'll come.

---

[1] Johnson used with Goldwater the same line of defense against charges of radicalism on civil rights that he had used with Russell Long in their conversation, above, of July 20, 1964.
[2] Machinery to enforce the Emancipation Proclamation.
[3] By citing the Eighteenth Amendment, which prohibited use of "intoxicating liquors," and the Volstead Act, its enforcement apparatus, Johnson means that he does not want the Civil Rights Act to be on the books but widely ignored.
[4] Dirksen had delivered Goldwater's nominating speech in San Francisco.
[5] Johnson wants more of Dirksen's help with his legislative program.

LBJ: Any time. Come down late in the evening and I'll buy you a drink. . . . It won't be Sanka, either.

DIRKSEN: [laughs] Hope not!

MONDAY, JULY 27, 1964

ROBERT KENNEDY
5:00 P.M.

> AFTER POLICE INTERCEDED in a dispute between two blacks, rioting had started on the evening of July 24 in Rochester, New York. Governor Nelson Rockefeller has called out a thousand National Guard troops to restore order.

KENNEDY: Obviously with the Communists, with the Black Muslims, just the no-gooders, you're not going to be able to do anything. But you know they talked about the city of Washington exploding three years ago. . . . What's been done here, through the opening up of the swimming pools and . . . the job program in the summer . . . has given at least the younger people the feeling that there are people in government . . . that are interested in them. . . . That makes a hell of a difference. Frequently these mayors are in touch with the Negro community only through the Democratic politicians . . . who are almost considered Uncle Toms.

. . . .

LBJ: Now you gonna be here tomorrow?

KENNEDY: Yes, I am.

LBJ: All right. . . . I want to talk to you about some other matters[1] and we can talk about this too.

HENRY LUCE
Editorial Chairman, Time Inc.
5:15 P.M.

> THE *Time-Life* founder has written Johnson about an article being prepared for *Life* on how he made his fortune.

LBJ: There's a lot of politics in this. Are you doing comparative articles on the investments of both candidates—or is it just me?

LUCE: Just you. We haven't gotten around to the other one yet.

[1] LBJ is about to lower the boom on Kennedy.

LBJ: Well, don't you want to do them together?

LUCE: [chuckles] We should.

. . . .

LBJ: I don't think that it's real important to the world whether land you paid sixty-five for is worth fifty-five or seventy-five.

LUCE: No, it isn't. . . . The main thing here, Mr. President . . . as you understand, is the enormous curiosity about anything about the President of the United States.

LBJ: I hadn't ever realized that. . . . I have no idea today what Ike has. He told me himself he was in partners with Sid Richardson[1] in the oil and gas business, and I didn't even know it. And Sid was one of my closest friends. . . . I talked to the President[2]—and I heard Mr. Joe Kennedy[3] tell him if he sold his oil and gas property, it would cost him ten million. Each one of the children. . . . I don't want to debate about the thing. But my curiosity has never gone to what a President owned and it doesn't make any difference because I'm worth three or four hundred thousand, and that's that.

WEDNESDAY, JULY 29, 1964

McGEORGE BUNDY
10:39 A.M.

>   JOHNSON HAS ARRANGED for Robert Kennedy to see him in the Oval Office at 1:00 P.M.

BUNDY: I think your meeting is very important today. I had quite a time last night.[4]

LBJ: What have you got to suggest?

BUNDY: Just be as clear and as open and candid and complete in your thinking as you can. . . . One question in my mind, Mr. President, is whether . . . you run the risk of his thinking that there's still room to divide . . . or whether if you say to him, "I want you to be the first to know who it is." . . .

LBJ: . . . But it gets out immediately. . . .

BUNDY: Not only that, but there is a finite chance . . . that an attack would be mounted on whoever you select.

LBJ: Yeah, I think that's right.

. . . .

---

[1] The Texas oil tycoon.
[2] Kennedy.
[3] JFK's father.
[4] Bundy had spoken to Robert Kennedy in the corner at a party the night before.

LBJ: I thought that I would just say that I've given a lot of thought to this thing, and have talked to practically every state in the union—either personally or my most trusted people—and that I thought that he had a bright future in the party, and I personally would be happy to see that successful. But that I couldn't this year. . . . Now what do you think his reaction is?

BUNDY: . . . My inclination . . . would be . . . to suggest that he think that over, and that you and he talk about it again. . . . There are two or three people . . . that could weigh in with him. I'm one. Bob McNamara is another. . . . There may be others who could say . . . "The President told us, because he knew how close we are to you, what he'd done, and we just want to say to you that we hope you'll accept this presidential judgment. . . . In a time when your brother's record is at stake . . . we honestly believe this is what your brother would want." . . .

LBJ: Yeah, except I've got to be final. I can't leave any doubts.

· · · ·

LBJ: Does he know what this meeting is about?

BUNDY: He guesses, yes. . . . And he knows—he really knows. And neither Bob[1] nor I in separate conversations have corrected him. He knows which way your mind is tending.

LBJ: Does he find fault with it?

BUNDY: Well, he *wants* that job.[2] . . . I don't think he finds fault with your right to have a *view*. I think he just plain *wants* it. . . . I think in some moods . . . he honestly doesn't know what his reaction is going to be. And just having watched him over the last nine months[3] . . . I would try not to ask him for a full comment at first flush. . . . I think there's a risk. . . .

LBJ: Who else does he talk to besides you two?

BUNDY: . . . He keeps his life pretty well compartmented. I assume he talks to Steve Smith.[4] I would suppose he would talk to Teddy, unless the doctors tell him not to.[5] . . . I think he talks in a sort of an "argue with us" way probably to a lot of people. . . .

LBJ: Kenny[6] said the other night that it had to be this or a big blowup.[7]

BUNDY: . . . My own judgment is that when he looks that one in the eye, it's going to be so destructive to him and to his brother's memory that he won't do it. Does Kenny think he will do it?

LBJ: He hasn't talked to me. He just, in one of those free moments at three or four o'clock in the morning made this observation, just between us—don't repeat it to a human. One of the Cabinet came in very upset about it and said that he had said that he had to do this "or there'd be hell to pay."

[1] McNamara.
[2] The vice presidency.
[3] Meaning in RFK's emotional mood following his brother's murder.
[4] Kennedy's brother-in-law.
[5] Bundy presumed that Edward Kennedy's doctors might want stressful subjects kept from him while he was recovering from his plane crash.
[6] O'Donnell.
[7] In other words, that Johnson had better choose Kennedy or risk a fight.

BUNDY: ... I don't myself believe it, Mr. President. I think that might be psychological warfare.[1]

CLARK CLIFFORD
11:45 A.M.

LBJ: How are you, my friend?

CLIFFORD: Fine, friend.

LBJ: I'm going to have that meeting today.

CLIFFORD: Yes sir.

LBJ: ... He's got the lady[2] thinking about going to the convention, and he put that out yesterday. He thinks that most of the delegations are for him, and this is the thing he wants more than anything else in his life. If he's denied it, it'll be "very cruel."

. . . .

CLIFFORD: Now I think it appropriate and courteous to give some reasons for your decision, but you are not asking him at any time for his reaction. ... You're calling him over because you owe him the courtesy to tell him you have reached a final and irrevocable decision, and you thought he ought to know it first. ... I would not make any reference to the fact that you have reached any conclusion.[3] I do not think that you're under any obligation to inform him ahead of time in that regard. It very likely would be as leaky as an open boat. ...

LBJ: I agree with you. ... They'll start working on whoever you suggested. If you name Mr. X, then they'd get the South against Mr. X.

CLARK CLIFFORD
2:17 P.M.

SIX MINUTES EARLIER, Robert Kennedy left the Oval Office. Now Johnson calls Clifford to report that he has done the deed.[4]

[1] By Kennedy to pressure Johnson to choose him.
[2] Jacqueline Kennedy.
[3] On who should be Vice President.
[4] Johnson had sat formally behind his desk, virtually reading from a memo prepared by Clifford, while Kennedy listened from a chair at the side. Kennedy suspected that "the whole conversation with Johnson was recorded." Not realizing how much LBJ had altered his brother's old taping system, RFK thought he saw "buttons on" that meant the Dictaphone was in play (quoted in Arthur M. Schlesinger, Jr., *Robert Kennedy and His Times*, p. 661). One reason that Johnson taped his private conversations was to provide evidence in case his interlocutor later disputed what was said. His encounter with Kennedy certainly qualified. But no tape of the conversation has ever surfaced. Kenneth O'Donnell later insisted that Johnson asked Walter Jenkins to "read" to O'Donnell "exactly" what Kennedy had said to him—and that, realizing "that he was revealing to me that their talk had been recorded," LBJ quickly said that what he had actually meant was for Jenkins to read from Johnson's notes on what he told Kennedy (*"Johnny, We Hardly Knew Ye,"* p. 397). If Johnson did not tape the RFK meeting and if O'Donnell's version is correct, LBJ may have been referring to his own account of the meeting, offered to Clark Clifford and others in telephone conversations that were taped and transcribed.

LBJ: He said, "Well, who have you decided on?" And I said, "I haven't made the final decision." . . . I told him that it was brought about by Goldwater's nomination, the strength in the Middle West and the border states, and I believed that a Democratic ticket should be made to try to appeal to those states. That I felt like I had an obligation to make this decision. I believe that President Kennedy had that obligation, that he made it—

CLIFFORD: Right.

LBJ: On the basis of what he thought was best for the country and for the party and for himself. . . . That I wanted to see his program carried out. . . . That I thought that he had a bright future in the party, would be willing to do what I could to contribute to it.

CLIFFORD: Good.

LBJ: . . . I told him that I would like for him to help in the campaign and help direct it. . . . He wanted me to know he would be glad to help out in the campaign —at least until November. . . . I said, "Would you like to stay on?"[1] He said no. . . . He said, "Have you thought about who you'd appoint?"[2] I said no. He said, "I see where you're considering this Leon Gronouski—or Jaworski—in Houston.[3] I said no. . . . He said, "I'd really like you to think of Nick Katzenbach."[4] "That's all right. Nice fellow. I'm impressed by him. I'll give thought to that. You don't think you could help the campaign and do that too?" He said no, he didn't think so. . . . I thought if he helped organize the campaign, it would be helpful to him and any future . . . ambitions that he might have. He said he would be glad to do that. He seemed to have expected what happened, but cherished the kind of hope. He kind of swallowed deeply a time or two. He wasn't combative in any way. I leaned over backwards not to be in the slightest arrogant. I was very firm and very positive and very final. . . . He said . . . "How are you going to announce this?" . . . I said, "I would be glad to handle it any way you want to." He said, "I would like to think about that a little."

· · · ·

LBJ: He got up, started for the door and I said, "Now, the campaign. We ought to get to work on it pretty soon." And he said he agreed. I said, "How do you feel about it?" And he—very significantly—said, "I think it's extremely dangerous. Every nut in the country is already lined up with this fellow."[5] And I said, "Yes, and a lot of young people and women that are not nuts." . . . Then he looked up at me and smiled and said, "Well, you didn't ask me. But I think I could have done a hell of a job for us." Meaning if he'd have gone on the ticket. "Well, I think you *will* do a hell of a job for us." I looked at him very straight, proud, and said, "And for yourself too."

CLIFFORD: Wonderful.

LBJ: And that's the way it ended.

[1] As Attorney General.
[2] To succeed RFK at the Justice Department.
[3] Johnson's friend Leon Jaworski, whom he had considered for the Court of Inquiry following the Kennedy assassination. (See LBJ conversation with Joseph Alsop, November 25, 1963.)
[4] RFK's deputy and friend.
[5] Goldwater.

CLIFFORD: Oh-h-h, I'm just so gratified. Let me say, right away, that this was not an easy task for you. It took courage and forthrightness and it just makes me very proud. This is the kind of President that I want.

. . . .

LBJ: Told him . . . "I want to be your friend. I want to carry out the Kennedy program. I think I'll get twenty-five of thirty-five bills that he left behind passed the first year. In the next four years, we'll carry out the other ten and extend it. I'd like to have your help in doing that. . . . Now on the vice presidency, President Kennedy asked me to do it. And I did it because I had had a lot of very active experience in the Senate and . . . I was ready to let up.[1] But I found it was very frustrating to sit there and not be able to do anything in the Senate, to sit in the Cabinet and not have any employees. . . . I don't think that anybody has really recognized how I felt, except President Kennedy. He said to me frequently that he couldn't understand how I could keep on with this frustrating experience. And he felt sorry for me. . . . I think that that's the way the vice presidency is. I think that there's much that you can do that will make yourself better understood and better prepared for any . . . ambitions you may have than just hearing the roll call in the Senate."

. . . .

LBJ: And now he said, "I think I ought to talk to you about the Bobby Baker thing. . . . I think that's going to give us some problems. There's something that showed up where it might be interpreted that he violated the law. They'll want to know why we haven't done something, and if we do do something, it might be embarrassing. I would like to talk to Jim Rowe,[2] who has your confidence. If it's all right with you, I'd like to have him talk with Katzenbach."[3] I said, "I want to do anything you want to do. I had no business relationship with Bobby. . . . I went to the Dominican Republic one time and he indicated he would like to go with me and I don't know, for some reason, I just thought it'd be better not to and I didn't fight him. And I'd have been in a hell of a shape if I had. But the last four years, I had no contact when these things were happening." . . . [to Clifford:] Now I think it would be a pretty good idea for you, after we hang up . . . to call Katzenbach and say . . . that I wanted you to talk to him, pursuant to the Attorney General's request.
CLIFFORD: Good. I shall do it at once.

. . . .

LBJ: [suggesting a message for Clifford to give RFK:] You could say very frankly that you believe that I would serve out one term. I might run for a second one, but if you're fifty-seven[4] years old, you wouldn't predict that. . . . You think that anybody could use four years . . . very valuably, particularly if he had a friendly President, which you believe me to be.
CLIFFORD: . . . I shall follow that meticulously.

[1] Meaning reduce his activity.
[2] The Washington lawyer who was Johnson's old New Deal friend.
[3] Johnson may have interpreted that as a veiled threat by Kennedy to dredge up Bobby Baker trouble that would damage LBJ in the fall. Had RFK no such intention, he could have chosen almost any other time to discuss the matter with Johnson.
[4] Actually Johnson was almost fifty-six.

McGEORGE BUNDY
2:30 P.M.

BUNDY: He came in here for a few minutes afterwards.[1] . . . I think you must have handled it just Grade A. . . . I was cheered up when he came in. . . . I did advise him beforehand, whatever his reaction, to say nothing in haste. He's worried about . . . running the campaign. He thinks it's a good way of making enemies.[2]

. . . .

LBJ: He wants to be President, and I think the best way for him to be President is to . . . be a little better understood. . . . I believe of the fifty states, there were three of 'em that indicated that some of their delegates would like to be for him. . . .

BUNDY: He's got enemies he doesn't need to have.

LBJ: And doesn't know about. And I've got 'em too.

. . . .

LBJ: What we got to do is find out a nice way and your great function now [is] . . . trying to pull us together . . . as close as he'll permit. I'm gonna have self-respect and I'm not gonna bow too much, but I'm gonna meet [him] 60 percent of the way.

BUNDY: Now that you've made this decision, you don't have any problem with self-respect. You're in charge.

LBJ: . . . You're gonna have to find a way today or tomorrow, that's agreeable to both of us, on how to get this cat out of the bag.[3] If I were a dictator, I'd just say that he'd indicated that he'd be glad to be helpful in the campaign . . . but he didn't choose to be a candidate.

. . . .

BUNDY: I think what actually happened, Mr. President, was that he looked hard at whether there was any other course that made any sense for anyone, himself included . . . and came out where I think we're going to be all right.

LBJ: I think it'd be very bad for me, for his brother's memory, and disastrous for him if he did anything else.

BUNDY: Disastrous for him.

LBJ: It'd mess up the whole Kennedy image and the whole Kennedy picture, trying to have a dynasty this quick and move right in and take over.

[1] Kennedy had called on Bundy after his meeting with Johnson.
[2] Bundy later discovered that Kennedy had taken his intervention in the matter as inexplicable disloyalty to him (McGeorge Bundy oral history, Kennedy Library). The breach was soon repaired.
[3] How Johnson's decision should be announced.

CLARK CLIFFORD
8:21 P.M.

CLIFFORD REPORTS THAT, as Johnson requested, he has arranged to see Katzenbach.

LBJ: I was hoping that the other man[1] would want to talk to you about other things. . . . He talked to McNamara. . . . McNamara suggested that he indicate by a statement that he didn't care to be Vice President. He said no, he wasn't ready to do that. . . . Kind of kicked up his heels. It worries McNamara a good deal.

. . . .

CLIFFORD: I think I'd give him tomorrow . . . to reach a conclusion. . . . If you haven't heard from him by the middle of the day tomorrow, I think we might consider the possibility of your checking in with him and saying that you fear the matter's going to get out. . . . You can say out of courtesy to him that the matter is getting hotter all the time and you believe the announcement should be made.

THURSDAY, JULY 30, 1964

McGEORGE BUNDY
10:01 A.M.

HAVING HEARD NOTHING from Robert Kennedy about how he should announce his decision to exclude him as running mate, Johnson asks Bundy what to do.

BUNDY: If you're getting near a clear-cut judgment in your own mind as to who you want,[2] why don't you just blitz that and tell the Cabinet and tell the leadership and tell the press, all in an hour and a half, between now and the weekend?
LBJ: [disagrees:] . . . Everybody that's left out concentrates their attentions on the fellow's deficiencies and the party men go to hitting at him.
BUNDY: [rebuts:] Everybody who comes to those meetings is going to say yes . . . and they're all on record.

. . . .

LBJ: I don't know what the delegates think about your doing that before they even get to the convention. They feel like they're kind of left out if you don't counsel with them.

[1] Robert Kennedy.
[2] For Vice President.

· · · ·

LBJ: If I don't hear from him by noon today I will think—

BUNDY: Something's cooking?

LBJ: They're putting out stories. I guess you saw the Evans and Novak story this morning.[1]

BUNDY: I did.

LBJ: Now that's disloyalty, Mac. . . . We're far ahead of where Kennedy was at this time. . . . I thought I'd wait until noon and if I didn't hear by noon, I'd say[2] . . . "It's all over the place and if you're not going to do it, why, I'm going to *have* to." . . . Do you have the feeling . . . that he wants me to say that I'm not gonna give it to him?

BUNDY: That was what he said yesterday. . . . He said, "I don't want my people who have been urging me to say that . . . I've changed my mind." I didn't say to him then—because he was in an edgy mood—that that's nonsense.

KENNETH O'DONNELL
Afternoon, Exact Time Unknown

>   AT JOHNSON'S BEHEST, O'Donnell has broached the subject of an announcement with the Attorney General.

LBJ: What was his reaction?

O'DONNELL: Whatever you want to do is all right with him. . . .

LBJ: Does he prefer that I announce it instead of him?

O'DONNELL: I think he does, Mr. President. He just sort of feels that it's rather arrogant of him to announce that he's decided not to allow himself to be a candidate. Whatever you want to do is fine with him and he will acknowledge it to be factual.

LBJ: [exhales] All right. . . . I dodged it all morning.[3] . . . I might be able to . . . let George Reedy say that the President . . . has reached one conclusion—that he's not going to . . . ask the convention to take any of his Cabinet members and put 'em on the ticket. Or anybody in the executive branch. That might include Shriver and McNamara and Stevenson and Kennedy.

O'DONNELL: I think that'd be good.

LBJ: . . . Then it would leave open the Senators and the Governors.

[1] Reporting that unlike the Kennedy organization four years ago, planning for Johnson's campaign "does not extend one minute beyond the convention at Atlantic City."
[2] To Robert Kennedy.
[3] At an Oval Office press conference at 12:05 P.M.

ROBERT McNAMARA
5:34 P.M.

JOHNSON HAS DECIDED to announce that he would not choose for Vice President "any member of the Cabinet or any of those who meet regularly with the Cabinet"[1]—specifically mentioning Rusk, McNamara, Kennedy, Secretary of Agriculture Orville Freeman, Adlai Stevenson, and Sargent Shriver. Before reading his statement for television cameras in the Fish Room at 6:00 P.M., he calls one of the victims.

LBJ: Bob, I hate to take the vice presidency away from you right after you're nominated, but I want to read you a statement.
McNAMARA: [laughs] I never had it!
LBJ: You did, as far as I'm concerned.

. . . .

LBJ: My thought was if we put Rusk and Stevenson and you in there, it was easier on Shriver and no family trouble. . . .
McNAMARA: I think it's an excellent approach. Very good indeed.
LBJ: While I'm thinking about naming him, I'm gonna try to get ahold of Rusk. [both laugh][2]

DEAN RUSK
5:42 P.M.

LBJ: I've gotta eliminate you from the Vice President's race. Do you care?
RUSK: Not at all. [both laugh] I eliminated myself.
LBJ: I saw that on Sunday.[3]

. . . .

LBJ: There have been stories this morning that Teddy wanted him[4] and Miz Kennedy was going to the convention . . . and that this means a war, and so I think I may as well lay it down right now.

JAMES ROWE
5:56 P.M.

FOUR MINUTES BEFORE his announcement, Johnson calls Hubert Humphrey's partisan and intimate Jim Rowe. In a message intended to unmistakably show Rowe and Humphrey which way he is turning, LBJ asks for a commitment that, if selected, Humphrey will be a loyal Vice President.

[1] The solution had been invented by Clark Clifford.
[2] They laugh because there has been no serious movement for Rusk, who is being used, like the others, as transparent camouflage for RFK's ouster.
[3] Appearing on ABC's *Issues and Answers* on July 26, Rusk had said that he had "absolutely no personal plans ever" to run for office.
[4] Robert Kennedy, to seek the vice presidency.

LBJ: Now, listen, we've got to decide between a good many people yet, but I want you to have a good set-to with this good man from Minnesota. . . . I want to be sure that they understand that ain't gonna be nobody running against me for eight years and gonna be following my platform and gonna be supporting me and gonna be as loyal to me, like I was to Kennedy.[1]

ROWE: I don't think you'd have a bit of problem on Hubert.

LBJ: I want him to understand it though. I want you to get it. . . . Just tell him that we're gonna be doing some exploring with other people. . . . That I told you to go on and get a couple of leaks about his strength, but that doesn't mean a commitment and it doesn't mean I'm a double-crosser if it doesn't come through that way, although you know that I'm very friendly. I didn't like that story in Drew Pearson the other day about what happened at my breakfast table about the Power Commission.[2] . . . He oughtn't to have done it.

· · · ·

LBJ: I just want you to say that Kennedy[3] sat down with me and said, "Now is there anything that'll keep you from being loyal to me as long as I'm in that office or running for it?" And that meant no campaigning against him and no disagreeing with him publicly and no . . . going off and growling, like Chester Bowles did on the Bay of Pigs.[4]

ROWE: And you wouldn't want any Jack Garners either.[5]

LBJ: That's right. Just say that he'd better make up his mind now whether he's ready to go way with me all the way on my platform, on my views, on my policies. Now I'm willing to always listen to him and always willing to consider what he's got to say. But when I make up my mind, I don't want to have to kiss the ass of a Vice President.

ROWE: That's right.

LBJ: Just see if he wants to be considered under those circumstances. Tell him that Kennedy sat down and had a cold one with me. He said, "Now I want you to understand. I know you don't believe in a lot of this integration in this platform.[6] But you've got to go with it whole hog or I don't want you to go." And I want him to know that if he goes, the first thing he'd better do is try to put a stop to this hell-raising so we don't throw out fifteen states. That'll defeat us.[7]

ROWE: You're damn right.

[1] President Kennedy.
[2] Pearson reported that Humphrey had complained to LBJ at a Democratic leadership breakfast that his Federal Power Commission had "too many oil and gas men" on it, and that Humphrey had proposed "a consumer's man" instead (Washington Post, July 27, 1964).
[3] John Kennedy, at the moment he chose LBJ for Vice President in 1960.
[4] After the Bay of Pigs failure in April 1961, Undersecretary of State Chester Bowles had leaked all over Washington that he had been against the idea.
[5] John Nance Garner was notoriously disloyal to Franklin Roosevelt, under whom he served for two terms as Vice President.
[6] This statement shows how far LBJ had come, at least publicly, on civil rights since July 1960.
[7] Johnson means the Mississippi Freedom Democratic Party's efforts to join the convention. In the context of this conversation, he is essentially establishing Humphrey's success in solving the problem as a test of whether or not he should get to be Vice President.

LBJ: He'd better get his Reuthers and the rest of 'em in here—and Joe Rauhs —and make 'em behave.[1] That's the first thing. But I got to see that he's loyal. I've got to be sure he's for me. I got to be sure he won't be running against me four years from now.

ROWE: You haven't any reason to think any of that now, have you?

LBJ: Except he sits there and then goes off and talks about how he tried to get a consumer man and I was playing with oil and gas people. That's not very complimentary.

ROWE: No, it ain't.

. . . .

LBJ: I'd just pick up the phone and call him and tell him you want him to come by and have a drink with you, that you have something important. There's an important announcement coming out and you've underwritten it[2] and you just want to be sure you're right. That you said, "He'll be loyal. He'll never run against you. He'll always support you. He'll take your platform. He'll be *your man*." And if he don't want to be my wife, he oughtn't to marry me.

RICHARD RUSSELL
6:10 P.M.

JOHNSON HAS JUST announced that no one in the Cabinet will be his Vice President.

RUSSELL: That'll eliminate a whole lot of 'em.

LBJ: [chuckles gleefully] I just had to eliminate one.

. . . .

RUSSELL: I think it's wise to get it out of the way now.

HUBERT HUMPHREY
6:46 P.M.

HUMPHREY: Now, Mr. President, I have a friend of yours in my office here by the name of Jim Rowe.

LBJ: [chuckles] Yes, sir.

HUMPHREY: He brought me over a little message that you sent along.

LBJ: Yeah.

HUMPHREY: And I want to come right to the point with you. If your judgment leads you to select me, I can assure you—unqualifiedly, personally, and with all the sincerity in my heart—complete loyalty.

[1] Actually, although Walter Reuther, United Auto Workers president, and Joseph Rauh, the Washington labor lawyer, were both great civil rights champions, only Rauh was directly involved in the Mississippi rebellion.
[2] Meaning that Rowe has vouched for Humphrey's selection.

LBJ: [speaking in murmur:] Yeah, I know that.

HUMPHREY: I just want you to know it.

LBJ: I know that.

HUMPHREY: And that goes for everything. All the way. The way you want it. Right to the end of the line.[1]

LBJ: Fine. Well—

HUMPHREY: I know these are difficult days for you and as I said before, I don't want to cause you any trouble.

LBJ: I know you don't.

. . . .

HUMPHREY: Have you seen that AP poll yet coming out tomorrow morning?

LBJ: No.

HUMPHREY: . . . Of the delegates they were able to get information on, it has Humphrey 341, Kennedy 230, Shriver 63, McCarthy 50, Brown[2] 35, Stevenson 27, McNamara 26. . . .

LBJ: That's good. Okay. He'll[3] talk to you about all of our problems and we'll have a good many, but we'll be talking in the days ahead. Bye.[4]

McGEORGE BUNDY
7:10 P.M.

BUNDY: What a day! [laughs] That was great. That[5] was a very, very smart formula. . . .

LBJ: . . . There were some upset people. Even Freeman was really upset.

BUNDY: I don't believe it.[6]

LBJ: Yeah, Walter Jenkins got right disturbed talking to him. And Shriver.

ROBERT ANDERSON
8:50 P.M.

> JOHNSON TOUCHES BASE with Eisenhower's last Treasury Secretary and close friend, who, in the wake of Goldwater's nomination, is corraling Republican businessmen for LBJ.

[1] In 1968, as Vice President and Democratic presidential nominee, Humphrey showed how seriously he took this private pledge of loyalty. By refusing to come out dramatically against LBJ's Vietnam policies, he probably cost himself the presidency.

[2] Governor Pat Brown of California.

[3] Rowe.

[4] Johnson truncates the conversation, almost as if he does not want to suggest that he is making an irrevocable commitment to Humphrey.

[5] Johnson's exclusion of the Cabinet from the vice presidency.

[6] Like Rusk, Secretary of Agriculture Orville Freeman was not widely thought to be a serious possibility.

LBJ: Stevenson and Shriver were upset. McNamara was pleased. He never did want to be considered. He's the best man available. . . . Bobby's out with Doug Dillon[1] tonight. I wonder why they're so close. . . . I think his strategy now is going to be—I don't believe he'll take this to the convention, but I think he'll sulk and sic 'em and hope that we are defeated and maybe contribute a little bit without getting caught, so we don't have the machinery. . . . I've got the Negroes now where they agree to behave themselves for a while, if he doesn't incite 'em and get 'em stirred up again.

ANDERSON: He'll try.

LBJ: Yeah, I think that's right.

FRIDAY, JULY 31, 1964

LAWRENCE O'BRIEN
6:10 P.M.

O'BRIEN: Didn't Sarge[2] feel that if it wasn't Bobby, it would be embarrassing for him to have it?

LBJ: Just the opposite.

O'BRIEN: You're kidding.

LBJ: Ken[3] heard him in here yesterday. He said that my information that Bobby wouldn't be strong for him if he didn't get it was completely in error—and that *he* ought to be it if Bobby wasn't.

O'BRIEN: I think that's the one ingredient, frankly, I've been lacking in my life —gall! [both laugh]

LBJ: Now they're all writing, Larry. I don't know how to stop these Rowland Evanses and Krafts.[4] I'm entitled to some loyalty . . . I don't want to start slashing and being wild . . . but . . . they[5] ought to accept the fact after nine months and give me the loyalty that I gave Kennedy.

• • • •

LBJ: If I'd give a little encouragement, I could start a real good brawl between columnists because there are a good many papers that are friendly to me.

[1] Secretary of the Treasury.
[2] Shriver.
[3] O'Donnell.
[4] Referring to columnist Joseph Kraft. Evans, Kraft, and other columnists close to RFK had been lamenting Johnson's decision.
[5] The Kennedy holdovers on the White House staff.

BILL MOYERS
8:02 P.M.

MOYERS: Mary McGrory[1] . . . is very much against it.[2] . . .

LBJ: . . . Wanted him named, Mary did?

MOYERS: Yes, sir. For almost the same reason that Kraft gave—that the young people have nowhere to go now. . . . She was almost in tears.

LBJ: I don't know why the younger generation can't come to *me* and to Humphrey as well as to him. He's been here ever since Joe McCarthy's days.[3] And the polls show that I'm higher with the young people than I am with any other age group.

.   .   .   .

MOYERS: Mary McGrory said he was very, very upset about the possibility of McCarthy.[4] . . . He said he would be very hurt if McCarthy were on the ticket.

LBJ: Why?

MOYERS: Because he's a Catholic. She said Bobby said, "If he wants a Catholic, he ought to take the number one Catholic in the country."

LBJ: [irritated:] Well, who in the hell gives *him* the right to appoint himself number one Catholic? . . . This guy's never done anything but cause all this backlash.[5] That's the only thing he's got to his credit.

.   .   .   .

LBJ: [on the troubled anti-poverty bill:] I think if you don't give twenty-four hours a day this time—and you don't get Shriver to do it—I think it's terrible for him to run off to Hyannis Port—but if you don't do it, both of you are gonna . . . destroy me. I think if we get beat on it, we've had it.

DOUGLASS CATER
Special Assistant to the President
8:47 P.M.

LBJ: I don't know of any finer, better way than to call 'em in and talk to 'em as I did. Let 'em hear it from my lips and say, "Now I like you, Cabinet, and that's not a second-rate position in this country. There's only ten men out of 190 million. And when the hell did you get the idea that the Vice President's going to be more than that? Who thought I was gonna die so quick? All of you were laughing about it . . . ten months ago, saying, 'What happened to Lyndon

---

[1] Of the *Washington Star*, who had seen RFK the previous evening.
[2] Kennedy's exclusion from the Vice Presidency.
[3] LBJ likes to connect RFK and Joseph McCarthy, for whom Kennedy worked in the early 1950s.
[4] Eugene McCarthy.
[5] LBJ is indulging his view that RFK is stirring up the Mississippi Freedom Democratic Party and other pro-black forces in order to generate white backlash that will smite Johnson in the fall.

Johnson?' And John Adams said so-and-so."[1] Now . . . here we got the problems
. . . that Bobby got us into. He's got 'em in Harlem and Rochester and Jackson
and Philadelphia, Mississippi . . . and Georgia. Hell, that's what he ought to be
doing instead of running around trying to drum up pressures to put on a poor
President to be Vice President. So I just thought I'd put a stop to it. So what's
wrong with that?

. . . .

LBJ: They say this is a convenient way of dumping Bobby. Well, we wanted to
dump the whole outfit and get 'em back to work!

JAMES ROWE
10:30 P.M.

TOLD THAT ROBERT KENNEDY has called a group of his political advisers to
Hyannis Port, an anxious Johnson worries that RFK will now wage an insur-
gent campaign for Vice President or even President.

LBJ: Are you where you can talk?
ROWE: Yes sir.
LBJ: Where did you hear about this meeting this weekend? . . . I understand
it's Hyannis Port.

. . . .

LBJ: I think we ought to watch that just like hawks. . . . They've got a bunch of
planted wires coming in now from three or four states.[2] And I think he's acting
very, very ugly and very mean. Because I told him to announce it any way he
wanted to. And then he ran off and sulked and never came back and hasn't
showed up.

. . . .

LBJ: What reaction did you get adversely to our announcement yesterday?
ROWE: None at all. Except the only reaction—you can't call this adverse—
was that your motivation was clear. You were just getting rid of Bobby.
LBJ: . . . Well, I was trying to stop Freeman from campaigning all over Kansas
and Iowa for Vice President. I was trying to stop people from saying that McNamara—every time I had him before a business group, with the Cabinet—that he
was doing it. I was trying to stop them from involving Rusk. Had him on TV
Sunday and raising hell with him. I was trying to stop Stevenson and those clubs
that were forming up in New Jersey.

[1] Adams called the vice presidency "the most insignificant office that ever the invention of
man contrived."
[2] At Johnson's request, Jenkins had asked DeLoach of the FBI to analyze the telegrams
received at the White House complaining about RFK's ouster: "He wants to know if you think
they're the real thing, or just something Bobby's people cooked up." DeLoach complied and
ruled them "a campaign orchestrated by some of Bobby's old supporters" (Cartha DeLoach,
Hoover's FBI, p. 383).

• • • •

LBJ: I thought we ought to take all of them at once and not leave the impression. . . . Rayburn told me in '40, "Roosevelt never has told me not to and it is all right."[1] And he had Rayburn and Jesse Jones[2] and everybody in the world running for Vice President . . . So I thought . . . if I don't say anything, they'll just keep on. They all think I'm encouraging them because they come in and I smile and treat 'em nice. So my judgment was that I ought to stop the whole goddamned thing so people wouldn't say that everybody in the Cabinet is running for Vice President and the government couldn't operate.

[1] At the 1940 Democratic convention in Chicago, LBJ had supported Speaker Rayburn's campaign to be FDR's Vice President. Roosevelt's method was to encourage dozens of Democrats to enter the race so that the field would be so divided that it would be easier to dictate his own choice.

[2] Of Houston, FDR's Secretary of Commerce from 1940 to 1945.

Chapter Ten
AUGUST 1964

SATURDAY, AUGUST 1, 1964

ROBERT McNAMARA
9:00 A.M.

LBJ: I've overloaded you now and I don't want you to have a breakdown. But I want you to think, with this administration coming up,[1] what you can do as my executive vice president to help me direct this Cabinet.

McNAMARA: Well, you're nice.

LBJ: No. . . . I need to issue instructions and see that they're carried out. . . . I told that Cabinet I didn't want them to get personal with Goldwater, didn't I?

McNAMARA: Yeah, absolutely.

LBJ: Now I've had two of them attack him this week.

• • • •

LBJ: Come in here now and be my number one executive. . . . Let's put this Cabinet to work on . . . what we want the next four years—what kind of administration it should be.

McNAMARA: [interpreting what he hears:] How do you get this Great Society?

• • • •

McNAMARA: Mr. President . . . I don't think it can be done by a Cabinet officer. I think it could be done by your Vice President. . . . But let me think about it and I'll have some ideas for you.

LBJ: . . . You just find out how to do it . . . if you have to covertly do it.

[1] The presidential term beginning in January 1965.

LAWRENCE O'BRIEN
5:42 P.M.

LBJ: [angry:] I'm getting a barrage of unnecessary heckling and harassing today from Hyannis Port—"Attorney General Kennedy received a barrage of . . . messages from supporters angered at the manner . . . in which the President eliminated him as a Democratic candidate." . . . Now will you talk to Ken[1] about that? Because . . . if they just keep on, I'm going to sock him[2] right in the puss, and I don't want to do that.

MONDAY, AUGUST 3, 1964

ROBERT ANDERSON
9:46 A.M.

THE PREVIOUS DAY, at 3:40 A.M. Washington time, the U.S. destroyer *Maddox*, on reconnaissance patrol, was attacked in the Gulf of Tonkin by North Vietnamese torpedo boats. The *Maddox*, joined by aircraft from the nearby aircraft carrier *Ticonderoga*, damaged two of the boats and left the third dead in the water. Concerned that the assault might have been a local commander's caprice,[3] suspecting that it was in response to United States–backed covert operations, Johnson did not retaliate. Instead he protested the attack to Hanoi. The *Maddox* and the destroyer *C. Turner Joy* were ordered to assert the right of freedom of the seas.[4] As this morning's papers reported, Secretary of State Dean Rusk downplayed the incident: "The other side got a sting out of this. If they do it again, they'll get another sting." During a conversation about which corporation leaders might be willing to support Johnson's election campaign, the President relates what happened.

LBJ: There have been some covert operations in that area that we have been carrying on[5]—blowing up some bridges and things of that kind, roads and so forth. So I imagine they wanted to put a stop to it. So they . . . fired and we respond immediately with five-inch [artillery shells] from the destroyer and with planes overhead. And we . . . knock one of 'em out and cripple the other two.

[1] O'Donnell.
[2] Robert Kennedy.
[3] General Nguyen Dinh Voc, director of the Institute of Military History in Hanoi, affirmed in 1997 that the assault was a local commander's initiative (*New York Times Magazine*, August 10, 1997).
[4] Ambassador Maxwell Taylor complained from Saigon that failure to respond to an unprovoked attack on a U.S. destroyer in international waters would be taken as a sign "that the U.S. flinches from direct confrontation with the North Vietnamese" (Taylor to Rusk, August 3, 1964, in *FRUS*, pp. 593–94).
[5] Johnson refers to Op Plan 34-A, the covert action program against North Vietnam he had approved at the start of 1964. On Thursday night, July 30, under 34-A, South Vietnamese patrol boats had shelled two North Vietnamese islands in the Gulf of Tonkin that were suspected to be bases for infiltration of the South.

Then we go right back where we were with that destroyer and with another one, plus plenty of planes standing by. . . .

ANDERSON: . . . You're going to be running against a man who's a wild man on this subject.[1] Any lack of firmness he'll make up. . . . You've got to do what's right for the country. . . . But whatever you can do to say, when they shoot at us from the back, we're not soft . . . we're going to protect ourselves, we'll protect our boys . . . I think it's all to the good.[2]

LBJ: Didn't it leave that impression yesterday?

ANDERSON: . . . I think a little emphasis on it would be worthwhile. . . . Don't take my advice on this, because I don't know a damned thing about what happened.

LBJ: What happened was we've been playing around up there[3] and they came out, gave us a warning, and we knocked hell out of 'em.

ANDERSON: That's the best thing in the world you could have done—just knock hell out of 'em.

LBJ: And we've got our people right there and we haven't pulled out. We've pulled *up*.

ANDERSON: . . . I haven't heard any adverse criticism from anybody. But I just know that this fellow's[4] going to play all of the angles.

ROBERT McNAMARA
10:20 A.M.

LBJ: I wonder if you don't think if it'd be wise for you and Rusk to get the Speaker and Mansfield[5] to call a group of fifteen or twenty people together from the Armed Services, Foreign Relations.[6] Tell 'em what happened. . . .

McNAMARA: Right. I've been thinking about this myself.

LBJ: They're gonna start an investigation if you don't. . . . You say, "They fired at us, we responded immediately and we took out one of their boats and put the other two running and we're putting out boats right there and we're not running 'em in."

McNAMARA: . . . We should also at that time, Mr. President, explain this Op

[1] In his San Francisco acceptance speech, Goldwater had complained that "failures infest the jungles of Vietnam. . . . Don't try to sweep this under the rug. We are at war in Vietnam. And yet the President . . . refuses to say . . . whether or not the objective over there is victory, and his Secretary of Defense continues to mislead and misinform the American people. . . . I needn't remind you, but I will, it has been during Democratic years that a billion persons were cast into Communist captivity and their fates cynically sealed."
[2] Johnson was especially affected by what Anderson said because he thought of him as, to some extent, the voice of Eisenhower. (See conversation with Anderson of June 2, 1964, above.) Anderson's suggestion may have shown Johnson what kind of criticism he could expect from even moderate Republicans (whose votes he hoped to win in November) if he did not demonstrate greater toughness at the Gulf of Tonkin.
[3] This refers to Op Plan 34-A and Operation DeSoto reconnaissance patrol vessels, which were collecting radio and radar signals from North Vietnam and China.
[4] Goldwater.
[5] The Senate Majority Leader.
[6] Committees of the House and Senate, in a closed-door session.

Plan 34-A, these covert operations. There's no question that that had bearing on it. On Friday night, as you probably know, we had four PT boats from Vietnam manned by Vietnamese or other nationals attack two islands. . . . Following twenty-four hours after that, with this destroyer[1] in that same area—undoubtedly led them[2] to connect the two events.

LBJ: Say that to Dirksen. You notice Dirksen says this morning that "we got to reassess our situation—do something about it."[3] I'd tell him that we're doing what he's talking about.

McNAMARA: . . . You want us to do it at the White House or would you rather do it at State or Defense?

LBJ: I believe it'd be better to do it up on the Hill. . . . I'd tell 'em awfully quiet though so they won't go in and be making a bunch of speeches.

· · · ·

LBJ: Now I wish that you'd give me some guidance on what we ought to say. I want to leave an impression on background . . . that we're gonna be firm as hell without saying something that's dangerous. . . . The people that're calling me up . . . all feel that the Navy responded wonderfully. And that's good. But they want to be damned sure I don't pull 'em out and run. . . . That's what all the country wants because Goldwater is raising so much hell about how he's gonna blow 'em off the moon. And they say that we oughtn't to do anything that the national interest doesn't require, but we sure ought to always leave the impression that if you shoot at us, you're gonna get hit.[4]

McNAMARA: I think you would want to instruct George Reedy this morning . . . to say that you personally have ordered the Navy to carry on the routine patrols off the coast of North Vietnam, to add an additional destroyer to the one that has been carrying on the patrols, to provide an air cap, and to issue instructions to the commanders to destroy any force that attacks our force in international waters.[5]

TUESDAY, AUGUST 4, 1964

ROBERT McNAMARA
9:43 A.M.

At 9:12 A.M., the Defense Secretary called Johnson and found him at his regular Tuesday breakfast with Democratic leaders of Congress. He told the

---

[1] The *Maddox*.

[2] The North Vietnamese.

[3] Dirksen had told reporters that the attack on the *Maddox* warranted a "new hard look" at American policy in Southeast Asia: "We must lay all of the cards on the table so that the American people will be fully informed and then take action to correct the situation."

[4] Johnson shows that he has taken Anderson's advice to heart.

[5] Seventy minutes after this talk with McNamara, Johnson told the press that he had "instructed the Navy" to continue the patrols off North Vietnam, add an additional destroyer, provide a combat air patrol over the destroyers, and order commanders of the combat aircraft

President that the *Maddox* was reporting the nearby presence of hostile ships. Drawing on U.S. intercepts of North Vietnamese communications, the *Maddox* had suspected that an attack seemed imminent, then radioed that its radar had picked up unidentified vessels and aircraft. In accordance with LBJ's previously issued orders, fighter aircraft had been launched from the *Ticonderoga*. Now that the breakfast is over, Johnson has returned to the Oval Office for a more extended telephone conversation with McNamara.

McNAMARA: Mr. President, General Wheeler and I are sitting here together. We just received a cable from Admiral Sharp.[1] . . . I have discussed this with Dean Rusk and he and I are in agreement. . . . Sharp recommends first that the track of the destroyer be shifted from eleven miles offshore to eight miles offshore. This makes no sense to us. . . . His purpose by shifting the track is simply to make clearer that we believe the twelve-mile limit is not an effective limit on us. . . . Secondly Sharp recommends that we authorize the—

LBJ: What reason does he give for his eight?

McNAMARA: Simply that it more clearly indicates our refusal to accept a twelve-mile restriction. We think we've clearly indicated our refusal to accept a twelve-mile restriction with the eleven-mile limit. . . .

LBJ: What other objections do you have?

McNAMARA: It changes a program that shouldn't be changed frequently. . . . This ship that's allegedly to be attacked tonight[2]—we don't like to see a change in operation plan of this kind at this time. . . . Certainly no military purpose is served by it.

LBJ: All right.

. . . .

McNAMARA: Secondly, he recommends that the task force commander be authorized to pursue any attacker and destroy the base of the attacker. In this instance, if he were attacked by patrol boats, it would mean that he would pursue the patrol craft into the shoreline, identify the base of the patrol craft, and destroy that base. Now this is an action that we might well wish to consider after the second attack, but I think it would be inappropriate . . . to provide the task force commander that authority. . . .

LBJ: What objections do you have to pursuing it?

McNAMARA: Only the objection that if we give such authority, you have in a sense lost control of the degree of our response to the North Vietnamese. . . . I personally would recommend to you, after a second attack on our ships, that we do retaliate against the coast of North Vietnam some way or other. And we'll be prepared.

LBJ: What I was thinking about when I was eating breakfast, but I couldn't talk it—I was thinking that it looks to me like the weakness of our position is that we respond only to an action and we don't have any of our own, but when they

---

and the two destroyers to "attack any force which attacks them in international waters" with the objective "not only of driving off the force but destroying it" (*FRUS*, p. 597).
  [1] Ulysses S. Grant Sharp, Jr., was American commander for the Pacific.
  [2] "Tonight" refers to local time in the Gulf of Tonkin.

move on us, and they shoot at us.[1] I think that we not only ought to shoot at them, but almost simultaneously pull one of these things that you've been doing —on one of their bridges, or something.

McNAMARA: Exactly. I quite agree with you, Mr. President. And I'm not sure that the response ought to be as Admiral Sharp suggests.

LBJ: I'm not either. . . . Unless I knew what base it was. . . . But I wish we could have something that we've already picked out and just hit about three of them damn quick and go right after them.

McNAMARA: We will have that. And I talked to Mac Bundy a moment ago and told him . . . we should . . . be prepared to recommend to you a response—a retaliation move against North Vietnam—in the event this attack takes place within the next six to nine hours.

LBJ: All right now. We better do that at lunch.[2] There's some things I don't want to go in with these other—I want to keep this close as I can. So let's just try to keep it to the two of us.

McNAMARA: I will be prepared to do so at lunch. . . . Now, thirdly, Sharp recommends that the task force commander be authorized to engage in hot pursuit beyond the eleven-mile limit. . . . At present, the instructions to the commander are—do not pursue an attacker closer to shore than eleven miles. . . . Dean[3] . . . agrees, as far as air pursuit is concerned. Pursue by air as close as three miles to shore. Do not pursue by sea closer than eleven miles. His reason for differentiating sea from air is that we can always argue that the air was further out than three miles and he's concerned about taking the ships in as close as three miles to shore. I'm willing to accept his point for a different reason however. . . . Our ships travel at about twenty-seven knots and these patrol boats travel at fifty knots, and the possibility of a ship being effective in that eleven- to three-mile area is not very great. The airpower is likely the most effective power anyhow. And I would therefore recommend that we accept Sharp's recommendation. But limit it to air.

LBJ: All right, okay.

ROBERT McNAMARA

10:53 A.M.

McNAMARA: Mr. President, we just had a report from the commander of that task force out there that they have sighted two unidentified vessels and three unidentified prop aircraft. And therefore the carrier launched two F-8s and two A-4Ds, and four A-1s.

LBJ: Go back over those again. What did we launch?

---

[1] With the criticism of such moderate Republicans as Anderson and Dirksen still ringing in his ears, Johnson is still worried about looking too soft on the Tonkin Gulf.

[2] Rusk, McNamara, CIA Director McCone, and Bundy were to lunch with Johnson after a noon meeting of the National Security Council.

[3] Rusk.

McNAMARA: We launched two F-8 fighter aircraft, two A-4Ds, which are jet attack aircraft, and four A-1Hs, which are prop-driven aircraft. So we have launched eight aircraft from the carrier to examine what is in the vicinity of the destroyers and to protect the destroyers. The report is that they have observed—and we don't know by what means. . . . I suspect this is radar—two unidentified vessels and three unidentified prop aircraft in the vicinity of the destroyers.

LBJ: Now what else do *we* have out there?

McNAMARA: We have only the *Ticonderoga*, with its aircraft and a protective destroyer screen. I think that there are three destroyers with the *Ticonderoga*. We have the *Constellation*[1] . . . which I sent orders to about an hour or two ago to move down towards South Vietnam. . . . We have ample forces to respond not only to these attacks on the destroyers but also to retaliate, should you wish to do so, against targets on the land. And when I come over at noontime I'll bring you a list. . . . There is a petroleum system that is concentrated. Seventy percent of the petroleum supply in North Vietnam, we believe, is concentrated in three dumps. And we can bomb or strafe those dumps and destroy their petroleum system. . . . In addition, there are certain prestige targets. . . . For example, there is one bridge that is the key bridge on the rail line south out of Hanoi and we could destroy that. . . .

LBJ: All right, good.

ROBERT McNAMARA
11:06 A.M.

McNAMARA: Mr. President, we just had word by telephone from Admiral Sharp that the destroyer is under torpedo attack.[2]

LBJ: [almost inaudible sound]

McNAMARA: I think I might get Dean Rusk and Mac Bundy and have them come over here and we'll go over these retaliatory actions and then we ought to—

LBJ: I sure think you ought to agree to that. Yeah. . . . Now where are these torpedoes coming from?

McNAMARA: We don't know. Presumably from these unidentified craft that I mentioned to you a moment ago. We thought that the unidentified craft might include one PT boat, which has torpedo capability, and two Swatow boats, which we don't credit with torpedo capability, although they may have it.

LBJ: What are these planes of ours doing around while they're being attacked?

McNAMARA: Presumably the planes are attacking the ships. We don't have any word from Sharp on that. The planes would be in the area at the present time. All eight of them.

LBJ: Okay, you get them over there and then you come over here.

[1] An aircraft carrier.
[2] McNamara wrote in his 1995 memoirs, "Did a second attack actually occur? . . . Visibility in the area at the time of the alleged attack was very limited. Because of that and because sonar soundings—which are often unreliable—accounted for most reports of the second attack,

JAMES ROWE
1:35 P.M.

IN THE MIDST of the new crisis over the Gulf of Tonkin, Johnson complains to Humphrey's partisan that the Minnesota Senator's garrulousness is endangering national security. His message is that if Humphrey does not stop it, he will not be Vice President.

LBJ: Our friend Hubert is just destroying himself with his big mouth.

ROWE: Is he talking again?

LBJ: Yeah, all the time. And you just can't stop it. . . . Every responsible person gets frightened when they see him. . . . Yesterday morning, he went on TV and . . . just blabbed everything that he had heard in a briefing.[1] . . . They said . . . "How would you account for these PT boat attacks on our destroyers when we are innocently out there in a gulf, sixty miles from shore?" . . . Humphrey said, "Well, we have been carrying on some operations in that area . . . where we have been going in and knocking out roads and petroleum things." And that is exactly what we *have* been doing![2]

ROWE: Good Lord!

LBJ: The damned fool . . . just ought to keep his goddamned big mouth shut on foreign affairs, at least until the election is over. . . . They don't *pay* him to do this. This is just not like he's getting a fee to speak to the *druggists.*[3] He is just doing this *free* and he's hurting his government. And he's hurting *us!*

· · · ·

LBJ: This by no way . . . a commitment . . . because I want to have lots of talks before *I* ever agree on who *I'm* going to recommend.[4] But . . . he ought to . . . pretty well stay out of the delicate, technical field of . . . what the Communists are thinking. . . . He just yak-yak-yak-yak. Just dancing around with the bald head. . . . That can ruin a man mighty quick.

ROBERT McNAMARA
5:09 P.M.

AS HE HAD SUGGESTED TO McNAMARA,[5] Johnson was too nervous about leaks and the ramifications of the Gulf of Tonkin events to allow a freewheeling

---

uncertainty remained about whether it had occurred" (*In Retrospect,* p. 133). In November 1995, when McNamara visited Hanoi, General Vo Nguyen Giap, who was North Vietnamese Vice Premier for Defense in 1964, convinced him that no second attack had ever occurred (*Washington Post,* November 11, 1995).

[1] On the August 2 actions in the Tonkin Gulf.

[2] Johnson refers to Op Plan 34-A.

[3] Johnson refers to the fact that in those days, Senators could speak to business groups for large honoraria. He might, perhaps subconsciously, also be alluding to the fact that Humphrey's South Dakota father was a druggist.

[4] As Vice President.

[5] See their 9:43 A.M. conversation, above.

discussion at the noon National Security Council meeting.[1] It was during a small luncheon afterward that Johnson told Rusk and McNamara that he agreed that a "firm, retaliatory strike" must be carried out.[2] They agreed on a plan that would strike North Vietnamese bases and the North Vietnamese oil depot at Vinh. But evidence that there had actually been an attack on the *Maddox* and *C. Turner Joy* remained cloudy.

At 4:47 P.M., McNamara and his deputy, Cyrus Vance, met with the Joint Chiefs "to marshal the evidence to overcome lack of a clear and convincing showing that an attack on the destroyers had in fact occurred."[3] During the discussion, McNamara discovered that someone—probably someone who knew of the meeting called by LBJ with congressional leaders for that evening—had leaked to the press that there has been a new attack in the Gulf of Tonkin. With the cat out of the bag, it would be very difficult for the administration now, should it be so inclined, to take the public position that evidence for the second attack was ambiguous or to withhold the proposed retaliation against North Vietnam without subjecting LBJ to election-year charges of cover-up and cowardice.[4]

McNAMARA: Mr. President, the story has broken on the AP and the UP.

LBJ: Yeah, I see it.[5]

McNAMARA: ... Anyway, it's broken. It seems to me ... we ... ought to agree now on a statement that could be made by one of the departments—I presume the Pentagon. ... The statement that we would make ... would simply say, that "during the night ... the two destroyers were attacked by the patrol boats. The attack was driven off. No casualties or damage to the destroyers. We believe several of the patrol boats were sunk. Details won't be available till daylight."

LBJ: That's okay. I'd just go on and put that out.

McNAMARA: All right. I'll take care of it.

LBJ: Anything else?

McNAMARA: No, I talked to Dillon.[6] And he fully agrees with the action. I

[1] Perhaps because Robert Kennedy was present.
[2] See *FRUS*, pp. 608–09.
[3] See *FRUS*, p. 609.
[4] Ultimately, the group agreed that the destroyers had been attacked, arguing that the *C. Turner Joy* had been illuminated when fired on by automatic weapons; one of the destroyers had spotted PT boat cockpit lights; anti-aircraft batteries had assaulted two American planes flying over the area; a North Vietnamese message suggesting the sinking of two boats had been intercepted; and Admiral Sharp had determined that an attack had taken place. (See *FRUS*, p. 609, and Robert McNamara, *In Retrospect*, p. 134.) Might the group's conclusion have been more tentative had their hand not been forced by the press leak?
[5] The dispatch read by Johnson said, "Congressional sources said leaders of both parties have been called at 6:45 for a White House leadership conference, presumably called to brief the lawmakers on the latest PT-boat attack."
[6] Secretary of the Treasury Douglas Dillon had complained at the noon NSC meeting, "There is a limit on the number of times we can be attacked by the North Vietnamese without hitting their naval bases" (*FRUS*, p. 608). This complaint from Dillon, another moderate Republican like Robert Anderson, coming on the heels of Anderson's insistence that LBJ not be too soft, may have nudged Johnson in the direction of toughness just before he had to decide what to do in the Tonkin Gulf. LBJ also knew that Robert Kennedy was close to Dillon and trusted him on foreign policy, so he may have taken Dillon's complaint as a sign that RFK might criticize him

couldn't get ahold of Bobby.[1] He's nowhere that he can be found. But I'll keep a call in for him.[2]

OLIN JOHNSTON

Democratic Senator from South Carolina

6:00 P.M.

JUST BEFORE LBJ joins his National Security Council to discuss the Gulf of Tonkin, he has this ironic exchange.

JOHNSTON: The newspapers called me today wanting to know if I was going to vote for you.

LBJ: [laughs]

JOHNSTON: I said yes. I'm for keeping us out of war and I'm voting for Lyndon Johnson.

LBJ: Well, I don't know whether I can do that. I'm going to do my best, Olin.

JOHNSTON: But the reason I said that—you are going to find in my state and in the South these mothers and people are *afraid* of *war*.

LBJ: They sure are.

JOHNSTON: And we got to stress that point down my way in order to get votes.

LBJ: We sure had, my friend.

CARTHA DeLOACH

8:01 P.M.

IN THE THICK of Johnson's Tonkin Gulf deliberations, the FBI's White House liaison reports that the mystery over the whereabouts of Michael Schwerner, Andrew Goodman, and James Chaney has apparently been solved.

DeLOACH: Mr. Hoover wanted me to call you, sir, immediately. . . . The FBI has found three bodies . . . southwest of Philadelphia, Mississippi—six miles west of where the civil rights workers were last seen on the night of June 21st. Our search party of agents turned up the bodies just about fifteen minutes ago. . . . We're going to get a coroner there right away, sir. . . . We have not identified them as yet as the three missing men but we have every reason to believe that they are. . . .

LBJ: When are you going to make the announcement?

---

for insufficient hawkishness. (For another example of this concern, see LBJ conversation with McGeorge Bundy of May 27, 1964, above.)

[1] Kennedy.

[2] At 5:19 P.M., the Joint Chiefs issued a message ordering execution of the attack on North Vietnam discussed by Johnson and McNamara over luncheon (*FRUS*, p. 610).

DeLOACH: Within ten minutes sir, if that is all right with you.

LBJ: . . . If you can hold it about fifteen minutes, I think we ought to notify these families.

DeLOACH: Mr. President, the only thing I'd suggest is to not . . . do that prior to the time that they're identified. . . .

LBJ: I think we could tell them that we don't know, but we found them and that kind of would ease it a little bit.[1]

LADY BIRD JOHNSON
8:35 P.M.

> AT 6:15 P.M., McNamara had told the National Security Council that North Vietnamese PT boats had "continued their attacks" on the *Maddox* and *C. Turner Joy*. Rusk added, "The unprovoked attack on the high seas is an act of war, for all practical purposes."[2] Now as Johnson prepares to announce the retaliation on television, the First Lady calls.

LBJ: Darling?

LADY BIRD: Yes, beloved.

LBJ: Did you want me?

LADY BIRD: I just wanted to see you whenever you're all alone, merely to tell you I loved you. That's all.

LBJ: I'll be over there. The Russells[3] still there?

LADY BIRD: No, they left at three-thirty this afternoon, dear.

LBJ: I'll be darned. Why didn't they tell me goodbye?

LADY BIRD: Because I guess they figured you just didn't have a moment.

LBJ: Any other news?

LADY BIRD: Nothing in comparison to yours, darling.

LBJ: I've been trying to get Senator Goldwater[4] and I'll come over just as soon as we get through.

LAWRENCE O'BRIEN
9:02 P.M.

LBJ: What effect is our asking Congress for a resolution to support us—Southeast Asia, and bombing the hell out of the Vietnamese tonight—what effect will that have on this bill?[5] Will it kill it or help us?

---

[1] Motivated by a $30,000 enticement approved by J. Edgar Hoover, two Ku Klux Klan informants had told the FBI that after the high-speed car chase Chaney, Schwerner, and Goodman had been shot to death and buried in a dam. The bodies were identified soon after this call.

[2] Robert Kennedy was absent. (See *FRUS*, pp. 611–12.)

[3] Senator Russell's nephew Bobby and his wife had been Johnson houseguests.

[4] Johnson was calling his opponent, who was yachting off California, to tell him in advance about his television broadcast.

[5] The poverty bill, which hangs in the balance in Congress.

O'BRIEN: It won't hurt us, but I just don't know whether it will help or not.

LBJ: I'd think they'd be a little more reluctant to vote against the President.

O'BRIEN: . . . It certainly is not going to hurt us.

LBJ: They ought not to be personally antagonistic too much.[1]

ROBERT McNAMARA
9:15 P.M.

McNAMARA: I just talked to Admiral Sharp again. He's been in contact with the carriers. . . . They won't launch for . . . about forty-five minutes. . . . I have this suggestion. . . . That you make your statement at approximately ten P.M. And that you leave out . . . the sentence . . . "Air action is now in execution against gunboats and supporting facilities in and near . . . North Vietnam." Without that sentence you don't disclose the targets, but you do disclose that action is presently under way.

. . . .

LBJ: What's delayed it[2] so?

McNAMARA: . . . They had to brief the crews and load the aircraft with specific types of weapons for these particular targets. . . .

LBJ: Now when they leave the carrier at ten, how long does it take them to get over the target?

McNAMARA: The last time over the target will be . . . about twelve o'clock, our time.

LBJ: Do we want to give them two hours' notice?

McNAMARA: I don't believe there's any reason not to, Mr. President. . . .

LBJ: Better check that, Bob.

. . . .

McNAMARA: They'll get the statement simultaneously, but they won't know what targets are being attacked.

LBJ: . . . I'd sure as hell hate to have some mother say, "You announced it and my boy got killed."

McNAMARA: I don't think there is much danger of that, Mr. President. How late would you be willing to hold the statement?

LBJ: I guess we could hold it until the eleven o'clock news. I don't know. We don't have to make it, do we?

McNAMARA: Oh, I think you need to make some kind of statement of this kind. . . . Something will have to be on the news tomorrow morning and it ought to come from you.

---

[1] Eager to "utilize" the crisis "in my own way," McCormack has asked House Majority Leader Albert and House Armed Services Chairman Vinson to "circulate around the lounge and say now here you can't let the President down with his own domestic measure with this international situation" (LBJ conversation with McCormack, August 4, 1964, not included in this volume).
[2] The attack.

BARRY GOLDWATER
Republican Senator from Arizona and Presidential Nominee
10:06 P.M.

> JOHNSON READS HIS STATEMENT aloud by telephone to Goldwater, who has been reached at the Balboa Bay Club in Newport Beach, California.

LBJ: Just very confidentially, we're going to take all the boats out that we can and all the bases in which they come.

GOLDWATER: . . . I think you've taken the right steps and I'm sure you'll find that everybody will be behind you.

LBJ: I thank you . . . I didn't want to say anything until I was able to reach you.

GOLDWATER: . . . Like always, Americans will stick together.[1]

WEDNESDAY, AUGUST 5, 1964

ROBERT McNAMARA
10:52 A.M.

> JUST ARRIVED at the Syracuse, New York, airport, Johnson is about to make a speech at Syracuse University. He takes a call from the Secretary of Defense, who reports on the retaliation against North Vietnam.

McNAMARA: The reaction from North Vietnam and China is slight so far. Less than I would have anticipated.

LBJ: How many planes did you lose?

McNAMARA: We lost two aircraft. . . . And possibly a third. . . . Two other aircraft were damaged.

· · · ·

McNAMARA: The estimate is still about twenty-five patrol boats damaged or destroyed. Ninety percent destruction of the petroleum area, which had about 10 percent of the total petroleum storage capacity of the country.

---

[1] After returning to the mansion to dine with Lady Bird, Bundy, and Jack Valenti, LBJ finally gave his televised statement from the Fish Room at 11:36 P.M., saying, "We seek no wider war." Lady Bird dictated into her diary, "Hold off as long as he did, and in spite of many assurances it was now safe to speak, it later appeared that there was uncertainty as to exactly where our planes were when he went on the air. What he was playing for, as I see it, was to wait until they had dropped their bombs, were safely on the way home, and then to make the announcement before the Communists made an announcement that this was an act of aggression on the part of the United States, getting their story to the world first. It must be said that the exact location of the planes was clouded in confusion and that is one of the many frightening things about his job" (August 4, 1964). In 1995, McNamara said that had he been certain that there had been no second Tonkin Gulf attack, "we would not have carried out that military attack" on North Vietnam (*Washington Post*, November 11, 1995).

. . . .

LBJ: Many people killed?

McNAMARA: I think probably not. . . . These bases were not in populated areas. . . . I think generally all here feel it was a success.

LBJ: Okay, Bob.[1]

ROBERT McNAMARA
6:00 P.M.

> BY NOW, Johnson has returned to the Oval Office. While being photographed, one by one, with Democratic Congressmen who are running for reelection, he steps aside to take McNamara's call.

McNAMARA: You remember that . . . we authorized the vessels and our aircraft to attack any North Vietnamese patrol boats outside the three-mile limit? The Chiefs and I would like to recommend that we withdraw that authority, so that we have a clear break in our pressure on North Vietnam—in order to see how they respond. . . .

LBJ: All right. . . . Why are things so quiet?

McNAMARA: I can't understand it. This is one of the reasons we want to change this order. We want to have a clear break here and see if it still stays quiet.

. . . .

LBJ: What do you think about this Russian statement? They just put out one saying we had no business being out in those waters.[2]

McNAMARA: I don't know. I thought they all day were rather calm about this. . . . As you know, even the North Vietnamese haven't claimed those waters as territorial waters. . . .

LBJ: O-o-kay. It's about daylight now out there now, isn't it?

McNAMARA: That's right. This is one of the reasons I wanted to change these orders, so that during this day we wouldn't be running patrols all over that ocean and shooting up everything we saw.[3]

---

[1] In his address at 11:30 A.M., Johnson declared that after a first attack on the *Maddox*, "that attack was repeated in those same waters against two United States destroyers. The attacks were deliberate. The attacks were unprovoked. The attacks have been answered. . . . The government of North Vietnam is today flouting the will of the world for peace."

[2] Khrushchev had complained to Johnson by letter that putting U.S. warships in the Gulf of Tonkin at all was a "military demonstration" to strengthen the "corrupt and rotten South Vietnamese" that might risk a "serious military conflict" (*FRUS*, pp. 635–37).

[3] Lady Bird dictated into her diary for that evening, "The tension lessens a little bit. At least the day is past and there is no response from Tonkin Bay. There seems to be a feeling in this country we have stood upon our hind legs and done the right thing" (August 5, 1964).

THURSDAY, AUGUST 6, 1964

ROBERT McNAMARA
12:46 P.M.

JOHNSON IS ASKING Congress for a joint resolution of support for his action in Vietnam, pronouncing the United States "prepared, as the President determines, to take all necessary steps, including the use of force," to assist any SEATO member "requiring assistance in defense of its freedom." This morning, Rusk, McNamara, and Wheeler have testified before closed-door sessions of the Senate and House committees dealing with foreign and military affairs. Rusk told the Senators that the "North Vietnamese attacks on our naval vessels" were "no isolated event" but "part and parcel of a continuing Communist drive to conquer South Vietnam . . . and eventually dominate and conquer other free nations of Southeast Asia."

LBJ: U Thant just said to me, how in the world do you reckon these folks are sending their PT boats out to shoot at us?[1] Humphrey said,[2] "I'll tell you why—because they thought we were launching—"

McNAMARA: I had a hell of a time with Morse this morning on that exact point. I think I finally shut him up.[3] . . .

LBJ: He said that on television last night. He said we were launching our PT boats from the destroyers.

McNAMARA: Yeah, well, I just absolutely denied it and I insisted the record be made clear. I just got back from the House and Senate.

LBJ: How did you get along?

McNAMARA: Very well. I think the vote in the Senate committee, as you probably know, was 16 to 1. And the vote in the House committee was unanimous, except for 2 present.[4]

LBJ: Who were they?

McNAMARA: The Iowa Congressman, you know.

LBJ: Gross?[5]

[1] Johnson had just received the U.N. Secretary-General in the Oval Office, where they both had dietetic orange drinks.
[2] On television.
[3] During the meeting with the Senate Foreign Relations and Armed Services Committees. Senator Wayne Morse of Oregon said, "I think we are kidding the world if you try to give the impression that when the South Vietnamese naval boats bombarded two islands a short distance off the coast of North Vietnam, we were not implicated." McNamara replied that the Maddox "so far as I know today had no knowledge of any possible South Vietnamese actions in connection with the two islands that Senator Morse referred to." In his memoirs, McNamara wrote that this reply, "I later learned, was totally incorrect" (In Retrospect, p. 137).
[4] McNamara refers to the Senate Foreign Relations and House Foreign Affairs Committees. Voting present allowed Congressmen to indicate some dissatisfaction without bearing the onus of opposing what seemed to be a patriotic cause.
[5] H.R. Gross, Republican.

McNAMARA: Gross and is it Dubinsky?[1] I've got the wrong name but it is another Republican.

LBJ: What was their theory? . . .

McNAMARA: . . . They didn't want a "no-win" policy and another Korea. Wayne Hays[2] was the one who first initiated that idea. . . . But when the vote came in, of course, Hays fell in line and voted in favor of the resolution. But on the whole, I think the hearings were very satisfactory. It was just near-unanimous support for not only for everything you've done—there was unanimous support for that—but near-unanimous support for everything you may do in the future, and generally a blank-check authorization for further action, with the exception of this "no-win" group. And there were one or two in the Senate. . . .

LBJ: Who besides Morse?

McNAMARA: . . . Thurmond[3] was on the "no-win" line. . . . Thurmond did not oppose. He just wanted to see stronger action. He opposed the current policy in South Vietnam. He insisted we ought to strike the North, if Khanh[4] wanted us to do so.

FRIDAY, AUGUST 7, 1964

ROBERT McNAMARA
1:40 P.M.

LBJ: [irritated:] You know this thing that I was worried about the other night? Looks like it's getting us in pretty hot water. You see what Foreman says on the floor?[5]

· · · ·

LBJ: I waited from seven o'clock until midnight to do something about it and then did it against my better judgment. But I think that we've got to make it clear that first of all, we didn't tell anybody what we were doing. Isn't that correct?

McNAMARA: That's correct.

---

[1] McNamara means Edward Derwinski, Republican of Illinois.

[2] Democratic Congressman from Ohio, a member of the House Foreign Affairs Committee.

[3] Senator Strom Thurmond from South Carolina, a member of the Senate Armed Services Committee. Elected as a Democrat in 1954 and 1960, Thurmond joined the Republicans in 1964, saying that the Democrats were turning the United States into a "socialist dictatorship."

[4] The South Vietnamese leader.

[5] Congressman Edgar Foreman, Republican of Odessa, Texas, had leveled exactly the criticism against the timing of LBJ's August 4 Fish Room statement that Johnson had feared. (See conversation with McNamara, 9:15 P.M., August 4, 1964, above.) Foreman said, "We have heard a lot about trigger-happy irresponsibility lately and an obvious reference to critical comments about Goldwater . . . But what kind of responsibility is this where the President goes on radio and TV and tells them, the Communists one and a half hours in advance, that the air strike is coming?"

LBJ: We said we were going to hit these bases but we cut that out of the statement and just said action is under way. And so we don't have to explain to any widows because when those planes took off, I guess, they could see them in radar, couldn't they?

McNAMARA: Oh, yes.

JOHN McCORMACK
3:01 P.M.

LBJ CONGRATULATES the Speaker on the House endorsement of what is now being called the Gulf of Tonkin Resolution.

LBJ: That was a good vote you had today.

McCORMACK: Yes, it was very good. Four hundred fourteen to nothing. One present.[1] What'd the Senate do?

LBJ: Eighty-eight to 2—Morse and Gruening.[2]

McCORMACK: Can't understand Gruening.

LBJ: Oh, he's no good. He's worse than Morse. He's just no good. I've spent millions on him up in Alaska.[3] . . . And Morse is just undependable and erratic as he can be.

McCORMACK: A radical.

LBJ: I just wanted to point out this little shit-ass Foreman today got up and said that we acted impulsively by announcing[4] that we had an answer on the way before the planes dropped their bombs. . . . It's just a pure lie and smoke screen.

SATURDAY, AUGUST 8, 1964

ROBERT McNAMARA
8:24 A.M.

JOHNSON HAS FLOWN for the weekend to the LBJ Ranch, where he is breakfasting in bed.

McNAMARA: All quiet on the Southeast Asia front, but a very serious crisis brewing in Cyprus.[5]

---

[1] Adam Clayton Powell had voted "present" on the grounds that he was a pacifist.
[2] Ernest Gruening, a Democratic Senator from Alaska. Morse and Gruening argued that the resolution constituted a "predated declaration of war power."
[3] Meaning federal assistance after the March 1964 Alaska earthquake.
[4] In his Tuesday night television statement.
[5] Greek and Turkish Cypriots were fighting again.

LBJ: Some of the reporters were quite critical about my coming down here last night. . . . Said that here's a war going on in two or three fronts here and he's walking off here to play for the weekend. . . .

McNAMARA: . . . You could say that you were advised by the Secretary of State and the Secretary of Defense that there was no reason for your continued presence in Washington this weekend.

· · · ·

LBJ: Now you got by without hearing any more from out in Southeast Asia?

McNAMARA: That's right. We have no reports of any imminent action. . . .

LBJ: You hear much more about our launching the planes too early?

McNAMARA: Oh I think that that's dead. You perhaps have seen the *New York Times* and the *Washington Post* this morning.

LBJ: No, I haven't seen either one of them.

McNAMARA: [chuckles] . . . Now we're getting credit for having been very statesmanlike. Because one of the five points I listed[1] was that we wanted to be certain that the North Vietnamese "and others" were aware of your decision that this would be a "firm but limited" response. The *Washington Post* said quite clearly it was intended that . . . Communist China would be alerted that although these planes were in the air . . . it was clear it was not our intention that they would go into China to bomb China. . . . I do think if you have a press conference today you're going to get questions on the claim of the North Vietnamese that their strike on the 2nd against the *Maddox* was retaliation for U.S. participation in the strike of July 30th and 31st against those islands. . . . This is a very delicate subject. . . .

LBJ: What's the net of it?

McNAMARA: The net of it is that you state categorically that U.S. forces did not participate in, were not associated with any alleged incident of that kind. . . .

LBJ: Is this an outgrowth of John's briefing?[2]

McNAMARA: . . . It's the outgrowth of a lot of conversation . . . in the press . . . and I think it's one that you have to disassociate yourself from and certainly not admit that any such incident took place. But neither should you get in a position of denying it. Because the North Vietnamese have asked the ICC[3] to come in there and examine the site and it would be very unfortunate if they developed proof that you in effect had misstated the case.

LBJ: Did the South Vietnamese launch an attack that period?

McNAMARA: On the night of the 30th and continuing into the morning of the 31st, the South Vietnamese ran one of these patrol boat raids against these two North Vietnamese islands. Part of that covert operational plan.[4] It was what John was alluding to when he talked to the leaders. . . . The *Washington Post* has

[1] In McNamara's statement, as reasons for the timing of Johnson's August 4 late-night retaliation announcement.
[2] Director of Central Intelligence John McCone's briefing of congressional leaders.
[3] The International Control Commission for Vietnam.
[4] Op Plan 34-A.

quite an article on it today.... "*Maddox* Incident Reexamined—Miscalculation Theory Weighed in Viet Crisis." This is by Murray Marder. He goes on to say that it's now thought it was probably a reprisal action by North Vietnam.

HALE BOGGS and CARL ALBERT
1:56 P.M.

WHILE LUNCHING on hamburgers at A.W. Moursund's neighboring ranch, LBJ hears from the House Majority Leader and Majority Whip, who are celebrating passage of the poverty bill.

BOGGS: We're just here toasting you all by ourselves....

LBJ: My gosh, I'm mighty proud of you.... I think you're the best! ... Wish you were here with me.

BOGGS: ... I think we had a great week. Don't you?

LBJ: Yeah. Couldn't have been better. I put out a good, strong statement a while ago.[1] ... How's Uncle Charlie feel?

BOGGS: ... Last seen going to Australia![2] [all laugh]

SUNDAY, AUGUST 9, 1964

WALTER REUTHER
8:50 A.M.

JOHNSON IMPLORES the United Auto Workers president to help avert a divisive floor fight over the Mississippi Freedom Democratic Party.

LBJ: If you and Hubert Humphrey have got any leadership, you'd get Joe Rauh[3] off that damn television. The only thing that can really screw us good is to seat that group of challengers from Mississippi.... He said he's going to take it to the convention floor. Now there's not a damn vote that we get by seating these folks. What we want to do is elect some Congressmen to keep 'em from repealing this act.[4] And who's seated at this convention don't amount to a damn. Only reason I would let Mississippi come in is because I don't want to run off fourteen

[1] "The goal is high. We shall not reach it swiftly."
[2] Boggs is joking that House Minority Leader Charles Halleck must be so disgruntled by the success of the bill that he wants to decamp for Australia.
[3] The Washington labor lawyer and MFDP counsel.
[4] Civil Rights Act.

border states, like Oklahoma and like Kentucky.[1] . . . Incidentally this Governor[2] has done everything I've asked him to do in Mississippi. We've broken that case.[3] I talk to him two or three times a week. Now he's not for Johnson.[4] But I can't say that he hasn't listened to us and he hasn't cooperated.

. . . .

REUTHER: Exactly. . . . We'll lose Mississippi, but the impact on the other Southern states—

LBJ: That's all I'm worried about. . . . I've got to carry Georgia . . . and Carl Sanders can't go if he throws 'em out. He has to go with 'em.[5] I've got to carry Texas. John Connally will go. . . . We don't want to cut off our nose to spite our face. If they give us four years, I'll guarantee the Freedom delegation somebody representing views like that will be seated four years from now. But we can't do it all before breakfast.

JOSEPH HAGGAR, JR.

Chairman of the Board, The Haggar Company, Dallas
1:16 P.M.

LBJ: You-all made me some real light slacks. . . . Now, I need about six pairs for summer wear.

HAGGAR: Yes, sir.

LBJ: I want . . . maybe three of the light brown. Kind of an almost powder color. Like a powder on a lady's face. . . . I need about six pairs to wear around in the evening when I come in from work.

. . . .

LBJ: I want them a half-inch larger in the waist than they were before . . . so that I can take them up. I vary about ten or fifteen pounds a month.

HAGGAR: All right, sir.

LBJ: . . . Make the pockets at least an inch longer. My money and my knife and everything fall out. . . . The crotch, down where your nuts hang, is always a little too tight. . . . Give me an inch that I can let out there because they cut me. They're just like riding a wire fence.

---

[1] Meaning that other delegations might walk out of the convention in sympathy with Mississippi, undermining Johnson's chances in the fall.
[2] Paul Johnson.
[3] The Goodman-Schwerner-Chaney case. In December 1964, nineteen men were charged in federal court, including Sheriff Lawrence Rainey and his deputy, Cecil Price. Eight were convicted, but all received relatively light sentences.
[4] Lyndon Johnson.
[5] If the Mississippi regulars are expelled, Sanders and his delegates will have to follow.

MONDAY, AUGUST 10, 1964

McGEORGE BUNDY
9:50 A.M.

RETURNED TO THE WHITE HOUSE, Johnson is in the mansion when Bundy calls.

BUNDY: We have no evidence of this talk from the Gulf of Tonkin which is in the papers this morning.[1] The situation is, in fact, quite quiet. We're more and more inclined to think that our problem is, having been so resolute in defense of our own ships, what are we going to do for General Khanh?[2] . . . You've probably seen how the Harris Poll treats this.[3] I don't think that that means we ought to get belligerent as hell. . . . I gather four o'clock is our signing ceremony.[4] That can be in the East Room, if you want a bigger crowd, Mr. President. I thought of the Treaty Room only because of the associations.[5] . . .

LBJ: I don't care. . . . I don't know how many would want to come for it.[6]

WEDNESDAY, AUGUST 12, 1964

ROBERT KENNEDY
9:00 A.M.

LATER THIS DAY, LBJ is to address the American Bar Association and see Mayor Robert Wagner in New York City. He has heard that RFK is now pondering a run for the Senate seat from New York held by Republican Kenneth Keating. Having struggled so hard to become Senator from Texas, Johnson is privately appalled at the prospect that Kennedy could tumble into a Senate seat from a powerful state where he does not live.[7] He fears that New York would give RFK a new power base from which to make political trouble for

[1] American jets had reportedly scrambled to meet Chinese Communist fighters flying south over the gulf.
[2] After the Gulf of Tonkin raids, Prime Minister Khanh, needing diversion from his domestic political problems, was more eager than ever for the Americans to extend the war to the North.
[3] The Harris Poll found that 85 percent of Americans endorsed Johnson's action in the Gulf of Tonkin.
[4] For the Gulf of Tonkin Resolution.
[5] In 1963, President Kennedy had signed the Partial Nuclear Test Ban Treaty in the Treaty Room, which was in the family quarters of the White House.
[6] Johnson signed the resolution in a muted East Room ceremony at 4:05 P.M.
[7] At that moment, Kennedy was still listed as a Massachusetts delegate to the convention in Atlantic City. His partisans were making the argument that he had lived with his family in Bronxville as a child.

LBJ. But he also understands, at least intellectually, that for Kennedy to plunge into an intensely fought Senate race would divert him from any lingering ambitions for the presidency or vice presidency in 1964. Wishing to discover Kennedy's intentions, Johnson reaches the Attorney General in Maine.

LBJ: I'm going up to New York about eleven o'clock. Some folks up there want to talk to me. . . . I don't want to say something or do something that might not be what you want done.

• • • •

KENNEDY: I thought that if I could work it out so that I wasn't just suddenly landing from Massachusetts into New York, that I would try to . . . run in New York. . . . If it looks plainly . . . that . . . I didn't become Vice President, and I decided to run in New York because it was the second best thing . . . it looks terrible to start out with such a burden. . . . Nobody likes to lose. But if I lose up there . . . it's a reflection on the whole family. . . .

LBJ: . . . I think from your standpoint, it would be, assuming that you have a reasonably good chance to win . . . the best possible base you could have. It would give you . . . more sense of achievement and more participation and leadership than you would expect from some of these other things we talked about.[1]

KENNEDY: Yes.

LBJ: Now how to wrap it up? I'm not close enough to know. I do know that there are three or four that have indicated to me an interest.[2] . . . I have said that I highly regarded you and I thought that you had a very bright future in the party . . . and a good deal of things they'd said about our relationship were without foundation. . . . If you can get me some indication of what might be appropriate, without their saying outsiders are coming in and telling them what they've got to do, I could say that I think we have a chance to pick up another seat if the New York people feel this way.[3] . . .

KENNEDY: . . . I think something like that would be very, very helpful.

• • • •

KENNEDY: I think it's damn tough up there. . . .

LBJ: . . . I just think you could win it hands down. I think you could have a position that you would enjoy and I think it would be very helpful to the party and the ticket. And to me.

KENNEDY: Thank you. I appreciate that. Thank you.

LBJ: And I just want to make it clear that I want to do what you want done. . . .

[1] Namely the vice presidency.

[2] In running for the New York Senate seat, including Adlai Stevenson, who wrote his friend Mary Lasker two days later, "Bobby is mad to run now and [RFK's brother-in-law] Steve Smith is making unctuous calls daily about getting together. . . . Bob Wagner is holding out but the K's have unleashed the mafia. . . . The avarice of the K's really makes me sick. I'd almost like to do it to challenge him" (August 14, 1964, Stevenson Papers, Princeton University). Although an Illinoisan, Stevenson believed he could claim New York residence on the grounds of having lived there for almost four years as U.N. Ambassador.

[3] Johnson knew that New York liberals, reformers, and civil libertarians had been suspicious of RFK since his days working for Joseph McCarthy and that others were averse to Kennedy as a carpetbagger.

KENNEDY: I think that would be damn helpful.

LBJ: All right, that's what will be done.

THURSDAY, AUGUST 13, 1964

EDWARD KENNEDY
1:10 P.M.

> EDWARD KENNEDY is still recovering from the broken back he had suffered in the June air crash.

KENNEDY: My son came up and was looking under the covers ... for my broken back and when he didn't see it, he thought I was sort of faking it out up here.

LBJ: [laughs] ... You can't keep a good man down.

KENNEDY: ... Mr. President, we have had a very nice invitation from Governor Harriman[1] to have a reception at the convention on Thursday after the selection of the presidential and vice presidential candidates ... for Mrs. Kennedy. ... Jackie has indicated that she would be delighted to accept this, but of course, we wanted to have this in complete accord with your wishes. ...

LBJ: ... I see no reason why it wouldn't work out fine. I don't know when I'm going to be there. I believe their plans were for me to come in that night and not go to the convention before that time, but ... I believe Miz Johnson will be there. ... Now you say Miz Kennedy. You're talking about Jackie—or your mother?

KENNEDY: Jackie ... Fredric March would do those readings again.[2] ... We wanted to ... make sure that this type of thing could be done with dignity. ... Too often it ... wouldn't have the kind of taste ... that Jackie would really like.

LBJ: ... I want to do anything and everything I can at any time to make her as happy and as pleased as she can be, under the circumstances. ...

KENNEDY: Thanks and congratulations on that South Vietnam—the Tonkin Gulf. ... I know you've received it from everyone, but one more voice.

LBJ: I appreciate it, Ted. I sure do. You got a mighty bright future and I'm mighty happy that things are coming so good and I want to help any way I can on it.

---

[1] Averell Harriman's friends referred to the Undersecretary of State by his old title of Governor of New York. Harriman was at that moment trying to use his old connections in the state to advance Robert Kennedy's Senate ambitions.

[2] March had read from JFK's favorite poetry at the June Kennedy Library dinner in New York.

FRIDAY, AUGUST 14, 1964

HUBERT HUMPHREY
11:05 A.M.

HUMPHREY: I've been just working the devil out of that Joe.[1] . . . And I understood that Dave Lawrence[2] and Kenny[3] met with Joe and had quite a talk with him . . . on the basis of seating both of these delegations.[4]

LBJ: You can't do that at all. There's no compromise. You can seat one or the other. You can't seat both of them because if you do, then the other one walks out. There's just no justification for messing with the Freedom Party at all in Mississippi.

• • • •

LBJ: If they want to elect Goldwater, that's not gonna make me cry one bit. I left the majority leadership to be Vice President, which no man would do unless he wanted to get away from activity. And I decided I wanted to get away from it. I didn't want to fall on my face and be dead there on the floor of the Senate some morning rasslin' with Wayne Morse and an old drunken John Butler.[5] . . . Now I'm back in it.[6] Through no fault of my own, but I'm in it. And I think that we have a pretty good party and I think that we have a chance to win—I don't think it's as good as anybody thinks it is. Last night the District Attorney in Dallas called me.[7] The Goldwater forces . . . and the Birch forces have rented about four thousand square feet there. They've put in the mail this week three million of these slanderous books about me.[8] . . . They're impeaching Earl Warren.[9] . . . And . . . your labor union people . . . are upset. Think that nigra's going to get his job.

HUMPHREY: Yeah.

LBJ: . . . They think a nigra's going to move next door to them. . . . And our organizations are tired and worn out and lazy and looking after themselves. They just think they've got labor and nigras and that's all there is to it. We're not appealing to the fresh people. So this is an extremely dangerous election. Now

[1] Rauh, on the Mississippi Freedom Democratic Party fight.
[2] Ex-Governor of Pennsylvania, head of that state's delegation, and chairman of the Democratic convention's Credentials Committee.
[3] O'Donnell.
[4] Both the white and predominantly black Mississippi delegations.
[5] After his apostasy on the Gulf of Tonkin Resolution, Wayne Morse is much on LBJ's mind. John Marshall Butler was a Republican Senator from Maryland from 1951 to 1963.
[6] Meaning active political life.
[7] Henry Wade, who would have been responsible for Lee Harvey Oswald's prosecution had Oswald survived.
[8] *A Texan Looks at Lyndon: A Study in Illegitimate Power* (Palo Duro Press, 1964), a paperback self-published by J. Evetts Haley, a Canyon, Texas, rancher who had run for Texas Governor in 1956 on a segregationist–states' rights platform. The book lambasted Johnson's "monumental egotism," his vindictive nature and his evil genius." Thanks in part to promotion by the John Birch Society, 7.3 million copies of Haley's tract were ultimately printed.
[9] One of the John Birch Society's notorious passions at the time was to impeach the Chief Justice for his liberal activism on the Supreme Court.

the thing that makes it more dangerous than anything else is—I am telling you, if I know anything I know this—if we mess with the group of Negroes that were elected to nothing, that met in a hotel room . . . and throw out the Governor and elected officials of the state[1]—if we mess with them, we will lose fifteen states without even campaigning.[2]

. . . .

LBJ: We've got to do something that will convince the CORE[3] crowd and Martin Luther King and Joe Rauh that if they want to help Goldwater, okay, they can go this way. . . . They'll have a roll call. The Northern states will probably prevail. New York and Pennsylvania and California and Ohio and Michigan cannot afford to have it said that they are for the Governor of Mississippi . . . against the Negroes in their own town, where they've got 20 percent Negroes.

HUMPHREY: That's right.

LBJ: . . . So we throw them out. And when we do, we write a blank check to him for fifteen states.

. . . .

HUMPHREY: I don't have as much control or influence with these people as I would like. . . . I have been in touch with Farmer.[4] I haven't been in touch lately with King.[5]

LBJ: King has gone to Europe today. His man Rustin[6] is calling. They are demanding that this be made the big fish.

. . . .

LBJ: Try to see if the Negroes don't realize that they've got the President, they'll have the Vice President, they've got the law, they'll have the government for four years. . . . Why in the living hell do they want to hand—*shovel*—Goldwater fifteen states? . . .

HUMPHREY: . . . We're just not dealing with . . . emotionally stable people on this, Mr. President.

. . . .

LBJ: Adam Clayton Powell[7] called up yesterday and said he's been looking up Goldwater's voting record and it wasn't too bad. He wants a little payoff. . . . Martin Luther King said, "I'll tell you this—between Mississippi and these things of Johnson, why, I don't know, maybe the Negroes won't vote."

[1] Mississippi.
[2] Meaning not only that the Democratic party will be divided but that Americans troubled by the Civil Rights Act will think that the Democrats have been taken over by the blacks. (See Johnson's conversation with Richard Russell, August 24, 1964, below.)
[3] Congress of Racial Equality.
[4] James Farmer, national director of CORE.
[5] Martin Luther King.
[6] Bayard Rustin.
[7] The maverick black Harlem Congressman.

JAMES RESTON
3:25 P.M.

LBJ: Scotty, the *Times* has got a story this morning saying that I had intervened up there[1] and endorsed Kennedy or recommended Kennedy and said he'd be "very valuable."

. . . .

LBJ: I'm not against the man and I'm not for him. I think if Wagner wants to be for him and New York wants to be for him, that's their privilege. Or against him! [chuckles]

SATURDAY, AUGUST 15, 1964

ROY WILKINS
9:50 A.M.

LBJ: Roy, do you know how much trouble I'm gonna have when I name this Vice President?[2] It's going to be almost like naming the Freedom Party to these folks.[3] They're just going to have hell swallowing it. Carl Vinson,[4] who's the best Democrat in the South . . . said, "We just cannot take any more civil rights advocates now." . . . And the ADA[5] sent out this thing with Hubert's name on it . . . for Vice President to every Southern delegate. . . . I'm not going to be panicky or desperate, but I'm just saying to you that the cause you fought for all your life is likely to be reversed and go right down the drain if you don't get Whitney or Walter[6] or some of these folks to . . . find some possible solution.

. . . .

LBJ: If I were the Negro . . . I'd just let Mississippi[7] sit up on the platform, if they wanted to, and I'd stand at attention and salute the son of a bitch. Then I'd nominate Johnson for President and my Vice President and I'd go out and elect my Congressman. . . . And the next four years, I'd see the promised land.

---

[1] In the New York Senate race.
[2] Presumably Johnson is referring, at least indirectly, to Humphrey, who has been a favorite of civil rights groups since before his speech as Mayor of Minneapolis to the 1948 Democratic convention: "The time has arrived for the Democratic party to get out of the shadow of states' rights and walk forthrightly into the bright sunshine of human rights."
[3] In the South.
[4] The House Armed Services Committee Chairman, of Georgia.
[5] The liberal Americans for Democratic Action.
[6] Whitney Young of the National Urban League and Walter Reuther.
[7] The all-white delegation.

518   TAKING CHARGE

CARTHA DeLOACH
5:03 P.M.

THROUGH WALTER JENKINS, Johnson has persuaded Hoover to mount an elaborate intelligence operation at Atlantic City that will keep track of the Mississippi Freedom Democratic Party rebels and other political leaders, to ensure that "there aren't any disruptions at the convention." William Sullivan of the FBI's Domestic Intelligence Division found the operation particularly concerned with "reporting on the activities of Bobby Kennedy."[1]

LBJ: Is he going to run for the Senate?

DeLOACH: Mr. President, I think he'll do anything if he thinks he can win. . . .

LBJ: They're giving a big party for Miz Kennedy on Thursday afternoon, after the nominations Wednesday night. Bringing her back from Europe.[2] At the convention.

DeLOACH: I still don't think he'll get anywhere there. I think that people realize, particularly the Democratic leaders, that if the President doesn't want him, they're not going to take him.

• • • •

DeLOACH: I think that it would be very wise if you could squeeze in fifteen or twenty minutes with about three or four Negro leaders. Not King alone. Get Wilkins, who's the leader of the entire Negro movement. He's the most rational statesman. . . . That would take the heat off and there wouldn't be any chance of them making any slurs against you between now and November.[3]

LBJ: Maybe I ought to follow that suggestion. . . . You let the record show that you recommended we get them all in there, so we can see what they're doing and so we can advise them to try to put a stop to these riots and demonstrations. And don't let the record show that I'm conniving with him alone.[4]

---

[1] By DeLoach's account, Hoover had at first said of the Atlantic City proposal, "Lyndon is way out of line," but quickly reconsidered: "Tell Walter we'll give him whatever help he wants." The FBI was already tracking Martin Luther King. (See Cartha DeLoach, *Hoover's FBI*, pp. 3–9; David J. Garrow, *Bearing the Cross*, Morrow, 1986, pp. 346–48; Sanford Ungar, *FBI*, Atlantic–Little, Brown, 1975, p. 289; William C. Sullivan, *The Bureau*, Norton, 1979, pp. 58–60; Arthur M. Schlesinger, Jr., *Robert Kennedy and His Times*, pp. 662–64.)

[2] Jacqueline Kennedy had been sailing off the coast of Yugoslavia.

[3] Here the spectacle of an FBI official presuming to advise Johnson on how to deal with civil rights leaders at a political convention.

[4] By "the record" Johnson means DeLoach's reports back to Hoover. He does not want Hoover to think that he is "conniving" alone with Martin Luther King, Hoover's nemesis. Four days later, Johnson indeed held an hour-long meeting with Wilkins, Farmer, A. Philip Randolph of the Brotherhood of Sleeping Car Porters, and John Lewis of the Student Nonviolent Coordinating Committee. King was invited but stayed away, assuming that he was unlikely to influence LBJ and that Johnson would exploit his presence nonetheless. King was right. Johnson used the session to praise his own civil rights achievements and refused to discuss Atlantic City.

MONDAY, AUGUST 17, 1964

DEAN RUSK
8:10 P.M.

As the Secretary of State knows, throughout the Kennedy administration Robert Kennedy complained to his brother about Rusk's orthodoxy and lassitude. Now Rusk evens scores.

RUSK: I think that if Bobby runs up there . . . it's going to be a drag on your own position in New York State.

. . . .

LBJ: This is a very, very ambitious young man. It's unbelievable how ambitious he is.

RUSK: Mr. President . . . I just can't wrap my mind around that kind of ambition. I don't know how to understand it.

LBJ: I don't either.

RUSK: This consuming passion is something that's just alien to my whole makeup.

LBJ: Yes, it is. Yes, it is.

RUSK: There's a ruthlessness about it that just scares the hell out of me.

LBJ: It is to me too. . . . He called me up at the ranch and demanded—just *demanded* that I send in the Internal Revenue agents all over Mississippi. And I just got shocked by it.[1] . . . I hope we get through this convention without any trouble. I'm very fearful.

THURSDAY, AUGUST 20, 1964

HUBERT HUMPHREY
9:20 A.M.

Edith Lehman, widow of New York Senator Herbert Lehman, who had died the previous December, has called LBJ to complain at length that her husband would not be honored at the Atlantic City convention.

---

[1] RFK had been groping for quiet ways to bring white Mississippi extremists to heel. LBJ here cites the suggestion as evidence for his private derision of Kennedy as an enemy of civil liberties. On other occasions, he mentioned Kennedy's work for Joseph McCarthy and his use of the FBI and IRS to harass steel executives during their confrontation with JFK over price increases in 1962.

LBJ: Miz Lehman calls up crying. . . . She said that . . . you thought it was an outrage. . . . I can't be handling it. . . . We have all the troubles in the world without chickenshit things coming up like a woman like that crying over the phone and getting every Jew in America mad at you.[1]

FRIDAY, AUGUST 21, 1964

KENNETH O'DONNELL
10:46 A.M.

THREE DAYS BEFORE the convention is to begin, Johnson has virtually settled in his own mind on Humphrey as his running mate. But he will not divulge his inclination to Humphrey or almost anyone else. He wants to see whether Humphrey can help settle the Mississippi Freedom Democratic Party dispute. And he wants to create some public suspense by suggesting that dark horses are in the running. Perhaps hoping that O'Donnell will leak what he hears, Johnson raises the possibility of Mike Mansfield, a Catholic whom the Kennedys like.[2]

LBJ: How much stronger are you for Hubert than you would be for Mansfield? . . .

O'DONNELL: I'd like to think about it.

LBJ: I'd think that Hubert would stir up the liberals more and get more applause from the Negroes and get a little bigger hand from the liberal columnists, the New Deal, and maybe a good deal of the New Frontier. . . . On the other hand, Mansfield has the respect and no one really hates him.

. . . .

LBJ: Mike, I would think, would give an awfully good answer to the Catholic question . . . if they . . . said, "We had our man[3] and they wouldn't let him serve but three years and he got killed." . . . Miller[4] might make something of it the last week or so.

. . . .

LBJ: He says he just won't take it, under any circumstances. . . . But I didn't think *I* wanted to.[5] . . . If you'd have bet me a million dollars, I'd have called it. Right quick. [chuckles]

---

[1] Lehman was Jewish.
[2] Johnson had to have realized that if he chose Mansfield as Vice President, he would have a sharp thorn in his side for the next four years if he escalated American involvement in Vietnam.
[3] President Kennedy.
[4] The Republican vice presidential nominee, a Catholic, whom Goldwater had chosen, he said, because "he drives Johnson nuts."
[5] Take the vice presidency in 1960.

O'DONNELL: I *bet* a million.

LBJ: That I wouldn't?

O'DONNELL: Yep.

LBJ: Well, you're bankrupt, aren't you?

. . . .

LBJ: There're some boys around here . . . talking that they ought to move the film back.[1] . . . We'd get more damned trouble by shifting it again. We'd get another series of stories. . . . Anybody that's done . . . these things before knows that . . . a little pathos and a little crying and a little sympathy and a little applauding . . . are good. . . .

O'DONNELL: I wouldn't shift it, Mr. President. . . .

LBJ: . . . We'll just leave it where it is.

WALTER JENKINS
8:30 P.M.

LBJ ASKS Jenkins to subtly suggest to Humphrey that if he cannot settle the Mississippi problem, he might not become Vice President.

LBJ: I think you ought to call Humphrey . . . and say, "You better get Reuther and you better get Rauh[2] and quit causing these goddamn troubles, Hubert, because this is going to make a bad convention if you don't tell them to quit doing stuff like this. Now if you haven't got any influence with any of this ADA[3] crowd, tell us who has."

JOHN STEINBECK
Novelist
8:45 P.M.

JOHNSON, who had once wept through the film version of *The Grapes of Wrath*, has asked the novelist, whose wife, Elaine, was a University of Texas schoolmate of Lady Bird's, to help on his acceptance speech. Steinbeck is at Sag Harbor, Long Island.

LBJ: How you getting along?

STEINBECK: I'm worried.

LBJ: What's the matter?

---

[1] The suggestion was to move the JFK memorial film back to Thursday afternoon from Thursday night, where it might cast a pall over LBJ's acceptance speech. Johnson had already been criticized by columnists for seeing to it that the film had been moved later in the week, after the President and Vice President had already been nominated, so that it could not start a groundswell for RFK.

[2] Walter Reuther and Joseph Rauh.

[3] Americans for Democratic Action.

. . . .

STEINBECK: My wishes go way beyond what can be accomplished. That goes with my own work too. . . . [slight chuckle]

LBJ: Why don't you come down here and I'll pep you up some? [chuckles]

. . . .

LBJ: I've got some stuff here that I would like for you to look at . . . and let us practice it kinda together. . . . "Peace should be the first concern of all governments, as it is the prayer of all men." That's a good sentence, isn't it?

STEINBECK: It's very good.[1] But it's not harsh enough.

LBJ: "In the second decade of the nuclear age, the preservation of peace requires the strength to wage war and the wisdom to avoid it."

STEINBECK: Why do you need me?

LBJ: I just thought that you were the ultimate and we'd improve it a little bit. . . . Why don't you get your wife to come down and spend the night with us Sunday? . . . You can spend Sunday afternoon, Sunday night, and as long as you can till you get through with it.[2]

BILL MOYERS
10:00 P.M.

JOHNSON'S AIDE REPORTS from the convention city.

MOYERS: People describing themselves as agents of McCarthy[3] were going around Atlantic City today, saying that he had it all wrapped up. . . .

LBJ: Just tell 'em that there's nobody got it wrapped up. . . . I wouldn't think that agents of McCarthy would say, "Our man is defeated. We're wrecked and we're ruined." Or agents of Humphrey. . . . Any guy that's running a campaign claims victory. . . . But there's four or five people being very, very seriously considered, and one of them is McCarthy. And one of them is Mansfield. And one of them is Humphrey. And one of them is Muskie. And one of them is Pastore. And one of them is Clark Kerr.[4] I'd just throw his name all over up there. Say they're liable to really get surprised. Because Humphrey hasn't got enough sense —he gets on the firing line, he's going to get shot at, you see, and destroyed. They'll make a real, full-grown Communist with a bastard baby out of him before Monday if he just keeps on.

---

[1] Obviously Steinbeck was very polite with Johnson.
[2] Steinbeck did go to the White House to help with Johnson's speech.
[3] Eugene McCarthy, Senator from Minnesota.
[4] Johnson hopes that someone will leak the last three very dark horse names to create suspense over the vice presidency and make Humphrey less of a sitting duck for his enemies. The inclusion of John Pastore, a journeyman Senator from Rhode Island whom LBJ had chosen as keynote speaker, shows how unserious Johnson really was. Muskie was a Senator from Maine. Clark Kerr was president of the University of California.

MONDAY, AUGUST 24, 1964

WALTER REUTHER
8:46 A.M.

As SENATE MAJORITY LEADER, Johnson's method of breaking deadlocks was to quietly suggest terms of compromise to loyal colleagues and then disappear while they worked it out. Now, on the first day of the Democratic National Convention, LBJ is publicly pretending to be aloof from the Mississippi Freedom Democratic Party struggles. But behind the scenes he is monitoring every twist and turn through Jenkins, Reuther, Humphrey, and others, not to mention the FBI. He hopes that the conflict will be solved if the convention does three things—seat the Jim Crow Mississippi delegation, as long as it will pledge to support the ticket; grant floor privileges but no votes to the MFDP; and promise that in 1968, delegate selection will be fully open to blacks. Reuther approves.[1]

REUTHER: Everybody thinks it's a way out. . . . When the convention meets tonight, the Credentials Committee makes a partial report, which means seating everybody but Mississippi. Tell the convention that . . . a subcommittee was set up. . . . The subcommittee is going to . . . study this thing further. . . . Our people down there believe that if we handle it this way, we can avoid a floor fight. And then the thing will get lost in the shuffle of the business of the convention. . . . I talked to Hubert about it about three o'clock this morning and he feels this is the way out. Joe Rauh is perfectly willing to break with these fellows,[2] but he says then you'll have no contact with them.[3] We went over at two o'clock this morning to talk with Martin Luther King at his hotel. . . . King was surrounded by a bunch of young people who were so emotional that you can't reach him.

· · · ·

LBJ: It's going to be a mighty hard four days. . . . My guess is this morning that you'll have a bunch of walkouts.[4] . . . If they see a legally elected delegation that's sitting there and not seated, it'll have the effect of just depriving them of representation. Alabama's done gone[5] and they tell me that Louisiana and Arkansas are going with them. And I'm afraid it's going to spread to eight or ten.

---

[1] Reuther is in Detroit, where he has been popping out of Ford, Chrysler, and General Motors contract talks to keep track of the bargaining in Atlantic City.

[2] The MFDP leaders. Rauh was worried about far-left influences on the Freedom Party.

[3] In other words, that Johnson would have no one in among the rebels personally well known to him.

[4] By white Southern delegations.

[5] A majority of Alabama delegates was still refusing a pledge to support the nominees chosen at Atlantic City.

RICHARD RUSSELL

11:10 A.M.

RUSSELL: If there's any exposé in the campaign and they[1] happen to get hold of anything that would tie the Communists all into that Mississippi crowd,[2] it would be mighty bad. . . . It could switch a couple of million votes or more.

LBJ: I think that I've got to decide, first, how I reply to his wire.[3] . . .

RUSSELL: I heard King addressing that crowd down there on the Boardwalk. . . . I heard him on my car radio coming down here, and he was just openly threatening. I don't see how you can possibly do business with a man—black, white, green, or yellow—that just comes out and intimidates. Says, "Don't do this, we are going to take it out of your hide." He said on the radio, "They say we niggers haven't got anywhere else to go. We'll show them we *have* got somewhere else to go."

LBJ: Yes, he's been saying that in private. . . . The question is what you do when they are getting ready to take charge of the convention. . . .

RUSSELL: You don't do a thing but say you're sorry, you think they are ill-advised. . . . Undoubtedly there may have been irregularities in selecting the white delegation, but . . . this Freedom delegation . . . didn't have . . . conventions but in about eighteen or twenty counties.[4] . . . I don't see how the hell they claim they represent the state. . . . It ain't going to hurt you any in the country to get run over.[5] It would hurt your pride like hell, I know, but it isn't going to hurt you politically.

LBJ: I would think that they'd say that hell, the Negroes have got more power in the Democratic party than the President has, and the damned nigras are taking it over—and to hell with the Democratic party.

RUSSELL: It would increase the backlash[6] a little bit. No question about that —whatever the backlash is. But this is August. It's over two months before the election. . . .

LBJ: They got the civil rights provision[7] agreed to unanimously.

RUSSELL: Yes? My God, that's a miracle of major proportions. . . .

LBJ: . . . There may have been a few no's, but I don't believe so. . . . What would you do about his wire?

RUSSELL: . . . If you've decided that the Mississippi delegation . . . the white delegation, ought to be seated, I think I'd say so to a press conference. I wouldn't say it in a wire to Martin Luther King. I don't think I would dignify him that much.

---

[1] The Republicans.
[2] The MFDP, should it be seated by the convention.
[3] Dr. King had wired Johnson to oppose seating of the white Mississippi regulars.
[4] Mississippi had eighty-two counties in all.
[5] By the Mississippi Freedom Democratic Party challengers.
[6] The national backlash that Johnson feared against civil rights and the Democrats that fall.
[7] Of the Democratic platform, which said that the Civil Rights Act of 1964 "deserves and requires full observance by every American and fair and effective enforcement."

. . . .

LBJ: It would be so much better if I'd stay out of the convention if I could. . . . And he's[1] trying to get me in it every way he can. And I think this is Bobby's *trap.*

. . . .

LBJ: I don't think there's any question but what Martin Luther King and that group wants me to be in a position of giving them an excuse to say that I have turned on the Negro.

RUSSELL: I don't believe they can sell that to the *Negro* even.

LBJ: Yeah, I think that's Bobby's strategy though, Dick.

RUSSELL: Suppose Bobby would like to see Goldwater elected President?

LBJ: No, but I think he'd like to see me caused all the damned trouble he can. And *maybe* elected. He told me, when he left me[2] with a sneer[3] on his face, "I think I would have been able to help you a lot." And I think he wants to prove that. . . .

RUSSELL: Well, the time was coming when King was going to come head-on into whoever was up there—whether it's you or Kennedy[4] or whoever. He's a very arrogant fellow.

LADY BIRD JOHNSON
Approximately 1:00 P.M.

JOHNSON IS EAGER to do anything that will divert the attention of news people from the Freedom Party controversy in Atlantic City.

LBJ: Would you like to take a walk with me and the press?

LADY BIRD: . . . I'm on my way to the foot doctor, honey. How about me taking a walk halfway around the grounds with you and then jump in my car and going to the foot doctor?

LBJ: Walk around once or twice and then go to the foot doctor. Come over here and start out from the office with me. There's no rush. In just five or ten minutes is all right. The press is ready. And put some lipstick on.[5]

---

[1] Robert Kennedy.
[2] On July 29, after LBJ told him that he would not be Vice President.
[3] LBJ told Clifford just after the RFK meeting that it was a smile, not a sneer. (See conversation of July 29, 1964, 2:17 P.M.)
[4] President Kennedy.
[5] At 1:27 P.M., the President and First Lady strolled the South Grounds with their dogs Him and Her and ample news coverage.

WALTER JENKINS
Approximately 4:30 P.M.

SITTING in the White House family quarters, Johnson is told that Humphrey has failed to solve the Mississippi problem.

JENKINS: He said, "I'm a hell of a salesman. I walked into the lion's den. . . . I argued fervently. I used all the heartstrings that I had and I made no headway. . . . I think we can forget now any possibility of them not trying for a floor fight unless they[1] have some votes." He said he asked some of the people there the result of giving them two votes. . . . Texas, Georgia, Florida, North Carolina would stay.[2] Arkansas, Louisiana doubtful. . . . He says he's racked his brain for anything further to do. He's not making a suggestion that you get into it. But he says this fellow Henry[3] is quite intelligent—he's more reasonable than some. . . . It may be they ought to come to Washington tonight.[4] . . . I said, "What could be done there that you haven't been able to do?" . . . He said, "Maybe you're right. I just don't know."

LBJ: [upset:] I don't want to see 'em at all. . . . If they're interested in the slightest in what concerns me, it is to go on and take the compromise that Rauh proposed. That's what they ought to do. . . . If they want Goldwater, they can have Goldwater.

WALTER REUTHER
8:25 P.M.

SITTING with Clark Clifford and Abe Fortas, Johnson is upstairs at the White House, watching the formal opening of the Democratic convention on television. On what should have been an exhilarating evening for LBJ, NBC co-anchors Chet Huntley and David Brinkley are instead talking about an impending floor fight and walkout by Southern delegations. Johnson is sinking into depression.

LBJ: [Clark] and Abe are . . . just distressed beyond words.[5]

REUTHER: I am too. I'm going to get in there and see if I can't help get ahold of this damned thing.

LBJ: I think the Negroes are going back to the Reconstruction period. Going right where they were then. They set themselves back a hundred years.

REUTHER: They're completely irrational. They don't know the victory they got is the proposition that next time no one can discriminate against Negroes. . . .

LBJ: And then I'm just trying to get a Vice President for 'em. And I want to try to get him accepted by the country.[6] . . . I don't know why they don't let us

[1] The MFDP challengers.
[2] At the convention.
[3] Aaron Henry, a Clarksdale, Mississippi, druggist and MFDP state chairman.
[4] To see Johnson.
[5] Johnson is really talking about himself.
[6] Johnson alludes to Humphrey.

do it. Then I want to try to get some appropriations to carry this thing[1] out. I haven't got a *dime*. . . . Hell, the Northerners are more upset about this. They call me and wire me, Walter . . . that the Negroes have taken over the country. They're running the White House. They're running the Democratic party. And it's not Mississippi and Alabama. . . . You're catching your hell from Michigan, Ohio, Philadelphia, and New York! . . . They're before that television. They don't understand that nearly every white man in this country would be frightened if he thought the Negroes were gonna take him over. . . . But they're on the television showing it. We can't ever buy spots that will equal this. We've got five million dollars budgeted, but we can't undo what they've done in the last two days— unless you do it tomorrow.[2]

TUESDAY, AUGUST 25, 1964

A.W. MOURSUND
10:05 A.M.

AFTER BREAKFASTING in bed and skipping his morning exercise, Johnson made his first call, at 7:50 A.M., to his close friend A.W. Moursund, in Atlantic City. His depression of last night has deepened. Frustrated by the cataclysm over Mississippi, he tells Moursund that he is inclined to announce that he will withdraw his name as a presidential candidate and retire to Texas.

Is he serious? Drawing on his vivid, emotional imagination, Johnson foresees a catastrophe in Atlantic City, with Southerners walking out and blacks furious that the Southern President has opposed the Mississippi rebels. He can imagine that in the fall of 1964, many white Americans will bray that the Democratic party has been seized by the blacks. Black voters, ungrateful for his championship of the Civil Rights Act, may sit on their hands out of anger at his turning on them over Mississippi. In Johnson's mind, there might be more riots in the cities, exploding into the raw open national conflict over race that he has feared for a year, with a Southern President powerless to stop it, perhaps even culminating in a November defeat by Goldwater.

Johnson also knows that perhaps the best way to force through a Mississippi compromise, if necessary, may be for him to threaten not to run. With delegates pledged to vote for him on the first ballot, he would probably be nominated against his stated wish. This would allow him to dictate his own terms before accepting a "draft." And he knows that the televised spectacle of LBJ being demanded by his party to run against his will could only strengthen him for the fall campaign.[3]

[1] The Civil Rights Act.
[2] In response to Johnson's plea, although still mired in union contract negotiations, Reuther chartered a plane and flew that evening from Detroit to Atlantic City in order to help settle the Mississippi problem.
[3] Johnson well remembered the Democratic convention of 1940, where his hero, Franklin Roosevelt, wishing to be "drafted" for a third term, sent the convention a message that he did not have "any desire" to serve again: delegates should feel "free to vote for any candidate."

Now in the family quarters, with the coverage from Atlantic City blaring out of his television, Johnson talks again to Moursund.[1]

MOURSUND: It's rough.

LBJ: I feel like I told you this morning. And I'm gonna do something like that during the day, unless I change my mind.

GEORGE REEDY
11:06 A.M.

By NOW, Johnson has gone to the Oval Office.

REEDY: I'm set to brief.

LBJ: Good.

REEDY: What should I tell 'em about this morning?

LBJ: I don't know, George. There's really not much to tell 'em. . . . I'm just writing out a little statement that I think I'm gonna make either at a press conference here or go up to Atlantic City this afternoon to make. But I don't think we can tell 'em about it now.

. . . .

REEDY: Incidentally the Attorney General just announced for the New York . . . Senate.

LBJ: Is he on TV, I wonder?

REEDY: I don't know . . . I saw the ticker.

. . . .

REEDY: I think the only other question they'll press me on is what the White House people are doing up there.[2]

LBJ: . . . Walter Jenkins is there seeing our old friends from various parts of the country. . . . And say I haven't talked to anybody at the convention this morning.

Then a demonstration—the Chicago Democratic machine's "voice from the sewers" shrieking by loudspeaker, "We Want Roosevelt!" After FDR's renomination, when delegates balked at his choice of the liberal Henry Wallace as running mate, FDR scrawled out a statement saying that he could not accept a Democratic party divided between liberalism and reaction. Better to let the convention choose by declining the nomination: "I so do." Delegates snapped immediately back into line. (See James MacGregor Burns, *Roosevelt: The Lion and the Fox*, Harcourt, 1956, pp. 425–30.) In March 1968, when Johnson said that he would not seek another term as President, Democrats took him at his word, but his close White House aide Joseph Califano felt that by that summer LBJ hoped for a convention draft—which he would turn down, but which would "validate his presidency" (*The Triumph and Tragedy of Lyndon Johnson*, pp. 319–21).
[1] Moursund had earlier made the absurd suggestion, perhaps to buck up Johnson's spirits, that LBJ take John Connally as his Vice President. Not only would this infuriate Northerners, but Connally's serious political background consisted of nineteen months as Governor of Texas. Furthermore, the Constitution says that if the President and Vice President come from the same state, they must forfeit that state's electoral votes. Thus a Johnson-Connally ticket would lose Texas's twenty-five electoral votes.
[2] In Atlantic City. The not-very-hidden implication was that Johnson was using his men to wheel and deal on his behalf to find a solution to Mississippi.

I don't plan to today. . . . Today I saw in the morning paper where Dave Lawrence[1] called me. I haven't talked to Dave Lawrence. They just write these damned lies! . . .

Here's what I'm gonna say to 'em. [reading from a handwritten statement:] Whatever number of months it is—forty-four months ago—"I was selected to be the Democratic Vice President. . . . On that fateful November day last year, I accepted the responsibility of the President, asking God's guidance and the help of all of our people. For nine months, I've carried on as effectively as I could. Our country faces grave dangers. These dangers must be faced and met by a united people under a leader they do not doubt. After thirty-three years in political life, most men acquire political enemies as ships accumulate barnacles. The times require leadership about which there is no doubt and a voice that men of all parties and sections and color can follow. I've learned, after trying very hard, that I am not that voice or that leader. Therefore . . . I suggest that the representatives from all states of this Union selected for the purpose of selecting a Democratic nominee for President and Vice President proceed to do their duty. And that no consideration be given to me because I am *absolutely unavailable.*". . .

Then they can just pick the two they want for the two places. We'll . . . do the best we can to help till January. Then, if he's elected . . . they can have a new and fresh fellow without any of the old scars. And I don't want this power of the Bomb. I just don't want these decisions I'm being required to make. I don't want the conniving that's required. I don't want the disloyalty that's around. I don't want the bungling and the inefficiencies of our people.

. . . .

REEDY: This will throw the nation into quite an uproar, sir.

LBJ: Yeah, I think so. And I think that now is the time, though. I don't know any better time. . . . I am absolutely positive that I cannot lead the South and the North. . . . And I don't want to lead the nation without my own state and without my own section.[2] I am very convinced that the Negroes will not listen to me.[3] They're not going to follow a white Southerner. And I think the stakes are too big to try to compromise.[4] I look at the *Herald Tribune.* There's nothing but the things that we've done terrible. I read the *New York Times.* We had a "pallid platform."[5] That was outrageous. I picked up every paper I had this morning, and we'd just played hell. There are just bound to be a lot of people that don't have these doubts and these angers . . . I have to carry. And the nation ought to have a chance to get the best available. That's who I want *my* children to have. And I know that I'm not.

REEDY: I think it's too late, sir. I know it's your decision, because you're the man that has to bear the brunt. But right now I think this just gives the country to Goldwater.

[1] The Pennsylvania Democratic leader.
[2] In other words, if Texas and the South oppose him that fall.
[3] As demonstrated to Johnson by their failure to fall into line on Mississippi.
[4] On Mississippi.
[5] A *New York Times* editorial that morning said that the Democrats had drafted a "pallid platform" that "blurs the nature of the contest" with Goldwater. This was the result of LBJ's demands for a document that would attract Republicans and independents.

LBJ: That's all right. I don't care. I'm just willing to—I don't *think* that. I don't *agree* with that a-tall. But I think that he could do better than I can because—

REEDY: He can't, sir. He's just a child. And look at our side. We don't have *anybody*. The only man around I'd trust to be President would be McNamara, and he wouldn't stand a chance.

LBJ: No, but we didn't trust any of the rest of 'em. You know, we didn't trust Eisenhower or Jack Kennedy. That's a matter for *them*.[1] Anyway they've been running their business for a couple hundred years, and I'll leave it up to them. And their processes can work without any dictation—without any influence from me.[2] And I don't feel like that I want to live with my wife and my daughters and the things they're going through, like *Time* magazine this week and the lies that they published.[3] I just don't want to be the center of attention enough that they're interested in publishing that stuff. I just want to be away from it. And I know that a man ought to have the hide of a rhinoceros to be in this job. But I don't. . . . And I'm not seeking happiness. I'm just seeking a little comfort once in a while. Getting away from it. I think I've earned it after thirty-three years. And I don't see any reason why I must die in it.[4]

REEDY: I think you've earned it too, sir. But I don't think it's a question of having a hide of a rhinoceros. It's kind of a question of rising above these things.

LBJ: Well, I can't do that. . . . I have a desire to unite people. And the South is against me and the North is against me. And the Negroes are against me. And the press doesn't really have an affection for me—or an understanding. And I'm unable to give it to 'em. I try, but I just look in that *Philadelphia Inquirer* this morning. Our friend Henry Brandon,[5] whom I do not know, but—"a textbook caricature of a fast-dealing politician. . . . He has not aroused any excitement as a person or any emotion or enthusiasm as a human being.". . .

REEDY: . . . Much worse things than that have been said about Presidents, sir. Abraham Lincoln was called a baboon.

LBJ: That's right. I'm not debating. I know that. I know another Johnson[6] sat in this same place and suffered more anguish than I'm suffering. But I don't see any reason why I *need* to. And I think it's a pretty peaceful period. . . . They can work it out. And I know that I'm *not* the best in the country and I have faith in the system that can select him so—*they* may not know I'm not the best. But if you got any thoughts, or any way that you can improve this—I'm not gonna make it very long—I'm just about ready to sign it off—I'd be glad to have 'em.

[1] The delegates.

[2] Johnson is still smarting from press criticism that he is dictating what happens at the convention.

[3] *Time* that week ran a long article on Johnson's fortune, "The Multimillionaire," and Lady Bird's role in it, which included a carping passage about her looks, clothes, manners, use of language, accent, and taste in music (August 28, 1964).

[4] Johnson was more aware of his own mortality than he ever let on in public. Not only had he suffered a massive coronary in 1955, but he was aware that men in his family had always died young.

[5] Washington correspondent for the *Sunday Times* of London.

[6] Andrew Johnson, who had suffered through Reconstruction. LBJ clearly understands the historical parallel. (See 8:25 P.M. Walter Reuther conversation, August 24, 1964, above.)

WALTER JENKINS
11:23 A.M.

LBJ: I don't believe there'll be many attacks on the orders I issue on Tonkin Gulf if I'm not a candidate.[1] And then I think the people will give the man that they want . . . a mandate. And he might continue the good work we've done. And I don't know who it would be. I expect it would be Bobby Kennedy and Hubert Humphrey. . . . But I believe they can get along with the Negroes better than I can. It's obvious to me that I haven't *got* any influence with 'em. Here at the crowning point in my life, when I need people's help, I haven't even got the loyal here—Ken O'Donnell and Larry O'Brien, my Attorney General. . . . So I just . . . don't see any reason why I ought to seek the right to endure anguish. . . . People I think have mistaken judgment. They think I want great power. And what I want is great solace—and a little love. That's all *I* want.

JENKINS: You have a lot more of that.

LBJ: I don't know. I looked at every paper this morning. . . . Jimmy Breslin's column had those two pictures that they put up for me—I never knew of it. I wish they didn't have a picture of me in the hall.[2] But it was the "arrogance run wild" and I'm "making every decision." . . . Humphrey—everything you say to Humphrey. . . . All of 'em working on the "Johnson compromise."[3] . . . I don't think a white Southerner is the man to unite this nation in this hour. I don't know who *is*, and I don't even want *that* responsibility. . . . I probably oughtn't to have told you about it, but I rather guess that if anybody's entitled to know, you are—what I'm thinking.

And I think that some of 'em will charge you with cowardice[4]—not wanting to face up to it. But I'd just as soon be charged with being a coward as being charged with being a thief.[5] Being charged with the things that they do say—being a manipulator and a conniver and a spendthrift. . . . Every column. . . . I've had doubts about whether a man born where I was born, raised like I was raised, could ever satisfy the Northern Jews and Catholics and union people. . . . And I don't feel good about throwing Alabama out and Mississippi and making them take an oath. . . . That don't make me happy either. . . . I don't want to have to *fight* to carry Texas. I just don't want Texas to have to say yes to me anymore. I've asked 'em the last time I wanna ask 'em. And if you don't know how that feels, why, you go out and start asking a man to please give you a quarter for a cup of coffee.

· · · ·

LBJ: I'd really honestly just say that "he believes that all of you've got more at stake than he has. And he has great respect for these people." So what I would suggest is that you get 'em in together this morning—they ought to be meeting

---

[1] This is just the argument that LBJ made for pulling out in 1968—that it would keep his decision-making on Vietnam from being viewed as partisan.

[2] The *New York Herald Tribune* columnist Jimmy Breslin had complained about the two huge LBJ portraits at the front of the convention hall, with much smaller pictures of Roosevelt, Truman, and Kennedy above them.

[3] Johnson is complaining that despite his admonition to conceal his role in the Mississippi negotiations, Humphrey's people have referred to LBJ's private formula for a solution as the "Johnson compromise."

[4] Meaning charge Johnson with cowardice.

[5] LBJ refers to the exposés of his private business dealings.

all day—and thinking about approaches.[1] . . . And then get the consensus there.
. . . And John[2] can go and talk to Sanders[3] and some of 'em. But I just don't want
Bill Moyer [*sic*] to call me up and say, "Sanders says that he's going to walk."
'Cause I don't *give* a goddamn whether he walks. . . . And I rather think that this
Freedom Party was born in the Justice Department.[4]

JENKINS: I don't agree with you on not winning.[5]

LBJ: . . . I just don't believe that you can ever carry a beer election in Blanco.
[chuckles] It's a prohibition town. . . . I just believe there's so much hatred of
Mississippi that nobody's really going to want to go on a roll call with 'em. And
I think they'll run just like quail.

. . . .

LBJ: I do not believe, Walter, that I can physically and mentally—Goldwater's
had a couple of nervous breakdowns and I don't want to be in this place like
Wilson.[6] And I do not believe I can physically and mentally carry the responsibilities of the bomb and the world and the Negroes and the South. . . . Now there
are younger men and better-prepared men and better-trained men and Harvard-
educated men. And I know my own limitations. . . . And I think the time to make
that decision is while they're there[7]—and not after they go home. I've thought
about it a good deal this morning. I haven't written a statement in twenty years,
but I'm just getting ready to write this one. I just got one more sentence on it,
and I told 'em to have a helicopter stand by. . . . I'll decide during the lunch hour
what I do about it—and either come on up there or call in a press conference
here. You have any idea which would be better, from your vantage point?

JENKINS: I would—

LBJ: From my standpoint, it'd be better here because you don't have to go
through any of the handshaking and the folderol. On the other hand, you kind
of hate for your managers to hear it through the press.

JENKINS: I don't think you ought to do it.

LBJ: If I'm gonna do it, I'm gonna *do* it! I *told* you that.

JENKINS: . . . If it's easier for you there, then I'd do it there.

LBJ: That's what *I* think it will be. Bird thought I ought to go up there because
it wasn't quite right to hold 'em up this long and have everybody guessing. I
think I've *got* to decide on the vice presidency today[8] 'cause Humphrey is just
being interviewed every ten minutes. . . . It's undignified.

---

[1] Meaning gather party leaders to solve the Mississippi problem.
[2] Connally.
[3] Governor Carl Sanders of Georgia.
[4] Meaning that Robert Kennedy has inspired the Freedom Party in order to damage Johnson.
[5] Johnson has insisted that a floor fight would result in the ouster of the white Mississippi regulars.
[6] Woodrow Wilson, the twenty-eighth President, who spent his last seventeen months in office paralyzed by a stroke. Since childhood Johnson had had nightmares of paralysis (Doris Kearns, *Lyndon Johnson and the American Dream*, p. 342). To make matters worse, in early August 1964, Lady Bird had read Gene Smith's *When the Cheering Stopped* (Morrow, 1964), which describes Wilson's decline. She dictated into her diary that the book was "proof" that the presidency was "a killing job" (August 1, 1964).
[7] While delegates are in Atlantic City.
[8] If Johnson does not withdraw from the race.

JENKINS: It's pretty hard for him not to. . . .

LBJ: I know, but I'm not gonna go through with *him* for four years, if I had to.[1]

A.W. MOURSUND
12:00 P.M.

> MOURSUND, in Atlantic City, tries to poison Johnson against Humphrey, whom he finds too liberal, for Vice President by saying that he has heard that Humphrey has asked Missouri Senator Stuart Symington to second his nomination.

MOURSUND: I thought you ought to know that. . . . Evidently he must feel kind of cocky about it.

LBJ: I guess so. I haven't heard it. There's no basis for it.

MOURSUND: I didn't figure there was. But he's always been that way.

LBJ: Yes, although not so much so. I'm just finishing this sentence. I'm going into the Security Council in about one minute.[2] I've just written me out a little statement. I'm just deciding whether I'm going to come up there and make it or make it at a three o'clock press conference here. [reads statement aloud, adding new ending:] "I shall carry forward, with your help, until a new President is sworn in next January, and then return to my home, as I have wanted to since the day I took this job."

• • • •

MOURSUND: I know your statement is on a hell of a lot higher level than 98 percent of the people think. They'll end up nominating this little bastard Bobby Kennedy, and he's a lightweight. Goldwater is a lightweight. And where we go, I don't know.

LBJ: . . . They've done it two hundred years though, and we've come through pretty well. And they have this machinery and it's not going to be assembled.[3] I'd hate like hell to try to reach them next September. . . . I think that clock's ticking.

MOURSUND: I'll be goddamned. I don't want to ever be in the position of saying that you ought to do this. Do you know a man who can do it right now?

LBJ: We'll see.

HUBERT HUMPHREY and WALTER REUTHER
2:31 P.M.

> AFTER THE NSC MEETING and lunch, Johnson went to his bedroom but could not sleep. He told Lady Bird that he did not want to accept the nomination. He would not go to Atlantic City. She did not take this lightly. Knowing

---

[1] In his glum mood, Johnson is unhappy with everybody.
[2] LBJ was about to meet with the National Security Council in the Cabinet Room.
[3] Meaning that at the end of this week, the convention delegates will disassemble.

how impetuous her husband was and how fast this convention could spin out of his control, she tried to talk him out of it. Later she dictated into her diary, "I do not remember hours I ever found harder."[1] But now, from Atlantic City, Humphrey and Reuther tell the President that a deal has been struck—Johnson's original formula, enhanced by a promise to give the MFDP insurgents two at-large convention votes.[2] There will be no floor fight over Mississippi.

REUTHER: Hubert and I have got a meeting set up at three-thirty with Dr. King and this fellow Henry[3] and I think we can . . . get this . . . fight off the television cameras. . . . We can all leave here together united and go back and do the hard work of winning this election behind your leadership.

HUMPHREY: Mr. President . . . we're not going to meet with Dr. Luther King or anybody else to negotiate.[4] . . . We've taken a position now. . . . We know it's right.

LBJ: Did you talk to any of their people[5] about this?

REUTHER: Yes, we have had some informal talks. . . . But I am confident that we can reduce the opposition to this to a microscopic faction so that they'll be completely unimportant.

· · · ·

LBJ: [immensely relieved:] I think it's a good solution. . . . Our party's always been a group that you can come to with any bellyache and injustice, whether it was a pecan-shelling plant that paid four cents an hour or sweatshop wages or usurious interest rates or discrimination to vote or Ku Klux Klan whipping somebody. . . . That's what the Democratic party's for. That's why it was born. And that's why it survives. . . . Long as the poor and the downtrodden and the bended know that they can come to us and be heard. And that's what we're doing. We're hearing 'em. . . . We passed a law back there in '57 and said it was the first time in eighty-five years that everyone was going to have a chance to vote. . . . And we're going to say it again in the convention in '64. . . . Get ahold of these people and say to 'em, "For God's sakes, we've tasted from the cup of injustice ourselves. . . . You're going to have a President and . . . a Vice President . . . that you trust. You're going to have Congress. . . . Let's all get out there in the precincts . . . we'll start out next January and do enough about . . . economic and

---

[1] Diary of Lady Bird Johnson, August 25, 1964, Johnson Library. Later in the afternoon, after a long walk with Lynda on the South Grounds, she wrote her husband, "You are as brave a man as Harry Truman—or FDR—or Lincoln. . . . To step out now would be wrong for your country. . . . Your friends would be frozen in embarrassed silence and your enemies jeering. I am not afraid of *Time* or lies or losing money or defeat." Earlier, in May, she had written him that should he not run, "I dread seeing you semi-idle, frustrated . . . seeing you look at Mr. X running the country and thinking you could have done it better. You may look around for a scape-goat. I do not want to be it. You may drink too much—for lack of a higher calling" (quoted in Lyndon Baines Johnson, *The Vantage Point*, pp. 93–94). As in August, LBJ's private talk about leaving the presidency in May came as Lady Bird was being publicly criticized—for the state of her Alabama property. This suggests that one factor in Johnson's August soliloquies was his desire to show his wife that he was ready to spare her any more such annoyances.
[2] Which are meaningless, since no issues will come for a roll call.
[3] Martin Luther King and MFDP chairman Aaron Henry.
[4] Meaning to negotiate further.
[5] Black leaders and MFDP members.

social and other interests that we can go in there and send a fellow like Humphrey down to make a speech now and then and cry with 'em a little."

• • • •

LBJ: [Now that Humphrey has helped to settle the Mississippi problem, Johnson cryptically suggests that he can expect to be Vice President:] Hubert, I'm not a sadistic person, as you well know. . . . I'm not just trying to play coy. . . . Since our conversation on the phone, I don't think we need to have any more—back there two or three weeks ago, a month ago, when Jim Rowe was here.[1] You don't have to spell out everything.

• • • •

LBJ: [warning that no one must learn that he was involved in the Mississippi solution:] Don't have people saying that I'm making you do this. I never heard of it. It's your proposal. . . . And my name's Joe Glutz. . . . We understand each other all right?

HUMPHREY: [elated:] We understand each other perfectly.

LBJ: I'll be in touch with you.

REUTHER: We'll go to work and put this in bed and we can relax. . . .

LBJ: . . . Don't tell anybody. Just you talked to Joe Glutz. That's my name.

JOHN CONNALLY
4:32 P.M.

> MARTIN LUTHER KING, Roy Wilkins, and other civil rights leaders tolerate the compromise, but two thirds of the MFDP delegation and the white Mississippi regulars do not. Nevertheless a floor fight has been thwarted. Johnson ceases all talk about withdrawing his name for President.

CONNALLY: How are you, sir?

LBJ: [chuckles, his good humor returned] Oh-h, doing the best I can.

• • • •

LBJ: John. . . . I'll take anything that any of you can work out anywhere to keep from showing our ass. I just—"nigger, nigger, nigger"—and I've got so much of it that I wrote out a statement this morning that *would* have solved it. I'm just harassed to death. . . . Mississippi's seated! She gets every damned vote she's entitled to. She oughtn't to be seated. She wouldn't let those nigras vote.[2] And that's not right. . . . Now she says, "I'm gonna be a goddamn dog in the manger."[3]

---

[1] See LBJ conversations with Rowe and Humphrey, July 30, 1964, above.
[2] LBJ refers to the Mississippi Democrats who prevented blacks from voting.
[3] That evening angry MFDP opponents of the compromise staged a heavily televised illegal "walk-in" and took the empty seats of the Mississippi delegation.

WALTER JENKINS
5:46 P.M.

LBJ: We might call McCormack[1] and ask him to tell the convention that I'm asking Senator Humphrey to run.[2] . . . Now would you call McCarthy first?

JENKINS: Yes, sir.

LBJ: Where do I stop then? . . .

JENKINS: . . . I think anybody who was ever seriously considered.

LBJ: . . . Who else would I call?

JENKINS: Brown.[3]

LBJ: Brown? He's nominating me. He knows he's out, doesn't he?

JENKINS: I think so, but I'm not sure.

LBJ: . . . Call Brown and Wagner[4] and just tell 'em I'm asking Humphrey to come down here tonight and go on the ticket.

WALTER JENKINS
5:51 P.M.

> DESPITE TELLING Humphrey three hours earlier that they didn't need any more conversation, Johnson has, through Walter Jenkins, asked Humphrey to study and comment on a *Washington Post* article of that day, based on a background interview with Johnson, in which LBJ outlines his demands of a Vice President.[5] Now Jenkins reports Humphrey's answer.

JENKINS: He said there was complete understanding and complete agreement. . . . He read the story in the newspaper and thought it was excellent. He said that . . . he could not beat how LBJ did for Kennedy in these various fields. . . . He would try to tie it. As far as timing,[6] he thought tonight was fine. He could get there on short notice. . . . If he left here,[7] he didn't believe he could do it without it being known he was leaving here.

. . . .

LBJ: I'd just tell him that the President had said he wanted to see him. . . .

JENKINS: Yeah, we told him if it gets out, he's off.

[1] The House Speaker and convention chairman.
[2] For Vice President. Johnson is beginning to lay the groundwork, but he wishes to keep the secret for another day in order to maintain dramatic tension and take the focus away from lingering problems over Mississippi.
[3] The California Governor.
[4] The New York Mayor.
[5] For instance, "He would have the Vice President make systematic trips . . . to explain Administration policies. . . . He would not look with favor on a Vice President who held news conferences."
[6] For the announcement of Johnson's running mate.
[7] Atlantic City.

LBJ: And just tell him . . . we'll just sit down and talk about some things and we'll decide how it is best for me to communicate it to the convention.

WALTER JENKINS
9:00 P.M.

A PLANE CHARTERED to fly Humphrey to Washington has been grounded by weather. Johnson is angry at Humphrey again after watching him on television, basking in the Mississippi compromise.

JENKINS: The weather has closed in and no planes are going to leave for a while.

LBJ: I don't think they ought to leave tonight anyway. . . . You've *got* to sit down . . . with him and tell him that he's just *got* to quit antagonizing the South. . . . He's just *got* to stay off that television, talking about he and Reuther are fixing this thing up. He doesn't say he did, but the commentators say he did. And I think we had better wait until the morning.

WEDNESDAY, AUGUST 26, 1964

BILL MOYERS
11:50 A.M.

MOYERS: There's a rumor . . . that you may make the announcement[1] on television tonight. . . . People are all standing around the hall expectantly awaiting some kind of announcement at the White House. . . . We've got the suspense going.

. . . .

LBJ: When Kennedy was nominated, he made a brief appearance that night.[2] Then he came back later to have his acceptance speech.

MOYERS: . . . Of course, he wasn't President.

LBJ: I don't want to sit around here though and let Bobby and them dominate that convention. . . . You know, he's got all these Irish Catholic girls writing for him. [reads aloud from newspaper:] "Bobby Sweeps Atlantic City—Kennedy Magic."[3]

MOYERS: Mr. President, we're building a hell of a reception tomorrow night.[4] Just the damnedest reception anybody's ever had.

[1] On the vice presidency.
[2] JFK had appeared at the Los Angeles convention hall on the night of his nomination.
[3] By Mary McGrory, in the *Washington Star*.
[4] For Johnson's acceptance speech.

•   •   •   •

MOYERS: Tomorrow needs to be the mark. It needs to become Lyndon Johnson's convention and Lyndon Johnson's party. And I think it will.

•   •   •   •

LBJ: I thought I might have Humphrey come down here late this afternoon.

WALTER JENKINS
12:30 P.M.

LBJ: I sure want Bobby to nominate me, if he will. I think even to the extent
of your calling him. But you ought to give Ken[1] one more time. Just say . . . if
. . . we're going to work as a team here—why, we see in the paper that we're
going to do campaign work for Bobby in New York—we want him to work with
us tonight and put an end to all this hell-raising. And he doesn't have to speak
but two minutes. . . .

JENKINS: All right.

LBJ: Tell Ken, by God, I want that done. If he doesn't want to do it, all right.
I'll remember that when he wants *me* to do something. . . . Say that's prime
television time and all he has to say is what he said yesterday—that he wants
the programs of his brother carried on. . . . President Johnson will carry them on
in the White House and he'll carry them on in New York. Second the nomination.

JENKINS: All right, sir.

LBJ: Number two, I would have that plane—try to have Hubert here about
four o'clock. . . . And let me know, so I can have my car meet him at the airport.
Tell Jack Valenti when you call to be sure my big Cadillac goes out and my
regular chauffeur, so they will know it is my car.

JENKINS: All right.

•   •   •   •

LBJ: But try to wind up that Bobby thing. . . . [then, on second thought:] Maybe
we oughtn't shove that. I don't know whether we need him to be seconding us
or not.

JENKINS: I don't think we need him, but we've got the question out and . . . I
think we ought to know whether he's going to say no or not.[2]

RICHARD DALEY
5:55 P.M.

THE PREVIOUS DAY, certain that he would not be chosen for Vice President,
convinced that Johnson had been toying with him, Eugene McCarthy wired

---

[1] O'Donnell, who had been asked to make this request of Kennedy.
[2] Robert Kennedy made no speech for Johnson that night.

LBJ and announced to the press that he was withdrawing his name.[1] Still eager to fabricate some mystery, Johnson has arranged for Connecticut Senator Thomas Dodd to fly with Humphrey to Washington. In Atlantic City, Mayor Daley is worried that the attention of the press and television will be riveted on a planned convention floor sit-in by the Mississippi Freedom Democratic Party that night. He calls Johnson to say that he had better do something to turn the spotlight back to himself.

DALEY: You know, we're at our peak tonight when you're nominated. . . . Hell, I'd really like to see you ride up there and surprise all of them and . . . walk into that hall. . . . Tonight . . . you're at your zenith.

• • • •

LBJ: The experts . . . thought that right after you're finished nominating, they'd switch to the White House office, where I'm working. . . . Then . . . they'd . . . let me recommend my man for Vice President . . .

DALEY: . . . Tonight I think the President belongs in the convention. . . . Sometimes these experts—all these guys that sell Campbell's Soup and Coca-Cola—they don't feel the human things.

LBJ: [chuckles] . . . I got Hubert here. . . . I'm going to see him in about thirty minutes. I'm probably going to try to have a meeting of the mind with Hubert.

DALEY: [ignoring news about Humphrey:] I would love to see you be in Atlantic City tonight. . . . What the hell—all this thing about the *Vice* President!

LBJ: [chuckles] Is it all right with you if I go along with Humphrey?

DALEY: Why, it is. I've told you a hundred times! Anything you want, I'm with you one hundred percent, and he's a good man. . . . I love him and I think he'll do a good job. Just as you did in '60 when the man[2] talked to me, like you are. He said, "What do you think of him?"[3] I said, "If you get him, it's the greatest choice you can make."

LBJ: God bless you.

GEORGE REEDY
6:04 P.M.

AFTER A BRIEF SHAM TALK with Dodd in the Cabinet Room, Johnson tells Reedy that Mayor Daley thinks that he should fly with Humphrey to announce his Vice President in Atlantic City tonight.

LBJ: Dick Daley just says to hell with everything—that "you're crazy not to do it." . . . And I don't like to get in an argument with Dick Daley when I need those votes in Chicago. . . . That messes up my birthday party with my press, doesn't it?[4]

[1] Some later wondered whether McCarthy's irritation with Johnson's treatment of him in 1964 was one reason behind his challenge to LBJ in 1968.
[2] John Kennedy.
[3] Johnson.
[4] On this, the night before his fifty-sixth birthday, there was a plan for Johnson to share a cake with reporters.

REEDY: Yes sir, and it'd get you some very bad reaction . . . because we can't bring the Washington press up with us if you go up tonight.

LBJ: Why can't we?

REEDY: Couldn't get a plane in time.

LBJ: I'd just call and see if you couldn't get one.

FRANCIS SMITH

Chairman, Philadelphia County Democratic Executive Committee
6:12 P.M.

> IN THE CABINET ROOM, Johnson asked Humphrey, "Do you want to be Vice President?" Humphrey said yes. LBJ said, "You have to understand that this is like a marriage with no chance of divorce." Humphrey said, "You can trust me, Mr. President."[1] With their troth sealed, Johnson takes his running mate into the Oval Office to share the news by telephone with powerful Democrats.

LBJ: I'm going to . . . probably ask him to help us on this ticket. And . . . I'd like to be able to tell him that I talked to Dick Daley, you and Bob Wagner and John Connally.

SMITH: Mr. President, I'm for anybody you're for and God bless the both of you.

LBJ: . . . I'll probably see you tonight. You got anybody there that can holler?

SMITH: . . . You can tell Humphrey that I'm a million percent for him.

LBJ: Wait just a minute. You tell him that yourself. [aside:] Hubert, mash that button—that top button.

HUMPHREY: Hello, Frank?

SMITH: God bless you and good luck to you.

HUMPHREY: . . . We'll be there working with you, friend.

· · · ·

LBJ: Say, Frank, don't say anything about this![2]

MURIEL HUMPHREY

Wife of Hubert Humphrey
6:34 P.M.

> JOHNSON AND HUMPHREY returned to the Cabinet Room, where Rusk, McNamara, and Bundy were waiting. LBJ told Humphrey that the three men had all been "pushing you" and installed him in the Vice President's place. Johnson had the White House operator find Muriel Humphrey in Atlantic City.

[1] As Humphrey recalled in his memoirs, *The Education of a Public Man* (Doubleday, 1976), pp. 301–03.
[2] Humphrey's selection or Johnson's trip to Atlantic City.

He told her, "We're going to nominate your boy!"[1] Then he put the excited Humphrey on the line.

HUMPHREY: The President's been wonderful and we're sitting together here with the Secretary of State and Secretary of Defense and Mr. McGeorge Bundy. . . . Are you ready to go over to the auditorium tonight?

MURIEL HUMPHREY: . . . The whole family is getting together and we're going to the Pageant[2] for dinner. . . . When will you be back?

HUMPHREY: . . . I'll be back for the convention. . . . There may be other things happening too.[3]

MURIEL HUMPHREY: We'll be in the seats at nine.

HUMPHREY: Fine. Wonderful, darling. You feel good?

MURIEL HUMPHREY: Oh, yes! This just about floored me is all. I sat down before I took the phone.

HUMPHREY: You did? [chuckling with delight] I'll tell him what you said. . . .

MURIEL HUMPHREY: You tell him if he pulls any more of these though, I'm not sure, if I don't have a chair under me![4]

FRIDAY, AUGUST 28, 1964

GEORGE REEDY
1:31 A.M.

ON THURSDAY EVENING, with LBJ absent from the hall, Robert Kennedy stepped before the delegates for the first and only time. For twenty-two minutes, they cheered, wept, and blew horns, just as Johnson had feared.[5] But it was too late for RFK to rob him of anything at this convention. The hall was darkened for the film, *The Thousand Days*, showing the late President teaching his delighted little son how to tickle his chin with a buttercup. After more weeping, LBJ entered the hall to listen to Humphrey's bracing, taunting accep-

[1] Quoted in Hubert Humphrey, *The Education of a Public Man*, pp. 303–04. Johnson's portion of the conversation with Mrs. Humphrey does not appear on the tape.

[2] The Pageant Motor Inn.

[3] To avoid Johnson's wrath, Humphrey will not divulge LBJ's secret plan to fly to the convention that night.

[4] That night, Johnson and Humphrey flew, along with Dodd, to Atlantic City. After being nominated by acclamation, LBJ told the convention, referring to the Mississippi fight, that they had found "a fair answer to honest differences among honorable men." Then he recommended Humphrey—"not a sectional choice . . . not merely the way to balance the ticket. This is simply the best man in America for the job."

[5] Reading a passage from *Romeo and Juliet* given him by Jacqueline, Kennedy said in remembrance of his brother, "When he shall die / Take him and cut him out in little stars / And he will make the face of heaven so fine / That all the world will be in love with night, /And pay no worship to the garish sun." Did Jacqueline and Robert intend the final line to refer to LBJ?

tance speech.[1] By contrast, Johnson's own oration seemed flat and endless. But this did not reduce his pleasure. After he turned from the rostrum, fireworks lit the sky. Carol Channing sang "Hello, Lyndon!" while the President ate a huge slice of birthday cake in the shape of the United States.

After midnight, Johnson returned to the house borrowed for his stay in Atlantic City. To his annoyance, it had no air conditioning. In the bedroom, he put on the television and raised a glass with Abe Fortas and Clark Clifford—in celebration and relief. Then Johnson took a rubdown, put on his pajamas, and downed sandwiches and ice cream. He is dropping off to sleep when his press secretary calls.

REEDY: Mr. President, I thought you should know about a *Houston Post* story tonight, which said that I resigned out of a dispute with you over coming to the convention last night[2]—that the idea originated with Pierre Salinger[3] and I objected to it, and that I then handed in my resignation. And it's the wildest thing I ever read. I told the *Houston Post* there was just flatly nothing to it.

LBJ: [faint:] Of course not. I never heard of it. Pierre Salinger never made any such suggestion to me.

· · · ·

LBJ: Just say you never heard of it and they must have been smoking marijuana or something.

· · · ·

LBJ: [yawns] The only man that I know of that really had anything legitimate to do with my coming up here was Dick Daley. . . . He thought we could really take charge if we'd make an appearance. . . . He didn't say so, but what he meant did happen—he wanted us to run the Freedom Party completely out of town. There was only nine of 'em they could locate after I got in.

REEDY: It was a damn good idea.

· · · ·

REEDY: Incidentally, one question they have been asking me is whether Senator Humphrey is going to fly down to Texas with you.[4]

LBJ: Yes, he is.

REEDY: I meant in the same plane. They're thinking of this President–Vice President thing.

LBJ: Fly on the same plane. I flew with Kennedy a good deal on the same plane.[5]

---

[1] "Most Democrats and most Republicans in the United States Senate voted for an $11.5 billion tax cut. . . . But not Senator Goldwater! . . . Most Democrats and most Republicans in the United States Senate . . . voted for the Civil Rights Act of 1964. But not Senator Goldwater!"

[2] Meaning Wednesday night. See LBJ's 6:04 P.M. conversation with Reedy, above, August 26, 1964.

[3] After winning the Democratic primary for Senator from California, Salinger had been appointed interim Senator on the death of Clair Engle.

[4] At noon on Friday.

[5] In November 1963, during a Florida trip, President Kennedy had told LBJ, "Get in my plane." Secret Service agents pleaded with him to reconsider. Laughing, Kennedy asked, "Don't you fellows want McCormack as President?" This was on the weekend before his assassination (William C. Sullivan memorandum, December 1, 1963, FBI).

REEDY: The schedule I have . . . is ten o'clock[1] for this breakfast in the ballroom . . . with the campaign workers. . . . Then the schedule shows you leaving Atlantic City at eleven-forty. . . .

LBJ: Okay. [joking:] Don't resign anymore!

WALTER JENKINS
8:28 A.M.

JOHNSON IS BEING SERVED breakfast in bed.

LBJ: You have a big time last night?

JENKINS: Very good.

LBJ: What troubles do we have?

JENKINS: . . . I think the convention came near to solving some. . . . Everybody's happy. Everybody thinks it was a great convention. Everybody thinks the speeches last night were wonderful.

LBJ: Good. Well, I believe I'll go home. Looks like Vietnam's in trouble. . . . Looks like they have a committee triumphant, ruling the country.[2] How long did I speak last night?

JENKINS: Forty-two minutes.

LBJ: God Almighty! With fifteen hundred words. Isn't that awful?

JENKINS: There was so much applause and so much demonstrating. . . .

LBJ: . . . How many applauses did I get?

JENKINS: Practically every sentence.

McGEORGE BUNDY
10:17 A.M.

BUNDY: Sir, that was great![3]

LBJ: Looks like you and Khanh got things messed up while I was up here looking after political affairs.

BUNDY: Oh, boy, Mr. President! We are keeping Max there, unless you've changed your mind.[4] . . .

[1] Friday morning.

[2] Emboldened by Johnson's Gulf of Tonkin reprisals, Prime Minister Khanh had declared a state of emergency, tightened censorship, drafted a new constitution, fired his chief rival, General Minh, the titular head of state, and appointed himself President of South Vietnam. Students and militant Buddhists marched through the capital. On August 25, Khanh quit, formed a temporary triumvirate with Generals Khiem and Minh, then flew off to the mountain retreat of Dalat, complaining of hemorrhoids and high blood pressure. In Saigon, Khanh's departure was followed by bloody riots.

[3] Bundy is speaking from the White House.

[4] Taylor, the new Ambassador in Saigon, had warned Khanh against "sweeping changes" that might provoke protests. He had been planning to come to Washington.

LBJ: Yeah, that's right. I would.[1]

BUNDY: Bob McNamara still thinks it's a mistake, but I've told him that just the appearance would be ruinous if Max came out of there and the thing came apart. . . .

LBJ: What happened?

BUNDY: . . . Our friend Khanh overplayed his hand and tried to get rid of Minh and set a situation in which he . . . allowed the Buddhists to trigger a lot of student parading. . . . Max Taylor has done an extraordinary job behind the scenes, quietly pressing home upon everybody, including Khanh, that this is no time to shake up the government. . . . Although Khanh . . . is not Napoleon, he is the strongest individual Max has yet seen. . . . So what we have to do is to live with this crowd. . . . The rioting . . . could get worse.

· · · ·

BUNDY: That was a great night last night, Mr. President!

LBJ: I thought we got out of this one all right.

BUNDY: . . . I won't tell you how long it[2] was because you probably don't want to be— [guffaws] —joked with.

LBJ: They told *me* it only had fifteen hundred words. . . .

BUNDY: It was twenty-four hundred words, Mr. President. We had it counted this morning.

LBJ: . . . Well, they just lied to me.

BUNDY: [laughs] But it was a *great job!*

LBJ: Forty-five minutes though, wasn't it?

BUNDY: It came across though. I was a simple TV viewer—Mary and I were. And we thought it was just great. . . . Well, sir, have a good weekend. When are you coming back? You don't know yet?

LBJ: Oh, about Tuesday, I guess, maybe.

BUNDY: Don't hurry. . . . We'll all be back here Monday and we'll keep business out of your hair, unless you want it.

GEORGE REEDY
5:50 P.M.

> THE JOHNSONS and Humphreys flew to the LBJ Ranch, where Jewel Malechek, wife of Johnson's ranch foreman, had baked him a chocolate birthday cake. The President ate a slice with milk, then retired for a nap. In the bedroom, he takes a call from Reedy, who has planned a press conference for tomorrow morning.

REEDY: I can offer them live television tomorrow at eleven or noon. . . .

LBJ: [sleepily:] . . . Doesn't look like to me like we're very prepared. Looks like everybody's pretty tired. We're pretty *bled* on the convention. I don't know

[1] Keep Taylor in Saigon.
[2] Johnson's acceptance speech.

what's happening in Vietnam and these other things. We ought to be prepared on it and I don't want to work getting it up.

REEDY: . . . If you and Senator Humphrey were to strike a few notes about a high-level campaign . . . I think it would go pretty well.

LBJ: I don't have a thing in the world to tell 'em. . . . We're just out here resting primarily. . . . I think we ought to just tell 'em that we've had a real long, difficult week and that we came in, we had a bite to eat, went to bed about four o'clock and just got up. And that everybody's tired and sleepy and we had a little nap. We're going over and ride in the boat in a while. . . . I don't believe it's good to get on live television if you got nothing to say.

· · · ·

REEDY: I'm going to be asked about this barbecue at Stonewall tomorrow.[1]

LBJ: . . . You don't know whether I'm going or not. . . . I resent the commercialness of it, and yet I don't want to turn down the poor sweet people. . . . [irritated:] I'd keep the White House press just as far away from Stonewall as I could. . . . They want to come up here and live, and I don't want 'em anywhere around. . . . They ought to be as far away from here as they can. All the time.

SATURDAY, AUGUST 29, 1964

DEAN RUSK
10:29 A.M.

> JOHNSON IS STAYING at his ranch, just as he had once planned to do on an earlier Saturday morning—November 23, 1963, when President and Mrs. Kennedy were to be his houseguests. Today his Secretary of State is calling about the new crisis in Vietnam, which is now more threatening.

RUSK: We're telling Max Taylor not to come on back until we have given him the word from here.

LBJ: I certainly agree.

RUSK: . . . He shouldn't rush back while there's still uncertainty and disorder out there. Are you meeting the press this afternoon?

LBJ: No.

RUSK: Because the situation in Saigon is a little difficult to handle. The leadership continues to be the same leadership, although there's some discussion of how they sort themselves out for the longer range. I think it would be important

---

[1] A birthday celebration by local Democrats.

for you to say as little as you think you can get away with, if you do see any
reporters today.

LBJ: I'm not going to say anything.

> Two days after this call, Johnson flew back to Washington. Bundy warned
> him by memo that the new crisis in South Vietnam "could hardly be more
> serious." There was a "drastic possibility" that Johnson would have to send
> "substantial armed forces" to Southeast Asia. Bundy wrote, "I myself believe
> that before we let this country go, we should have a hard look at this grim
> alternative, and I do not at all think that it is a repetition of Korea."[1]
>
> The second volume of *The Johnson White House Tapes* will begin with
> LBJ operating behind the scenes of the 1964 campaign, winning the greatest
> presidential election victory in modern times, and then plunging into war in
> Vietnam.

[1] Bundy to LBJ, August 31, 1964, Johnson Library.

Editor's Note

ONE DAY in mid-January 1973, in the presidential suite atop his presidential library, Lyndon Baines Johnson asked to see his longtime aide Mildred Stegall. She arrived to find her boss sitting in his gargantuan custom-built white corduroy reclining chair, his back to the commanding view of Austin.[1]

Johnson's white hair curled over his collar. His face was blotchy pink and gray from heart disease. He reminded Stegall that he was feeling ill and did not expect to live long. If he died, she must ensure that the recordings and transcripts of conversations he had secretly made as President, now in her custody, not be opened for at least fifty years. As far as he was concerned, he said, most of them should never be opened. It was her responsibility to carry out his instructions.

On Monday afternoon, January 22, 1973, in his bedroom at the LBJ Ranch, the thirty-sixth President of the United States reached for his telephone and asked a Secret Service agent to rush over. When the agent arrived, he found Johnson lying on the floor, stricken by a massive coronary.

A week after Johnson's death, Stegall signed a document ceding the sealed boxes of tapes[2] and transcripts to the Johnson Library. Her edict said that only after fifty years could the Archivist of the United States or the library director listen to the recordings. Then, in the year 2023, they must decide whether the tapes should be "promptly resealed or examined by the appropriate security officials of the government for possible clearance."[3]

---

[1] Chief sources for this Editor's Note are Mildred Stegall memoranda of January 29, 1973, and July 17, 1973 (Johnson Library); interviews with Mildred Stegall, July 17, 1997, and Johnson Library officials and archivists; and other Johnson Library materials.

[2] The word "tapes" is used here and throughout this book to refer both to the reel-to-reel recordings and to the Dictabelts made by Johnson.

[3] Mildred Stegall memorandum, January 29, 1973. The President's Daily Diary (Johnson Library) refers to the destruction of one Johnson tape—of a November 24, 1966, conversation with Abe Fortas—saying "belt destroyed on President's instruction." Neither Stegall nor Harry Middleton, director of the Johnson Library since its founding in 1971, know of any other effort by LBJ or his aides, during either the Johnson presidency or his retirement, to destroy tapes or otherwise sanitize the collection (Stegall and Middleton interviews). The absence of such an effort is almost impossible to prove. But it is given credence by other records and the frankness of much of the material on these tapes.

• • • •

Johnson began keeping exact records of his private conversations while Senate Major-ity Leader in the 1950s. He asked close aides—usually Walter Jenkins—to listen in on a dead-key telephone extension and keep a shorthand account of what LBJ and other senators told each other. This enabled Johnson later to remember what promises they had made and confront those who double-crossed him or said one thing in private and another in public. No doubt he also wished to create a historical record of his mastery as one of the most robust parliamentary leaders in American history.

As Vice President, walking around Room 274 of the Executive Office Building, Johnson used an Edison Voicewriter to record some of his private telephone conversa-tions on round red plastic platters. LBJ did not tell those with whom he spoke that they were being recorded. Presumably he drew no distinction between taping and letting Jenkins listen in with his stenographic pad. But like others at the time who were swept up by new recording technology without pondering its impact on privacy, he had crossed a Rubicon. Participants in conversations secretly transcribed in short-hand could always deny that their words were noted accurately. Not so for those who appeared on a tape.

So seized was Johnson by the historical and managerial importance of secretly recording his conversations that on his first night as President, despite all of his other worries, he apparently had the presence of mind to ensure that his first conversations in his new job were captured on a new IBM magnetic belt taping system. Once he moved to the Oval Office, Johnson used the Dictaphone system employed by John Kennedy, which recorded conversations on plastic Dictabelts.

Johnson thus became the only President to record himself from his first month in office to the last. Between November 1963 and January 1969, LBJ taped about 9,500 conversations, totaling about 643 hours.[1] (During the period covered by this volume, LBJ taped about 240 hours of conversation.)

Earlier Presidents had sporadically recorded themselves in private, but nowhere near so profusely. During his 1940 campaign against Wendell Willkie, Franklin Roo-sevelt accidentally preserved his request to start a whispering campaign about Will-kie's mistress on a three-foot-wide wire recorder located in the West Wing basement and attached to a microphone in the lamp on his desk. The device was intended to record his Oval Office press conferences. FDR almost never used it.[2] His successor, Harry Truman, was appalled by the idea of secret recording and had it yanked out.

Dwight Eisenhower installed a Dictaphone device to record himself in the Oval Office, but apparently used it very little. He told his Cabinet, "There are some guys I just don't trust in Washington and I want to have myself protected so they can't later report that I said something else."[3] A 1955 Dictabelt unearthed in 1997 lets us hear Ike inveighing to the Senate Foreign Relations Committee chairman, Walter George, against a proposed constitutional amendment to reduce his treaty-making power, blaming it on the national turn of mood against FDR, whom Eisen-hower considered "almost an egomaniac."[4] John Kennedy recorded about 250 hours of meetings and about 12 hours of telephone conversations during the last half of his presidency.

After Johnson moved into the Oval Office on the day after Kennedy's funeral, he ordered JFK's taping system expanded. New Dictaphone equipment appeared in

[1] Richard Nixon taped only from February 1971 to July 1973, less than half of his presidency, but because his system was voice-activated, roughly 3,700 hours were recorded.
[2] See *American Heritage*, February-March 1982.
[3] Quoted in William Bragg Ewald, Jr., *Eisenhower the President* (Prentice Hall, 1981), p. 89.
[4] January 7, 1955, Eisenhower Library. See also *Washington Post*, March 15, 1997.

the kneeholes of the desks of presidential secretaries, in the Situation Room, on the nightstand in the President's second-floor bedroom in the family quarters, at Camp David, in his bedroom and home office at the LBJ Ranch.

Before a telephone conversation that Johnson wished to be recorded, he might tell a secretary, "Take this," or "Get this down." If he was in the midst of an exchange going unrecorded and wanted it preserved, he might "mash a button" (Johnson's phrase[1]) to summon a secretary and then twirl his finger in the air. Dictaphones in LBJ's White House and ranch bedrooms were generally operated by Johnson or one of his valets. The great preponderance of tapes capture Johnson in telephone conversation, but the hands-free "squawk box" on LBJ's desk also recorded many face-to-face Oval Office encounters.[2] Often, after the exchange that Johnson had wished to record was over, the Dictaphone ground on, capturing other conversations that LBJ almost certainly did not intend to have preserved either for daily business or for history.

Johnson demanded that some of the tapes be immediately transcribed for his reference.[3] This put Johnson staff members under excruciating pressure. The secrecy, haste, and difficulty of the work made them nervous and they had other tasks to do. LBJ's secretary Yolanda Boozer recalled that during his early months in the White House she often worked at night, when there was less chance that an outsider might discover what she was doing. Transcripts were slipped into the President's bedroom night reading.

From early in his presidency, there were rumors that Johnson was taping some of his conversations. Robert Kennedy and the few others close to the slain President who knew about JFK's taping system had no reason to presume that Johnson would not use it. But no outsider could know how much more voraciously Johnson was taping than his predecessor.

In December 1967, Johnson ordered his taping system expanded to include the small room off the Oval Office that he used for naps and intimate meetings, as well as the Cabinet Room. Eight holes were drilled into the coffin-shaped Cabinet table to implant small microphones that ran to a Tandberg reel-to-reel tape recorder housed in a locked cabinet in the West Wing basement and operated by a switch on a table next to the President's armchair.

Anxious about leaks and the danger that a tape or transcript might fall into sinister hands, Johnson had made Mildred Stegall custodian of his fast-growing audio archive, which she kept in her West Wing office vault. By Stegall's recollection, about once every six months—much more often during the last year of Johnson's life, when he was certain that he was about to die—LBJ asked her for assurance that the collection was secure and "repeatedly stressed that no one was to have access to it."[4]

On November 12, 1968, Richard Nixon called at the White House, a week after

---

[1] LBJ used the same phrase to refer to a President issuing the command for nuclear war against the Soviet Union.

[2] In this book, "OFFICE CONVERSATION" refers to an exchange among Johnson and people who work for him—usually in the Oval Office or the adjoining lounge, occasionally with one of the aides by telephone from elsewhere. Other face-to-face conversations in this book are identified as such where that information provides an additional dimension of understanding.

[3] Other Presidents who taped, including Richard Nixon, did not use their recordings as a management tool. Nixon intended his taping system almost purely as a means of capturing exchanges that might be used later to burnish his historical reputation. In contrast, the preamble to a January 29, 1964, talk with Senate Majority Leader Mike Mansfield included in this book shows how LBJ sometimes used the transcripts of previous conversations: LBJ: "Yes?" SECRETARY: "I have the recordings of the Mansfield calls, but they are not transcribed. They will take a few minutes. And he is holding on 92."

[4] Mildred Stegall memorandum, July 17, 1973.

his election as President. Johnson showed him the taping equipment in his office and bedroom. He told Nixon that such a system would be vital in writing his memoirs and keeping abreast of daily business: "You've got to know what's happening, and the only way you can do that is to have a record of it."[1] Nixon listened politely but soon told his aide Robert Finch that the first thing he would do as President would be to rip out Johnson's taping system.[2]

Returned to the LBJ Ranch in January 1969, Johnson started work on his presidential memoirs, *The Vantage Point*. He reread old transcripts and had new ones made of some untranscribed conversations for possible use in the book. But still he kept the secret of his taping close to his vest. Doris Kearns, then a young political scientist and ex–White House Fellow helping to draft his memoirs, was kept sufficiently in the dark that in her own 1976 book on Johnson she refers to "a dozen or so typed transcripts apparently made from phone conversations which Johnson showed to me with the suggestion that from these I 'could learn more about the way government really works than from a hundred political science textbooks.' "[3] *The Vantage Point*, published in 1971, includes a number of brief quotations from Johnson's cache of transcripts but does not hint at their provenance.

· · · ·

The American people knew little about LBJ's taping until July 1973. Six months after Johnson's death, on national television, Nixon White House aide Alexander Butterfield told the Senate Watergate Committee that Nixon had been taping his private conversations. The public was furious to learn that their President had taped people without their knowledge. Lunging for self-protection, Nixon tried to hide behind LBJ's skirts. He had his lawyer, Fred Buzhardt, write committee chairman Sam Ervin that the Nixon recording system was "similar to that employed by the last administration."[4] But Americans remained ignorant of the full extent of Johnson's taping.[5]

By 1990, Harry Middleton, the LBJ White House speechwriter who was Director of the Johnson Library, Lady Bird Johnson, and other members of the Johnson circle were pondering whether they should overrule LBJ's insistence that the tapes be sealed until at least 2023. They established that they had the legal right to do so. They realized that the tapes might deteriorate if left untouched. And they knew that historians and the public had acquired a far more harshly demanding attitude about archival openness than they had when Johnson died, before Watergate. It was not hard to imagine that scholars suing for release of Richard Nixon's tapes and papers as historical documents paid for by taxpayers might turn their fire on Johnson's.

---

[1] Christopher Matthews interview with Nixon aide H.R. Haldeman, cited by Matthews in his *San Francisco Examiner* column, December 5, 1993.

[2] Nixon had the system removed on February 15, 1969. His post-presidential aide Monica Crowley quotes Nixon as saying in 1991 that "Johnson was obsessed with recording everything. . . . We know what my problems were with that crap, but Kennedy was the one to put it in, and Johnson worshipped it" (*Nixon Off the Record*, Random House, 1996, p. 17). It was in February 1971 that Nixon quietly installed his voice-activated system. Aides and admirers had convinced him that LBJ was right in arguing that a secret taping apparatus would help to ensure his place in history. Nixon had first asked for a system like Johnson's. But his Chief of Staff, H.R. Haldeman, worried that his boss would forget to have it turned on and off. He also felt that "this President was far too inept with machinery ever to make a success of a switch system" (*Prologue*, Summer 1988).

[3] *Lyndon Johnson and the American Dream*, p. 412.

[4] Buzhardt to Ervin, July 16, 1973, Sam Ervin Papers, University of North Carolina.

[5] In one of the first clues, the *Washington Post*'s Austin correspondent Dan Balz reported in 1982 that the Johnson tapes "may be more extensive than is generally believed" (February 4, 1982).

The John F. Kennedy Assassination Records Collection Act of 1992, passed by Congress in the wake of the furor generated by Oliver Stone's film *JFK*, required the Johnson Library, like all U.S. government archives, to open virtually all of its holdings dealing with the Dallas murder. Seizing the moment, Middleton and his colleagues pledged to open not only those recordings related to the assassination, but, to their great credit, the entire collection of Johnson White House tapes, covering the full Johnson presidency from November 1963 to January 1969, as swiftly as possible.[1]

. . . .

In creating this book, I have listened to virtually every Johnson White House tape for the period from November 1963 through August 1964—often many times—and have personally transcribed most of the conversations that appear here. The main reason for this is accuracy. The transcripts that LBJ's secretaries made of some of the tapes are fragmentary, inaccurate, and unreliable for the historian. Those created in the White House were intended to help the President in daily business. Those made in his retirement were intended chiefly to harvest quotations for *The Vantage Point*.

The pressure that LBJ imposed on his White House secretaries to get the transcripts done fast caused many mistakes. Perhaps the classic example appears in a secretarial transcript made of his talk with John McCormack of November 29, 1963, in which LBJ complains that he has a "pack them bastards" waiting to speak with him. Close listening to the tape and examination of Johnson's Daily Diary reveal that he actually said that he had the "Pakistan Ambassador" waiting to speak with him.[2] (It was an understandable error for the transcriber to make. Before Johnson became President, packs of bastards were probably more of a staple among his daily visitors than Pakistan ambassadors.)[3]

None of the tapes is easy to decipher. The Dictaphone of the 1960s was designed not for historiography but to record an executive's dictation. Sound quality is often flat and scratchy. Many of the people on these tapes have accents that are difficult to understand—not least LBJ himself, especially when he is tired. Some of Johnson's Oval Office recordings feature the President talking while beverage glasses are rattling, papers are being shuffled, toothpaste commercials are blaring out of a television set, and aides are chattering in the background. Thus the only way to make these tapes a reliable source is for a historian to be steeped in the daily history of LBJ's

[1] With the exception of the assassination openings, which include some conversations from 1966 and 1967, the Johnson White House tapes are being opened chronologically. Like all government holdings, the tapes are subject to a government classification process. Portions of tapes may be closed for reasons of national security or to conform to the donor's deed of gift, usually to avoid damaging living persons or releasing private family, medical, or financial information. The Johnson Library and the government have withheld less than 4 percent of the taped material for the period thus far released. Unlike the Richard Nixon estate, which is, as of this writing, demanding to have roughly one quarter of the Nixon White House tapes snipped out and returned to the Nixon family as "personal and private," the Johnson circle has made no effort to have any portions of the LBJ tapes permanently deleted on grounds of privacy. The only other body of taped Johnson conversations to be closed are six of the eight conversations that LBJ recorded with Jacqueline Kennedy during the period covered by this volume. As a courtesy, Lady Bird Johnson and Harry Middleton gave Mrs. Kennedy's daughter, Caroline, the option of keeping these tapes closed. Perhaps not surprisingly for the author of a book on privacy rights, but unfortunately for history, she has exercised it. Nevertheless, the library has released LBJ's conversations with Jacqueline Kennedy of June 20 and July 4, 1964, as they are part of larger exchanges. They appear in this volume.
[2] See the rendering in Chapter One of this book.
[3] Another mistaken secretarial transcript has LBJ telling Katharine Graham that her late husband was "pathetic," when in fact he had said "prophetic." (See conversation of December 2, 1963.)

presidency, armed with names, issues, and context, and to listen hard to every syllable —sometimes over and over again. Readers should remember that transcription of any historical recording will be, at least to some extent, subjective—especially from tapes whose quality is often poor.

As a historical source, the tape of a conversation has a towering advantage over a memorandum of the same exchange. Meaning is conveyed through not just language but tone, intensity, pronunciation, pauses, and other aspects of sound. In transforming the conversations from tape into the words that appear in this book, I have tried to render these elements as faithfully as possible.

One obvious issue is dialect. It would be easy to render LBJ, with his Hill Country accent (more noticeable when he was in Texas or talking to other Southerners), as some kind of country-and-western character. But that would be just as misleading as filling a volume of John Kennedy's conversations with similarly literal renderings of his Brookline accent—"Cuber," "heah," "leadah"—which would make that President, much admired for his eloquence, sound like a nightclub comedian.

What I have done in the case of Johnson and others on these tapes who speak with unusual accents, stresses, or pronunciations is to use italics or show the words phonetically only when these instances are conspicuous or when the more literal rendering adds meaning. Only occasionally in this book, for example, does LBJ say "fella" instead of "fellow" or drop Gs from his participles. (He does consistently say "you-all"—not the Alabaman's "y'all" or the Northerner's "you all.") I do show where Johnson and his interlocutors laugh and chuckle, and I use bracketed adjectives to convey the tone of some of the statements. Where Johnson or another figure uses incorrect grammar or pronunciation, I have in most cases simply rendered it as heard, without adding the interjection "[sic]."[1]

I have edited each conversation to exclude extraneous material and repetition, but not where that might change the meaning. Ellipses appear where shorter parts of conversations have been pared; a larger break is used for longer deletions. The only words to be eliminated without some kind of indication are "uhs," "wells," and similar interjections, but only in cases where they do not add meaning.

. . . .

The Johnson White House tapes allow us to listen in on an American presidency from beginning to end. This is the first time we have done so, and it will almost certainly be the last. Since the uproar over the Nixon tapes in 1973, Presidents have shrunk from that kind of comprehensive secret recording.[2]

Like any fresh primary source, secret White House tapes must be analyzed with skepticism. As Richard Nixon showed while trying to maneuver his White House counsel, John Dean, into taking the blame for Watergate, a President who knows he is taping a conversation can manipulate or entrap an interlocutor who does not.[3] He can also try to present the best face for history.[4]

---

[1] *Sic* is used in some cases where LBJ mangles proper names.

[2] While working on this volume, I asked President Clinton (for the record) whether he taped his conversations in the style of Presidents Johnson and Nixon. He chuckled and shook his head.

[3] As I suggest in Chapter Seven of this book, for instance, Johnson may be doing this when he tries to get Richard Russell to agree that Congress might "impeach" a President who failed to defend South Vietnam—and McGeorge Bundy to insist on firmness in Southeast Asia. Knowing (as he avows in other taped private conversations) the odds against victory in Southeast Asia, LBJ may have thought that such conversations might exculpate him with later historians should Vietnam end, as it did, in calamity.

[4] As Johnson did, for instance, when he recounted Oval Office confrontations with Robert Kennedy to others (such as Richard Maguire, February 11, 1964, and Clark Clifford and

The tapes opened thus far reveal surprisingly few efforts by Johnson to preen himself on them for history. Not only were many made for another purpose—to help him in his daily business—but beleaguered as he seemed to feel, even at the best of times, LBJ was unlikely to have often been willing to impair an effort to work his will over someone in order to impress some distant historian. And during many of these conversations, as earlier noted, Johnson had forgotten or was unaware that the hidden recorder was still running.

I have conceived this book in the style of an edited and annotated anthology of private letters written by a public figure in the days when leaders did business on paper, revealing their private purposes, methods, and obsessions. In the manner of such a collection, the conversations appear here in chronological order, suggesting the variety of issues and people with which a President has to deal almost simultaneously, how he obtains information and reacts to it, the pressures on him, and the flow of his hourly decision-making. My chief standard in deciding which conversations to include in the book is whether they add something of historical importance to what we knew before and whether they show us a heretofore unseen facet of Lyndon Johnson and the people with whom he dealt.

The mandate for a historian writing a book of his own prose is to draw on all sources available—tapes, letters, memos, cables, memoirs, oral histories, and other material—and strive to make lasting judgments. The editor of a volume of new primary source material, like this one, has a different responsibility—not to drown out the subject's voice with his own or pretend that final judgments can be based solely on a single category of source material, however rich. His task instead is preeminently to explain what the new material means and what it tells us beyond what we know already.

In the case of the Johnson White House tapes, that is a lot. More even than most Presidents, LBJ was famous for concealing himself. In an early draft of *The Death of a President*, William Manchester wrote that for Johnson, the shortest distance between two points was a tunnel.[1] Despite his expressed wish (at the May 1971 opening of his presidential library) to have history written "with the bark off," LBJ had a nineteenth-century notion of how a President should look and sound.[2] His speeches, press conferences, television interviews, and memoirs were almost designed to conceal the earthy, vulnerable, suspicious, affectionate, devious, explosive, funny, domineering, sometimes threatening private man who strides across the pages of this book. That the tapes might one day offer later generations a sustained look at the more primal Lyndon Johnson may have bothered him. But it is safe to assume that one thing would bother him more—being forgotten.

McGeorge Bundy, July 29, 1964)—demonstrating the audio equivalent of Dean Acheson's maxim that no man comes out of his own memorandum of conversation looking second best.

[1] See William Manchester, *Controversy* (Little, Brown, 1976), pp. 21–22. This was the kind of statement that was reported back to Johnson and made him so angry at Manchester and his book.

[2] Doris Kearns wrote that after she drafted a passage from LBJ's private anecdotes for *The Vantage Point*, he told her, "For Christ's sake, get that vulgar language of mine out of there. What do you think this is, the tale of an uneducated cowboy? It's a Presidential memoir, damn it, and I've got to come out looking like a statesman, not some backwoods politician" (*Lyndon Johnson and the American Dream*, p. 355).

Cast of Characters

Here are key figures who appear in this volume of *The Johnson White House Tapes*, identified by the principal title(s) they held during the period it covers.

CARL ALBERT (1908–   ). House Majority Leader, Democrat of Oklahoma.

JOSEPH ALSOP (1910–1989). Columnist, *Washington Post*.

CLINTON ANDERSON (1895–1975). Democratic Senator from New Mexico.

ROBERT ANDERSON (1910–1989). Former Secretary of the Treasury, Eisenhower administration.

JOHN BAILEY (1904–1975). Democratic National Chairman.

BOBBY BAKER (1928–   ). Former Secretary to the Majority, U.S. Senate.

GEORGE BALL (1909–1994). Undersecretary of State.

HALE BOGGS (1914–1972). House Majority Whip, Democrat of Louisiana.

JACK BROOKS (1922–   ). Democratic Congressman from Texas.

EDMUND "PAT" BROWN (1906–1996). Democratic Governor of California.

GEORGE BROWN (1898–1983). Board chairman, Brown & Root, Inc.

McGEORGE BUNDY (1919–1996). Special Assistant to the President for National Security Affairs.

WILLIAM BUNDY (1917–   ). Assistant Secretary of State for Far Eastern Affairs.

HORACE BUSBY (1924–   ). Special Assistant to the President.

HARRY BYRD, SR. (1887–1966). Democratic Senator from Virginia and Chairman, Senate Finance Committee.

ROBERT BYRD (1917–   ). Democratic Senator from West Virginia.

LIZ CARPENTER (1920–   ). Press Secretary and Staff Director to the First Lady.

CLIFTON CARTER (1918–1971). Liaison to the President, Democratic National Committee.

FIDEL CASTRO (1926–   ). Premier of Cuba.

JAMES CHANEY (1943–1964). Civil rights worker.

ROBERTO CHIARI (1905–1981). President of Panama.

CLARK CLIFFORD   (1906–   ). Partner, Clifford & Miller, Washington, D.C.
JOHN CONNALLY   (1917–1993). Democratic Governor of Texas.
NELLIE CONNALLY   (1919–   ). Wife of John Connally.
PAUL CORBIN   (1914–1990). Assistant to the Democratic National Chairman.
RICHARD DALEY   (1902–1976). Democratic Mayor of Chicago.
CHARLES DE GAULLE   (1890–1969). President of France.
CARTHA "DEKE" DELOACH   (1920–   ). Assistant Director, Federal Bureau of Investigation, and Liaison to the President.
C. DOUGLAS DILLON   (1909–   ). Secretary of the Treasury.
EVERETT DIRKSEN   (1896–1969). Senate Minority Leader, Republican of Illinois.
THOMAS DODD   (1907–1971). Democratic Senator from Connecticut.
HELEN GAHAGAN DOUGLAS   (1900–1980). Actress, former Democratic Congresswoman from California.
ALEC DOUGLAS-HOME   (1903–1995). Prime Minister of the United Kingdom.
RALPH DUNGAN   (1923–   ). Special Assistant to the President.
JAMES EASTLAND   (1904–1986). Democratic Senator from Mississippi and Chairman, Senate Judiciary Committee.
DWIGHT EISENHOWER   (1890–1969). Thirty-fourth President of the United States.
ROWLAND EVANS   (1921–   ). Syndicated columnist.
MYER "MIKE" FELDMAN   (1917–   ). Deputy Special Counsel to the President.
GERALD FORD   (1913–   ). Republican Congressman from Michigan.
ABE FORTAS   (1910–1982). Partner, Arnold, Fortas & Porter, Washington, D.C.
ORVILLE FREEMAN   (1918–   ). Secretary of Agriculture.
ALFRED FRIENDLY   (1911–1983). Managing editor, *Washington Post.*
J. WILLIAM FULBRIGHT   (1905–1995). Chairman, Senate Foreign Relations Committee, Democrat of Arkansas.
ROSWELL GILPATRIC   (1904–1996). Deputy Secretary of Defense (until January 1964).
ARTHUR GOLDBERG   (1908–1990). Associate Justice, U.S. Supreme Court.
BARRY GOLDWATER   (1909–   ). Republican Senator from Arizona, Republican nominee for President.
ANDREW GOODMAN   (1943–1964). Civil rights worker.
RICHARD GOODWIN   (1931–   ). Presidential speechwriter.
KERMIT GORDON   (1916–1976). Director, Bureau of the Budget.
KATHARINE GRAHAM   (1917–   ). President, Washington Post Company.
CHARLES HALLECK   (1900–1986). House Minority Leader, Republican of Indiana.
W. AVERELL HARRIMAN   (1891–1986). Undersecretary of State for Political Affairs.
HOUSTON HARTE   (1893–1972). Owner, *San Angelo Standard Times,* San Angelo, Texas.
ANDREW HATCHER   (1925–1990). Assistant Press Secretary to the President.
WALTER HELLER   (1915–1987). Chairman, Council of Economic Advisers.
J. EDGAR HOOVER   (1895–1972). Director, Federal Bureau of Investigation.
HUBERT HUMPHREY   (1911–1978). Senate Majority Whip, Democrat of Minnesota, Democratic nominee for Vice President.
WALTER JENKINS   (1918–1985). Special Assistant to the President.
LADY BIRD JOHNSON   (1912–   ). Wife of Lyndon Johnson.

LUCI BAINES JOHNSON (1947–   ). Daughter of Lyndon Johnson.

LYNDA BIRD JOHNSON (1944–   ). Daughter of Lyndon Johnson.

LYNDON BAINES JOHNSON (1908–1973). Thirty-sixth President of the United States.

PAUL JOHNSON (1916–1985). Democratic Governor of Mississippi.

OLIN JOHNSTON (1896–1965). Democratic Senator from South Carolina.

JOHN JONES (1917–1994). President, Houston Chronicle Publishing Company.

B. EVERETT JORDAN (1896–1974). Democratic Senator from North Carolina, Chairman, Senate Rules Committee.

NICHOLAS KATZENBACH (1922–   ). Deputy Attorney General.

JESSE KELLAM (1900–1977). General manager, Texas Broadcasting Company.

EDWARD KENNEDY (1932–   ). Democratic Senator from Massachusetts.

JACQUELINE BOUVIER KENNEDY (1929–1994). Widow of John F. Kennedy.

JOHN FITZGERALD KENNEDY (1917–1963). Thirty-fifth President of the United States.

JOSEPH KENNEDY (1888–1969). Former Ambassador to the Court of St. James's, father of John F. Kennedy.

ROBERT KENNEDY (1925–1968). Attorney General.

ROSE FITZGERALD KENNEDY (1890–1995). Mother of John F. Kennedy.

NGUYEN KHANH (1927–   ). Leader of South Vietnam (beginning January 1964).

NIKITA KHRUSHCHEV (1894–1971). Chairman, Council of Ministers, Union of Soviet Socialist Republics.

MARTIN LUTHER KING, JR. (1929–1968). President, Southern Christian Leadership Conference.

DAVID LAWRENCE (1889–1966). Former Governor of Pennsylvania.

WALTER LIPPMANN (1889–1974). Columnist, *Washington Post.*

HENRY CABOT LODGE, JR. (1902–1985). U.S. Ambassador to South Vietnam (until June 1964).

RUSSELL LONG (1918–   ). Democratic Senator from Louisiana.

CLARE BOOTHE LUCE (1903–1987). Playwright and former Republican Congresswoman from Connecticut.

HENRY LUCE (1898–1967). Editor-in-Chief, Editorial Chairman, Time Incorporated.

EUGENE MCCARTHY (1916–   ). Democratic Senator from Minnesota.

JOHN MCCLELLAN (1896–1977). Democratic Senator from Arkansas.

JOHN MCCLOY (1895–1989). President, Chase Manhattan Bank.

JOHN MCCORMACK (1891–1980). Speaker of the House, Democrat of Massachusetts.

ROBERT MCNAMARA (1916–   ). Secretary of Defense.

MARSHALL MCNEIL (1904–1981). Reporter, Scripps-Howard Newspapers.

RICHARD MAGUIRE (1917–1983). Treasurer, Democratic National Committee.

THOMAS MANN (1912–   ). Assistant Secretary of State for Inter-American Affairs.

MIKE MANSFIELD (1903–   ). Senate Majority Leader, Democrat of Montana.

MARIANNE MEANS (1934–   ). Correspondent, Hearst Newspapers.

WILLIAM MILLER (1914–1983). Republican Congressman from New York, Republican National Chairman, Republican nominee for Vice President.

DUONG VAN "BIG" MINH (1916–). Leader of South Vietnam (until January 1964).

A.W. MOURSUND (1919–). Banker, rancher, lawyer, businessman, Johnson City, Texas.

BILL MOYERS (1934–). Special Assistant to the President.

EDMUND MUSKIE (1914–1996). Democratic Senator from Maine.

RICHARD NIXON (1913–1994). Former Vice President of the United States and Partner, Nixon, Mudge, Rose, Guthrie & Alexander, New York.

ROBERT NOVAK (1931–). Syndicated columnist.

LAWRENCE O'BRIEN (1917–1990). Special Assistant to the President.

KENNETH O'DONNELL (1924–1977). Special Assistant to the President.

THOMAS "TIP" O'NEILL (1912–1994). Democratic Congressman from Massachusetts.

LEE HARVEY OSWALD (1939–1963). Accused assassin of John F. Kennedy.

OTTO PASSMAN (1900–1988). Democratic Congressman from Louisiana.

JOHN PASTORE (1907–). Democratic Senator from Rhode Island.

DREW PEARSON (1897–1969). Syndicated columnist.

ADAM CLAYTON POWELL, JR. (1908–1972). Chairman, House Education and Labor Committee, Democrat of New York.

JOSEPH RAUH (1911–1992). Partner, Rauh & Silard, Washington, D.C.

GEORGE REEDY (1917–). Special Assistant to the President, Press Secretary to the President.

JAMES RESTON (1909–1995). Washington Bureau Chief and columnist, *New York Times*.

WALTER REUTHER (1907–1970). President, United Auto Workers.

ABRAHAM RIBICOFF (1910–). Democratic Senator from Connecticut.

JUANITA ROBERTS (1913–1983). Personal secretary to the President.

NELSON ROCKEFELLER (1908–1979). Republican Governor of New York.

WALT ROSTOW (1916–). Director, Policy Planning Staff, Department of State.

JAMES ROWE (1909–1984). Partner, Corcoran, Foley, Youngman & Rowe, Washington, D.C.

JAMES ROWLEY (1908–1992). Chief, U.S. Secret Service.

JACK RUBY (1911–1967). Convicted murderer of Lee Harvey Oswald.

DEAN RUSK (1909–1994). Secretary of State.

RICHARD RUSSELL (1897–1971). Democratic Senator from Georgia, Chairman, Senate Armed Services Committee.

PIERRE SALINGER (1925–). Press Secretary to the President, Democratic candidate for the Senate, Senator from California.

ARTHUR SCHLESINGER, JR. (1917–). Historian, Special Assistant to the President (until January 1964).

MICHAEL SCHWERNER (1939–1964). Civil rights worker.

WILLIAM SCRANTON (1917–). Republican Governor of Pennsylvania.

SARGENT SHRIVER (1915–). Director, Peace Corps and War on Poverty.

GEORGE SMATHERS (1913–). Democratic Senator from Florida.

HOWARD SMITH (1883–1976). Chairman, House Rules Committee, Democrat of Virginia.

STEPHEN SMITH (1927–1990). President, John F. Kennedy Library Corporation.

THEODORE SORENSEN   (1928–   ). Special Counsel to the President (until February 1964).

JOHN STENNIS   (1901–1995). Democratic Senator from Mississippi.

ADLAI STEVENSON   (1900–1965). 1952 and 1956 Democratic nominee for President, U.S. Ambassador to the United Nations.

MAXWELL TAYLOR   (1901–1987). Chairman, Joint Chiefs of Staff, U.S. Ambassador to South Vietnam (beginning July 1964).

ALBERT THOMAS   (1898–1966). Democratic Congressman from Texas.

J.D. TIPPIT   (1924–1963). Dallas policeman, allegedly killed by Lee Harvey Oswald.

HARRY TRUMAN   (1884–1972). Thirty-third President of the United States.

JACK VALENTI   (1921–   ). Special Assistant to the President.

CYRUS VANCE   (1917–   ). Deputy Secretary of Defense (beginning January 1964).

CARL VINSON   (1883–1981). Chairman, House Armed Services Committee, Democrat of Georgia.

ROBERT WAGNER   (1910–1991). Democratic Mayor of New York.

GEORGE WALLACE   (1919–   ). Democratic Governor of Alabama.

EARL WARREN   (1891–1974). Chief Justice of the United States.

EDWIN WEISL, SR.   (1896–1972). Partner, Simpson, Thacher & Bartlett, New York.

EARLE WHEELER   (1908–1975). Chairman, Joint Chiefs of Staff (beginning July 1964).

LEE WHITE   (1923–   ). Associate Counsel to the President.

WILLIAM S. WHITE   (1905–1994). Syndicated columnist.

GERALDINE WHITTINGTON   (1931–1993). Personal secretary to the President.

ROY WILKINS   (1901–1981). Executive Secretary, National Association for the Advancement of Colored People.

RALPH YARBOROUGH   (1903–1996). Democratic Senator from Texas.

WHITNEY YOUNG   (1921–1971). Executive Director, National Urban League.

RUFUS YOUNGBLOOD   (1921–1996). Secret Service agent.

Appendix

The Warren Report and
the Garrison Investigation

THROUGHOUT HIS TIME in the White House, Johnson was forced to deal with questions raised by the assassination that ushered in his presidency. In September 1964, the Warren Commission released its controversial report, finding that the thirty-fifth President had been killed by a lone sniper, Lee Harvey Oswald, that Oswald had been killed by another lone gunman, Jack Ruby, and that no conspiracy, foreign or domestic, was involved. By 1967, New Orleans District Attorney James Garrison was pursuing the possibility of a conspiracy to kill President Kennedy that originated in his city.

FRIDAY, SEPTEMBER 18, 1964

RICHARD RUSSELL
7:54 P.M.

AT THE END of the Warren Commission's deliberations, nine days before its report was released, Johnson calls Senator Russell at his home in Winder, Georgia, to ask about what it contains.

RUSSELL: That danged Warren Commission business, it whupped me down so. We got through today. You know what I did? I . . . got on the plane and came home. I didn't even have a toothbrush. I didn't bring a shirt. . . . Didn't even have my pills—antihistamine pills to take care of my em-fy-see-ma.

LBJ: Why did you get in such a rush?

RUSSELL: I'm just worn out, fighting over that damned report.

LBJ: Well, you ought to have taken another hour and gone get your clothes.

RUSSELL: No, no. They're trying to prove that the same bullet that hit Kennedy first was the one that hit Connally, went through him and through his hand, his bone, and into his leg. . . . I couldn't hear all the evidence and cross-examine all of 'em. But I did read the record. . . . I was the only fellow there that . . . suggested any change whatever in what the staff got up.[1] This staff business always scares me. I like to put my own views down. But we got you a pretty good report.

LBJ: Well, what difference does it make which bullet got Connally?

RUSSELL: Well, it don't *make* much difference.[2] But they said that . . . the commission believes that the same bullet that hit Kennedy hit Connally. Well, I don't believe it.

LBJ: I don't either.

RUSSELL: And so I couldn't sign it. And I said that Governor Connally testified directly to the contrary and I'm not gonna approve of that. So I finally made 'em say there was a difference in the commission, in that part of 'em believed that that wasn't so. And 'course if a fellow was accurate enough to hit Kennedy right in the neck on one shot and knock his head off in the next one—and he's leaning up against his wife's head—and not even wound her—why, he didn't miss completely with that third shot. But according to their theory, he not only missed the whole automobile, but he missed the street! Well, a man that's a good enough shot to put two bullets right into Kennedy, he didn't miss that whole automobile. . . . But anyhow, that's just a little thing.

LBJ: What's the net of the whole thing? What's it[3] say? Oswald did it? And he did it for any reason?

RUSSELL: Just that he was a general misanthropic fellow, that he had never been satisfied anywhere he was on earth—in Russia or here. And that he had a desire to get his name in history. . . . I don't think you'll be displeased with the report. It's too long. . . . Four volumes.

LBJ: Unanimous?

RUSSELL: Yes, sir. I tried my best to get in a *dis*-sent, but they'd come 'round and trade me out of it by giving me a little old threat.[4]

---

[1] Russell was not the only commission member who questioned the "single bullet" theory. So did Hale Boggs and John Sherman Cooper. But Russell was the only one who felt so strongly that he balked at signing a report affirming full confidence in the theory. Insistent on a unanimous report, John McCloy brokered a deal to use compromise language, saying that there was "very persuasive evidence from the experts to indicate that the same bullet which pierced the President's throat also caused Governor Connally's wounds." McCloy's language, which Russell approved, went on to say that testimony by Connally had "given rise to some difference of opinion as to this probability," but all commission members agreed that all of the bullets that struck Kennedy and Connally "were fired from the sixth floor window of the Texas School Book Depository." (See Kai Bird, *The Chairman,* Simon & Schuster, 1992, pp. 564–66.)

[2] Actually it could have meant a world of difference. For Kennedy and Connally to have been struck by separate bullets, with another shot missing the car, suggested that there may have been two gunmen firing at them in Dallas, and hence a conspiracy.

[3] The Warren Report.

[4] McCloy had insisted that a report that was not unanimous would damage the national interest. He thus fashioned the aforementioned compromise that allowed the commission to call itself unanimous in its conclusions.

MONDAY, SEPTEMBER 28, 1964

MIKE MANSFIELD
7:22 A.M.

LBJ: There's a good deal of feeling that maybe the Cuban thing—they don't quite understand why he[1] was messing back and forth with Cuba and what connection that had with it. And they don't quite find the motive yet that this fellow had for wanting to kill him.[2] He was going back and forth to Russia. He was messing around in Mexico with the Cubans.

· · · ·

LBJ: I'm going to . . . try to get Hoover and the Secret Service together. . . . They[3] had the stuff on Oswald but didn't give it to the Secret Service.

· · · ·

LBJ: Honestly, just 'tween us, on the whole I'd rather have you protected or my daughter protected and my wife—somebody I love—by FBI. They're sharp, fast, and quick.

SATURDAY, FEBRUARY 18, 1967

RAMSEY CLARK
Acting Attorney General
10:39 A.M.

CLARK, who was about to become LBJ's third Attorney General, and Cartha "Deke" DeLoach, the FBI liaison to the Johnson White House, helped LBJ keep discreet track of Jim Garrison's freewheeling investigation of Kennedy's murder.

CLARK: I talked to Deke further about it yesterday. . . . What he[4] is working on must be the associations that Oswald had in the three, four months he was down there[5] in '62, '63. . . . I think that the subject is so volatile and emotional though that it could get confused and obscured. I had heard that Hale Boggs[6] was saying that Garrison was saying—privately around town—if he traced back

[1] Oswald.
[2] What motive Oswald had to kill Kennedy.
[3] The FBI.
[4] Garrison.
[5] In New Orleans.
[6] House Majority Whip, of Louisiana.

or if *you* could be found in it someplace, which—I can't believe he's been saying that. The Bureau says they haven't heard any such thing and they've got lots of eyes and ears. . . . Either that or this guy Garrison is completely off his rocker.

LBJ: Who did Hale tell this to?

CLARK: Apparently Marvin.[1]

LBJ: [to Watson:] Hale tell you . . . that this fellow—the district attorney down there—said that this was traced to me, or something?

MARVIN WATSON: Privately he was using your name as having known about it.

* * * *

LBJ: You know this story going around about the CIA and their trying to get —sending in the folks to get Castro?

CLARK: To assassinate Castro.

LBJ: . . . Has anybody ever told you all the story?

CLARK: No.

LBJ: I think you ought to have that. It's incredible. I don't believe there's a thing in the world to it.[2] I don't think we ought to seriously consider it. But I think you ought to know about it.

CLARK: Who would I get it from?

LBJ: I've had it from three or four. I've forgotten who's come in here. I'll have to check.

CLARK: Does the Bureau have it?

LBJ: No, I don't think so. . . . Drew Pearson[3] came and gave it to me. Said Morgan told him—Hoffa's lawyer.[4] He says that they have a man that was involved that was brought in to the CIA with a number of others and instructed by the CIA and the Attorney General to assassinate Castro after the Bay of Pigs.

CLARK: You know, I've heard that much. I just haven't heard names, places.

LBJ: . . . I think it would look bad on us if we'd had it reported to us a number of times and we . . . just laughed, if this is true. . . . He said that the limitation[5] runs out in November. . . .

[1] Marvin Watson of the Johnson White House staff.

[2] This refers to CIA-Mafia efforts to have the Cuban leader murdered under Presidents Eisenhower and Kennedy. By deflecting the story so airily, Johnson may not be leveling with Clark. He had suspected Cuban involvement in the assassination from almost the moment Kennedy was killed. (See Chapter One.) He later said that he was shocked to be informed "that we were running a damn Murder, Incorporated, in the Caribbean" and that "Kennedy was trying to get Castro, but Castro got him first" (*Atlantic*, July 1973, and *New York Times*, June 25, 1976).

[3] The syndicated columnist.

[4] Edward P. Morgan, lawyer to Teamsters union president James Hoffa. Pursued since 1957 by Robert Kennedy, in his drive against union corruption, Hoffa had been convicted in 1964 of jury tampering and mail fraud. He had appealed the verdict. Morgan had been told of the CIA effort against Castro by another of his clients, the Mafia boss John Roselli, who was involved. Morgan had confided what he had learned to Drew Pearson, who conveyed it to LBJ—including Robert Kennedy's possible role in authorizing the murder attempts, which Johnson may have considered a lever for use against RFK, if it ever became necessary.

[5] Edward P. Morgan, referring to the statute of limitations.

CLARK: It'd be six years, all right, which would mean November probably. But not for a concealed situation.

LBJ: That's what I'd think. But anyway he says in November he's going to tell it.

CLARK: Pearson is?

LBJ: No, this individual. . . . There's just all kinds of things that come to me every day. I don't pay any attention to 'em, but maybe I was a little worried this morning because one of my lawyer friends told me I ought to call you and talk to you about it so you'll have a file that protects you, that you don't just look like they report these things to us and we just throw them overboard. . . . But anyway, that following this, Castro said they had these pills and they were supposed to take 'em when he caught 'em. And they didn't get to take their pills. So he tortured 'em and they told him all about it. . . . So he said, "Okay, we'll just take care of that." So then he called Oswald and a group in and told them about this meeting and go set it up and get the job done. Now that's their story and I talked to Abe[1] about it first and he just said, "Well, it's so incredible." . . . Then they also claim that you-all[2] have tapped . . . Hoffa's lawyers' telephones and haven't admitted that yet and that they're going to have to explode that. . . . There have been two or three here circulating it to me and Pearson was just one of 'em. But I've forgotten who the others are. They were reputable people or they wouldn't have gotten in here.

· · · ·

LBJ: He[3] came to see me in the mansion, I would say, a month ago. . . . It sounded just like you're telling me that Lady Bird was taking dope. I just wouldn't pay much attention to it. . . . Anyway, I'll try to think of the other names and give 'em to you. He's the only one I can remember now. . . . I credit it 99.99 percent untrue. But that's something I think we ought to know has been reported and you-all ought to do what you think ought to be done to protect yourself.

· · · ·

LBJ: You can be your own judge about it, but I would think what you ought to do is either write or call Deke—and take notes on what you say to him—and say the President has seen this on television and read of it and he says to tell you —without interfering or obstructing in any way the local investigation—to be sure that if there's anything to this or any scintilla of evidence that should be considered that you be sure that it is presented to me. . . . I think that his local people there are watching it anyway probably, but I think that would show that you weren't . . . totally uninterested in pursuing it.

CLARK: I did everything that you said last week, except I didn't mention your name in it. . . . I didn't document it, but I can do that.

LBJ: Maybe you don't need to do either. You be the judge. I'm just telling you what Abe told me he thought we ought to do. This had a pretty good run this morning on NBC.

[1] Fortas, appointed by LBJ in 1965 to the Supreme Court.
[2] The Justice Department.
[3] Pearson.

WEDNESDAY, FEBRUARY 22, 1967

RAMSEY CLARK
6:40 P.M.

> EARLIER IN THE DAY, David Ferrie, whom Garrison was about to have
> arrested as a conspirator in the Kennedy assassination, was discovered dead in
> New Orleans.

CLARK: The Special Agent in Charge[1] down there . . . says that they are quite
convinced the death was by natural causes, that it was a small cerebral hemor-
rhage. . . . The only part of the autopsy that's not complete is the toxicology, and
it'll take two to three days to complete that. . . . The FBI interviewed Ferrie in
November of '63 because he had known Oswald in New Orleans. He was a
commercial pilot and there was some allegation at the time that he may have
flown Oswald to Dallas. All the evidence at that time indicated that that had not
happened. The plane that he had was not suited for the purpose. Any idea that
the plane would be used to take Oswald to Cuba after he did this[2] is just not a
real possibility. In addition to that, of course, Oswald had left New Orleans and
gone to Dallas long before President Kennedy's trip was known of. . . .
   Ferrie denied it all quite vociferously. He called the Bureau Saturday and said
that he was quite a sick man and he was just disgusted with Garrison. He was
going to sue him for slander. . . . He wanted to know what the Bureau could do
to help him with this nut. Garrison has apparently said that Ferrie wasn't involved, that he's checked it out, his plane wasn't suited . . . that while he may
have been part of the discussions, he wasn't one of the people that he was
referring to. So fortunately, unless he tries to change, he's apparently cut himself
off from using Ferrie as his way out of what I think is his predicament.
   Ferrie was a homosexual. He had a long list of arrests. And there was an
eleven-year-old boy with him when he was discovered, but they don't have any
evidence of foul play. It's all a pretty sordid mess. . . . I'd given kind of a background to some press people yesterday, saying that I thought Garrison had to
bear responsibility for anything he had to the Secret Service and the FBI immediately, that I couldn't imagine any half-responsible district attorney in the country
in a situation vaguely comparable to this not immediately reporting to them. . . .
The SAC[3] down there just can't talk with him. He just has no confidence in
Garrison. He's afraid that Garrison would try to use him. . . . I had thought at
one time for me to call on him . . . myself. But I'm afraid he would use that to
try to escalate the thing. . . . That's what we have on Ferrie. It sure took a bad
turn today.

LBJ: [chuckles grimly]

---

[1] Of the FBI.
[2] Kennedy's assassination.
[3] Special Agent in Charge.

THURSDAY, MARCH 2, 1967

JOHN CONNALLY
9:22 P.M.

THE TEXAS GOVERNOR CALLS Johnson from New York with more conspiracy rumors about the Kennedy assassination.

CONNALLY: All day today, I have been interviewed up here. They continue to break some stories on this conspiracy thing, based on what this fellow, this D.A. in New Orleans talked about—Mr. Garrison. . . . Of course, I just simply say I know nothing about it. But a newsman named Paul Smith has just been here to interview me again. They have a long story on the radio tonight, over WINS, the radio station here in New York . . . from a man who saw the files in Garrison's office . . . that Garrison has information that would prove that there were four assassins in the United States sent here by Castro or Castro's people. Not Castro himself, but one of his lieutenants. One was picked up in New York . . . and interviewed by the FBI and the Secret Service, but did not reveal a great deal of information. . . . One of the teams was composed of Lee Harvey Oswald, this fellow Shaw[1] that has just been arrested in New Orleans yesterday and the man Ferrie, plus one other man. . . . And there were two other teams that I know nothing about.

WINS Radio has had some reporters . . . in Cuba working on various angles of this thing for the past day. . . . In Cuba they found . . . and all of this is not going on the air at all . . . that after the Missile Crisis, President Kennedy and Khrushchev had made a deal to leave Castro in power. But about six months after the Missile Crisis was over, the CIA was instructed to assassinate Castro and sent into Cuba. Some of 'em were captured and tortured by Castro and his people. . . . President Kennedy did not give the order to the CIA but that some other person extremely close to President Kennedy did. They did not name the man, but the inference was very clear . . . that it was his brother[2] who ordered the CIA to send a team into Cuba to assassinate Castro. That then one of Castro's lieutenants, as a reprisal measure, sent four teams into the United States to assassinate President Kennedy. That Lee Harvey Oswald was a member of the team operating out of New Orleans. . . .

LBJ: Good. This is confidential too. We've had that story on about three occasions and the people here say that there's no basis for it. . . . I've given a lot of thought to it. First, one of Hoffa's lawyers went to one of our mutual friends and asked him to come and relay that to us. . . . A week or two passed, and Pearson came to me—Drew Pearson. Told me that the lawyer Edwin [sic] Morgan here had told him the same thing and . . . they would tell all the story after November, when the limitation[3] ran out. . . . Our lawyers said they couldn't believe there

---

[1] Clay Shaw, a New Orleans businessman who was another Garrison target. He was later tried for and acquitted of conspiring to assassinate Kennedy.
[2] Robert Kennedy.
[3] Statute of limitations.

was any limitation on a conspiracy. I talked to another one or two of our good lawyers . . . a few months ago. He evaluated it pretty carefully and said that it was ridiculous.

Now with the CIA thing breaking and the thing turning, as it did, and reconstructing the requests that were made of me back there right after I became President,[1] I have talked some more about it and I've got the A.G.[2] coming down to see me tomorrow night to spend the weekend with me. I thought I'd go over it with him again . . . so Hoover and them could watch it very carefully. They say that there's not anything to the Garrison story. At least, Hoover[3] says so, as near as he can tell. He says that they interviewed Ferrie and they interviewed this other fellow very carefully and closely and the fellow claims that he got a call from Oswald, but that they can't find any record of it. And the doctor that had him under surveillance said that he wasn't in a position to talk on November the 23rd, and he was under very heavy sedation. And that the Shaw thing is a phony, and that Ferrie died of natural causes and that that was a phony. But that some of these same sources that were preventing trying to involve this jail thing[4] have been feeding stuff to Garrison, as they did here. I don't know whether there's any basis for it or not. . . . It's pretty hard to see how we would know directly what Castro did. . . . As Abe[5] said, who is it that's seen Castro and heard from Castro and knows Castro that could be confirming all this? . . . So we will look into it and I appreciate very much your calling me and I'll try to bear this in mind.

· · · ·

LBJ: The FBI thinks that both Ferrie and Shaw are frauds—I mean, that Garrison using them is a fraud. . . . They do not give any credit to it. But we can't ever be sure and we just want to be sure.

[1] This may refer to requests for Johnson to resume covert action against Castro.
[2] The Attorney General, Ramsey Clark.
[3] J. Edgar Hoover.
[4] LBJ refers to the desire of Morgan and other Hoffa allies to keep the Teamsters leader out of prison. They may have hoped that Johnson might be willing to intervene at the last minute as the price of tamping down public revelations about the CIA-Mafia conspiracy against Castro. But five days after this conversation, Hoffa entered prison to begin a thirteen-year sentence, which was commuted in 1971 by President Nixon. Four years later, Hoffa disappeared.
[5] Fortas.

Acknowledgments

THE NOTION of this book sprang from a dinner I had at the Jockey Club in Washington, D.C., in June 1994, with Harry Middleton, Director of the Johnson Library, and the Washington lawyer Harry McPherson, who worked for LBJ in both the Senate and White House, and his wife. Middleton mentioned that having opened a series of Johnson White House tape recordings in response to the John F. Kennedy Assassination Records Collection Act of 1992, the Library had decided, as its highest priority, to open its entire collection of tapes, from 1963 to 1969. I replied that if so, some historian should transcribe, edit, and annotate a selection of the conversations in book form. Not only was this the only time a President had ever taped himself from the beginning until the end of his presidency (or almost certainly ever would, in light of the public outrage when Richard Nixon's recording system was revealed in 1973). It would also be a vital new means of understanding Lyndon Johnson, who, as we have known from a rich offering of journalism, memoir, history, and biography, was such a different person in private from in public.

My literary agent, Esther Newberg, shared my view of the potential importance of a multivolume edition of the Johnson tapes, with annotation and historical commentary. My editor, Alice Mayhew, instantly agreed, observing that the Johnson years were a pivotal moment in American history and that the private LBJ could not be anything but riveting. In September 1994, we three flew down to Austin to view shelf after shelf of Dictabelts and reel-to-reel tapes in their large, walk-in vault, speak with archivists who were processing them, and listen, with rising enthusiasm, to the private Johnson in some of the conversations that the Library had opened. During a talk with Middleton in his office, we all concurred that my book would be strictly independent and unauthorized. I would have no privileged access to the tapes. No Library official or other member of the Johnson circle would see the book before it emerged from the printer.

From Harry Middleton and his colleagues—Patrick Borders, Tina Houston, Barbara Biffle, Juanita Hannusch, Yolanda Boozer, Claudia Anderson, Regina Greenwell, Linda Hanson, Mary Knill, Philip Scott, Ted Gittinger, and the others in the Johnson Library—I have for three years experienced nothing but high archival professionalism. Processing a collection with such complex demands as the five years of Johnson tapes would strain the resources of any presidential library. Throwing these conversations open will almost certainly irritate some of those around LBJ who would have preferred distant, embellished memories of what he said and what others said to him, instead of reality. There is no better evidence of Middleton's commitment to openness than his insistence on opening all of the recordings as quickly and fully as possible. A different kind of library director might have attempted to hide behind LBJ's spoken instructions to keep the tapes under seal until at least 2023 and used lawyers to thwart whatever legal challenges historians might have raised to their closure.

The incomparable Esther Newberg was a constant source of enthusiasm and wisdom—practical, literary, and historical. In this she was abetted by Jack Horner, Sloan Harris, David Schmerler, John DeLaney, and Jessica Green. And I now know firsthand why so many authors I admire insist that there is no better editor in America than Alice Mayhew. She made it possible for me to interrupt work on another book in order to create this volume and made working on it a pleasure from beginning to end, as did all of her superb colleagues at Simon & Schuster—particularly Roger Labrie, who met the challenges of a complicated publication process with judgment and sangfroid. Stephen Messina oversaw the book's copy editing with extreme skill and good humor. I am grateful also to Liz Stein and Lisa Weisman, as well as Jonathan Newcomb, Jack Romanos, Carolyn Reidy, Michele Martin, Michael Selleck, Victoria Meyer, Pamela Duevel, Marcella Berger, Eric Rayman, George Turianski, Michael Accordino, Edith Fowler, Wendy Nicholson, and Theresa Horner—and Fred Chase, of Laredo, Texas, who copyedited the manuscript. Don Reuben generously gave me the benefit of his long and distinguished history in literary and copyright law. Dolores Figiel oversaw much of the word processing, to which Lisa Spodak contributed. Maryam Mashayekhi helped the author to assemble research materials, Sandi Fox to check facts.

Most of all I thank my wife, Afsaneh Mashayekhi Beschloss, and our two sons, to whom this book is dedicated—Alexander and Cyrus (who was born two thirds through the work on this volume)—for tolerating the many distractions and interruptions that the relentless, demanding voice of Lyndon Baines Johnson imposed on their lives.

MICHAEL R. BESCHLOSS
Washington, D.C.
August 1997

Index

Fehmer, Marie, 15, 122
Feinberg, Abe, 348
Feldman, Myer "Mike," 102, 205, 278–79, 289
Ferguson, Jim, 295
Ferrie, David, 564–66
Fine, John, 420
Finland, Lasker's proposed appointment to, 171–72
Ford, Gerald, 51–52, 59, 64–65
foreign aid and foreign affairs, 37, 86, 88, 104, 134–35, 199–200
    Albert on, 110n, 112–13
    Fulbright and, 134
    for Indonesia, 157–58
    JFK assassination and, 64, 67
    McCormack on, 110–11, 113
    Mansfield and, 110n, 120, 123
    O'Brien on, 99–100, 121
    Passman and, 62, 99–100, 110–14
    press coverage of, 182, 201n, 225
    Rusk and, 174
    Russell on, 94–95, 174
    Thomas on, 113–14
    Valeo on, 123
Foreman, Edgar, 507–8
Forrestal, Michael, 293, 371
Fortas, Abe, 11n, 35n, 74n, 82, 171, 286, 547n, 563, 566
    on Baker scandal, 166, 186, 188–89, 196–99
    JFK assassination and, 49–51
    and LBJ's address to Joint Session of Congress, 82–83
    LBJ's finances and, 166, 298, 325, 335–336, 358, 393
    LBJ's presidential campaign and, 526, 542
    Warren Commission and, 66
France:
    in Indochina, 367, 373n, 377
    Vietnam and, 214, 293, 414
Frank, Irving, 143–44
Frederika, Queen of Greece, 187, 270
Freedom Summer 1964, 313n, 425
Freeman, Orville, 244, 484, 487, 490
Friendly, Alfred:
    Baker scandal and, 166, 186
    JFK assassination and, 34–35
    Reynolds file and, 235
Friendly Sons of St. Patrick, LBJ's speech to, 288n, 289
Fulbright, Betty, 65–66, 87, 265
Fulbright, J. William, 60, 86–88, 192, 264–265, 292, 297–98

on Alliance for Progress, 87
budget and, 25
civil rights and, 333–35
Copenhagen and The Hague visit of, 333–34
on Cuba, 87–88
foreign aid and, 134
JFK assassination and, 65
LBJ's relationship with, 65–66
on Mann appointment, 101
on National Cultural Center, 87
Panama and, 252, 297n, 298
and successor to Lodge, 408
Vietnam War and, 88, 264, 294n, 297n, 298

Galbraith, John Kenneth, 38–41, 82n, 457
Gargan, Ann, 302–3, 345–46
Garner, John Nance, 485
Garrison, Jim, JFK assassination investigated by, 559, 561–66
Garwood, John, 33
Gemmill, Henry, 325
Geneva Accords, 387
Gilpatric, Roswell:
    on firing of military aides, 116–18
    on leaks, 165–66
    as Lodge's successor, 407–11, 416
Glass, Alice, 251
Goldberg, Arthur, 20–21, 236
Goldenson, Leonard, 275
Goldwater, Barry, 400
    Baker scandal and, 181–82, 184n, 223n, 290
    civil rights and, 419–20, 457n, 459, 464–66, 474
    Guantánamo crisis and, 229
    LBJ's meetings with, 472, 474
    on LBJ's State of the Union address, 154
    on Lodge's resignation, 426n, 427
    presidential campaign of, 81, 133n, 154n, 172, 190, 231, 239, 241, 272, 344, 383–84, 388, 417, 419–20, 427, 444, 446, 451, 456–59, 462, 464–68, 470, 474, 478–79, 487, 492, 494, 502, 504, 515–16, 520n, 525–27, 529, 532–533, 542n
    Vietnam War and, 213, 264, 272, 368–369, 373, 402, 414, 494–95, 502, 504, 507n
Goldwyn, Sam, 335
Goodman, Andrew, 425–26, 431–35, 458n, 501, 502n, 511n
Goodwin, Richard, 280, 384, 404
Gordon, Kermit, 38, 163–64

Photo Credits